CLYMER®

KAWASAKI

KX60 & KX80 • 1983-1990

The world's finest publishers of mechanical how-to manuals

INTERTEC PUBLISHING
P.O. Box 12901, Overland Park, Kansas 66282-2901

Copyright ©1990 Intertec Publishing

FIRST EDITION
First Printing October, 1990
Second Printing February, 1994
Third Printing May, 1996
Fourth Printing January, 1998
Fifth Printing June, 2000

Printed in U.S.A.

CLYMER and colophon are registered trademarks of Intertec Publishing.

ISBN: 0-89287-535-6

Library of Congress: 90-55659

MEMBER

MIC   MOTORCYCLE
      INDUSTRY
      COUNCIL, INC.

AMA

Technical photography by Ron Wright.

Technical assistance provided by Curt Jordan, Jordan Engineering, Santa Ana, California.

Technical illustrations by Steve Amos.

COVER: Photographed by Mark Clifford, Mark Clifford Photography, Los Angeles, California.

CONTENTS

QUICK REFERENCE DATA

GENERAL ENGINE SPECIFICATIONS

Bore × stroke	
KX60	43 × 41.6 mm (1.69 × 1.64 in.)
KX80	
U.S.	48 × 45.8 mm (1.89 × 1.80 in.)
All other	47 × 45.8 mm (1.85 × 1.80 in.)
Displacement	
KX60	60cc (3.66 cu. in.)
KX80	
U.S.	82 cc (5.06 cu. in.)
All other	79 cc (4.84 cu. in.)
Compression ratio	
KX60	8.3:1
KX80	
U.S.	8.4:1
All other	8.3:1
U.S.	9.4:1
All other	9.1:1
Port timing	
KX60	
1983-1984	
Intake open	—
Intake close	—
Transfer open	61° BBDC
Transfer close	61° ABDC
Exhaust open	90.5° BBDC
Exhaust close	90.5° ABDC
KX60	
1985-on	
Intake open	—
Intake close	—
Transfer open	62.5° BBDC
Transfer close	62.5° ABDC
Exhaust open	92° BBDC
Exhaust close	92° ABDC
KX80	
1983-1985	
Intake open	—
Intake open	—
Transfer open	63° BBDC
Transfer close	63° ABDC
Exhaust open	94° BBDC
Exhaust close	94° ABDC
1986	
Intake open	—
Intake close	—
Transfer open	65.5° BBDC
Transfer close	65.5° ABDC
Exhaust open	94.5° BBDC
Exhaust close	94.5° ABDC
1987-on	
Intake open	—
Intake close	—
Transfer open	62.5° BBDC
Transfer close	62.5° ABDC
Exhaust open	93.5° BBDC
Exhaust close	93.5° ABDC

RECOMMENDED LUBRICANTS AND FUEL

Engine oil	Kawasaki 2-stroke racing oil
Transmission oil	SAE 10W-30 or 10W-40 transmission oil
Front fork oil	
KX60	SAE 5W-20
KX80	
1983-1985	SAE 10W-20
1986-on	SAE 10W
Air filter	Foam air filter oil
Drive chain	Chain lube
Brake fluid (KX80)	DOT 3
Fuel	Premium grade-research octane 87 or higher
Control cables	Cable lube

SPARK PLUG TYPE AND GAP

	Type	Gap mm (in.)
KX60		
1983-1984	NGK B9ES	0.7-0.8 (0.028-0.032)
1985-on	NGK B9EG	0.6-0.7 (0.024-0.028)
KX80		
1983-1985	NGK B9EV	0.6-0.7 (0.024-0.028)
1986-on		
U.S.	NGK B9EG	0.6-0.7 (0.024-0.028)
All except U.S.	NGK BR9EG	0.6-0.7 (0.024-0.028)

MAINTENANCE TORQUE SPECIFICATIONS

	N·m	ft.-lb.
Cylinder head bolts or nuts	25	18
Handlebar	21	15
Front fork crown pinch bolts or nuts		
KX60		
Upper	20	14
Lower	25	18
KX80		
Upper		
1983	20	14
1984	—	—
1985	17	12
1986-1987	20	14
1988-on	17	12
Lower		
1983-1985	28	18
1986-1987	20	14
1988-on	17	12
Steering stem (KX60)		
Nut	35	25
Locknut		
1983-1986	29	22
1987-1988	19	14

(continued)

MAINTENANCE TORQUE SPECIFICATIONS (continued)

	N·m	ft.-lb.
Steering stem (KX80)		
1983-1985		
Nut	34	25
Locknut		
1983	—	—
1984	—	—
1985	29	22
1986-on		
Nut	44	33
Locknut	4.0	35 in.-lb.
Rear axle nut	69	51

TRANSMISSION/CLUTCH OIL CAPACITY

Model	cc	qt.
KX60		
1983-1985	550	0.58
1986-on	600	0.63
KX80		
1983-1985	600	0.63
1986-on	700	0.74

FRONT FORK OIL

	Capacity cc (oz.)	Oil level mm (in.)	Range mm (in.)
KX60			
1983-1985	178.5-183.6	127-137	*
	(6.04-6.21)	(5.0-5.4)	*
1986-on	178.5-183.6	127-137	100-165
	(6.04-6.21)	(5.0-5.4)	3.9-6.5
KX80			
1983	254.5-259.5	161-169	*
	(8.60-8.77)	(6.34-6.65)	*
1984	284-292	118-122	*
	(9.60-9.87)	(4.65-4.80)	*
1985	271.5-279.5	138-142	*
	(9.18-9.45)	(5.43-5.59)	*
1986	317-325	128-132	100-160
	(10.7-11.0)	(5.0-5.2)	(3.9-6.3)
1987			
G, H	322-328	123-127	95-155
	(10.9-11.1)	(4.8-5.0)	(3.7-6.1)
J, K	366-374	108-112	80-140
	(12.4-12.6)	(4.3-4.4)	(3.1-5.5)
1988			
L, M	330-336	110-120	90-145
	(11.1-11.4)	(4.3-4.7)	(3.5-5.7)
N, P	349-355	95-105	90-130
	(11.8-12.0)	(3.7-4.11)	(3.5-5.1)
1989			
L, M	327-333	100-110	90-145
	(11.0-11.3)	(3.9-4.3)	(3.5-5.7)

* Not specified.

FRONT FORK AIR PRESSURE

	kg/cm²	psi
KX60		
1983-1985	0-2.51	0-36
1986-on	0-0.4	0-6
KX80		
1983-1985	0-2.51	0-36
1986-on	0-0.4	0-6

COOLANT CAPACITY

	cc	qt.
KX60	500	0.53
KX80		
1985	610	0.64
1986-on	650	0.69

TIRE INFLATION PRESSURE

Front	1.0 kg/cm² (14 psi)
Rear	1.0 kg/cm² (14 psi)

DRIVE CHAIN SLACK

Model	mm	in.
KX60	15-30	0.6-1.2
KX80	40-50	1.6-2.0

CHAPTER ONE

GENERAL INFORMATION

This Clymer shop manual covers all 1983-on Kawasaki KX60 and KX80 motocross bikes.

Troubleshooting, tune-up, maintenance and repair are not difficult, if you know what tools and equipment to use and what to do. Step-by-step instructions guide you through jobs ranging from simple maintenance to complete engine and suspension overhaul.

This manual has been specifically written for the home mechanic. The text is complete enough, however, for use by the professional mechanics. For example, engine service includes basic repair information as well as complete engine overhaul and crankshaft rebuilding. All procedures, tables, photos, etc., in this manual assume that the reader may be working on the bike or using this manual for the first time.

For the most frequently used general information and maintenance specifications refer to the *Quick Reference Data* pages in the front of the book. Readily accessible information can help prevent serious and expensive mechanical errors. Also note that the *Quick Reference Data* pages contain general tuning information that you can refer to while at the race track.

To save time on all maintenance tasks, use the index at the end of this manual. It has been carefully prepared and lists all major maintenance tasks by paragraph heading. Whether you want to remove the piston or simply adjust the drive chain, a quick look in the index will tell you exactly what page it is on.

For a better understanding of manual contents refer to *Manual Organization* in this chapter.

To save yourself time, energy and possible future aggravation, finish reading this entire chapter. If you acquaint yourself with all the special features of this manual it can become a valuable and indispensable tool. This manual can help make your repairs more successful and your machine better maintained and race ready.

Table 1 lists model coverage with engine serial numbers.

Table 2 lists general dimension specifications and **Table 3** lists dry weight specifications for all models.

Metric and U.S. standards are used throughout this manual. U.S. to metric conversion is given in **Table 4**.

General torque specifications are listed in **Table 5**.

Technical abbreviations are listed in **Table 6**.

Metric tap drill sizes are listed in **Table 7**.

Tables 1-7 are found at the end of the chapter.

MANUAL ORGANIZATION

This chapter provides general information useful to Kawasaki owners and mechanics. In addition, information in this chapter discusses the tools and techniques for preventive maintenance, troubleshooting and repair.

Chapter Two provides methods and suggestions for quick and accurate diagnosis and repair of problems. Troubleshooting procedures discuss typical symptoms and logical methods to pinpoint the trouble.

Chapter Three explains all periodic lubrication and routine maintenance necessary to keep your Kawasaki operating well. Chapter Three also includes recommended tune-up procedures, eliminating the need to constantly consult other chapters on the various assemblies.

Subsequent chapters describe specific systems, providing disassembly, repair, assembly and adjustment procedures in simple step-by-step form. If a repair is impractical for a home mechanic, it is so indicated. It is usually faster and less expensive to take such repairs to a dealer or competent repair shop. Specifications concerning a specific system are included at the end of the appropriate chapter.

NOTES, CAUTIONS AND WARNINGS

The terms *NOTE, CAUTION* and *WARNING* have specific meanings in this manual. A *NOTE* provides additional information to make a step or procedure easier or clearer. Disregarding a *NOTE* could cause inconvenience, but would not cause damage or personal injury.

A *CAUTION* emphasizes areas where equipment damage could occur. Disregarding a *CAUTION* could cause permanent mechanical damage; however, personal injury is unlikely.

A *WARNING* emphasizes areas where personal injury or even death could result from negligence. Mechanical damage may also occur. *WARNINGS* are to be taken *seriously*. In some cases, serious injury and death has resulted from disregarding similar warnings.

SAFETY FIRST

Professional mechanics can work for years and never sustain a serious injury. If you observe a few rules of common sense and safety, you can enjoy many safe hours servicing your own machine. If you ignore these rules you can hurt yourself or damage the equipment.

1. Never use gasoline as a cleaning solvent.
2. Never smoke or use a torch in the vicinity of flammable liquids, such as cleaning solvent, in open containers.
3. If welding or brazing is required on the machine, remove the fuel tank to a safe distance, at least 50 feet away.
4. Use the proper sized wrenches to avoid damage to fasteners and injury to yourself.
5. When loosening a tight or stuck nut, be guided by what would happen if the wrench should slip. Be careful; protect yourself accordingly.
6. When replacing a fastener, make sure to use one with the same measurements and strength as the

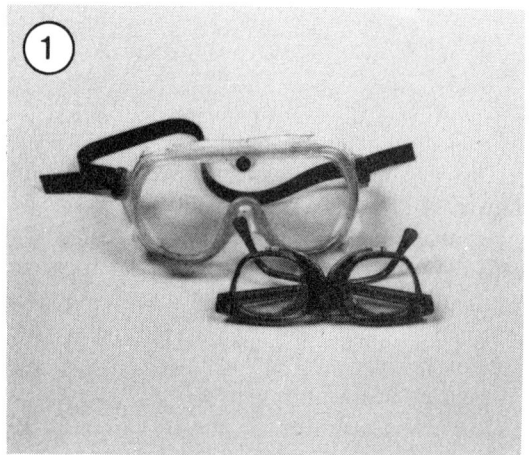

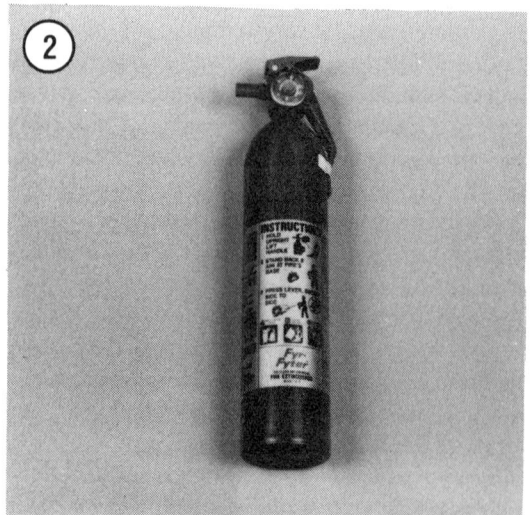

old one. Incorrect or mismatched fasteners can result in damage to the motorcycle and possible personal injury. Beware of fastener kits that are filled with cheap and poorly made nuts, bolts, washers and cotter pins. Refer to *Fasteners* in this chapter for additional information.

7. Keep all hand and power tools in good condition. Wipe off greasy and oily tools after using them. They are difficult to hold and can cause injury. Replace or repair worn or damaged tools.

8. Keep your work area clean and uncluttered.

9. Wear safety goggles (**Figure 1**) during all operations involving drilling, grinding, the use of a cold chisel or *anytime* you feel unsure about the safety of your eyes. Safety goggles should also be worn anytime solvent and compressed air is used to clean parts.

10. Keep an approved fire extinguisher (**Figure 2**) near your workbench and in your tow vehicle while at the race track. Be sure it is rated for gasoline (Class B) and electrical (Class C) fires.

11. When drying bearings or other rotating parts with compressed air, never allow the air jet to rotate the bearing or part. The air jet is capable of rotating the bearing at speeds far in excess of those for which they were designed. The bearing or rotating part is very likely to disintegrate and cause serious injury and damage. To prevent bearing damage when using compressed air, hold the inner bearing race by hand (**Figure 3**).

SERVICE HINTS

Most of the service procedures covered are straightforward and can be performed by anyone reasonably handy with tools. It is suggested, however, that you consider your own capabilities carefully before attempting any operation involving major disassembly.

1. "Front," as used in this manual, refers to the front of the motorcycle; the front of any component is the end closest to the front of the motorcycle. The "left-" and "right-hand" sides refer to the position of the parts as viewed by a rider sitting on the seat and facing forward. For example, the throttle control is on the right-hand side. These rules are simple, but confusion can cause a major inconvenience during service. See **Figure 4**.

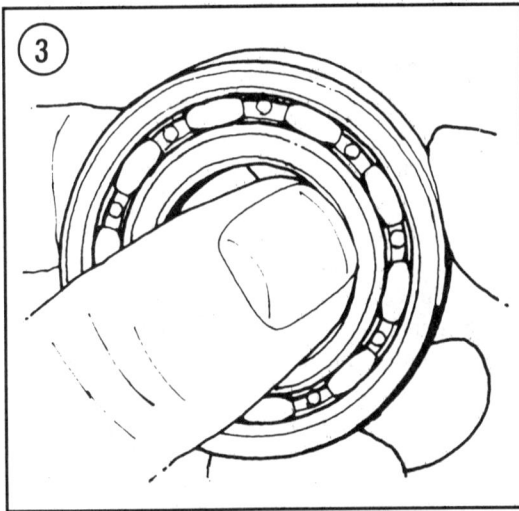

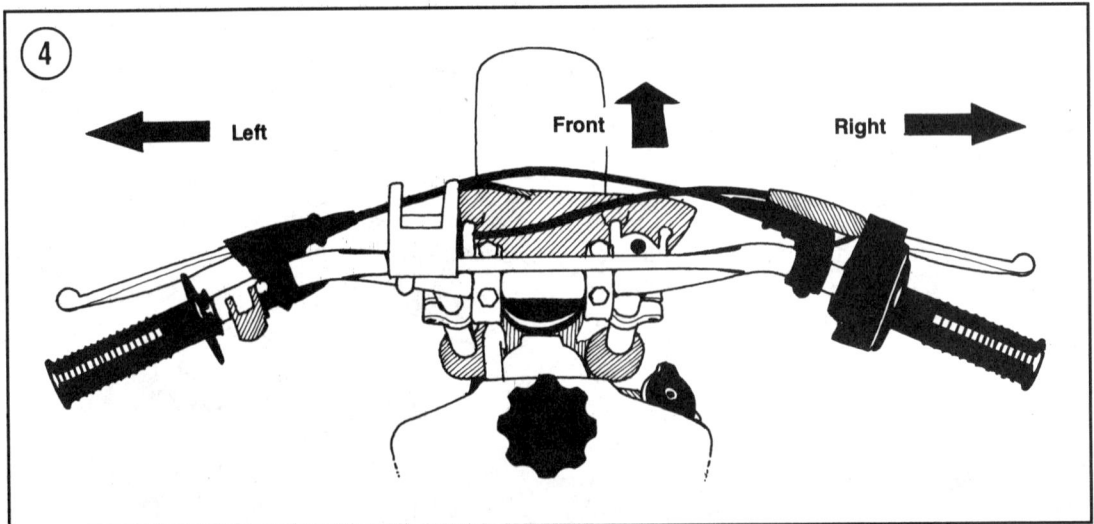

2. When disassembling any engine or drive component, mark the parts for location and mark all parts which mate together. Small parts, such as bolts, can be identified by placing them in plastic sandwich bags (**Figure 5**). Seal the bags and label them with masking tape and a marking pen. When reassembly is going to take place immediately, an accepted practice is to place nuts and bolts in a cupcake tin or egg carton in the order of disassembly.

3. Finished surfaces should be protected from physical damage or corrosion. Keep gasoline off painted surfaces.

4. Use penetrating oil on frozen or tight bolts, then strike the bolt head a few times with a hammer and punch (use a screwdriver on screws). Avoid the use of heat where possible, as it can warp, melt or affect the temper of parts. Heat also ruins finishes, especially paint and plastics. Additional information on removing frozen fasteners, repairing stripped threads and removing broken bolts and screws is described under *Mechanic's Tips* in this chapter.

5. No parts removed or installed (other than bushings and bearings) in the procedures given in this manual should require unusual force during disassembly or assembly. If a part is difficult to remove or install, find out why before proceeding.

6. Cover all openings after removing parts or components to prevent dirt, small tools, etc. from falling in.

7. Read each procedure *completely* while looking at the actual parts before starting a job. Make sure you *thoroughly* understand what is to be done and then carefully follow the procedure, step-by-step.

8. Recommendations are occasionally made to refer service or maintenance to a Kawasaki dealer or a specialist in a particular field. In these cases, the work will be done more quickly and economically than if you performed the job yourself.

9. In procedural steps, the term "replace" means to discard a defective part and replace it with a new or exchanged unit. "Overhaul" means to remove, disassemble, inspect, measure, repair or replace defective parts, reassemble and install major systems or parts.

10. Some operations require the use of a hydraulic press. It would be wiser to have these operations performed by a shop equipped for such work, rather than to try to do the job yourself with makeshift equipment that may damage your machine.

11. Repairs go much faster and easier if your machine is clean before you begin work. There are many special cleaners on the market, like Bel-Ray Degreaser, for washing the engine and related parts. Follow the manufacturer's directions on the container for the best results. Clean all oily or greasy parts with cleaning solvent as you remove them.

> *WARNING*
> *Never use gasoline as a cleaning agent. It presents an extreme fire hazard. Be sure to work in a well-ventilated area when using cleaning solvent. Keep a fire extinguisher, rated for gasoline fires, handy in any case.*

12. Much of the labor charges for repairs made by dealers are for the time involved during the removal, disassembly, assembly and reinstallation of other parts in order to reach the defective part. It is frequently possible to perform the preliminary operations yourself and then take the defective unit to the dealer for repair at considerable savings.

13. If special tools are required, make arrangements to get them before you start. It is frustrating and time-consuming to get partly into a job and then be unable to complete it.

14. Make diagrams (or take a Polaroid picture) wherever similar-appearing parts are found. For instance, crankcase bolts are often not the same length. You may think you can remember where everything came from, but mistakes are costly.

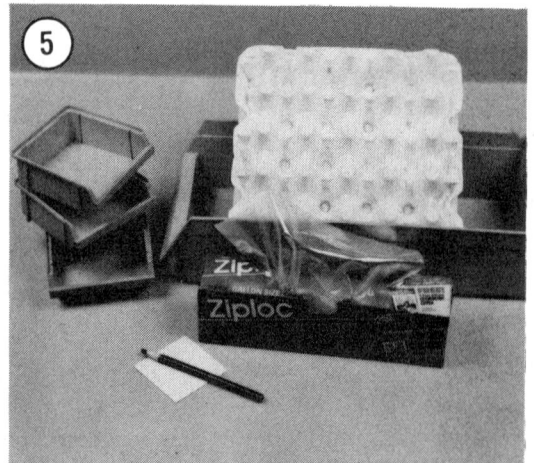

There is also the possibility that you may be sidetracked and not return to work for days or even weeks, in which the time carefully laid out parts may have become disturbed.

15. When assembling parts, be sure all shims and washers are installed exactly as they came out.

16. Whenever a rotating part butts against a stationary part, look for a shim or washer. Use new gaskets if there is any doubt about the condition of the old ones. A thin coat of silicone sealant on non-pressure type gaskets may help them seal more effectively.

17. When installing engine gaskets, always use Kawasaki replacement gaskets *without* sealer, unless specifically designated in the text. Kawasaki gaskets are designed to swell when in contact with oil. Gasket sealer prevents the gaskets from swelling as intended, which can result in oil leaks. Kawasaki gaskets are also cut from material of the precise thickness needed. Installation of a too thick or too thin gasket in a critical area could cause engine damage.

NOTE
If you're in a jam and your dealer does not have the correct gasket, you can purchase gasket material from an automotive parts store and make a gasket. When purchasing gasket material, measure the thickness of the old gasket and purchase gasket material with the same approximate thickness. Do not attempt to make a replacement head gasket with a gasket material.

18. Heavy grease can be used to hold small parts in place if they tend to fall out during assembly. However, keep grease and oil away from electrical components.

19. A carburetor is best cleaned by disassembling it and cleaning the parts with a carburetor cleaner. Never soak gaskets and rubber parts in any cleaners. Never use wire to clean out jets and air passages. They are easily damaged. Use compressed air to blow out the carburetor only if the float has been removed first.

20. When installing the "fold-over" type locking washers always use a new washer if possible. If a new washer is not available always fold-over a part of the washer that has not been previously folded. Reusing the same fold may cause the washer to break, resulting in a loose piece of metal adrift in the engine and also no locking action. When folding the washer over, start the fold with a screwdriver and finish it with a pair of pliers. If a punch or chisel is used to make the fold, the fold may be too sharp, thereby increasing the chances of the washer breaking under stress. Because these washers are inexpensive, it is recommended to keep several on hand.

21. Take your time and do the job right. Do not forget that a newly rebuilt engine must be broken in just like a new one.

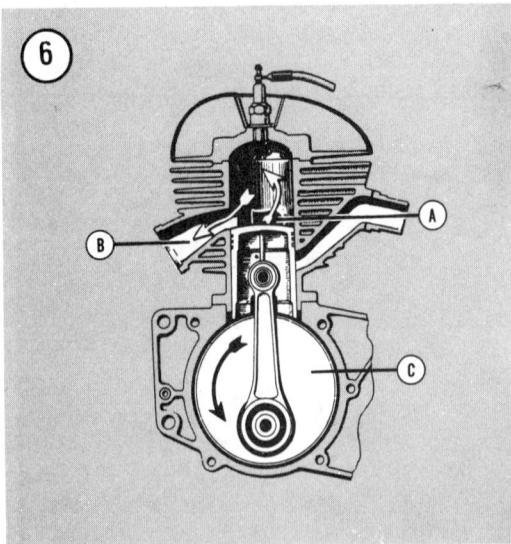

ENGINE OPERATION

All Kawasaki KX models are equipped with 2-stroke engines. During this discussion, assume that the crankshaft is rotating counterclockwise in **Figure 6**. As the piston travels downward, a transfer port (A) between the crankcase and the cylinder is uncovered. The exhaust gases leave the cylinder through the exhaust port (B), which is also opened by the downward movement of the piston. A fresh fuel/air charge, which has previously been compressed slightly, travels from the crankcase (C) to the cylinder through the transfer port (A) as the port opens. Since the incoming charge is under pressure, it rushes into the cylinder quickly and helps to expel the exhaust gases from the previous cycle.

Figure 7 illustrates the next phase of the cycle. As the crankshaft continues to rotate, the piston moves upward, closing the exhaust and transfer ports. As the piston continues upward, the air/fuel mixture in the cylinder is compressed. Notice also that a vacuum is created in the crankcase at the same time. Further upward movement of the piston uncovers the intake port (D). A fresh fuel/air charge is then drawn into the crankcase through the intake port because of the vacuum created by the upward piston movement.

The third phase is shown in **Figure 8**. As the piston approaches top dead center, the spark plug fires, igniting the compressed mixture. The piston is then driven downward by the expanding gases.

When the top of the piston uncovers the exhaust port, the fourth phase begins, as shown in **Figure 9**. The exhaust gases leave the cylinder through the exhaust port. As the piston continues downward, the intake port is closed and the mixture in the crankcase is compressed in preparation for the next cycle.

It can be seen from this discussion that every downward stroke of the piston is a power stroke.

WASHING THE BIKE

Dirt bikes get dirty. If you are riding your bike and maintaining it properly, you will spend a good deal of time cleaning it. After each riding session, wash the bike. It will make maintenance and service procedures quick and easy. More important, proper cleaning will prevent dirt from falling into critical areas undetected. Failing to clean the bike or cleaning it incorrectly will add to your maintenance costs and shop time because dirty parts wear out prematurely. It's unthinkable that your bike could break during a moto because of improper cleaning, but it can happen.

When cleaning your bike, you will need a few tools, shop rags, scrub brush, bucket, liquid cleaner and access to water. Many riders use a coin-operated car wash. Coin-operated car washes are convenient and quick, but with improper use, the high water pressure can do your bike more damage than good.

NOTE
A safe biodegradable, non-toxic and non-flammable liquid cleaner that
works well for washing your bike as well as removing grease and oil from engine and suspension parts is Simple Green. Simple Green can be purchased through some supermarket, hardware, garden and discount supply houses. Follow the directions on the container for recommended dilution ratios.

When cleaning your bike, and especially when using a spray type degreaser, remember that what goes on the bike will rinse off and drip onto your driveway or into your yard. If you can, use a degreaser at a coin-operated car wash. If you are cleaning your bike at home, place thick cardboard or newspapers underneath the bike to catch the oil and grease deposits that are rinsed off.

1. Place the bike on a stand.
2. Remove the air filter unit as described in Chapter Three. Insert a dry rag into the carburetor throat to keep water from getting inside the engine.
3. Check the following before washing the bike:
    a. Make sure the gas cap is screwed on tightly.
    b. Make sure the oil fill cap is tight.
    c. Plug the silencer opening with a large cork or rag.
    d. Make sure the radiator cap is correctly installed on *liquid-cooled* models.
4. Wash the bike from top to bottom with soapy water. Use the scrub brush to get excess dirt out of the wheel rims and engine crannies. Concentrate on the upper controls, engine, side panels and gas

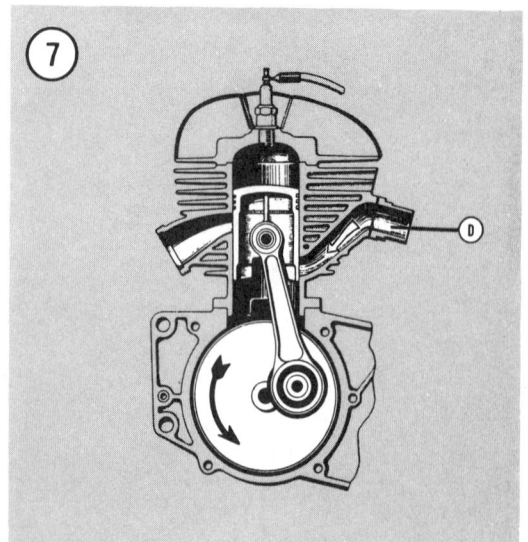

tank during this wash cycle. Don't forget to wash dirt and mud from underneath the fenders.

5. Remove the gas tank, side panels and seat. Wrap a plastic bag around the ignition coil and CDI unit. Concentrate the second wash cycle on the frame tube members, outer air box areas, suspension linkage, rear shock and swing arm.

6. Direct the hose underneath the engine and swing arm. Wash this area thoroughly. If this area is extremely dirty, you may want to lay the bike on its side.

7. The final wash is the rinse. Use cold water without soap and spray the whole motorcycle

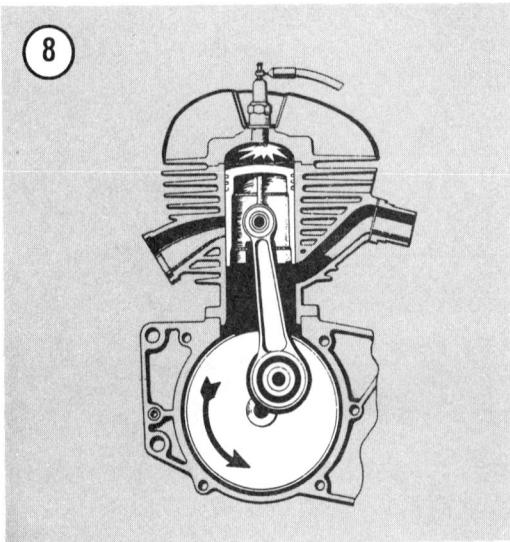

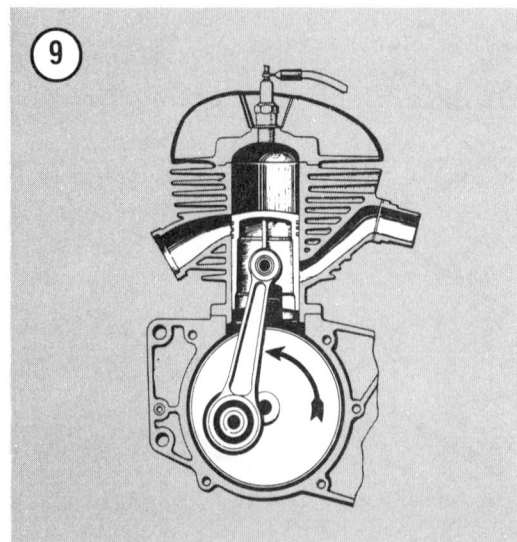

again. Use as much time and care when rinsing the bike as when washing it. Builtup soap deposits will quickly corrode electrical connections and remove the natural oils from tires, causing premature cracks and wear. Make sure you thoroughly rinse the bike off.

8. Before taking the bike into the garage, wipe it dry with a shop rag. Inspect the machine as you dry it for further signs of dirt and grime. Make a quick visual inspection of the frame and other painted pieces. Spray any worn-down spots with WD-40 or Bel-Ray 6-in-1 to prevent rust from building on the bare metal. When the bike is back at your work area you can repaint the bare areas with touch-up paint. A quick shot from a paint can each time you work on the bike will keep it looking sharp and stop rust from building and weakening parts.

TORQUE SPECIFICATIONS

The materials used in the manufacture of your bike can be subjected to uneven torque stresses if the fasteners used to hold the sub-assemblies are not installed and torqued correctly. Improper bolt tightening can cause cylinder head warpage, crankcase leaks, premature bearing and seal failure and suspension failure from loose or missing fasteners. An accurate torque wrench (described in this chapter) should be used together with the torque specifications listed at the end of most chapters.

Torque specifications throughout this manual are given in Newton-meters (N·m) and foot-pounds (ft.-lb.).

Table 5 lists general torque specifications for nuts and bolts that are not listed in the respective chapters. To use the table, first determine the size of the nut or bolt by measuring it with a vernier caliper. **Figure 10** and **Figure 11** show how to do this.

FASTENERS

The materials and designs of the various fasteners used on your bike are not arrived at by chance or accident. Fastener design determines the type of tool required to work the fastener. Fastener material is carefully selected to decrease the possibility of physical failure.

Nuts, bolts and screws are manufactured in a wide range of thread patterns. To join a nut and bolt, the diameter of the bolt and the diameter of the hole in the nut must be the same. It is just as important that the threads on both be properly matched.

The best way to tell if the threads on 2 fasteners are matched is to turn the nut on the bolt (or the bolt into the threaded hole in a piece of equipment) with fingers only. Be sure both pieces are clean. If much force is required, check the thread condition on each fastener. If the thread condition is good, but the fasteners jam, the threads are not compatible. A thread pitch gauge (**Figure 12**) can also be used to determine pitch. Kawasaki motorcycles are manufactured with ISO (International Organization for Standardization) metric fasteners. The threads are cut differently than that of American fasteners (**Figure 13**).

Most threads are cut so that the fastener must be turned clockwise to tighten it. These are called right-hand threads. Some fasteners have left-hand threads; they must be turned counterclockwise to be tightened. Left-hand threads are used in locations where normal rotation of the equipment would tend to loosen a right-hand threaded fastener.

ISO Metric Screw Threads

ISO (International Organization for Standardization) metric threads come in 3 standard thread sizes: coarse, fine and constant pitch. The ISO coarse pitch is used for most all common fastener applications. The fine pitch thread is used on certain precision tools and instruments. The constant pitch thread is used mainly on machine parts and not for fasteners. The constant pitch thread, however, is used on all metric thread spark plugs.

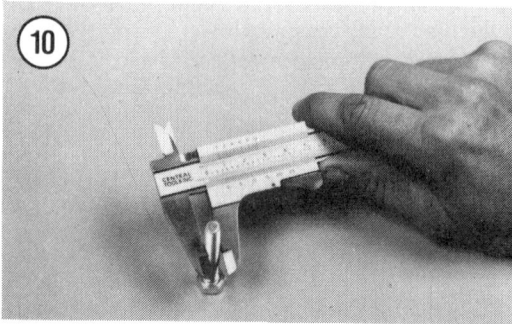

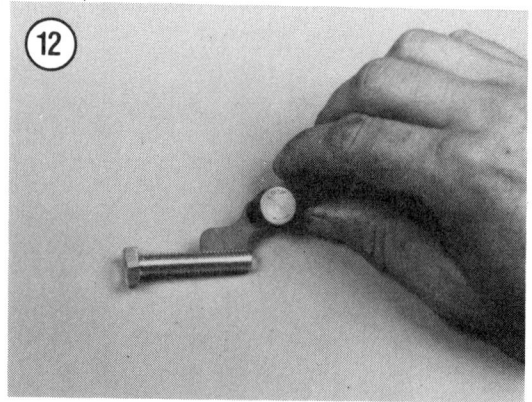

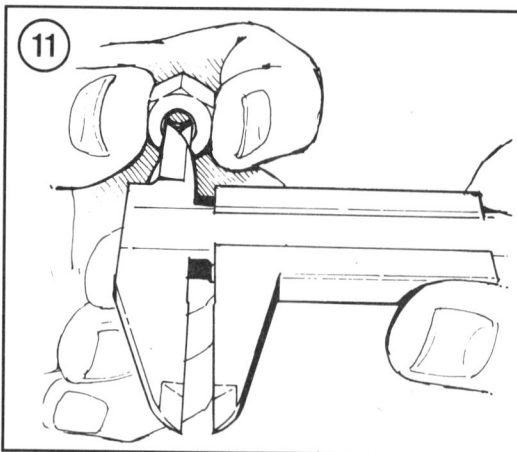

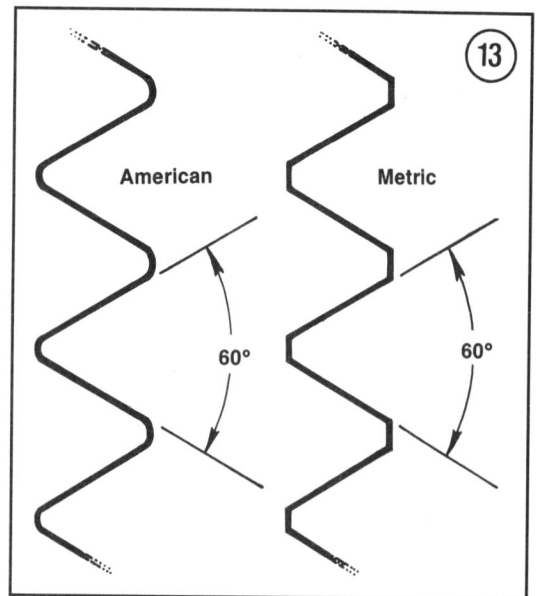

ISO metric threads are specified by the capital letter M followed by the diameter in millimeters and the pitch (or the distance between each thread) in millimeters separated by the sign "—". For example a M—1.25 bolt is one that has a diameter of 8 millimeters with a distance of 1.25 millimeters between each thread. The measurement across 2 flats on the head of the bolt (**Figure 14**) or nut indicates the proper wrench size to be used. **Figure 10** shows how to determine bolt diameter.

NOTE
*When purchasing a bolt from a dealer or parts store, it's important to know how to specify bolt length. The correct way to measure bolt length is by measuring the length starting from underneath the bolt head to the end of the bolt (**Figure 15**). Installing a bolt that is too long in a blind hole can cause damage. Always measure bolt length in this manner to prevent from purchasing bolts that are the incorrect length.*

Machine Screws

There are many different types of machine screws. **Figure 16** shows a number of screw heads requiring different types of turning tools. Heads

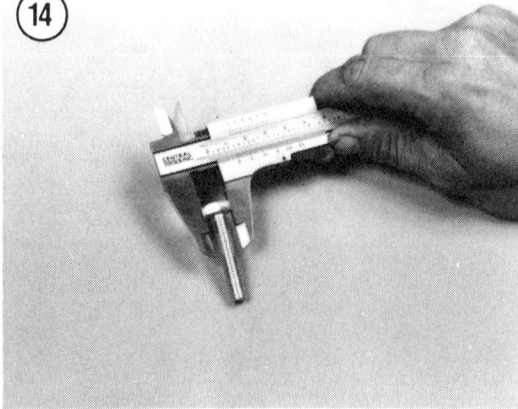

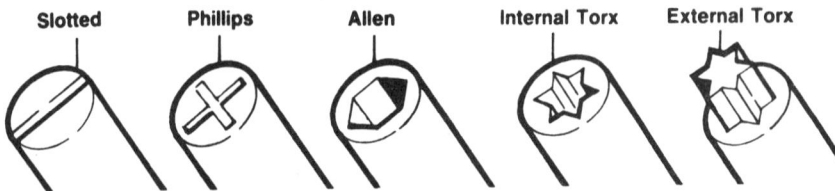

OPENINGS FOR TURNING TOOLS

Slotted   Phillips   Allen   Internal Torx   External Torx

are also designed to protrude above the metal (round) or to be slightly recessed in the metal (flat). See **Figure 17**.

Bolts

Commonly called bolts, the technical name for these fasteners is cap screw. Metric bolts are described by the diameter and pitch (or the distance between each thread).

Nuts

Nuts are manufactured in a variety of types and sizes. Most are hexagonal (6-sided) and fit on bolts, screws and studs with the same diameter and pitch.

Figure 18 shows several types of nuts. The common nut is generally used with a lockwasher. Self-locking nuts have a nylon insert which prevents the nut from loosening; no lockwasher is required. Wing nuts are designed for fast removal by hand. Wing nuts are used for convenience in non-critical locations.

To indicate the size of a metric nut, manufacturers specify the diameter of the opening and the thread pitch. This is similar to bolt specifications, but without the length dimension. The measurement across 2 flats on the nut indicates the proper wrench size to be used.

Prevailing Torque Fasteners

Commonly referred to as self-locking fasteners, prevailing torque fasteners (bolts, screws and nuts) incorporate a system that develops an interference between the bolt, screw, nut or tapped hold threads. Interference is achieved in various ways: by distorting threads, coating threads with dry adhesive or nylon, distorting the top of an all-metal nut, using a nylon insert in the center or at the top of a nut, etc.

Prevailing torque fasteners offer greater holding strength and better vibration resistance. Some prevailing torque fasteners can be reused if in good condition. Others, like the nylon insert nut, form an initial locking condition when the nut is first installed; the nylon forms closely to the bolt thread pattern, thus reducing any tendency for the nut to loosen. When the nut is removed, the locking efficiency is greatly reduced. For greatest safety, it is recommended that you install new prevailing torque fasteners whenever they are removed.

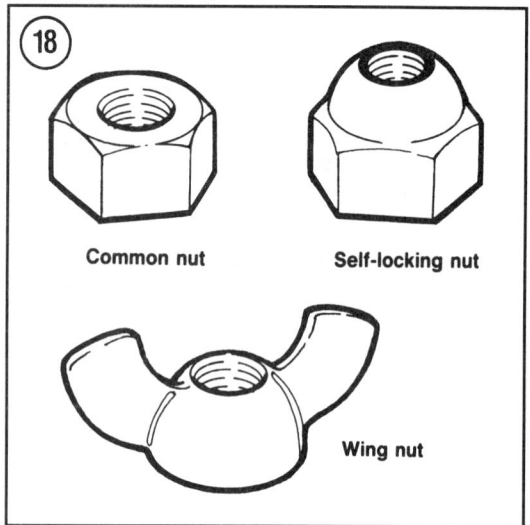

Common nut   Self-locking nut

Wing nut

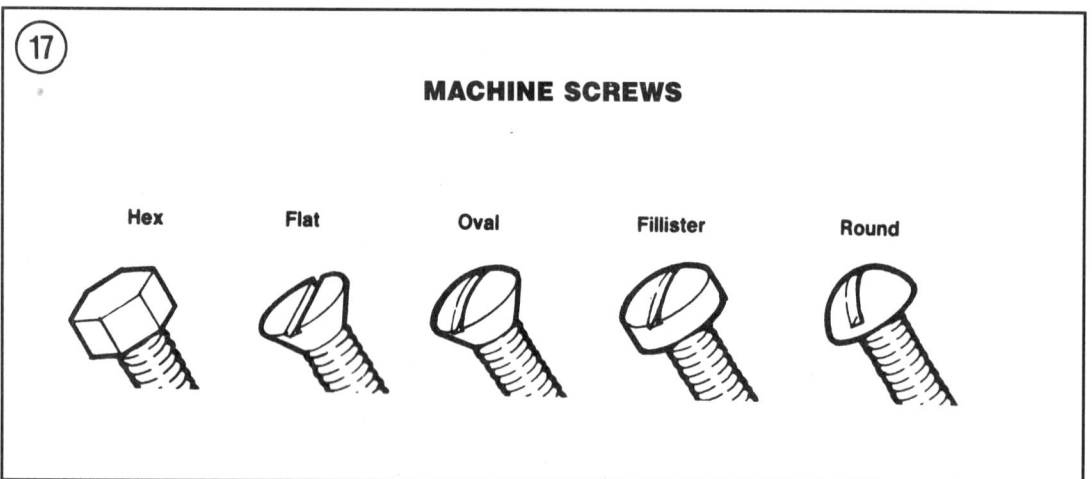

MACHINE SCREWS

Hex   Flat   Oval   Fillister   Round

Washers

There are 2 basic types of washers: flat washers and lockwashers. Flat washers are simple discs with a hole to fit a screw or bolt. Lockwashers are designed to prevent a fastener from working loose due to vibration, expansion and contraction. **Figure 19** shows several types of washers. Washers are also used in the following functions:

a. As spacers.

b. To prevent galling or damage of the equipment by the fastener.

c. To help distribute fastener load during torquing.

d. As seals.

Note that flat washers are often used between a lockwasher and a fastener to provide a smooth bearing surface. This allows the fastener to be turned easily with a tool.

Cotter Pins

Cotter pins are used in critical areas where a loosened fastener could cause severe component damage or result in personal injury. When using a cotter pin, the threaded stud, shaft or bolt must have a hole in it. The mating nut or locknut normally has castellations around its outer edge (**Figure 20**). When the nut is tightened, the castellations on the edge of the nut must align with the hole in the stud or bolt. The cotter pin is then inserted through the nut and the threaded part.

> *NOTE*
> *If after tightening a nut to a specific torque specification you find that the nut castellations do not align with the hole in the threaded part, tighten the nut so that the holes align. Do **not** loosen the nut.*

Figure 20 shows a correctly installed cotter pin. Note how the head of the cotter pin fits into the nut and how the legs are bent. An improperly installed cotter pin will have less holding power. During reassembly, do not reuse a cotter pin. The legs could break and allow the cotter pin to fall out and perhaps the fastener to unscrew itself. If a cotter pin is too long, trim the legs with wire cutters before locking it in place.

Circlips

Circlips (or snap rings) can be internal or external design. They are used to retain items on shafts (external type) or within tubes (internal type). In some applications, circlips of varying thicknesses are used to control the end play of parts assemblies. These are often called selective circlips. Circlips should be replaced during installation, as removal weakens and deforms them.

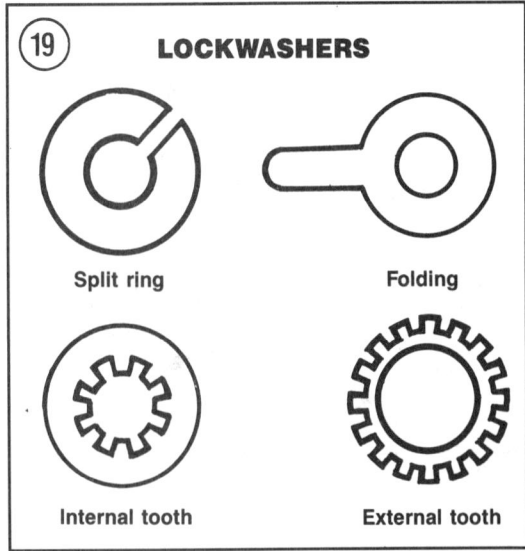

19 LOCKWASHERS

Split ring   Folding

Internal tooth   External tooth

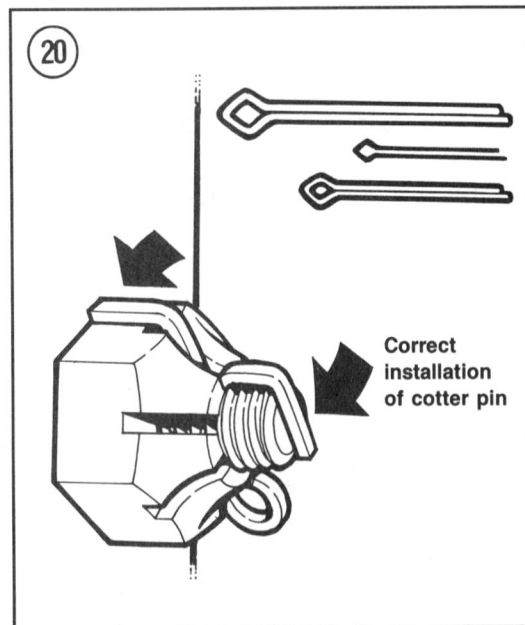

20

Correct installation of cotter pin

Two basic styles of circlips are available: machined and stamped circlips. Machined circlips (**Figure 21**) can be installed in either direction (shaft or housing) because both faces are machined, thus creating two sharp edges. Stamped circlips (**Figure 22**) are manufactured with one sharp edge and one rounded edge. When installing stamped circlips in a thrust situation, the sharp edge must face away from the part producing the thrust. When installing circlips, observe the following:

a. Compress or expand circlips only enough to install or remove them.

b. After the circlip is installed, make sure it is completely seated in its groove.

c. Transmission circlips become worn with use and increase gear side play. For this reason, it is generally better to replace all transmission circlips whenever the transmission is disassembled.

LUBRICANTS

Periodic lubrication assures long life for any type of equipment. The *type* of lubricant used is just as important as the lubrication service itself, although in an emergency the wrong type of lubricant is better than none at all. The following paragraphs describe the types of lubricants most often used on motorcycle equipment. Be sure to follow the manufacturer's recommendations for lubricant types.

Generally, all liquid lubricants are called "oil." They may be mineral-based (including petroleum bases), natural-based (vegetable and animal bases), synthetic-based or emulsions (mixtures). "Grease" is an oil to which a thickening base has been added so that the end product is semi-solid. Grease is often classified by the type of thickener added; lithium soap is commonly used.

Engine Oil

Four-stroke oil

Four-stroke oil for motorcycle and automotive engines is graded by the American Petroleum Institute (API) and the Society of Automotive Engineers (SAE) in several categories. Oil containers display these ratings on the top or label.

API oil grade is indicated by letters; oils for gasoline engines are identified by an "S".

Viscosity is an indication of the oil's thickness. The SAE assigns numbers which indicate viscosity; thin oils have low numbers while thick oils have high numbers. A "W" after the number, such as 5W or 10W, indicates that the viscosity testing was done at a low temperature to simulate cold weather operation.

Multi-grade oil, such as 10W-40, maintains the same viscosity during different temperatures. This allows the oil to perform efficiently across a wide range of temperatures.

Four-stroke oil used in your KX lubricates the transmission and clutch components. Gears tend to shear the polymers within the oil which control viscosity. For this reason, you should always use an oil designed specifically for motorcycles. Motorcycle gear oil contains additional amounts of EP (extreme pressure) additives to prevent oil shear. The SAE and API oil ratings do not address this unique need.

NOTE
The oil viscosity numbers on motorcycle designated gear oils differ from regular SAE numbers. Refer to the application numbers on the back of the

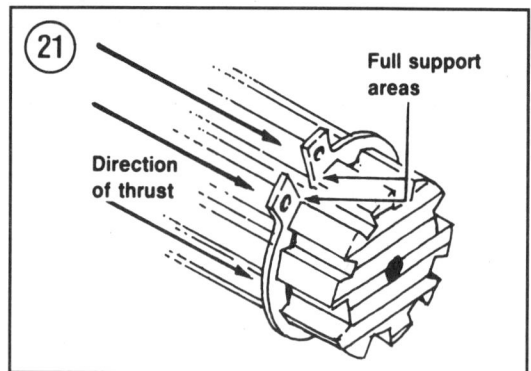

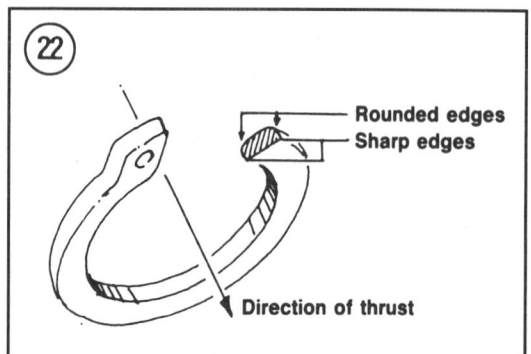

oil can (specified for motorcycle use) when cross-referencing oil viscosity.

Two-stroke engine oil

Lubrication for a 2-stroke engine is provided by oil mixed with the incoming fuel/air mixture. Some of the oil mist settles out in the crankcase, lubricating the crankshaft and the connecting rod lower end. The rest of the oil enters the combustion chamber to lubricate the piston rings and cylinder walls. This oil is burned during the combustion process.

Engine oil must have several special qualities to work well in a 2-stroke engine. It must mix easily and stay in suspension in gasoline. When burned, it can't leave behind excessive deposits. It must be appropriate for the high temperatures associated with 2-stroke engines.

In addition to oil grade, manufacturer's specify the ratio of gasoline to oil required during break-in and normal engine operation. Using too little oil will cause excessive engine wear and

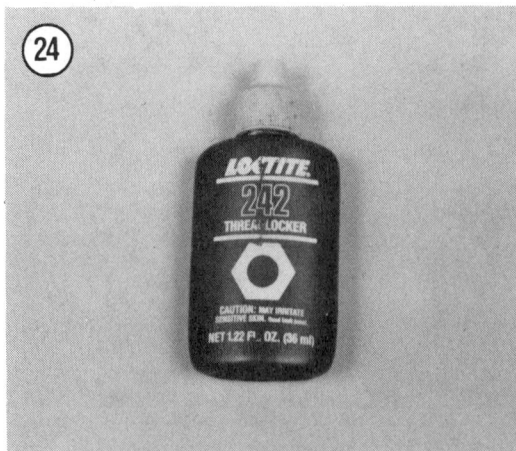

overheating and result in seizure. Too much oil will cause spark plug fouling and excessive carbon buildup in the combustion chamber and exhaust port.

Grease

Greases are graded by the National Lubricating Grease Institute (NLGI). Greases are graded by number according to the consistency of the grease; these range from No. 000 to No. 6, with No. 6 being the most solid. A typical multipurpose grease is NLGI No. 2. For specific applications, equipment manufacturers may require grease with an additive such as molybdenum disulfide (MOS2). See **Figure 23.**

RTV GASKET SEALANT

Room temperature vulcanizing (RTV) sealant is used on some pre-formed gaskets and to seal some components. RTV is a silicone gel supplied in tubes and can be purchased in a number of different colors.

Moisture in the air causes RTV to cure. Always place the cap on the tube as soon as possible when using RTV. RTV has a shelf life of one year and will not cure properly when the shelf life has expired. Check the expiration date on RTV tubes before using and keep partially used tubes tightly sealed.

Applying RTV Sealant

Clean all gasket residue from mating surfaces. Surfaces should be clean and free of oil and dirt. Remove all RTV gasket material from blind attaching holes, as it can cause a "hydraulic" effect and affect bolt torque.

Apply RTV sealant in a continuous bead 2-3 mm (0.08-0.12 in.) thick. Circle all mounting holes unless otherwise specified. Torque mating parts within 10 minutes after application.

THREADLOCK

A threadlock should be used to help secure many of the fasteners used on the bike. A threadlock will lock fasteners against vibration loosening and seal against leaks. Loctite 242 (blue) and 271 (red) are recommended for many threadlock requirements described in this manual (**Figure 24**).

Loctite 242 (blue) is a medium strength threadlock and component disassembly can be performed with normal hand tools. Loctite 271 (red) is a high strength threadlock and heat or special tools, such as a press or puller, may be required for component disassembly.

Applying Threadlock

Surfaces should be clean and free of oil and dirt. If a threadlock was previously applied to the component, this residue should also be removed.

Shake the Loctite container thoroughly and apply to both parts. Assemble parts and/or tighten fasteners.

PARTS REPLACEMENT

Kawasaki makes frequent changes during a model year, some minor, some relatively major. When you order parts from the dealer or other parts distributor, always order by frame and engine numbers. The frame number is stamped on the frame steering neck (**Figure 25**). The engine number is stamped on the crankcase (**Figure 26**). Write the numbers down and carry them with you. Compare new parts to old before purchasing them. If they are not alike, have the parts manager explain the difference to you. **Table 1** lists engine serial numbers for all KX models covered in this manual.

OPTIONAL PARTS

Depending on model year and availability, Kawasaki sells optional carburetor jets (**Figure 27**), sprockets and suspension components through their dealer parts departments. Contact your dealer for additional information.

BASIC HAND TOOLS

Many of the procedures in this manual can be carried out with simple hand tools and test equipment familiar to the average home mechanic. Keep your tools clean and in a tool box. Keep them organized with the sockets and related drives together, the open-end combination wrenches together, etc. After using a tool, wipe off dirt and grease with a clean cloth and return the tool to its correct place in your tool box.

Top quality tools are essential; they are also more economical in the long run. If you are now starting to build your tool collection, stay away from the "advertised specials" featured at some parts houses, discount stores and chain drug stores. These are usually a poor grade tool that can be sold cheaply and that is exactly what they are—*cheap*. They are usually made of inferior material, and are thick, heavy and clumsy. Their rough finish makes them difficult to clean and they usually don't last very long. If it is ever your misfortune to use such tools, you will probably find out that the wrenches do not fit the heads of bolts and nuts correctly and will damage the fastener.

Quality tools are made of alloy steel and are heat treated for greater strength. They are lighter and

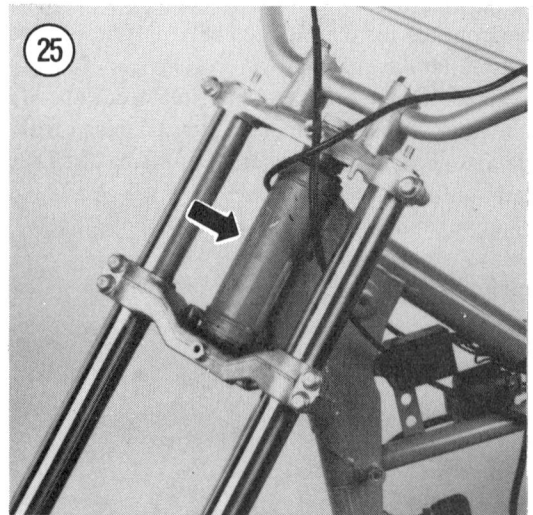

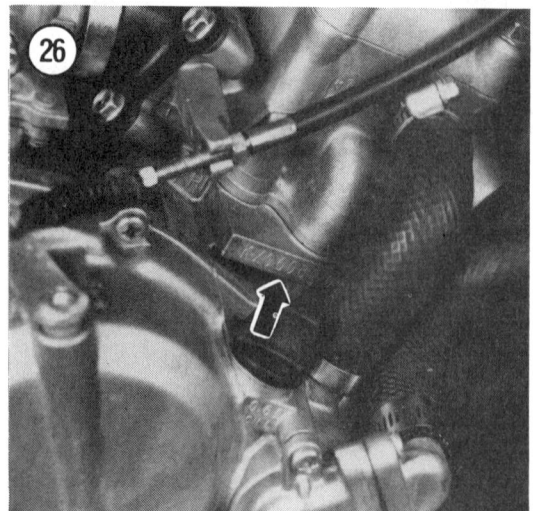

better balanced than cheap ones. Their surface is smooth, making them a pleasure to work with and easy to clean. The initial cost of good quality tools may be more but they are cheaper in the long run. Don't try to buy everything in all sizes in the beginning; do it a little at a time until you have the necessary tools.

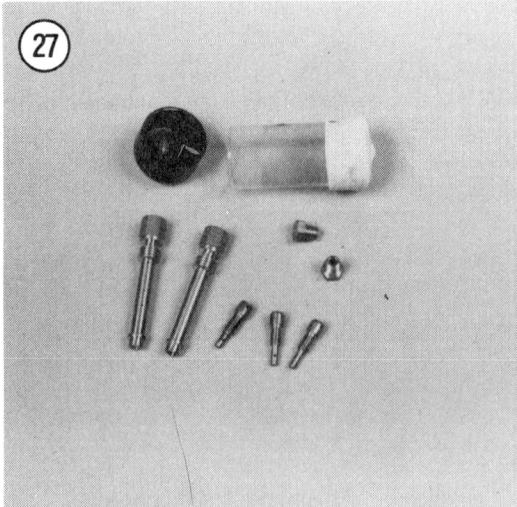

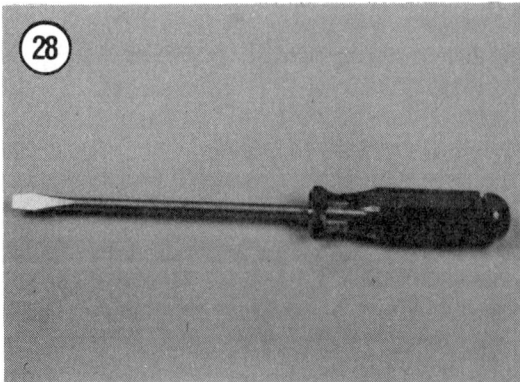

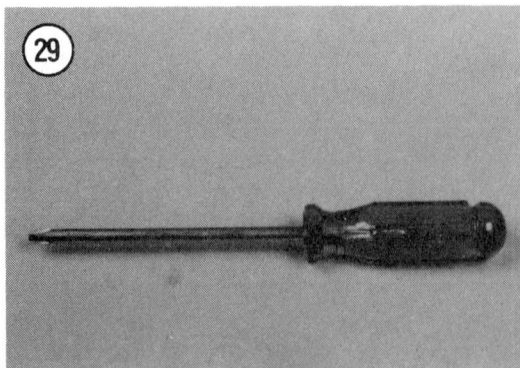

The following tools are required to perform virtually any repair job. Each tool is described and the recommended size given for starting a tool collection. Additional tools and some duplicates may be added as you become familiar with the vehicle. The KX model is built with metric standard fasteners, so if you are starting your collection now, buy metric sizes.

Screwdrivers

The screwdriver is a very basic tool, but if used improperly it will do more damage than good. The slot on a screw has a definite dimension and shape. A screwdriver must be selected to conform with that shape. Use a small screwdriver for small screws and a large one for large screws or the screw head will be damaged.

Two basic types of screwdriver are required: common (flat-blade) screwdrivers (**Figure 28**) and Phillips screwdrivers (**Figure 29**).

Screwdrivers are available in sets which often include an assortment of common and Phillips blades. If you buy them individually, buy at least the following:

a. Common screwdriver—5/16 × 6 in. blade.
b. Common screwdriver—3/8 × 12 in. blade.
c. Phillips screwdriver—size 2 tip, 6 in. blade.

Use screwdrivers only for driving screws. Never use a screwdriver for prying or chiseling metal. Do not try to remove a Phillips or Allen head screw with a common screwdriver (unless the screw has a combination head that will accept either type); you can damage the head so that the proper tool will be unable to remove it.

Keep screwdrivers in the proper condition and they will last longer and perform better. Always keep the tip of a common screwdriver in good condition. **Figure 30** shows how to grind the tip to the proper shape if it becomes damaged. Note the symmetrical sides of the tip.

Pliers

Pliers come in a wide range of types and sizes. Pliers are useful for cutting, bending and crimping. They should never be used to cut hardened objects or to turn bolts or nuts. **Figure 31** shows several pliers useful in motorcycle repair.

Each type of pliers has a specialized function. Slip-joint pliers and are used mainly for holding things and for bending. Needlenose pliers are used to hold or bend small objects. Water pump pliers (commonly referred to as channel locks) can be adjusted to hold various sizes of objects; the jaws remain parallel to grip around objects such as pipe or tubing. There are many more types of pliers.

CAUTION
Pliers should not be used for loosening or tightening nuts or bolts. The pliers sharp teeth will grind off the nut or bolt corners and damage the fastener.

CAUTION
If slip-joint pliers are going to be used to hold an object with a finished surface that can be easily damaged, wrap the object with tape or cardboard for protection.

Vise Grips

Vise Grips (**Figure 32**) are used to hold objects very tightly while another task is performed on the object. While Vise Grips work well, caution should be followed with their use. Because Vise Grips exert more force than regular pliers, their sharp jaws will permanently scar the object. In addition, when Vise Grips are locked in position, they can crush or deform thin wall material.

Vise Grips are available in many types for more specific tasks.

Circlip Pliers

Circlip pliers (**Figure 33**) are special in that they are only used to remove circlips from shafts or within engine or suspension housings. When purchasing circlip pliers, there are two kinds to distinguish from. External pliers (spreading) are used to remove circlips that fit on the outside of a shaft. Internal pliers (squeezing) are used to remove circlips which fit inside a housing.

Box-end, Open-end and Combination Wrenches

Box-end and open-end wrenches are available in sets or separately in a variety of sizes.

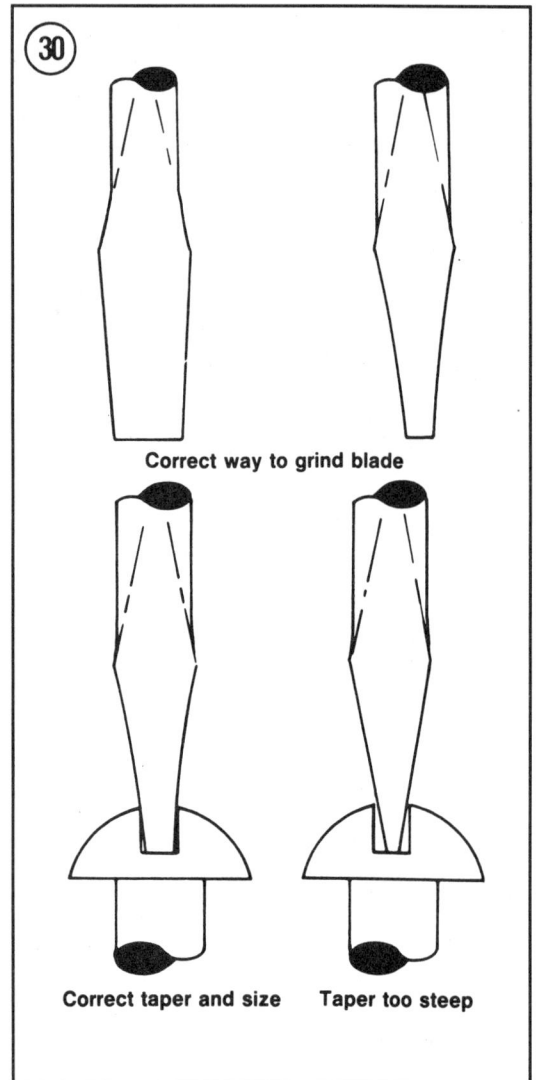

Correct way to grind blade

Correct taper and size   Taper too steep

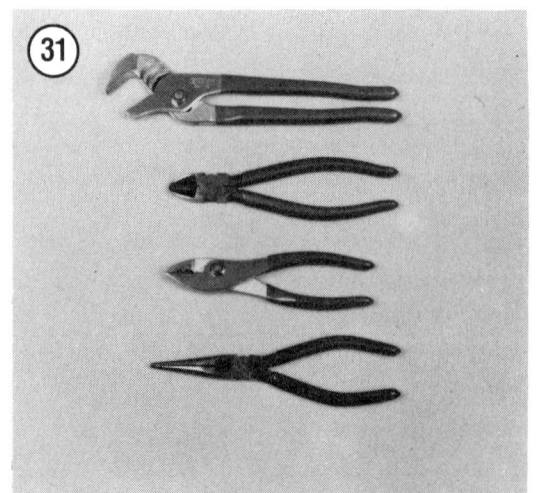

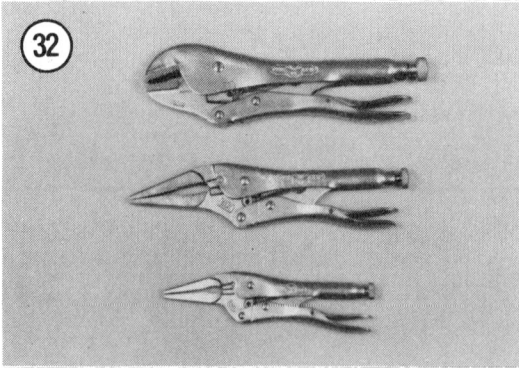

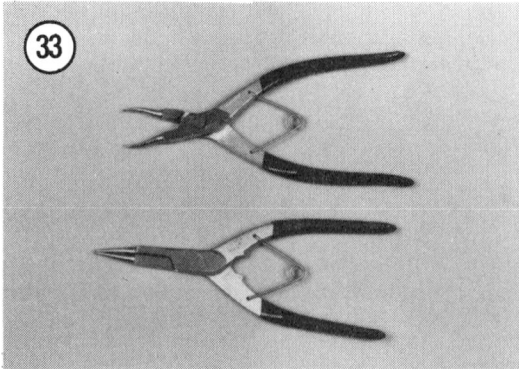

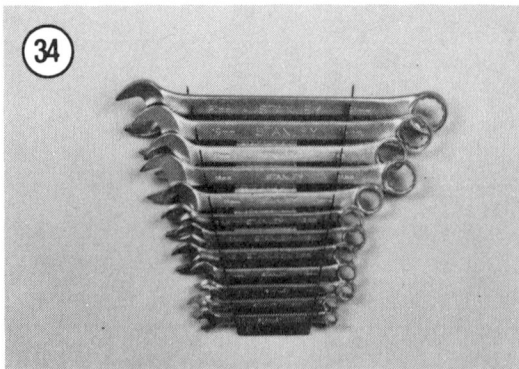

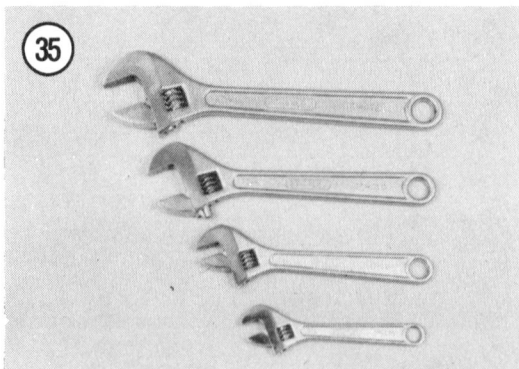

On open-end and box-end wrenches, the number stamped near the end refers to the distance between 2 parallel flats on the head of a nut or bolt. On combination wrenches, the number is stamped near the center.

Open-end wrenches are speedy and work best in areas with limited overhead access. Their wide jaws make them unsuitable for situations where the bolt or nut is sunken in a well or close to the edge of a casting. These wrenches only grip on two flats of a fastener so if either the fastener head or wrench jaws are worn, the wrench may slip off.

Box-end wrenches require clear overhead access to the fastener, but can work well in situations where the fastener head is close to another part. They grip on all six edges of a fastener for a very secure grip. They are available in either 6-point or 12-point. The 6-point gives superior holding power and durability but requires a greater swinging radius. The 12-point works better in situations with limited swinging radius.

Combination wrenches (**Figure 34**) have open end on one side and box-end on the other with both ends being the same size. These wrenches are favored by professionals because of their versatility.

No matter what style of wrench you choose, proper use is important to prevent personal injury. When using a wrench, get in the habit of pulling the wrench toward you. This reduces the risk of injuring your hand should the wrench slip. If you have to push the wrench away from you to loosen or tighten a fastener, open and push with the palm of your hand. This technique gets your fingers and knuckles out of the way should the wrench slip. Before using a wrench, always think ahead as to what could happen if the wrench should slip or if the bolt should strip out or break.

Adjustable Wrenches

An adjustable wrench (sometimes called a Crescent wrench) can be adjusted to fit nearly any nut or bolt head which has clear access around its entire perimeter. Adjustable wrenches are best used as a backup wrench to keep a large nut or bolt from turning while the other end is being loosened or tightened with a proper wrench. See **Figure 35**.

Adjustable wrenches have only two gripping surfaces which makes them more subject to slipping off the fastener and damaging the part and possibly your hand. Refer to *Box-end, Open-end and Combination Wrenches* in this chapter.

These wrenches are directional; the solid jaw must be the one transmitting the force. If you use the adjustable jaw to transmit the force, it will loosen and possibly slip off.

Adjustable wrenches come in all sizes but something in the 6 to 8 inch range is recommended as an all-purpose wrench.

Socket Wrenches

This type is undoubtedly the fastest, safest and most convenient to use. Sockets which attach to a ratchet handle (**Figure 36**) are available with 6-point or 12-point openings and 1/4, 3/8, 1/2 and 3/4 in. drives (**Figure 37**). The drive size indicates the size of the square hole which mates with the ratchet handle.

Torque Wrench

A torque wrench (**Figure 38**) is used with a socket to measure how tightly a nut or bolt is installed. They come in a wide price range and with either 3/8 or 1/2 in. square drive. The drive size indicates the size of the square drive which mates with the socket.

Impact Driver

This tool makes removal of tight fasteners easy and eliminates damage to bolts and screw slots. Impact drivers and interchangeable bits (**Figure 39**) are available at most large hardware and motorcycle dealers. Sockets can also be used with a hand impact driver. However, make sure the socket is designed for impact use. Do not use regular hand type sockets, as they may shatter.

Hammers

The correct hammer (**Figure 40**) is necessary for repairs. Use only a hammer with a face (or head) of rubber or plastic or the soft-faced type that is filled with buckshot. These are sometimes necessary in engine teardowns. *Never* use a metal-faced hammer on engine or suspension parts, as severe damage will result in most cases. You can always produce the same amount of force with a soft-faced hammer. A metal-faced hammer, however, will be required when using a hand impact driver.

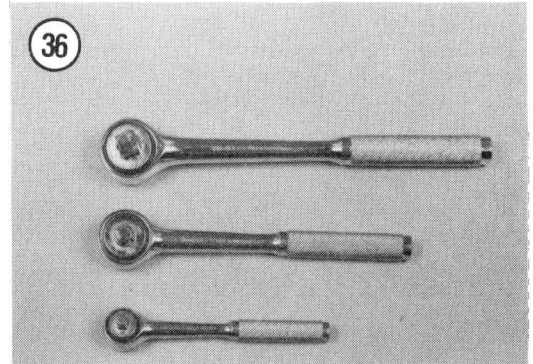

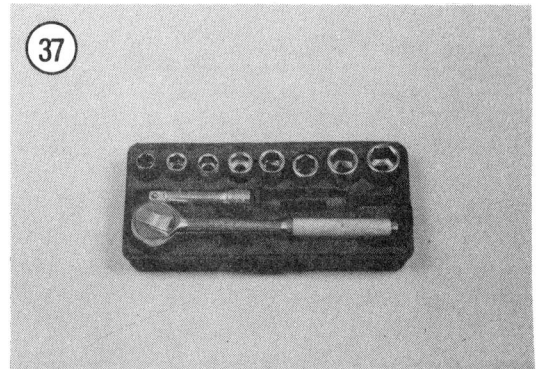

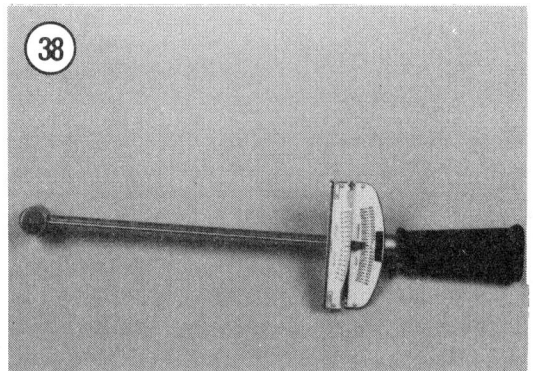

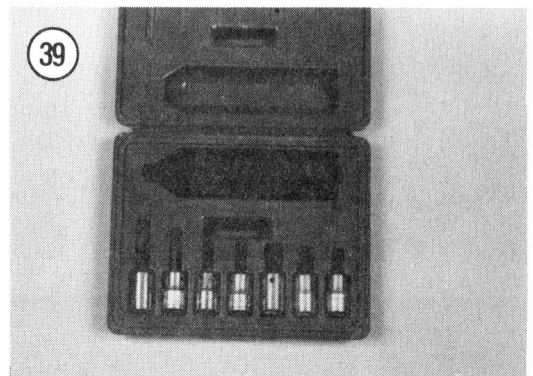

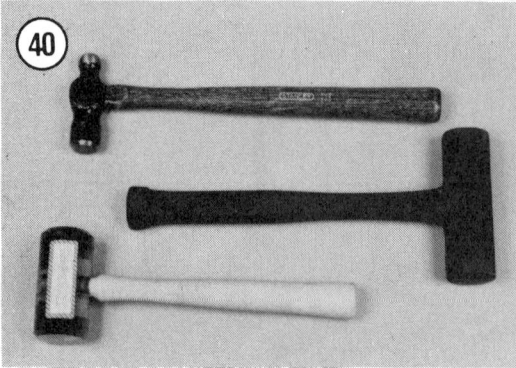

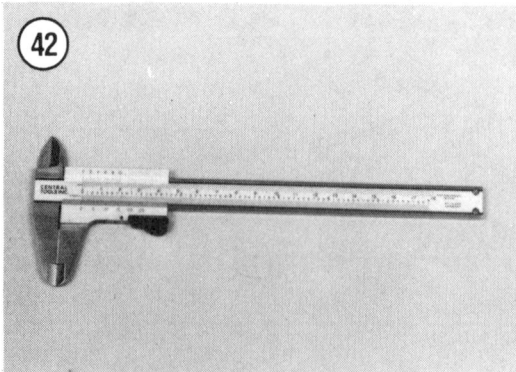

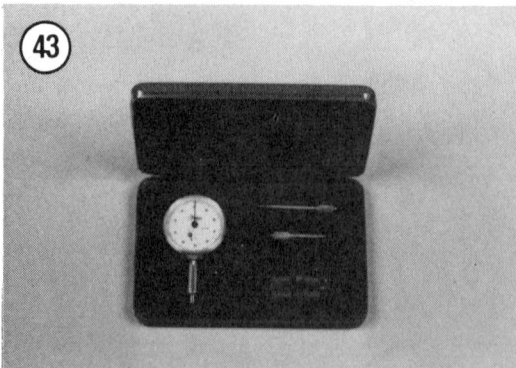

PRECISION MEASURING TOOLS

Measurement is an important part of motorcycle service. When performing many of the service procedures in this manual, you will be required to make a number of measurements. These include basic checks such as engine compression and spark plug gap. As you get deeper into engine disassembly and service, measurements will be required to determine the condition of the piston and cylinder bore, crankshaft runout and so on. When making these measurements, the degree of accuracy will dictate which tool is required. Precision measuring tools are expensive. If this is your first experience at engine service, it may be more worthwhile to have the checks made at a dealer. However, as your skills and enthusiasm increase for doing your own service work, you may want to begin purchasing some of these specialized tools. The following is a description of the measuring tools required in order to perform engine and suspension service on the KX.

Feeler Gauge

The feeler gauge (**Figure 41**) is made of either a piece of a flat or round hardened steel of a specified thickness. Wire gauges are used to measure spark plug gap. Flat gauges are used for all other measurements.

Vernier Caliper

This tool is invaluable when reading inside, outside and depth measurements to within close precision. See **Figure 42**.

Outside Micrometers

One of the most reliable tools used for precision measurement is the outside micrometer. Outside micrometers will be required to measure piston and piston pin outside diameters. Outside micrometers are also used with other tools to measure various bore diameters. Micrometers can be purchased individually or as a set.

Dial Indicator

Dial indicators (**Figure 43**) are precision tools used to check ignition timing and runout limits. For motorcycle repair, select a dial indicator with a continuous dial face (**Figure 44**). This type of dial is required to accurately measure ignition timing.

Cylinder Bore Gauge

The cylinder bore gauge is a very specialized precision tool. The gauge set shown in **Figure 45** is comprised of a dial indicator, handle and a number of length adaptors to adapt the gauge to different bore sizes. The bore gauge can be used to make cylinder bore measurements such as bore size, taper and out-of-round. An outside micrometer must be used together with the bore gauge to determine bore dimensions.

Small Hole Gauges

A set of small hole gauges (**Figure 46**) allow you to measure a hole, groove or slot ranging in size up to 13 mm (0.500 in.). An outside micrometer must be used together with the small hole gauge to determine bore dimensions.

Compression Gauge

An engine with low compression cannot be properly tuned and will not develop full power. A compression gauge (**Figure 47**) measures engine compression. The one shown has a flexible stem with an extension that can allow you to hold it while kicking the engine over. Open the throttle all the way when checking engine compression. See Chapter Three.

Strobe Timing Light

A strobe timing light (**Figure 48**) is used to check ignition timing. By flashing a light at the precise instant the spark plug fires, the firing point can be seen by checking the relationship of marks on the flywheel with a fixed mark on the crankcase.

Suitable lights range from inexpensive neon bulb types to powerful xenon strobe lights. The light from a neon bulb type is very weak and requires dark conditions to see easily while xenon strobe lights can be used outdoors in bright sunlight. Both types will work on the motorcycle when used in accordance with the manufacturer's instructions.

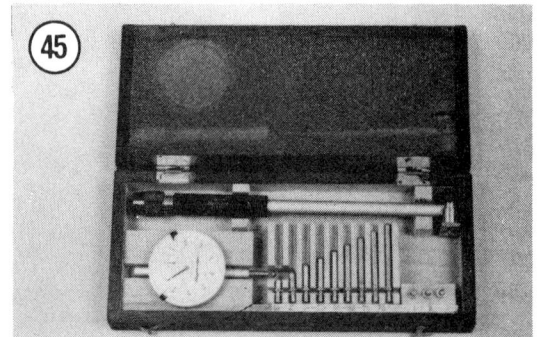

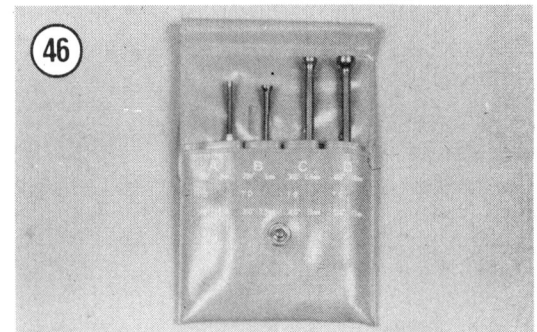

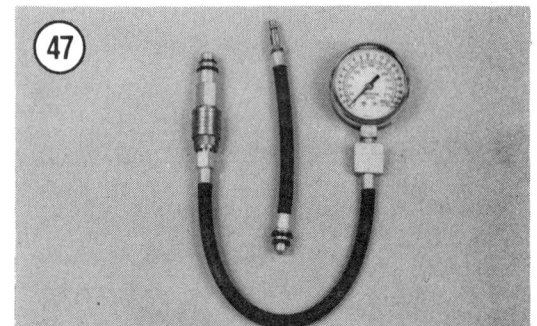

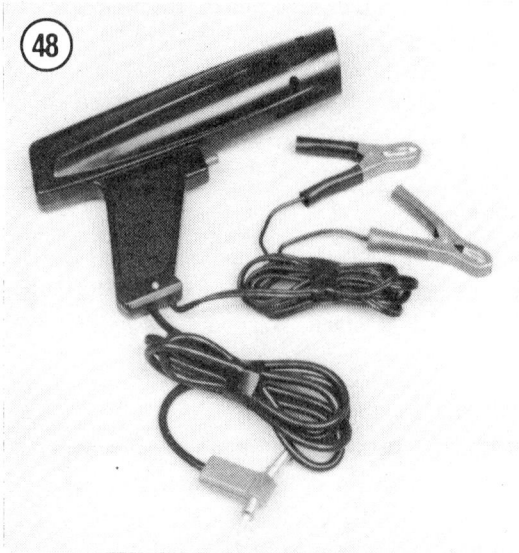

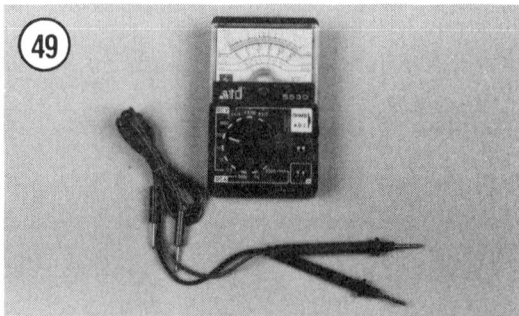

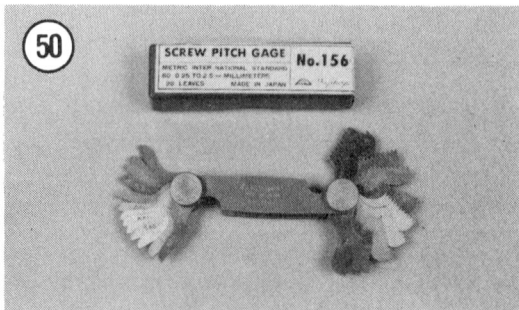

Multimeter or VOM

This instrument (**Figure 49**) is invaluable for electrical system troubleshooting. See *Electrical Troubleshooting* in Chapter Nine for its use.

Screw Pitch Gauge

A screw pitch gauge (**Figure 50**) determines the thread pitch of bolts, screws, studs, etc. The gauge is made up of a number of thin plates. Each plate has a thread shape cut on one edge to match one thread pitch. When using a screw pitch gauge to determine a thread pitch size, try to fit different blade sizes onto the thread until both threads match.

Magnetic Stand

A magnetic stand is used to securely hold a dial indicator when checking the runout of a round object or when checking the end play of a shaft.

V-blocks

V-blocks (**Figure 51**) are precision ground blocks used to hold a round object when checking its runout or condition.

SPECIAL TOOLS

This section describes special tools unique to motorcycle service and repair.

Flywheel Puller

A flywheel puller (**Figure 52**) will be required whenever it is necessary to remove the flywheel and service the stator plate assembly or when

adjusting the ignition timing. In addition, when disassembling the engine, the flywheel must be removed before the crankcases can be split. There is no satisfactory substitute for this tool. Because the flywheel is a taper fit on the crankshaft, makeshift removal often results in crankshaft and flywheel damage. Don't think about removing the flywheel without this tool.

Flywheel Holder

The flywheel holder is used to hold the flywheel during flywheel removal. While most flywheel pullers are of a universal design that allows their use on a number of different models, the Kawasaki flywheel puller designed for use on KX models in this manual is pretty much non-universal. This is due mainly to the design of the KX flywheel. Substitute tools are described in Chapter Nine.

Pressure Cable Lube Tool

A cable luber is used to help force cable lubricant throughout a control cable.

This tool (**Figure 53**) is clamped to one end of a control cable and has a tube fitting to allow a cable lubricant to be forced throughout the length of the cable.

Spoke Wrench

This special wrench is used to tighten wheel spokes (**Figure 54**). Always use the correct size spoke wrench to prevent from rounding out and damaging the spoke nipple.

Tire Levers

When riding and maintaining a dirt bike, get use to changing tires. To prevent from pinching tubes during tire changing, purchase a good set of tire levers (**Figure 55**). Never use a screwdriver in place of a tire lever; refer to Chapter Eleven for its use. Before using a tire lever, check the working end of the tool and remove any burrs with a fine-cut file. Don't use a tire lever for prying anything but tires.

The Grabbit

This is a special tool that is very useful as a holding tool, especially in the removal and installation of the clutch nut and the drive sprocket nut. It is called the Grabbit (**Figure 56**) and can be ordered through your Kawasaki dealer or from Joe Bolger Products, Inc., Summer Street, Barre, MA 01005

Bike Stand

One of the most important tools you can own for servicing the bike at home and race track is a portable bike stand. A good stand will be both

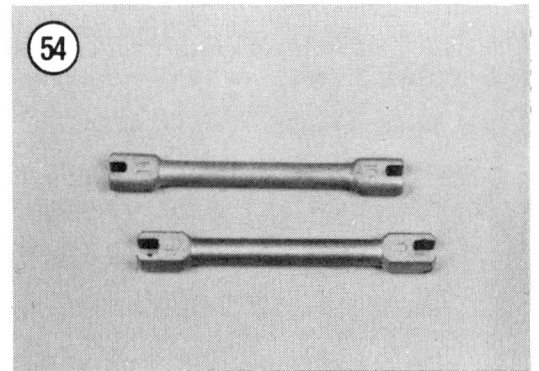

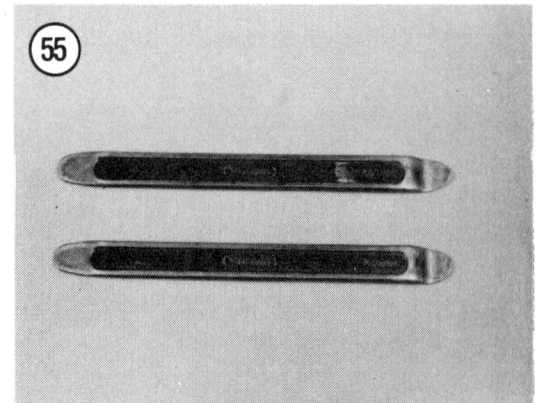

lightweight and sturdy. These features will allow you to remove both wheels when the stand is in use as well as preventing the bike from toppling over when major parts are being serviced. The bike stand shown in **Figure 57** has a tool shelf that can be used to hold tools and parts during service.

NOTE
*The bike stand shown in **Figure 57** can be purchased through Fett Brothers Manufacturing, RR 4 Box 383C, Frazee, MN 56544.*

Special Tools

A few special tools may be required for major service. These are described in the appropriate chapters and are available either from Kawasaki dealers or other manufacturer's as indicated.

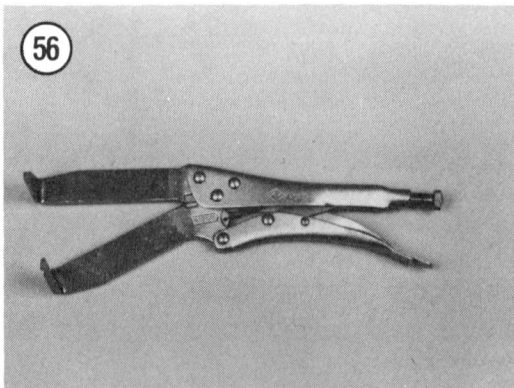

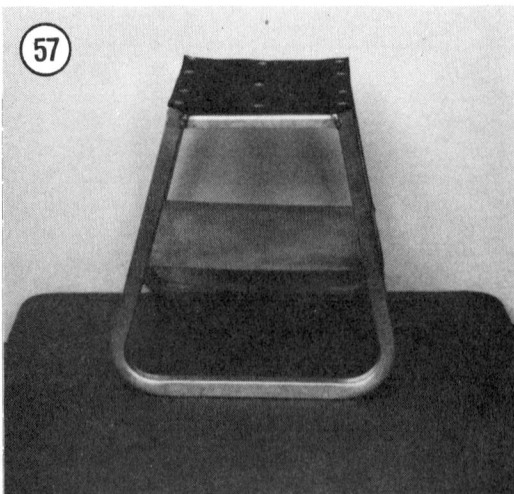

FABRICATING TOOLS

Some of the procedures in this manual require the use of special tools. The resourceful mechanic can, in many cases, think of acceptable substitutes for special tools. This can be as simple as using a few pieces of threaded rod, washers and nuts to remove or install a bearing or fabricating a tool from scrap material. However, using a substitute for a special tool is not recommended as it can be dangerous to and may damage the part. If you find that a tool can be designed and safely made, but will require some type of machine work, you may want to search out a local community college or high school that has a machine shop curriculum. Some shop teachers welcome outside work that can be used as practical shop applications for advanced students.

EXPENDABLE SUPPLIES

Certain expendable supplies are also required. These include grease, oil, gasket cement, shop rags and cleaning solvent. Ask your dealer for the special locking compounds, silicone lubricants and lube products which make vehicle maintenance simpler and easier. Cleaning solvent is available at some service stations.

WARNING
Having a stack of clean shop rags on hand is important when performing engine work. However, oil and solvent soaked rags can become a fire hazard. To prevent spontaneous combustion from a pile of solvent soaked rags, store them in a lid sealed metal container until they can be washed or discarded.

WARNING
To prevent the absorption of solvent and other chemicals into your skin while cleaning parts, wear a pair of petroleum-resistant rubber gloves. These can be purchased through industrial supply houses or well-equipped hardware stores.

MECHANIC'S TIPS

Removing Frozen Nuts and Screws

When a fastener rusts and cannot be removed, several methods may be used to loosen it. First, apply penetrating oil such as Liquid Wrench or WD-40 (available at hardware or auto supply stores). Apply it liberally and let it penetrate for 10-15 minutes. Rap the fastener several times with a small hammer; do not hit it hard enough to cause damage. Reapply the penetrating oil if necessary.

For frozen screws, apply penetrating oil as described, then insert a screwdriver in the slot and rap the top of the screwdriver with a hammer. This

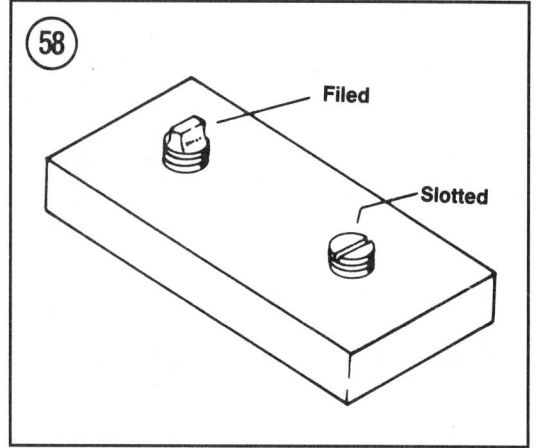

Filed

Slotted

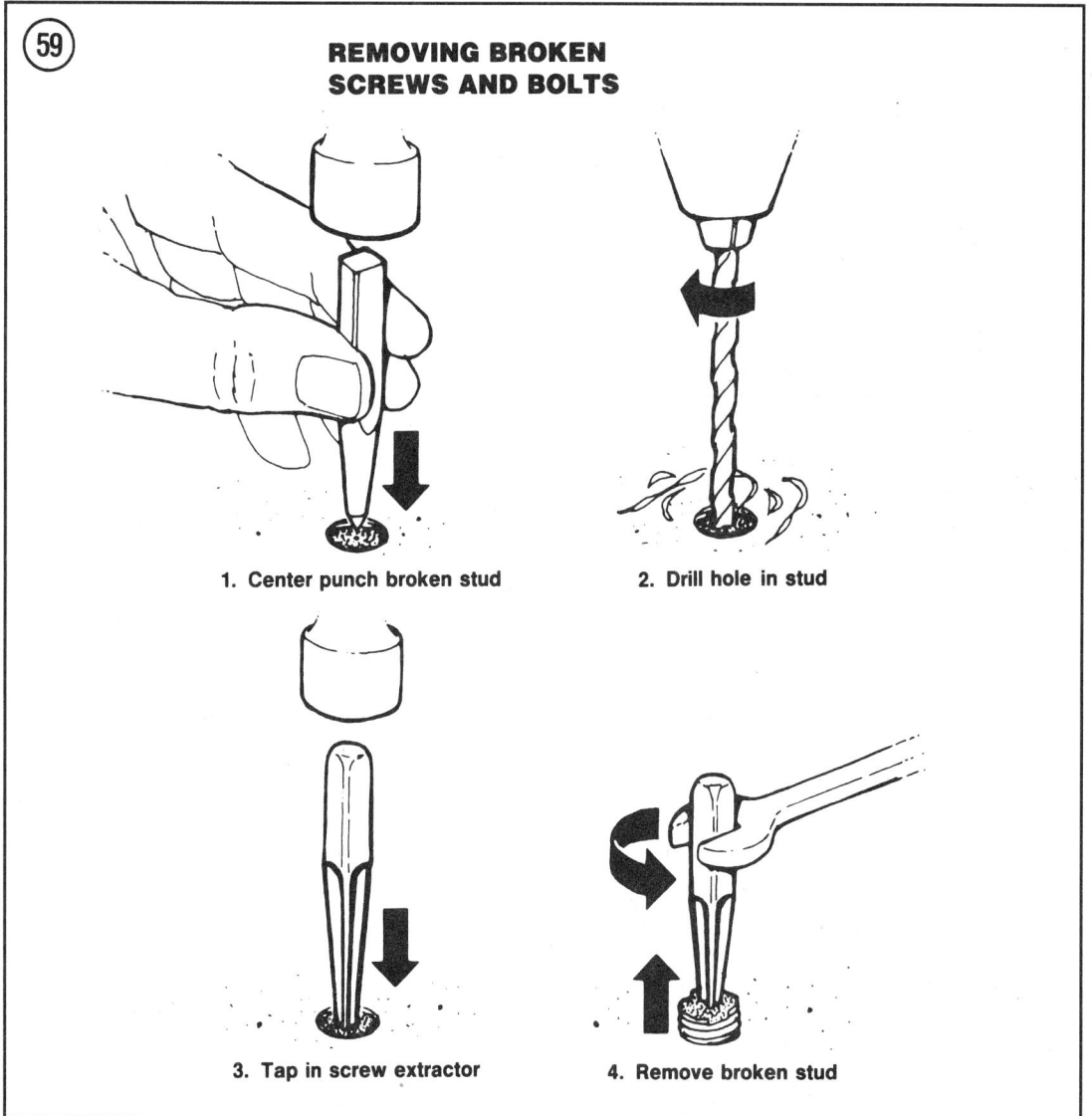

REMOVING BROKEN SCREWS AND BOLTS

1. Center punch broken stud

2. Drill hole in stud

3. Tap in screw extractor

4. Remove broken stud

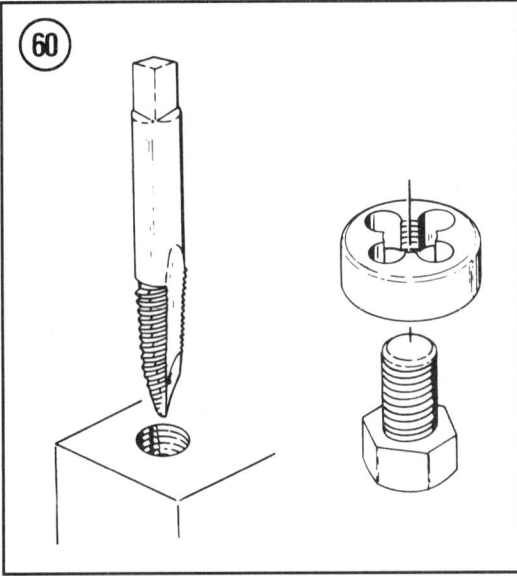

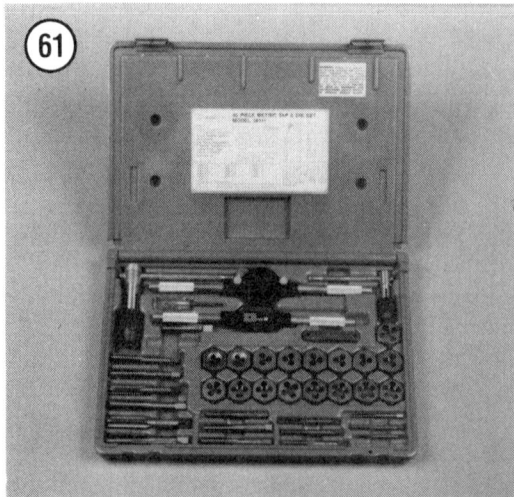

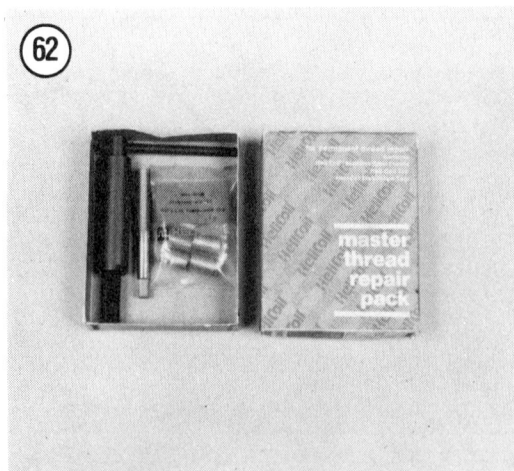

loosens the rust so the screw can be removed in the normal way. If the screw head is too chewed up to use this method, grip the head with Vise Grip pliers and twist the screw out.

Avoid applying heat unless specifically instructed, as it may melt, warp or remove the heat temper from parts.

Removing Broken Screws or Bolts

When the head breaks off a screw or bolt, several methods are available for removing the remaining portion.

If a large portion of the remainder projects out, try gripping it with Vise Grips. If the projecting portion is too small, file it to fit a wrench or cut a slot in it to fit a screwdriver. See **Figure 58**.

If the head breaks off flush, use a screw extractor. To do this, centerpunch the exact center of the remaining portion of the screw or bolt. Drill a small hole in the screw and tap the extractor into the hole. Back the screw out with a wrench on the extractor. See **Figure 59**.

Remedying Stripped Threads

Occasionally, threads are stripped through carelessness or impact damage. Often the threads can be cleaned up by running a tap (for internal threads on nuts) or die (for external threads on bolts) through the threads. See **Figure 60**. To clean or repair spark plug threads, a spark plug tap can be used.

NOTE
Tap and dies can be purchased individually or in a set as shown in **Figure 61**.

If an internal thread is damaged, it may be necessary to install a Helicoil (**Figure 62**) or some other type of thread insert. Follow the manufacturer's instructions when installing their insert.

If it is necessary to drill and tap a hole, refer to **Table 7** for metric tap drill sizes.

Removing Broken or Damaged Studs

If a stud is broken or the threads severely damaged, perform the following. A tube of Loctite 271 (red), 2 nuts, 2 wrenches and a new stud will be required during this procedure.

1. Thread two nuts onto the damaged cylinder stud. Then tighten the 2 nuts against each other so that they are locked.

NOTE
If the threads on the damaged stud do not allow installation of the 2 nuts, you will have to remove the stud with a pair of Vise Grips.

2. Turn the bottom nut counterclockwise and unscrew the stud.

3. Clean the threads on the new stud and the threaded hole in the component with solvent or electrical contact cleaner and allow to thoroughly dry.

4. Install 2 nuts on the top half of the new stud as in Step 1. Make sure they are locked securely.

5. Coat the bottom half of a new stud with Loctite 271 (red).

6. Turn the top nut clockwise and thread the new stud securely.

7. Remove the nuts and repeat for each stud as required.

8. Follow Loctite's directions on cure time before assembling the component.

SAFETY

General Tips

1. Read your owner's manual and know your machine.

2. Check the throttle and brake controls before starting the engine.

3. Know all state, federal and local laws concerning your vehicle's operation.

NOTE
*The Kawasaki KX60 and KX80 models are designed and manufactured for **off-road use only**. It does not conform to Federal Motor Vehicle Safety Standards and it is illegal to operate it on public streets, roads or highways.*

4. Know how to make an emergency stop.

5. Never ride on private property without having received permission.

6. Never add fuel while anyone is smoking in the area or when the engine is running.

7. Never wear loose scarves, belts or boot laces that could catch on moving parts or tree limbs.

8. Always wear appropriate riding clothing, eye protection and a helmet.

9. Never allow anyone to operate the motorcycle without proper instruction.

10. Use the "buddy system" for long trips, just in case you have a problem or run out of gas.

11. Never attempt to repair your machine with the engine running.

12. Check all machine components and hardware frequently, especially wheels and steering.

13. The KX60 and KX80 motorcycles are designed for a rider only. Do not carry a passenger.

Table 1 ENGINE SERIAL NUMBERS

Model number and year	Engine serial No. start to end
1983 KX60-A1	KX060AE000001-001800
1984 KX60-A2	KX060AE001801-003800
1985 KX60-B1	KX060BE000001-002400
1986 KX60-B2	KX060BE002401-004900
1987 KX60-B3	KX060BE004901-007300
1988 KX60-B4	KX060BE007301-on
1989*	
1990 KX60-B6	KX060BE009201-on
1983 KX80-E1	KX080EE000001-005300
1984 KX80-E2	KX080EE005301-012800
1985 KX80-E3	KX080EE012801-021000
1986 KX80-G1	KX080EE023501-035000
1987 KX80-G2	KX080EE035001-on
1987 KX80-J2	KX080EE035001-on
1988 KX80-L1	KX080EE042301-on
1988 KX80-N1	KX080EE042301-on
1989 KX80-L2	KX080EE046801-on
1989 KX80-N2	KX080EE046801-on
1990 KX80-L3	KX080EE054301-on
1990 KX80-N3	KX080EE054301-on

* No 1989 model sold in U.S. European numbers not available.

Table 2 GENERAL DIMENSIONS

	mm	In.
Overall length		
KX60	1,560	61.42
KX80		
1983	1,783	70.20
1984	1,785	70.28
1985	1,800	70.87
1986	1,815	71.5
1987		
G, H	1,815	71.5
J, K	1,895	74.6
1988-on		
L, M	1,810	71.26
N, P	1,905	75.00
Overall width		
KX60	705	27.76
KX80		
1983-1985	710	27.95
1986-on	745	29.3

(continued)

Table 2 GENERAL DIMENSIONS (continued)

	mm	in.
Overall height		
KX60	915	36.02
KX80		
1983-1986	1,050	41.34
1987		
G, H	1,050	41.34
J, K	1,080	42.5
1988-on		
L, M	1,050	41.34
N, P	1,080	42.5
Wheelbase		
KX60	1,080	42.52
KX80		
1983	1,224	48.19
1984	1,225	48.23
1985	1,240	48.82
1986-1987	1,225	48.23
1988-on		
L, M	1,250	49.21
N, P	1,290	50.79
Clearance		
KX60	250	9.84
KX80		
1983	307	12.09
1984-1985	310	12.20
1986-1987	335	13.2
1988-on		
L, M	335	13.2
N, P	365	14.4
Seat height		
KX60		
1983-1987	*	*
1988-on	710	27.9
KX80		
1983-1987	*	*
1988-on		
L, M	840	33.1
N, P	870	34.3

* Specification not specified for these models years.

Table 3 DRY WEIGHT SPECIFICATIONS

	kg	lb.
KX60		
1983-1984	51	112
1985-on	50.5	111
KX80		
1983-1984	61	134
1985-1987	60.5	133
1988-on		
L, M	61	134
N, P	64	141

Table 4 U.S. STANDARDS AND METRIC EQUIVALENTS

Fractions	Decimal in.	Metric mm	Fractions	Decimal in.	Metric mm
1/64	0.015625	0.39688	33/64	0.515625	13.09687
1/32	0.03125	0.79375	17/32	0.53125	13.49375
3/64	0.046875	1.19062	35/64	0.546875	13.89062
1/16	0.0625	1.58750	9/16	0.5625	14.28750
5/64	0.078125	1.98437	37/64	0.578125	14.68437
3/32	0.09375	2.38125	19/32	0.59375	15.08125
7/64	0.109375	2.77812	39/64	0.609375	15.47812
1/8	0.125	3.1750	5/8	0.625	15.87500
9/64	0.140625	3.57187	41/64	0.640625	16.27187
5/32	0.15625	3.96875	21/32	0.65625	16.66875
11/64	0.171875	4.36562	43/64	0.671875	17.06562
3/16	0.1875	4.76250	11/16	0.6875	17.46250
13/64	0.203125	5.15937	45/64	0.703125	17.85937
7/32	0.21875	5.55625	23/32	0.71875	18.25625
15/64	0.234375	5.95312	47/64	0.734375	18.65312
1/4	0.250	6.35000	3/4	0.750	19.05000
17/64	0.265625	6.74687	49/64	0.765625	19.44687
9/32	0.28125	7.14375	25/32	0.78125	19.84375
19/64	0.296875	7.54062	51/64	0.796875	20.24062
5/16	0.3125	7.93750	13/16	0.8125	20.63750
21/64	0.328125	8.33437	53/64	0.828125	21.03437
11/32	0.34375	8.73125	27/32	0.84375	21.43125
23/64	0.359375	9.12812	55/64	0.859375	21.82812
3/8	0.375	9.52500	7/8	0.875	22.22500
25/64	0.390625	9.92187	57/64	0.890625	22.62187
13/32	0.40625	10.31875	29/32	0.90625	23.01875
27/64	0.421875	10.71562	59/64	0.921875	23.41562
7/16	0.4375	11.11250	15/16	0.9375	23.81250
29/64	0.453125	11.50937	61/64	0.953125	24.20937
15/32	0.46875	11.90625	31/32	0.96875	24.60625
31/64	0.484375	12.30312	63/64	0.984375	25.00312
1/2	0.500	12.70000	1	1.00	25.40000

Table 5 GENERAL TORQUE SPECIFICATIONS

Thread diameter	N·m	ft.-lb.
5 mm	3.4-4.9	30-43 in.-lb.
6 mm	5.9-7.8	52-69 in.-lb.
8 mm	14-19	10.0-13.5
10 mm	25-39	19-25
12 mm	44-61	33-45
14 mm	73-98	54-72
16 mm	115-155	83-115
18 mm	165-225	125-165
20 mm	225-325	165-240

Table 6 TECHNICAL ABBREVIATIONS

ABDC	After bottom dead center
ATDC	After top dead center
BBDC	Before bottom dead center
BDC	Bottom dead center
BTDC	Before top dead center
C	Celsius (Centigrade)
cc	Cubic centimeters
CDI	Capacitor discharge ignition
cu. in.	Cubic inches
F	Fahrenheit
ft.-lb.	Foot-pounds
gal.	Gallons
hp	Horsepower
in.	Inches
kg	Kilogram
kg/cm²	Kilograms per square centimeter
kgm	Kilogram meters
km	Kilometer
l	Liter
m	Meter
mm	Millimeter
N·m	Newton-meters
oz.	Ounce
psi	Pounds per square inch
pts.	Pints
qt.	Quarts
rpm	Revolutions per minute

Table 7 METRIC TAP DRILL SIZES

Metric tap (mm)	Drill size	Decimal equivalent	Nearest fraction
3×0.50	No. 39	0.0995	3/32
3×0.60	3/32	0.0937	3/32
4×0.70	No. 30	0.1285	1/8
4×0.75	1/8	0.125	1/8
5×0.80	No. 19	0.166	11/64
5×0.90	No. 20	0.161	5/32
6×1.00	No. 9	0.196	13/64
7×1.00	16/64	0.234	15/64
8×1.00	J	0.277	9/32
8×1.25	17/64	0.265	17/64
9×1.00	5/16	0.3125	5/16
9×1.25	5/16	0.3125	5/16
10×1.25	11/32	0.3437	11/32
10×1.50	R	0.339	11/32
11×1.50	3/8	0.375	3/8
12×1.50	13/32	0.406	13/32
12×1.75	13/32	0.406	13/32

CHAPTER TWO

TROUBLESHOOTING

Diagnosing mechanical problems is relatively simple if you use orderly procedures and keep a few basic principles in mind. The first step in any troubleshooting procedure is to define the symptoms as closely as possible and then localize the problem. Subsequent steps involve testing and analyzing those areas which could cause the symptoms. A haphazard approach may eventually solve the problem, but it can be very costly in terms of wasted time and unnecessary parts replacement.

Proper lubrication, maintenance and periodic tune-ups as described in Chapter Three will reduce the necessity for troubleshooting. Even with the best of care, however, all motorcycles are prone to problems which will require troubleshooting.

Never assume anything. Do not overlook the obvious. If the engine won't start, is the kill switch shorted out? Is the engine flooded with fuel from using the choke too much.

If the engine suddenly quits, check the easiest, most accessible problem first. Is there gasoline in the tank? If so, is the fuel reaching the carburetor? Has the spark plug wire fallen off? Is the fuel vent allowing air to enter the tank as it should?

If nothing obvious turns up in a quick check, look a little further. Learning to recognize and describe symptoms will make repairs easier for you or a mechanic at the shop. Describe problems accurately and fully.

Gather as many symptoms as possible to aid in diagnosis. Note whether the engine lost power gradually or all at once, what color smoke came from the exhaust and so on. Remember that the more complicated a machine is, the easier it is to troubleshoot because symptoms point to specific problems.

After the symptoms are defined, areas which could cause problems are tested and analyzed. Guessing at the cause of a problem may provide the solution, but it can easily lead to frustration, wasted time and a series of expensive, unnecessary parts replacements.

You do not need fancy equipment or complicated test gear to determine whether repairs can be attempted at home. A few simple checks could save a large repair bill and lost time while the bike sits in a dealer's service department. On the other hand, be realistic and do not attempt repairs beyond your abilities. Service departments tend to charge heavily for putting together a disassembled engine that may have been abused. Some won't even take on such a job—so use common sense, don't get in over your head.

OPERATING REQUIREMENT

An engine needs 3 basics to run properly: correct fuel/air mixture, compression and a spark at the right time (**Figure 1**). If one basic requirement is missing, the engine will not run. Two-stroke engine operating principles are described in Chapter One under *Engine Operation*.

If the bike has been sitting for any length of time and refuses to start, check and clean the spark plug. If this is okay, then look to the gasoline delivery system. This includes the tank, fuel shutoff valve, in-line fuel filter and fuel line to the carburetor. Gasoline deposits may have gummed up carburetor jets and air passages. Gasoline tends to lose its potency after standing for long periods. Condensation may contaminate it with water. Drain the old gas and try starting with a fresh tankful.

TROUBLESHOOTING INSTRUMENTS

Chapter One lists the instruments needed and instruction on their use.

STARTING THE ENGINE

When your engine refuses to start, frustration can cause you to forget basic starting principles and procedures. The following outline will guide you through basic starting procedures.

Starting a Cold Engine

1. Shift the transmission into NEUTRAL.
2. Apply the front brake and rock the bike back and forth. This will help to mix the fuel in the tank.
3. Turn the fuel valve to ON.
4. Open the choke. Depending on model and year; pull the choke knob out (**Figure 2**) or push the choke lever down.
5. With the throttle completely *closed,* kick the engine over with the kickstarter.
6. When the engine starts, work the throttle slightly to keep it running.

7. Idle the engine approximately for a minute or until the throttle responds cleanly and the choke can be closed.

Starting a Warm or Hot Engine

1. Shift the transmission into NEUTRAL.
2. Turn the fuel valve to ON.
3. Make sure the choke is closed. Depending on model and year; the choke knob should be pushed down or in (**Figure 2**) or the choke lever should be pulled up.

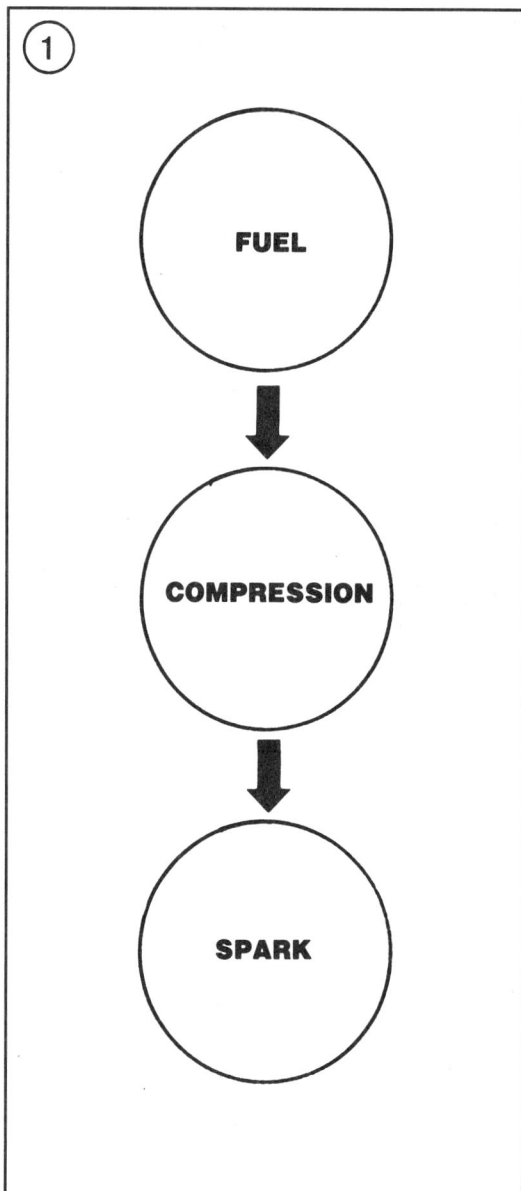

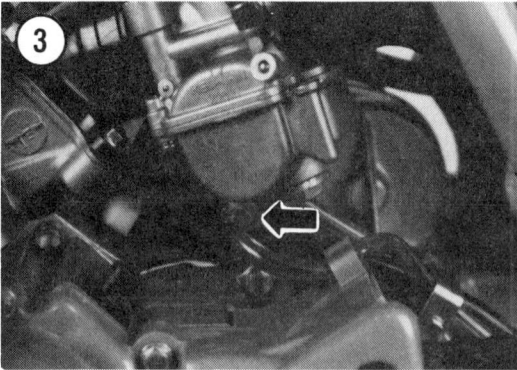

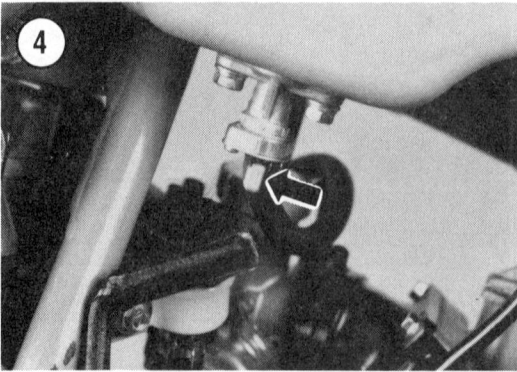

4. Open the throttle slightly and kick the engine over.

Starting a Flooded Engine

If the engine is flooded, open the throttle all the way and kick the engine over with the kickstarter until it starts. Do not open the choke.

NOTE
If the engine refuses to start, check the carburetor overflow hose attached to the fitting at the bottom of the float bowl (Figure 3). If fuel is running out of the hose, the floats may be stuck open.

STARTING DIFFICULTIES

When the bike is difficult to start, or won't start at all, it does not help to kick away at the kick starter. Check for obvious problems even before getting out your tools. Go down the following list step-by-step. Do each one. If the bike still will not start, refer to the appropriate troubleshooting procedures which follow in this chapter.

1. Is there fuel in the tank? Remove the filler cap and rock the bike from side-to-side. Listen for fuel sloshing around.

WARNING
Do not use an open flame to check in the tank. A serious explosion is certain to result.

2. If there is fuel in the tank, pull off a fuel line at the carburetor. Turn the fuel valve to RES (**Figure 4**) and see if fuel flows freely. If none comes out and there is a fuel filter installed in the fuel line, turn the fuel valve off, remove the filter and turn the fuel valve to RES again. If fuel flows, the filter is clogged and should be replaced. If no fuel comes out, the fuel valve may be blocked by foreign matter, or the fuel cap vent may be plugged. If the carburetor is getting usable fuel, turn to the electrical system next.

3. Make sure the kill switch button (**Figure 5**) is not stuck or working improperly or that the wire is broken and shorting out.

4. Is the spark plug wire on tight (**Figure 6**)? Push it on and slightly rotate it to clean the electrical connection between the plug and the connector. Also check that the high-tension lead ends at the coil and plug cap are pushed in all the way.

5. Is the choke knob or lever in the right position? Refer to *Starting the Engine* in this chapter.

ENGINE STARTING TROUBLE

An engine that refuses to start or is difficult to start is very frustrating. More often than not, the problem is very minor and can be found with a simple and logical troubleshooting approach.

The following items show a beginning point from which to isolate engine starting problems.

Engine Fails to Start

Perform the following spark test to determine if the ignition system is operating properly.

> *CAUTION*
> *Before removing the spark plug in Step 1, clean all dirt and debris from the plug base. Dirt that falls into the cylinder will cause rapid piston, piston ring and cylinder wear.*

> *NOTE*
> *If you are checking the spark plug while at the track or on the trail, dirt has probably clogged underneath the fuel tank. When the spark plug is removed, some of this dirt could fall into the cylinder. If you do not have time to remove the fuel tank, wrap a large clean cloth (or a riding jacket) around the fuel tank. Then remove the spark plug and check or replace it as required. Remove the cloth after reinstalling the spark plug.*

1. Remove the spark plug (**Figure 6**).

2. Connect the spark plug wire and connector to the spark plug and touch the spark plug base to the cylinder head to ground it (**Figure 7**). Position the spark plug so you can see the electrode.

3. Crank the engine over with the kickstarter. A fat blue spark should be evident across the spark plug electrode.

> *WARNING*
> *Do not hold the spark plug, wire or connector or a serious electrical shock may result. If it is necessary to hold onto the high voltage lead, do so with an insulated pair of pliers.*

4. If the spark is good, check for one or more of the following possible malfunctions:
    a. Obstructed fuel line or fuel filter.
    b. Leaking cylinder head or cylinder base gasket.

5. If spark is not good, check for one or more of the following:
    a. Weak ignition coil.
    b. Weak CDI unit.

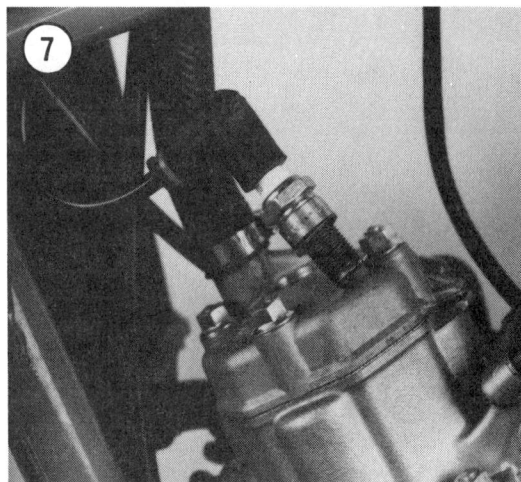

c. Loose electrical connections.

d. Dirty electrical connections.

e. Loose or broken ignition coil ground wire.

Engine is Difficult to Start

Check for one or more of the following possible malfunctions:

a. Fouled spark plug.

b. Improperly operating choke.

c. Contaminated fuel system.

d. Improperly adjusted carburetor.

e. Loose electrical connections.

f. Dirty electrical connections.

g. Weak CDI unit.

h. Weak ignition coil.

i. Poor compression

Engine Will Not Crank

If the engine will not crank because of a mechanical problem, check for one or more of the following possible malfunctions.

a. Defective kickstarter and/or gear.

b. Seized piston.

c. Seized crankshaft bearings.

d. Broken connecting rod.

ENGINE

Engine problems are generally symptoms of something wrong in another system, such as ignition, fuel or starting.

Preignition

Preignition is the premature burning of fuel and is caused by hot spots in the combustion chamber (**Figure 8**). The fuel actually ignites before it is supposed to. Glowing deposits in the combustion chamber, inadequate cooling or an overheated spark plug can all cause preignition. This is first noticed in the form of a power loss but will eventually result in extended damage to the internal parts of the engine because of higher combustion chamber temperatures.

Detonation

Commonly called "spark knock" or "fuel knock," detonation is the violent explosion of fuel in the combustion chamber prior to the proper time of combustion (**Figure 9**). Severe damage can result. Use of low octane gasoline is a common cause of detonation.

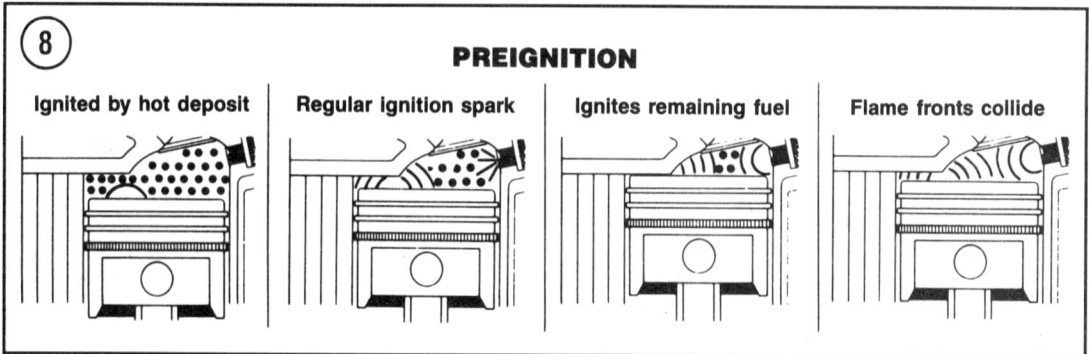

(8) PREIGNITION

| Ignited by hot deposit | Regular ignition spark | Ignites remaining fuel | Flame fronts collide |

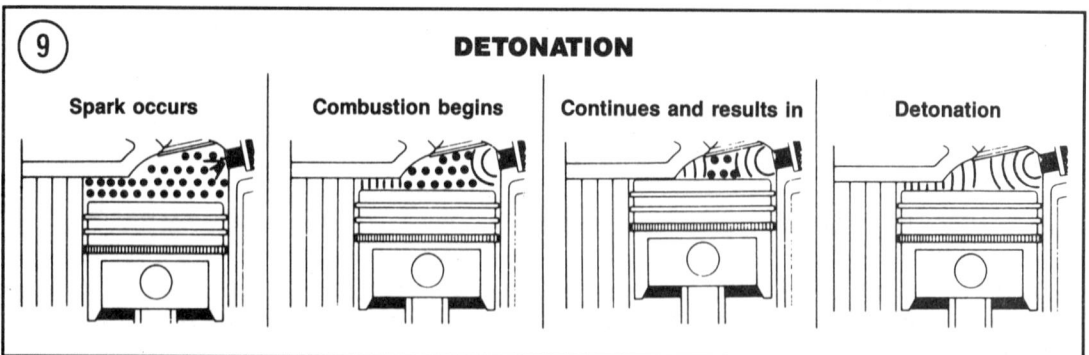

(9) DETONATION

| Spark occurs | Combustion begins | Continues and results in | Detonation |

Even when high octane gasoline is used, detonation can still occur if the engine is improperly timed. Other causes are over-advanced ignition timing, lean fuel mixture at or near full throttle, inadequate engine cooling, or the excessive accumulation of deposits on piston and combustion chamber.

Power Loss

Several factors can cause a lack of power and speed. Look for a clogged air filter or a fouled or damaged spark plug. Dynamically (engine running) check the ignition timing at full advance. See Chapter Three. This will allow you to make sure that the ignition system is operating properly. If the ignition timing is incorrect dynamically, but was properly set with a dial indicator, there may be a problem with an ignition component.

A piston or cylinder that is galling has an incorrect piston clearance or worn or sticky piston rings may be responsible. Look for loose bolts, defective gaskets or leaking machined mating surfaces on the cylinder head, cylinder or crankcase. Also check the crankshaft seals; refer to *Two-stroke Pressure Testing* in this chapter.

If the engine seems to operate correctly, but you are experiencing performance related problems, check the front and rear brakes for signs of dragging.

Piston Seizure

This is caused by incorrect bore clearance, piston rings with an improper end gap, compression leak, incorrect type of oil, spark plug of the wrong heat range, incorrect ignition timing or the use of an incorrect fuel/oil mixture. Overheating from any of these problems may result in piston seizure.

ENGINE PERFORMANCE

In the following check list, it is assumed that the engine runs, but is not operating at peak performance. This will serve as a starting point from which to isolate a performance malfunction.

The possible causes for each malfunction are listed in a logical sequence and in order of probability.

Engine Will Not Idle

a. Carburetor incorrectly adjusted.
b. Pilot jet clogged.
c. Obstructed fuel line or fuel shutoff valve.
d. Fouled or improperly gapped spark plug.
e. Cylinder head gasket leaking.

Engine Misses at High Speed

a. Fouled or improperly gapped spark plug.
b. Improper carburetor main jet selection.
c. Carburetor main jet and/or needle jet clogged.
d. Obstructed fuel line or fuel shutoff valve.
e. Ignition timing incorrect.

Engine Overheating

a. Incorrect carburetor jetting or fuel/oil ratio mixture.
b. Incorrect ignition timing.
c. Improper spark plug heat range.
d. Intake system or crankcase air leak.
e. Dragging brake(s).
f. Malfunction with liquid cooling system.
g. Radiator damage.

Black Exhaust and Engine Runs Roughly

a. Clogged air filter element.
b. Carburetor adjustment incorrect—mixture too rich.
c. Carburetor floats damaged or incorrectly adjusted.
d. Choke not operating correctly.
e. Water or other contaminants in fuel.
f. Excessive piston-to-cylinder clearance.

Engine Loses Power

a. Carburetor incorrectly adjusted.
b. Engine overheating.
c. Ignition timing incorrect due to improper timing or defective ignition component(s).
d. Incorrectly gapped spark plug.
e. Obstructed silencer.
f. Dragging brake(s).

Engine Lacks Acceleration

a. Carburetor adjustment incorrect.
b. Clogged fuel line.

c. Ignition timing incorrect due to improper timing or faulty ignition component(s).
d. Dragging brake(s).

ENGINE NOISES

1. *Knocking or pinging during acceleration—* Caused by using a lower octane fuel than recommended. May also be caused by poor fuel available at some "discount" gasoline stations. Pinging can also be caused by a spark plug of the wrong heat range and incorrect carburetor jetting. Refer to *Correct Spark Plug Heat Range* in Chapter Three.
2. *Slapping or rattling noises at low speed or during acceleration—*May be caused by piston slap, i.e., excessive piston-cylinder wall clearance.
3. *Knocking or rapping while decelerating—* Usually caused by excessive rod bearing clearance.
4. *Persistent knocking and vibration—*Usually caused by worn main bearings.
5. *Rapid on-off squeal—*Compression leak around cylinder head gasket or spark plug.

EXCESSIVE VIBRATION

This can be difficult to find without disassembling the engine. Usually this is caused by loose engine or suspension mounting hardware.

FUEL SYSTEM

Many riders owners automatically assume that the carburetor is at fault when the engine does not run properly. While fuel system problems are not uncommon, carburetor adjustment is seldom the answer. In many cases, adjusting the carburetor only compounds the problem by making the engine run worse.

Fuel system troubleshooting should start at the gas tank and work through the system, reserving the carburetor as the final point. Most fuel system problems result from an empty fuel tank, a plugged fuel filter or fuel valve or sour fuel.

Carburetor chokes can also present problems. A choke stuck open will show up as a hard starting problem; one that sticks closed will result in a flooding condition. Check choke operation.

TWO-STROKE PRESSURE TESTING

Many owners of 2-stroke bikes are plagued by hard starting and generally poor running, for which there seems to be no cause. Carburetion and ignition may be good, and compression tests may show that all is well in the engine's upper end.

What a compression test does not show is lack of primary compression. The crankcase in a 2-stroke engine must be alternately under pressure and vacuum. After the piston closes the intake port, further downward movement of the piston causes the entrapped mixture to be pressurized so that it can rush quickly into the cylinder when the scavenging ports are opened. Upward piston movement creates a slight vacuum in the crankcase, enabling the fuel/air mixture to be drawn in from the carburetor.

NOTE
The operational sequence of a 2-stroke engine is illustrated in Chapter One.

If crankcase seals or cylinder gaskets leak, the crankcase cannot hold pressure or vacuum, and proper engine operation becomes impossible. Any other source of leakage such as a defective cylinder base gasket or porous or cracked crankcase castings will result in the same conditions. See **Figure 10**.

It is possible, however, to test for and isolate engine pressure leaks. The test is simple but requires special equipment. A typical two-stroke pressure test kit is shown in **Figure 11**. Briefly, what is done is to seal off all natural engine openings, then apply air pressure. If the engine does not hold air, a leak or leaks is indicated. Then it is only necessary to locate and repair all leaks.

The following procedure describes a typical pressure test.
1. Remove the flywheel (Chapter Nine) to gain access to the left-hand oil seal (**Figure 12**).
2. Remove the primary drive gear (Chapter Six) to gain access to the right-hand oil seal (**Figure 13**).
3. Remove the carburetor.

NOTE
Do not remove the intake manifold. The manifold should remain on the engine during this test as it may be causing the leak.

4. Take a rubber plug and insert it tightly in the intake manifold.

5. Remove the exhaust pipe and block off the exhaust port, using suitable adapters and fittings.

6. Remove the spark plug and install the pressure gauge adaptor into the spark plug hole. Connect the pressurizing lever and gauge to the pressure fitting installed where the spark plug was, then continue to squeeze the lever until the gauge indicates approximately 6-8 psi.

CAUTION
Do not apply more than 8 psi. or the crankcase seals may be damaged.

7. Observe the pressure gauge. If the engine is in good condition, the pressure should hold for 3-5 minutes. If the pressure starts to immediately drop, there is a leak.

Before condemning the engine, first be sure that there are no leaks in the test equipment or sealing plugs. If the equipment shows no signs of leakage, go over the entire engine carefully. Large leaks can be heard; smaller ones can be found by going over every possible leakage source with a small brush and soap suds solution. Possible leakage points are listed below:

a. Crankshaft seals. See **Figure 12** (left-hand seal) or **Figure 13** (right-hand seal).

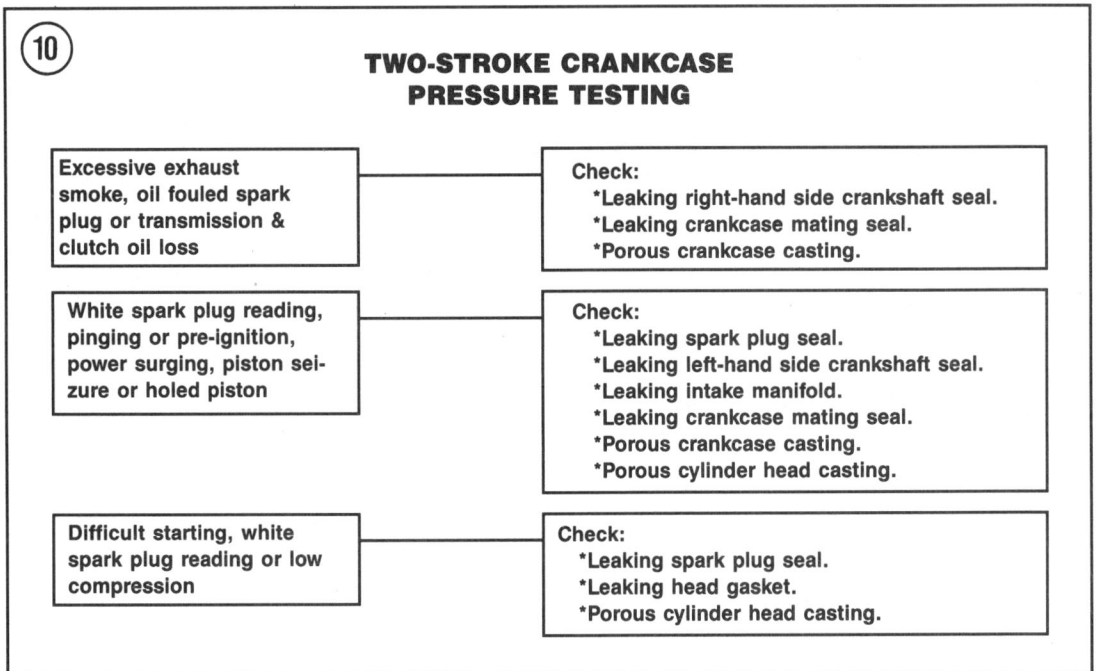

TWO-STROKE CRANKCASE PRESSURE TESTING

Excessive exhaust smoke, oil fouled spark plug or transmission & clutch oil loss	Check: *Leaking right-hand side crankshaft seal. *Leaking crankcase mating seal. *Porous crankcase casting.
White spark plug reading, pinging or pre-ignition, power surging, piston seizure or holed piston	Check: *Leaking spark plug seal. *Leaking left-hand side crankshaft seal. *Leaking intake manifold. *Leaking crankcase mating seal. *Porous crankcase casting. *Porous cylinder head casting.
Difficult starting, white spark plug reading or low compression	Check: *Leaking spark plug seal. *Leaking head gasket. *Porous cylinder head casting.

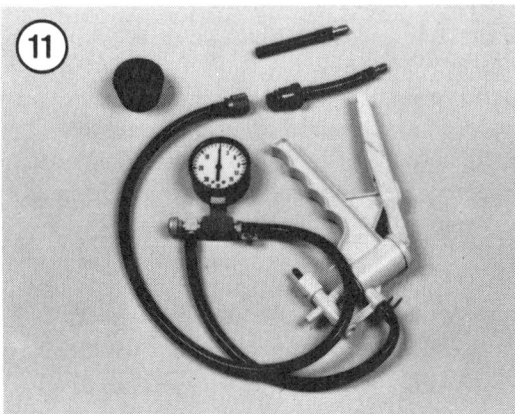

b. Spark plug (**Figure 6**).
c. Cylinder head joint.
d. Cylinder base joint.
e. Carburetor base joint.

f. Crankcase joint.
g. Porous crankcase, cylinder or cylinder head casting.

CLUTCH

The three basic clutch troubles are:
a. Clutch noise.
b. Clutch slipping.
c. Improper clutch disengagement.

All clutch troubles, except adjustments, require partial engine disassembly to identify and cure the problem. Refer to Chapter Six for procedures.

The troubleshooting procedures outlined in **Figure 14** will help you solve the majority of clutch troubles in a systematic manner.

TRANSMISSION

The basic transmission troubles are:
a. Excessive gear noise.
b. Difficult shifting.

CLUTCH TROUBLESHOOTING

Clutch slipping — Check:
*Worn clutch plates
*Weak clutch springs
*Incorrect clutch adjustment
*Damaged pressure plate

Clutch dragging — Check:
*Incorrect clutch adjustment
*Worn clutch housing or boss assemblies
*Worn or uneven clutch springs
*Worn clutch plates

Excessive clutch noise — Check:
*Damaged gear teeth
*Worn clutch plates
*Excessive backlash between the primary drive and driven gears

⑮

TRANSMISSION TROUBLESHOOTING

| Excessive gear noise |

Check:
*Worn bearings
*Worn or damaged gears
*Excessive gear backlash

| Difficult shifting |

Check:
*Damaged gears
*Damaged shift forks
*Damaged shift drum
*Damaged shift lever assembly
*Incorrect mainshaft and countershaft
  engagement
*Incorrect clutch disengagement

| Gears pop out of mesh |

Check:
*Worn gear or transmission shaft splines
*Shift forks worn or bent
*Worn dog holes in gears
*Insufficient shift lever spring tension
*Damaged shift lever linkage

| Incorrect shift lever operation |

Check:
*Bent shift lever
*Bent or damaged shift lever shaft
*Damaged shift lever linkage or gears

| Incorrect shifting after engine
  reassembly |

Check:
*Missing transmission shaft shims
*Incorrectly installed parts
*Shift forks bent during reassembly
*Incorrectly assembled crankcase
  assembly
*Incorrect clutch adjustment
*Incorrectly assembled shift linkage
  assembly

c. Gears pop out of mesh.

d. Incorrect shift lever operation.

Transmission symptoms are sometimes hard to distinguish from clutch symptoms. Be sure that the clutch is not causing the trouble before working on the transmission.

The troubleshooting procedures outlined in **Figure 15** will help you solve the majority of transmission troubles.

IGNITION SYSTEM

All models are equipped with a capacitor discharge ignition (CDI) system. This solid state system uses no contact breaker point or other moving parts. Because of the solid state design, problems with the capacitor discharge system are relatively few. However, when problems arise they stem from one of the following:

a. Weak spark.

b. No spark.

It is possible to check CDI systems that:

a. Do not spark.

b. Have broken or damaged wires.

c. Have a weak spark.

It is difficult to check CDI system that malfunction due to:

a. Vibration problems.

b. Components that malfunction only when the engine is hot or under a load.

The troubleshooting procedures in **Figure 16** will help you isolate the ignition problem fast. When troubleshooting the ignition system, consider the following:

1. Remove the fuel tank and locate the kill switch connectors at the ignition coil. Disconnect the kill switch (**Figure 5**) electrical connectors and see if the problem still exists.

2. Remove the flywheel (Chapter Nine) and make sure that the stator plate screws (A, **Figure 17**) are

tight. If the screws are loose, recheck the ignition timing as described in Chapter Three.

3. With the fuel tank removed, untape all electrical connectors. Make sure the connectors are connected properly. If necessary, clean the connectors with electrical contact cleaner.

4. Check the left- and right-hand crankshaft bearings for excessive play. See **Figure 12** and **Figure 13**. Remove the magneto rotor as described in Chapter Nine. Grab the end of the crankshaft and try to move it up and down. Any noticeable play indicates worn crankshaft bearings. Refer to Chapter Five.

5. Check the stator plate (B, **Figure 17**) for cracks or damage that would cause the pulser coil and magneto to be out of alignment.

FRONT SUSPENSION AND STEERING

Poor handling may be caused by improper front or rear tire pressure, a damaged or bent frame or front steering components, worn swing arm bushings, worn wheel bearings or dragging brakes.

BRAKES

Disc Brakes

The disc brake is critical to riding performance and safety. It should inspected frequently and any problems located and repaired immediately. When replacing or refilling the brake fluid, use only DOT 3 brake fluid from a closed and sealed container. See Chapter Twelve for additional information of brake fluid and disc brake service. The troubleshooting procedures in **Figure 18** will help you isolate the majority of front disc brake troubles.

Drum Brakes

The front and rear drum brakes are relatively simple in design and operation. However many riders do not get full stopping power because of a glaze residue that builds on the linings surface. To work properly, the drum brakes must be cleaned and serviced weekly. Periodic maintenance will also allow inspection of parts so that they can be replaced before a part fails.

Refer to the troubleshooting chart in **Figure 19** for drum brake problems and checks to make.

(16)

IGNITION SYSTEM DIAGNOSIS
PROBLEM: WEAK SPARK OR NO SPARK AT ALL

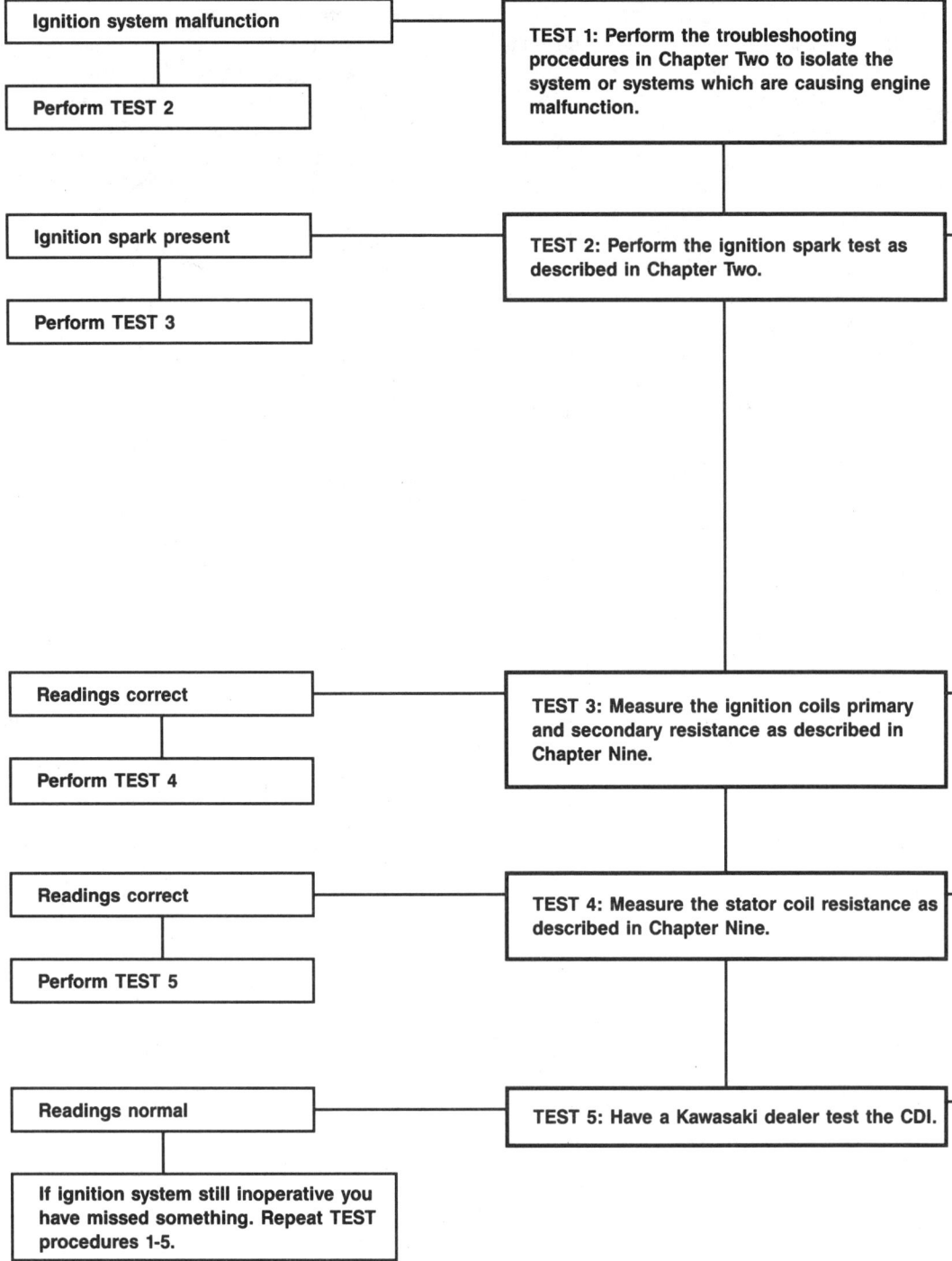

Ignition system malfunction

Perform TEST 2

TEST 1: Perform the troubleshooting procedures in Chapter Two to isolate the system or systems which are causing engine malfunction.

Ignition spark present

Perform TEST 3

TEST 2: Perform the ignition spark test as described in Chapter Two.

Readings correct

Perform TEST 4

TEST 3: Measure the ignition coils primary and secondary resistance as described in Chapter Nine.

Readings correct

Perform TEST 5

TEST 4: Measure the stator coil resistance as described in Chapter Nine.

Readings normal

If ignition system still inoperative you have missed something. Repeat TEST procedures 1-5.

TEST 5: Have a Kawasaki dealer test the CDI.

2

```
┌─────────────────────────────────┐
│  No spark or weak spark         │
└─────────────────────────────────┘
            │
┌──────────────────────────────────────────────────────┐
│  Have a Kawasaki dealer perform an ignition coil      │
│  spark plug gap test.                                 │
└──────────────────────────────────────────────────────┘
         │                                    │
┌──────────────────┐              ┌──────────────────┐
│  Spark           │              │  No spark        │
└──────────────────┘              └──────────────────┘
         │                                    │
┌──────────────────────┐    ┌──────────────────────────────────────┐
│  Perform Test 3      │    │  Check for poor contact at the spark  │
└──────────────────────┘    │  plug cap and all ignition connectors │
                            └──────────────────────────────────────┘
```

```
┌──────────────────────────────────────┐
│  Replace the bad coil(s) and retest   │
└──────────────────────────────────────┘
```

```
┌──────────────────────────┐
│  Readings incorrect       │
└──────────────────────────┘
            │
┌──────────────────────────────────────┐
│  Replace the stator coil and retest   │
└──────────────────────────────────────┘
```

```
┌──────────────────────────┐
│  Readings abnormal        │
└──────────────────────────┘
            │
┌──────────────────────────┐
│  Replace the CDI.         │
└──────────────────────────┘
```

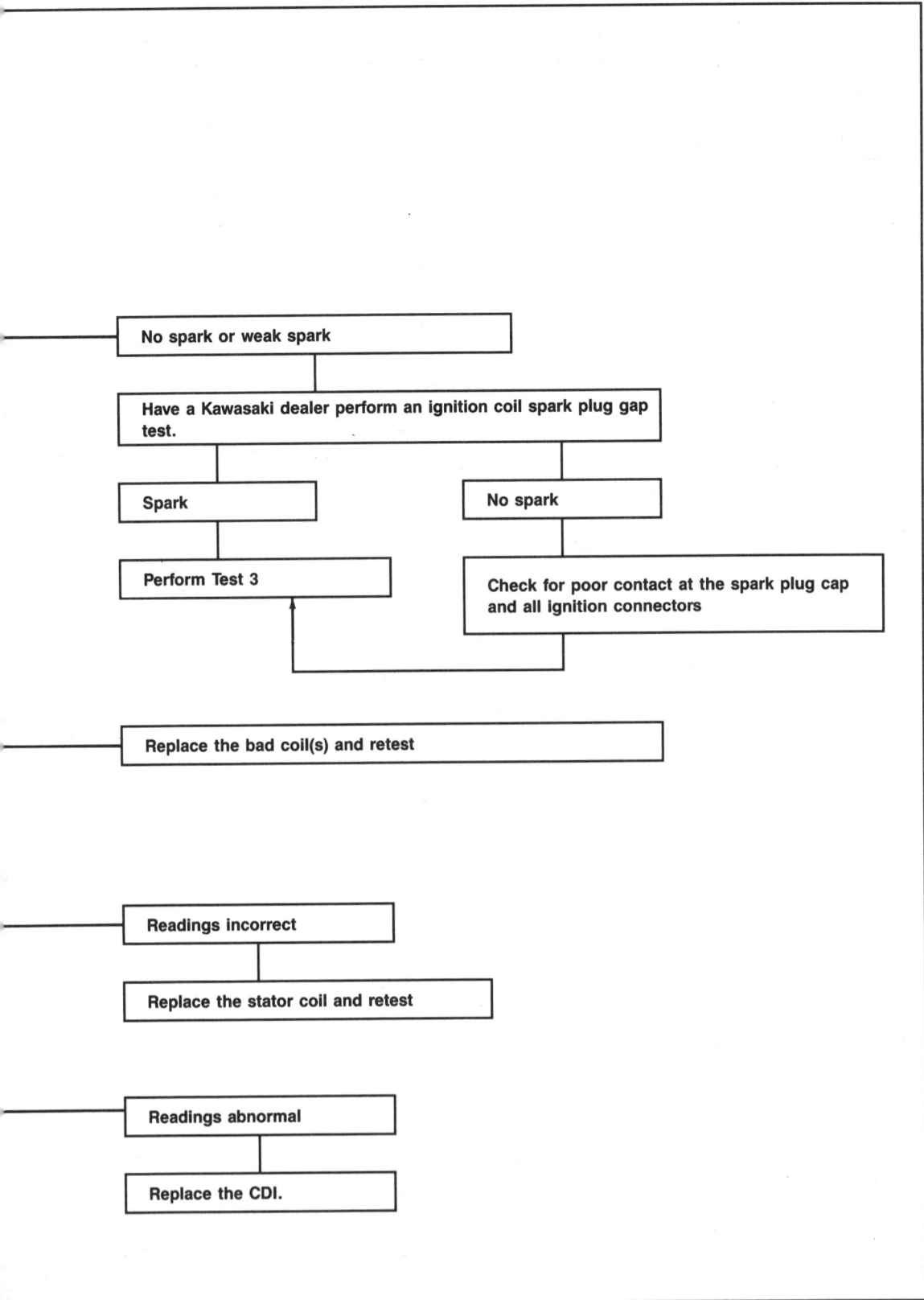

(18) **DISC BRAKE TROUBLESHOOTING**

| Disc brake fluid leakage |

Check:
*Loose or damaged line fittings
*Worn caliper piston seals
*Scored caliper piston and/or bore
*Loose banjo bolts
*Damaged washers
*Leaking master cylinder diaphragm
*Leaking master cylinder secondary seal
*Cracked master cylinder housing
*Too high brake fluid level
*Loose master cylinder cover

| Brake overheating |

Check:
*Warped brake disc
*Incorrect brake fluid
*Caliper piston and/or brake pads hanging up
*Riding brakes during riding

| Brake chatter |

Check:
*Warped brake disc
*Loose brake disc
*Incorrect caliper alignment
*Loose caliper mounting bolts
*Loose front axle nut and/or clamps
*Worn wheel bearings
*Damaged front hub
*Restricted brake hydraulic line
*Contaminated brake pads

| Brake locking |

Check:
*Incorrect brake fluid
*Plugged passages in master cylinder
*Incorrect front brake adjustment
*Caliper piston and/or brake pads hanging up
*Warped brake disc

| Insufficient brakes |

Check:
*Air in brake lines
*Worn brake pads
*Low brake fluid level
*Incorrect brake fluid
*Worn brake disc
*Worn caliper piston seals
*Glazed brake pads
*Leaking primary cup seal in master cylinder
*Contaminated brake pads and/or disc

| Brake squeal |

Check:
*Contaminated brake pads and/or disc
*Dust or dirt collected behind brake pads
*Loose parts

(19)

DRUM BRAKE
TROUBLESHOOTING

2

Brakes do not hold

Check:
*Worn brake linings.
*Glazed brake linings.
*Worn brake drum.
*Glazed brake drum.
*Incorrect brake adjustment.
*Worn or damaged brake cable.
*Worn or defective brake return springs.

Brakes grab

Check:
*Worn or damaged brake return springs.
*Incorrect brake adjustment.
*Brake drum out-of-round.
*Warped brake lining web.
*Loose or worn wheel bearings.

Brakes squeal or scrape

Check:
*Worn brake linings.
*Brake drum out-of-round or scored.
*Contaminated brake linings and/or drum.
*Broken, loose or damaged brake components.
*Loose or worn wheel bearing.

Brake chatter

Check:
*Brake drum out-of-round.
*Brake linings worn unevenly.
*Warped brake lining web.
*Incorrect brake adjustment.
*Loose or worn wheel bearing.
*Worn or damaged brake return springs.

CHAPTER THREE

LUBRICATION, MAINTENANCE, AND TUNE-UP

DNF (did not finish) is a very unpopular but nonetheless often repeated phrase heard throughout race tracks world wide. The cause of a rider's DNF could have been from a crash, but usually it is caused by a mechanical breakdown or failure. This chapter covers all of the regular maintenance required to keep your KX in top shape. Regular maintenance is something you can't afford to ignore if you are racing competitively or trail riding on the weekends. Because the KX is designed and built primarily for motocross competition, it is rugged and reliable and will handle difficult terrain at fast speeds. However, because competition motorcycles are subjected to tremendous heat, stress and vibration, they must be inspected and serviced at regular intervals.

When neglected, any bike becomes unreliable and actually dangerous to ride. By maintaining a routine service schedule as described in this chapter, costly mechanical problems and unexpected breakdowns can be prevented.

This chapter explains lubrication, maintenance and tune-up procedures required for 1983 and later Kawasaki KX60 and KX80 models. **Table 1** and **Table 2** are suggested maintenance schedules. **Tables 1-15** are at the end of the chapter.

NOTE
Due to the number of models and years covered in this book, be sure to follow the correct procedure and specifications for the specific model and year. Also use the correct quantity and type of fluid as indicated in the tables.

PRE-CHECKS

The following checks should be performed prior to each race or before the first ride of the day.
1. Inspect the fuel line and fittings for wetness.
2. Make sure the fuel tank is full and has the correct fuel/oil mixture. Refer to *Engine Lubrication* in this chapter.
3. Make sure the air filter element is clean and that the cover is securely in place.
4. Check the clutch/transmission oil level.

5. Check the operation of the clutch and adjust if necessary.

6. Check that the clutch and brake levers operate properly with no binding. Replace broken levers.

CLYMER RACE TIP
*When checking the clutch and brake lever housings for tightness, do not tighten the lever housing screws (**Figure 1**) so tight that the lever assembly cannot be turned by hand. If the bike is dropped or if you crash, the lever housing will turn around the handlebar. If the housing is too tight,*

the lever will probably bend or break off.

WARNING
While checking the brake and clutch levers, also check the ball on the end of the lever. If the ball is broken off, replace the lever immediately. The lever balls help to prevent the lever from puncturing your hand or arm during a crash.

7. Inspect the front and rear suspension. Make sure it has a good solid feel with no looseness.

8. Check the drive chain for wear and correct tension.

9. Check tire pressure (**Table 3**).

NOTE
*While checking tire pressure, also check the position of the valve stem. If the valve stem is cocked sideways like that shown in **Figure 2**, your riding time could end quickly because of a flat tire. Refer to **Tires and Wheels** in this chapter.*

10. Check the exhaust system for damage.

11. Check the tightness of all fasteners, especially engine and suspension mounting hardware.

12. Check the rear sprocket and bolts as follows:
    a. Check the sprocket holes for signs of egg-shaping. If the sprocket is found in this condition, the sprocket bolts have loosened. Replace the sprocket before the hub is destroyed.
    b. Check the sprocket bolts for tightness.
    c. Replace nuts that have started to round at their head corners.

WARNING
*Never remove the radiator cap (**Figure 3**) or cylinder drain plug when the engine is hot. The coolant is under pressure and removal of the cap or plug can cause severe coolant burns.*

13. *Liquid cooled models:* Remove the radiator cap (**Figure 3**) and check the coolant level. Top off the coolant as described in this chapter. If the coolant level is low, check the hoses for leaks or damage.

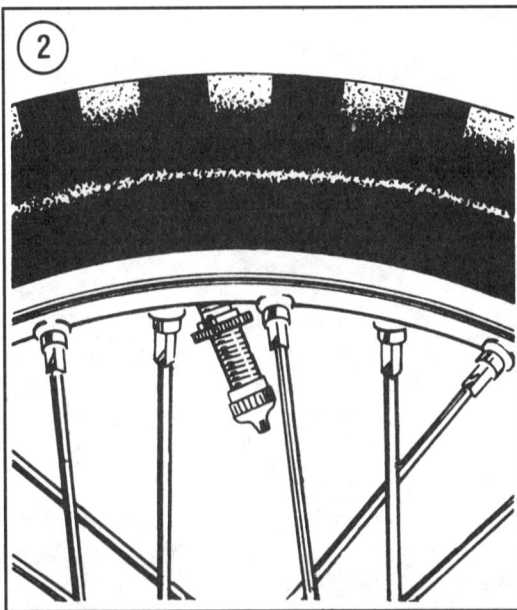

TIRES AND WHEELS

Tire Pressure

Tire pressure should be checked and adjusted to maintain good traction and handling. An accurate gauge should be carried in your tool box. The approximate tire inflation pressure specification for all models is listed in **Table 3**. When racing, track conditions usually dictate tire air pressure. Lower air pressures can be used for soft, smooth or muddy track conditions. If the track is rougher with a number of big jumps or rocks, you may need a higher air pressure.

Tire Inspection

Tires take a lot of punishment due to the variety of terrain they are subjected to. Inspect them periodically for excessive wear, cuts, abrasions, etc. Sidewall tears are the most common cause of tire failure in motocross. This type of damaged is usually caused by sharp rocks or other rider's footpegs. Often times, sidewall tears cannot be seen from the outside. If necessary, remove the tire from the rim as described in Chapter Eleven. Run your hand around the inside tire casing to feel for tears or sharp objects imbedded in the casing. The outside of the tire can be inspected visually.

CLYMER RACE TIP
If a regular standard inner tube is used, replace it every 10 races. A stronger heavy-duty tube will last longer and is not as easy to puncture. The stronger tube weighs more but it's a sacrifice that's worth the durability.

Wheel Spoke Tension

Tap each spoke with a wrench. The higher the pitch of sound it makes, the tighter the spoke. The lower the sound frequency, the looser the spoke. A "ping" is good, a "clunk" says the spoke is too loose.

If one or more spokes are loose, tighten them as described in Chapter Eleven.

NOTE
Most spokes loosen as a group rather than individually. Extra-loose spokes should be tightened carefully. Burying just a few spokes tight into the rim will put improper pressure across the wheel. Refer to Chapter Eleven.

Rim Inspection

Frequently inspect the condition of the wheel rims. If a rim has been damaged it may be enough to cause excessive side-to-side play. Refer to Chapter Eleven.

Tube Alignment

Before each riding day, check the tube's valve stem alignment. **Figure 2** shows a valve stem that has slipped. If the tube is not repositioned, the valve stem will eventually pull away from the tube, causing a flat. However, don't get your tire irons out yet, the tube can be realigned without removing the tire.

1. Wash the tire if it is very dirty or caked with mud.
2. Remove the valve stem core and release all air pressure from the tube.
3. Loosen the rim locknut(s). See **Figure 4**.
4. With an assistant steadying the bike, squeeze the tire and break the tire-to-wheel seal all the way around the wheel. If the tire seal is very tight, it may be necessary to lay the bike on its side and break the tire seal with your foot or a rubber hammer. Use care though; have an assistant steady the bike so that it doesn't rock and damage the handlebars or a control lever.
5. After the tire seal is broken, put the bike on a stand so that the wheel clears the ground.

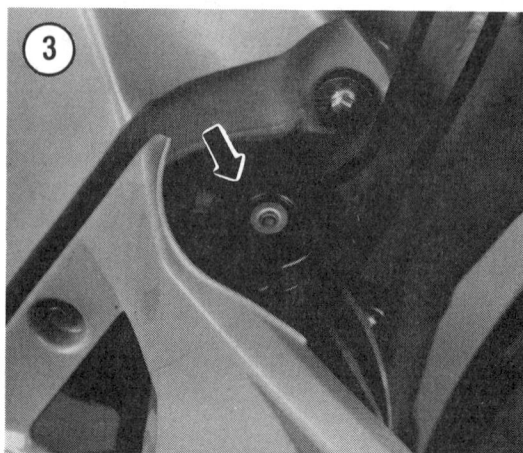

6. Apply a mixture of soap and water from a spray container (like that used when changing a tire) along the tire bead on both sides of the tire.

7. Have an assistant apply the brake "hard." If the wheel turns on drum brakes, tighten the front or rear brake adjuster until the brake will hold.

8. Using both of your hands, grab hold of the tire and turn it and the tube until the valve stem is straight up (90°). See **Figure 5**.

9. When the valve stem is straight up, install the valve stem core and inflate the tire. If the soap and water solution has dried, reapply it to help the tire seat on the rim. Check the tire to make sure it seats all the way around the rim.

WARNING
Do not overinflate the tire and tube. If the tire will not seat properly remove the valve stem core and re-lubricate the tire.

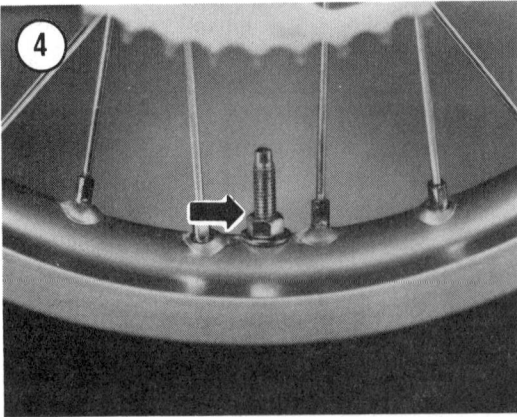

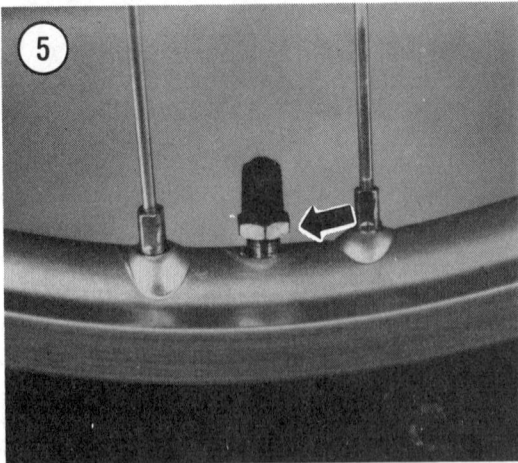

10. Tighten the rim lock(s) securely.

11. Adjust the tire pressure (**Table 3**). When installing the valve stem nut, do not tighten it against the rim. If the tube tire and tube slips again, the valve stem will pull away from the tube and cause a flat. Instead, tighten the nut against the valve cap as shown in **Figure 5**. This will allow the valve stem to slip without damage until you can reposition the tire and tube.

LUBRICANTS

Clutch/Transmission Oil

Oil is graded according to its viscosity, which is an indication of how thick it is. The Society of Automotive Engineers (SAE) system distinguishes oil viscosity by numbers, called "weights." Thick (heavy) oils have higher viscosity numbers than thin (light) oils. For example, a 5 weight (SAE 5) oil is a light oil while a 90 weight (SAE 90) oil is relatively heavy. The viscosity of the oil has nothing to do with its lubricating properties.

Grease

A good quality grease—preferably waterproof—should be used for many of the parts on the KX. Water does not wash grease off parts as easily as it washes off oil. In addition, grease maintains its lubricating qualities better than oil on long and strenuous events.

CLEANING SOLVENT

A number of solvents can be used to remove old dirt, grease, and oil. Kerosene is readily available and comparatively inexpensive. Another inexpensive solvent similar to kerosene is ordinary diesel fuel. Both of these solvents have a very high temperature flash point and can be used safely in any adequately ventilated area away from open flames.

WARNING
Never use gasoline. Gasoline is extremely volatile and contains tremendously destructive potential energy. The slightest spark from metal parts accidentally hitting, or a tool slipping, could cause a fatal explosion.

ENGINE LUBRICATION

WARNING
Serious fire hazards always exist around gasoline. Do not allow any smoking in areas where fuel is being mixed or while refueling the machine. Always have a fire extinguisher, rated for gasoline and electrical fires, within reach just to play it safe.

Proper Fuel Selection

Two-stroke engines are lubricated by mixing 2-stroke oil with the fuel. The various components of the engine are thus lubricated as the fuel/oil mixture passes through the crankcase and cylinders.

Kawasaki recommends the use of any gasoline with a minimum posted pump rating of 87 to prevent engine knock and assure proper operation.

Sour Fuel

Fuel should not be stored for more than a week. Gasoline forms gum and varnish deposits as it ages. Such fuel will cause carburetion and engine deposit troubles that will result in engine starting problems. Make sure to keep the fuel tank cap tight; otherwise some of the fuel could evaporate and result in a too rich oil mixture.

Recommended Fuel Mixture

The engines on all KX60 and KX80 models are lubricated by 2-stroke oil mixed with gasoline. **Table 4** lists the recommended 2-stroke oil. **Table 5** lists fuel/oil mixture ratios for all models. Fuel tank capacity is listed in **Table 6.**

CAUTION
Do not, under any circumstances, use multi-grade or other high detergent automotive oils, or oils containing metallic additives. Such oils are harmful to 2-stroke engines. Since they do not mix properly with gasoline, they will not not burn as 2-stroke oils do and they will leave an ash residue, their use may result in piston scoring, bearing failure or engine damage.

Correct Fuel Mixing

Mix the fuel and oil outdoors. Mix the fuel in a separate container and pour the mixture into the fuel tank after it is properly mixed.

WARNING
Gasoline is an extreme fire hazard. Never use gasoline near sparks, heat or flame. Do not smoke while mixing fuel. Always have a fire extinguisher, rated for gasoline and electrical fires, within reach to play it safe.

Using less than the specified amount of oil can result in insufficient lubrication and serious engine damage. Using more oil than specified causes spark plug fouling, erratic carburetion, excessive smoking and rapid carbon accumulation which can cause preignition.

Cleanliness is of prime importance. Even a very small particle of dirt can cause carburetion problems. Always use fresh gasoline with an octane rating of 87 or higher. Gum and varnish deposits tend to form in gasoline stored in a tank for any length of time. Use of sour fuel can result in carburetor problems and spark plug fouling.

Mix the oil and gasoline thoroughly in a separate clean, sealable container larger than the quantity being mixed to allow room for agitation. Always measure the quantities exactly. See **Table 4** and **Table 5**.

Use a discarded baby bottle with graduations in both cubic centimeters (cc) or fluid ounces (oz.) on the side. Pour the required amount of oil into

the mixing container and add approximately 1/2 the required amount of gasoline. Agitate the mixture thoroughly, then add the remaining fuel and agitate again until all is mixed well.

To avoid any contaminants entering into the fuel system, use a funnel with a filter when pouring the fuel into the tank.

Consistent Fuel Mixtures

The carburetor idle adjustment is sensitive to fuel mixture variations which result from the use of different oils and gasolines or from inaccurate measuring and mixing. This may require readjustment of the idle needle. To prevent the necessity for constant readjustment of the carburetor from one batch of fuel to the next, always be consistent. Prepare each batch of fuel exactly the same as previous ones.

PERIODIC LUBRICATION

Transmission Oil
Checking and Changing

The transmission oil lubricates both the transmission and the clutch. Proper operation and long service for the clutch and transmission require clean oil. Oil should be changed at the intervals indicated in **Table 1** or **Table 2**. Check the oil level frequently and add as necessary to maintain the correct level. Refer to **Table 7** for oil capacities for the various models.

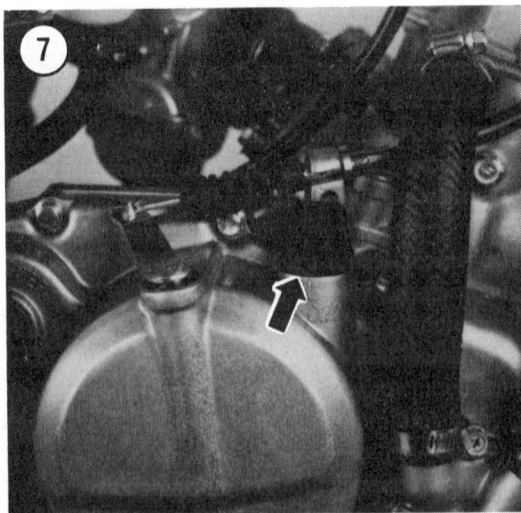

Try to use the same brand of oil. Do not mix 2 brand types at the same time as they all vary slightly in their composition. Use of oil additives is not recommended as it may cause clutch slippage.

Checking

1. Start the engine and let it warm up approximately 2-3 minutes. Shut it off. Wait a few minutes to allow the oil to drain down into the engine.
2. Place the bike in an upright position.
3. Locate the oil level gauge mounted in the clutch cover. See **Figure 6**, typical.
4. The oil level should register between the upper and lower gauge (**Figure 6**) lines. If necessary remove the oil fill cap (**Figure 7**) and add the recommended weight of oil to correct the level.

> *NOTE*
> *If the oil level is too high, remove the oil fill cap and remove excess oil with a siphon. A plunger cap and tube from a discarded hand lotion bottle can be used as a siphon.*

Changing

To drain the oil you will need the following:
a. Drain pan.
b. Funnel.
c. Can opener or pour spout.
d. 1 quart of oil.

There are a number of ways to discard the old oil safely. The easiest way is to pour it from the drain pan into a half-gallon plastic bleach or milk bottle. Tighten the cap and take the oil to a service station or oil retailer for recycling. *Do not* discard the oil in your household trash or pour it onto the ground.

1. Start the engine and let it reach operating temperature.
2. Shut it off and place a drip pan under the engine.
3. Wipe all dirt and debris from around the drain plug. Then remove the drain plug. Remove the oil fill cap to help speed up the flow of oil.
4. Let the oil completely drain.
5. Inspect the sealing washer on the drain plug. Replace if necessary.

6. Replace the drain plug if the corners are starting to round out.

7. Install the drain plug and tighten securely.

8. Fill the transmission with the correct weight and quantity oil. Refer to **Table 4** and **Table 7**.

9. Screw in the oil fill cap and start the engine. Let it idle for 2-3 minutes. Check for leaks.

10. Turn the engine off and check for correct oil level. Adjust as necessary.

Front Fork Oil Change (KX60)

On KX60 models, it is necessary to remove the front forks in order to drain the fork oil. These fork tubes are not fitted with drain screws.

1. Remove the front wheel as described in Chapter Eleven.

2. Disconnect the front brake cable clamp at the left-hand fork tube.

> *CAUTION*
> *Release the air pressure gradually. If released too fast, oil may spurt out with the air. Protect your eyes accordingly.*

3. Remove the air valve cap from each fork tube. Then depress the air valve with a screwdriver.

4. Measure the height distance from the top of the fork crown to the top of the fork tube (not the fork cap) (**Figure 8**). Record this distance so that the fork tubes can be reinstalled into the same position.

5. Loosen the upper fork crown pinch bolt.

> *NOTE*
> *The fork cap is under spring pressure. Remove the cap slowly and don't let it fly off when it is released from the fork tube.*

> *WARNING*
> *If the fork tubes are bent, the fork cap may be under considerable spring pressure. Do not attempt to remove the fork cap. Allow a qualified mechanic to remove the cap and repair the forks for you.*

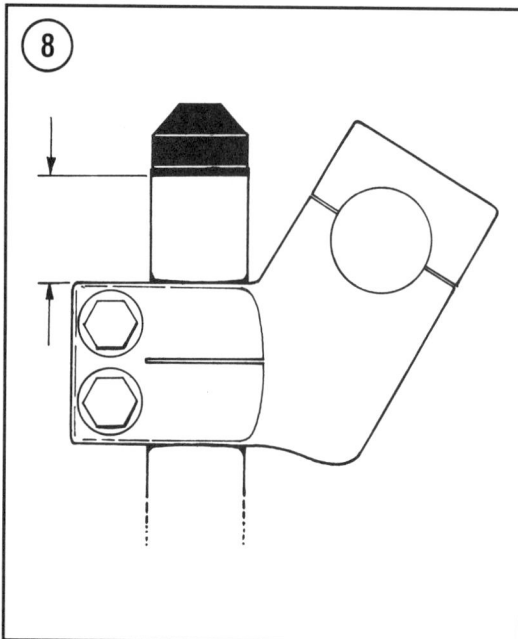

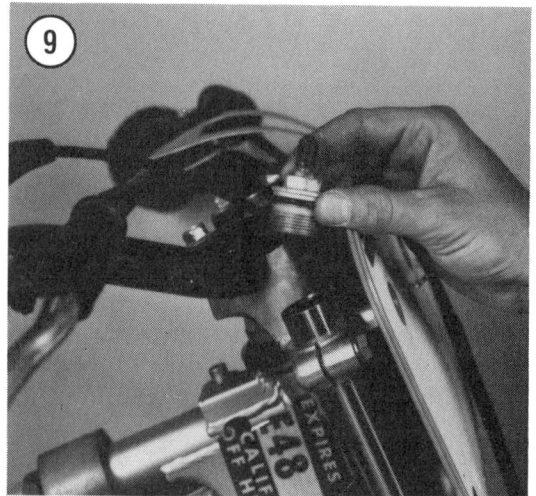

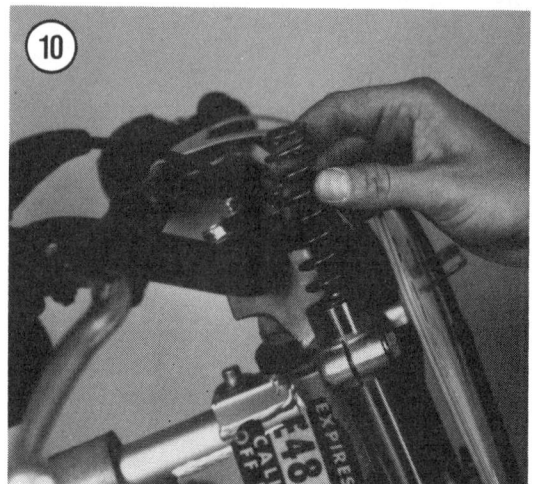

3

6. Loosen and remove the upper fork cap (**Figure 9**) with a socket and a speeder bar or long T-handle.

7. Remove the fork spring (**Figure 10**). Immediately wrap the end of the spring with a rag to prevent oil from dripping onto the floor or bike. Place the fork spring on newspapers laid over the workbench.

8. Loosen the lower fork crown pinch bolt and remove the fork assembly. If necessary, rotate the fork tube while removing it.

9. Turn the fork assembly upside down and pour the fork oil into a pan.

NOTE
Hold the fork assembly upside down and pump it a couple of times to expel any remaining oil trapped in the lower portion of the slider.

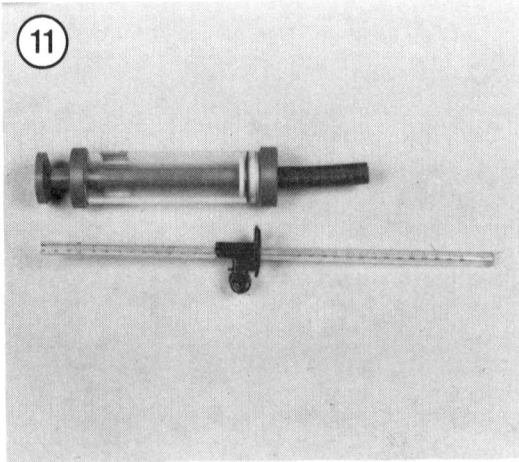

10. Repeat for the opposite fork tube.

11. Fill each fork with the specified weight and quantity fork oil. Refer to **Table 4** and **Table 9**.

NOTE
The weight of the oil can vary according to your own preference and the conditions of the track (lighter weight for less damping and heavier for more damping action). Do add the correct amount of oil as this specification should be followed.

NOTE
In order to measure the correct amount of fluid, use a discarded baby bottle. These have measurements in cubic centimeters (cc) and fluid ounces (oz.) on the side.

12. Using a fork oil level gauge (**Figure 11**), measure the distance from the top of the fork tube to the top of the oil (**Figure 12**). See **Figure 13**. Refer to **Table 9** for the correct specifications. Repeat for the opposite fork. If the oil level is too high, use the gauge to siphon some of the oil out of the fork tube. If the oil level is too low, pour some fork oil into the fork tube. Measure the fork oil level.

NOTE
A tape measure or ruler can be used to perform Step 12. However, to assure a precise oil level, you may want to invest in a fork oil level gauge offered

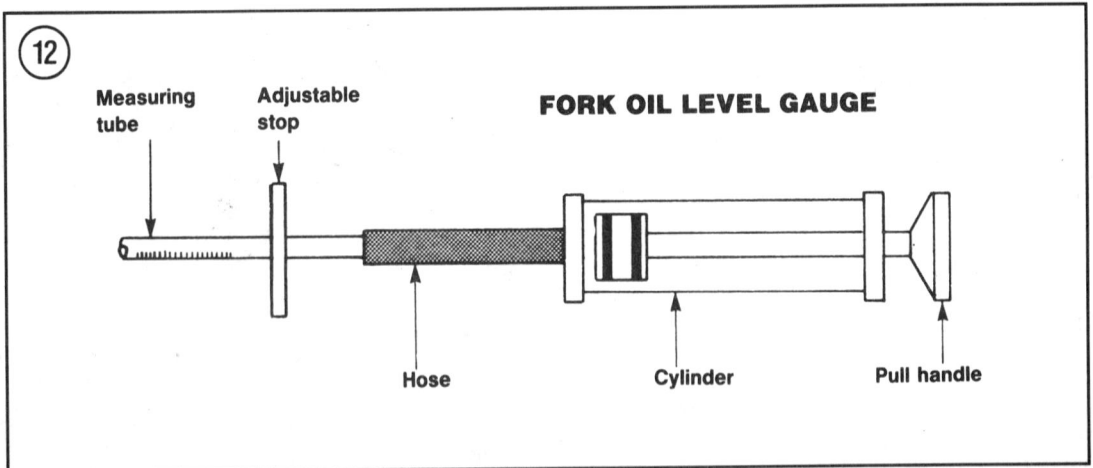

FORK OIL LEVEL GAUGE

Measuring tube

Adjustable stop

Hose

Cylinder

Pull handle

by Kawasaki or one of the numerous companies dealing in motocross accessories. This type of tool works well when you are trying to adjust the suspension at the race track.

13. Reinstall the fork tube into the steering stem assembly so that the top of the fork tube is reinstalled to the dimension recorded in Step 4. Tighten the lower fork crown pinch bolt to the torque specification in **Table 8**.

14. Install the fork spring (**Figure 10**).

15. Inspect the O-ring seal on the upper fork cap (**Figure 14**) and replace if necessary.

16. ·Install the fork cap while pushing down on the spring. Start the fork cap slowly and don't cross-thread it. Tighten it securely.

17. Tighten the upper fork crown pinch bolt to the torque specification in **Table 8**. This bolt must be tightened after the fork cap has been installed and tightened.

18. Install the front wheel as described in Chapter Eleven.

19. *Air assist forks:* Inflate each fork tube to the correct amount of air pressure as described in this chapter.

Front Fork Oil Change (KX80)

The fork oil should be changed at the interval described in **Table 2**. If it becomes contaminated with dirt or water, change it immediately.

1. Support the motorcycle so that the front wheel clears the ground.

2. Remove the fork tube air valve cap. Use a small screwdriver or punch and release all air pressure in the fork (A, **Figure 15**).

CAUTION
Release the air pressure gradually. If released too fast, oil may spurt out with the air. Protect your eyes accordingly.

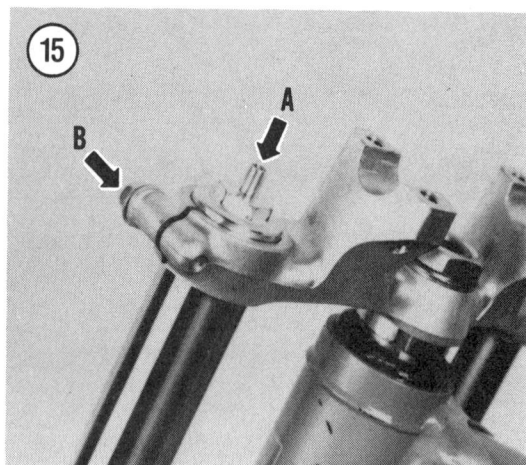

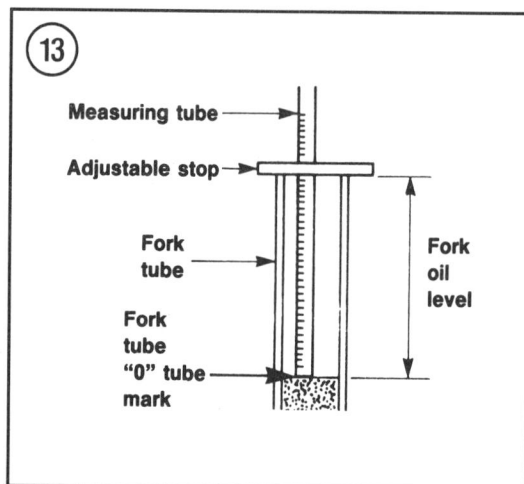

3. Place a drip pan underneath the drain screw (**Figure 16**). Remove the drain screw and allow the oil to drain. Never reuse the oil.

CAUTION
Do not allow the fork oil to contact any of the brake components or to run onto the front tire.

4. Remove the stand or blocks from underneath the bike. With both of the bike's wheels on the

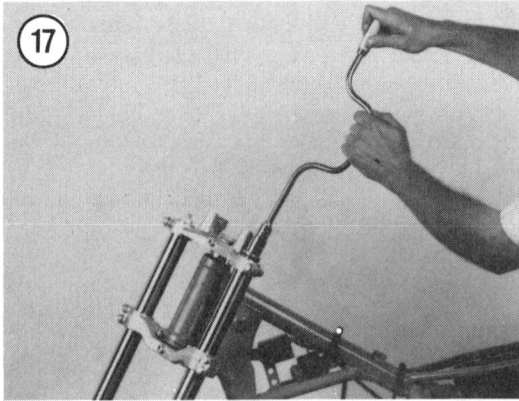

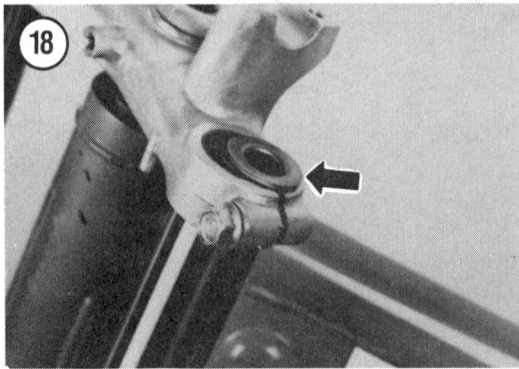

ground, apply the front brake lever and push down on the handlebar. Repeat this action until all the oil is released from the fork tube.
5. Check the drain screw seal. Replace it if worn or damaged.
6. Reinstall the drain screw. Tighten it securely.
7. Repeat Steps 2-6 for the opposite fork tube.
8. Place the motorcycle on a stand so that the front wheel clears the ground.
9. Loosen the upper fork crown pinch bolt (B, **Figure 15**).

NOTE
The fork cap is under spring pressure. Remove the cap slowly and don't let it fly off when it is released from the fork tube.

WARNING
If the fork tubes are bent, the fork cap may be under considerable spring pressure. Do not attempt to remove the fork cap. Allow a qualified mechanic to remove the cap and repair the forks for you.

10. Loosen and remove the upper fork cap with a socket and a speeder bar or long T-handle (**Figure 17**).
11A. *1983:* Remove the fork spring (**Figure 10**).
11B. *1984-1987:* Remove the following:
  a. Spacer.
  b. Spring seat.
  c. Fork spring (**Figure 10**).
11C. *1988-on:* Remove the following:
  a. Spring seat (**Figure 18**).
  b. Spacer (**Figure 19**).
  c. Spring seat (**Figure 20**).
  d. Fork spring (**Figure 20**).

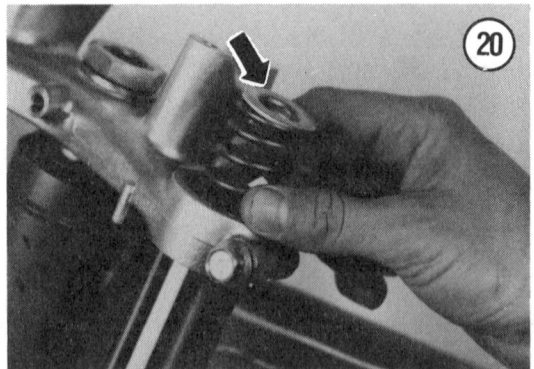

12. Immediately wrap the end of the spring with a rag to prevent oil from dripping onto the floor or bike. Place the fork spring on newspapers laid over the workbench.

13. Fill the fork tube with the specified weight and quantity fork oil. See **Table 4** and **Table 9**.

14. Repeat Steps 10-13 for the opposite fork.

15. Allow the oil to settle for a few minutes. With an assistant's help, roll the bike off of the stand so that the forks are placed in a vertical position.

16. Using a fork oil level gauge (**Figure 11**) measure the distance from the top of the fork tube to the top of the oil (**Figure 12**). Refer to **Table 9** for the correct specifications. Repeat for the opposite fork. **Figure 13** shows a fork oil level gauge being used with the forks removed. If the oil level is too high, use the gauge to siphon some of the oil out of the fork tube. If the oil level is too low, pour some fork oil into the fork tube. Measure the fork oil level.

NOTE
A tape measure or ruler can be used to perform Step 16. However, to assure a precise oil level, you may want to invest in a fork oil level gauge offered by Kawasaki or one of the numerous companies dealing in motocross accessories. This type of tool works well when you are trying to adjust the suspension at the race track.

17. Place the bike onto the stand so that the front wheel clears the ground. Push down on the front wheel so that the forks are completely extended.

18. Check the O-ring in the fork cap (**Figure 14**). Replace it if worn or damaged.

19A. *1983:* Install the fork spring.

19B. *1984-1987:* Install the fork spring, spring seat and spacer.

19C. *1988-on:* Install the fork spring, spring seat, spacer and spring seat.

20. Place the fork cap in position and push it down with a speeder bar and sprocket (**Figure 17**). Install the fork cap by carefully threading it into the fork. Don't cross-thread it. Tighten the fork cap securely.

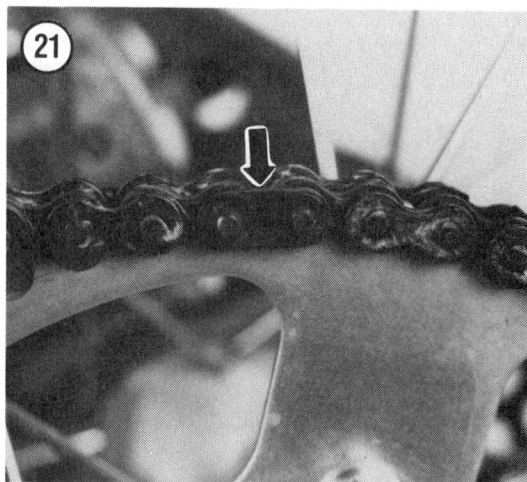

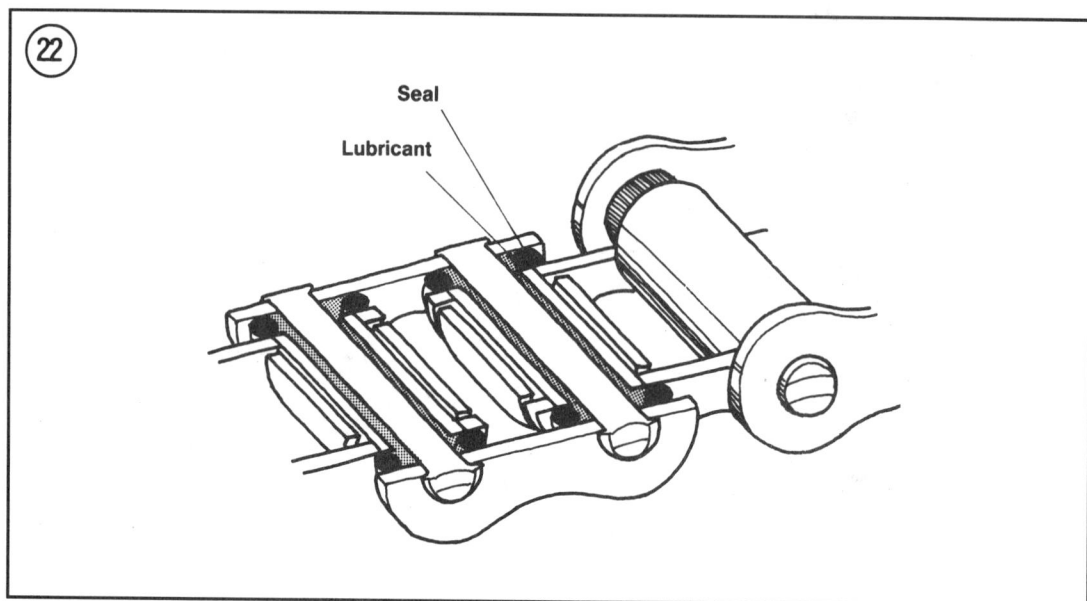

Seal

Lubricant

21. Tighten the upper fork crown pinch bolt to the torque specification in **Table 8**. This bolt must be tightened after the fork cap has been installed and tightened.

22. Inflate each fork tube to the correct amount of air pressure as described in this chapter.

Drive Chain
Cleaning/Lubrication

The drive chain should be cleaned after each race or weekend trail ride. The chain should be lubricated before each ride and during the day as required. A properly maintained chain will provide maximum service life and reliability.

1. Support the bike with a bike stand so that the rear wheel clears the ground.

2. Turn the rear wheel until the master link rides on the rear sprocket. Disconnect the master link (**Figure 21**) and remove the chain from the motorcycle.

CAUTION
*If a drive chain has been installed that is equipped with O-rings between the side plates (**Figure 22**), use only kerosene for cleaning. This is to prevent O-ring damage. Do not use gasoline or other solvents that will cause the O-rings to swell or deteriorate.*

3. Immerse the chain in a pan of cleaning solvent and allow it to soak for about a half hour. Move it around and flex it during this period so that the

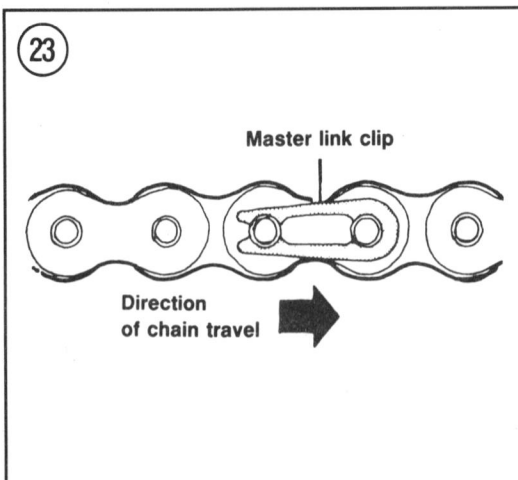

Master link clip

Direction of chain travel

dirt between the pins and rollers may work its way out.

4. Scrub the rollers and side plates with a stiff brush and rinse away loosened dirt. Rinse it a couple of times to make sure all dirt and grit are washed out. Hang up the chain and allow it to thoroughly dry.

5. Lubricate the chain with a good grade of chain lubricant, carefully following the manufacturer's instructions.

6. Reinstall the chain on the motorcycle. Use a new master link clip and install it so that the closed end of the clip is facing the direction of chain travel (**Figure 23**).

WARNING
Always check the master link clip after the bike has been rolled backwards such as unloading from a truck or trailer. The master link clip may have snagged on the chain guide or tensioner and become disengaged. Losing a chain while riding can cause a serious spill not to mention the chain damage which may occur.

Control Cables

The control cables should be lubricated at the general lubrication intervals as described in **Table 1** or **Table 2**. Also they should be inspected at this time for fraying, and the cable sheath should be checked for chafing. The cables are relatively inexpensive and should be replaced when found to be faulty.

A can of cable lube and a cable lubricator will be required for this procedure.

CLYMER RACE TIP
If you are having trouble with the stock cables, you may want to install Teflon-lined cables, such as Terry cables. These cables are smoother than the stock cables and can be washed in warm soapy water. They don't require any oiling and will last longer than the standard cables.

1. Disconnect the cables from the clutch lever and the throttle grip assembly and from where they attach to the carburetor and clutch mechanism.

2. Attach a cable lubricator following the manufacturer's instructions (**Figure 24**).

3. Insert the nozzle of the lubricant can into the lubricator, press the button on the can and hold down until the lubricant begins to flow out of the other end of the cable.

> *NOTE*
> *Place a shop cloth at the end of the cable to catch the oil as it runs out the end or place the end in an empty container. Discard this oil as it is dirty and should not be reused.*

4. Remove the lubricator, reconnect the cable(s) and adjust the cable(s) as described in this chapter.

Miscellaneous Lubrication Points

Lubricate the clutch lever, front brake lever, rear brake pedal pivot point and the sidestand pivot point (if so equipped).

PERIODIC MAINTENANCE

Drive Chain Adjustment

The drive chain should be checked and adjusted prior to each race or weekend ride. Note the following for your model before adjusting the chain. Drive chain free play is listed in **Table 10**.

  a. On 1983-1987 models, drive chain slack is measured on the top chain run.

  b. On 1988 and later models, drive chain slack is measured on the bottom chain run (**Figure 25**).

> *WARNING*
> *Always spin the drive chain in the proper direction. If the wheel is turned in the opposite direction, the master link clip may by pulled off by the chain guide.*

1. Place the bike on a stand so that the rear wheel clears the ground. Spin the rear wheel and check the chain for tightness at several spots. Check and adjust the chain at its tightest point.

2. Lower the bike so that both wheels are on the ground. Support the bike by a sidestand. There should not be a rider on the bike when performing this adjustment.

3. Measure the drive chain slack for your model at a point midway between the 2 sprockets with both wheels on the ground.

4. Compare the drive chain slack with the specifications for your model listed in **Table 10**. If necessary, adjust the drive chain as follows.

5. Place the bike back on the stand so that the rear wheel clears the ground.

6. Remove the rear axle cotter pin (if so equipped). Discard the cotter pin.

7. See **Figure 26** or **Figure 27**. Loosen the axle adjuster locknut (A) and turn the adjuster bolt or

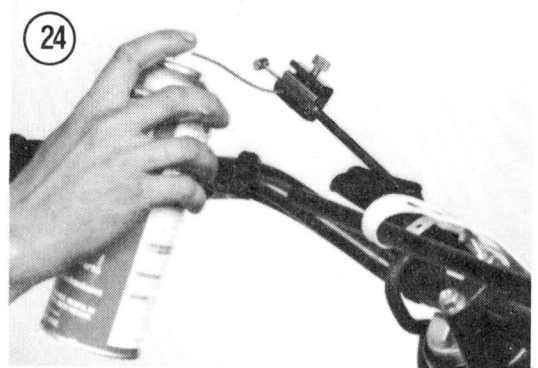

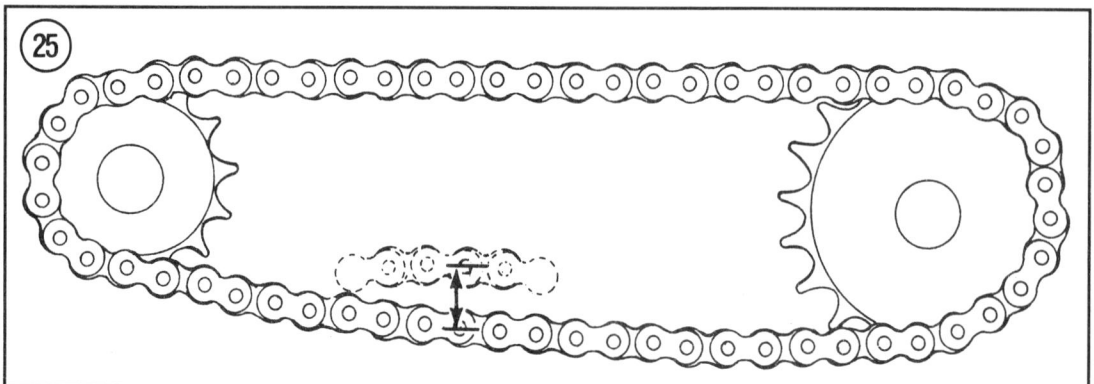

nut (B). Turn the adjuster in or out as required in equal amounts. Be sure that the marks on both adjusters align with the same marks on each side of the swing arm.

8. Sight along the top of the drive chain from the rear sprocket to see that it is correctly aligned. It should leave the top of the rear sprocket in a straight line (A, **Figure 28**). If it is cocked to one side or the other (B and C, **Figure 28**) the wheel is incorrectly aligned and must be corrected. Refer to Step 7.

9. Tighten the rear axle nut to the tightening torque in **Table 8**.

10. If so equipped, install a new cotter pin and bend it over completely.

NOTE
Always install a new cotter pin. Never reuse an old one.

11. After the drive chain has been adjusted, the rear brake pedal free play has to be adjusted as described in this chapter.

12. Check that the drive chain master link is installed properly and that the outer clip is tight on the chain.

13. Lower the bike from the stand.

Drive Chain Inspection

Kawasaki recommends replacing the drive chain when it has stretched longer than 2% of its original length.

A quick check will give you an indication of when to actually measure chain wear. At the rear sprocket, pull one of the links away from the sprocket. If the link pulls away more than ½ the height of a sprocket tooth, the chain has probably worn out (**Figure 29**).

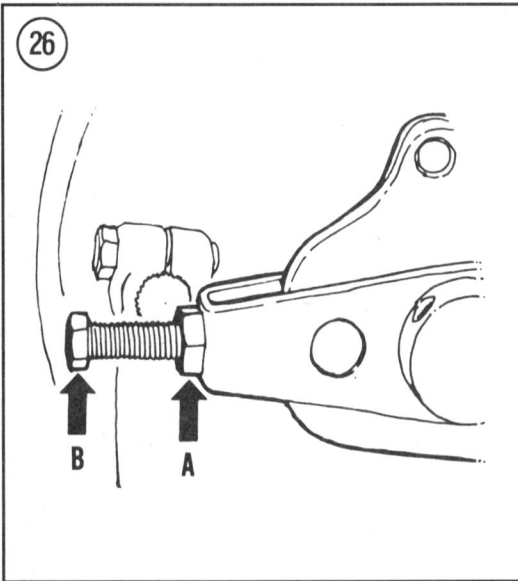

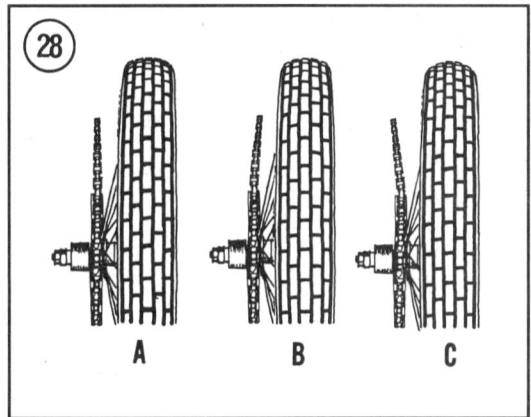

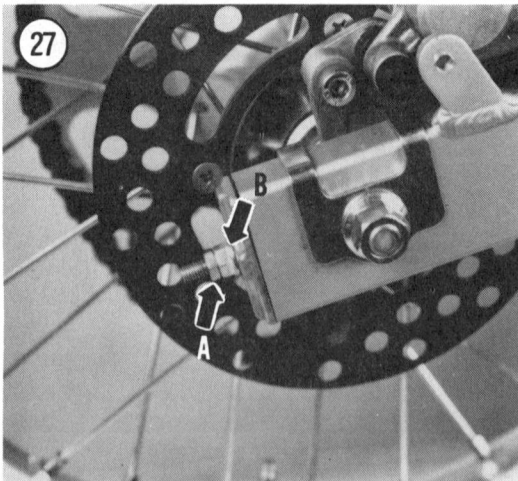

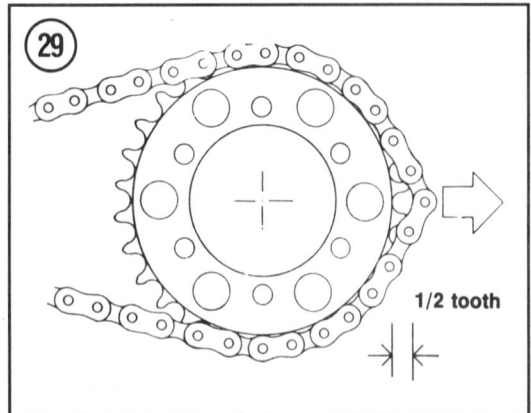

To measure chain wear, perform the following:

1. Loosen the axle nut and tighten the chain adjusters to move the wheel rearward until the chain is taut.

2. Lay a scale along the top chain run, and measure the length of any 20 links in the chain, from the center of the first pin you select to the 21st pin (**Figure 30**). If the link length is more than the limit given in **Table 11**, install a new drive chain.

3. If the drive chain is worn, inspect the rear wheel and engine drive sprockets for undercutting or sharp teeth (**Figure 31**). If wear is evident, replace the sprockets too, or you'll soon wear out a new drive chain.

NOTE
*Check the inner faces of the inner plates (**Figure 32**). They should be lightly polished on both sides. If they show considerable wear on both sides, the sprockets are not aligned. Adjust*

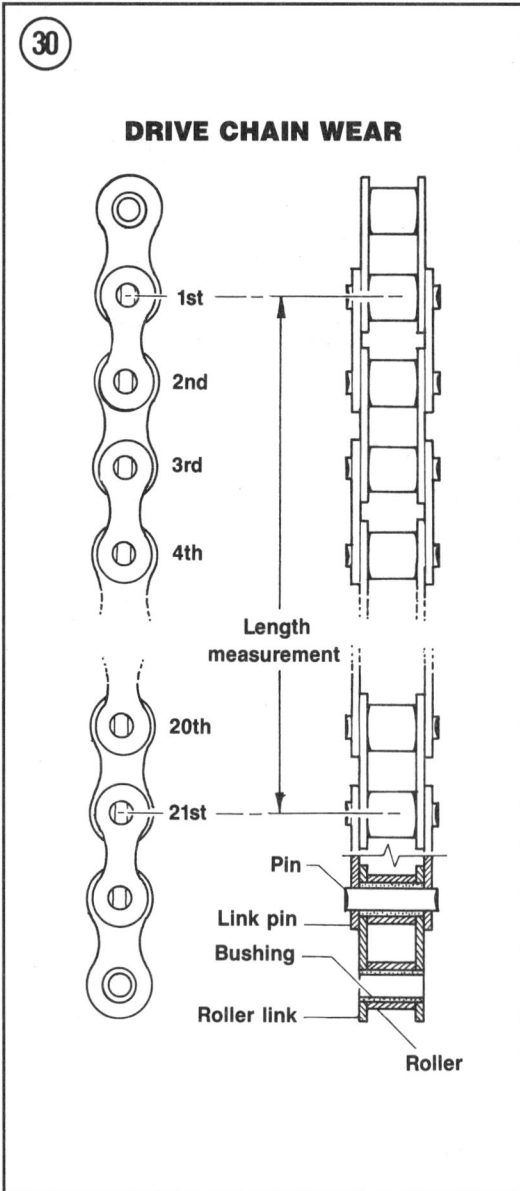

DRIVE CHAIN WEAR

1st
2nd
3rd
4th
Length measurement
20th
21st
Pin
Link pin
Bushing
Roller link
Roller

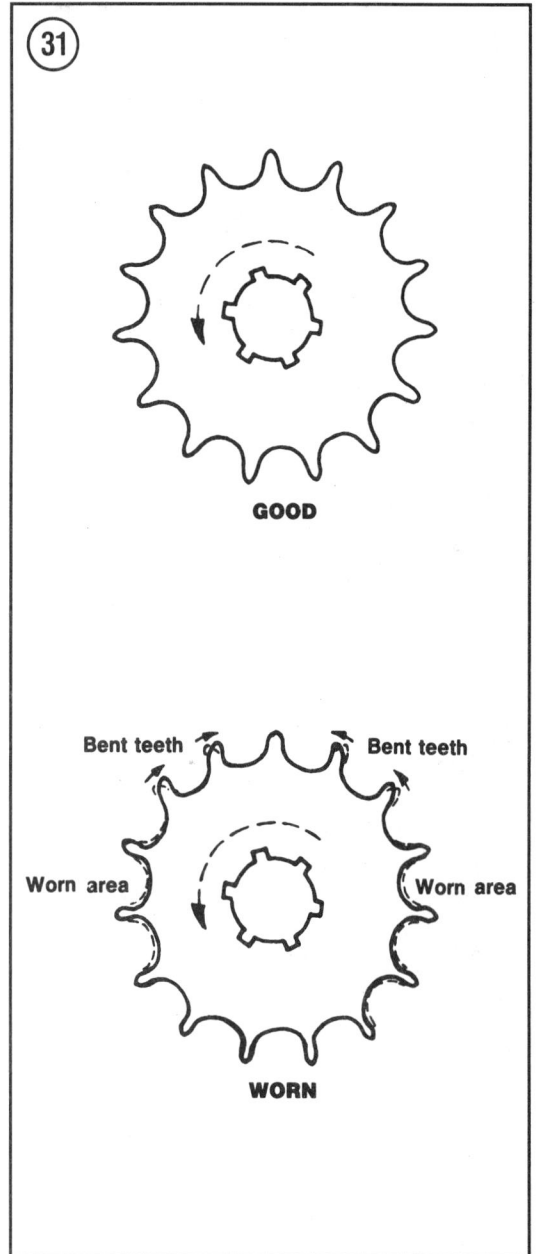

GOOD

Bent teeth — Bent teeth
Worn area — Worn area

WORN

*alignment as described under **Drive Chain Adjustment** in this chapter.*

Drive Chain Guard and Rollers Replacement

The drive chain rollers (**Figure 33**) and guides (**Figure 34**) should be inspected and replaced as necessary. It is a good idea to inspect them prior to each race. Worn or damaged chain rollers or guard can allow the drive chain to damage the rear swing arm.

Front Brake Lever Adjustment (Drum Brakes)

The front brake lever should be adjusted to suit your own personal preference, but should maintain a minimum cable slack of 4-5 mm (5/32-3/16 in.).

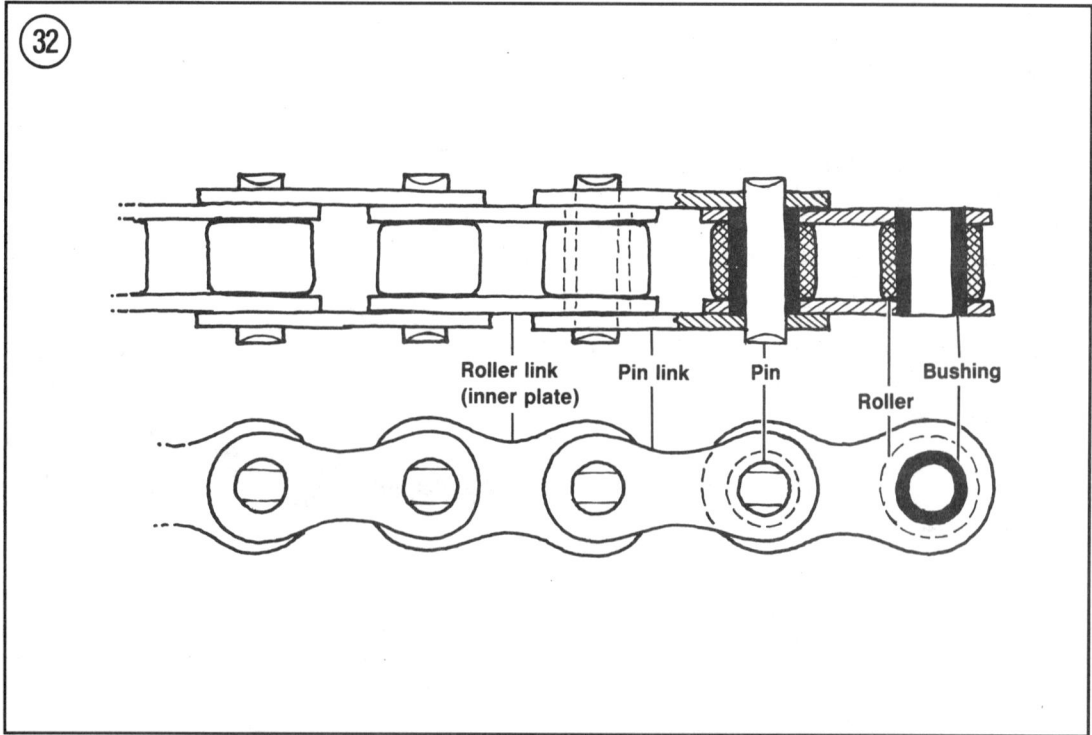

Roller link (inner plate)   Pin link   Pin   Bushing   Roller

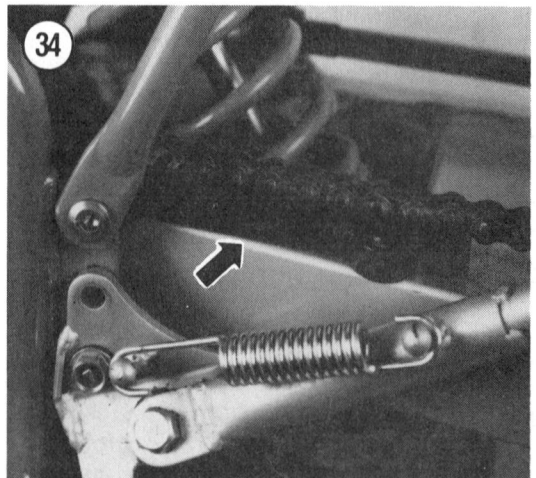

Refer to **Figure 35**. The brake lever should travel this amount before the brake shoes come in contact with the drum, but it must not be adjusted so closely that the brake shoes contact the drum with the lever relaxed. The primary adjustment should be made at the hand lever.

1. Slide back the rubber boot.

2. Loosen the locknut (A, **Figure 36**) and turn the adjusting barrel (B, **Figure 36**) in or out to achieve the correct amount of free play. Tighten the locknut.

3. Because of normal brake wear, this adjustment will eventually be "used up." It is then necessary to loosen the locknut (A) and screw the adjusting barrel (B) all the way in toward the hand grip. Tighten the locknut (A).

4. At the adjuster on the brake panel, loosen the locknut (A, **Figure 37**) and turn the adjuster nut (B, **Figure 37**) until the brake lever can be used once again for the fine adjustment. Be sure to tighten the locknut (A).

5. If proper adjustment cannot be achieved by the use of these adjustment points, the cable has stretched and must be replaced as described in Chapter Thirteen.

> *WARNING*
> *Insufficient brake cable free play will cause the front wheel to lockup.*

Front Brake Lever Adjustment (Disc Brake)

Brake pad wear in the caliper is automatically adjusted as the piston moves forward in the caliper. However, the front brake lever free play must be maintained to prevent excessive brake drag. This would cause premature brake pad wear.

1. Slide back the rubber boot (A, **Figure 38**).

2. Loosen the locknut and turn the adjuster bolt (B, **Figure 38**) in or out to achieve a free play that best suits you.

3. Tighten the locknut and reposition the rubber boot.

> *WARNING*
> *A too tight adjuster position would reduce free play and cause the brake pads to drag on the disc. Brake drag creates excessive heat buildup and*

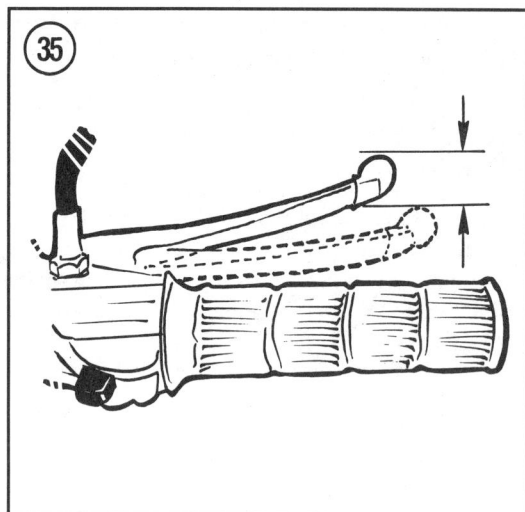

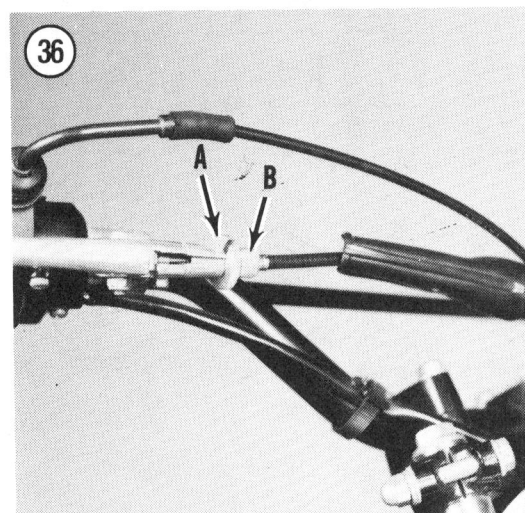

premature pad wear. These conditions could cause the brake to lockup.

4. Support the bike so that the front wheel clears the ground and spin the front wheel. If the wheel does not spin freely, the free play is too tight. Repeat Steps 2 and 3.

Rear Brake Pedal Adjustment (Drum Brake)

Rear brake adjustment is largely a matter of personal preference.

To adjust the rear brake, turn the brake adjusting nut on the brake rod at the rear wheel (**Figure 39**). Normal pedal travel is approximately 20-30 mm (25/32-1 3/16 in.).

The brake pedal height (**Figure 40**) can be changed to suit riding habits. Loosen the adjuster bolt locknut and turn the bolt as required to reposition the brake pedal. Tighten the locknut. See **Figure 41**.

Rotate the rear wheel and check for brake drag. Also operate the pedal several times to make sure it returns to the at-rest position immediately after release.

NOTE
Brake drag can sometimes be difficult to check because of the drag induced by the drive chain. If you are having brake problems and you want to be sure you have removed all brake drag, remove the master link and slip the drive chain off of the rear sprocket. Spin the rear wheel and check the rear brake. Adjust the rear brake as required and reconnect the drive chain and master link.

WARNING
Insufficient brake free play will cause the rear wheel to lock up.

Rear Brake Pedal Adjustment (Disc Brake)

Rear brake adjustment is largely a matter of personal preference.

1. The brake pedal height (**Figure 42**) can be changed to suit riding habits. Loosen the adjuster bolt locknut and turn the bolt (A, **Figure 43**) as required to reposition the brake pedal. Tighten the locknut.

2. To adjust the rear brake, loosen the pushrod locknut at the master cylinder (B, **Figure 43**) and turn the adjuster as required. Tighten the locknut and recheck the adjustment.

> *WARNING*
> *A too tight adjuster position would reduce free play and cause the brake pads to drag on the disc. Brake drag creates excessive heat buildup and premature pad wear. These conditions could cause the brake to lockup.*

3. Support the bike so that the rear wheel clears the ground and spin the wheel. If the wheel does not spin freely, the free play is too tight. Repeat Step 2.

Brake Fluid Level Check (1984-on KX80)

The brake fluid level in the reservoir should always be kept more than half full. See **Figure 44** (front) and **Figure 45** (rear). If the brake fluid drops below half-full, correct by adding fresh DOT 3 brake fluid.

> *NOTE*
> *If the brake fluid level lowers rapidly, check the disc brake line and fittings. Replace the brake line or tighten the fitting(s) if necessary.*

1. Place the bike on level ground.
2. Clean any dirt from the cover prior to removing the cover.
3A. *Front brake:* Perform the following:
  a. Turn the handlebar so that the master cylinder reservoir is level.
  b. Remove the top cover screws and remove the cover and diaphragm (**Figure 44**).
3B. *Rear brake:* Perform the following:
  a. Remove the left-hand side cover.
  b. Unscrew the cover and remove it and the diaphragm (**Figure 45**).

4. Add fresh DOT 3 brake fluid from a sealed container.

> *WARNING*
> *Use brake fluid clearly marked DOT 3 and specified for disc brakes. Others may vaporize and cause brake failure. Do not intermix different brands or types of brake fluid as they may not be compatible. Do not intermix a silicone based (DOT 5) brake fluid as it can cause brake component damage leading to brake system failure.*

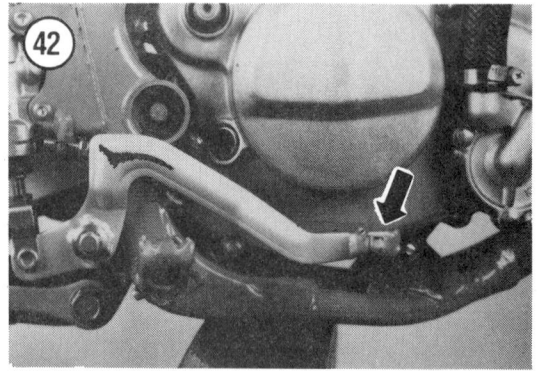

CAUTION
Be careful when handling brake fluid.
Do not spill it on painted or plastic
surfaces as it will destroy the surface.
Wash the area immediately with soap
and water and thoroughly rinse it off.

5. Reinstall the diaphragm and top cover. Install the screws and tighten securely.

Disc Brake Lines

Check the brake line between the master cylinder and the brake caliper. If there is any leakage, tighten the connections and bleed the brake as described in Chapter Thirteen. If this does not stop the leak or if a brake line is obviously damaged, cracked or chafed, replace the brake line and bleed the system (Chapter Thirteen).

Disc Brake Pad Wear

Inspect brake pads for excessive or uneven wear, scoring and oil or grease on the friction surface. Refer to Chapter Thirteen.

Disc Brake Fluid Change

Every time the reservoir cap is removed, a small amount of dirt and moisture enters the brake fluid. The same thing happens if a leak occurs or any part of the hydraulic system is loosened or disconnected. Dirt can clog the system and cause unnecessary wear. Water in the brake fluid vaporizes at high temperature, impairing the hydraulic action and reducing the brake's stopping ability.

To maintain peak performance, change the brake fluid once a year. To change brake fluid, follow the *Brake Bleeding* procedure in Chapter Thirteen.

WARNING
Use brake fluid clearly marked DOT 3
only. Others may vaporize and cause
brake failure.

Clutch Adjustment

Continuous use of the clutch lever causes the clutch cable to stretch. For the clutch to operate correctly, the clutch cable free play (**Figure 46**) must be maintained at 2-3 mm (3/32-1/8 in.). If there is no clutch cable free play, the clutch cannot disengage completely. This would cause clutch slippage and rapid clutch plate wear.

1. Pull the clutch lever toward the handlebar. When cable resistance is felt, hold the lever and measure the distance traveled, shown in **Figure 46**, with a ruler; this is clutch cable free play. If resistance was felt as soon as you pulled the clutch lever, there is no cable free play.

2. See **Figure 47**. At the hand lever, loosen the locknut (A) and turn the adjusting barrel (B) in or out to obtain the correct amount of free play. Tighten the locknut.

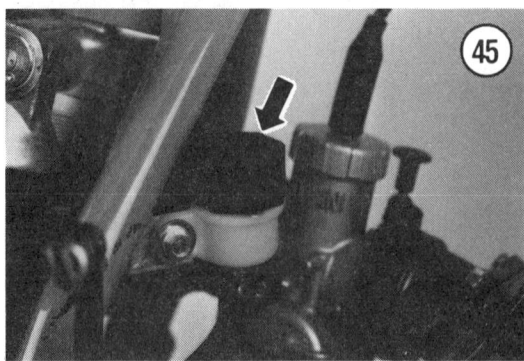

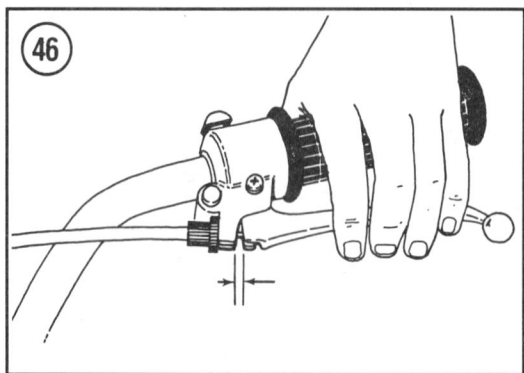

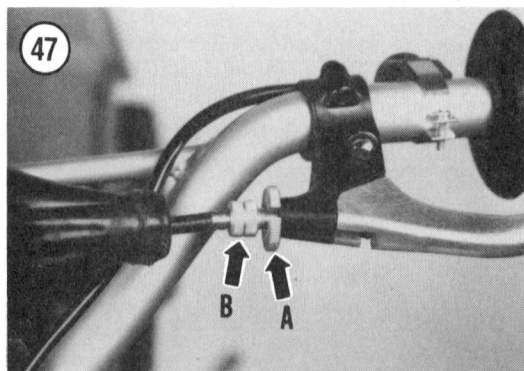

3. If the proper amount of free play cannot be achieved at this adjustment point, loosen the cable's midline adjuster locknut and turn the adjusting barrel in or out. See **Figure 48** or **Figure 49**. Tighten the locknut.

4. If the clutch cable free play cannot be achieved using these adjustment points, the clutch cable has stretched excessively and must be replaced as described in Chapter Six.

Throttle Cable Adjustment and Operation

For correct operation, the throttle cable should have 2-3 mm (3/32-1/8 in.) free play. In time, the throttle cable free play will become excessive from cable stretch. This will delay throttle response and affect low speed operation. On the other hand, if there is no throttle cable free play, an excessively high idle can result.

1. Start the engine and allow it to idle.

2. With the engine at idle, twist the throttle to raise engine speed.

3. Determine the amount of movement (free play) required to raise the engine speed from idle. If the free play is incorrect, perform the following. Turn the engine off.

4. Depending on the model year, throttle cable adjusters are found at the throttle grip (**Figure 50**) and at the top of the carburetor (**Figure 51**).

5. Loosen the adjuster locknut at the throttle grip and turn the adjuster in or out to achieve proper free play. Tighten the locknut securely.

6. If the adjustment cannot be corrected at the throttle grip adjuster, turn the throttle grip adjuster all the way in. Then loosen the locknut at the carburetor (**Figure 51**, if so equipped) and turn the adjuster as required; tighten the locknut. If the adjustment is still incorrect, complete by turning the adjuster at the throttle grip. Tighten the locknut.

7. If the throttle cable cannot be adjusted properly, the cable has stretched excessively and must be replaced.

8. Make sure the throttle grip rotates freely from a fully closed to fully open position.

> *NOTE*
> *If the throttle grip turns slowly, and you feel the cable is adjusted properly and it is not damaged, check the throttle*

grip at the handlebar for damage. A spill on the right-hand side may have damaged the throttle grip assembly.

9. Start the engine and allow it to idle. Turn the handlebar from side-to-side. If the idle increases, the throttle cable is incorrectly routed or there is not enough cable free play.

Throttle Grip

After each race, the throttle grip and throttle housing should be cleaned and serviced.

1. Remove the Phillips screws securing the throttle housing (**Figure 52**).
2. Separate the throttle housings.
3. Disconnect the throttle cable at the twist grip.
4. Clean the inner twist grip bore with aerosol electrical contact cleaner.
5. Clean the throttle housings thoroughly.
6. Check the end of the handlebar for burrs or other damage that would cause the twist grip to stick or rotate slowly. If necessary, smooth the end of the handlebar with sandpaper or a file.
7. Install by reversing these steps. Make sure the throttle grip rotates freely from a fully closed to fully open position.

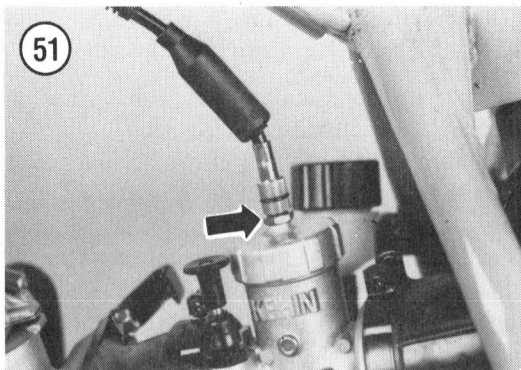

> *WARNING*
> *Do not ride the bike if the throttle grip is not operating correctly. A stuck throttle may cause you to crash.*

Air Filter

The air filter element should be removed, cleaned, and re-oiled at intervals indicated in **Table 1** or **Table 2**.

The air filter removes dust and abrasive particles from the air before it enters the carburetor and engine. Very fine particles that may enter into the engine will cause rapid wear to the piston rings, cylinder and bearings and may clog small passages in the carburetor. Never run the KX without the air filter element installed.

Proper air filter servicing can do more to ensure long service from your engine than any other single item.

> *CLYMER RACE TIP*
> *While preparing your bike for a race, you should have 1 or 2 extra air filter elements on hand and stored in a plastic bag so that if race conditions are extremely dusty or muddy, the dirty element can be replaced after practice or between motos.*

Removal/installation

Due to the number of different KX models covered in this manual, the following should be used as a basic guide to removal and installation.
1A. *KX60:* Remove the left-hand side cover.
1B. *1983-1985 KX80:* Remove the left-hand side cover.
1C. *1986-1987 KX80:* Remove the right-hand side cover.
1D. *1988-on KX80:* Remove the seat.
2. *All models except 1988-on KX80:* Remove the air filter cover screws and remove the cover (**Figure 53**, typical). On some models, it will be necessary to loosen the air filter housing hose

clamp at the carburetor. Then remove the air filter housing/air filter element assembly. Take the filter out of the housing.

3. *1985-on:* Remove the screws or wing nuts securing the air filter element to the housing. Remove the element. See **Figure 54** or **Figure 55**.

4. Inspect all fittings, hoses and connections from the air box to the carburetor. Make sure that all are airtight and that they will not let in any unfiltered air.

5. Clean the air filter element as described in this chapter.

6. Install the filter element by reversing these steps.

Foam filter cleaning

All models are equipped with a foam air filter element. To work properly, the filter element must be properly cleaned and oiled with a foam air filter oil.

1. Remove the air filter element as described in this chapter.

2. Stuff a clean shop rag into the carburetor opening to prevent the entry of foreign matter.

3. Examine the inside of the air box. There should be no signs of dust or dirt on the inside of the air box that is properly protected by the air filter. If dirt is noticeable, the air filter may be damaged or it was improperly serviced.

4. Clean the inside of the air box with a clean shop rag soaked in solvent or soap and water.

5. After the air box has dried, coat the inside of the air box with a layer of wheel bearing grease. Apply the grease with your hands so that it covers all of the air box inside surfaces. The grease works like an additional filter and will help to catch passed dirt.

6. If your filter element uses a plastic guide, remove it from the filter element (**Figure 55**).

> *CAUTION*
> *Do not clean the air filter element with gasoline. Besides being a fire hazard, gasoline will break down the filter's seam glue and corrode the seam stitching. This will cause the filter to leak.*

7. Fill a clean pan with liquid cleaner and warm water. If you are using an accessory air filter, the manufacturer may sell a special air filter cleaner.

8. Submerge the filter into the cleaning solution and gently work the cleaner solution into the filter pores. Soak and squeeze (gently) the filter element to clean it.

> *CAUTION*
> *Do not wring or twist the filter element when cleaning it. This harsh action could damage a pore or tear the filter element loose at a seam. This would allow unfiltered air to enter the engine and cause severe and rapid wear.*

9. Rinse the filter element under warm water while soaking and gently squeezing it.

10. Repeat Step 8 and Step 9 two or three times or until there are no signs of dirt being rinsed from the filter element.

11. After cleaning the filter element, inspect it. If it is torn or broken in any area, it should be replaced. Do not run the engine with a damaged

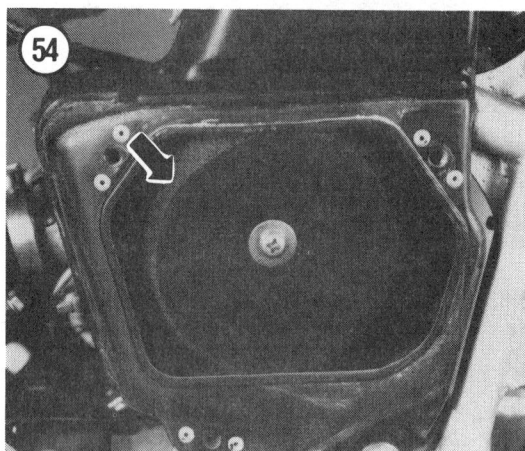

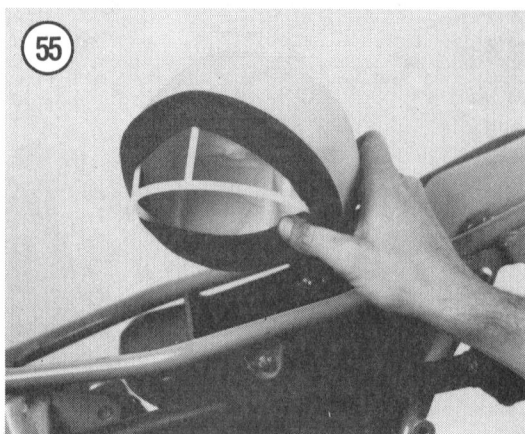

filter element as it may allow dirt to enter the engine and cause severe engine wear.

12. Set the filter element aside and allow it to dry thoroughly.

> *CAUTION*
> *A damp filter element will not trap fine dust. Make sure the filter element is **completely** dry before oiling it.*

13. Properly oiling an air filter element is a messy job. You may want to wear a pair of disposable rubber gloves when performing this procedure. Oil the filter as follows:

   a. Purchase a box of gallon size resealable plastic storage bags. The bags can be used when cleaning the filter as well as for storing engine and carburetor parts during disassembly.

   b. Place the cleaned filter element into a storage bag.

   c. Pour foam air filter oil onto the filter element to soak it.

   d. Gently squeeze and release the filter element to soak filter oil into the filter's pores. Repeat until all of the pores are discolored with the oil.

   e. Remove the filter element from the bag and check the pores for uneven oiling. This is indicated by light or dark areas. If necessary soak the filter element and squeeze it again.

   f. When the filter element oiling is even, squeeze the filter element a final time.

14. Remove the filter element from the bag. Install the plastic filter support inside the filter element, if so equipped.

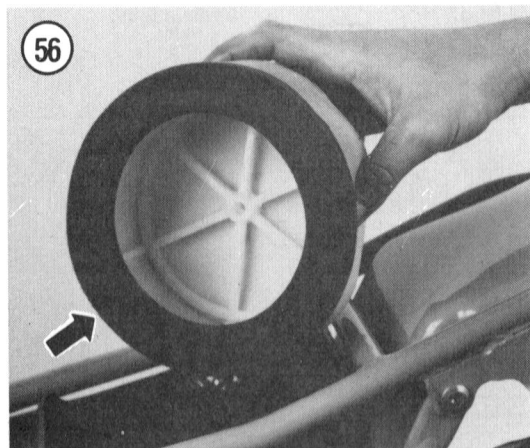

15. Apply a coat of thick wheel bearing grease to the filter's sealing surface (**Figure 56**).

16. Install the air filter assembly as described in this chapter.

17. Pour the left over filter oil from the bag back into the bottle for reuse.

18. Dispose of the plastic bag.

Fuel Line Inspection

Inspect the fuel line from the fuel tank to the carburetor. If it is cracked or starting to deteriorate it must be replaced. Make sure the small hose clamps are in place and holding securely. Also make sure that the overflow and vent tubes are in place.

> *WARNING*
> *A damaged or deteriorated fuel line presents a very dangerous fire hazard to both the rider and the machine if fuel should spill⁻ onto a hot engine or exhaust pipe.*

> *CLYMER RACE TIP*
> *If you have been experiencing fuel contamination that is plugging carburetors jets (especially the pilot jet), install a fuel filter in the fuel line between the fuel tank and the carburetor. Use the stock Kawasaki fasteners to hold the fuel line to the filter.*

Wheel Bearings

The wheel bearings should be cleaned and repacked at the interval listed in **Table 1** or **Table 2** or more often if the vehicle is operated often in water (especially salt water). The correct service procedures are covered in Chapter Eleven (front) or Chapter Twelve (rear).

Steering Head Adjustment Check

The steering head pivot assembly on all KX60 and 1983-1985 KX80 models consists of upper and lower inner and outer bearing races separated by loose ball bearings. On 1986 and later KX80 models, tapered roller bearings are used. Because the KX models are subjected to rough terrain and

3

conditions, bearing play should be checked and adjusted at the interval listed in **Table 1** or **Table 2**. A loose bearing adjustment will hamper steering and cause premature bearing and race wear. In severe conditions, a loose bearing adjustment can cause loss of control.

1. Place the bike on a stand so that the front wheel clears the ground.

2. Hold onto the front forks tubes and gently rock the fork assembly back and forth. If you can feel looseness, adjust the steering head bearings as described in Chapter Eleven.

Liquid Cooling System Inspection (Models so Equipped)

WARNING
When performing any service work to the engine or cooling system, never remove the radiator cap, coolant drain screws or disconnect any hose while the engine and radiator are hot. Scalding fluid and steam may be blown out under pressure and cause serious injury.

Once a year, or whenever troubleshooting the cooling system, the following items should be checked. If you do not have the test equipment, the tests can be done by a Kawasaki dealer, radiator shop or service station.

1. Remove the radiator cap (**Figure 57**).

2. Check the rubber washers on the radiator cap. Replace the cap if the washers show signs of deterioration, cracking or other damage. If the radiator cap washers are okay, perform Step 3.

CAUTION
Do not exceed 1.25 kg/cm² (17.8 psi) when performing Steps 3 and 4 or damage to the cooling system will occur.

3. Have the radiator cap pressure tested (**Figure 58**). The specified radiator cap relief pressure is 0.95-1.25 kg/cm² (13.5-17.8 psi). The cap must be able to sustain this pressure for 6 seconds. Replace the radiator cap if it does not hold pressure.

4. Leave the radiator cap off and have the entire cooling system pressure tested. The entire cooling system should be pressurized to 0.95-1.25 kg/cm² (13.5-17.8 psi). The system must be able to hold this

pressure for 10 seconds. Replace or repair any components that fail this test.

5. Check all cooling system hoses for damage or deterioration. Replace any hose that is questionable. Make sure all hose clamps are tight.

6. Carefully clean any dirt, mud, bugs, etc. from the radiator core. Use a whisk broom, compressed air or low-pressure water. If the radiator has been hit by a rock, *carefully* straighten out the fins with a flat-bladed screwdriver.

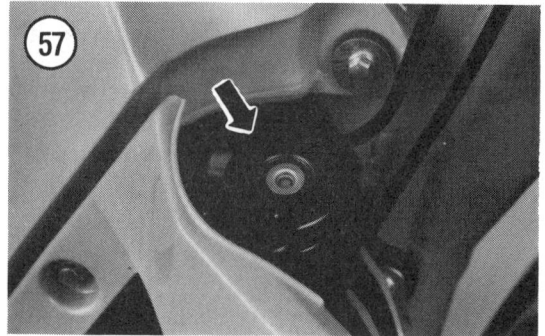

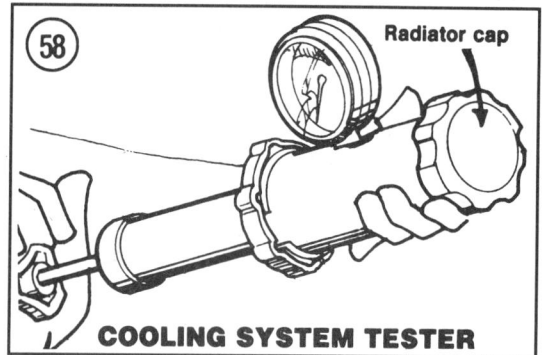

COOLING SYSTEM TESTER

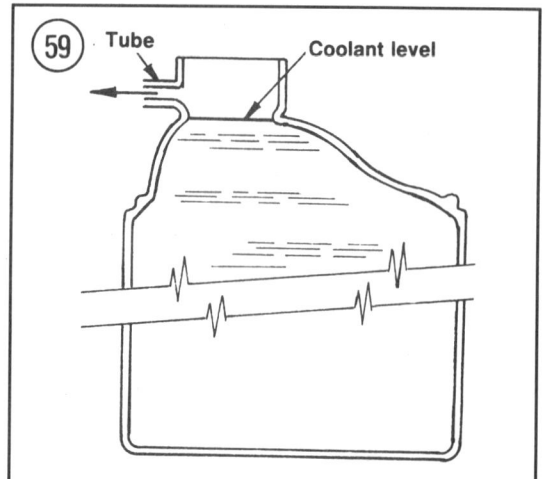

NOTE
If the radiator has been damaged across 20% or more of the frontal area, the radiator should be replaced.

Coolant Check

WARNING
Do not remove the radiator cap when the engine is hot.

Before starting the bike, check the coolant level in the radiator. Remove the radiator cap (**Figure**

57). The coolant should be at the bottom of the radiator filler neck as shown in **Figure 59**. If the level is low, add a sufficient amount of coolant and distilled water (in a 50:50 ratio) as described under *Coolant*. Reinstall the radiator cap.

Coolant

Only a high quality ethylene glycol-based coolant compounded for aluminum engines should be used. The coolant should be mixed with distilled water in a 50:50 ratio. Coolant capacity is listed in **Table 12**. When mixing antifreeze with distilled water, make sure to use only distilled water. Never use tap or salt water as this will damage engine parts. Distilled water can be purchased at supermarkets in gallon containers.

Coolant Change

The cooling system should be completely drained and refilled at the intervals indicated in **Table 1** or **Table 2**.

CAUTION
Use only a high quality ethylene glycol antifreeze coolant specifically labeled for use with aluminum engines. Do not use an alcohol-based antifreeze.

The following procedure must be performed when the engine is *cold*.

CAUTION
Be careful not to spill antifreeze coolant on painted surfaces as it will destroy the surface. Wash immediately with soapy water and rinse thoroughly with clean water.

1. Place a clean container under the water pump.
2. Remove the radiator cap (**Figure 57**). This will speed up the draining process.
3. Remove the water pump drain bolt and allow the coolant to drain into a pan. See **Figure 60** (KX60) or **Figure 61** (KX80).
4. *1986-on KX80:* Place a rag underneath the cylinder coolant drain plug (**Figure 62**). Remove the bolt and lean the bike over to allow the coolant to drain into a pan.

5. Do not install the drain bolts.

6. Flush the cooling system with clean tap water directed through the radiator filler neck. Allow this water to drain completely.

7. Install the drain bolt(s).

8. Refill the radiator. Add the coolant through the radiator filler neck. Use a 50:50 mixture of antifreeze coolant and distilled water. Radiator capacity for all models is listed in **Table 12**. Do not install the radiator cap at this time.

9. Start the engine and let it run at idle speed until the engine reaches normal operating temperature. Make sure there are no air bubbles in the coolant and that the coolant level stabilizes at the correct level (**Figure 59**). Add coolant as necessary until the correct level is reached.

10. Install the radiator cap.

11. After the engine has cooled, remove the radiator cap and check the coolant level. Add coolant up to the filler neck, if necessary. Reinstall the radiator cap.

Handlebars

Inspect the handlebars weekly for any signs of damage. A bent or damaged handlebar should be replaced; do not attempt to straighten or weld a handlebar. These procedures can weaken the handlebar and cause it to break.

The knurled section on carbon steel and chrome-moly handlebars should be kept very rough. Keep the clamps clean with a wire brush. Any time that the bars slip in the clamps (like when you land flat and they move forward slightly) they should be removed and wire brushed clean to prevent small balls of aluminum from gathering in the clamps and reducing their gripping abilities. Checking the condition of aluminum bars is especially critical because they are not knurled at the mounting position. If an aluminum bar slips, its gripping power is reduced. Remove the bar and check the mounting area thoroughly.

If you are going to install a new handlebar and the KX has a front disc brake, make sure the handlebar is long enough to accept the master cylinder reservoir; the reservoir assembly is longer than the brake lever setup used on drum brakes.

Check the handlebar mounting bolts for tightness. Refer to **Table 8** for torque specifications.

CLYMER RACE TIP

Some riders find it preferable to "tune" the handlebar width by cutting up to 2 inches from each end. This will allow the smaller rider to more easily handle the machine. There are many excellent aftermarket handlebars available which come in a variety of sizes, shapes and colors. When looking for handlebars, look for a comfortable bend and strong material, preferably chrome-moly, which is stronger than steel and won't bend easily. You also should purchase a cross bar pad to protect your face and teeth.

Handlebar Grips

Handlebar grips (**Figure 63**) should be tight on the handlebar. During a spill, the handlebar usually catches the brunt of the accident and consequently one of the grips is damaged. A common problem is having the grip tear or rip at the end of the handlebar. This condition reduces the grip's holding power. If a grip is damaged, it should be replaced.

To remove a grip, insert a thin-tipped screwdriver underneath the grip and squirt some aerosol electrical contact cleaner between the grip and handlebar or twist grip. Quickly remove the screwdriver and twist the grip to break its hold on the handlebar or twist grip; slide the grip off. Remove any burrs from the end of the handlebar with a file and clean the handlebar thoroughly. When installing new grips, squirt aerosol electrical

contact cleaner into the grip as used during removal and quickly push and twist it onto the handlebar or twist grip. Allow plenty of time for the aerosol electrical contact cleaner to evaporate and the grip to take hold before riding the bike. Some riders wrap safety wire at both ends of the grips for additional holding power.

> *WARNING*
> *Loose grips can cause you to crash. Always replace damaged or loose grips before riding.*

Nuts, Bolts and Other Fasteners

Constant vibration can loosen many of the fasteners on the motorcycle. Check the tightness of all fasteners, especially those on:
  a. Engine mounting hardware.
  b. Engine crankcase covers.
  c. Handlebar and front forks.
  d. Gearshift lever.
  e. Kickstarter lever.
  f. Brake pedal and lever.
  g. Exhaust system.

ENGINE TUNE-UP

The number of definitions of the term "tune-up" is probably equal to the number of people defining it. For the purposes of this book, a tune-up is general adjustment and maintenance to insure peak engine performance.

The following paragraphs discuss each facet of a proper tune-up which should be performed in the order given. Unless otherwise specified, the engine should be thoroughly cool before starting any tune-up procedure.

Have the new parts on hand before you begin.

To perform a tune-up on the KX, you will need the following tools and equipment:
  a. 14 mm spark plug wrench.
  b. Socket wrench and assorted sockets.
  c. Phillips head screwdriver.
  d. Spark plug wire feeler gauge and gapper tool.

Cylinder Head Nuts or Bolts

The engine must be at room temperature for this procedure.
1. Support the bike on a stand.

2. Tighten each nut or bolt equally in a crisscross pattern to the tightening torque in **Table 8**.

Cylinder Compression

A cylinder cranking compression check is one of the quickest ways to check the internal condition of the engine: rings, head gasket, etc. It's a good idea to check compression at each tune-up, write it down, and compare it with the reading you get at the next tune-up. This will help you spot any developing problems.
1. Warm the engine to normal operating temperature. Shut the engine off.
2. Remove the spark plug.
3. Insert the tip of a compression gauge into the hole. Make sure the gauge is seated properly.

> *NOTE*
> *You may have to remove the fuel tank to provide clearance for the gauge. See Chapter Eight.*

> *NOTE*
> *Press the kill switch while performing Step 4.*

4. Hold the throttle wide open and crank the engine several revolutions until the compression gauge gives its highest reading. Record the reading. Refer to **Table 13** for compression readings. If the reading is only slightly below normal, ring or cylinder wear is likely. If the compression is very low, it's likely that a ring is broken or there is a hole in the piston crown.

Correct Spark Plug Heat Range

Spark plugs are available in various heat ranges, hotter or colder than the plugs originally installed at the factory.

Select plugs of the heat range designed for the loads and conditions under which the KX will be run. Use of incorrect heat ranges can cause a seized piston, scored cylinder wall, or damaged piston crown.

In general, use a hot plug for low speeds, low engine loads and low temperatures. Use a cold plug for high speeds, high engine loads and high temperatures. The plug should operate hot enough to burn off unwanted deposits, but not so hot that they burn themselves or cause preignition. A spark of the correct heat range will show a light tan color on the portion of the insulator within the cylinder after the plug has been in service.

The reach (length) of a plug is also important. A longer than normal plug could interfere with the piston, causing permanent and severe damage. Refer to **Figure 64**.

The standard heat range spark plug for the various models is listed in **Table 14**.

Spark Plug Removal

CAUTION
Whenever the spark plug is removed, dirt around the plug or underneath the fuel tank can fall into the plug hole. This can cause expensive engine damage.

1. Grasp the spark plug cap (**Figure 65**) as near the plug as possible and pull it off the plug. If it is stuck to the plug, twist it slightly to break it loose. Pulling on the lead instead of the cap may cause the cap and lead to separate.

2. Blow out any foreign matter from around the base of the spark plug with compressed air. If you do not have a compressor, use a can of compressed inert gas, available from photo stores.

NOTE
If there is a lot of dirt collected underneath the fuel tank, wrap a large cloth around the tank. The cloth will prevent dirt from falling into the cylinder head plug hole when the plug is removed.

3. Remove the spark plug with a 14 mm spark plug wrench.

NOTE
If the plug is difficult to remove, apply penetrating oil, like WD-40 or Liquid Wrench, around the base of the plug and let it soak in about 10-20 minutes.

4. Inspect the plug carefully as described under *Reading Spark Plugs* in this chapter. Look for a broken center porcelain, excessively eroded electrodes and excessive carbon or oil fouling.

5. If necessary, discard the plug after inspection. Cleaning spark plugs is not recommended. A new plug is inexpensive and is far more reliable.

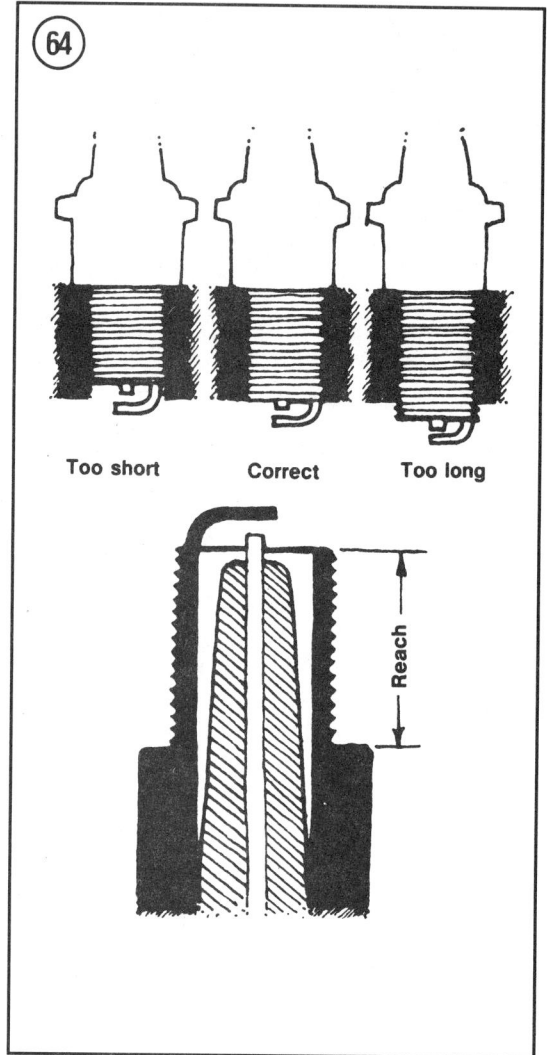

Too short   Correct   Too long

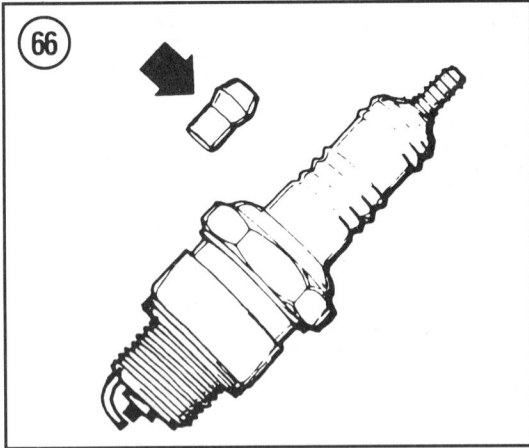

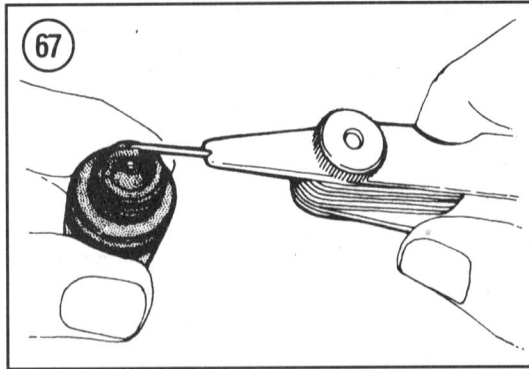

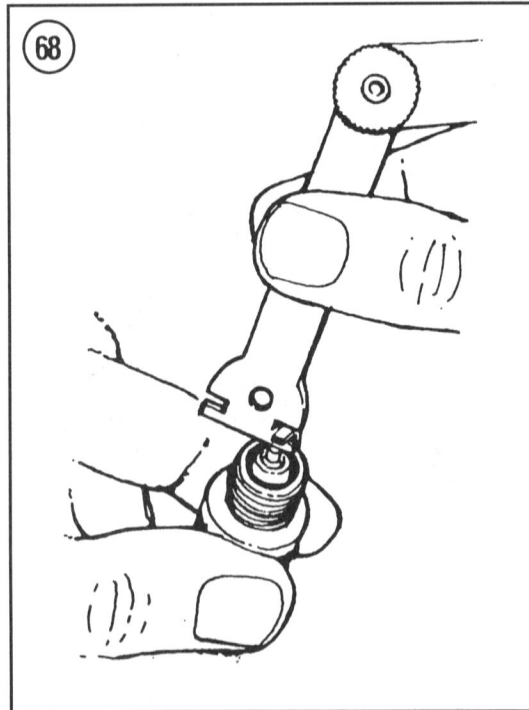

Gapping the Plug

A new spark plug should be carefully gapped to ensure a reliable, consistent spark. You must use a special spark plug gapping tool and a wire feeler gauge.

1. Remove the new spark plug from the box. Screw on the small piece that is loose in the box (**Figure 66**).

2. Insert a wire feeler gauge between the center and side electrode (**Figure 67**). The correct gap is listed in **Table 14**.

If the gap is correct, you will feel a slight drag as you pull the wire through. If there is no drag, or the gauge won't pass through, bend the side electrode with a gapping tool (**Figure 68**) to set the proper gap.

> *CAUTION*
> *Never try to close the electrode gap by tapping the spark plug on a solid surface. This can damage the plug internally. Always use the gapping tool to open or close the gap.*

Spark Plug Installation

Improper spark plug installation is a common cause of poor spark plug performance. The gasket on the plug must be fully compressed against a clean plug seat in order for heat transfer to take place effectively. This requires close attention to proper tightening during installation.

1. Inspect the spark plug hole threads. If the threads appear contaminated or if plug removal was difficult, clean them with a thread chaser. Apply grease to the threads of the chaser before use. Wipe the cylinder head seat clean before installing the plug.

2. Apply anti-seize to the plug threads before installing the spark plug.

> *NOTE*
> *Anti-seize can be purchased at most automotive parts stores.*

3. Screw the spark plug in by hand until it seats. Very little effort is required. If force is necessary, you have the plug cross-threaded. Unscrew it and try again.

4. Use a spark plug wrench and tighten the plug an additional 1/4 to 1/2 turn after the gasket has

made contact with the head. If you are installing an old, regapped plug and reusing the old gasket, only tighten an additional 1/4 turn.

NOTE
Do not overtighten. This will only squash the gasket and destroy its sealing ability.

5. Install the spark plug cap. Make sure it is on tight.

CAUTION
Make sure the spark plug wire is positioned away from the exhaust pipe.

Reading Spark Plugs

Because the firing end of a spark plug operates in the combustion chamber, it reflects the operating condition of the engine. Much information about engine and spark plug performance can be determined by careful examination of the spark plug. This information is only valid after performing the following steps.
1. Ride the bike a short distance at full throttle in any gear.
2. Push on the kill switch before closing the throttle and simultaneously pull in the clutch or shift to neutral; coast and brake to a stop.
3. Remove the spark plug and examine it. Compare it to **Figure 69** and note the following:

Normal condition

If the plug has a light tan- or gray-colored deposit and no abnormal gap wear or erosion, good engine, carburetion and ignition condition are indicated. The plug in use is of the proper heat range and may be serviced and returned to use.

Carbon fouled

Soft, dry, sooty deposits covering the entire firing end of the plug are evidence of incomplete combustion. Even though the firing end of the plug is dry, the plug's insulation decreases. An electrical path is formed that lowers the voltage from the ignition system. Engine mis-firing is a sign of carbon fouling. Carbon fouling can be caused by one or more of the following:
   a. Too rich fuel mixture.

   b. Spark plug heat range too cold.
   c. Clogged air filter element.
   d. Over-retarded ignition timing.
   e. Ignition component failure.
   f. Low engine compression.
   g. Prolonged idling.

Oil fouled

The tip of an oil fouled plug has a black insulator tip, a damp oily film over the firing end and a carbon layer over the entire nose. The electrodes will not be worn. Common causes for this condition are:
   a. Too much oil in the fuel.
   b. Poorly mixed fuel.
   c. Wrong type of oil.
   d. Low idle speed or prolonged idling.
   e. Ignition component failure.
   f. Spark plug heat range too cold.
   g. Engine still being broken in.
Oil fouled spark plugs may be cleaned in an emergency, but it is better to replace them. It is important to correct the cause of fouling before the engine is returned to service.

Gap bridging

Plugs with this condition exhibit gaps shorted out by combustion deposits between the electrodes. If this condition is encountered, check for an improper oil type, excessive carbon in combustion chamber or a clogged exhaust port and pipe. Be sure to locate and correct the cause of this condition.

Overheating

Badly worn electrodes and premature gap wear are signs of overheating, along with a gray or white "blistered" porcelain insulator surface. The most common cause for this condition is using a spark plug of the wrong heat range (too hot). If you have not changed to a hotter spark plug and the plug is overheated, consider the following causes:
   a. Lean fuel mixture.
   b. Ignition timing too advanced.
   c. Cooling system malfunction.
   d. Engine air leak.
   e. Improper spark plug installation (overtightening).
   f. No spark plug gasket.

(69)

SPARK PLUG CONDITIONS

NORMAL USE

OIL FOULED

CARBON FOULED

OVERHEATED

GAP BRIDGED

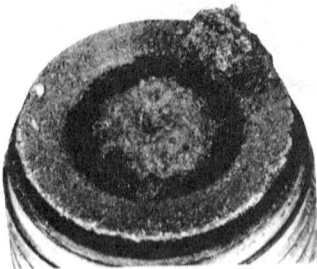

SUSTAINED PREIGNITION

WORN OUT

Worn out

Corrosive gases formed by combustion and high voltage sparks have eroded the electrodes. A spark plug in this condition requires more voltage to fire under hard acceleration. Replace with a new spark plug.

Preignition

If the electrodes are melted, preignition is almost certainly the cause. Check for carburetor mounting or intake manifold leaks and overadvanced ignition timing. It is also possible that a plug of the wrong heat range (too hot) is being used. Find the cause of the preignition before returning the engine into service.

Ignition Timing

All models are equipped with a capacitor discharge ignition (CDI). This system uses no breaker points and greatly simplifies ignition timing and makes the ignition system much less susceptible to failures caused by dirt, moisture and wear.

Since there are no components to wear, adjusting the ignition timing is only necessary after the engine has been disassembled or if the stator base plate screws have worked loose.

1. Place the bike on a stand.
2. Remove the crankcase left-hand side cover (**Figure 70**).

> *NOTE*
> *If the bike is a KX80 and was purchased used, there may be 3 timing marks on the stator plate. The center timing mark is the stock factory timing mark. The other 2 marks were made by a previous owner for altering the ignition timing. The 2 additional timing marks are a factory approved modification. However, you may want to check the accuracy of the new marks. This procedure is described under Timing Mark Verification following this procedure.*

3. Check the stator plate-to-crankcase timing mark alignment (**Figure 71**). Both marks should align.

> *NOTE*
> *On some models it will be necessary to remove the flywheel to gain access to the stator plate screws. Refer to Chapter Nine.*

4. If the marks are not aligned, loosen the stator plate screws (A, **Figure 72**) and turn the stator plate (B, **Figure 72**) to align the marks. Tighten the screws and recheck.
5. If necessary, install the flywheel as described in Chapter Nine.

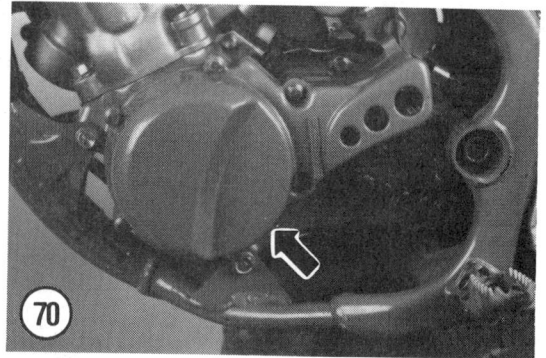

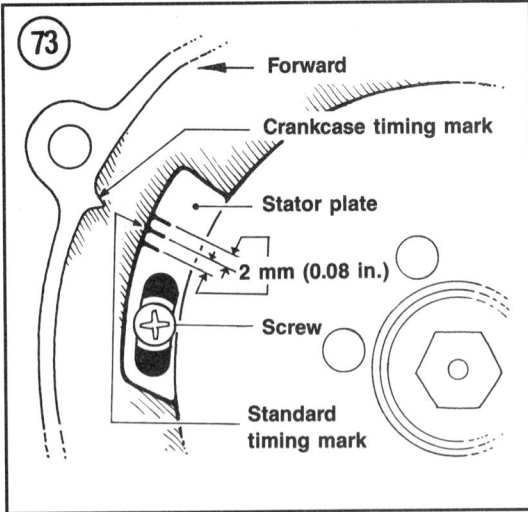

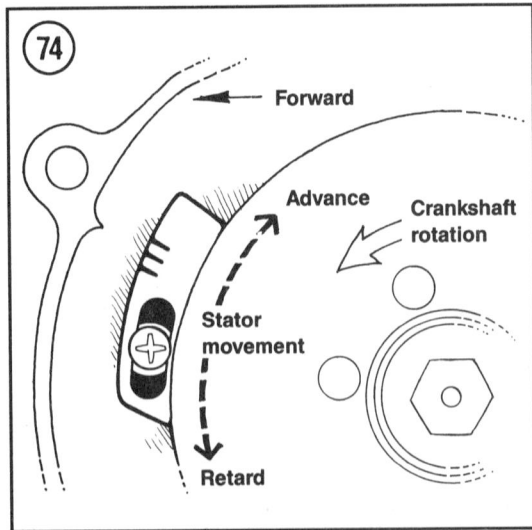

6. Reinstall the crankcase left-hand side cover (**Figure 70**).

Timing Mark Verification (KX80)

The ignition timing on all KX80 models can be retarded or advanced from the stock setting to change the power band to suit race conditions.

1. Place the bike on a stand.
2. Remove the crankcase left-hand side cover (**Figure 70**).
3. The stator plate has a single timing mark (**Figure 71**). If you wish to alter the timing, it will be necessary to scribe 2 new marks on the stator plate. Referring to **Figure 73**, scribe a timing mark 2 mm (0.08 in.) apart from the standard timing mark on both sides.
4. After scribing the new timing marks, the timing can be adjusted by loosening the stator plate mounting screws and moving the stator plate so that the crankcase mark aligns within the area outlined by the 2 new lines. Moving the stator plate clockwise advances the ignition timing; moving the stator plate counterclockwise retards ignition timing. See **Figure 74**.

CAUTION
Do not adjust the ignition timing outside of the range listed in Step 4 or engine damage may occur.

5. Reinstall the crankcase left-hand side cover (**Figure 70**).

Carburetor Idle Speed Adjustment (KX60 and 1983-1987 KX80)

Proper idle speed is a balance between a low enough idle to give adequate compression braking and a high enough idle to prevent engine stalling (if desired). The idle air/fuel mixture affects transition from idle to part throttle openings.

1. Make sure that the throttle cable free play is correct as described in this chapter.
2. Warm up the engine completely. Then turn the throttle adjust screw (**Figure 75**) to set the idle at the desired speed.

NOTE
After this adjustment is completed, test ride the bike. Throttle response from

idle should be rapid and without any hesitation. If there is any hesitation, the pilot jet may be slightly clogged.

> *WARNING*
> *With the engine idling, move the handlebar from side-to-side. If idle speed increases during this movement, the throttle cable needs adjusting or it may be incorrectly routed through the frame. Correct this problem immediately. Do not ride the bike in this unsafe condition.*

Carburetor Idle Speed Adjustment (1988-on KX80)

Proper idle speed is a balance between a low enough idle to give adequate compression braking and a high enough idle to prevent engine stalling (if desired). The idle air/fuel mixture affects transition from idle to part throttle openings.

1. Make sure that the throttle cable free play is correct as described in this chapter.
2. Turn the pilot air screw (**Figure 76**) in until it seats lightly, then back it out 2 turns.

> *CAUTION*
> *Never turn the pilot air screw in tight. You'll damage the screw or the soft aluminum screw seat in the carburetor.*

3. Warm up the engine completely. Then turn the idle speed screw (**Figure 76**) to set the idle as low as possible without stalling the engine.
4. Turn the pilot air screw (**Figure 76**) until the engine drops off quickly one way and then where the idle shoots up when its turned the other way. The midpoint between high and low engine idle is the correct pilot air screw adjustment.

> *NOTE*
> *The pilot air screw should not be opened more than 3 turns or it may vibrate loose and fall out. If you cannot get the bike to idle properly, check that the air filter is clean. If air filter is okay and other engine systems are operating correctly, the pilot jet size may be incorrect. Refer to Chapter Eight.*

5. Reset the idle speed (**Figure 76**) as desired.

> *NOTE*
> *After this adjustment is completed, test ride the bike. Throttle response from idle should be rapid and without any hesitation. If there is any hesitation, turn the pilot air screw in or out in ¼ turn increments until this problem is solved.*

> *WARNING*
> *With the engine idling, move the handlebar from side-to-side. If idle speed increases during this movement, the throttle cable needs adjusting or it may be incorrectly routed through the frame. Correct this problem immediately. Do not ride the bike in this unsafe condition.*

Decarbonizing

The carbon deposits should be removed from the piston, cylinder head, exhaust port and muffler as indicated in **Table 1** or **Table 2**. If it is not cleaned off, it will cause reduced performance, preignition (ping) or overheating.

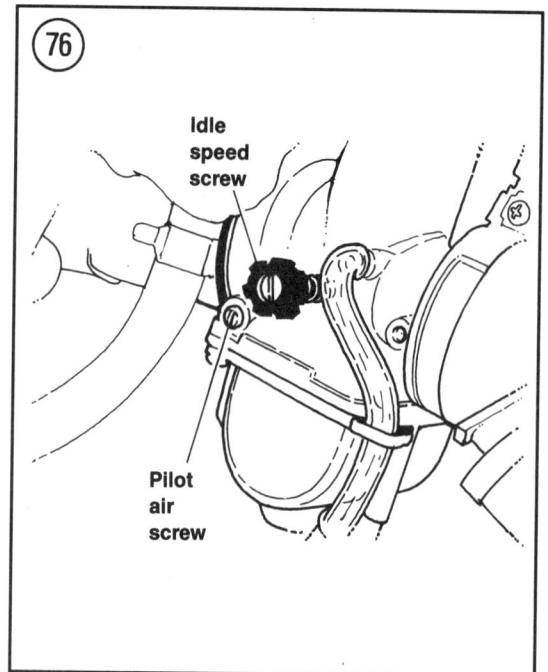

(76)

Idle speed screw

Pilot air screw

Engine Decarbonizing

1. Remove the cylinder head and cylinder as described under *Cylinder Removal/Installation* in Chapter Four.

2. Stuff a clean shop cloth into the opening in the crankcase to keep any foreign matter from entering into it.

3. Gently scrape off carbon deposits from the top of the piston and cylinder head with a block of hardwood. Do not scratch the surface.

4. Wipe the surfaces clean with a cloth dipped in cleaning solvent.

5. Scrape off the carbon in the exhaust port with a dull screwdriver or end of a hacksaw blade. Do not scratch the surfaces.

6. Install the cylinder and cylinder head (Chapter Four).

Exhaust System Decarbonizing

1. Remove the exhaust pipe assembly as described under *Exhaust System Removal/Installation* in Chapter Eight.

2. On some models, the packing in the silencer can be replaced (**Figure 77**). Remove the bolt at the end of the silencer and pull the packing assembly out. Pull off the old packing and wrap new packing around the pipe. Install after first cleaning the exhaust pipe as described in this section.

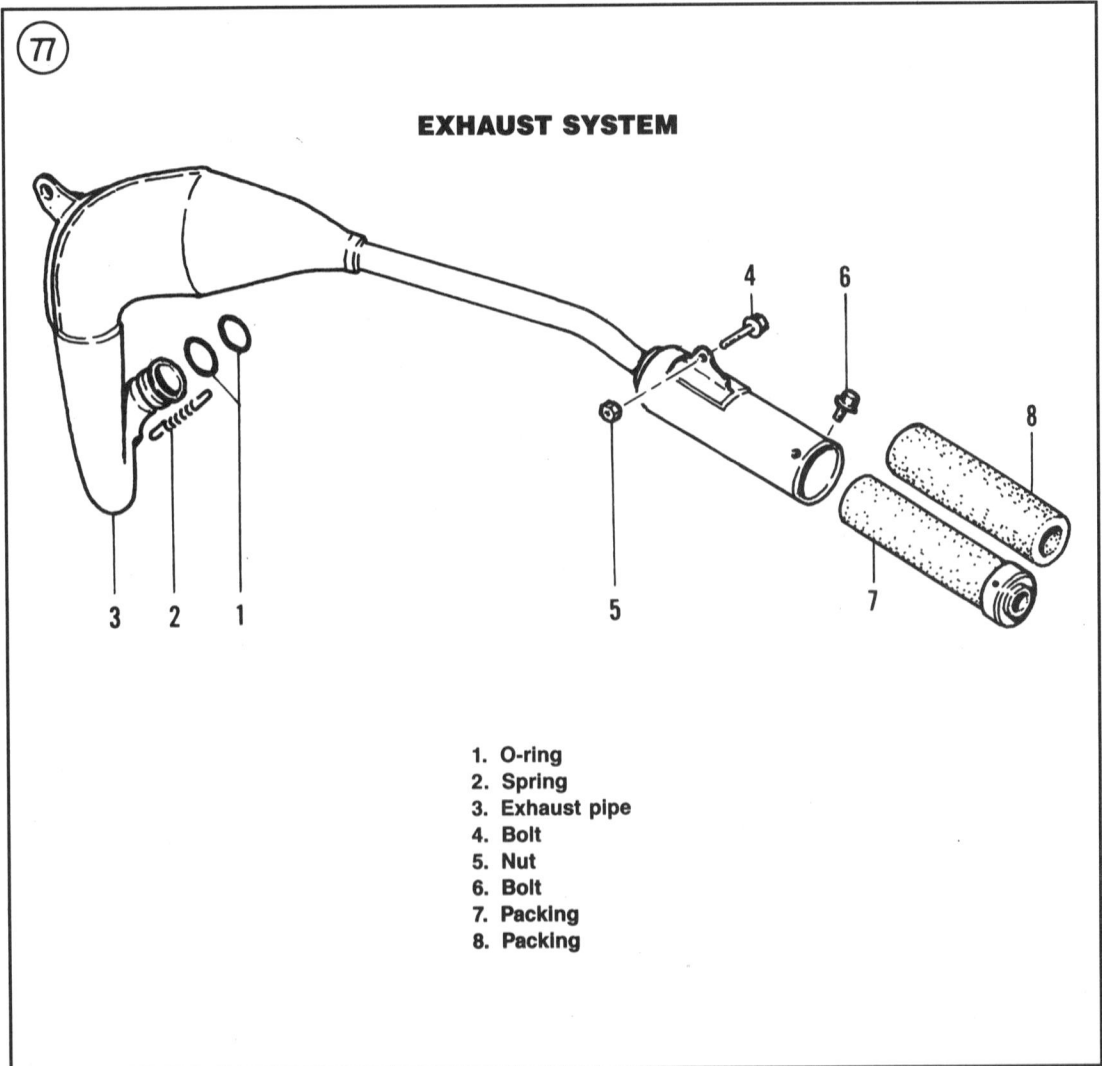

EXHAUST SYSTEM

1. O-ring
2. Spring
3. Exhaust pipe
4. Bolt
5. Nut
6. Bolt
7. Packing
8. Packing

3. Gently scrape off carbon deposits from the interior of the head pipe where it attaches to the cylinder.

> **WARNING**
> *If a length of cable is used in an electric drill to clean the inside of the exhaust pipe, do not start the drill **until** the cable is inserted into the exhaust pipe. Operating the drill with the cable out of the pipe could cause serious injury if the cable should whip against your face or body.*

4. Clean out the rest of the interior of the expansion chamber by running a piece of used motorcycle drive chain around in it. Another way is to chuck a length of wire cable, with one end frayed, in an electric drill (**Figure 78**). Run it around in the front portion a couple of times. Shake out all loose carbon. Also tap on the outer shell of the exhaust pipe assembly with a plastic mallet to break any additional carbon loose.

5. Blow out the expansion chamber with compressed air.

6. Visually inspect the entire exhaust pipe assembly, especially in the many areas of welds, for cracks or other damage. Replace if necessary, or repair as described in Chapter Eight.

7. Reinstall the silencer assembly, if removed.

8. Install the assembly.

FRONT FORK AIR PRESSURE MEASUREMENT

Air pressure will increase or decrease pressure through the entire fork travel range. Because air pressure makes the forks hard, many riders do not pressurize their forks. Instead, they use the air valves on the fork caps to bleed off air that builds up inside the forks after each ride. When bleeding off air pressure, prop the front wheel up so that it clears the ground. Then depress the air valve (**Figure 79**) and bleed off all air pressure. Raising the front wheel off the ground prevents a vacuum from building in the fork tubes.

If your front forks seem soft and are bottoming harshly, you may want to add a small amount of air pressure. Consider the following when adjusting fork air pressure:

a. Decreasing air pressure will soften fork travel.
b. Increasing air pressure will stiffen fork travel.

> **CAUTION**
> *Do not exceed the air pressure specifications in **Table 15** or the fork seals will be damaged.*

1. Place the bike on a stand so that the forks are fully extended and the front wheel clears the ground.

2. Remove the air valve caps.

3. Use a small manual air pump. Attach it to the air fitting and inflate the fork to the desired setting.

4. Repeat for the opposite side.

> **WARNING**
> *Use only compressed air or nitrogen— do **not** use any other type of compressed gas as an explosion may result. Never heat the front forks with a torch or place them near an open flameor extreme heat.*

> **NOTE**
> *The air pressure difference between the 2 fork tubes should be 0.1 kg/cm² (1.4 psi) or less.*

5. Reinstall the air caps.

6. Test ride the bike.

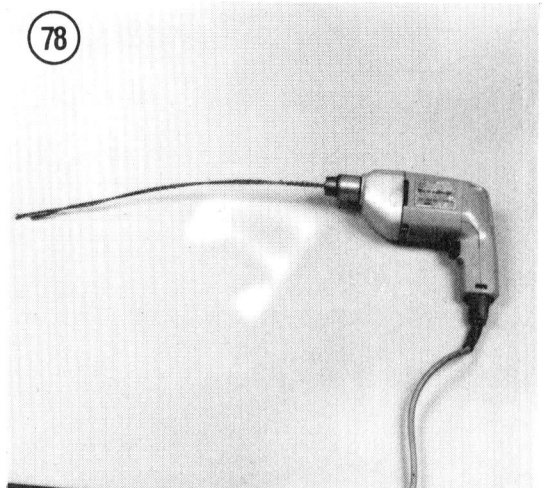

STORAGE

Several months of inactivity can cause serious problems and a general deterioration of your bike's condition. This is especially true in areas of weather extremes. During the winter months it is advisable to specially prepare the bike for lay-up.

Selecting a Storage Area

Most riders store their bikes in their home garages. If you do not have a home garage, facilities suitable for long-term motorcycle storage are readily available for rent or lease in most areas. In selecting a building, consider the following points.

1. The storage area must be dry, free from dampness and excessive humidity. Heating is not necessary, but the building should be well insulated to minimize extreme temperature variations.

2. Buildings with large window areas should be avoided, or such windows should be masked (also a good security measure) if direct sunlight can fall on the bike.

3. Buildings in industrial areas, where factories are liable to emit corrosive fumes, are not desirable, nor are facilities near bodies of salt water.

4. The area should be selected to minimize the possibility of loss from fire, theft, or vandalism. The area should be fully insured, perhaps with a package covering fire, theft, vandalism, weather, and liability. Talk this over with your insurance agent and get approval on these matters. The building should be fireproof and items such as the

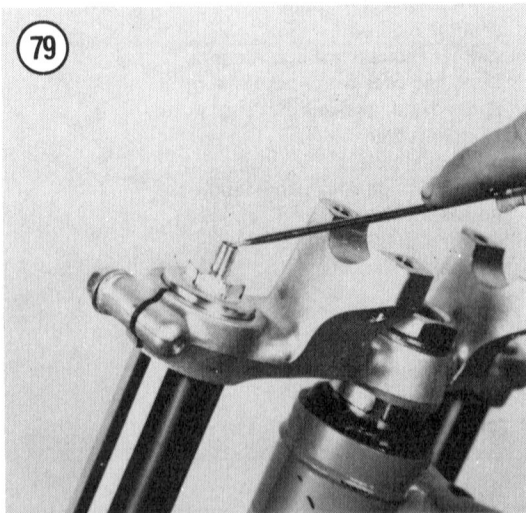

security of doors and windows, alarm facility, and proximity of police should be considered.

Preparing Bike for Storage

Careful preparation will minimize deterioration and make it easier to restore the bike to service later. Use the following procedure.

1. Wash the bike completely. Make certain to remove all dirt in all the hard to reach parts like the cooling fins (models so equipped) on the head and cylinder. Completely dry all parts of the bike to remove all moisture. Wax all painted and polished surfaces, including any chromed areas.

2. Run the bike for about 20-30 minutes to warm up the oil in the clutch and transmission. Drain the oil, regardless of the time since the last oil change. Refill with the normal quantity and type of oil.

3. Drain all gasoline from the fuel tank, interconnecting hose, and the carburetor. Leave the fuel shutoff valve in the ON position. As an alternative, a fuel preservative may be added to the fuel. This preservative is available from many motorcycle shops and marine equipment suppliers.

4. Lubricate the drive chain and control cables; refer to specific procedures in this chapter.

5. Remove the spark plug and add about one teaspoon of 2-stroke engine oil into the cylinder. Reinstall the spark plug and turn the engine over to distribute the oil to the cylinder walls and piston. Depress the engine kill switch while doing this to prevent it from starting.

6. Tape or tie a plastic bag over the end of the silencer to prevent the entry of moisture.

7. Check the tire pressure, inflate to the correct pressure and move the bike to the storage area. Place it securely on a stand or wood blocks with both wheels off the ground.

8. Cover the bike with a tarp, blanket or heavy plastic drop cloth. Place this cover over the bike mainly as a dust cover—do not wrap it tightly, especially any plastic material, as it may trap moisture causing condensation. Leave room for air to circulate around the bike.

Inspection During Storage

Try to inspect the bike weekly while in storage. Any deterioration should be corrected as soon as possible. For example, if corrosion of bright metal parts is observed, cover them with a light coat of grease or silicone spray after a thorough polishing.

Turn the engine over a couple of times. Don't start it; use the kickstarter and hold the kill switch on. Pump the front forks to keep the seals lubricated.

Restoring Bike to Service

A bike that has been properly prepared and stored in a suitable area requires only light maintenance to restore to service. It is advisable, however, to perform a spring tune-up.

1. Before removing the bike from the storage area, reinflate the tires to the correct pressures. Air loss during storage may have nearly flattened the tires, and moving the bike can cause damage to tires, tubes and rims.

2. When the bike is brought to the work area, turn the fuel shutoff valve to the OFF position, and refill the fuel tank with the correct fuel:oil mixture. Remove the main jet cover on the base of the carburetor, turn the fuel shutoff valve to the ON position, and allow several cups of fuel to pass through the fuel system. Turn the fuel shutoff valve to the OFF position and install the main jet cover.

3. Remove the spark plug and squirt a small amount of fuel into the cylinder to help remove the oil coating.

4. Install a fresh spark plug and start up the engine.

5. Perform the standard tune-up as described earlier in this chapter.

6. Check the operation of the engine kill switch. Oxidation of the switch contacts during storage may make it inoperative.

7. Clean and test ride the motorcycle.

WARNING
Place a metal container under the carburetor to catch all expelled fuel— this presents a real fire danger if allowed to drain onto the bike and the floor. Dispose of the fuel properly.

WARNING
If any type of preservative (Armor All or equivalent) has been applied to the tire treads, be sure the tires are well ''scrubbed-in'' prior to any fast riding or cornering on a hard surface. If not, they will slip right out from under you.

Table 1 PERIODIC MAINTENANCE (KX60)*

Before each race	Check clutch adjustment
	Check throttle cable adjustment
	Check spark plug gap
	Check carburetor adjustment
	Clean air filter element
	Check radiator hoses and connections
	Check front and rear brake adjustment
	Check spoke tightness and rim runout
	Lubricate drive chain
	Check drive chain slack
	Check front fork operation and condition
	Clean the fuel system
	Check steering play and adjust
	Perform general lubrication
Every 3 races	Change transmission oil
	Check piston and cylinder condtion
	Check piston clearance
	Decarbonize top end
	Check top end bearing
	(continued)

Table 1 PERIODIC MAINTENANCE (KX60)* (continued)

Every 5 races	Check clutch plate condition
	Replace the exhaust pipe O-ring
	Check the front and rear sprockets
	Check drive chain wear
	Change the front fork oil
	Grease the steering stem
	Grease the brake camshafts
	Grease the rear shock sleeve
	Check the Uni-trak link bearing and sleeve for wear
	Lubricate the swing arm
	Check brake wear
Every 10 races	Check the crankshaft main bearings
	Check the connecting rod lower bearing
	Grease the wheel bearings
Every year	Inspect entire cooling system
Every 4 years	Replace fuel hose
As required	Change coolant
	Replace the air filter element
	Replace swing arm chain protectors and pads

*The service intervals should be performed more frequently if the bike is ridden often or if the bike is used in competition or whenever it is operated in very dusty conditions.

3

Table 2 PERIODIC MAINTENANCE (KX80)*

Before each race	Check clutch adjustment
	Check throttle cable adjustment
	Check spark plug gap
	Check carburetor adjustment
	Clean air filter element
	Check radiator hoses and connections
	Check front and rear brake adjustment
	Check spoke tightness and rim runout
	Lubricate drive chain
	Check drive chain slack
	Check front fork operation and condition
	Clean the fuel system
	Check steering play and adjust
	Perform general lubrication
	Check brake fluid level
After 2nd race; thereafter every 5 races	Change rear shock oil**
Every 3 races	Change transmission oil
	Check piston and cylinder condition
	Check piston clearance
	Decarbonize top end
	Check top end bearing

(continued)

Table 2 PERIODIC MAINTENANCE (KX80)* (continued)

Every 5 races	Check clutch plate condition
	Replace the exhaust pipe O-ring
	Check the front and rear sprockets
	Check drive chain wear
	Change the front fork oil
	Grease the steering stem
	Grease the brake camshafts
	Grease the rear shock sleeve
	Check the Uni-trak link bearing and sleeve for wear
	Lubricate the swing arm
	Check brake wear
Every 10 races	Check the crankshaft main bearings
	Check the connecting rod lower bearing
	Grease the wheel bearings
Every year	Inspect entire cooling system
	Change brake fluid
Every 2 years	Replace brake master cylinder cup and dust seal
	Replace brake caliper piston and dust seals
Every 4 years	Replace brake hose
	Replace fuel hose
As required	Change coolant
	Replace the air filter element
	Replace swing arm chain protectors and pads

* The service intervals should be performed more frequently if the bike is ridden often or if the bike is used in competition or whenever it is operated in very dusty conditions.
** Rebuildable shocks only.

Table 3 TIRE INFLATION PRESSURE

Front	1.0 kg/cm^2 (14 psi)
Rear	1.0 kg/cm^2 (14 psi)

Table 4 RECOMMENDED LUBRICANTS AND FUEL

Engine oil	Kawasaki 2-stroke racing oil
Transmission oil	SAE 10W-30 or 10W-40 transmission oil
Front fork oil	
KX60	SAE 5W-20
KX80	
1983-1985	SAE 10W-20
1986-on	SAE 10W
Air filter	Foam air filter oil
Drive chain	Chain lube
Brake fluid (KX80)	DOT 3
Fuel	Premium grade-research octane 87 or higher
Control cables	Cable lube

Table 5 FUEL:OIL PREMIX RATIO

Model	Premix ratio	
KX60		
1983	20:1	
1984	30:1	
1985-on	32:1	
KX80		
1983	20:1	
1984	30:1	
1985-on	32:1	
Gasoline U.S. gal.	**Oil oz.**	**Oil cc**
RATIO 20:1		
1	6.4	190
2	12.8	380
3	19.2	570
4	25.6	760
5	32	945
RATIO 30:1		
1	4.3	127
2	8.5	251
3	12.8	379
4	17.1	506
5	21.3	630
RATIO 32:1		
1	4	118
2	8	237
3	12	355
4	16	473
5	20	591

Table 6 FUEL TANK CAPACITY

Model	U.S. gal.	Liters
KX60	0.9	3.5
KX80		
1983-1985	1.2	4.5
1986-1987	1.1	4.1
1988-on	1.3	4.9

Table 7 TRANSMISSION/CLUTCH OIL CAPACITY

Model	cc	qt.
KX60		
1983-1985	550	0.58
1986-on	600	0.63
KX80		
1983-1985	600	0.63
1986-on	700	0.74

3

Table 8 MAINTENANCE TORQUE SPECIFICATIONS

	N·m	ft.-lb.
Cylinder head bolts or nuts	25	18
Handlebar	21	15
Front fork crown pinch bolts or nuts		
KX60		
Upper	20	14
Lower	25	18
KX80		
Upper		
1983	20	14
1984	—	—
1985	17	12
1986-1987	20	14
1988-on	17	12
Lower		
1983-1985	28	18
1986-1987	20	14
1988-on	17	12
Steering stem (KX60)		
Nut	35	25
Locknut		
1983-1986	29	22
1987-1988	19	14
Steering stem (KX80)		
1983-1985		
Nut	34	25
Locknut		
1983	—	—
1984	—	—
1985	29	22
1986-on		
Nut	44	33
Locknut	4.0	35 in.-lb.
Rear axle nut	69	51

Table 9 FRONT FORK OIL

	Capacity cc (oz.)	Oil level mm (in.)	Range mm (in.)
KX60			
1983-1985	178.5-183.6 (6.04-6.21)	127-137 (5.0-5.4)	* *
1986-on	178.5-183.6 (6.04-6.21)	127-137 (5.0-5.4)	100-165 (3.9-6.5)
KX80			
1983	254.5-259.5 (8.60-8.77)	161-169 (6.34-6.65)	* *
1984	284-292 (9.60-9.87)	118-122 (4.65-4.80)	* *
1985	271.5-279.5 (9.18-9.45)	138-142 (5.43-5.59)	* *
1986	317-325 (10.7-11.0)	128-132 (5.0-5.2)	100-160 (3.9-6.3)

(continued)

Table 9 FRONT FORK OIL (continued)

	Capacity cc (oz.)	Oil level mm (in.)	Range mm (in.)
KX80 (continued)			
1987			
G, H	322-328 (10.9-11.1)	123-127 (4.8-5.0)	95-155 (3.7-6.1)
J, K	366-374 (12.4-12.6)	108-112 (4.3-4.4)	80-140 (3.1-5.5)
1988			
L, M	330-336 (11.1-11.4)	110-120 (4.3-4.7)	90-145 (3.5-5.7)
N, P	349-355 (11.8-12.0)	95-105 (3.7-4.11)	90-130 (3.5-5.1)
1989			
L, M	327-333 (11.0-11.3)	100-110 (3.9-4.3)	90-145 (3.5-5.7)
* Not specified.			

Table 10 DRIVE CHAIN SLACK

Model	mm	in.
KX60	15-30	0.6-1.2
KX80	40-50	1.6-2.0

Table 11 DRIVE CHAIN LENGTH MEASUREMENT

	Standard mm (in.)	Wear limit mm (in.)
All models	254 (10.0)	259 (10.2)

Table 12 COOLANT CAPACITY

	cc	qt.
KX60	500	0.53
KX80		
1985	610	0.64
1986-on	650	0.69

Table 13 ENGINE COMPRESSION

Model	Standard kg/cm^2 (psi)	Min./max. range kg/cm^2 (psi)
KX60	10-12 (142-171)	7.7-12 (109-171)
KX80		
1983-1985	10-12 (142-171)	7.7-12 (109-171)
1986-on	11-13 (156-185)	8.4-13 (119-185)

Table 14 SPARK PLUG TYPE AND GAP

	Type	Gap mm (in.))
KX60		
1983-1984	NGK B9ES	0.7-0.8 (0.028-0.032)
1985-on	NGK B9EG	0.6-0.7 (0.024-0.028)
KX80		
1983-1985	NGK B9EV	0.6-0.7 (0.024-0.028)
1986-on		
U.S.	NGK B9EG	0.6-0.7 (0.024-0.028)
All except U.S.	NGK BR9EG	0.6-0.7 (0.024-0.028)

Table 15 FRONT FORK AIR PRESSURE

	kg/cm·	psi
KX60		
1983-1985	0-2.51	0-36
1986-on	0-0.4	0-6
KX80		
1983-1985	0-2.51	0-36
1986-on	0-0.4	0-6

CHAPTER FOUR

ENGINE TOP END

This chapter covers information to service the cylinder head, cylinder, piston, piston rings and reed valve. Engine lower end service (crankshaft, transmission removal and installation, shift drum and shift forks) is covered in Chapter Five. Clutch and kickstarter service is covered in Chapter Six. Transmission overhaul is covered in Chapter Seven.

Before removing and disassembling the engine top end, clean the entire engine and frame with a good grade commercial degreaser, like Gunk or Bel-Ray engine degreaser or equivalent. It is easier to work on a clean engine and you will do a better job.

Make certain that you have all the necessary tools available and purchase replacement parts prior to disassembly. Also make sure you have a clean place to work.

It is a good idea to identify and mark parts as they are removed so that errors will be avoided during assembly and installation. Clean all parts thoroughly upon removal, then place them in trays or boxes with their associated mounting hardware. Do not rely on memory alone as it may be days or weeks before you complete the job. In the text there is frequent mention of the left-hand and right-hand side of the engine. This refers to the engine as it sits in the bike's frame, not as it sits on your workbench.

General engine specifications are listed in **Table 1**. Engine service specifications are listed in **Table 2** (KX60) and **Table 3** (KX80). **Tables 1-4** are at the end of the chapter.

ENGINE LUBRICATION

Engine lubrication is provided by the fuel:oil mixture used to power the engine. There is no oil supply in the crankcase, as it would be drawn into the cylinder causing the spark plug to foul.

ENGINE COOLING

Air-cooled Engines (1983-1984 KX60)

Cooling is provided by air passing over the cooling fins on the engine cylinder head and cylinder. To prevent engine damage from overheating, it is important to keep these fins free from a buildup of dirt, oil, grease, and other foreign matter. Brush out the fins with a whisk broom or small stiff paint brush.

CAUTION
Remember cooling fins are thin and may be damaged if struck too hard.

Liquid-cooled Engines
(1985-on KX60 and KX80)

The cylinder head and cylinder on these models is liquid-cooled. A radiator is mounted at the front of the bike and a water pump is mounted behind the clutch cover. The cylinder head and cylinder are cast without cooling fins.

CLEANLINESS

Repairs go much faster and easier if your engine is clean before you begin work. This is especially important when servicing the engine's top end. If the top end is being serviced while the engine is installed in the frame, note that dirt trapped underneath the fuel tank or upper frame tube can fall into cylinder or crankcase opening. There are special cleaners for washing the motor and related parts. Just spray or brush on the cleaning solution, let it stand, then rinse it away with a garden hose. See Chapter One. If you are servicing the bike at a race track, you may not have access to soap and water to clean the bike. Instead, wrap a large clean cloth or plastic around the gas tank and upper

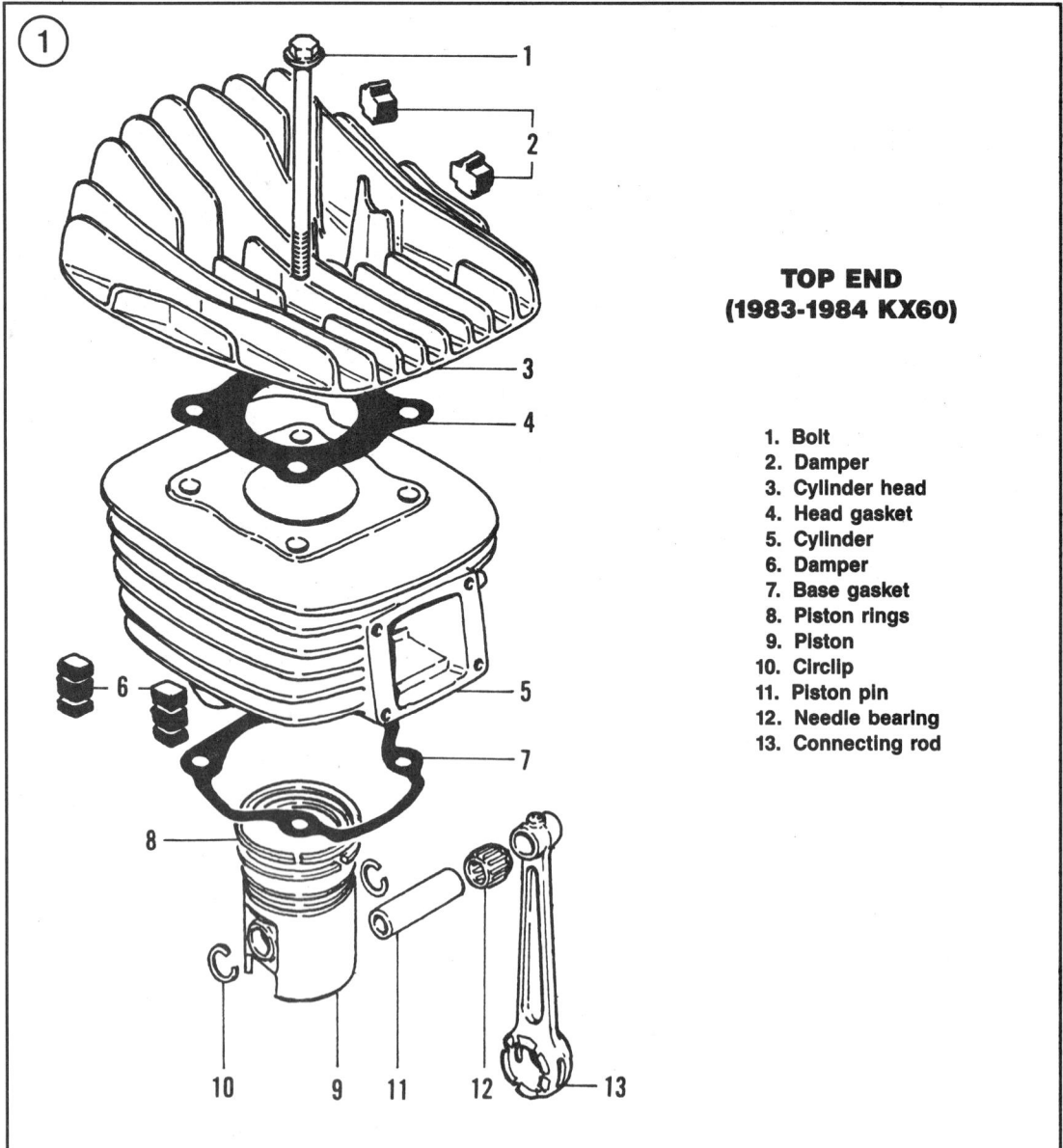

**TOP END
(1983-1984 KX60)**

1. Bolt
2. Damper
3. Cylinder head
4. Head gasket
5. Cylinder
6. Damper
7. Base gasket
8. Piston rings
9. Piston
10. Circlip
11. Piston pin
12. Needle bearing
13. Connecting rod

frame tube. This will prevent dirt from falling into the engine with the top end removed.

SERVICING ENGINE IN FRAME

Some of the components can be serviced while the engine is mounted in the frame (the bike's frame is a great holding fixture—especially for breaking loose stubborn bolts and nuts):

a. Cylinder head.
b. Cylinder.
c. Piston.
d. Carburetor.
e. Flywheel.
f. Clutch.
g. External shift mechanism.

CYLINDER HEAD

The cylinder head is bolted to the top of the cylinder with either 4 nuts or bolts depending on model and year. A gasket separates the cylinder head and cylinder.

Removal/Installation (Air-cooled)

CAUTION
To prevent warpage and damage to any component, remove the cylinder head only when the engine is at room temperature.

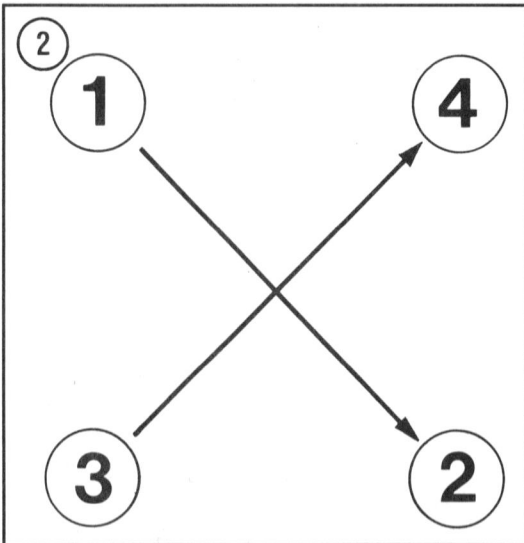

Refer to **Figure 1** for this procedure.

1. Remove the seat, side covers and fuel tank.
2. Remove the exhaust system as described under *Exhaust System Removal/Installation* in Chapter Eight.
3. Disconnect the spark plug wire and move it out of the way.

NOTE
If you think that it may be necessary to remove the spark plug later, loosen it now while the cylinder head is bolted down.

4. Loosen the bolts securing the cylinder head in a crisscross pattern (**Figure 2**). Loosen the bolts a quarter of a turn until they are all loose.
5. Loosen the cylinder head by tapping around the perimeter with a rubber or plastic mallet.

CAUTION
Remember, the cooling fins are fragile and may be damaged if tapped or pried on too hard. Never use a metal hammer.

NOTE
Do not pry the cylinder head if it is stuck. Sometimes it is possible to loosen the head with engine compression. Rotate the engine with the kickstarter (with the spark plug installed). As the piston reaches TDC on the compression stroke, it may pop the cylinder head loose.

6. Remove the cylinder head by pulling straight up and off the cylinder (**Figure 1**). Store the cylinder head with the gasket surface placed on a thick piece of cardboard.
7. Remove the cylinder head gasket and discard it.
8. Bring the piston to top dead center (TDC). Lay a rag over the cylinder to prevent dirt from falling into the cylinder.
9. Inspect the cylinder head as described in this chapter.
10. Install the cylinder head by reversing these steps. Note the following.
11. Install the head gasket (**Figure 1**).
12. Install the cylinder head.

13. Install the 4 cylinder head bolts (**Figure 1**). Tighten the bolts in a crisscross pattern (**Figure 2**) to the torque specification in **Table 4**.

14. Install the exhaust system, tighten the spark plug and install the spark plug wire seat, side covers and fuel tank.

**Removal/Installation
(Water-cooled)**

Refer to **Figure 3** (1985-on KX60), **Figure 4** (1983-1985 KX80) or **Figure 5** (1986-on KX80) for this procedure.

1. Remove the seat, frame side covers and fuel tank.

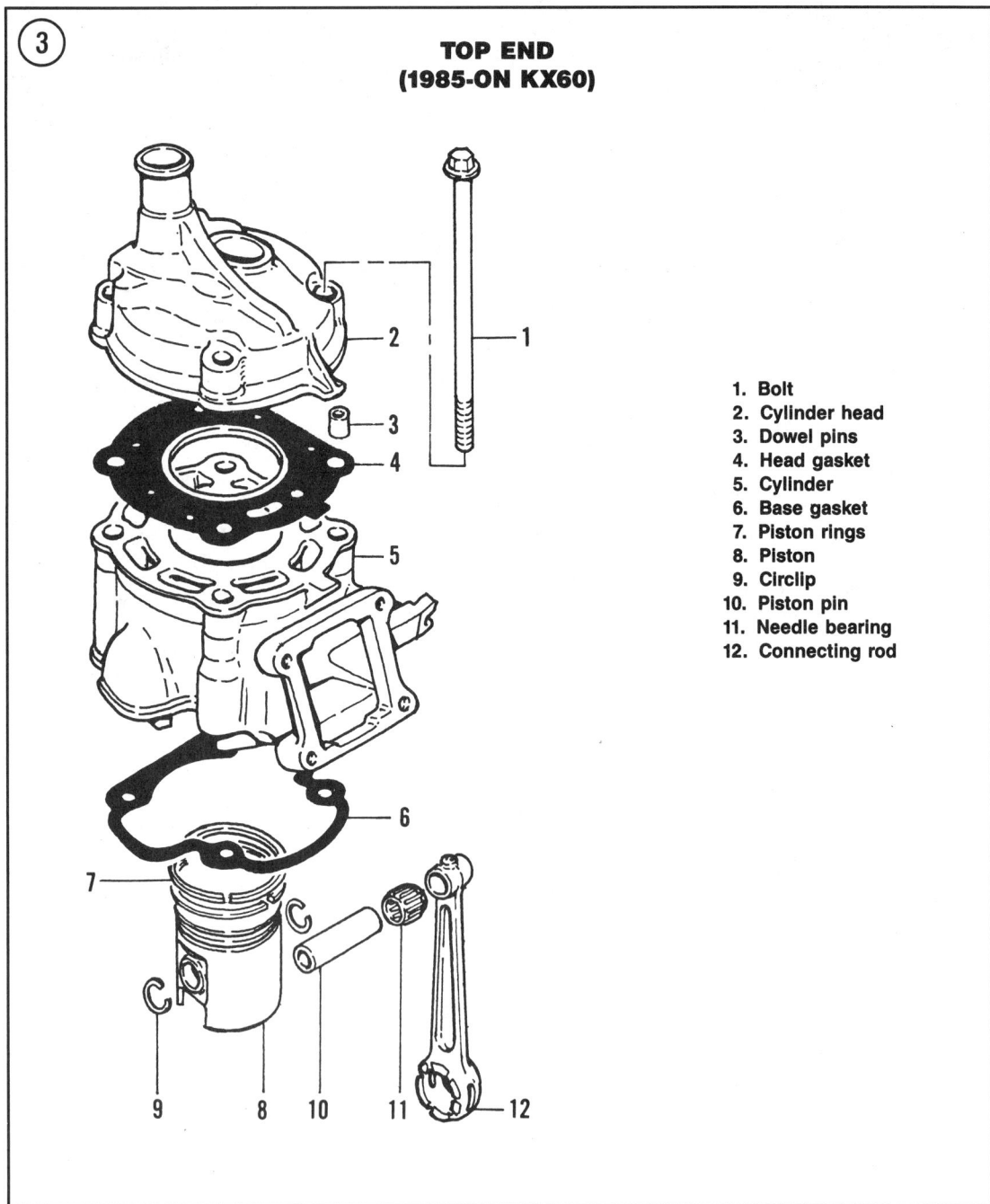

**TOP END
(1985-ON KX60)**

1. Bolt
2. Cylinder head
3. Dowel pins
4. Head gasket
5. Cylinder
6. Base gasket
7. Piston rings
8. Piston
9. Circlip
10. Piston pin
11. Needle bearing
12. Connecting rod

④

TOP END
(1983-1985 KX80)

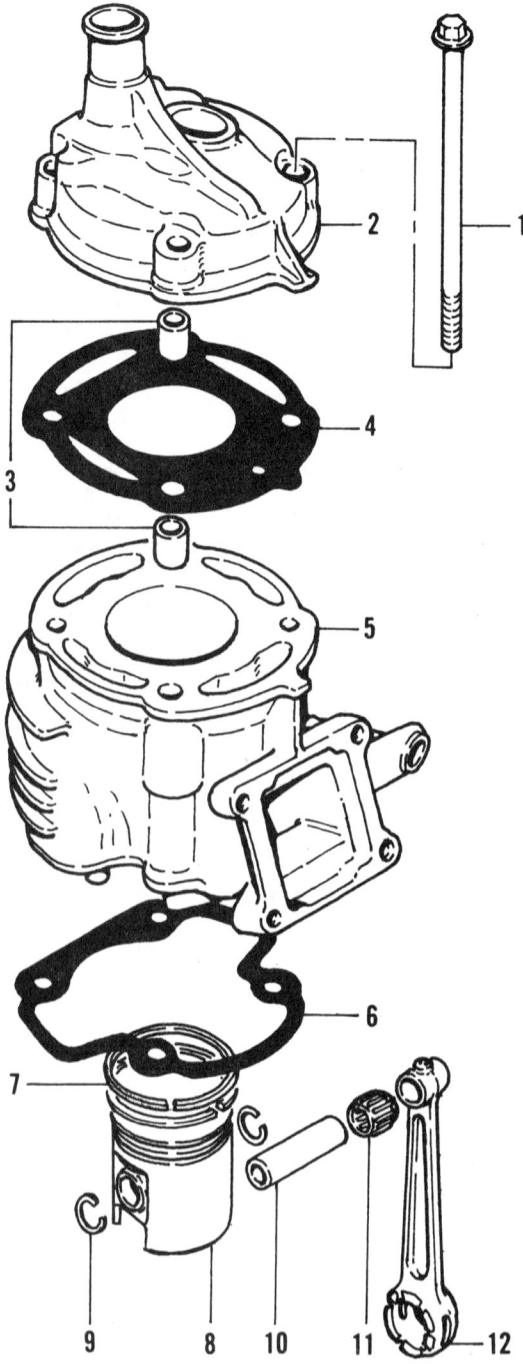

1. Bolt
2. Cylinder head
3. Dowel pins
4. Head gasket
5. Cylinder
6. Base gasket
7. Piston rings
8. Piston
9. Circlip
10. Piston pin
11. Needle bearing
12. Connecting rod

4

⑤

**TOP END
(1986-ON KX80)**

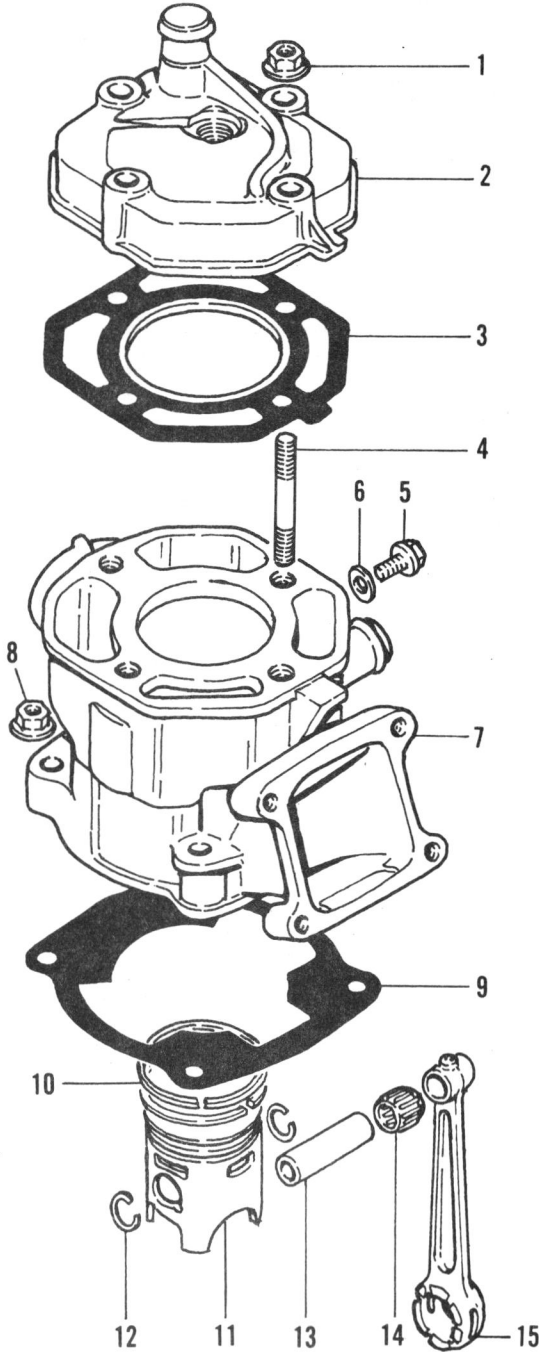

1. Nut
2. Cylinder head
3. Head gasket
4. Studs
5. Drain screw
6. Washer
7. Cylinder
8. Nut
9. Base gasket
10. Piston rings
11. Piston
12. Circlip
13. Piston pin
14. Needle bearing
15. Connecting rod

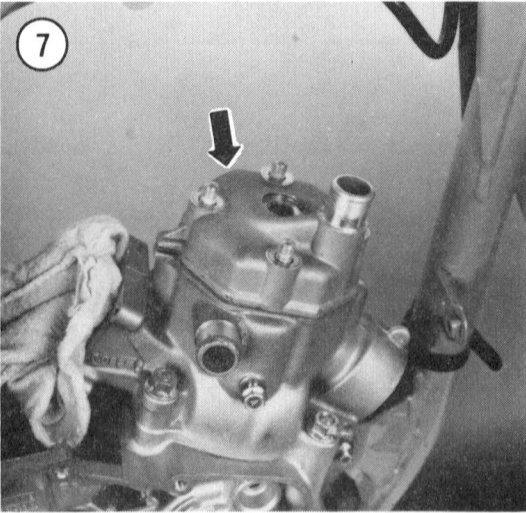

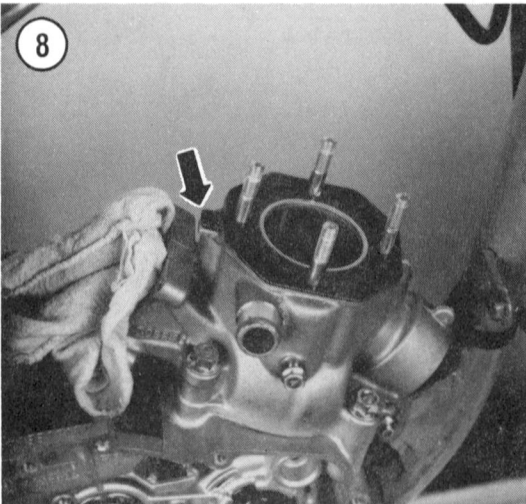

2. Remove the exhaust system as described under *Exhaust System Removal/Installation* in Chapter Eight.

NOTE
If you think that it may be necessary to remove the spark plug later, loosen it now while the cylinder head is bolted down.

3. Disconnect the spark plug wire (A, **Figure 6**) and move it out of the way.
4. Drain the cooling system as described in Chapter Three.
5. Disconnect the radiator hose at the cylinder head (B, **Figure 6**).
6. Loosen the bolts or nuts securing the cylinder head in a crisscross pattern (**Figure 2**). Loosen the bolts or nuts a quarter of a turn until they are all loose. Then remove the fasteners.
7. Loosen the cylinder head by tapping around the perimeter with a rubber or plastic mallet. Never use a metal hammer.
8. Remove the cylinder head (**Figure 7**) by pulling straight up and off the cylinder.
9. Remove the cylinder head gasket.
10. Remove the dowel pins, if so equipped. See **Figure 3** or **Figure 4**.
11. Installation is the reverse of these steps. Note the following.
12. Install the dowel pins, if so equipped.
13. Install a new cylinder head gasket.

NOTE
*On 1986 and later KX80 models, install the cylinder head gasket so that the tab on the gasket faces to the rear and aligns with the boss on the rear of the cylinder **Figure 8**.*

14. Place the cylinder head on the cylinder with the radiator hose coupling facing toward the front (**Figure 7**). Screw on the cylinder head nuts or bolts finger-tight.
15. Tighten the nuts or bolts in a crisscross pattern to the torque specification in **Table 4**.
16. Reinstall the radiator hose at the cylinder head and tighten the hose clamp securely (B, **Figure 6**).
17. Fill the radiator as described in Chapter Three under *Coolant Change*.

18. Install the exhaust system, tighten the spark plug and install the spark plug wire, seat, side covers and fuel tank.

**Inspection
(All Models)**

1. Clean the cylinder head as described under *Engine Decarbonizing* in Chapter Three.
2. Use a straightedge and feeler gauge and measure the flatness of the cylinder head (**Figure 9**). If the cylinder head warpage exceeds 0.03 mm (0.0012 in.), resurface the cylinder head as follows:
   a. Tape a piece of 400-600 grit wet emery sandpaper onto a piece of thick plate glass or surface plate.
   b. Slowly resurface the head by moving it in figure-eight patterns on the sandpaper.
   c. Rotate the head several times to avoid removing too much material from one side. Check the progress often with the straightedge and feeler gauge.
   d. If the cylinder head warpage still exceeds the service limit excessively, it will be necessary to have the head resurfaced by a machine shop. Note that removing excessive amounts of material from the cylinder head mating surface will increase the compression ratio. Consult with the machinist on how much material was removed; it may be necessary to use 2 cylinder head gaskets to compensate for the material that was removed.
3. With the spark plug removed, check the end of the spark plug threads in the cylinder head (A, **Figure 10**) for any signs of carbon buildup or

cracking. The carbon can be removed with a 14 mm spark plug tap (**Figure 11**).

> *NOTE*
> *Always use an aluminum thread fluid or kerosene on the tap and cylinder head threads when performing Step 3.*

4. Check the flatness of the 4 cylinder head nut or bolt surfaces (**Figure 12**). Remove any burrs with a file or sandpaper.

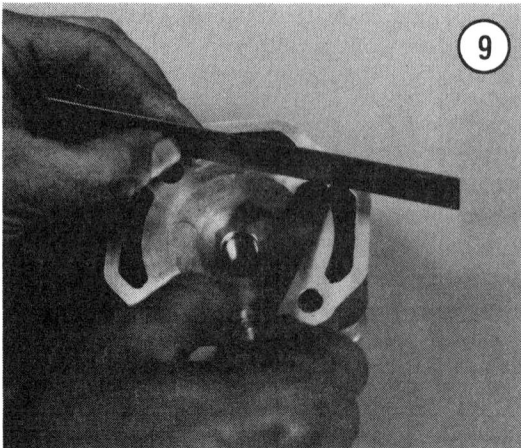

5. *Water-cooled engines:* Check the coolant passages in the head (B, **Figure 10**) for sludge buildup. Clean with a soft wood dowel.

6. Wash the cylinder head in hot soapy water and rinse thoroughly before installation.

CYLINDER

Removal/Installation

Refer to **Figure 1** (1983-1984 KX60), **Figure 3** (1985-on KX60), **Figure 4** (1983-1985 KX80) or **Figure 5** (1986-on KX80) for this procedure.

1. *Liquid-cooled models:* Drain the coolant as described under *Coolant Change* in Chapter Three.

2. Remove the cylinder head as described in this chapter.

3. Remove the carburetor as described in Chapter Eight.

4. *Liquid cooled models:* Disconnect the coolant hose at the cylinder (**Figure 13**).

5. *1986-on KX80:* Loosen the cylinder base nuts in a crisscross pattern (**Figure 14**). Then remove the nuts.

6. Loosen the cylinder by tapping around the perimeter with a rubber or plastic mallet.

> *CAUTION*
> *When removing the cylinder in Step 7, do not twist the cylinder so far that would allow the piston rings to snap into the intake port. This would cause the cylinder to bind and may damage the piston rings and piston. If this should happen, remove the reed valve assembly and push the rings back into position.*

7. Rotate the engine so the piston is at the bottom of its stroke. Pull the cylinder (**Figure 15**) straight up and off the piston.

8. Remove the cylinder base gasket and discard it. Install a piston holding fixture under the piston to protect the piston skirt from damage. This fixture may be purchased or may be a homemade unit of wood. See **Figure 16**.

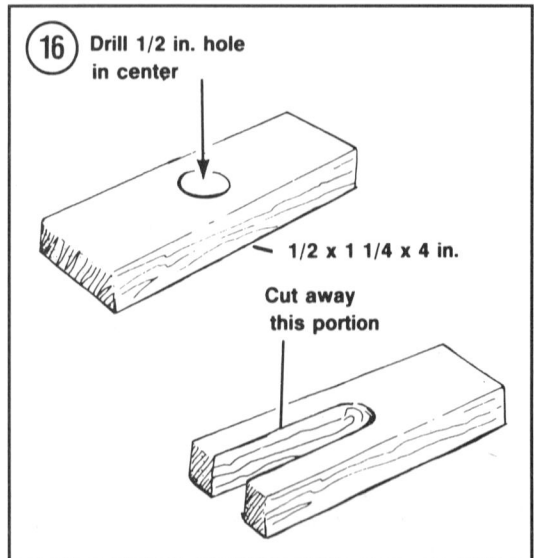

(16) Drill 1/2 in. hole in center

1/2 x 1 1/4 x 4 in.

Cut away this portion

9. Place a clean shop cloth into the crankcase opening to prevent the entry of foreign material.
10. Inspect the cylinder bore as described under *Inspection* in this chapter.
11. Before installing the cylinder, clean the bore as described under *Inspection* in this chapter.
12. Check that the top surface of the crankcase and the bottom surface of the cylinder (**Figure 17**) are clean prior to installation.
13. Install a new base gasket.
14. Make sure the end gap of the piston ring(s) are lined up with the locating pin(s) in the ring groove(s) (**Figure 18**). Lightly oil the piston rings and the inside of the cylinder bore. Rotate the crankshaft to bring the piston in contact with the piston holding fixture.

CAUTION
Do not rotate the cylinder while installing it. A piston ring could snag in the cylinder intake port and break. If a ring does snag, try to reach through the intake port and push it back into place.

15. Start the cylinder down over the piston *with the exhaust port facing forward*.
16. Compress each ring, with your fingers, as the cylinder starts to slide over it. See **Figure 19**.

NOTE
Make sure the ring(s) are still properly aligned with the locating pin(s) in the piston.

17. Slide the cylinder down until it bottoms on the piston holding fixture.
18. Remove the piston holding fixture and shop cloth and slide the cylinder into place on the crankcase (**Figure 15**).
19. Hold the cylinder in place with one hand and push the kickstarter lever down with the other hand. If the piston catches or stops in the cylinder, the piston ring(s) were not lined up properly. The piston should move up and down the cylinder bore smoothly.
20. *1986-on KX80:* Install the cylinder base nuts (**Figure 14**) and tighten them securely in a crisscross pattern (**Figure 2**) to the torque specification in **Table 4**.

21. Install the cylinder head as described under *Cylinder Head Removal/Installation* in this chapter.

22. *Liquid-cooled models:* Reconnect the coolant hose at the cylinder (**Figure 13**).

23. Install the carburetor as described under *Carburetor Removal/Installation* in Chapter Eight.

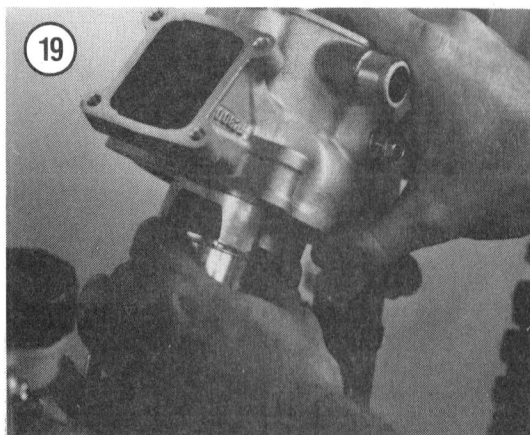

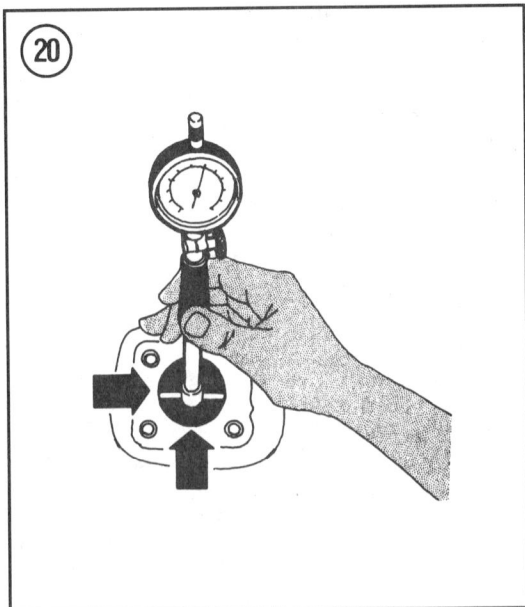

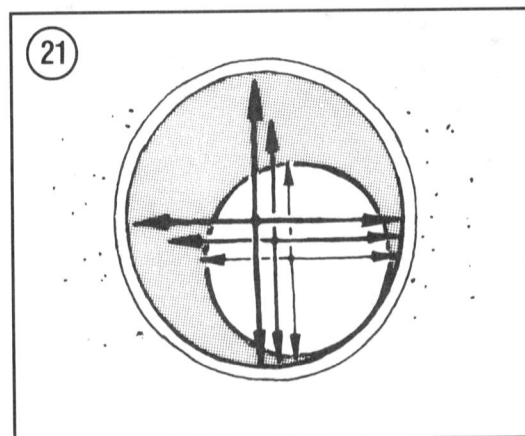

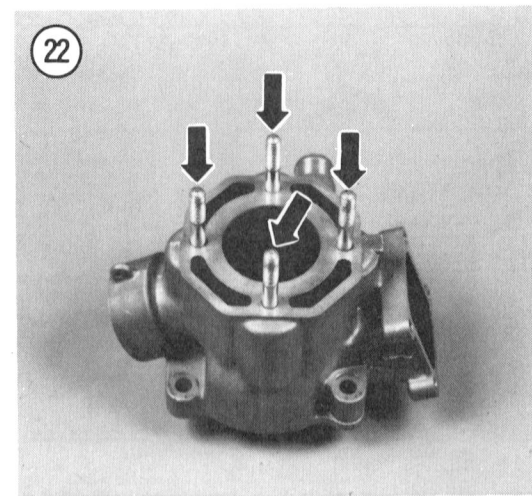

24. Follow the *Break-in Procedure* in this chapter if a new set of rings, a new piston or a new cylinder were installed.

Inspection
(All Models)

The KX60 and KX80 Kawasaki cylinders are aluminum with a molybdenum coated bore called Electro-Fuse. Cylinder measurement requires a precision bore gauge, inside micrometer or equivalent. If you don't have the right tools, have your dealer or a machine shop make the measurements.

> *NOTE*
> *The Electro-Fuse cylinder bore is extremely hard and durable and should last a long time. However, the quickest way to damage the bore surface is to run the bike with a dirty or damaged air filter. To insure long service from your bike's cylinder, service the air filter as described in Chapter Three.*

1. Remove and inspect the reed valve as described in this chapter.

> *CAUTION*
> *Electro-fuse cylinders cannot be bored oversize. The cylinder coating would be removed, and the engine would quickly seize.*

2. Measure the cylinder bore with a bore gauge (**Figure 20**) at the points shown in **Figure 21**. Measure in 2 axes—in line with the piston pin and at 90° to the pin. Then measure the bore gauge with an outside micrometer to determine the bore diameter. If the bore exceeds the wear limit in **Table 2** or **Table 3**, the cylinder must be replaced.
3. When installing a new cylinder, give the bike the same break-in procedure you would use on a new machine.
4. *1986-on:* Check the cylinder studs (**Figure 22**) for thread damage or looseness. If thread damage is minor, they may be cleaned up with a M8 × 1.25 metric die. If the studs are damaged or loose, replace them as described in Chapter One.
5. Before installing the cylinder, wash the bore in hot soapy water. Then after drying the cylinder, immediately lubricate the bore with two-stroke oil.

PISTON, PISTON PIN AND PISTON RINGS

The piston is made of an aluminum alloy. The piston pin is a precision fit and is held in place by a clip at each end. A caged needle bearing is used on the small end of the connecting rod.

Refer to **Figure 1** (1983-1984 KX60), **Figure 3** (1985-on KX60), **Figure 4** (1983-1985 KX80) or **Figure 5** (1986-on KX80) when performing procedures in this section.

Piston and Piston Rings Removal

1. Remove the cylinder head and cylinder as described under *Cylinder Removal* in this chapter.
2. Before removing the piston, hold the rod tightly and rock the piston as shown in **Figure 23**. Any rocking motion (do not confuse with the normal sliding motion) may indicate excessive wear on the piston pin, needle bearing, piston pin bore, or more likely a combination of all three.

NOTE
Wrap a clean shop cloth under the piston so that the clip will not fall into the crankcase.

WARNING
Wear safety glasses when performing Step 3.

3. Remove the clips from each side of the piston pin bore (**Figure 24**) with a small screwdriver or scribe. Hold your thumb over one edge of the clip when removing it to prevent it from springing out.
4. Use a proper size wooden dowel or socket extension and push out the piston pin (A, **Figure 25**).

CAUTION
If the engine ran hot or seized, the piston pin may be difficult to remove. However, do not drive the piston pin out of the piston with a rod and

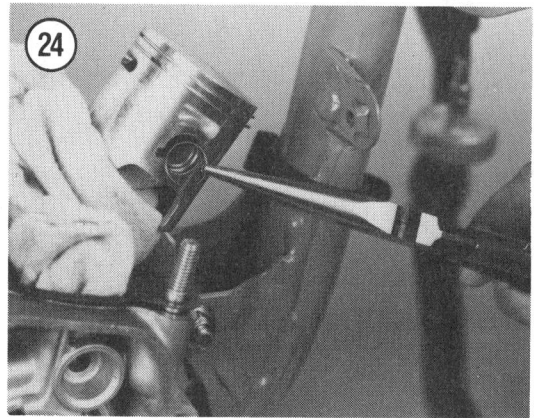

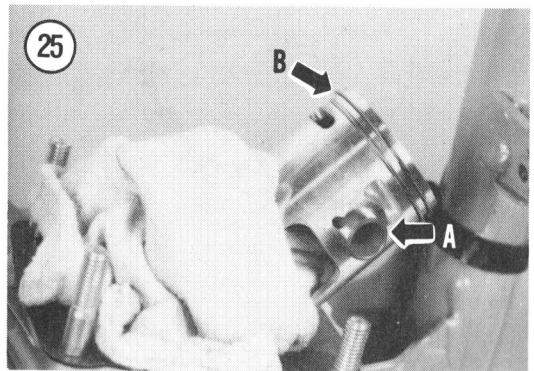

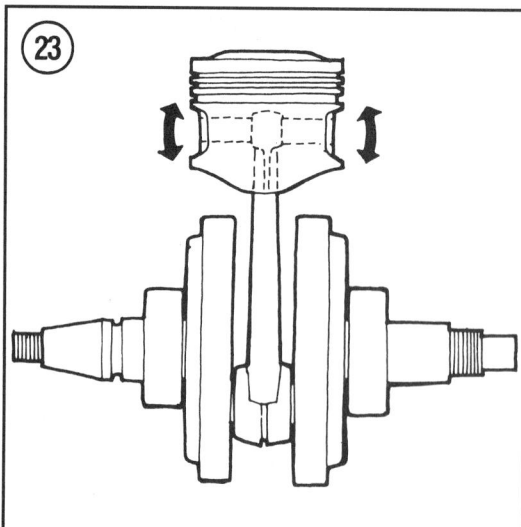

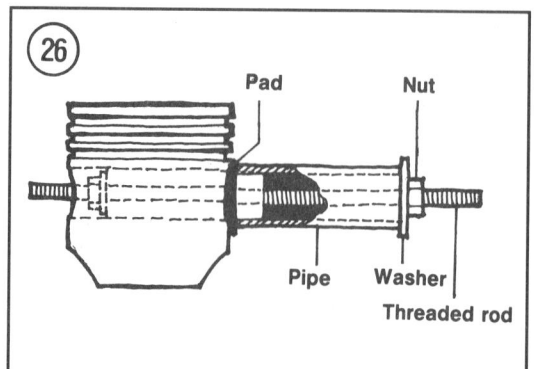

hammer. This will damage the piston, needle bearing and connecting rod. If the piston pin will not push out by hand, remove it as described in Step 5.

NOTE
The parts required to assemble the special tool in Step 5 can be purchased from a well stocked hardware store.

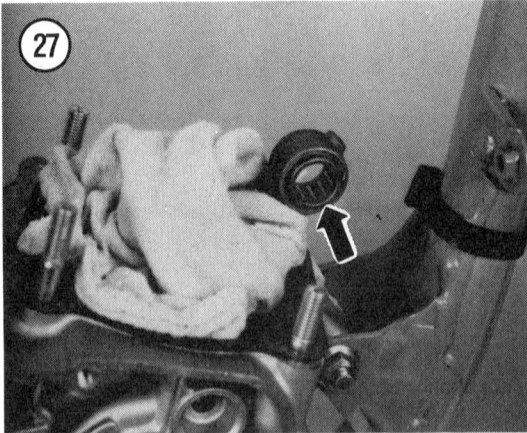

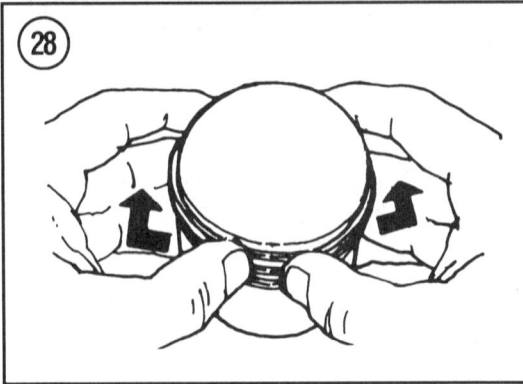

5. If the piston pin is tight, fabricate the tool shown in **Figure 26**. Assemble the tool onto the piston and pull the piston pin out of the piston. Make sure to install a pad between the piston and piece of pipe to prevent it from scoring the side of the piston.
6. Lift the piston (B, **Figure 25**) off the connecting rod.
7. Remove the needle bearing from the connecting rod (**Figure 27**).
8. If the piston is going to be left off for some time, place a piece of foam insulation tube, or shop cloth, over the end of the rod to protect it.

NOTE
Always remove the top piston ring first.

9. First remove the top ring by spreading the ends with your thumbs just enough to slide it up over the piston (**Figure 28**).Repeat for the other ring.

Piston Pin and Needle Bearing Inspection

1. Clean the needle bearing (**Figure 29**) in solvent and dry it thoroughly. Use a magnifying glass and inspect the bearing cage for cracks at the corners of the needle slots and inspect the needles themselves for cracking. If any cracks are found, the needle bearing must be replaced.
2. Check the piston pin for severe wear, scoring or chrome flaking. Also check the piston pin for cracks along the top and side. Replace the piston pin if necessary.
3. Oil the needle bearing and pin and install them in the connecting rod. Slowly rotate the pin and check for radial (up and down) play (**Figure 30**).

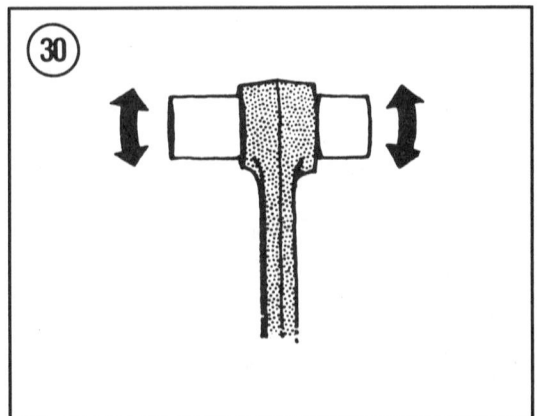

If any play exists, the pin and bearing should be replaced, providing the rod bore is in good condition. If the condition of the rod bore is in question, the old pin and bearing should be checked in a new connecting rod.

4. Measure the piston pin outside diameter with a micrometer (**Figure 31**). Replace the piston pin if the diameter is less than the service limit in **Table 2** or **Table 3**.

5. Measure the piston pin bore inside diameter with a small hole gauge (**Figure 32**). Then measure the gauge with an outside micrometer to determine the pin bore diameter (**Figure 33**). Replace the piston if the pin bore diameter exceeds the wear limit in **Table 2** or **Table 3**.

CAUTION
If there are signs of piston seizure or overheating, replace the piston pin and bearing. These parts have been weakened from excessive heat and may fail later.

Connecting Rod Inspection

1. Wipe the piston pin bore in the connecting rod with a clean rag and check it for galling, scratches, or any other signs of wear or damage. If any of these conditions exist, replace the connecting rod as described in this chapter.

2. Check the connecting rod big end bearing play. You can make a quick check by simply rocking the connecting rod back and forth (**Figure 34**). If there is more than a very slight rocking motion (some side-to-side sliding is normal), you should measure the connecting rod side clearance with a feeler gauge (**Figure 35**). If the play exceeds the wear limit specified in **Table 2** or **Table 3**, refer to crankshaft disassembly in Chapter Five and have the connecting rod and bearing replaced by a qualified dealer or service repair shop experienced in rebuilding crankshafts.

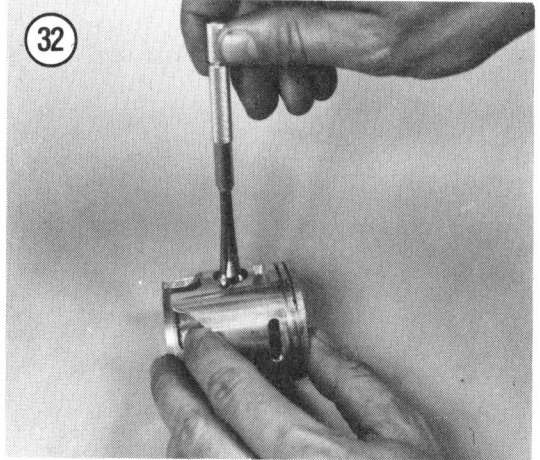

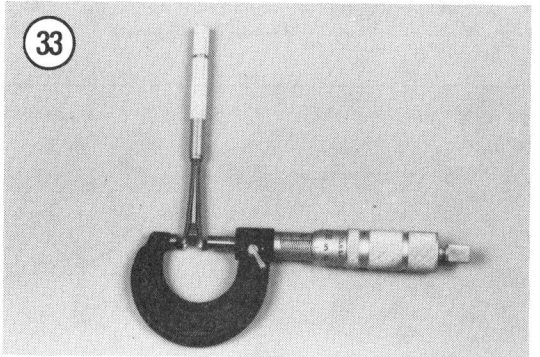

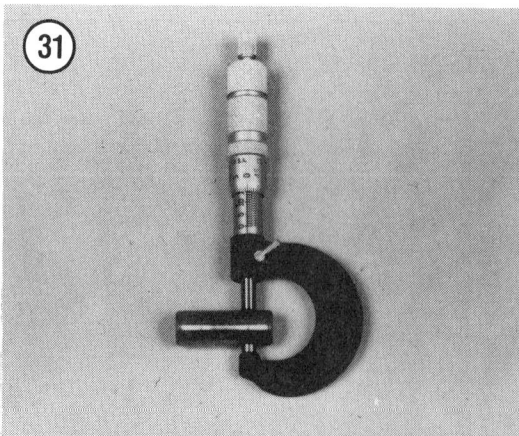

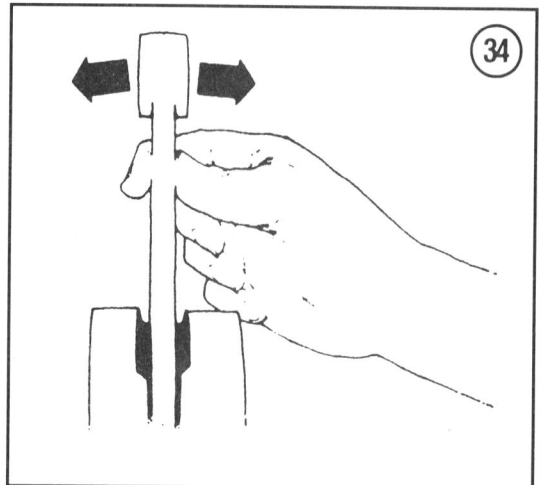

NOTE
Figure 35 shows the connecting rod side clearance being checked with the crankshaft removed. The clearance can be checked with the lower end assembled and the cylinder removed.

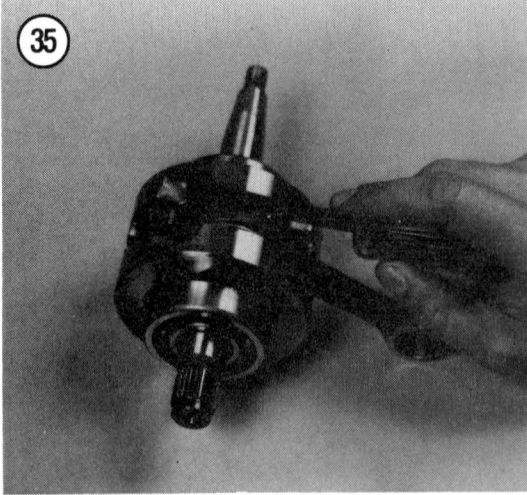

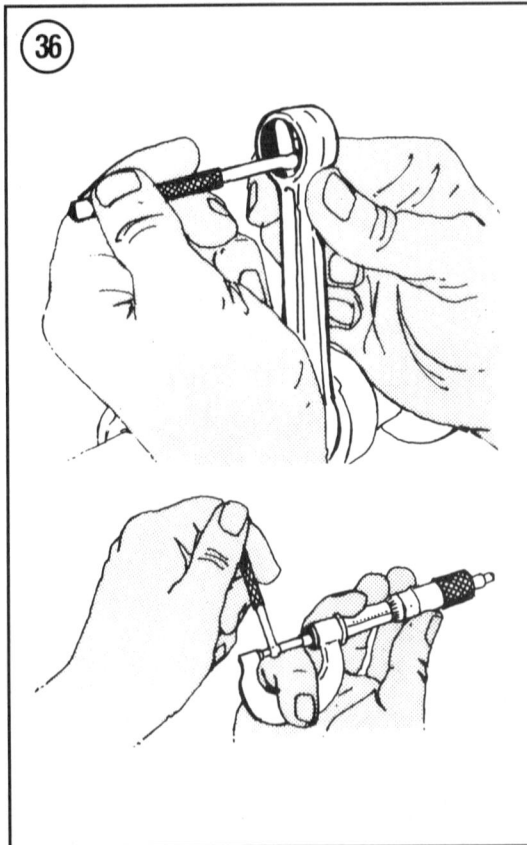

4. Measure the inside diameter of the small end of the connecting rod with a telescoping gauge (**Figure 36**). Then measure the gauge with an outside micrometer to determine the bore diameter. If the diameter exceeds the wear limit specified in **Table 2** or **Table 3**, replace the connecting rod.

Piston and Ring Inspection

1. Carefully check the piston for cracks at the top edge of the transfer cutaways (**Figure 37**) and replace if found. Check the piston skirt (**Figure 38**) for brown varnish buildup. More than a slight amount is an indication of worn or sticking rings which should be replaced.

2. Check the piston skirt for galling and abrasion which may have resulted from piston seizure. If light galling is present, smooth the affected area with No. 400 emery paper and oil or a fine

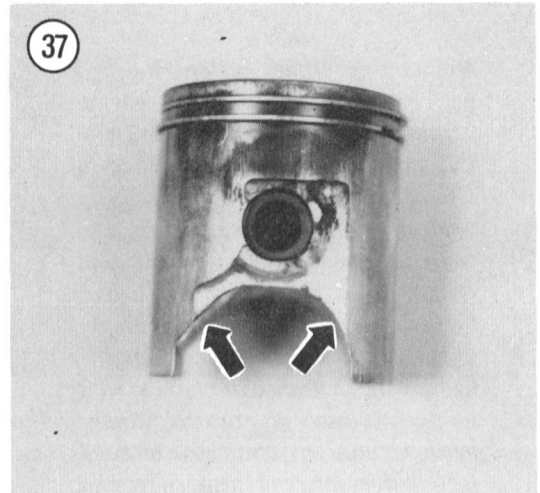

oilstone. However if galling is severe or if the piston is deeply scored, replace it.

CAUTION
Attempting to clean and then use a badly damaged or seized piston will result in seizure and possibly severe cylinder bore damage.

3. Check the piston ring locating pins in the piston (**Figure 39**). The pins should be tight and the piston should show no signs of cracking around the pins. If a locating pin is loose, replace the piston. A loose pin will fall out and cause severe engine damage.

4. Check the piston pin clip grooves in the piston for cracks or other damage that could allow a piston pin clip to fall out. This would cause severe engine damage. Replace the piston if any one groove shows signs of wear or damage.

NOTE
Maintaining proper piston ring end gap helps to ensure peak engine performance. Always check piston ring end gap at the intervals specified in Chapter Three. Excessive ring end gap reduces engine performance and can cause overheating. Insufficient ring end gap will cause the ring ends to butt together and cause the ring to break. This would cause severe engine damage. So that you don't have to wait for parts, always order extra cylinder head and base gaskets to have on hand for routine top end inspection and maintenance.

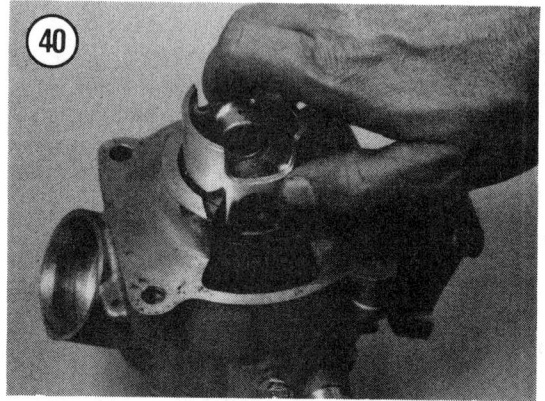

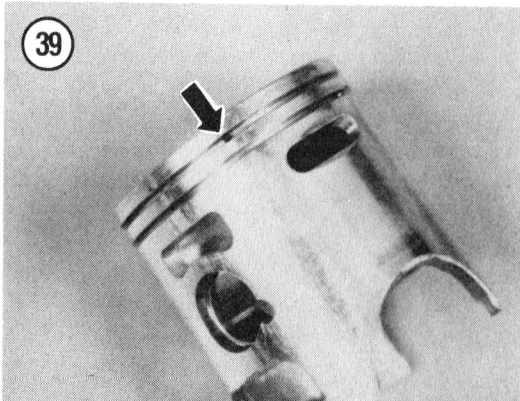

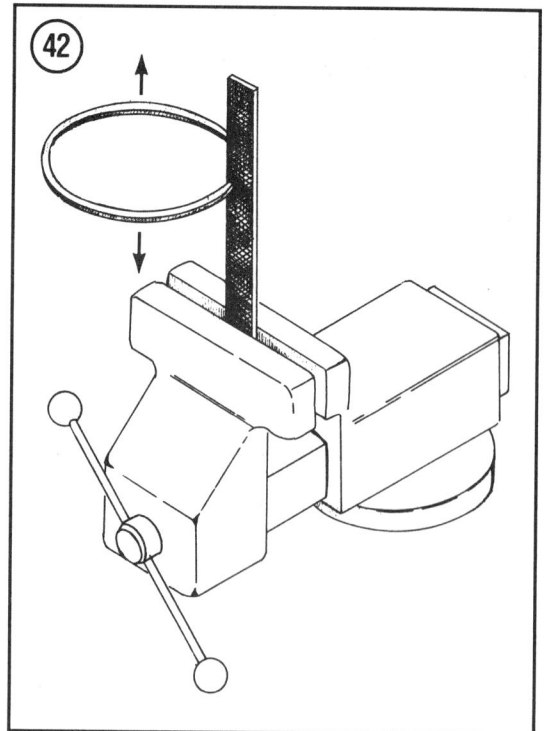

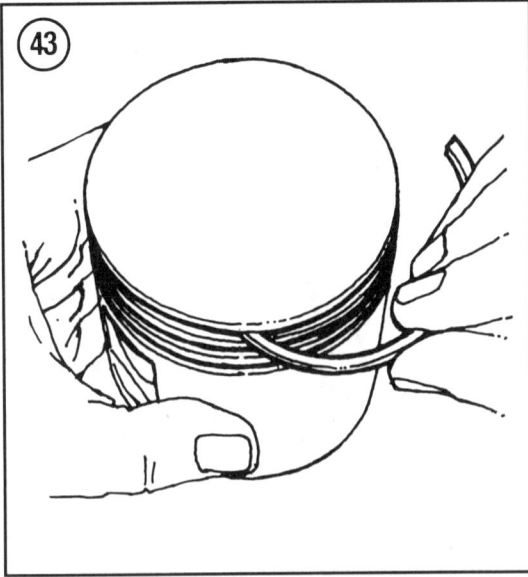

5. Measure piston ring end gap. Place a ring into the bottom of the cylinder and push it in about 20 mm (3/4 in.) with the crown of the piston (**Figure 40**). This ensures that the ring is square in the cylinder bore. Measure the gap with a flat feeler gauge (**Figure 41**) and compare to the wear limit in **Table 2** or **Table 3**. If the gap is greater than specified, the ring(s) should be replaced.

NOTE
*When installing new ring(s), measure the end gap in the same manner as for old ones. If the gap is less than specified, make sure you have the correct piston rings. If the replacement rings are correct but the end gap is too small, carefully file the ends with a fine cut file until the gap is correct (*Figure 42*).*

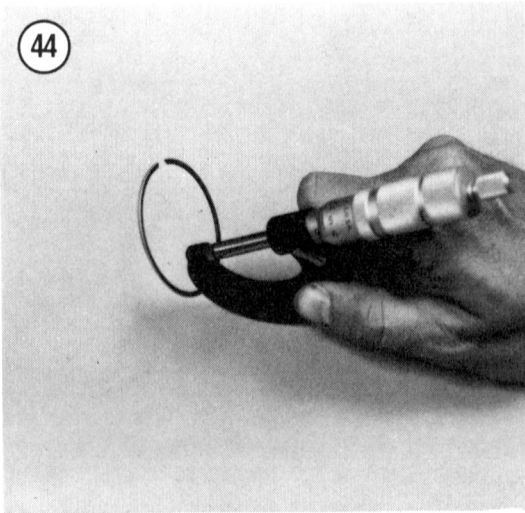

6. Carefully remove all carbon buildup from the ring grooves with a broken ring (**Figure 43**) ground to a point. Inspect the grooves carefully for burrs, nicks, or broken and cracked lands. Recondition or replace the piston if necessary.

7. Measure the thickness of each ring with a micrometer (**Figure 44**) at the points indicated in **Figure 45**. If the thickness is less than the wear limit specified in **Table 2** or **Table 3**, replace the piston rings as a set.

8. Install the piston rings onto the piston as described in this chapter. Then measure the side clearance of each ring in its groove with a flat feeler gauge (**Figure 46**) and compare to the wear limit in **Table 2** or **Table 3**. If the clearance is greater than specified, the rings must be replaced, and if the clearance is still excessive with the new rings, the piston must also be replaced.

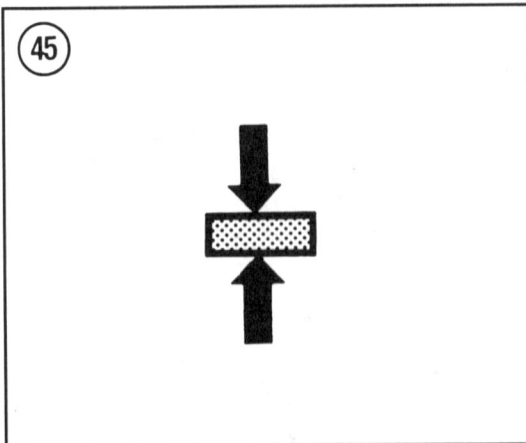

9. Observe the condition of the piston crown (**Figure 47**). Normal carbon buildup can be removed with a wire wheel mounted in a drill press. If the piston shows signs of overheating, pitting or other abnormal conditions, the engine may be experiencing preignition or detonation; both conditions and solutions are discussed in Chapter Two.

10. If the piston checked out okay after performing these inspection procedures, measure the piston outside diameter as described under *Piston/Cylinder Clearance* in this chapter.

11. If new piston rings are required, follow *Break-in Procedure* in this chapter.

Piston/Cylinder Clearance

The following procedure requires the use of a bore gauge and a micrometer. If these tools are not available, have the measurements performed by a dealer or machine shop.

1. Measure the outside diameter of the piston with a micrometer at the approximate height (**Table 2** or **Table 3**) above the bottom of the piston skirt, at a 90 degree angle to the piston pin (**Figure 48**). If the diameter exceeds the wear limit in **Table 2** or **Table 3**, install a new piston.

> *NOTE*
> *Always replace both pistons at the same time. Always install new rings when installing a new piston.*

2. Wash the cylinder in solvent to remove any oil and carbon particles. The cylinder bore must be cleaned thoroughly before attempting any measurement as incorrect readings may be obtained.

3. Measure the cylinder bore with a bore gauge (**Figure 20**) at the points shown in **Figure 21**. Measure in 2 axes—in line with the piston pin and at 90° to the pin. Then measure the bore gauge with an outside micrometer to determine the bore diameter. If the bore exceeds the wear limit in **Table 2** or **Table 3**, the cylinder must be replaced.

> *NOTE*
> *When installing a new cylinder, always install a new piston and new rings.*

4. Piston clearance is the difference between the maximum piston diameter and the minimum cylinder diameter. Subtract the dimension of the piston from the cylinder dimension. If the clearance exceeds the dimension in **Table 2** or **Table 3**, the cylinder and/or piston should be replaced.

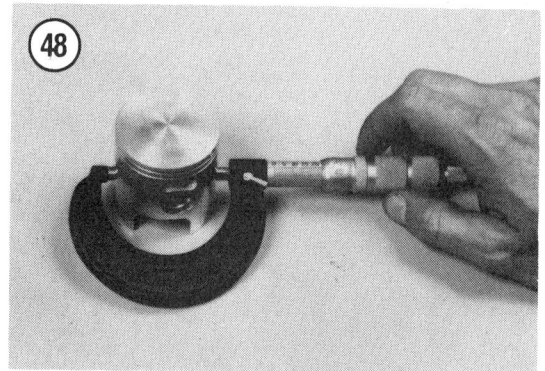

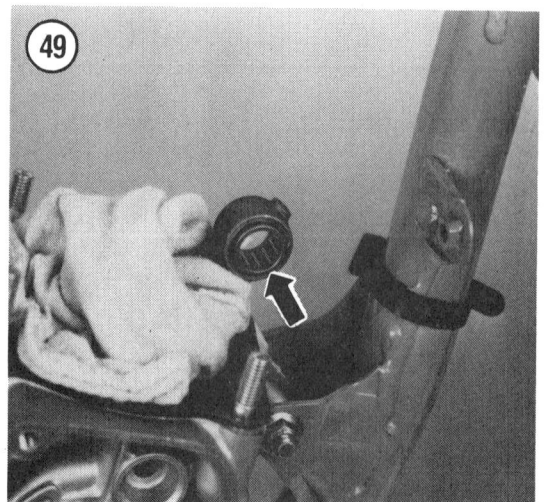

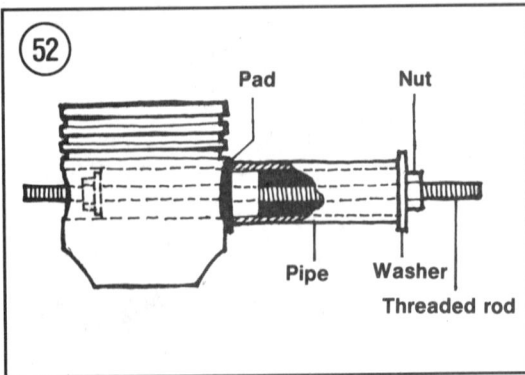

Pad   Nut

Pipe   Washer

Threaded rod

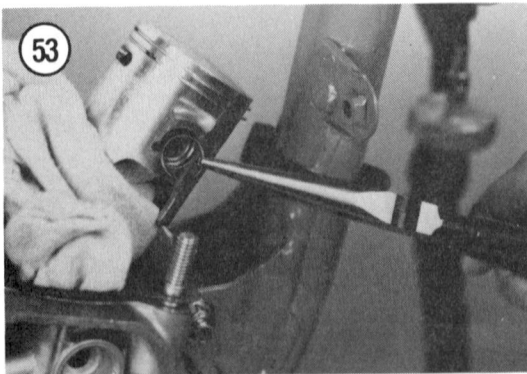

NOTE

As described under **Cylinder Inspection,** *all Kawasaki KX60 and KX80 cylinders use a coated bore called Electro-Fuse. Electro-Fuse cylinders cannot be bored oversize. The cylinder coating would be removed, and the engine would quickly seize.*

Piston and Piston Rings Installation

1. Apply assembly oil to the needle bearing and install it in the connecting rod (**Figure 49**).
2. Oil the piston pin and install it in the piston until the end of it extends slightly beyond the inside of the boss (**Figure 50**).
3. Place the piston over the connecting rod with the arrow on the piston crown pointing forward. Line up the pin with the needle bearing and push the pin into the piston until it is even with the piston pin clip grooves.

NOTE

If the arrow on the piston crown cannot be seen, note the locating rings in the piston ring grooves. The locating rings must face toward the **back** *of the bike when the piston is installed. See* **Figure 51**.

CAUTION

If the piston pin will not slide into the piston smoothly, use the homemade tool described during **Piston Removal** *to install the piston pin (**Figure 52**). When using the homemade tool, the pipe and pad is not required. Instead, run the threaded rod through the piston pin. Secure the end of the piston pin next to the piston with the small washer and nut. Slide the large washer onto the threaded rod so that it is next to the piston pin. Install the nut next to the large washer and tighten the nut to push the piston pin into the piston.*

4. Install new piston pin clips (**Figure 53**) in the piston clip grooves. Make sure they are seated in the grooves (**Figure 54**).

5. Check installation by rocking the piston back and forth around the pin axis and from side-to-side along the axis.

6. Install the piston rings—first the bottom one, then the top—by carefully spreading the ends of the ring with your thumbs and slipping the ring over the top of the piston. If the piston rings are marked on one side, the marked side should face up.

7. Make sure the rings are seated completely in the grooves, all the way around the circumference, and that the ends are aligned with the locating pins. See **Figure 51**.

8. Follow the *Break-in Procedure* in this chapter if new piston and rings were installed.

BREAK-IN PROCEDURE

If the rings were replaced, a new piston installed or the cylinder replaced, the engine must be run in at moderate speeds and loads for no less than 2 hours. Don't exceed 75 percent of normal allowable rpm during run in. After the first half hour, remove the spark plug and check its condition. The electrode should be dry and clean and the color of the insulation should be light to medium tan. If the insulation is white (indicating a too lean fuel:air mixture) or if it is dark and oily (indicating a too rich fuel:air mixture ratio), correct the condition with a main jet change; both incorrect conditions produce excessive engine heat and can lead to damage to the rings, piston and cylinder before they have had a chance to seat in.

Refer to Chapter Three for further information on how to read a spark plug and to Chapter Eight for carburetor jetting.

REED VALVE ASSEMBLY

All models are equipped with a reed valve assembly (**Figure 55**) installed in the intake tract between the carburetor and crankcase. The reed is a thin flexible diaphragm made of stainless steel or fiber material. The reed valve regulates the air:fuel mixture drawn from the carburetor into the crankcase.

Particular care must be taken when handling and repairing the reed valve assembly.

Removal/Installation

The reed valve can be removed with the cylinder removed or installed on the bike.

1. If the reed valve is going to be removed with the cylinder installed on the bike, note the following:

   a. Wash the bike thoroughly before disassembly.

   b. Remove the carburetor.

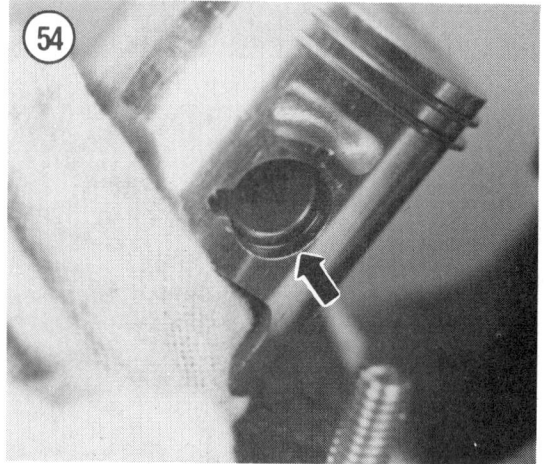

2. Remove the bolts securing the intake manifold (**Figure 56**) to the cylinder. Remove the manifold.
3. Pull the reed cage assembly (**Figure 57**) out of the cylinder intake tract.

NOTE
Some mechanics seal the reed cage against the cylinder with a chemical sealer. This is not necessary (unless mating surfaces are damaged) and it

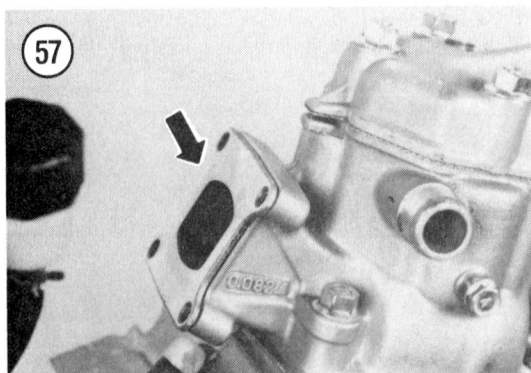

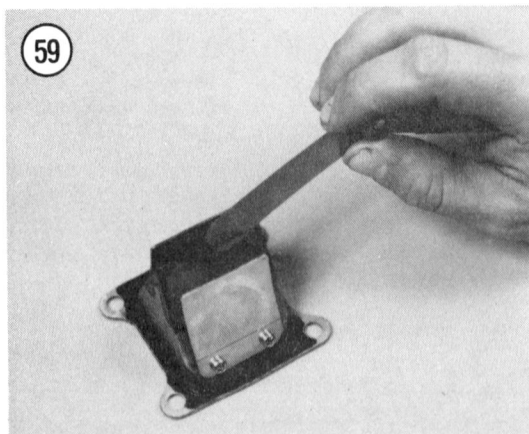

can make removal of the reed cage difficult. If the reed cage on your model is secured with a sealer, do not pry the cage off. This will damage the mating surfaces and may cause an air leak. Instead, tap the side (non-gasket area) of the cage with a rubber mallet or soft-faced drift until the cage breaks free of the sealer. Do not use a hard-faced drift or screwdriver to tap the reed cage off; this will flare the edge of the reed cage surface and cause an air leak. If you are working on a bike in which a sealer was used, check the reed cage carefully for pry marks or other damage.

4. *1983 KX80:* Remove and discard the reed cage gasket. If a sealer was used, carefully scrape all gasket residue from the cylinder mating surface.
5. Inspect the reed valve assembly as described in this chapter.
6. Install a new gasket and insert the reed valve assembly into the cylinder (**Figure 57**). The assembly is not marked or indexed so it can be installed either way.
7. *1983 KX80:* Be sure to install a new manifold gasket.
8. Install the rubber intake manifold with the carburetor locating notch (**Figure 56**) facing UP.
9. Hand tighten the bolts in a crisscross pattern.

NOTE
If you are concerned about an air leak at the reed cage, apply silicone sealant around the outside mating areas. Fill the depression formed by the edge of the cylinder, reed cage and manifold completely with sealant. Follow the manufacturer's sealant cure time recommendations before starting the engine.

Inspection

1. Carefully examine the reed valve assembly (**Figure 58**) for visible signs of wear, distortion or damage.
2. Use a flat feeler gauge and check the clearance between the reed plate and the gasket (**Figure 59**). Refer to the service limits in **Table 2** or **Table 3**.

If the clearance exceeds this dimension, the reed plate(s) must be replaced.

3. Remove the screws securing the reed stop to the reed body. Be careful that the screwdriver does not slip off and damage the reed plate.

4. Carefully examine the reed plate, reed stop and gasket. Check for signs of cracks, metal fatigue, distortion, or foreign matter damage. Pay particular attention to the rubber gasket seal. The reed stops and reed plates are available as replacement parts, but if the rubber gasket seal is damaged the entire assembly should be replaced.

5. Check the thread holes in the reed cage. If the threads are stripped, do not repair the threads.

Instead, it will be safer to replace the reed cage. Loose screws can fall into the engine and cause expensive damage.

6. Install the reed plates. Apply Loctite 242 (blue) to the threads prior to installation and tighten securely.

NOTE
Make sure that all parts are clean and free of any small dirt particles or lint from a shop cloth as they may cause a small amount of distortion in the reed plate.

7. Reinstall the reed valve assembly as described in this chapter.

Table 1 GENERAL ENGINE SPECIFICATIONS

Bore × stroke	
KX60	43 × 41.6 mm (1.69 × 1.64 in.)
KX80	
U.S.	48 × 45.8 mm (1.89 × 1.80 in.)
All other	47 × 45.8 mm (1.85 × 1.80 in.)
Displacement	
KX60	60cc (3.66 cu. in.)
KX80	
U.S.	82 cc (5.06 cu. in.)
All other	79 cc (4.84 cu. in.)
Compression ratio	
KX60	8.3:1
KX80	
U.S.	8.4:1
All other	8.3:1
U.S.	9.4:1
All other	9.1:1
Port timing	
KX60	
1983-1984	
Intake open	—
Intake close	—
Transfer open	61° BBDC
Transfer close	61° ABDC
Exhaust open	90.5° BBDC
Exhaust close	90.5° ABDC
KX60	
1985-on	
Intake open	—
Intake close	—
Transfer open	62.5° BBDC
Transfer close	62.5° ABDC
Exhaust open	92° BBDC
Exhaust close	92° ABDC
KX80	
1983-1985	
Intake open	—
Intake open	—
Transfer open	63° BBDC
Transfer close	63° ABDC
Exhaust open	94° BBDC
Exhaust close	94° ABDC
1986	
Intake open	—
Intake close	—
Transfer open	65.5° BBDC
Transfer close	65.5° ABDC
Exhaust open	94.5° BBDC
Exhaust close	94.5° ABDC
1987-on	
Intake open	—
Intake close	—
Transfer open	62.5° BBDC
Transfer close	62.5° ABDC
Exhaust open	93.5° BBDC
Exhaust close	93.5° ABDC

4

Table 2 ENGINE SPECIFICATIONS (KX60)

	New mm (in.)	Service limit mm (in.)
Cylinder head warp limit	—	0.03 (0.0012)
Cylinder inside diameter	43.000-43.015 (1.6929-1.6935)	43.10 (1.697)
Piston diameter	42.965-42.980 (1.6915-1.6921)	42.83 (1.686)
Piston-to-cylinder clearance	0.030-0.050 (0.0012-0.0020)	—
Piston ring/side clearance	0.02-0.06 (0.0008-0.0024)	0.16 (0.006)
Piston ring thickness	0.97-0.99 (0.0382-0.0390)	0.9 (0.035)
Piston ring groove thickness	1.01-1.03 (0.0398-0.0406)	1.10 (0.0433)
Piston ring end gap	0.15-0.35 (0.006-0.014)	0.7 (0.028)
Piston pin diameter	11.995-12.000 (0.4722-0.4724)	11.96 (0.471)
Piston pin bore diameter	12.000-12.006 (0.4724-0.4727)	12.07 (0.475)
Connecting rod small end inside diameter	16.002-16.013 (0.6300-0.6304)	16.05 (0.6319)
Piston measuring height	5.0 (0.2)	—
Connecting rod side clearance	0.35-0.45 (0.0138-0.0178)	0.70 (0.028)
Reed warp limit		
1983-1985	*	*
1986-1988	—	0.7 (0.028)
* Not specified.		

Table 3 ENGINE SPECIFICATIONS (KX80)

	New mm (in.)	Service limit mm (in.)
Cylinder head warp limit	—	0.03 (0.0012)
Cylinder inside diameter		
KX80E, G, J, L, N	48.000-48.015 (1.8898-1.8904)	48.10 (1.894)
KX80F, H, K, M, P	47.000-47.015 (1.8504-1.8510)	47.10 (1.854)
Piston diameter		
KX80E	47.955-47.97 (1.8880-1.8886)	47.83 (1.883)
KX80F	46.955-46.970 (1.8486-1.8492)	46.83 (1.844)
KX80G, J, L, N	47.939-47.954 (1.8874-1.8880)	47.82 (1.883)
(continued)		

Table 3 ENGINE SPECIFICATIONS (KX80) (continued)

	New mm (in.)	Service limit mm (in.)
KX80H, K, M, P	46.939-46.954 (1.8480-1.8486)	46.82 (1.843)
Piston-to-cylinder clearance		
1983	0.035-0.045 (0.0014-0.0018)	—
1984-1985	0.040-0.060 (0.0016-0.0024)	—
1986-on	0.050-0.070 (0.0020-0.0028)	—
Piston ring/side clearance	0.02-0.06 (0.0008-0.0024)	0.16 (0.006)
Piston ring thickness	0.97-0.99 (0.0382-0.0390)	0.9 (0.035)
Piston ring groove thickness	1.01-1.03 (0.0398-0.0406)	1.10 (0.0433)
Piston ring end gap	0.15-0.35 (0.006-0.014)	0.7 (0.028)
Piston pin diameter	13.995-14.000 (0.5510-0.5512)	13.96 (0.5496)
Piston pin bore diameter	14.000-14.006 (0.5512-0.5514)	14.07 (0.5539)
Connecting rod small end inside diameter	18.002-18.013 (0.7087-0.7092)	18.05 (0.7106)
Piston measuring height		
1983-1985	6.0 (0.24)	—
1986-on	17.0 (0.67)	—
Connecting rod side clearance	0.35-0.45 (0.0138-0.0178)	0.70 (0.028)
Reed warp limit		
1983-1985	*	*
1986-1987	—	0.7 (0.028)
1988-on	—	0.2 (0.008)

* Not specified.

Table 4 ENGINE TIGHTENING TORQUES

	N·m	ft.-lb.
Cylinder head bolts	25	18
Cylinder base nuts		
1986-on KX80	25	18
Cylinder drain bolt		
1986-on KX80	8.8	78 in.-lb.
Spark plug	27	20

CHAPTER FIVE

ENGINE LOWER END

This chapter describes service procedures for the following lower end components of the engine:
a. Crankcases.
b. Crankshaft.
c. Connecting rod.
d. Transmission (removal and installation).
e. Internal shift mechanism (removal and installation).

Before removing and disassembling the crankcase, clean the entire engine and frame with a good grade commercial degreaser, like Gunk or Bel-Ray engine degreaser or equivalent. It is easier to work on a clean engine and you will do a better job.

Make certain that you have all the necessary tools available, especially any special tool(s) and purchase replacement parts before disassembly. Also make sure you have a clean place to work.

It is a good idea to identify and mark parts as they are removed so that errors will be avoided during assembly and installation. Clean all parts thoroughly upon removal, then place them in trays or boxes with their associated mounting hardware.

Do not rely on memory alone as it may be days or weeks before you complete the job. In the text there is frequent mention of the left-hand and right-hand side of the engine. This refers to the engine as it sits in the bike's frame, not as it sits on your workbench.

Crankshaft specifications are listed in **Table 1**. **Table 1** and **Table 2** are at the end of the chapter.

SERVICING ENGINE IN FRAME

Some of the components can be serviced while the engine is mounted in the frame (the bike's frame is a great holding fixture—especially for breaking loose stubborn bolts and nuts):
a. Cylinder head.
b. Cylinder.
c. Piston.
d. Carburetor.
e. Flywheel.
f. Clutch.
g. External shift mechanism.

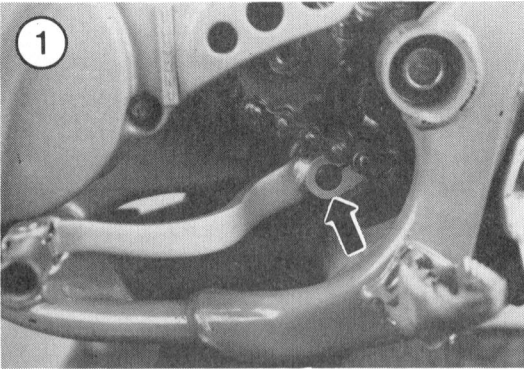

ENGINE

Removal/Installation

If the engine is going to be removed for non-engine related service, engine disassembly is not required. Instead, remove the engine as a unit. If service requires crankcase disassembly, use the frame as a holding tool and remove all of the engine sub-assemblies while the engine is mounted in the frame. After the sub-assemblies are removed, the crankcase can be removed as a unit and then serviced as required.

1. Support the bike on a bike stand.
2. Remove the seat and both frame side covers.
3. Remove the fuel tank as described in Chapter Eight.
4. Remove the exhaust system as described under *Exhaust System Removal/Installation* in Chapter Eight.
5. Remove the carburetor as described under *Carburetor Removal/Installation* in Chapter Eight.
6. Remove the shift lever pinch bolt and slide the lever (**Figure 1**) off of the shift shaft. If the lever is tight, pry the lever slot open with a screwdriver and pull the lever off.
7. See **Figure 2**. Loosen the clutch cable adjuster locknut at the handlebar and turn the adjuster to loosen the clutch cable.
8. Disconnect the clutch cable at the engine (**Figure 3**). On some models, it will be necessary to loosen the clutch cable locknuts (**Figure 4**) before removing the cable.
9. Remove the master link on the drive chain (**Figure 5**). Then disconnect the drive chain and remove it.
10. *Liquid-cooled engines:* Perform the following:
   a. Drain the coolant as described under *Coolant Change* in Chapter Three.

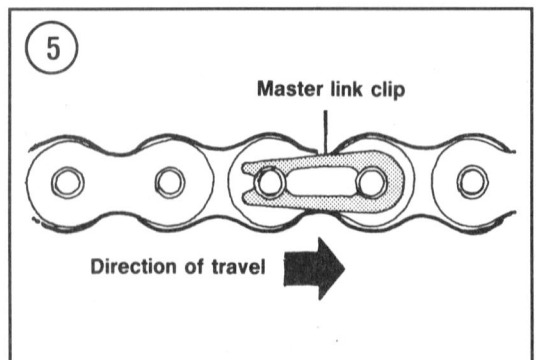

Master link clip

Direction of travel

b. Disconnect the water hose at the cylinder head (A, **Figure 6**).

c. Disconnect the water hose at the water pump (B, **Figure 6**).

11. If you are going to disassemble the crankcases, remove the following engine sub-assemblies:

   a. Cylinder head (Chapter Four).

   b. Cylinder (Chapter Four).

   c. Piston (Chapter Four).

   d. Flywheel (Chapter Nine).

   e. Clutch (Chapter Six).

   f. Kickstarter (Chapter Six).

   g. Primary drive gear (Chapter Six).

   h. Drive sprocket (this chapter).

12. Remove the engine assembly as follows:

   a. Remove the front and lower engine mount bolts (**Figure 7**).

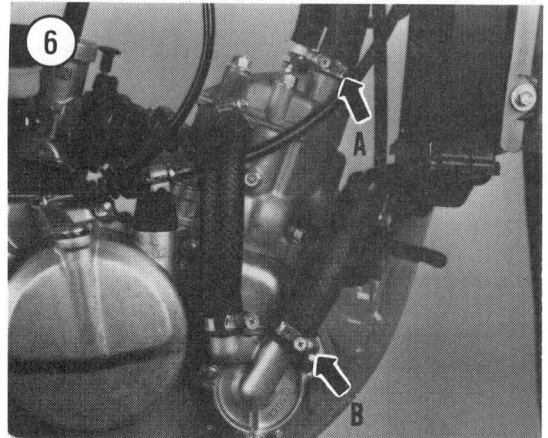

NOTE
*On some models, it will be necessary to remove the rear brake pedal (**Figure 8**) to gain access to the swing arm pivot shaft.*

   b. Remove the engine-to-swing arm pivot shaft nut (A, **Figure 9**) and withdraw the pivot shaft.

   c. Lift the engine (B, **Figure 9**) out of the frame from the right-hand side.

   d. The swing arm is now loose from its mounting on the frame. If it is necessary to move the bike, align the swing arm with the frame and install the pivot shaft and nut.

13. Check the front and lower engine mount brackets on the frame for damage.

14. Installation is the reverse of these steps. Note the following.

15. Tighten the pivot shaft to the torque specification in **Table 2**.

16. Tighten the engine mount bolts to the torque specification in **Table 2**.

17. If the engine oil was drained, fill the clutch/transmission with the correct type and quantity oil as described under *Transmission Oil* in Chapter Three.

18. *Liquid-cooled engines:* Refill the cooling system as described under *Coolant Change* in Chapter Three.

19. Reinstall the drive chain. Connect the master link so that the closed end of the chain faces the direction of chain travel (**Figure 5**).

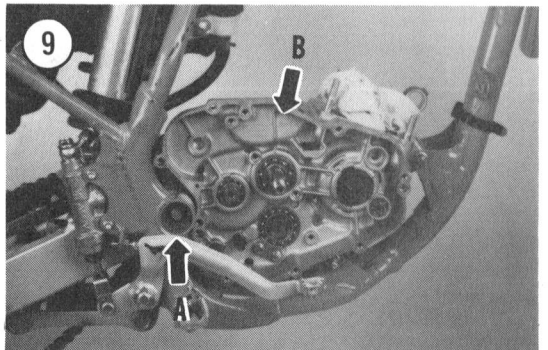

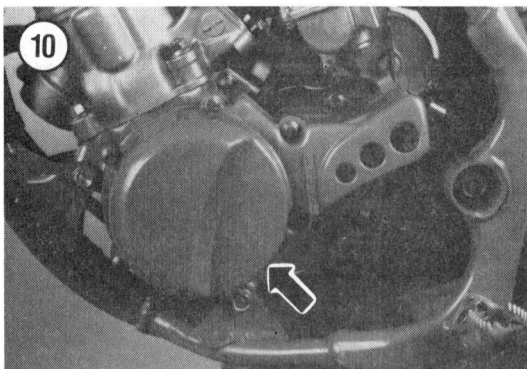

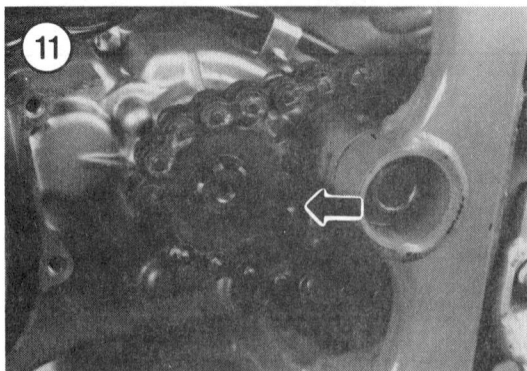

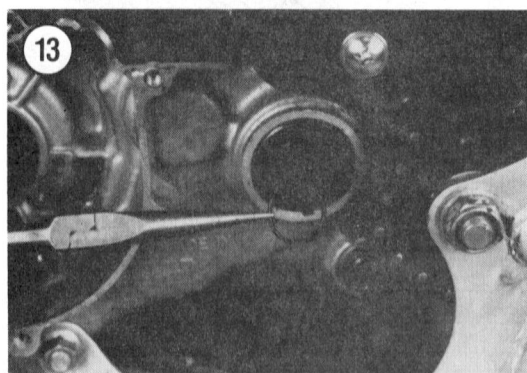

20. Adjust the clutch, drive chain and rear brake pedal as described in Chapter Three.
21. Start the engine and check for leaks.

ENGINE SPROCKET

The engine sprocket is mounted on the left end of the transmission countershaft, with a sleeve and O-ring inside of it. The sprocket is secured with a circlip.

Removal/Installation

1. Remove the engine sprocket cover (**Figure 10**).
2. Remove the circlip securing the engine sprocket with circlip pliers.
3. Remove the engine sprocket (**Figure 11**). If necessary, remove the spacer (**Figure 12**) and O-ring (**Figure 13**).
4. Installation is the reverse of these steps. Always install a new circlip and make sure it is correctly seated in the transmission shaft groove.

CRANKCASE AND CRANKSHAFT

Disassembly of the crankcase—splitting the cases—and removal of the crankshaft assembly require that the engine be removed from the frame. However, the cylinder head, cylinder and all other attached assemblies should be removed with the engine in the frame.

The crankcase is made in 2 halves of precision diecast aluminum alloy and is of the "thin-walled" type. To avoid damage to them, do not hammer or pry on any of the interior or exterior projected walls. These areas are easily damaged if stressed beyond what they are designed for. They are assembled without a gasket; only gasket sealer is used while dowel pins align the crankcase halves when they are bolted together. The crankcase halves are sold as a matched set only (**Figure 14**). If one crankcase half is damaged, both must be replaced.

The crankshaft assembly is made up of 2 full-circle flywheels pressed together on a hollow crankpin. The connecting rod big end bearing on the crankpin is a needle bearing assembly (**Figure 15**). The crankshaft assembly is supported by 2 ball bearings in the crankcase.

The procedure which follows is presented as a complete, step-by-step major lower end rebuild that should be followed if an engine is to be completely reconditioned.

Remember that the right- and left-hand side of the engine relates to the engine as it sits in the bike's frame, not as it sits on your workbench.

Special Tools

When splitting the crankcase assembly, a few special tools are required. These tools allow easy disassembly and reassembly of the crankcase without prying or hammer use. Remember, the crankcase halves can be easily damaged by improper disassembly or reassembly techniques.

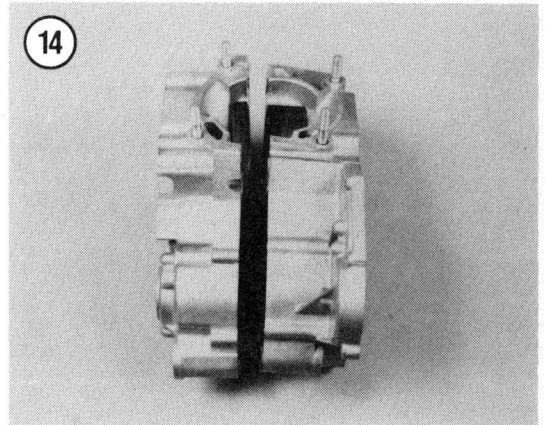

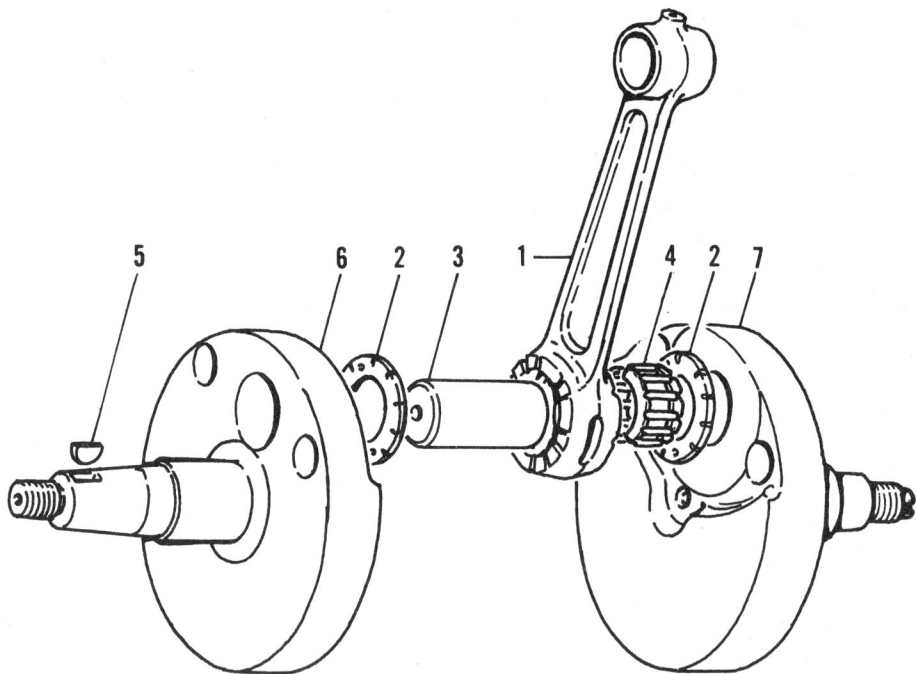

CRANKSHAFT

1. Connecting rod
2. Shims
3. Pin
4. Needle bearing
5. Woodruff key
6. Left-hand crank half
7. Right-hand crank half

The following tools are required:

a. Kawasaki crankcase separating tool (part No. 57001-1098) (**Figure 16**) or equivalent. This tool threads into the crankcase threaded holes and is used to separate the crankcase halves and to press the crankshaft out of the crankcase. The tool is very simple in design and a similar type of tool, such as a steering wheel puller can be substituted.

b. Some type of press will be required to assemble the crankcase assembly.

c. Kawasaki crankshaft jig (part No. 57001-1174) (**Figure 17**). This tool is used to prevent the crankcase halves from pressing inward when reassembling the crankcase halves.

Crankcase Disassembly
(All Models)

This procedure describes disassembly of the crankcase halves and removal of the crankshaft, transmission and internal shift mechanism.

1. Remove all exterior engine assemblies as described in this chapter and other related chapters.

NOTE
Drain the clutch/transmission oil as described in Chapter Three. To avoid misplacing the drain bolt, reinstall it after the oil is completely drained.

2. Slide the spacer off the transmission countershaft (**Figure 18**). Then remove the O-ring (**Figure 19**) from its groove in the transmission countershaft.

NOTE
Make sure to remove the entire external shift mechanism assembly as described in Chapter Six for your model.

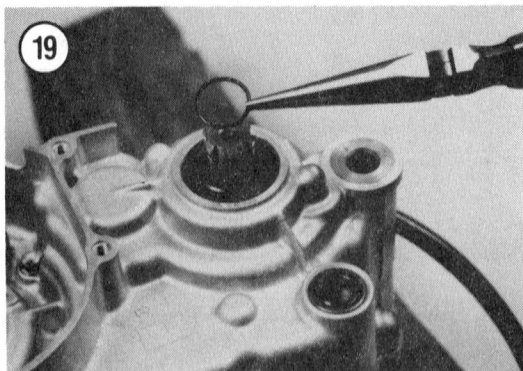

3. Place the engine assembly on a couple of wood blocks with the left-hand side facing up (**Figure 20**).

4. Loosen all bolts securing the crankcase halves together one-quarter turn. To prevent warpage, loosen them in a crisscross pattern.

5. Remove all bolts loosened in Step 4. Be sure to remove all of the bolts.

NOTE
To prevent loss and to ensure proper location during assembly, draw the crankcase outline on cardboard, then punch holes to correspond with bolt locations. Insert the bolts in their appropriate locations. Also record the position of any clips that hold electrical wires or drain tubes.

CAUTION
*Perform this operation over and close down to the work bench as the crankcase halves may easily separate. **Do not** hammer on the crankcase halves.*

6. Install the crankcase separating tool (**Figure 21**) into the threaded holes on the left-hand crankcase. Center the center pressure bolt on the end of the crankshaft. Tighten the securing bolts into the crankcase, making sure the tool body is parallel with the crankcase. If necessary, back out one of the separating tool bolts.
7. Screw the center pressure bolt *clockwise* until both cases begin to separate.

CAUTION
*While tightening the puller bolt make sure the puller body is kept parallel to the crankcase surface during this operation (**Figure 22**). Otherwise it will put an uneven stress on the case halves and may damage them.*

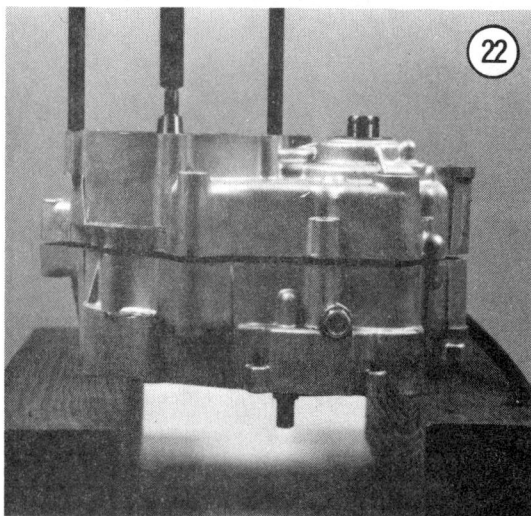

8. Use a plastic or rubber mallet and tap the crankcase half and transmission shaft to help during separation. Continue to operate the puller

until the left-hand crankcase half is free (**Figure 23**). Remove the puller and lift the left-hand crankcase half (**Figure 24**) off of the lower crankcase. Make sure the left-hand case oil seal doesn't grab and pull the transmission countershaft assembly up when removing the case half.

CAUTION
Crankcase separation requires only hand pressure on the puller center pressure bolt. If extreme pressure seems to be needed, or if both halves will not remain parallel, stop immediately. Check for crankcase bolts not removed, or any part that is still attached, or transmission shafts hung up in a bearing. Relieve puller pressure immediately.

CAUTION
Never pry between case halves. Doing so may result in oil leaks, requiring replacement of the case halves.

9. Remove the 2 dowel pins after removing the left-hand crankcase half. See **Figure 25** (KX60 and 1983-1985 KX80) or **Figure 26** (1986-on KX80).
10. The transmission assemblies and the crankshaft assemblies will usually stay in the right-hand case half. See **Figure 25** or **Figure 26**.
11A. *KX60 and 1983-1985 KX80:* Remove the transmission assembly as follows:
   a. Remove the 2 shift fork shafts (**Figure 27**). If the shafts are tight, rotate the shift drum to release tension.
   b. Pivot the shift forks away from the shift drum grooves and remove the shift drum (**Figure 28**).

c. Remove the 3 shift forks (**Figure 29**).

d. Lift and remove both transmission shafts (**Figure 30**) at the same time.

11B. *1986-on KX80:* Remove the transmission assembly as follows:

a. Remove the shift fork shafts (**Figure 31**). If the shafts are tight, rotate the shift drum to release tension.

b. Pivot the shift forks away from the shift drum grooves and remove the shift drum (**Figure 32**).

c. Remove the 3 shift forks (**Figure 33**).

d. Lift and remove both transmission shafts (**Figure 34**) at the same time.

12. Remove the breather grommet (**Figure 35**) from the left-hand crankcase.

NOTE
*Step 13 describes crankshaft (**Figure 36**) removal. As explained under **Special Tools** in this chapter, a press*

will be required to remove and install the crankshaft. If you do not have a press or access to one, have the crankshaft removed by a dealer or machine shop.

NOTE
*If the Kawasaki crankshaft jig is not used when removing the crankshaft in Step 14, the crankshaft may be forced out of alignment. **Figure 37** shows the crankshaft jig in position between the crankshaft wheels.*

13. Support the right-hand crankcase/crankshaft assembly in a press bed (**Figure 38**). Make sure the blocks used underneath the crankcase half are wide enough to allow complete removal of the crankshaft. Fit the crankshaft jig between the crankshaft wheels. Check that the crankshaft jig and the connecting rod cannot catch on a support block as the crankshaft is pressed out. Insert a soft metal spacer (aluminum or brass) between the press ram and the end of the crankshaft. Press the crankshaft out of the crankcase (**Figure 39**). Make sure to catch the crankshaft as it is pressed out or it may fall to the floor.

14. Remove the crankshaft jig from the crankshaft.

15. Clean and inspect the crankcase and crankshaft as described in this chapter.

16. Service to the transmission and internal shift mechanism is described in Chapter Seven.

Crankcase Assembly

1. Pack all of the crankcase oil seals with a heat durable grease.
2. Apply engine oil to both crankshaft main bearings.

> *NOTE*
> *Before installing the crankshaft in Step 3, install the Kawasaki crankcase jig onto the crankshaft as shown in (**Figure 37**).*

> *CAUTION*
> *If the crankcase jig is not used, the crankshaft may be forced out of alignment during installation.*

> *NOTE*
> *When installing the crankshaft in Step 3, make sure that the crankshaft is pressed into the crankcase half evenly. After aligning the crankshaft with the crankcase half, apply pressure from the press until the crankshaft moves a small amount and then stop. Recheck crankshaft alignment. If the crankshaft is pinched to one side, stop and release pressure from the crankshaft. Realign the crankshaft before continuing. When the crankshaft is aligned correctly, reapply pressure so that the crankshaft moves a small amount. Then stop and recheck the alignment. Continue until the crankshaft is pressed in all the way.*

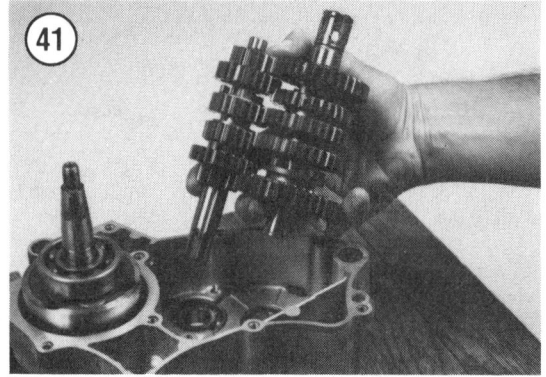

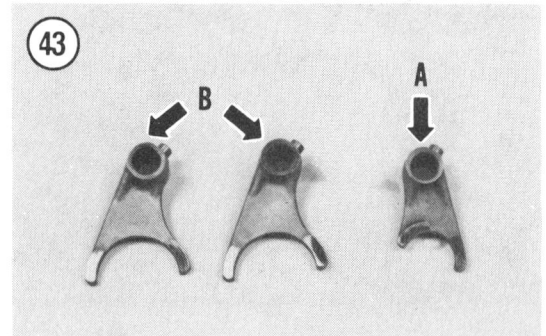

3. If the crankshaft was removed, press it into the right-hand crankcase (**Figure 40**) with a press. Remove the crankshaft jig (**Figure 37**) from the crankshaft.

CAUTION
If you do not have access to a press, have the crankshaft installed by a dealer or machine shop. Do not drive the crankshaft into the bearing. Do not drive the crankshaft into the crankcase with a hammer.

4. Place the right-hand crankcase assembly onto wood blocks.

5. Apply transmission oil to the inner race of all bearings in the right-hand crankcase half.

6A. *KX60 and 1983-1985 KX80:* Install the transmission and the internal shift mechanism as follows:

  a. Coat all sliding surfaces with transmission oil.

  b. Mesh the mainshaft and countershaft assemblies together (**Figure 41**) and install them into the right-hand crankshaft. See **Figure 42**.

  c. The shift forks used in this transmission can be identified by the length of their shift fingers. The mainshaft shift fork fingers (A, **Figure 43**) are shorter than the fingers used on the 2 countershaft shift forks (B, **Figure 43**). The 2 countershaft shift forks (B) are identical.

  d. Install the mainshaft third/fourth gear shift fork (A, **Figure 43**). See **Figure 44**.

  e. Install the countershaft sixth gear shift fork (B, **Figure 43**). See **Figure 45**.

  f. Install the countershaft fifth gear shift fork (B, **Figure 43**). See **Figure 46**.

  g. Install the shift drum (**Figure 47**) into the right-hand crankcase.

  h. Viewing the shift drum as it sits in the right-hand crankcase, you will note that it has 3 machined slots. Engage the shift fork pins with the shift drum slots as follows. Engage the countershaft sixth gear shift fork with the bottom shift drum slot. Engage the mainshaft third/fourth gear shift fork with the middle shift drum slot. Engage the countershaft fifth gear shift fork with the top shift drum slot.

  i. Install the shift fork shafts (**Figure 48**) through the shift fork(s). Make sure the shafts engage the shaft holes in the right-hand crankcase.

5

6B. *1986-on KX80:* Install the transmission as follows:

  a. Coat all sliding surfaces with transmission oil.

  b. Mesh the mainshaft and countershaft assemblies together (**Figure 49**) and install them into the right-hand crankshaft. See **Figure 50**.

  c. The shift forks are identified in **Figure 51**: Mainshaft third/fourth gear shift fork (A), countershaft fifth gear shift fork (B) and countershaft sixth gear shift fork (C).

  d. Install the mainshaft third/fourth gear shift fork (A, **Figure 51**). See **Figure 52**.

  e. Install the countershaft fifth gear shift fork (B, **Figure 51**). See **Figure 53**.

  f. Install the countershaft sixth gear shift fork (C, **Figure 51**). See **Figure 54**.

  g. Install the shift drum (**Figure 55**) into the right-hand crankcase.

  h. Viewing the shift drum as its sits in the right-hand crankcase, you will note that it has 2 machined slots. Engage the shift fork pins with the shift drum slots as follows. Engage the countershaft sixth gear shift fork with the bottom shift drum slot. Engage the mainshaft third/fourth gear shift fork with the top shift drum slot. Engage the countershaft fifth gear shift fork with the top shift drum slot.

  i. Install the shift fork shafts (**Figure 56**). Make sure the shafts engage the shaft holes in the right-hand crankcase.

NOTE
Step 7 is best done with the aid of a helper as the assemblies are loose and

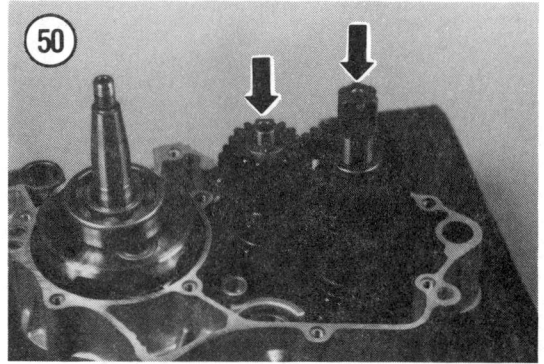

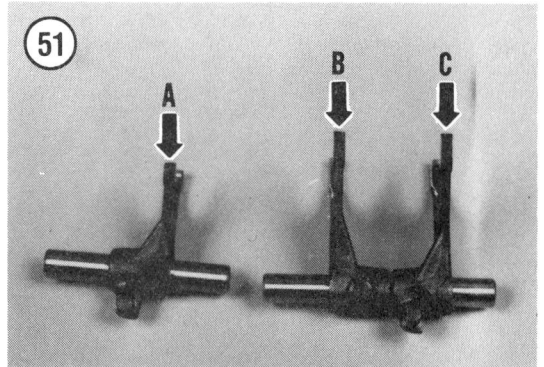

don't want to spin very easily. Have the helper spin the transmission shaft while you turn the shift drum through all the gears.

7. Spin the transmission shafts and shift through the gears using the shift drum. Make sure you can shift into all gears. This is the time to find that something may be installed incorrectly—not after the crankcase is completely assembled.

8. Shift the transmission assembly into NEUTRAL.

9. Set the crankcase assembly in the press bed.

10. Install the Kawasaki crankcase jig into position on the crankshaft.

11. Install the 2 locating dowels into the right-hand crankcase half. See **Figure 57** (KX60 and 1983-1985 KX80) or **Figure 58** (1986-on KX80).

12. Install the breather grommet (**Figure 59**) into the left-hand crankcase.

13. Apply a light coat of *non-hardening liquid gasket* such as 4-Three Bond, or equivalent, to the mating surfaces of both crankcase halves.

> *NOTE*
> *Make sure the mating surfaces are clean and free of all old gasket material. This is to make sure you get a leak free seal.*

14. Set the upper crankcase half over the one on the blocks. Push it down squarely into place until it reaches the crankshaft bearing, usually with about 1/2 inch left to go. Install the Kawasaki Crankshaft Jig onto the crankshaft.

15. Use a press and press the upper crankcase half over the main bearing (**Figure 60**). After the cases are assembled, make sure each shaft rotates smoothly.

> *CAUTION*
> *Crankcase halves should fit together without force. If the crankcase halves do not fit together completely, do not attempt to pull them together with the crankcase screws. Separate the crankcase halves and investigate the cause of the interference. If the transmission shafts were disassembled, recheck to make sure that a gear is not installed backwards. Also check that the shift drum neutral detent is not installed—it must be removed during this procedure. Crankcase halves are a matched set and are very expensive. Do not risk damage by trying to force the cases together.*

16. Remove the crankcase jig (**Figure 60**).

17. Install all the crankcase bolts and tighten only finger-tight at first. Place any clips under the bolts in the locations recorded during disassembly.

18. Securely tighten the bolts in 2 stages in a crisscross pattern until they are firmly hand-tight.

19. After the crankcase halves are completely assembled, rotate the crankshaft and check for binding; the crankshaft should rotate freely. If the crankshaft is tight, it is not centered correctly (**Figure 61**). Center the crankshaft as follows:

   a. Carefully tap the appropriate end of the crankshaft with a piece of soft metal (aluminum or brass) and a hammer.

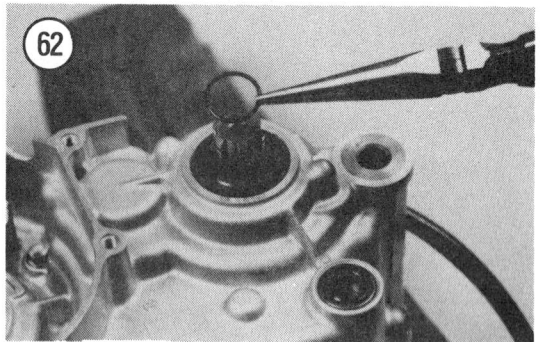

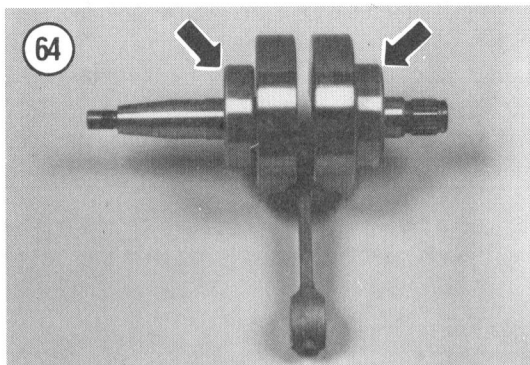

5

b. Repeat until the crankshaft rotates freely.

20. Spin the countershaft while operating the shift drum and check that the shafts turn smoothly and all gears engage properly.

21. Install a new O-ring over the countershaft as shown in **Figure 62**. Seat the O-ring with the spacer (**Figure 63**).

22. Install all exterior engine assemblies as described in this chapter and other related chapters.

Crankcase Inspection

1. Remove the crankcase oil seals as described under *Bearing and Oil Seal Replacement* in this chapter.

2. Clean both crankcase halves inside and out with cleaning solvent. Thoroughly dry with compressed air and wipe off with a clean shop cloth. Be sure to remove all traces of old gasket sealer from all mating surfaces.

3. Oil the crankshaft main bearings (**Figure 64**) with clean 2-stroke engine oil before checking the bearings in Steps 4 and 5.

4. Check the crankshaft main bearings (**Figure 64**) for roughness, pitting, galling, and play by rotating them slowly by hand. If any roughness or play can be felt in the bearing, it must be replaced.

NOTE
Always replace both crankcase main bearings as a set.

5. Inspect the other bearings as described in the previous step. See **Figure 65**, typical.

6. Replace any worn or damaged bearings as described under *Bearing and Oil Seal Replacement* in this chapter.

7. Carefully inspect the cases (**Figure 66**) for cracks and fractures, especially in the lower areas where they are vulnerable to rock damage. Also check the areas around the stiffening ribs, around bearing bosses and threaded holes. If any are found, have them repaired by a shop specializing in the repair of precision aluminum castings or replace them as a set.

8. *1986-on KX80:* Check the shift shaft pin (**Figure 67**) for looseness. Tighten the pin if necessary.

Bearing and Oil Seal Replacement

On 1986 and later KX80 models, the main bearing oil seal is installed between the bearing and a shoulder on the case half. Thus the bearing and oil seal must be removed at the same time. During assembly, the oil seal must be installed first, then the bearing.

1. *Crankshaft oil seals:* Drive out the oil seals with a suitable size socket (**Figure 68**) or pry them out with a screwdriver (**Figure 69**). Place a rag or wood block underneath the screwdriver to prevent from damaging the crankcase. If the seals are old and difficult to remove, heat the cases as described later and use an awl and punch a small hole in the steel backing of the seal. Install a small sheet metal screw into the seal and pull the seal out with a pair of pliers.

> **CAUTION**
> *Do not install the screw too deep or it may contact and damage the bearing behind it.*

2. Some transmission bearings are held in position by a retainer plate (**Figure 70**) or with bolts and washers. Remove the retainers before removing the bearings. If it is not necessary to remove the bearings, check the retainer plate bolts for tightness.

> **CAUTION**
> *Before heating the crankcases in this procedure to remove the bearings, wash the cases thoroughly with detergent and water. Rinse and rewash the cases as required to remove all traces of oil and other chemical deposits.*

3. The bearings are installed with a slight interference fit. The crankcase must be heated to a temperature of about 212° F (100° C) in an oven or on a hot plate (**Figure 71**). An easy way to check to see that it is at the proper temperature is to drop tiny drops of water on the case; if they sizzle and evaporate immediately, the temperature is correct. Heat only one case at a time.

> **CAUTION**
> *Do not heat the cases with a torch (propane or acetylene)—never bring a flame into contact with the bearing or case. The direct heat will destroy the case hardening of the bearing and will likely warp the case half.*

4. Remove the case from the oven or hot plate and hold onto the 2 crankcase studs with a kitchen pot holder, heavy gloves, or heavy shop cloths—*it is hot*.

5. Remove the oil seals if not already removed.

> **NOTE**
> *A suitable size socket and extension works well for removing and installing bearings.*

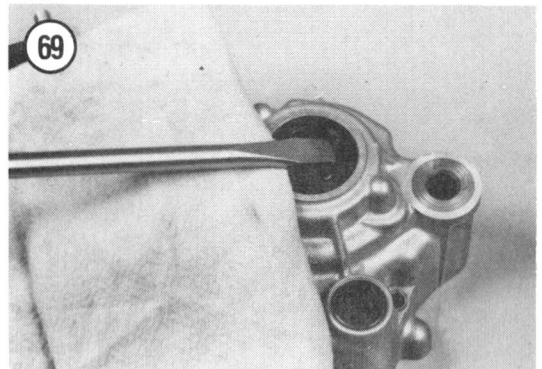

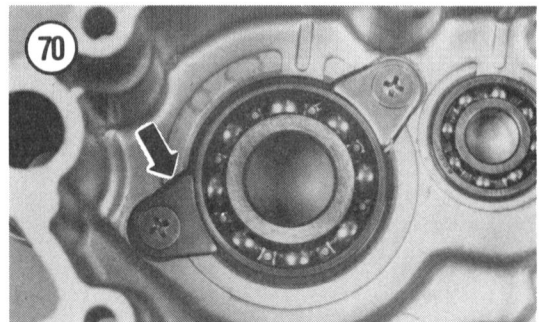

6. Hold the crankcase with the bearing side down and tap the bearing out (**Figure 72**). Repeat for all bearings in that case half.

NOTE
A special bearing remover may be required to remove blind bearings

(Figure 65) installed in the crankcases. Occasionally you can remove a blind bearing by heating the crankcase and then tapping the crankcase on a soft wooden surface. If the bearing does not fall out, remove it with the proper tool. Do not force or pry the bearing out or crankcase damage could occur.

NOTE
On 1986 and later KX80 models, it is necessary to install the main bearing oil seals before installing the bearings. Refer to oil seal installation as described in this procedure.

7. While heating up the crankcase halves, place the new bearings in a freezer if possible. Chilling them will slightly reduce their overall diameter while the hot crankcase is slightly larger due to heat expansion. This will make installation much easier.

NOTE
Before installing new bearing(s) or oil seal(s) apply a light coat of lithium based grease to the inside and outside to aid in installation. Be sure to apply the same grease to the lips of new oil seals.

NOTE
Always install bearings with the manufacturer's mark or number facing outward or so that after the crankcase is assembled you can still see these marks.

8. While the crankcase is still hot, install the new bearing(s) into place in the crankcase. Install the bearings by hand, if possible. If necessary, lightly tap the bearing(s) into the case with a socket placed on the outer bearing race. *Do not* install new bearings by driving on the inner bearing race. Install the bearing(s) until it seats completely.

NOTE
Pack all crankcase oil seals with a heat durable grease before installation.

9. Oil seals can be installed with a suitable size socket and extension (**Figure 73**). **Figure 74** and

Figure 75 show the correct way to install main bearing oil seals on 1986 and later KX80 models. When installing oil seals, it is important to drive the seal in squarely. Drive the seals in until they are flush with the case.

10. Align the bearing retainers with the crankcase. Apply Loctite 242 (blue) to the retainer screws and tighten them securely.

NOTE
Sometimes a main bearing will come off with the crankshaft instead of staying in the crankcase. If it is necessary to replace a bearing mounted on the crankshaft, a bearing adapter and a hydraulic press will be required.

Crankshaft Inspection

1. Clean the crankshaft thoroughly with solvent. Dry the crankshaft thoroughly. Then lubricate all bearing surfaces with a light coat of two-cycle engine oil.
2. Check the crankshaft journals and crankpin for scratches, heat discoloration or other defects.
3. Check flywheel taper, threads and keyway for damage. If one crankshaft half is damaged, the crankshaft can be disassembled and the damaged part replaced as described in this chapter.
4. Check crankshaft oil seal surfaces for grooving, pitting or scratches.
5. Check crankshaft bearing surfaces for chatter marks and excessive or uneven wear. Minor cases of chatter mark may be cleaned up with 320 grit carborundum cloth. If 320 cloth is used, clean crankshaft in solvent and recheck surfaces. If they did not clean up properly, disassemble the crankshaft and replace the damaged part.

6. Check the lower end bearing and connecting rod (**Figure 76**) for signs of heat or damage.
7. Slide the connecting rod to one side and check the connecting rod to crankshaft side clearance with a flat feeler gauge (**Figure 77**). Compare to dimensions given in **Table 1**. If the clearance is greater than specified the crankshaft assembly must be disassembled and the connecting rod replaced.
8. Check crankshaft runout with a dial indicator and V-blocks as shown in **Figure 78**. Retrue the

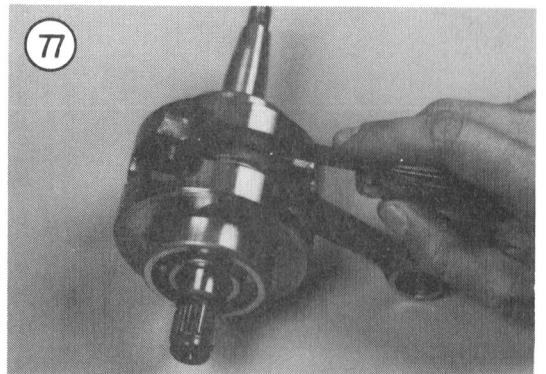

crankshaft if the runout exceeds the service limit in **Table 1**.

9. Place the crankshaft in V-blocks and attach a dial indicator to the bottom of the connecting rod big end as shown in **Figure 79**. While holding the crankshaft in position, push the connecting forward and then push it in the opposite direction. The difference in the high and low readings is crankshaft radial clearance. If the radial clearance exceeds the service limit in **Table 1**, replace the connecting rod.

10. If necessary, overhaul the crankshaft as described in this chapter.

Crankshaft Overhaul

Crankshaft overhaul requires a hydraulic press of 32 ton capacity, holding jigs, crankshaft alignment jig and dial indicators. A typical crankshaft is shown in **Figure 80**.

1. Measure the crank wheel width with a micrometer or vernier caliper (**Figure 81**). Record

5

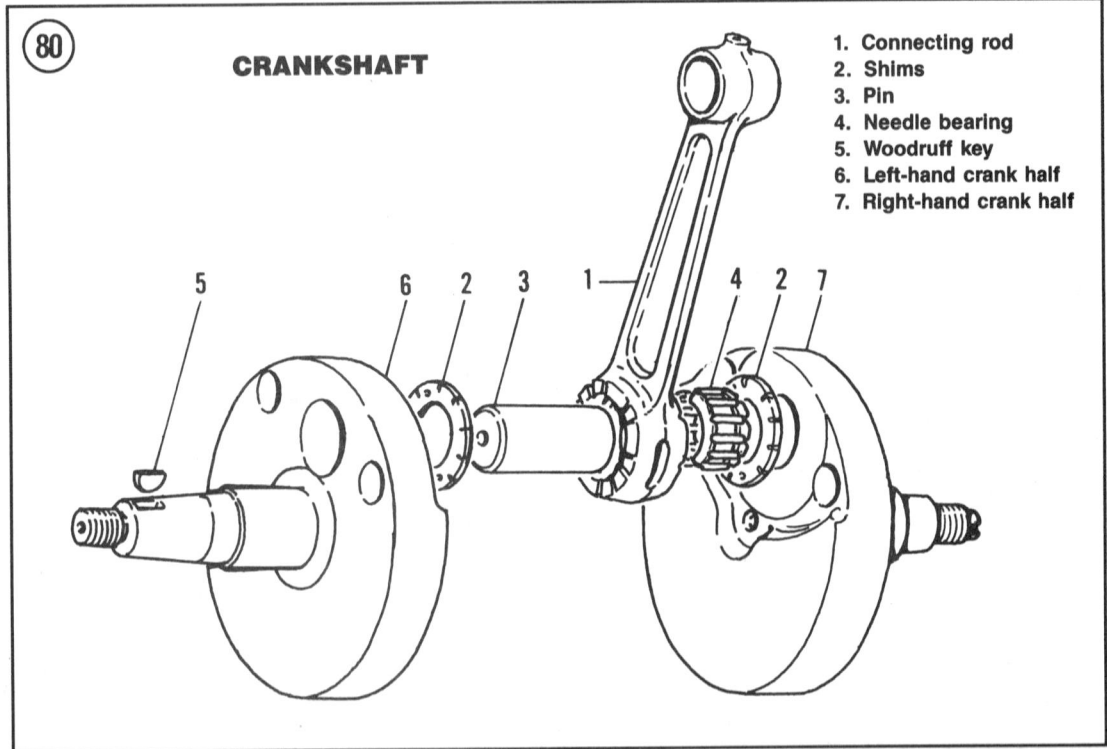

CRANKSHAFT

1. Connecting rod
2. Shims
3. Pin
4. Needle bearing
5. Woodruff key
6. Left-hand crank half
7. Right-hand crank half

the measurement so that it can be used during crankshaft reassembly.

2. Apply machinist blue across both crank halves. Then lay a square across both crank halves and mark them with a scribe. During reassembly, these marks can be used for initial alignment.

3. Place the crankshaft assembly in a suitable jig. Then press out the crankpin. Use an adapter between the press and crankpin. See **Figure 82**. Make sure to catch the lower crank half and crankpin assembly.

4. Remove the spacers, connecting rod and lower end bearing (**Figure 83**).

5. Press out the crankpin (**Figure 84**).

6. Wash the crank halves thoroughly in solvent.

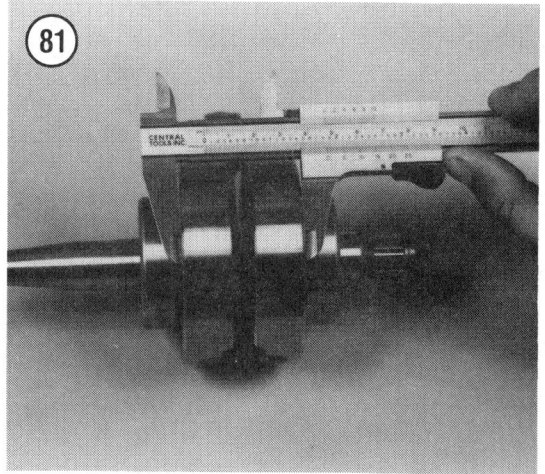

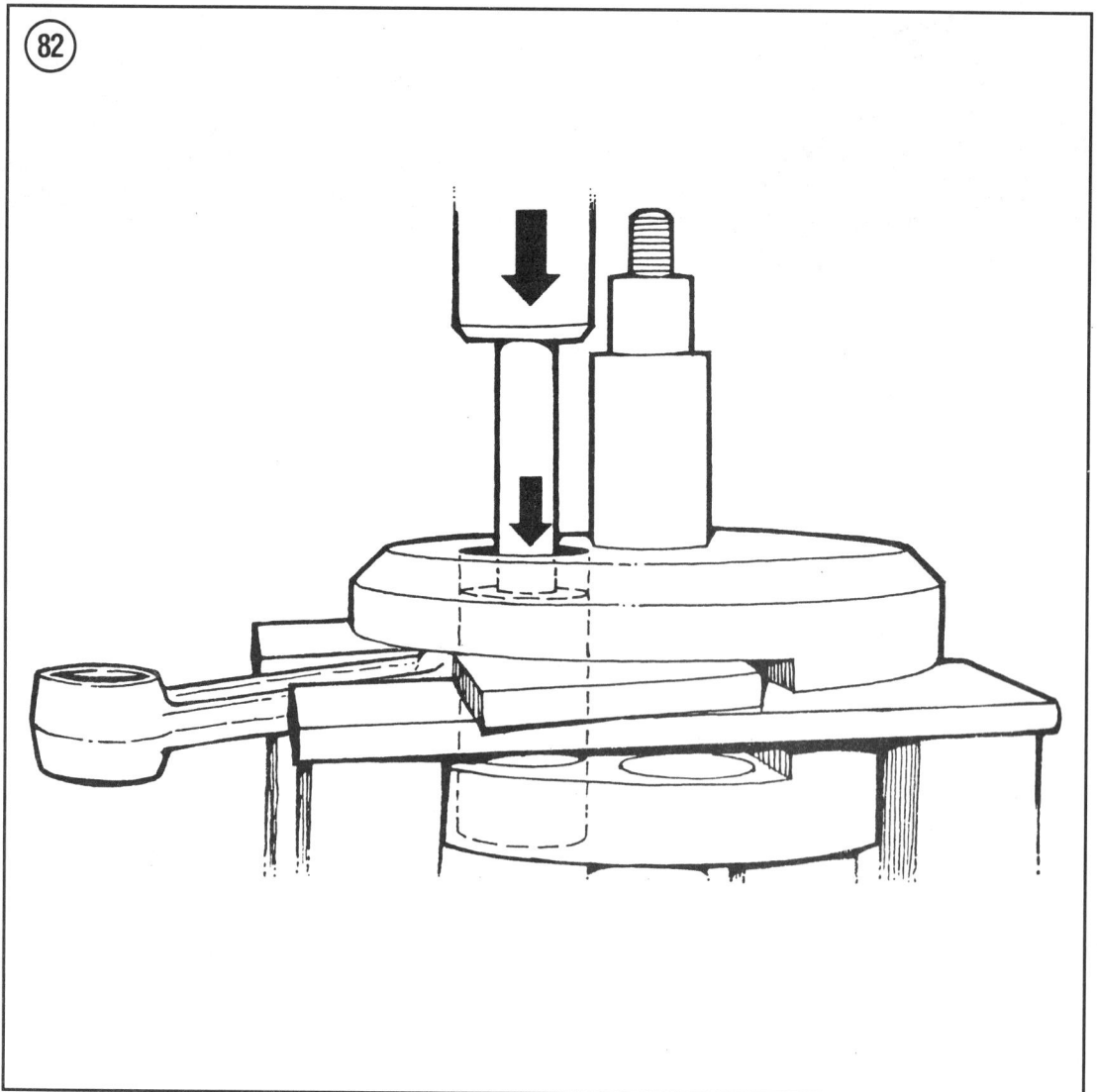

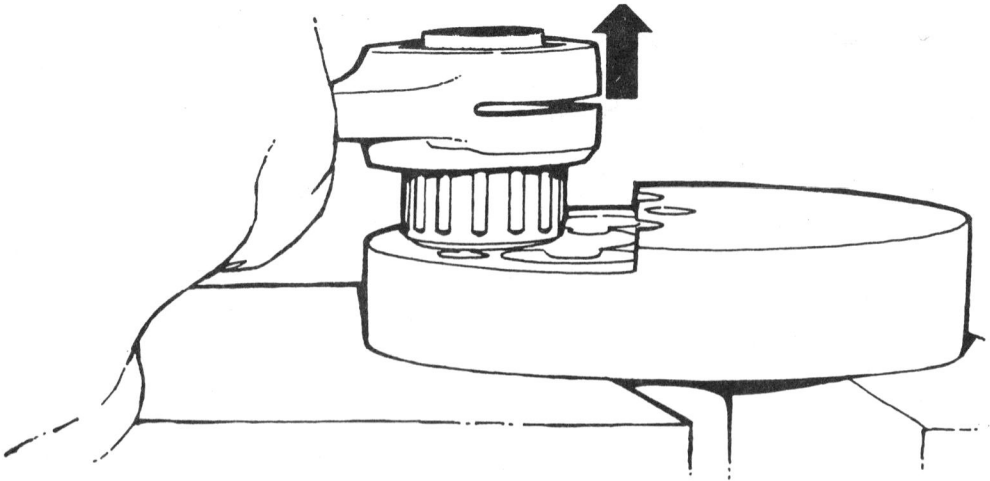

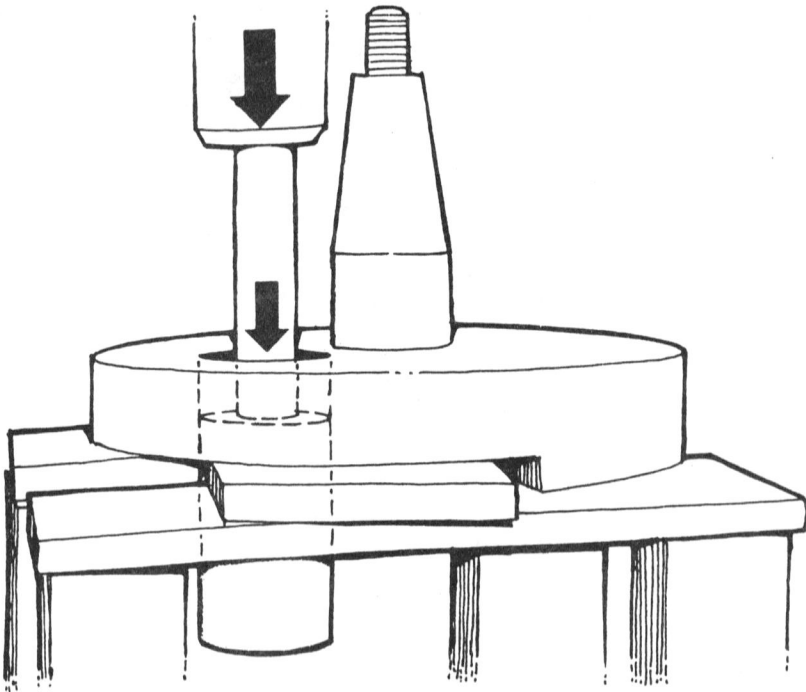

5

7. Using a suitable alignment fixture, press the replacement crankpin into one crank half (**Figure 85**) until the crankpin is flush with the outside of the crank half.

8. Install a spacer and the needle bearing over the crankpin (**Figure 86**).

9. Install the connecting rod (**Figure 87**) and the remaining spacer. There is no front or back to the connecting rod; it fits either way.

10. Use a square and align the marks (Step 2) made before disassembly (**Figure 88**). Then start pressing the crank half onto the crankpin.

11. Insert a suitable size feeler gauge between the upper thrust washer and the crank half (**Figure 89**). Then continue pressing the crank half onto the crankpin until the feeler gauge fits tightly. Refer to connecting rod side clearance in **Table 1** for clearance.

12. Release all pressure from the press. The feeler gauge will then slip out easily.

13. Measure crank wheel width (**Figure 81**) and compare to the specifications recorded in Step 1. Use this measurement as a guide only. The connecting rod side clearance should be the determining factor when assembling the crankshaft assembly.

14. Check and adjust crankshaft alignment as described in this chapter.

Crankshaft Alignment

After overhauling the crankshaft or when disassembling the engine, it is important to check crankshaft alignment and adjust as required so that both crank halves and the shafts extending from them all rotate on a common center. The crankshaft

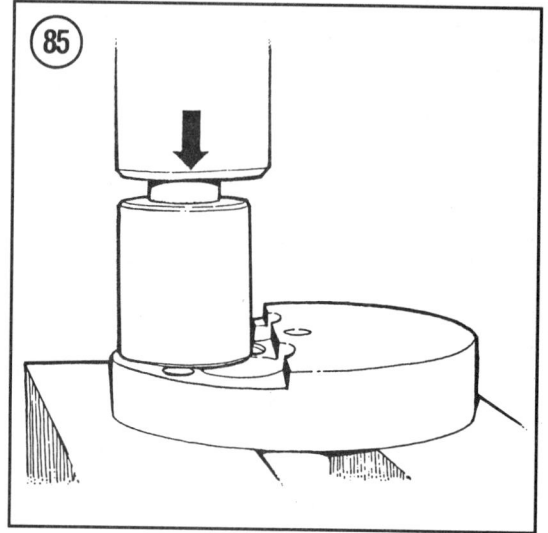

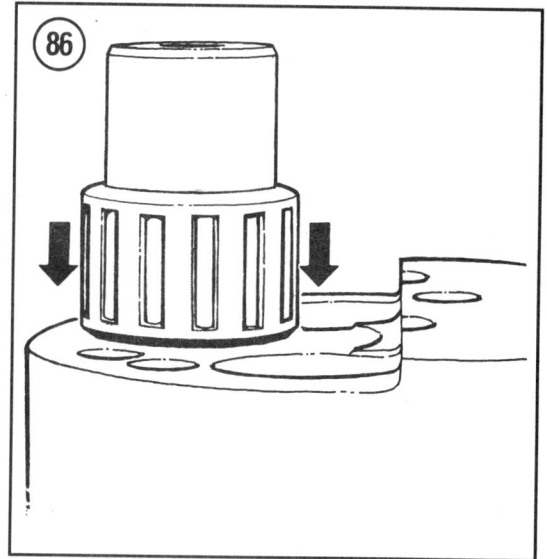

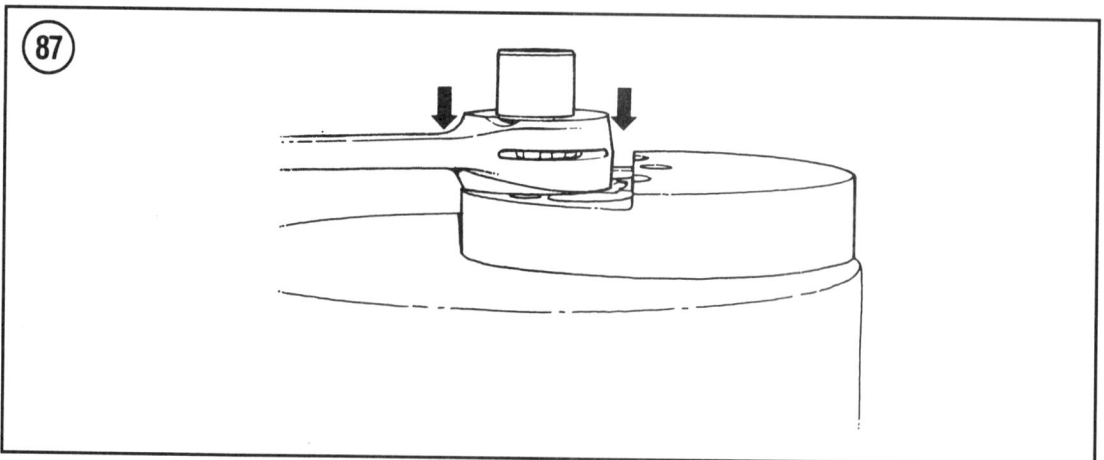

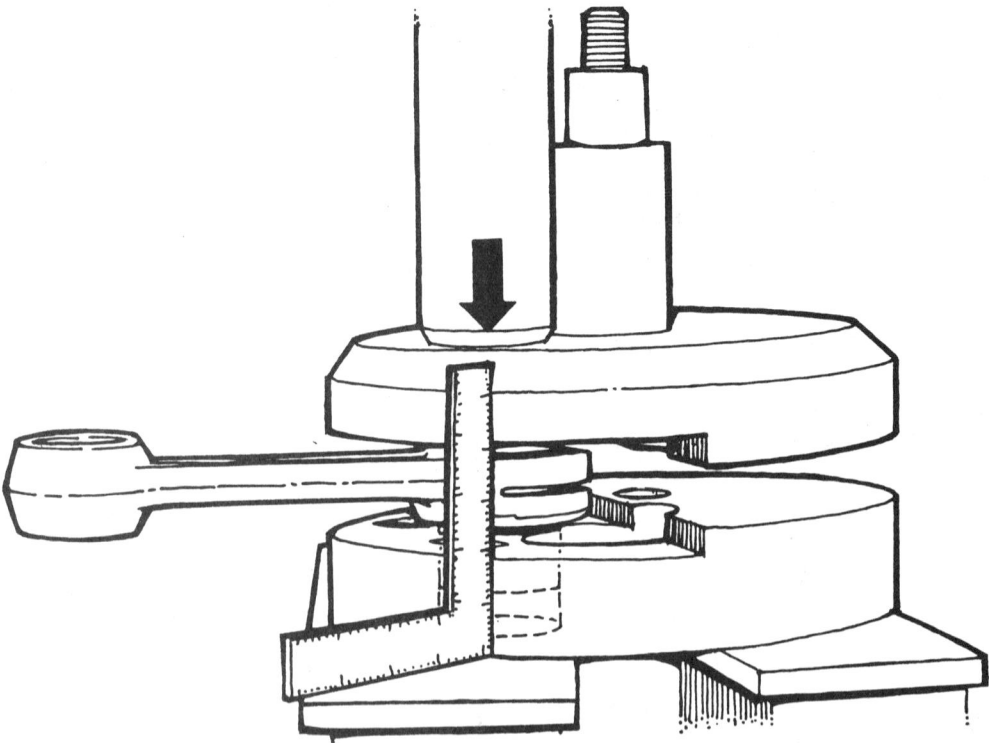

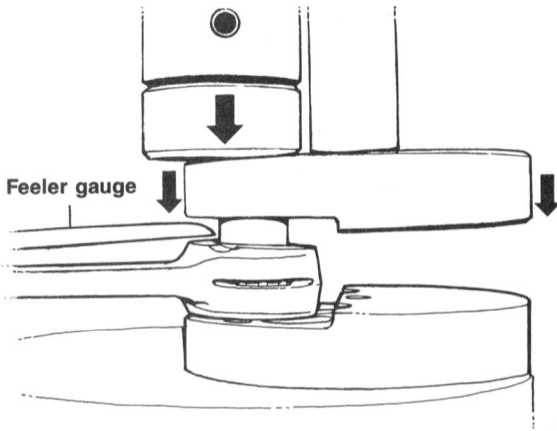

Feeler gauge

should be checked for runout and wheel deflection as follows.

Mount the assembled crankshaft in a suitable fixture or on V-blocks using 2 dial indicators (**Figure 90**). Slowly rotate the crankshaft through one or more complete turns and observe both dial indicators. One of several conditions will be observed:

1. *Runout:* Neither dial indicator needle begins its swing at the same time, and the needles will move in opposite direction during part of the crankshaft rotation cycle. Each needle will probably indicate a different amount of total travel. This condition is caused by eccentricity (both crank wheels not being on the same center), as shown in **Figure 90**. To correct, slowly rotate the crankshaft assembly until the drive side dial gauge indicates its maximum. Mark the rim of the drive side crank wheel at the point in line with the plungers on both dial indicators.

Remove the crankshaft assembly. Then, while holding one side of the crankshaft, strike the chalk mark a sharp blow with a brass hammer (**Figure 91**). Recheck alignment after each blow, and continue this procedure until both dial gauges begin and end their swings at the same time.

CAUTION
Make sure that only a brass faced hammer is used to strike the crankshaft wheels. A lead hammer will damage

the crankshaft wheels, requiring replacement.

2. *Wheel deflection:* The crank wheels can become pinched or spread. This conditioned can be checked by measuring crank wheel width (**Figure 81**) at various spots or by checking runout with 2 dial indicators (**Figure 92** and **Figure 93**). When checking in an alignment jig, both dial indicators will indicate maximum travel when the crankpin is toward the dial gauges if the crank wheels are pinched. Correct the condition by removing the crankshaft assembly from the fixture. Then drive a wedge or chisel between the two crank wheels

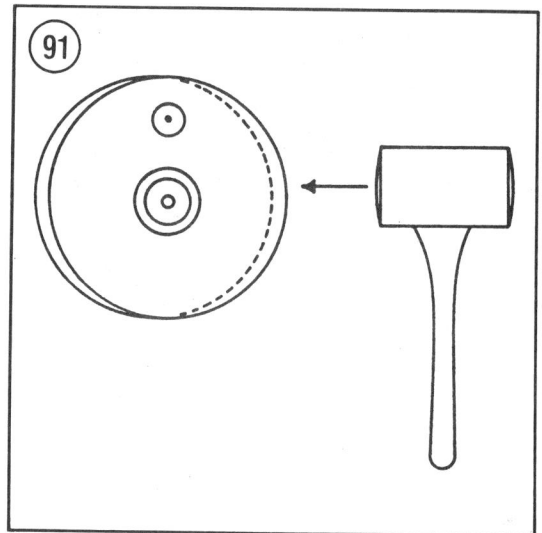

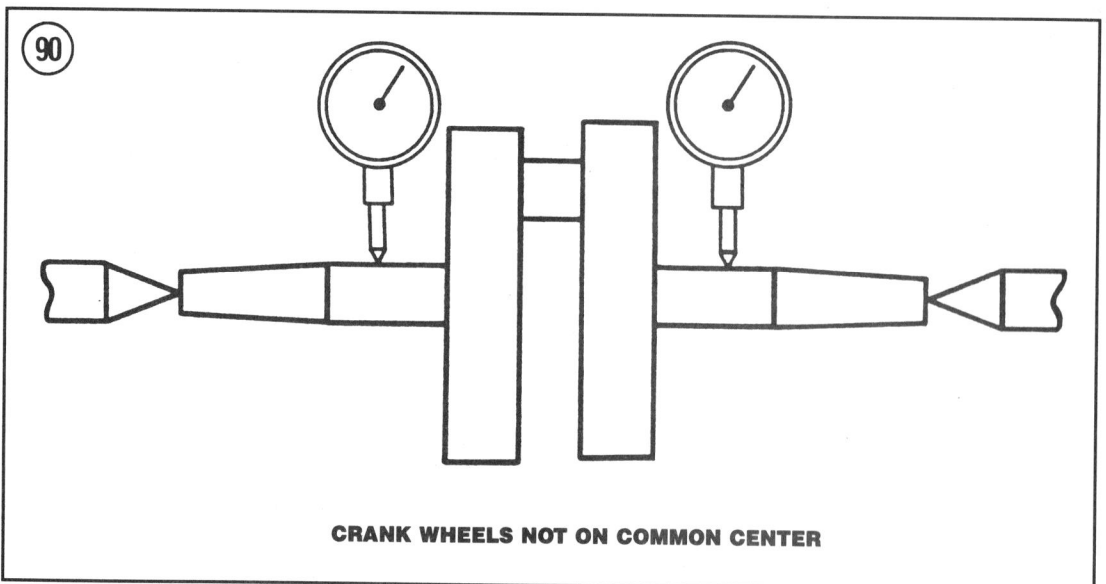

CRANK WHEELS NOT ON COMMON CENTER

at a point opposite maximum dial gauge indication. Recheck alignment after each adjustment. Continue until the dial gauges indicate no more than 0.01 mm (0.0004 in.) runout.

If the dial gauges indicated their maximum when the crankpin was on the side of the alignment jig away from the dial gauges, the crank wheels are spread. Correct this condition by tapping the outside of one of the wheels toward the other with a brass hammer. Recheck alignment after each blow. Continue adjustment until runout is within 0.01 mm (0.0004 in.) runout.

NOTE
When adjusting wheel deflection, it will be necessary to check and adjust runout as required.

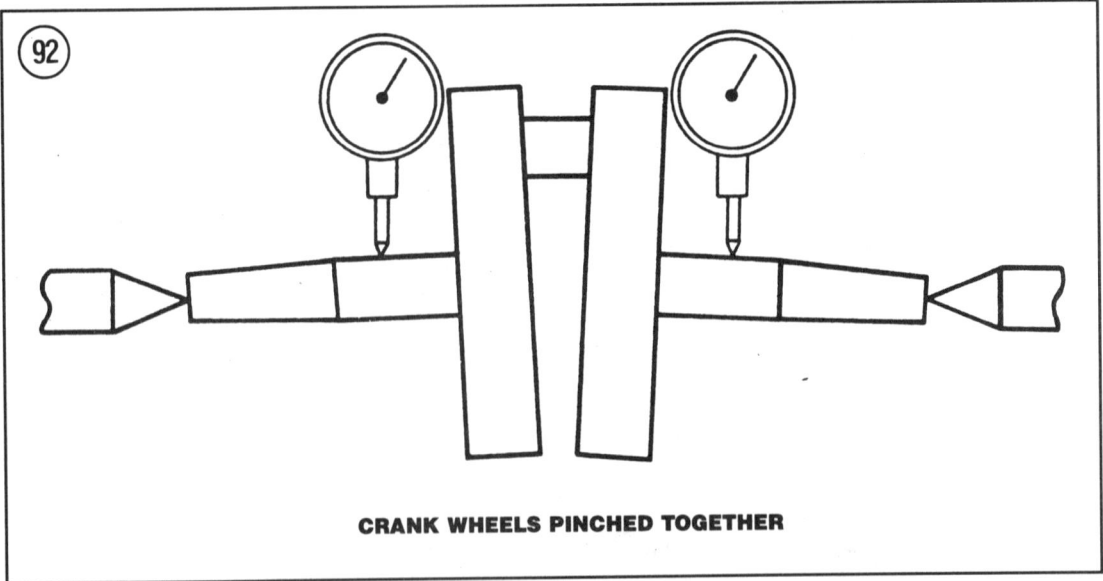

CRANK WHEELS PINCHED TOGETHER

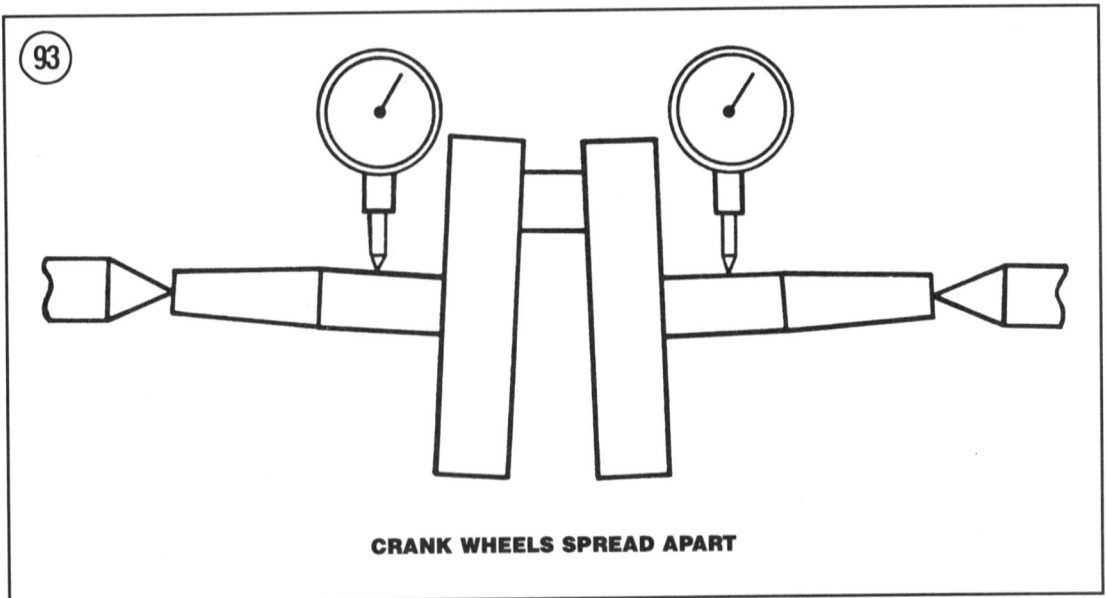

CRANK WHEELS SPREAD APART

Tables are on the following page.

Table 1 CRANKSHAFT SPECIFICATIONS

	New mm (in.)	Service limit mm (in.)
Connecting rod big end radial clearance		
KX60	0.021-0.033 (0.0008-0.0013)	0.08 (0.0032)
KX80	0.023-0.035 (0.0009-0.0014)	0.08 (0.0032)
Connecting rod side clearance		
KX60	0.35-0.45 (0.0138-0.0178)	0.70 (0.028)
KX80	0.35-0.45 (0.0138-0.0178)	0.70 (0.028)
Crankshaft runout		
KX60	0-0.03 (0-0.0012)	0.10 (0.004)
KX80	0-0.03 (0-0.0012)	0.05 (0.002)

Table 2 TIGHTENING TORQUES

	N·m	ft.-lb.
Engine mount bolts		
KX60	25	18
KX80		
1983-1988	25	18
1989	29	22
Swing arm pivot shaft nut	69	51

CHAPTER SIX

CLUTCH, KICKSTARTER AND EXTERNAL SHIFT MECHANISM

This chapter contains removal, inspection and installation of the clutch, primary drive gear, kickstarter and external shift mechanism.

Clutch specifications are listed in **Table 1**. **Tables 1** and **2** are found at the end of the chapter.

CLUTCH COVER

Removal/Installation

1. Drain the clutch/transmission oil as described in Chapter Three.
2. Place a bike stand under the frame to support the bike securely.
3. *Water-cooled models:* Perform the following:
   a. Drain the coolant as described under *Coolant Change* in Chapter Three.
   b. Disconnect the coolant hoses at the clutch cover. See **Figure 1**, typical.
4. Remove the rear brake pedal as follows:
   a. *Drum brake models:* Loosen the rear brake rod wing nut (**Figure 2**) and remove it. Then remove the spring from the brake rod and the collar from the brake arm on the hub.

b. Remove the rear brake pedal pivot bolt and remove the brake pedal. See **Figure 3** or **Figure 4**.

c. Remove the return spring.

5. Remove the kickstarter lever pinch bolt and pull the lever off of the kickstarter shaft.

6. If it is necessary to disconnect the clutch cable from the clutch cover, perform the following:

a. Loosen the clutch cable adjuster locknut and loosen the adjuster at the handlebar (**Figure 5**).

b. Loosen the clutch cable adjuster locknuts at the engine (**Figure 6**), if so equipped.

c. Disconnect the clutch cable at the engine.

7. Remove the oil fill cap.

NOTE
On models equipped with Phillips screws, an impact driver with a Phillips bit (described in Chapter One) is required to loosen the clutch cover screws in Step 8. Attempting to loosen Phillips screws with a Phillips screwdriver may ruin the screw heads.

8. Remove the Phillips screws or bolts securing the water pump cover onto the clutch cover. Remove the water pump cover. Remove the dowel pins (if so equipped).

9. Remove the impeller mounting bolt and remove the impeller.

10. Remove the clutch cover mounting Phillips screws or bolts (**Figure 7**).

11. Turn the clutch release lever toward the rear of the bike and remove the clutch cover (**Figure 7**).

12. Remove and discard the gasket.

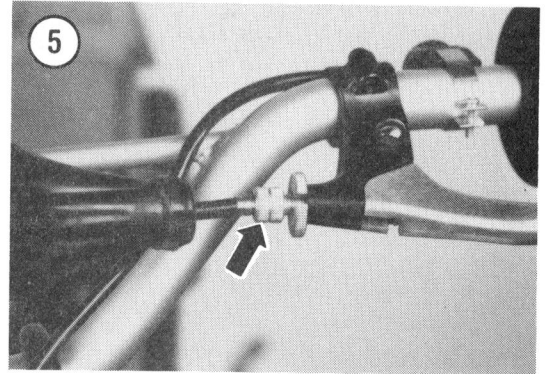

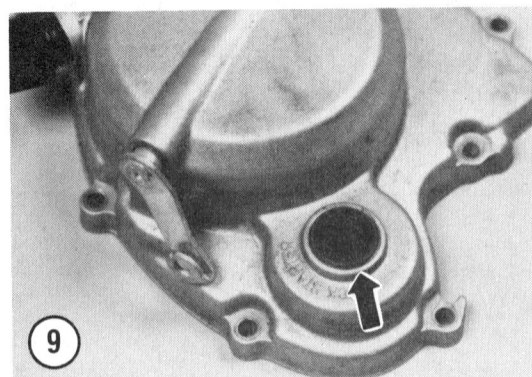

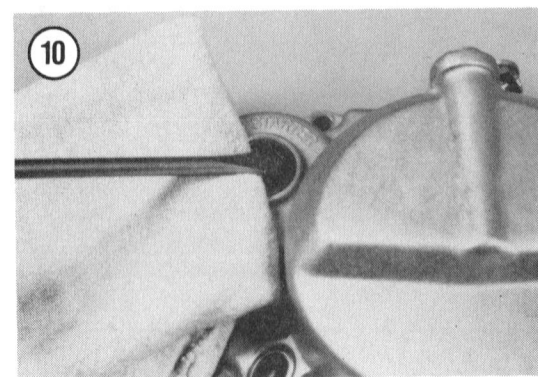

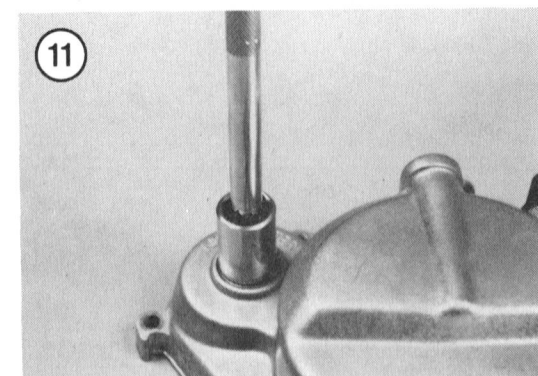

13. Remove the 2 dowel pins. See **Figure 8**, typical.

14. Check the clutch cover oil seal (**Figure 9**). If the lip is damaged or if there are signs of oil leakage, replace as follows:

    a. Pry the oil seal out of the cover with a large flat-tipped screwdriver. Place a rag or block of wood underneath the screwdriver to prevent clutch cover damage (**Figure 10**). If the seal is tight, lift the screwdriver and work it around the seal at different points. Applying heavy pressure at one point could damage the cover.

    b. Clean the seal bore with solvent and thoroughly dry.

    c. Apply a lightweight multipurpose grease to the lips of the new seal before installation.

    d. Align the seal with the seal bore and drive it into place with a suitable size socket placed on the outer portion of the seal (**Figure 11**). Install the seal until it bottoms out or when it is flush with the cover.

15. Installation is the reverse of these steps. Note the following.

16. Tighten the impeller bolt securely.

17. Install a new water pump cover O-ring.

18. Make sure to install the 2 dowel pins and a new cover gasket.

19. Turn the clutch release lever toward the rear of the bike when installing the clutch cover.

20. Tighten the cover Phillips screws or bolts securely.

21. Refill the clutch/transmission oil as described in Chapter Three.

22. *Water-cooled models*. Perform the following:

    a. Reconnect the coolant hoses at the clutch cover.

    b. Refill the engine coolant as described under *Coolant Change* in Chapter Three.

23. Adjust the clutch as described in Chapter Three.

24. Apply wheel bearing grease to the rear brake pedal pivot shaft before installation.

25. Adjust the rear brake as described in Chapter Three.

Clutch Release Shaft and Oil Seal Removal/Installation

1A. *1983 KX60:* Remove the bolt securing the clutch release shaft to the clutch cover. Remove the release shaft and its O-ring.

1B. *1984-on KX60 and KX80:* Remove the circlip (**Figure 12**) securing the clutch release shaft. Then remove the release shaft (**Figure 13**).

2. Visually inspect the release shaft surfaces for cracks, deep scoring or excessive wear. Replace the release shaft if necessary.

3. Check the release shaft O-ring (if so equipped). Replace if necessary.

4. Check the release shaft oil seal (**Figure 14**) in the clutch cover, if so equipped. If the lip is damaged or if there are signs of oil leakage, replace as follows:

   a. Pry the oil seal out of the cover with a flat-tipped screwdriver. Place a rag or block of wood underneath the screwdriver to prevent clutch cover damage. If the seal is tight, lift the screwdriver and work it around the seal at different points. Applying heavy pressure at one point could damage the cover.

   b. Clean the seal bore with solvent and thoroughly dry.

   c. Apply a lightweight multipurpose grease to the lips of the new seal before installation.

   d. Align the seal with the seal bore and drive it into place with a suitable size socket placed on the outer portion of the seal. Install the seal until it bottoms out or when it is flush with the cover.

5. Installation is the reverse of these steps. Note the following:

   a. Install a new release shaft O-ring, if so equipped.

   b. Install a new release shaft circlip, if so equipped.

   c. On 1983 KX60 models, tighten the bolt securely.

CLUTCH

The clutch is a wet multi-plate type which operates immersed in the oil supply it shares with the transmission. The clutch boss is splined to the transmission mainshaft and the clutch housing can rotate freely on the mainshaft. The clutch housing is geared to the primary drive gear attached to the crankshaft.

The clutch release mechanism is mounted within the left-hand crankcase cover on the opposite side of the clutch mechanism.

The clutch can be removed with the engine in the frame.

Removal/Disassembly

Refer to **Figure 15** or **Figure 16** for this procedure.

1. Remove the clutch cover as described in this chapter.

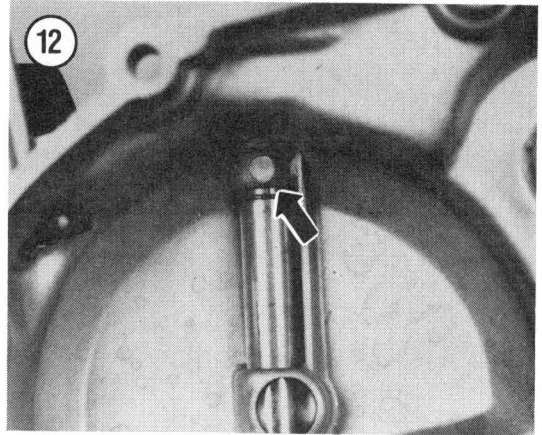

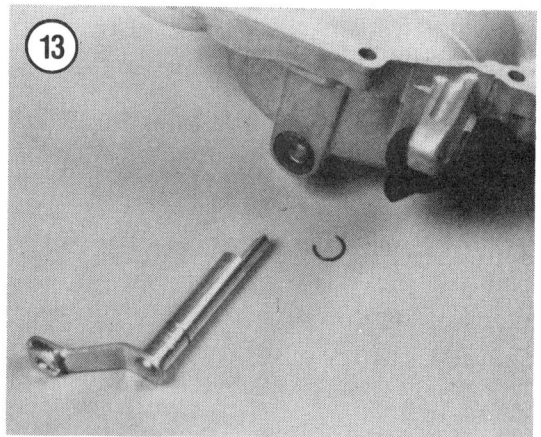

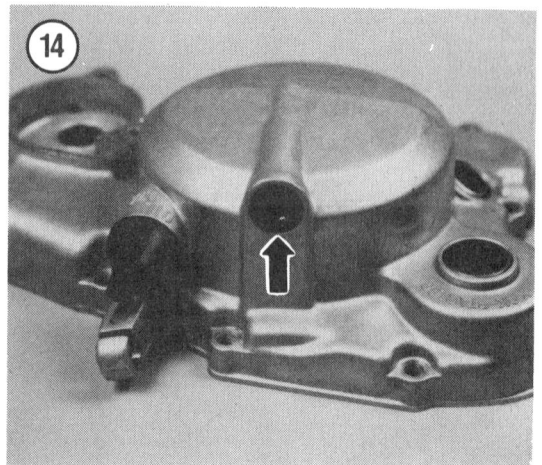

⑮

CLUTCH
(KX60 AND 1983-1984 KX80)

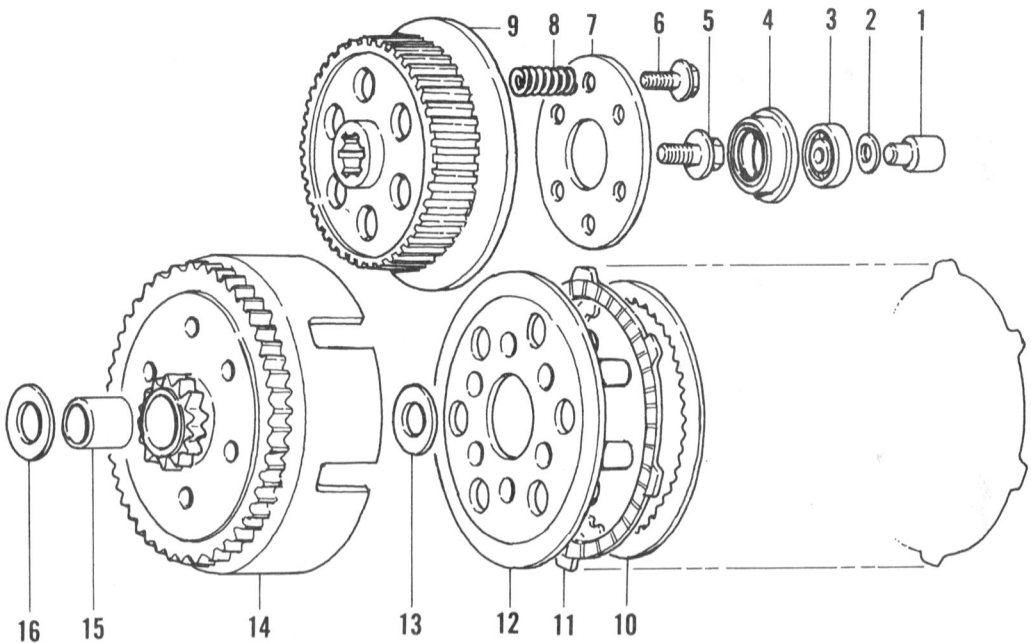

6

1. Pusher
2. Washer
3. Bearing
4. Pusher plate
5. Clutch hub bolt
6. Bolts
7. Clutch spring holder
8. Springs
9. Clutch hub
10. Clutch friction plate
11. Clutch steel plate
12. Clutch wheel
13. Thrust washer
14. Clutch housing
15. Spacer
16. Washer

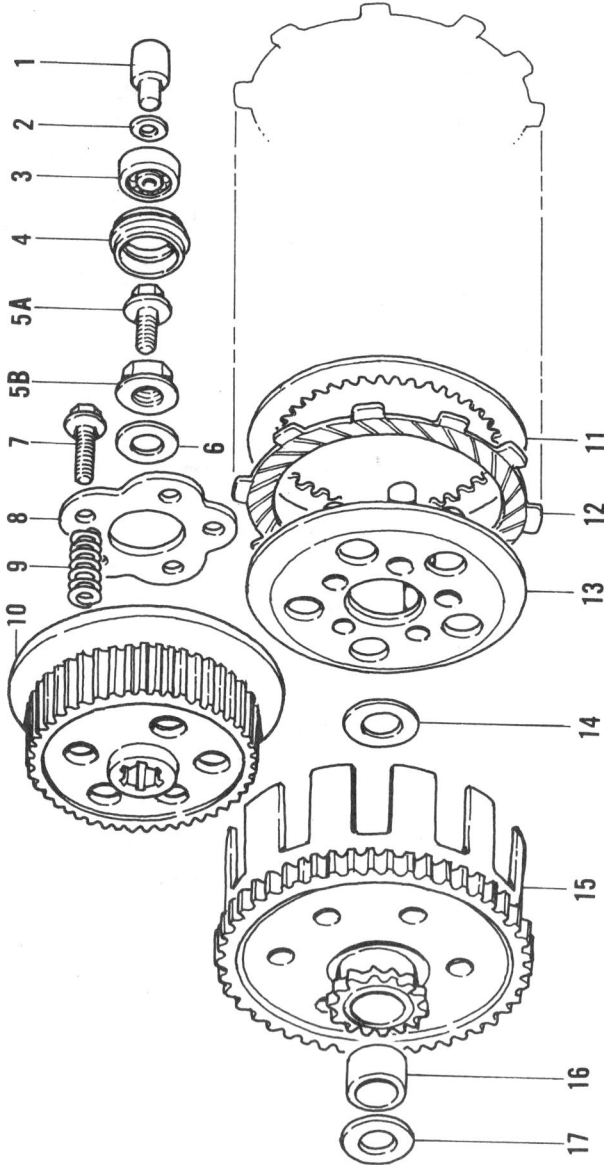

CLUTCH (1985-ON KX80)

1. Pusher
2. Washer
3. Bearing
4. Pusher plate
5A. Clutch hub bolt (1985-1987)
5B. Clutch hub nut (1988-on)
6. Washer (1988-on)
7. Bolts
8. Clutch spring holder
9. Springs
10. Clutch hub
11. Clutch friction plate
12. Clutch steel plate
13. Clutch wheel
14. Thrust washer
15. Clutch housing
16. Spacer
17. Washer

17

18

19

20

2. Remove the pusher (**Figure 17**), washer, bearing and pusher plate (**Figure 18**) from the clutch spring holder.

3. Loosen and remove the clutch hub bolt or the nut and washer (**Figure 19**).

NOTE
*You can lock the clutch by shifting the transmission into gear and stepping on the brake pedal, by inserting a piece of copper between the primary gear and the clutch housing ring gear teeth (**Figure 20**), or by holding the flywheel with a holding tool.*

4. See **Figure 21**. Loosen the spring holder bolts (A) gradually in a crisscross pattern, then remove the bolts and spring holder (B).

5. Remove the clutch springs (**Figure 22**).

6

A B
21

22

NOTE
If it is not necessary to disassemble the clutch hub/plate assembly, install one clutch spring, a large washer and one spring plate bolt as shown in Figure 23. The bolt will allow you to remove the hub assembly without having to align the plates during assembly.

6. Remove the clutch/plate assembly (**Figure 24**).
7. Remove the thrust washer (**Figure 25**).
8. Remove the clutch housing (**Figure 26**).
9. Remove the spacer (**Figure 27**).
10. Remove the washer (**Figure 28**).
11. Disassemble the clutch hub/plate assembly. See **Figure 15** or **Figure 16**.

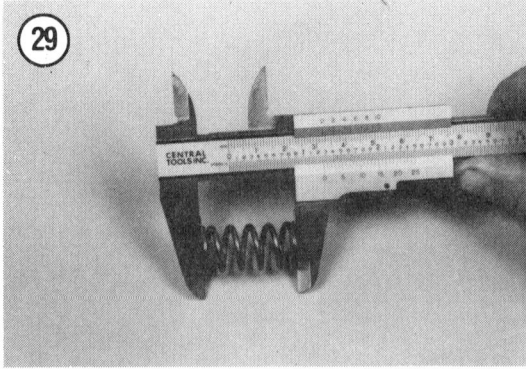

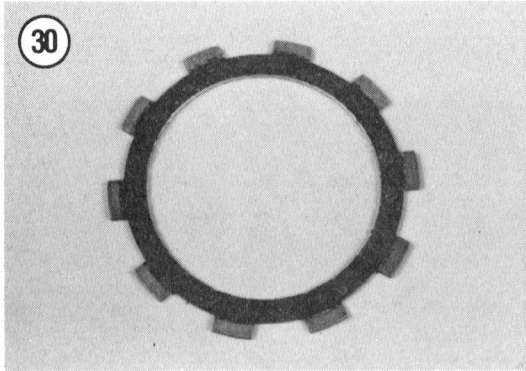

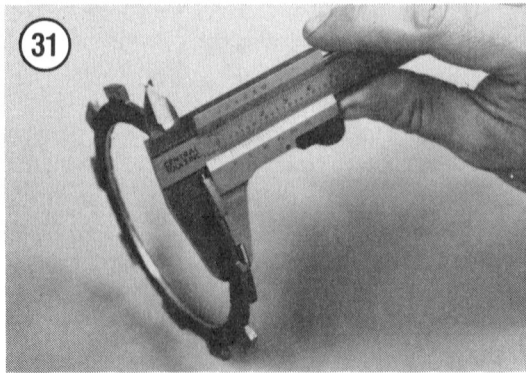

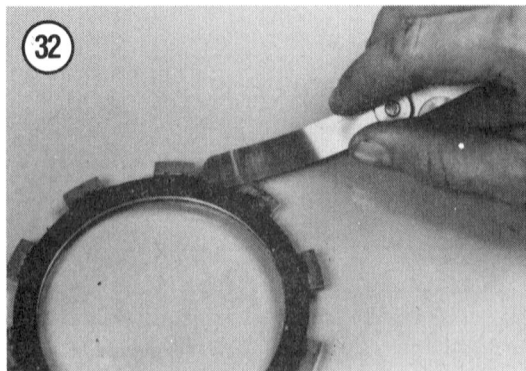

Inspection

Clutch service specifications and wear limits are listed in **Table 1**. Replace those parts which are excessively worn, defective, cracked or damaged in any way.

1. Clean all parts in a solvent and dry thoroughly.
2. Measure the free length of each clutch spring (**Figure 29**) with a vernier caliper. Replace the springs as a set if any one spring is too short.
3. **Table 1** lists the number of stock friction discs (**Figure 30**) used in each model. The friction material is made of cork that is bonded onto an aluminum plate for warp resistance and durability. Measure the thickness of each friction disc at several places around the disc (**Figure 31**) with a vernier caliper. Replace all friction discs if any one is found too thin. Do not replace only 1 or 2 discs.
4. Place each friction disc on a surface plate or a thick piece of glass and check for warpage with a feeler gauge (**Figure 32**). If any disc is warped more than specified, replace the entire set of discs. Do not replace only 1 or 2 discs.
5. The friction discs (**Figure 30**) have tabs that slide in the clutch housing grooves. Inspect the grooves for cracks or galling in the grooves. They must be smooth for chatter-free clutch operation. Light damage can be repaired with an oilstone. Replace the clutch housing if damage is severe.
6. Place a friction disc into the clutch housing and measure the clearance between the friction disc tang and the clutch housing finger with a feeler gauge (**Figure 33**). Check the clearance at each friction disc tang. If the clearance exceeds the

6

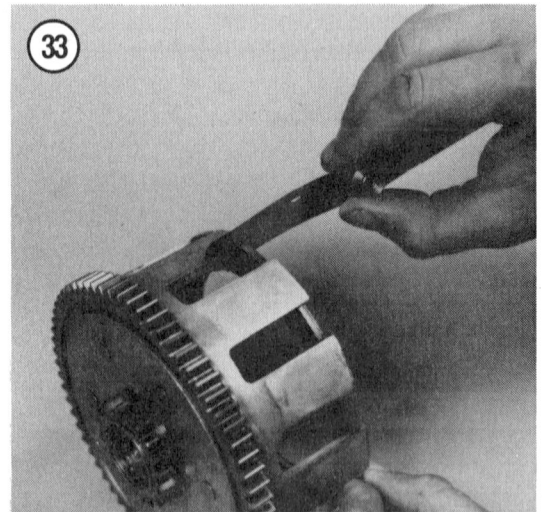

service limit in **Table 1**, replace the friction discs. Repeat for each friction disc.

7. **Table 1** lists the number of stock clutch metal plates (**Figure 34**) used in each model. Place each clutch metal plate on a surface plate or a thick piece of glass and check for warpage with a feeler gauge (**Figure 35**). If any plate is warped more than specified, replace the entire set of plates. Do not replace only 1 or 2 plates.

8. The clutch metal plate inner teeth (**Figure 34**) mesh with the clutch hub splines (A, **Figure 36**). Check the splines for cracks or galling. They must be smooth for chatter-free clutch operation. If the clutch hub splines are worn, check the clutch metal plate teeth for wear or damage.

9. Inspect the shaft splines (B, **Figure 36**) in the clutch hub assembly. If damage is only a slight amount, remove any small burrs with a fine cut file. If damage is severe, replace the assembly.

10. Inspect the clutch wheel studs (**Figure 37**) for thread damage or cracks at the base of the studs. Thread damage may be repaired with a M6 × 1 metric tap. Use kerosene on the tap threads. If a bolt stud is cracked, the clutch wheel must be replaced.

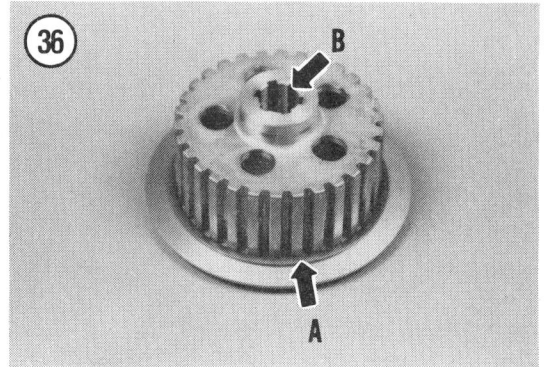

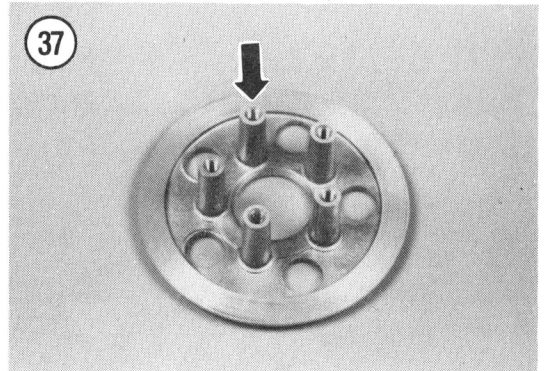

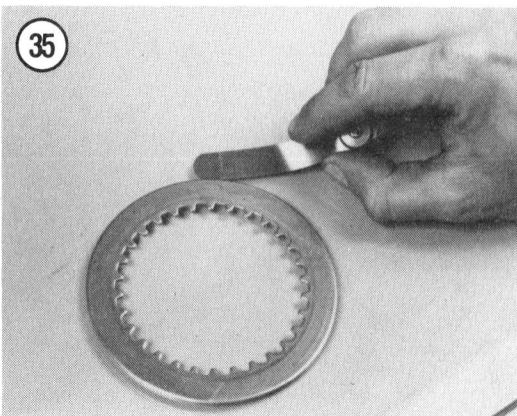

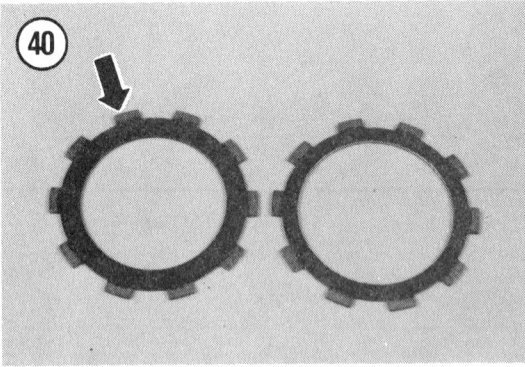

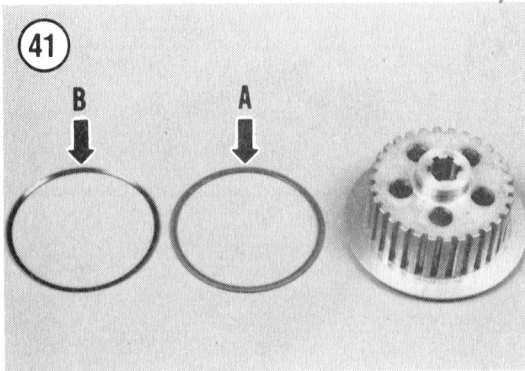

11. Check the clutch housing bearing bore (A, **Figure 38**) for cracks, deep scoring, excessive wear or heat discoloration. If the bearing bore is damaged, also check the mainshaft for damage. Replace worn or damaged parts.

12. Check the clutch housing gear teeth (B, **Figure 38**) for tooth wear, damage or cracks. Replace the clutch housing if necessary.

NOTE
If the clutch housing gear teeth are damaged, the gear teeth on the primary drive gear and the kickstarter idler gear may also be damaged. Inspect them also.

13. Check the bearing in the pusher plate (**Figure 39**) for roughness or damage. Replace the bearing if necessary.

14. *1989 KX80:* These models use an additional friction plate (**Figure 40**) and a thrust plate (A, **Figure 41**) and spring (B, **Figure 41**). Check these parts for wear and damage.

Assembly/Installation

Refer to **Figure 15** or **Figure 16** for this procedure.

1. Coat all clutch parts with transmission oil before reassembly.

2A. *1989 KX80:* Assemble the clutch hub/plate assembly as follows:

   a. Place the clutch hub onto the workbench so that it faces as shown in **Figure 42**.

   b. Install the flat thrust plate (A, **Figure 41**) over the clutch hub (**Figure 43**). Then install the spring (**Figure 44**) and the special friction plate. See **Figure 40** and **Figure 45**.

c. Install a steel plate (**Figure 46**) and then a friction disc. Alternate until all of the clutch plates and discs are installed. The last part installed should be a friction disc (**Figure 47**).

d. Position the friction plates so that all of the plate tabs align as shown in **Figure 47**.

e. Install the clutch wheel (**Figure 48**).

f. Install a clutch spring bolt, spring and washer as shown in **Figure 49**. The bolt will hold the assembly together during installation.

2B. *All models except 1989 KX80:* Assemble the clutch hub/plate assembly as follows:

a. Place the clutch hub onto the workbench so that it faces as shown in **Figure 42**.

b. Install a friction disc and then a steel plate (**Figure 46**). Alternate until all of the clutch plates and discs are installed. The last part installed should be a friction plate (**Figure 47**).

c. Position the friction discs so that all of the plate tabs align as shown in **Figure 47**.

d. Install the clutch wheel (**Figure 48**).

e. Install a clutch spring bolt, spring and washer as shown in **Figure 49**. The bolt will hold the assembly together during installation.

3. Slide the washer (**Figure 50**) onto the mainshaft.

4. Install the spacer (**Figure 51**) onto the mainshaft.

5. Install the clutch housing.

6. Install the thrust washer (**Figure 52**).

7. Align the clutch hub/plate assembly (**Figure 49**) with the clutch housing and install the hub assembly.

8. Remove the bolt, spring and washer (**Figure 53**) installed in sub-step 2a or sub-step 2b.

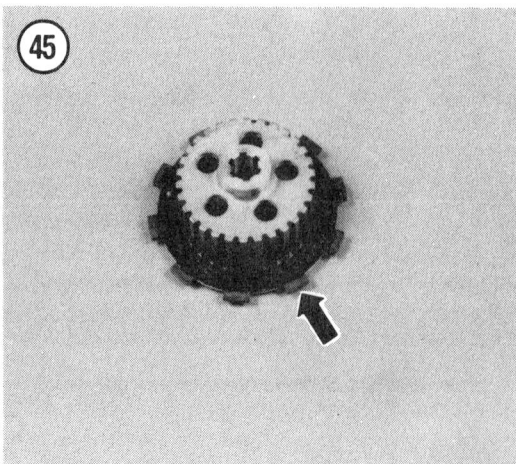

9. Install the clutch springs (**Figure 54**), spring holder and clutch spring bolts. Tighten the bolts in a crisscross pattern.

10. Referring to **Figure 15** or **Figure 16**, install the clutch hub bolt or the washer and nut.

11. Secure the clutch housing with the same tool used during removal. Tighten the clutch hub bolt or nut (**Figure 55**) to the torque specification in **Table 2**.

12. Install the washer onto the pusher. Then insert the pusher/washer into the pusher holder.

13. Install the pusher plate assembly.

14. Install the clutch cover as described in this chapter.

PRIMARY DRIVE PINION GEAR

The primary drive pinion gear is part of the primary drive gear system where power flows from the crankshaft to the transmission.

Removal/Installation

Removal of the primary drive pinion gear is not required except for replacement, crankcase disassembly or when checking the right-hand crankshaft oil seal during a pressure test.

1. Remove the clutch cover as described in this chapter.

2A. *KX60 and 1983-1985 KX80:* Perform the following:

   a. Pry the lockwasher tab away from the pinion gear nut (A, **Figure 56**).

   b. Place a piece of copper between the pinion gear and the clutch housing drive gear (B, **Figure 56**) or hold the flywheel with a holding tool.

   c. Loosen the pinion gear nut (A, **Figure 56**).

   d. Remove the pinion gear washer and nut.

   e. Slide the pinion gear off of the crankshaft (**Figure 57**).

   f. Remove the Woodruff key (**Figure 58**) from the crankshaft.

2B. *1986-on KX80:* Remove the circlip (**Figure 59**) and slide the pinion gear off of the crankshaft (**Figure 60**).

> *NOTE*
> *On 1986 and later KX80 models, the water pump drive and driven gears are installed behind the pinion gear (**Figure 61**). If necessary, remove them at this time. During reassembly, don't forget to install them.*

3. Installation is the reverse of these steps. Note the following.

4A. *KX60 and 1983-1985 KX80:* Perform the following:

   a. Install the Woodruff key into the crankshaft (**Figure 58**).

b. The pinion gear has a hole drilled into one side; install the gear so that the hole faces outward (right-hand side). See **Figure 57**.

c. Align the slot in the gear with the Woodruff key and install the gear.

d. Install a new lockwasher.

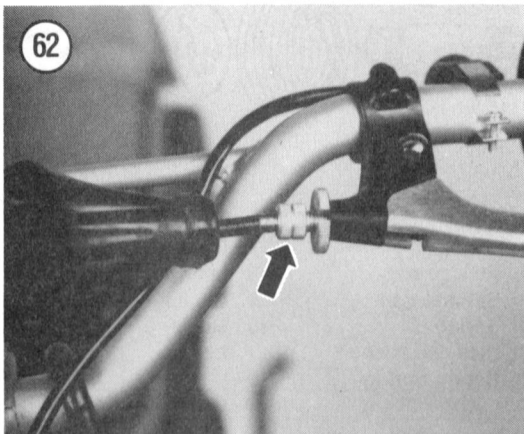

e. Use the same tool to lock the clutch housing when tightening the pinion gear nut.

f. Tighten the pinion gear nut to the tightening torque in **Table 2**.

4B. *1986-on KX80:* Install the pinion gear onto the crankshaft so that the cut side of the gear faces out. Secure the gear with a new circlip. Make sure the circlip seats completely in the crankshaft groove. See **Figure 59**.

5. Install the clutch cover as described in this chapter.

CLUTCH CABLE

Replacement

In time the clutch cable will stretch to the point that it is no longer useful and will have to be replaced.

1. Remove the fuel tank.

NOTE
Some of the following figures are shown with the engine partially disassembled for clarity. It is not necessary to remove these components for cable replacement.

2. Pull the protective boot away from the clutch lever and loosen the locknut and adjusting barrel. See **Figure 62**.

3. Slip the cable end out of the hand lever.

4. Disconnect the clutch cable at the clutch release mechanism on the right-hand side of the engine.

NOTE
Prior to removing the cable make a drawing (or take a Polaroid picture) of the cable routing through the frame. It is very easy to forget its routing after it has been removed. Replace the cable exactly as it was, avoiding any sharp turns.

5. Pull the cable out of any retaining clips on the frame.

6. Remove the cable and replace it with a new one.

7. Install by reversing these removal steps. Make sure it is correctly routed with no sharp turns. Adjust the clutch cable as described in Chapter Three.

KICKSTARTER

Refer to **Figure 63** when servicing the kickstarter assembly.

Removal/Installation

1. Remove the clutch as described in this chapter.
2. Using a pair of needlenose pliers, pull the end of the return spring out of the hole in the crankcase (**Figure 64**). Slowly allow the spring to unwind before releasing it.
3. Remove the screws or bolts securing the ratchet guide to the crankcase. Remove the ratchet guide. See **Figure 65** (KX60 and 1983-1985 KX80) or **Figure 66** (1986-on KX80).
4. Pull the kickstarter assembly (**Figure 67**) out of the crankcase.
5. Remove the idler gear as follows:
   a. Remove the circlip (**Figure 68**).
   b. Remove the idler gear (**Figure 69**).
6. If necessary, disassemble the kickstarter assembly and service it as described in this chapter.
7. Install the idler gear a follows:
   a. Apply molybdenum disulfide grease to the inside of the idler gear.

   b. Install the idler gear (**Figure 69**).
   c. Install a new circlip (**Figure 68**). Make sure the circlip seats in the groove completely.
8. Install the kickstarter assembly as follows.
9. Insert the kickstarter assembly into the crankcase (**Figure 70**).
10. Install the ratchet guide and secure it with the 2 mounting bolts or screws. See **Figure 65** or **Figure 66**. Apply Loctite 242 (blue) to the bolts before assembly. Tighten the bolts securely.

NOTE
Make sure the return spring is properly installed on the kickstarter assembly before installing the kickstarter. The short end of the spring should engage the spring hole in the shaft and the opposite end of the spring should face in the direction shown in **Figure 71***. If you are unsure about spring alignment, refer to* **Disassembly/Inspection/ Assembly** *in this chapter.*

11. While holding the kickstarter assembly with one hand, grab the return spring with needlenose

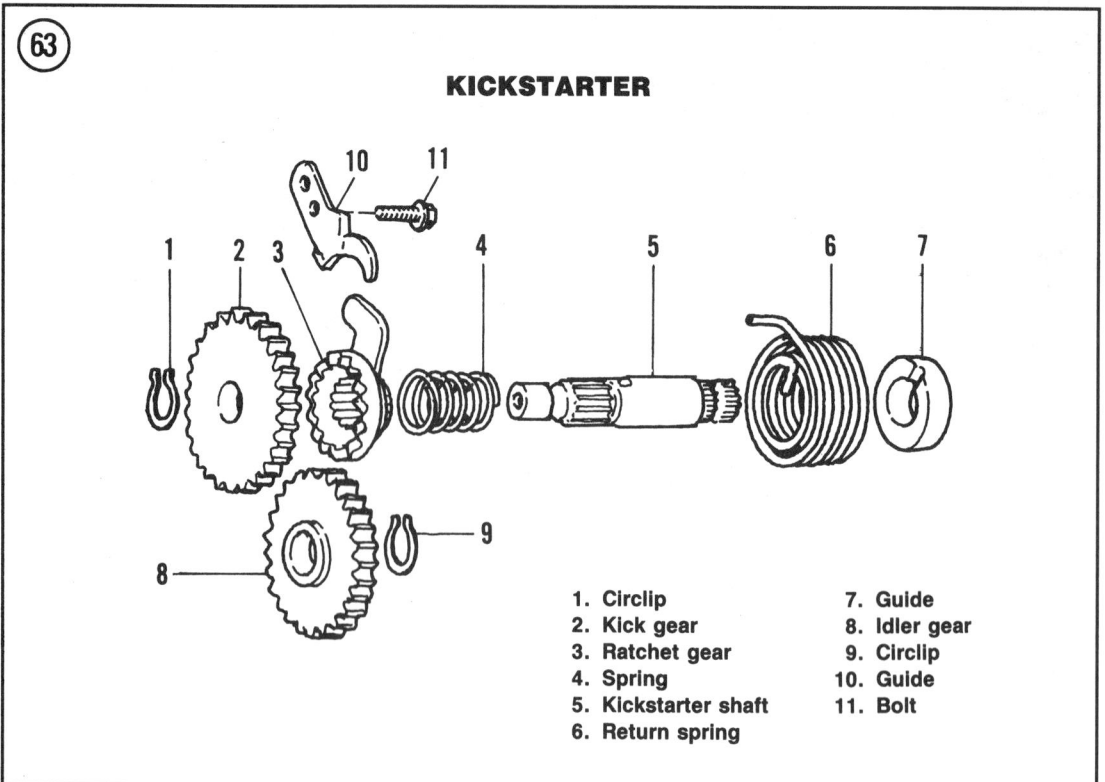

KICKSTARTER

1. Circlip
2. Kick gear
3. Ratchet gear
4. Spring
5. Kickstarter shaft
6. Return spring
7. Guide
8. Idler gear
9. Circlip
10. Guide
11. Bolt

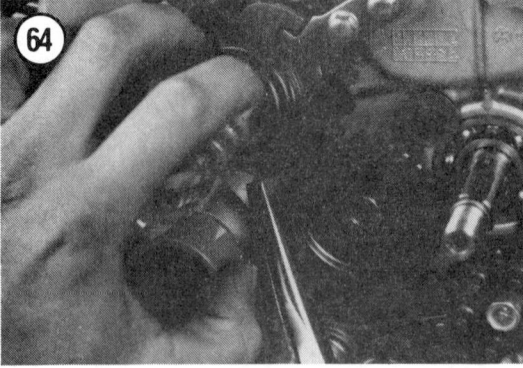

6

pliers and hook the end of the spring into the hole in the crankcase (**Figure 64**). **Figure 72** shows the kickstarter assembly properly installed.

12. Slip the kickstarter lever onto the kickstarter axle. Hold the kickstarter assembly in place and work the lever to check kickstarter operation. Remove the lever.

13. Install the clutch cover as described in this chapter. Operate the kickstarter to make sure it works correctly.

Disassembly/Inspection/Assembly

Refer to **Figure 63** for this procedure.

1. Remove the spring guide (**Figure 73**).
2. Remove the return spring (**Figure 74**).
3. Remove the small spring (**Figure 75**).
4. Remove the circlip (**Figure 76**).
5. Remove the kick gear (**Figure 77**).
6. Remove the ratchet gear (**Figure 78**).
7. Wash all parts thoroughly in solvent (**Figure 79**).
8. See **Figure 80**. Check for broken, chipped, or missing teeth on the kick gear (A) and ratchet gear (B).
9. Check the kickstarter shaft (**Figure 81**) as follows:

    a. Check the kickstarter lever splines for damage that would allow the lever to slip when the kickstarter is used.

    b. Check the shaft surface for cracks, deep scoring or other damage.

    c. Check the return spring hole in the shaft for cracks, wallowing or other conditions that

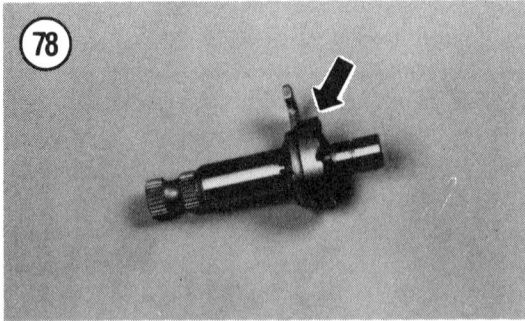

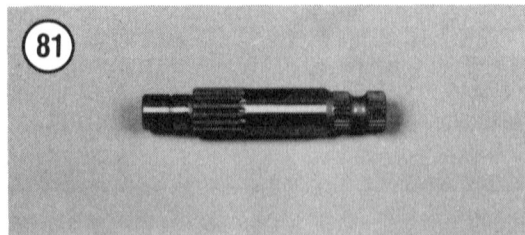

would allow the spring to slip out when using the kickstarter.

d. Install the ratchet gear onto the shaft and check that the gear operates smoothly on the shaft. Check the shaft splines for cracks or other damage.

e. Replace the kickstarter shaft if necessary.

10. See **Figure 82**. Check the return spring (A) and the small spring (B) for cracks, breakage or other damage. Replace if necessary.

11. Apply assembly oil to the sliding surfaces of all parts.

12. See **Figure 83**. Align the notch on the ratchet gear (A) with the hole (B) in the kickstarter shaft. Install the ratchet gear so that if faces in the direction shown in **Figure 78**.

13. Install the kick gear (**Figure 77**) and secure it with the circlip (**Figure 76**).

14. Install the small spring (**Figure 75**).

6

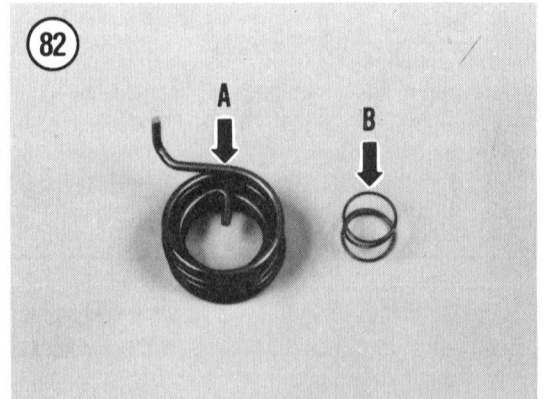

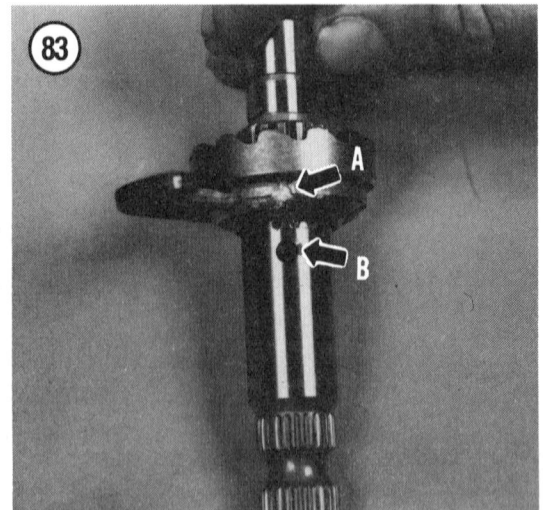

15. Install the return spring (**Figure 74**). Align the small end of the spring (A, **Figure 84**) with the hole (B) in the kickstarter shaft.

16. Install the spring guide (**Figure 73**) as follows:
   a. Align the notch in the spring guide with the portion of the return spring that fits into the shaft and install the spring guide.
   b. Push the spring guide all the way down until it bottoms (**Figure 85**).

EXTERNAL SHIFT MECHANISM

The external shift mechanism is located on the same side of the crankcase as the clutch assembly. To remove the shift drum and shift forks it is necessary to remove the engine and split the crankcases.

NOTE
The gearshift lever is subject to a lot of abuse under race conditions. If the motorcycle has been in a hard spill, the gearshift lever may have been hit and the shaft may have been bent. If the shaft is bent, it is very hard to straighten without subjecting the crankcase to abnormal stress where the shaft enters the case.

If the shaft is bent enough to prevent it from being withdrawn from the

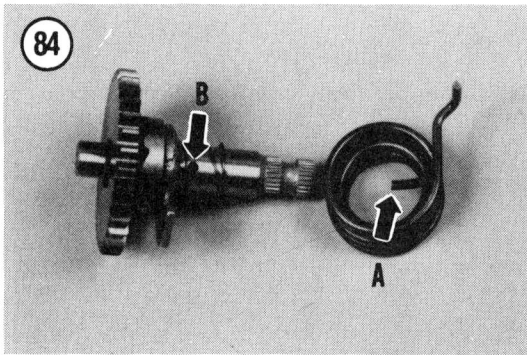

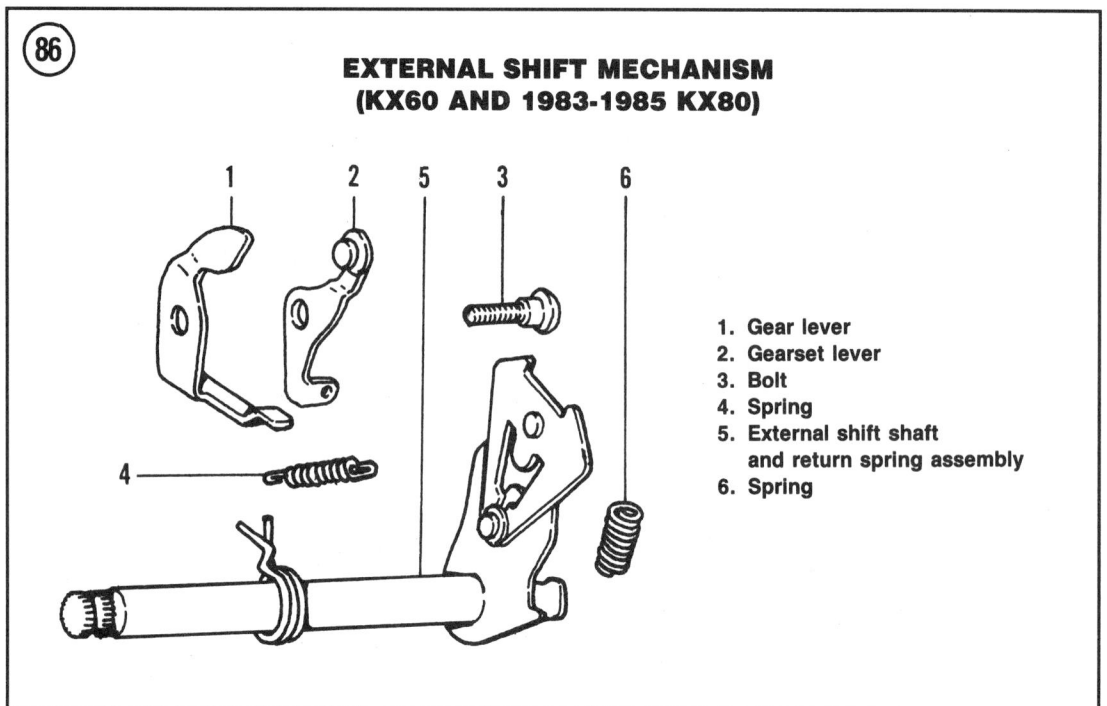

**EXTERNAL SHIFT MECHANISM
(KX60 AND 1983-1985 KX80)**

1. Gear lever
2. Gearset lever
3. Bolt
4. Spring
5. External shift shaft and return spring assembly
6. Spring

crankcase, there is little recourse but to cut the shaft off with a hacksaw very close to the crankcase. It is much cheaper in the long run to replace the shaft than risk damaging a set of expensive crankcases. After cutting off the end of the shaft, use a file or rotary grinder to remove all burrs from the shaft before removing it.

Removal/Installation (KX60 and 1983-1985 KX80)

Refer to **Figure 86** for this procedure.

1. Remove the pinch bolt and remove the shift lever from the left-hand side.

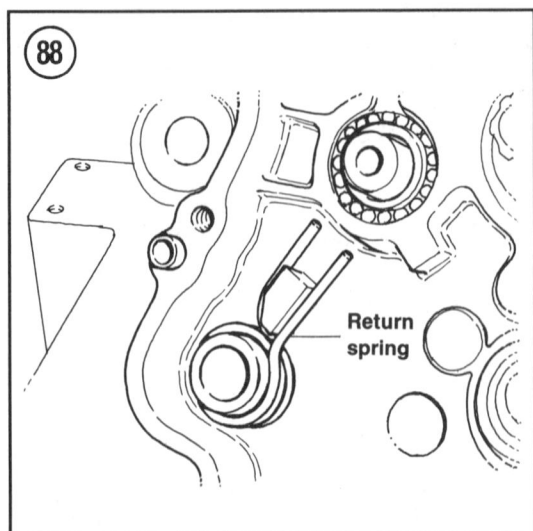

Return spring

2. Remove the clutch as described in this chapter.
3. Remove the idler gear as described under *Kickstarter Removal* in this chapter.

> *CAUTION*
> *On some models, the right-hand footpeg bracket interferes with removal of the external shift shaft (A, **Figure 87**). Do not attempt to remove the shift shaft by prying it out of the case as severe crankcase damage will result. On these models, it will be necessary to remove the engine as described in Chapter Five.*

4. Remove the external shift shaft (A, **Figure 87**) from the crankcase. Remove the return spring from behind the shaft (**Figure 88**).
5. Disconnect the spring and remove the screw holding the gear set lever to the crankcase. Remove the lever (B, **Figure 87**).
6. Inspect the external shift mechanism assembly as follows. Replace worn or damaged parts.
   a. Check the shift shaft for cracks or bending. Check the splines on the end of the shaft for damage.
   b. Check the return spring for fatigue, cracks or other damage. Replace if necessary.
   c. Check the engagement arms on the shift pawl for wear or damage. Damage or severe wear with the engagements will cause shifting problems.
7. Install the gear set lever (B, **Figure 87**) and secure it with the screw. Install the lever spring.
8. Install the return spring (**Figure 88**) so that the large rounded edge faces in.
9. Install the external shift shaft (A, **Figure 87**). Make sure the engagement arms on the shift pawl engage with the shift drum pins.
10. Reverse Steps 1-3 to complete assembly.

Removal/Installation (1986-on KX80)

Refer to **Figure 89** for this procedure.

1. Remove the pinch bolt and remove the shift lever from the left-hand side.
2. Remove the clutch as described in this chapter.
3. Remove the idler gear as described under *Kickstarter Removal* in this chapter.

4. Remove the external shift shaft (A, **Figure 90**) from the crankcase.

5. Disconnect the spring (B, **Figure 90**) and remove the screw (C, **Figure 90**) holding the neutral set lever to the crankcase. Remove the lever.

NOTE
Loctite is used to help secure the segment bolt (A, Figure 91). If necessary, loosen the bolt with a hand impact driver and socket.

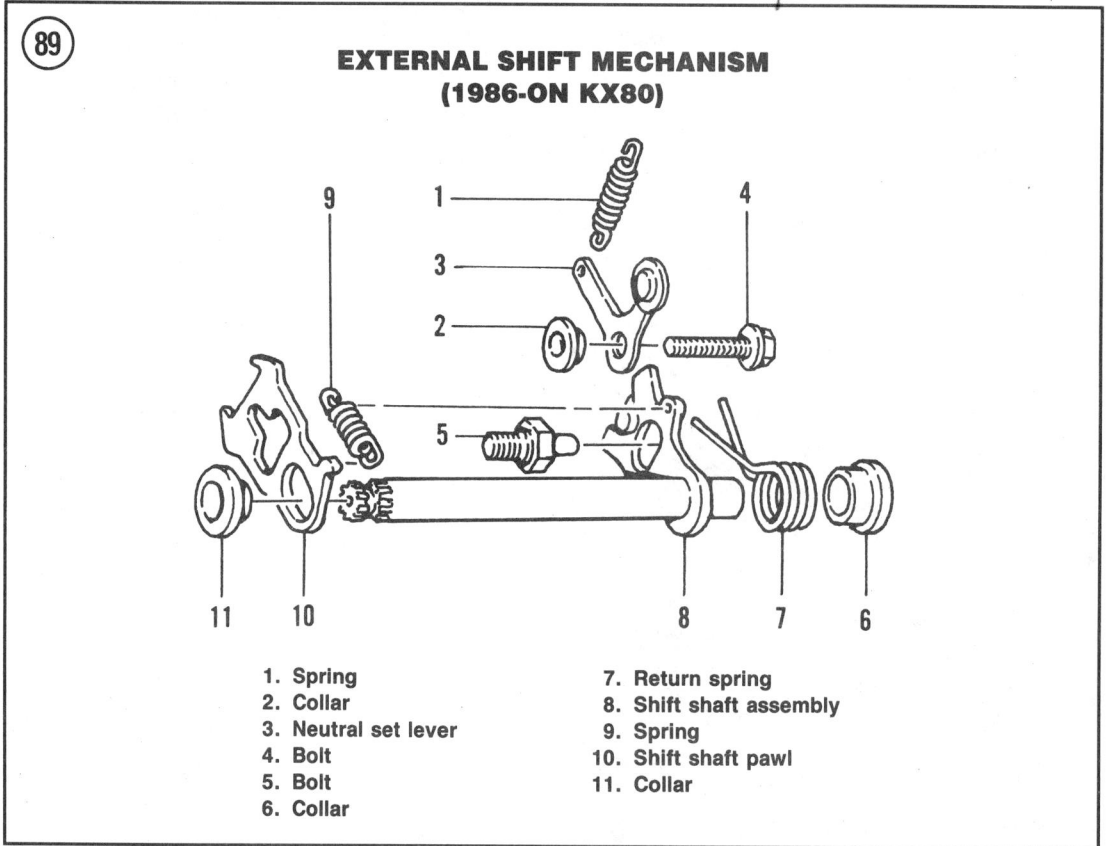

**EXTERNAL SHIFT MECHANISM
(1986-ON KX80)**

1. Spring
2. Collar
3. Neutral set lever
4. Bolt
5. Bolt
6. Collar
7. Return spring
8. Shift shaft assembly
9. Spring
10. Shift shaft pawl
11. Collar

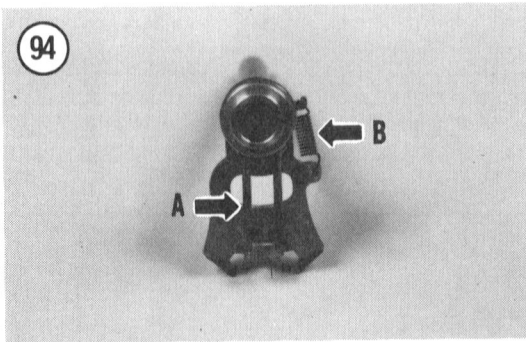

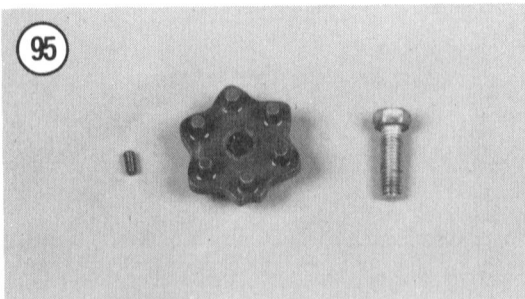

6. Remove the shift drum segment as follows:
   a. Remove the bolt (A, **Figure 91**) holding the segment to the shift drum. Remove the segment (B, **Figure 91**).
   b. Remove the pin (**Figure 92**) from the shift drum.

7. Inspect the external shift mechanism assembly as follows. Replace worn or damaged parts.
   a. Check the shift shaft (**Figure 93**) for cracks or bending. Check the splines on the end of the shaft for damage.
   b. Check the return spring on the shift shaft. The return spring arms should be installed on the shaft arm as shown in A, **Figure 94**. Replace the return spring if it shows signs of fatigue or if it is cracked.
   c. Check the small spring (B, **Figure 94**) on the shift shaft pawl.
   d. Check the engagement arms on the shift pawl for wear or damage. Damage or severe wear with the engagements will cause shifting problems.
   e. Check the segment (**Figure 95**) for cracks, severe wear or other damage. Replace if necessary.

8. Install the shift drum segment as follows:
   a. Insert the pin (**Figure 92**) into the shift drum hole. Then align the hole in the segment with the pin and install the segment (B, **Figure 91**). **Figure 96** shows the segment pin hole.
   b. Clean the segment bolt threads to remove all traces of old Loctite. Then wipe the bolt threads with Loctite 242 (blue) and install the bolt. Tighten the bolt securely.

6

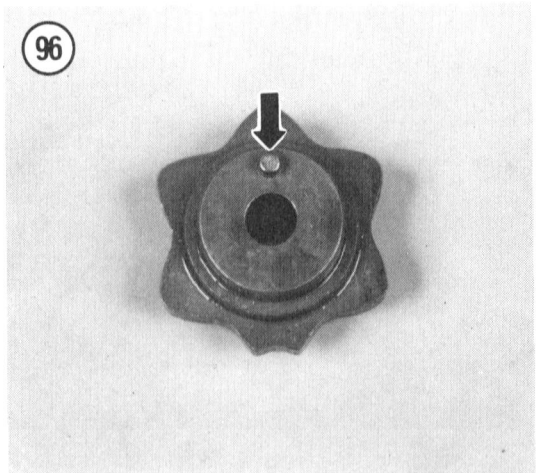

9. Insert the shift shaft into the crankcase, making sure the return spring on the shaft centers with the crankcase stud (**Figure 97**).

10. Install the neutral set lever and bolt (**Figure 98**). Tighten the bolt securely.

11. Attach the spring to the neutral set lever and the crankcase pin as shown in **Figure 99**.

12. Reverse Steps 1-3 to complete assembly.

Table 1 CLUTCH SPECIFICATIONS

	New mm (in.)	Service limit mm (in.)
Friction plate thickness	3.1-3.3 (0.12-0.13)	2.9 (0.11)
Clutch plate warpage*	0-0.15 (0-0.006)	0.3 (0.012)
Friction plate/clutch housing clearance		
KX60	—	—
KX80	0.35-0.60 (0.014-0.024)	0.9 (0.035)
Clutch spring free length		
1988-on		
KX60	26.6 (1.05)	25.3 (0.996)
KX80	33.5 (1.32)	31.8 (1.25)
Number of clutch plates and friction discs		
KX60		
Steel	4	—
Friction disc	5	—
KX80		
Steel		
1983-1984	4	—
1985-1987	5	—
1988	6	—
1989	6	—
Friction disc		
1983-1984	5	—
1985-1987	6	—
1988	7	—
1989	7**	—

* Warpage limit for friction disc and steel clutch plates.
** 1989 models use 6 regular friction discs and 1 extra thick disc for a total of 7 discs.

6

Table 2 TIGHTENING TORQUES

	N·m	ft.-lb.
Clutch hub bolt		
1983	59	43
1984-1986	69	51
1987	64	47
Clutch hub nut		
1988-on KX80	78	58
Primary pinion gear nut*	49	36
Engine drain plug	20	14.5

* A circlip is used to secure the primary gear on 1986 and later KX80 models.

CHAPTER SEVEN

TRANSMISSION AND
INTERNAL SHIFT MECHANISM

The transmission and internal shift mechanism (shift drum and forks) are all basically the same. The transmission on all models is a 6-speed unit. To gain access to the transmission and internal shift mechanism it is necessary to remove the engine and split the crankcase (Chapter Five). Once the crankcase has been split, the transmission, shift drum and forks can easily be removed as described in Chapter Five.

Transmission ratios are listed in **Table 1**. **Table 1** and **Table 2** are found at the end of the chapter.

NOTE
If disassembling a used, well run-in engine for the first time by yourself, pay particular attention to any additional shims that may have been added by a previous owner. These may have been added to take up the tolerance of worn components and must be reinstalled in the same position since the shims have developed a wear pattern. If new parts are going to be installed, these shims may be eliminated. This is something you will have to determine upon reassembly.

TRANSMISSION OPERATION

The basic transmission has 6 pairs of constantly meshed gears (**Figure 1**) on the mainshaft (A) and countershaft (B). Each pair of meshed gears gives one gear ratio. In each pair, one of the gears is locked to its shaft and always turns with it. The other gear is not locked to its shaft and can spin freely on it. Next to each free spinning gear is a third gear which is splined to the same shaft, always turning with it. This third gear can slide from side-to-side along the shaft splines. The side of the sliding gear and the free spinning gear have mating "dogs" and slots." When the sliding gear moves up against the free spinning gear, the 2 gears are locked together, locking the free spinning gear to its shaft. Since both meshed mainshaft and countershaft gears are now locked to their shafts, power is transmitted at that gear ratio (**Table 1**).

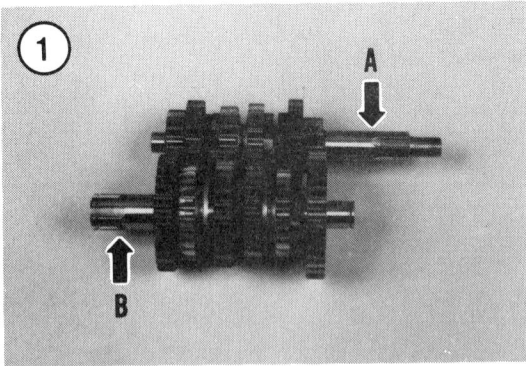

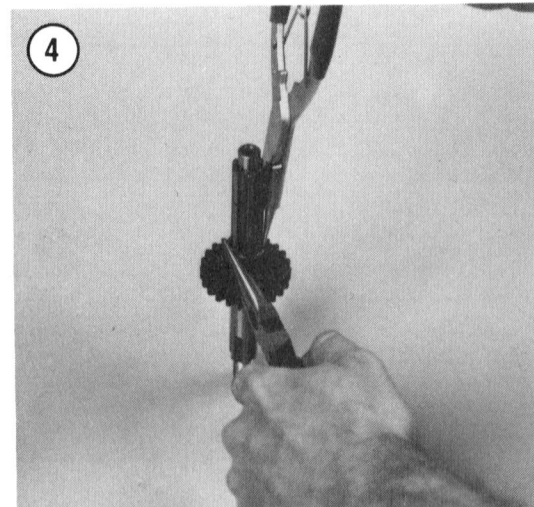

Shift Drum and Forks

Each sliding gear has a deep groove machined around its outside (**Figure 2**). The curved shift fork arm rides in this groove, controlling the side-to-side sliding of the gear, and therefore the selection of different gear ratios. Each shift fork slides back and forth on a guide shaft, and has a peg that rides in a groove machined in the shift drum (**Figure 3**). When the shift linkage rotates the shift drum, the zigzag grooves move the shift forks and sliding gears back and forth.

TRANSMISSION TROUBLESHOOTING

Refer to *Transmission* in Chapter Two.

TRANSMISSION OVERHAUL

A 6-speed transmission is used on all KX60 and KX80 models.

7

Removal/Installation

Remove and install the transmission and internal shift mechanism as described under *Crankcase Disassembly/Reassembly* in Chapter Five.

Transmission Service Notes

1. The circlips are a tight fit on the transmission shafts. They should all be replaced during reassembly.
2. Circlips will turn and fold over, making removal and installation difficult. To ease removal, open the circlip with a pair of circlip pliers while at the same time holding the back of the circlip with a pair of pliers and remove it. See **Figure 4**.

Mainshaft
Disassembly/Assembly
(KX60 and 1983-1985 KX80)

Refer to **Figure 5** for this procedure.

NOTE
A divided container such as an egg carton can be used to help maintain correct alignment and position of the parts as they are removed from the mainshaft (Figure 6).

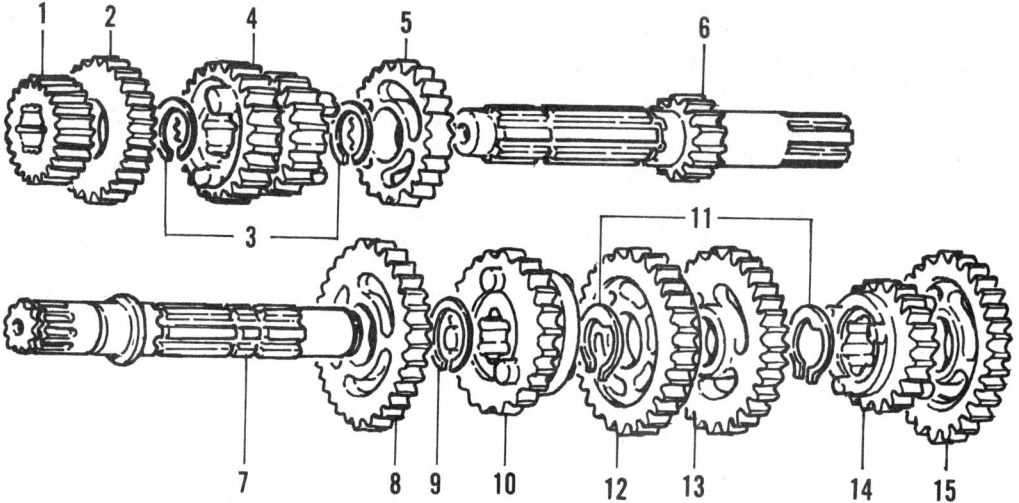

**TRANSMISSION
(KX60 AND 1983-1985 KX80)**

1. Mainshaft second gear
2. Mainshaft fifth gear
3. Circlip
4. Mainshaft third/fourth combination gear
5. Mainshaft sixth gear
6. Mainshaft/first gear
7. Countershaft
8. Countershaft second gear
9. Circlip
10. Countershaft fifth gear
11. Circlip
12. Countershaft fourth gear
13. Countershaft third gear
14. Countershaft sixth gear
15. Countershaft first gear

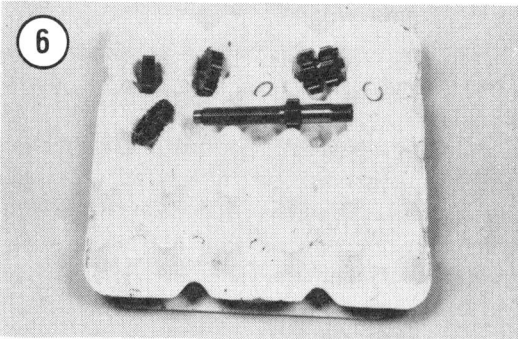

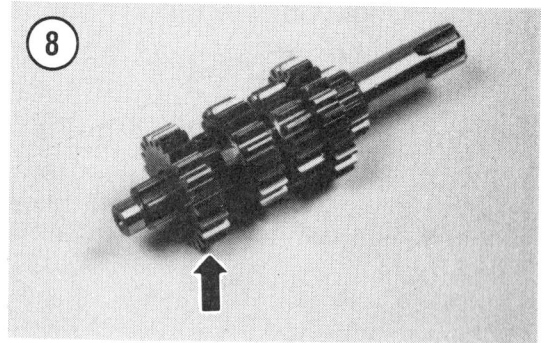

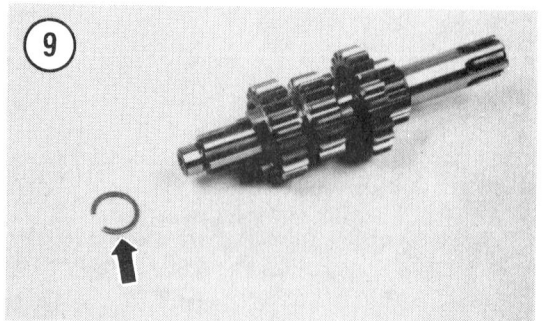

1. Place the assembled shaft into a large can or plastic bucket and thoroughly clean with solvent and stiff brush. Dry with compressed air if available.

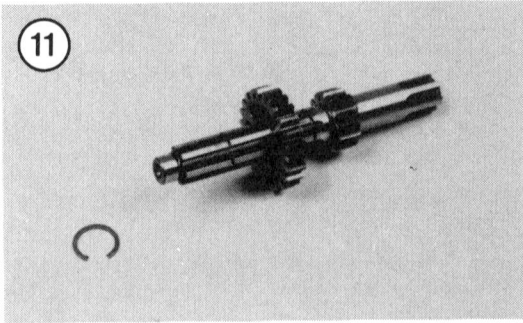

2. Remove second gear (**Figure 7**).
3. Remove fifth gear (**Figure 8**).
4. Remove the circlip (**Figure 9**).
5. Remove the third/fourth combination gear (**Figure 10**).
6. Remove the circlip (**Figure 11**).
7. Remove sixth gear (**Figure 12**).
8. Inspect the mainshaft parts as described under *Transmission Inspection* in this chapter.

NOTE
*When installing circlips during transmission assembly, make sure to align the circlip opening with a spline groove and not a spline. If a circlip has a notch, the notch should fit into a transmission shaft groove (**Figure 13**).*

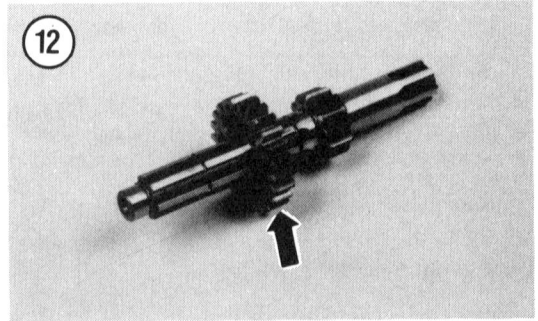

7

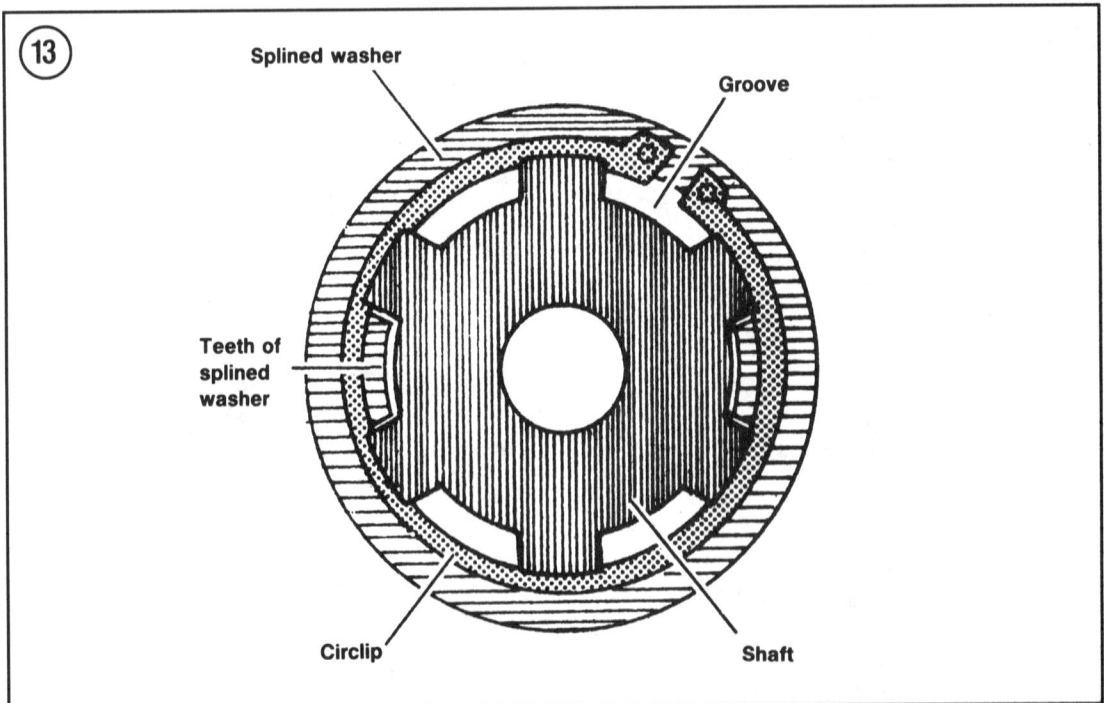

9. Slide on sixth gear (**Figure 12**) so that the plain side faces toward first gear. Then install the circlip (**Figure 11**) into the groove next to the gear. Make sure the circlip seats in the groove completely (**Figure 14**).

10. Slide on third/fourth combination gear so that the smaller gear faces toward sixth gear (**Figure 10**).

11. Install the circlip into the groove closest to the third/fourth combination gear (**Figure 9**). Make sure the circlip seats in the groove completely (**Figure 15**).

12. Slide on fifth gear (**Figure 8**) so that the slotted side faces toward the third/fourth combination gear.

NOTE
Second gear can be installed with either side facing toward fifth gear.

13. Slide on second gear (**Figure 7**).

14. After assembly is complete, refer to **Figure 16** for the correct placement of all gears.

Countershaft Disassembly/Assembly (KX60 and 1983-1985 KX80)

Refer to **Figure 5** for this procedure.

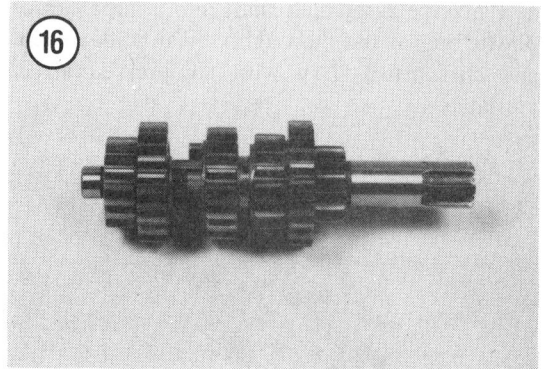

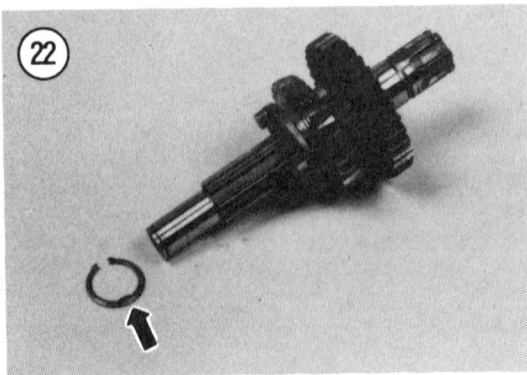

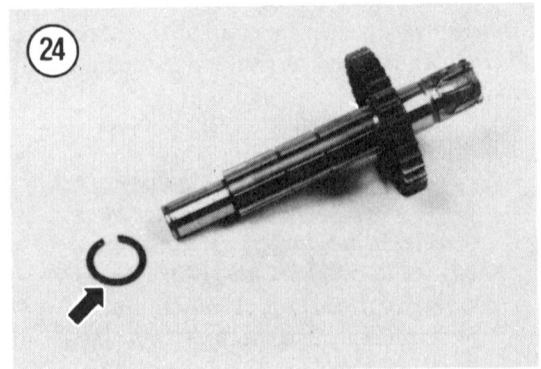

NOTE

A divided container such as an egg carton can be used to help maintain correct alignment and position of the parts as they are removed from the countershaft.

1. Place the assembled shaft into a large can or plastic bucket and thoroughly clean with solvent and stiff brush. Dry with compressed air or let it sit on rags to drip dry.
2. Remove first gear (**Figure 17**).
3. Remove sixth gear (**Figure 18**).
4. Remove the circlip (**Figure 19**).
5. Remove third gear (**Figure 20**).
6. Remove fourth gear (**Figure 21**).
7. Remove the circlip (**Figure 22**).
8. Remove fifth gear (**Figure 23**).
9. Remove the circlip (**Figure 24**).
10. Remove second gear (**Figure 25**).
11. Check the countershaft assembly as described under *Transmission Inspection* in this chapter.

NOTE

When installing circlips during transmission assembly, make sure to

7

*align the circlip opening with a spline groove and not a spline. If a circlip has a notch, the notch should fit into a transmission shaft groove (**Figure 13**).*

12. Slide on second gear (**Figure 25**) so that the flat side faces toward the left-hand side. Then install the circlip (**Figure 24**) in the groove next to second gear. Make sure the circlip (**Figure 26**) seats in the groove completely.

13. Slide on fifth gear (**Figure 23**) so that the shift fork groove faces away from second gear. Then install the circlip (**Figure 22**) in the groove closest to fifth gear. Make sure the circlip (**Figure 27**) seats in the groove completely.

14. Slide on fourth gear (**Figure 21**) so that the dog recess faces toward fifth gear.

15. Slide on third gear (**Figure 20**) so that the dog recess faces toward the right-hand side. Then install the circlip (**Figure 19**) in the groove closest to third gear. Make sure the circlip seats in the groove completely (**Figure 28**).

16. Slide on sixth gear (**Figure 18**) so that the shift fork groove faces toward third gear.

17. Install first gear (**Figure 17**) so that the plain side faces toward the right-hand side.

18. After assembly is complete, refer to **Figure 29** for the correct placement of all gears. Make sure all circlips are seated correctly in the countershaft grooves.

NOTE
*After both transmission shafts have been assembled, mesh the 2 assemblies together in the correct position (**Figure 30**). Check that all gears meet correctly. This is your last check prior to installing the assemblies into the crankcase to make sure they are correctly assembled.*

Mainshaft
Disassembly/Assembly
(1986-on KX80)

Refer to **Figure 31** for this procedure.

NOTE
*A divided container such as an egg carton can be used to help maintain correct alignment and position of the parts as they are removed from the mainshaft (**Figure 3**).*

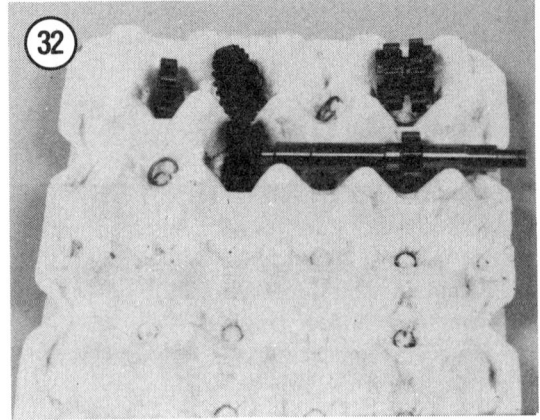

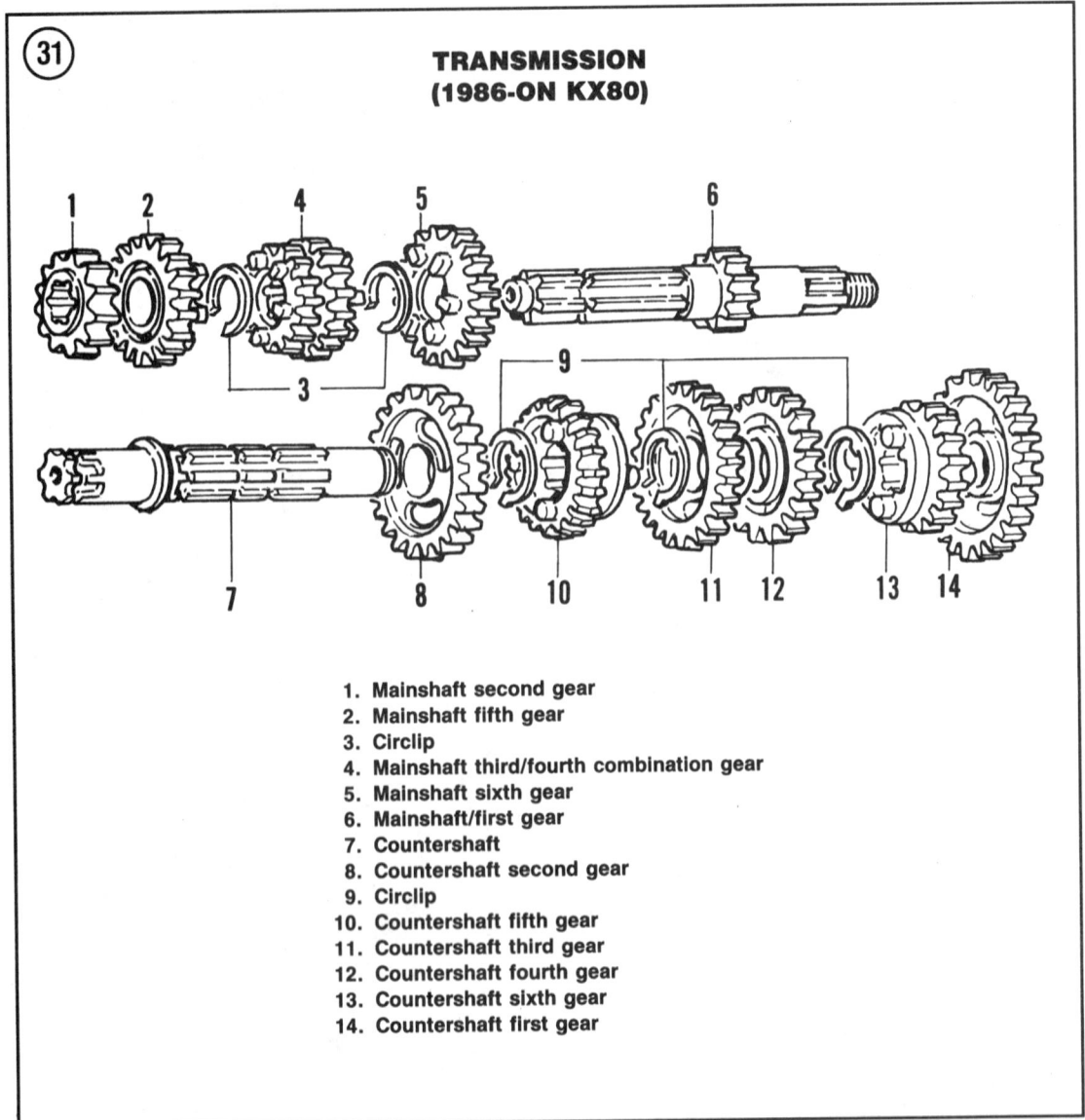

TRANSMISSION (1986-ON KX80)

1. Mainshaft second gear
2. Mainshaft fifth gear
3. Circlip
4. Mainshaft third/fourth combination gear
5. Mainshaft sixth gear
6. Mainshaft/first gear
7. Countershaft
8. Countershaft second gear
9. Circlip
10. Countershaft fifth gear
11. Countershaft third gear
12. Countershaft fourth gear
13. Countershaft sixth gear
14. Countershaft first gear

7

1. Place the assembled shaft into a large can or plastic bucket and thoroughly clean with solvent and stiff brush. Dry with compressed air or let sit on rags to drip dry.
2. Remove second gear (**Figure 33**).
3. Remove fifth gear (**Figure 34**).
4. Remove the circlip (**Figure 35**).
5. Remove the third/fourth combination gear (**Figure 36**).
6. Remove the circlip (**Figure 37**).
7. Remove sixth gear (**Figure 38**).
8. Inspect the mainshaft parts as described under *Transmission Inspection* in this chapter.

NOTE
*When installing circlips during transmission assembly, make sure to align the circlip opening with a spline groove and not a spline. If a circlip has a notch, the notch should fit into a transmission shaft groove (**Figure 39**).*

9. Slide on sixth gear (**Figure 38**) so that the plain side faces toward first gear. Then install the circlip (**Figure 37**) into the groove next to the gear. Make sure the circlip seats in the groove completely (**Figure 40**).
10. Slide on third/fourth combination gear so that the larger gear faces toward sixth gear (**Figure 36**).
11. Install the circlip (**Figure 35**) into the groove closest to the third/fourth combination gear. Make sure the circlip seats in the groove completely (**Figure 41**).
12. Slide on fifth gear (**Figure 34**) so that the plain side faces toward the circlip.

NOTE
Second gear can be installed with either side facing toward fifth gear.

13. Slide on second gear (**Figure 33**).
14. After assembly is complete, refer to **Figure 42** for the correct placement of all gears.

Countershaft Disassembly/Assembly (1986-on KX80)

Refer to **Figure 31** for this procedure.

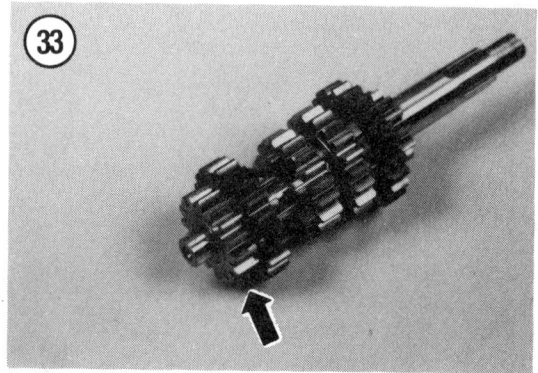

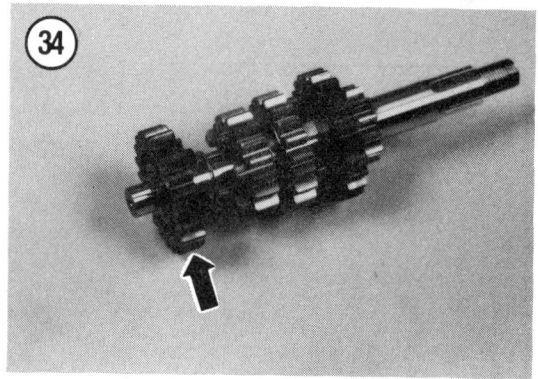

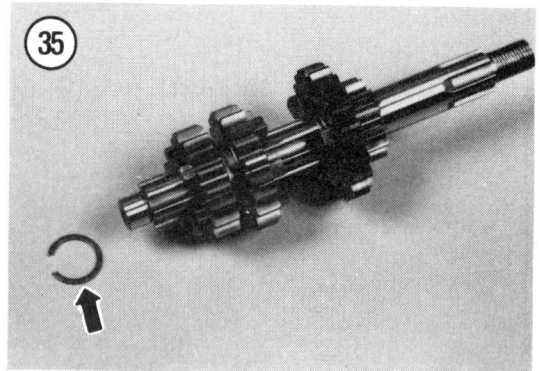

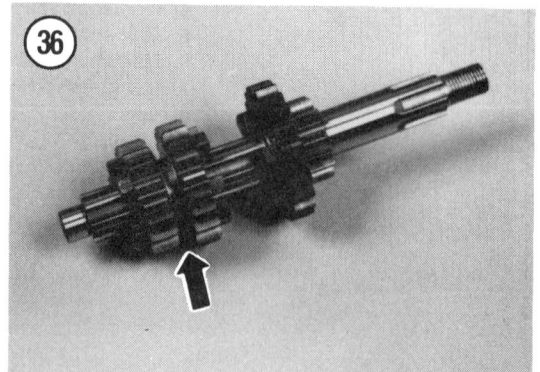

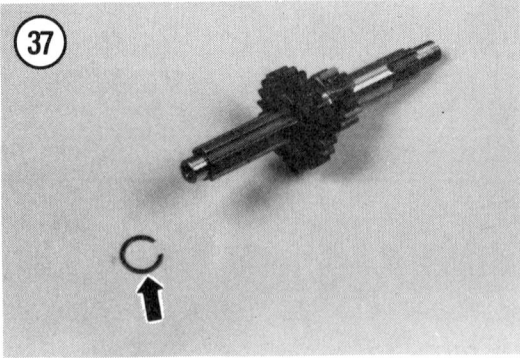

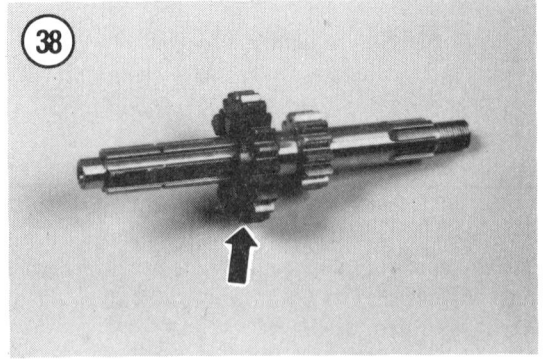

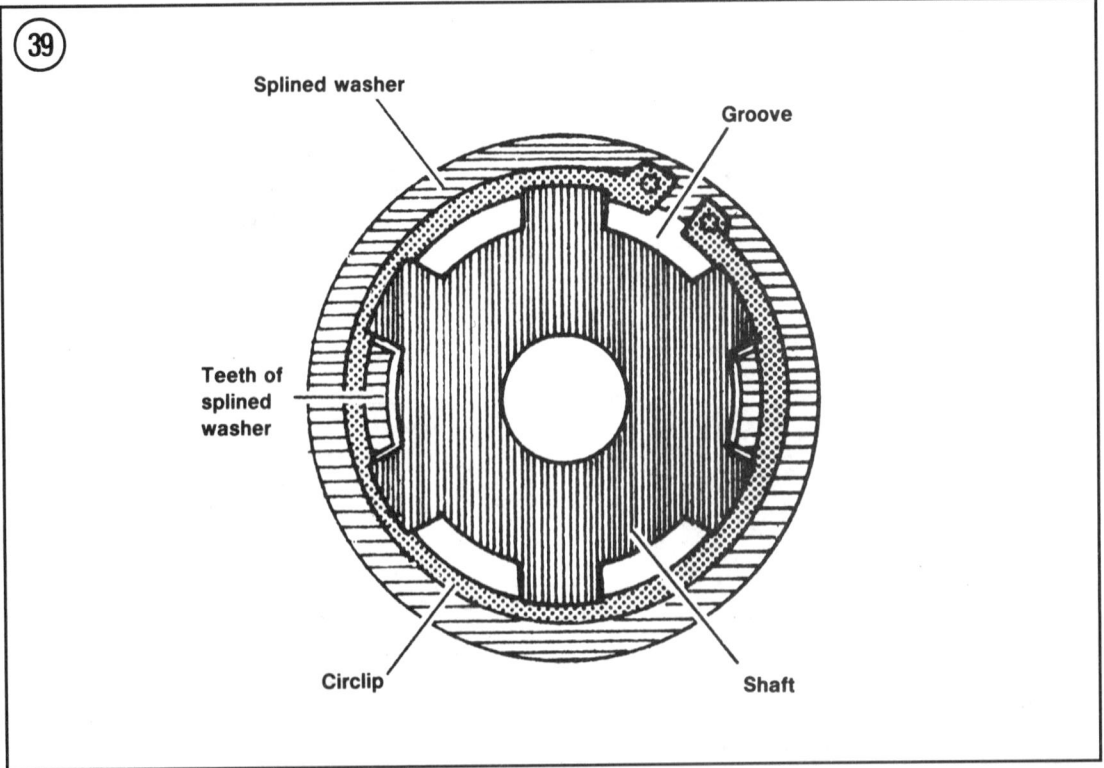

Splined washer

Groove

Teeth of
splined
washer

Shaft

Circlip

7

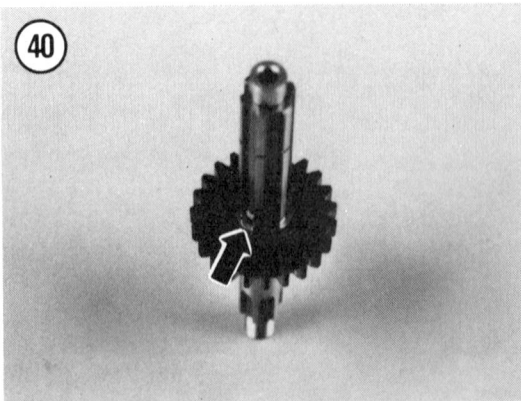

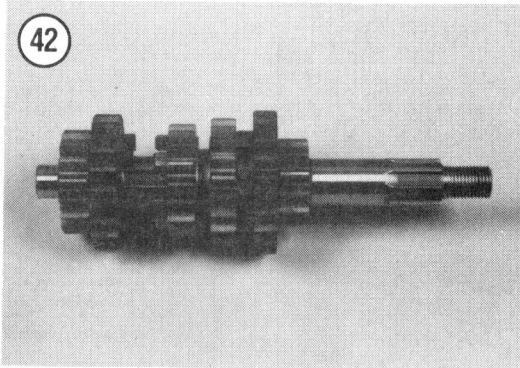

NOTE
A divided container such as an egg carton can be used to help maintain correct alignment and position of the parts as they are removed from the countershaft.

1. Place the assembled shaft into a large can or plastic bucket and thoroughly clean with solvent and stiff brush. Dry with compressed air or let sit on rags to drip dry.
2. Remove first gear (**Figure 43**).
3. Remove sixth gear (**Figure 44**).
4. Remove the circlip (**Figure 45**).
5. Remove fourth gear (**Figure 46**).
6. Remove third gear (**Figure 47**).
7. Remove the circlip (**Figure 48**).
8. Remove fifth gear (**Figure 49**).
9. Remove the circlip (**Figure 50**).
10. Remove second gear (**Figure 51**).
11. Check the countershaft assembly as described under *Transmission Inspection* in this chapter.

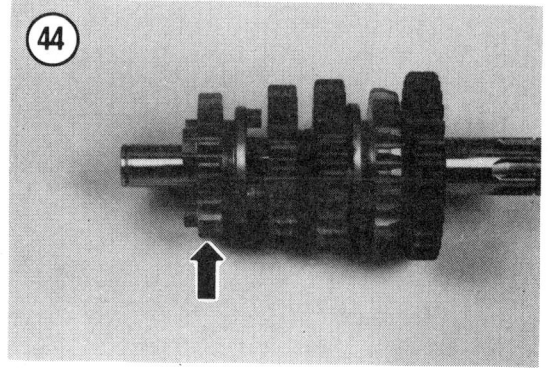

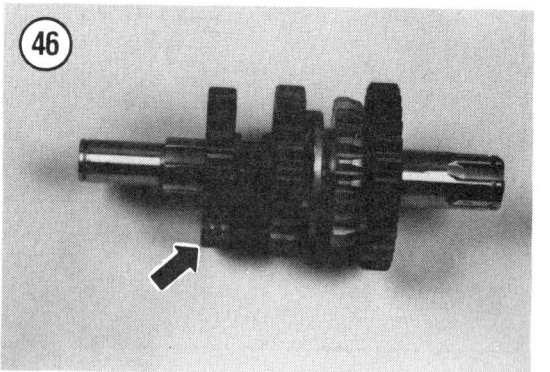

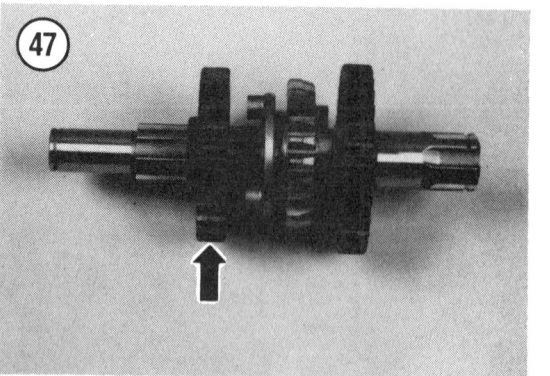

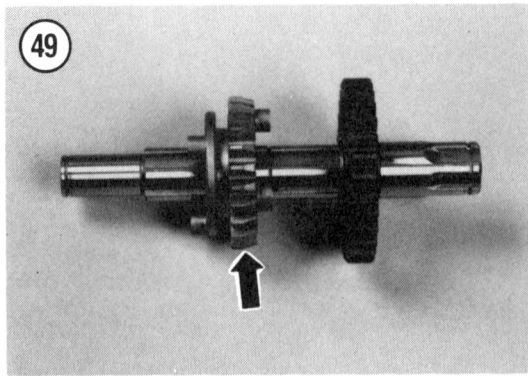

NOTE

*When installing circlips during transmission assembly, make sure to align the circlip opening with a spline groove and not a spline. If a circlip has a notch, the notch should fit into a transmission shaft groove (**Figure 39**).*

12. Slide on second gear (**Figure 51**) so that the flat side faces toward the left-hand side. Then install the circlip (**Figure 50**) in the groove next to second gear. Make sure the circlip (**Figure 52**) seats in the groove completely.

13. Slide on fifth gear (**Figure 49**) so that the shift fork groove faces toward the right-hand side. Then install the circlip (**Figure 48**) in the groove closest to fifth gear. Make sure the circlip (**Figure 53**) seats in the groove completely.

14. Slide on third gear (**Figure 47**) so that the dog recess faces toward fifth gear.

7

15. Slide on fourth gear (**Figure 46**) so that the dog recess faces toward the right-hand side. Then install the circlip (**Figure 54**) in the groove closest to third gear.

16. Slide on sixth gear (**Figure 44**) so that the shift fork groove faces toward fourth gear.

17. Install first gear (**Figure 43**) so that the plain side faces toward the right-hand side.

18. After assembly is complete, refer to **Figure 55** for the correct placement of all gears. Make sure all circlips are seated correctly in the countershaft grooves.

NOTE
After both transmission shafts have been assembled, mesh the 2 assemblies together in the correct position (Figure 56). Check that all gears meet correctly. This is your last check prior to installing the assemblies into the crankcase to make sure they are correctly assembled.

**Transmission Inspection
(All Models)**

1. Check each gear for excessive wear, burrs, pitting, or chipped or missing teeth.

2. Make sure the dogs (A, **Figure 57**) on the gears are in good condition. If the dogs are rounded, the mating shift fork and/or shift fork shaft is probably bent or damaged.

3. Check the shift fork groove in the sliding gears (B, **Figure 57**) for wear, scuffing or other abnormal conditions.

4. Check each stationary gear dog slot (**Figure 58**). The slots should not be rounded or worn severely.

5. Measure the width of each sliding gear shift fork groove (**Figure 59**) with a vernier caliper and compare to the wear limit specification in **Table 2**.

6. Make sure that all gears slide on their respective shafts smoothly.

NOTE
Defective gears should be replaced, and it is a good idea to replace the mating gear even though it may not show as much wear or damage.

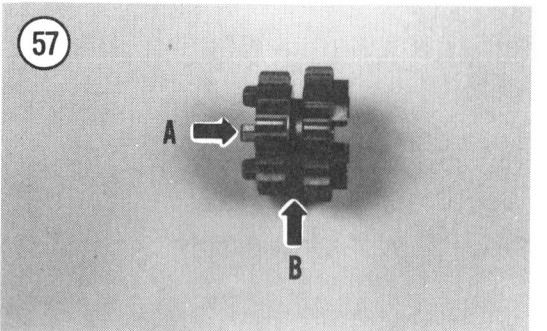

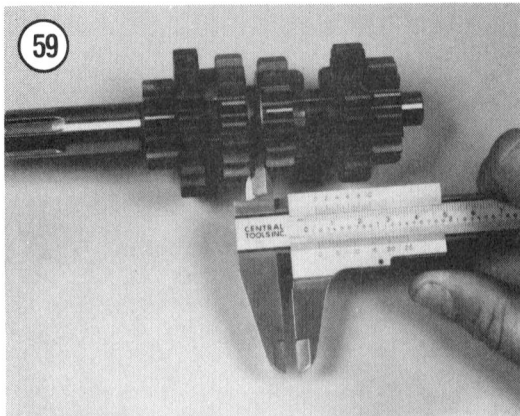

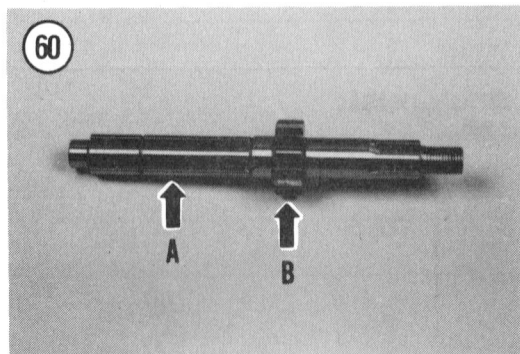

A B

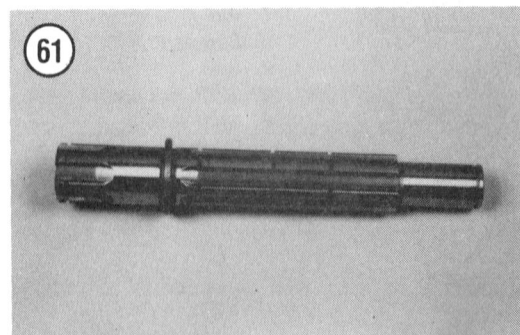

7. Check the mainshaft (A, **Figure 60**) and countershaft (**Figure 61**) splines for wear, cracks or other damage. Check the circlip grooves in the shafts for cracks or wear that could allow a circlip to pop out. Also check the mainshaft first gear (B, **Figure 60**). If the gear is damaged, replace the mainshaft assembly.

8. Replace all circlips during reassembly.

9. If there is any doubt as to the condition of any part, replace it with a new one.

INTERNAL SHIFT MECHANISM

Removal/Installation

Remove and install the transmission and internal shift mechanism as described under *Crankcase Disassembly/Reassembly* in Chapter Five.

Inspection

Refer to **Figure 62** (KX60 and 1983-1985 KX80) or **Figure 63** (1986-on KX80) for this procedure.

1. Inspect each shift fork (**Figure 64**) for signs of wear or cracking. Examine the shift forks at the points where they contact the slider gear (**Figure 64**). This surface should be smooth with no signs of wear or damage. Make sure the forks slide smoothly on their respective shaft. See **Figure 65** (KX60 and 1983-1985 KX80) or **Figure 66** (1986-on KX80).

2. Check the shift fork shaft for bending. Remove the shift forks from their shafts and roll each shaft on a piece of glass. Any clicking noise detected indicates that the shaft is bent.

3. Check for any arc-shaped wear or burn marks on the shift forks. This indicates that the shift fork has come in contact with the gear. The fork fingers have become excessively worn and the fork must be replaced.

4. Measure the diameter of each shift fork guide pin with a vernier caliper (**Figure 67**) and compare to the wear limit in **Table 2**.

5. Measure the thickness of each shift fork finger with a vernier caliper (**Figure 68**) and compare to the wear limit in **Table 2**.

6. Check grooves in the shift drum (**Figure 69**) for wear or roughness. Then measure each groove width with a vernier caliper (**Figure 70**) and compare to the wear limit in **Table 2**.

7. Replace worn or damaged parts.

7

**Shift Drum
Disassembly/Reassembly
(KX60 and 1983-1985 KX80)**

*NOTE
The screw (Figure 71) used to secure
the shift drum plate and pin assembly*

*is normally held in position with
Loctite. Use a hand impact driver with
a Phillips bit to loosen the screw.*

1. Loosen the screw (**Figure 71**) holding the plate
to the shift drum. Remove the screw and plate
(**Figure 72**).

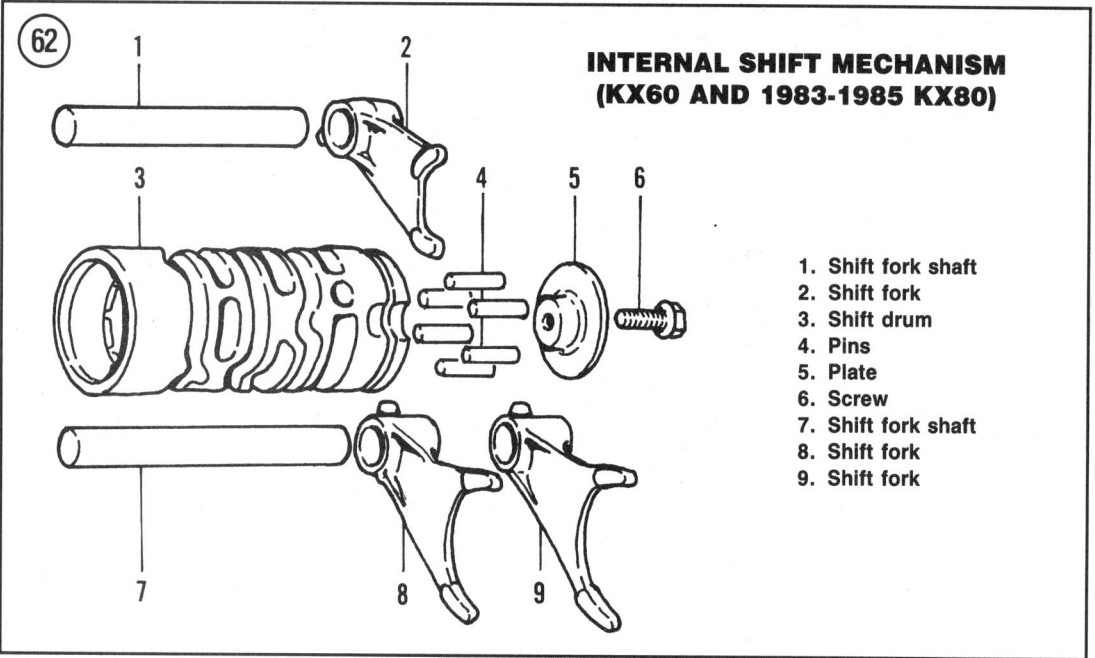

**INTERNAL SHIFT MECHANISM
(KX60 AND 1983-1985 KX80)**

1. Shift fork shaft
2. Shift fork
3. Shift drum
4. Pins
5. Plate
6. Screw
7. Shift fork shaft
8. Shift fork
9. Shift fork

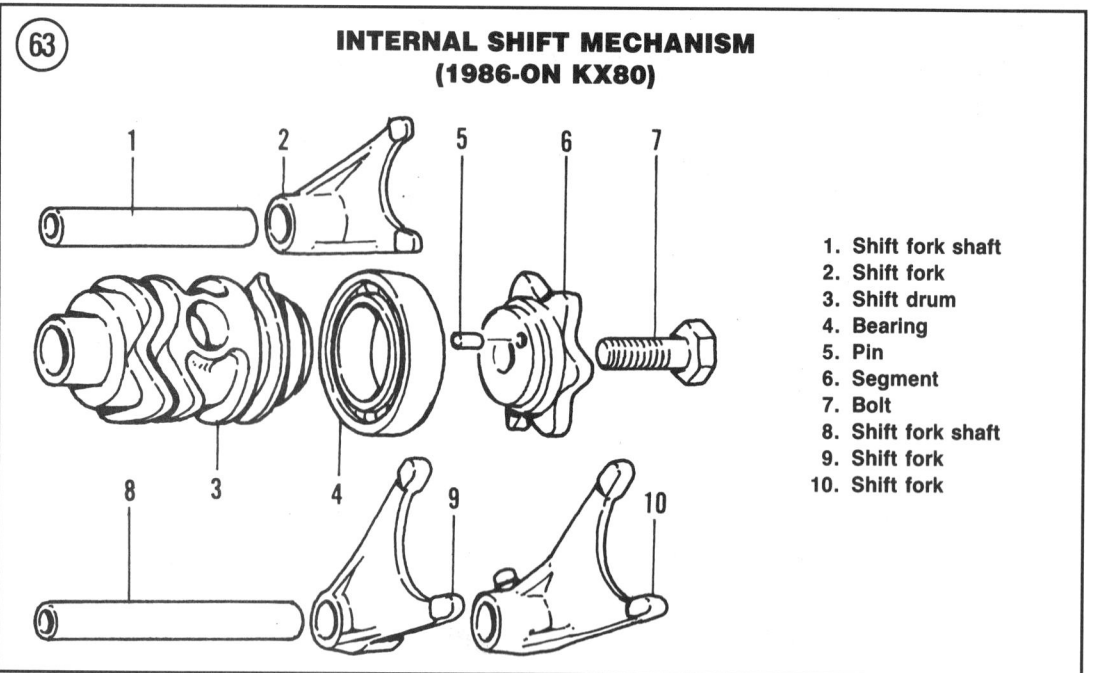

**INTERNAL SHIFT MECHANISM
(1986-ON KX80)**

1. Shift fork shaft
2. Shift fork
3. Shift drum
4. Bearing
5. Pin
6. Segment
7. Bolt
8. Shift fork shaft
9. Shift fork
10. Shift fork

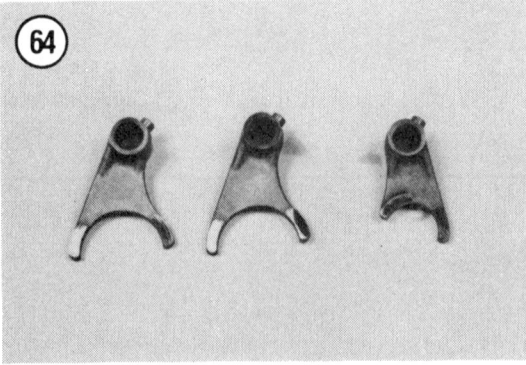

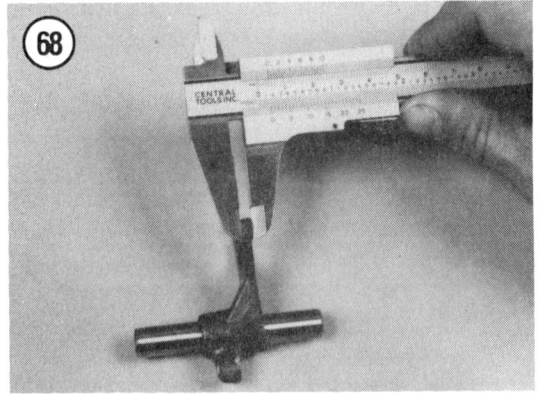

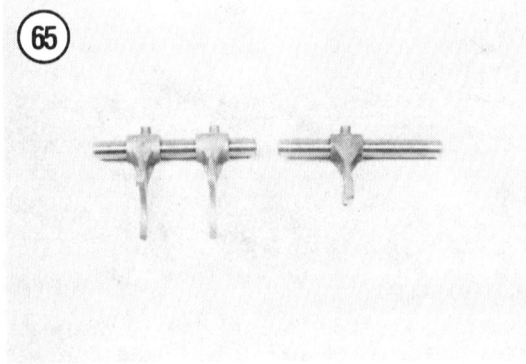

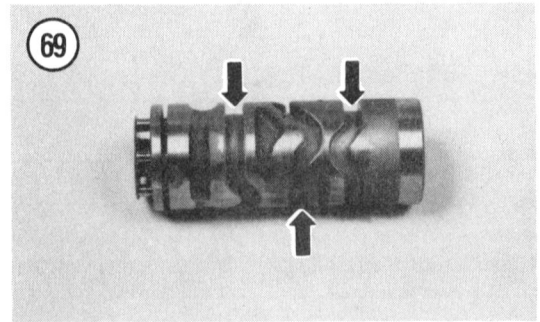

7

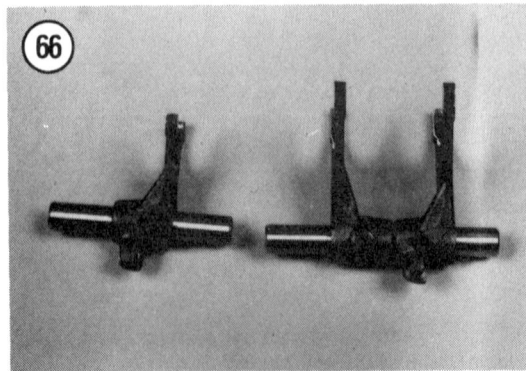

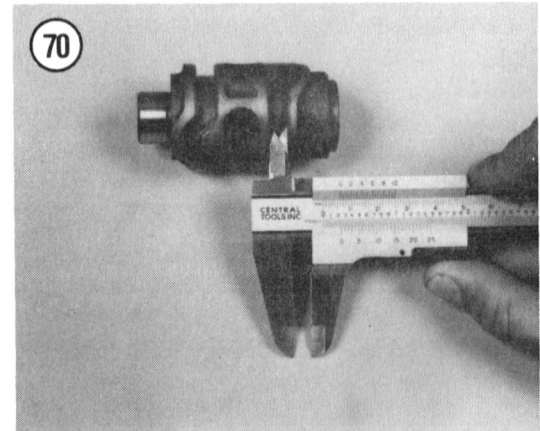

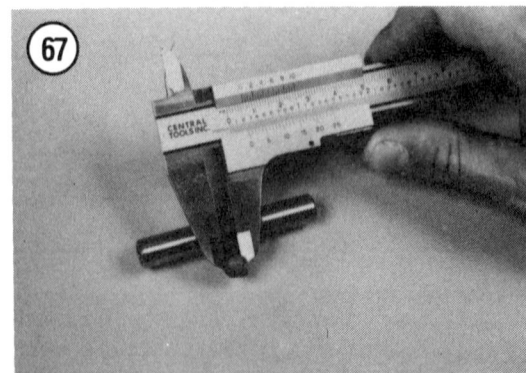

2. Remove the 6 shift drum pins (**Figure 73**).

3. Check the shift drum pins for damage; replace all pins as a set if necessary.

4. Install the 6 shift drum pins into the shift drum pin holes (**Figure 74**).

5. Install the plate.

6. Apply Loctite 242 (blue) to the screw and install it. Tighten the screw securely.

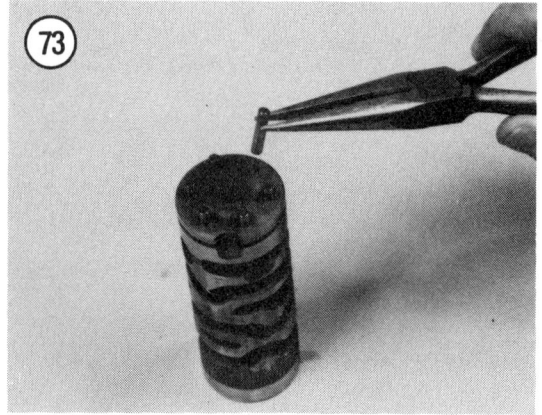

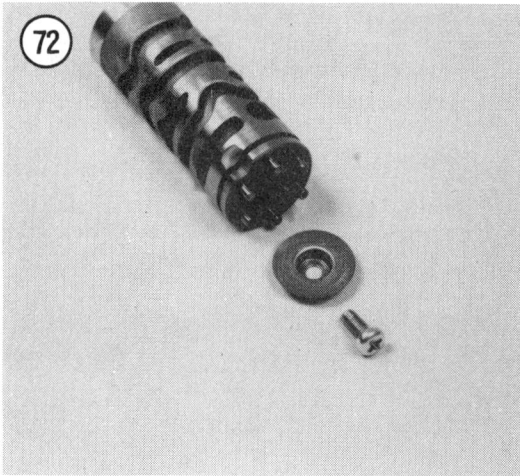

Table 1 TRANSMISSION GEAR RATIOS

KX60	
1st	2.846 (37:13)
2nd	2.125 (34:16)
3rd	1.722 (31:18)
4th	1.428 (30:21)
5th	1.217 (28:23)
6th	1.083 (26:24)
Final reduction ratio	3.384 (44:13)
Overall drive ratio	12.833 (top)

(continued)

Table 1 TRANSMISSION GEAR RATIOS (continued)

KX80	
1983-1985	
1st	2.846 (37:13)
2nd	2.125 (34:16)
3rd	1.722 (31:18)
4th	1.428 (30:21)
5th	1.217 (28:23)
6th	1.083 (26:24)
Final reduction ratio	
1983	3.500 (49:14)
1984-1985	3.571 (50:14)
Overall drive ratio	
1983	11.691 (top)
1984-1985	11.929 (top)
1986	
1st	2.538 (33:13)
2nd	1.875 (30:16)
3rd	1.500 (27:18)
4th	1.250 (25:20)
5th	1.090 (24:22)
6th	0.956 (22:23)
Final reduction ratio	3.769 (49:13)
Overall drive ratio	12.258 (top)
1987-on	
1st	2.538 (33:13)
2nd	1.875 (30:16)
3rd	1.500 (27:18)
4th	1.250 (25:20)
5th	1.090 (24:22)
6th	0.956 (22:23)
Final reduction ratio	
G, H	3.769 (49:13)
J, K	4.153 (54:13)
L, M	3.692 (48:13)
N, P	4.076 (53:13)
Overall drive ratio	
G, H	12.258 (top)
J, K	13.509 (top)
L, M	12.008 (top)
N, P	13.258 (top)

7

Table 2 SHIFT FORK/SHIFT DRUM SERVICE SPECIFICATIONS

	New mm (in.)	Service Limit mm (in.)
Shift fork finger thickness	3.90-4.00 (0.154-0.157)	3.80 (0.150)
Gear shift fork groove width	4.05-4.15 (0.159-0.163)	4.25 (0.167)
Shift fork guide pin diameter	5.90-6.00 (0.232-0.236)	5.85 (0.230)
Shift drum groove width	6.05-6.20 (0.238-0.244)	6.25 (0.246)

CHAPTER EIGHT

FUEL AND EXHAUST SYSTEMS

The fuel system consists of the fuel tank, shutoff valve, and a single Mikuni (1983-1987) or Keihin (1988-on) carburetor and air cleaner. There are slight differences among the various models and they are noted in the various procedures.

The exhaust system consists of an exhaust pipe assembly and a silencer.

This chapter includes service procedures for all parts of the fuel system and exhaust system.

Carburetor specifications are listed in **Tables 1-3** at the end of the chapter.

AIR FILTER

The air filter must be cleaned frequently. Refer to Chapter Three for specific procedures and service intervals.

CARBURETOR OPERATION

For proper operation, a gasoline engine must be supplied with fuel and air mixed in proper proportions by weight. A mixture in which there is an excess of fuel is said to be rich. A lean mixture is one which contains insufficient fuel. A properly adjusted carburetor supplies the proper mixture to the engine under all operating conditions.

The carburetors installed on all **KX** models consist of several major systems. A float and float valve mechanism maintain a constant fuel level in the float bowl. The pilot system supplies fuel at low speeds. The main fuel system supplies fuel at medium and high speeds. Finally a starter (choke) system supplies a rich mixture needed to start a cold engine.

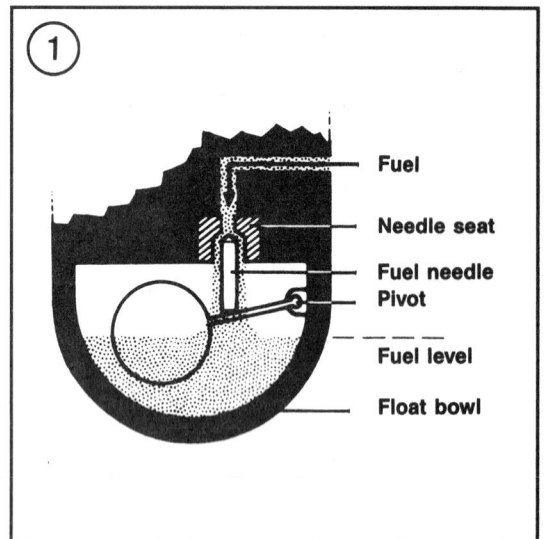

Float Mechanism

To assure a steady supply of fuel, the carburetor is equipped with a float valve through which fuel flows by gravity from the gas tank into the float bowl (**Figure 1**). Inside the bowl is a combined float assembly that moves up and down with the fuel level. Resting on the float arm is a float needle, which rides inside the float valve. The float valve regulates fuel flow into the float bowl. The float needle and float valve contact surfaces which are accurately machined to ensure correct fuel flow calibration. As the float rises, the float needle rises inside the float valve and blocks it, so that when the fuel has reached the required level in the float bowl, no more fuel can enter.

Pilot and Main Fuel Systems

The carburetor's purpose is to supply and atomize fuel and mix it in correct proportions with air that is drawn in through the air intake. At primary throttle openings (from idle to 1/8 throttle) a small amount of fuel is siphoned through the pilot jet by suction from the incoming air (**Figure 2**).

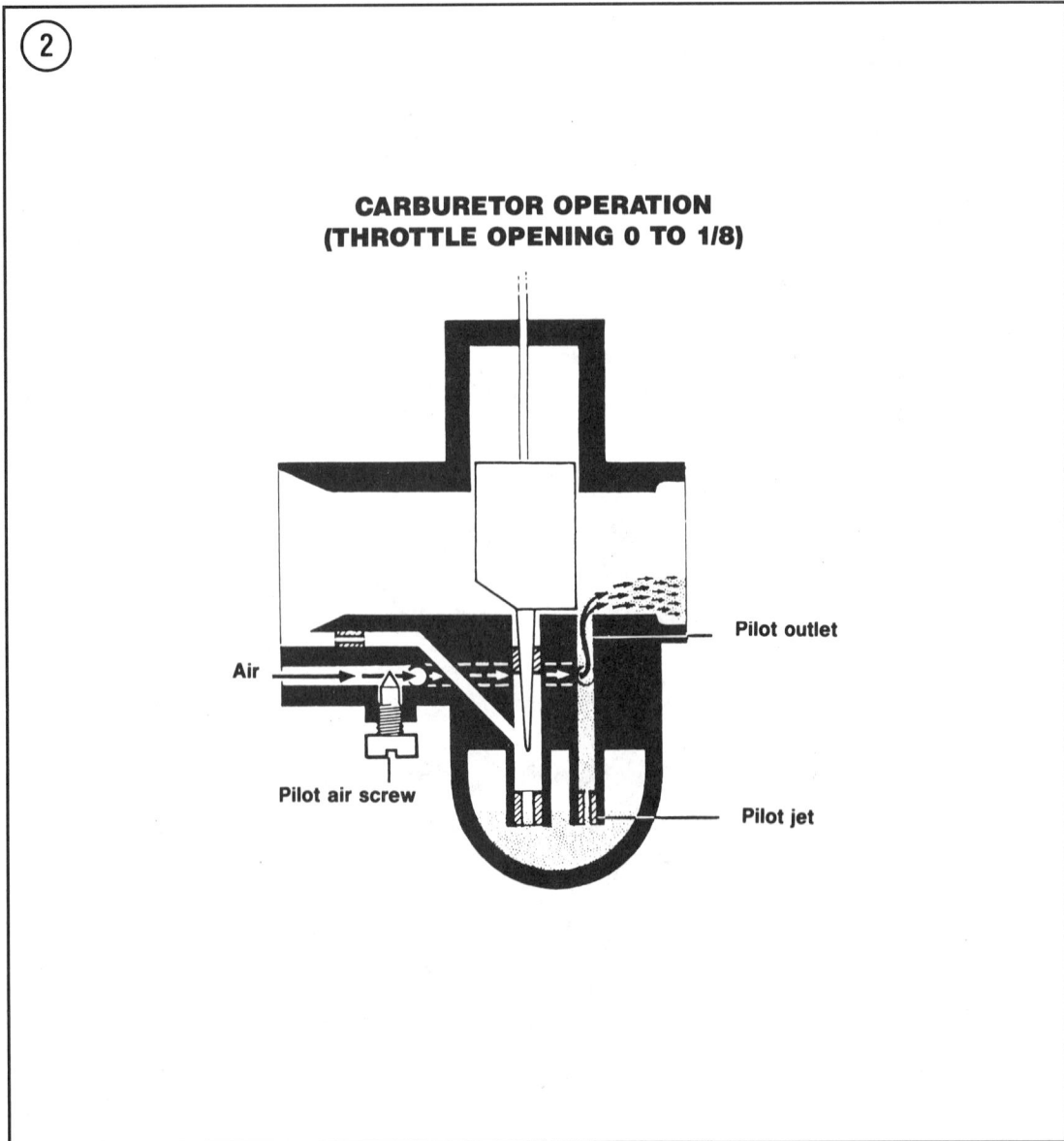

(2)

**CARBURETOR OPERATION
(THROTTLE OPENING 0 TO 1/8)**

Pilot outlet

Air

Pilot air screw

Pilot jet

8

As the throttle is opened further, the air stream begins to siphon fuel through the main jet and needle jet. The tapered needle increases the effective flow capacity of the needle jet as it rises with the throttle slide, in that it occupies decreasingly less of the area of the needle jet (**Figure 3**). In addition, the amount of cutaway in the leading edge of the throttle slide aids in controlling the fuel/air mixture during partial throttle openings.

At full throttle, the carburetor venturi is fully open and the needle is lifted far enough to permit the main jet to flow at full capacity. See **Figure 4** and **Figure 5**.

Starting System (Choke)

The starting system consists of a starter plunger, mixing tube, starter jet and air passage. When the plunger valve is lifted, it opens the air passage permitting air to flow through the passage where it siphons fuel through the starter jet, into the mixing tube and then into the air passage where it is mixed (fuel-rich) and discharged into the throttle bore.

CARBURETOR SERVICE
(1983-1987)

Major carburetor service (removal and cleaning) should be performed after every race on competition bikes. On a bike that is used for fun on weekends, it should be performed whenever the engine is decarbonized or when poor engine performance, hesitation, and little or no response to mixture adjustment is observed. The service interval time will become natural to you after owning and running the bike for a period of time.

Carburetor Identification

Refer to **Table 1** (KX60) or **Table 2** (1983-1987 KX80) at the end of this chapter for carburetor specifications.

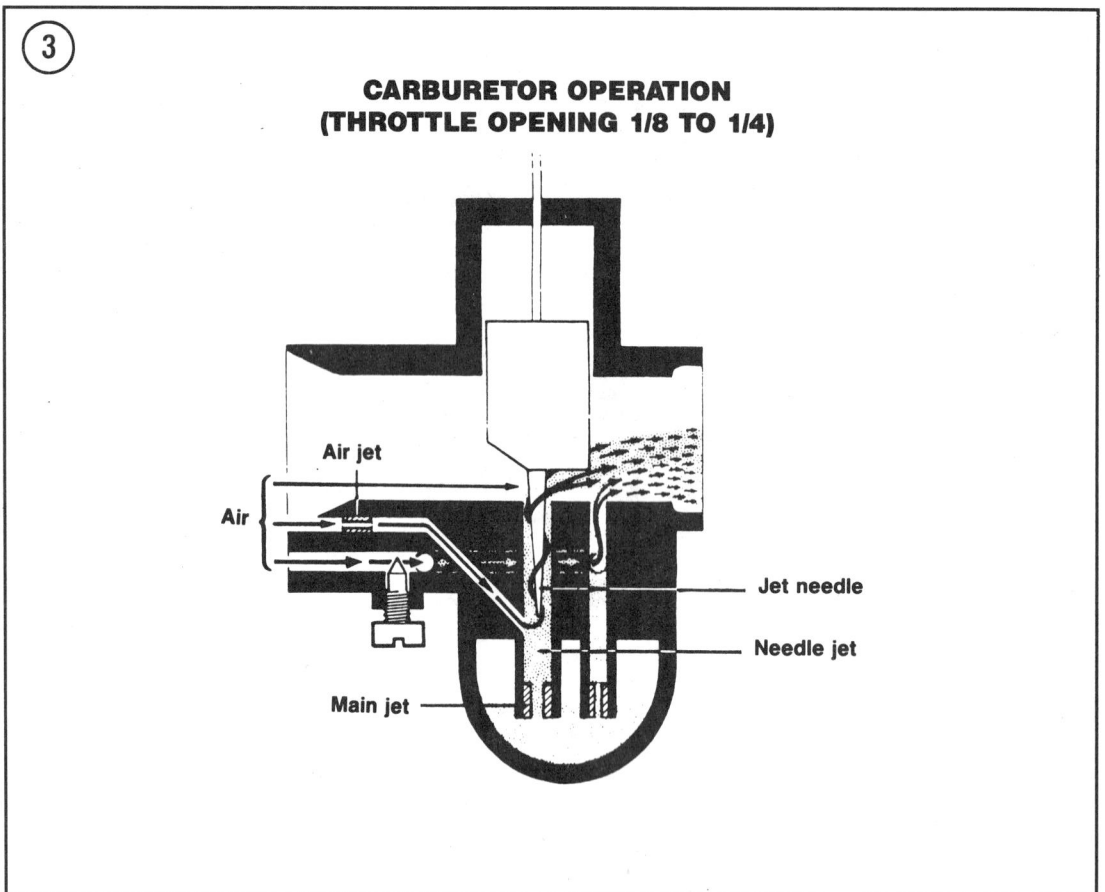

(3)

**CARBURETOR OPERATION
(THROTTLE OPENING 1/8 TO 1/4)**

Air jet

Air

Jet needle

Needle jet

Main jet

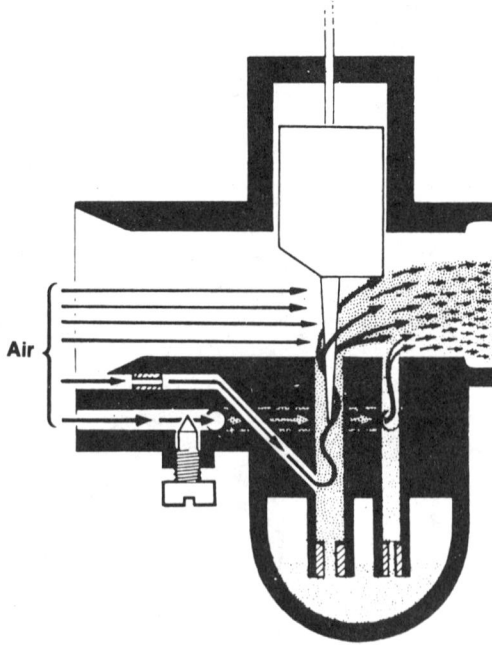

4

**CARBURETOR OPERATION
(THROTTLE OPENING 1/4 TO 3/4)**

Air

8

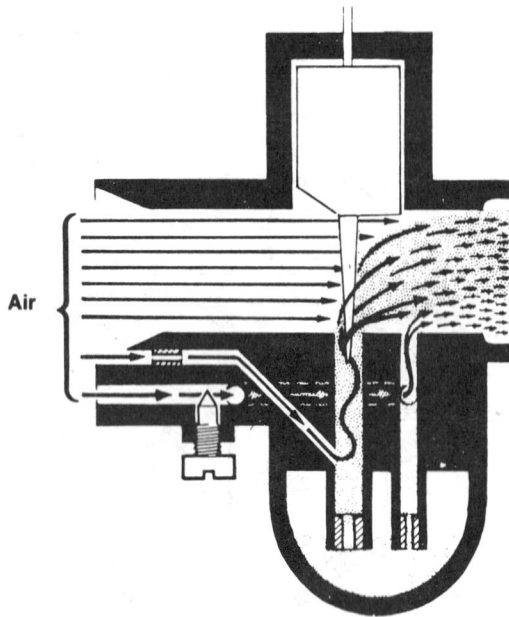

5

**CARBURETOR OPERATION
(THROTTLE OPENING 3/4 TO FULL)**

Air

Removal/Installation

1. Support the bike on a bike stand.
2. Turn the fuel shutoff valve to the OFF position and disconnect the fuel line at the carburetor.
3. If necessary, remove the fuel tank as described in this chapter.

> *NOTE*
> *Before removing the top cap, thoroughly clean the area around it so no dirt will fall into the carburetor.*

4. Unscrew the carburetor top cap (A, **Figure 6**) and pull the throttle valve assembly up and out of the carburetor (**Figure 7**).

> *NOTE*
> *If the top cover and slide assembly are not going to be removed for cleaning, wrap them in a clean shop cloth or place them in a resealable plastic bag to help keep them clean.*

5. Loosen the screws on both clamps (B, **Figure 6**) on the rubber boots. Slide the clamps away from the carburetor.
6. Make sure all overflow and drain tubes are free.
7. Carefully work the carburetor free from the rubber boots and remove it.
8. Take the carburetor to a workbench for disassembly and cleaning.
9. Install by reversing these removal steps. Install the throttle valve so that the groove in the valve aligns with the pin in the carburetor bore. Operate the throttle grip and check valve operation. It should move smoothly with no signs of sticking or dragging.

> *WARNING*
> *Do not ride the bike if the throttle valve does not operate correctly. Remove the carburetor cap and pull the valve back out. Check parts before starting the bike.*

Disassembly/Assembly

Refer to the exploded drawing for your model and year:
  a. **Figure 8** (1983 KX60).
  b. **Figure 9** (1984-on KX60).
  c. **Figure 10** (1983-1985 KX80).
  d. **Figure 11** (1986-1987 KX80).

The carburetors are basically the same even though minor variations exist between different models. Where differences occur, they are identified.

1. Remove the fuel line and all drain and overflow tubes.

2A. *All models except 1986-1987 KX80:* Unscrew the nut and remove the choke assembly (**Figure 12**).

2B. *1986-1987 KX80:* Referring to **Figure 11**, remove the screw and washer securing the choke lever. Then remove the choke assembly. Don't loose the small spring and ball located behind the choke lever.

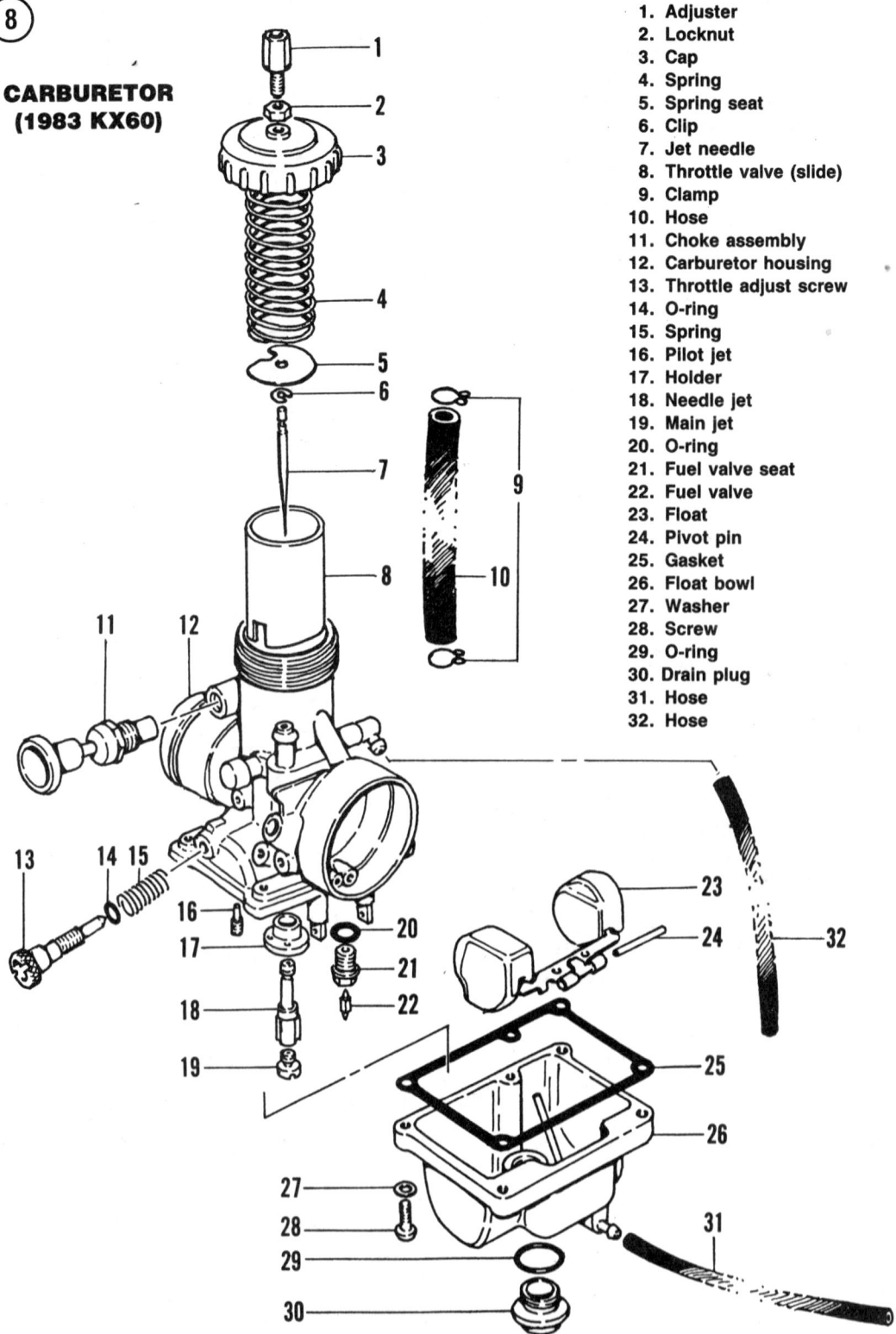

CARBURETOR (1983 KX60)

1. Adjuster
2. Locknut
3. Cap
4. Spring
5. Spring seat
6. Clip
7. Jet needle
8. Throttle valve (slide)
9. Clamp
10. Hose
11. Choke assembly
12. Carburetor housing
13. Throttle adjust screw
14. O-ring
15. Spring
16. Pilot jet
17. Holder
18. Needle jet
19. Main jet
20. O-ring
21. Fuel valve seat
22. Fuel valve
23. Float
24. Pivot pin
25. Gasket
26. Float bowl
27. Washer
28. Screw
29. O-ring
30. Drain plug
31. Hose
32. Hose

8

⑨

**CARBURETOR
(1984-ON KX60)**

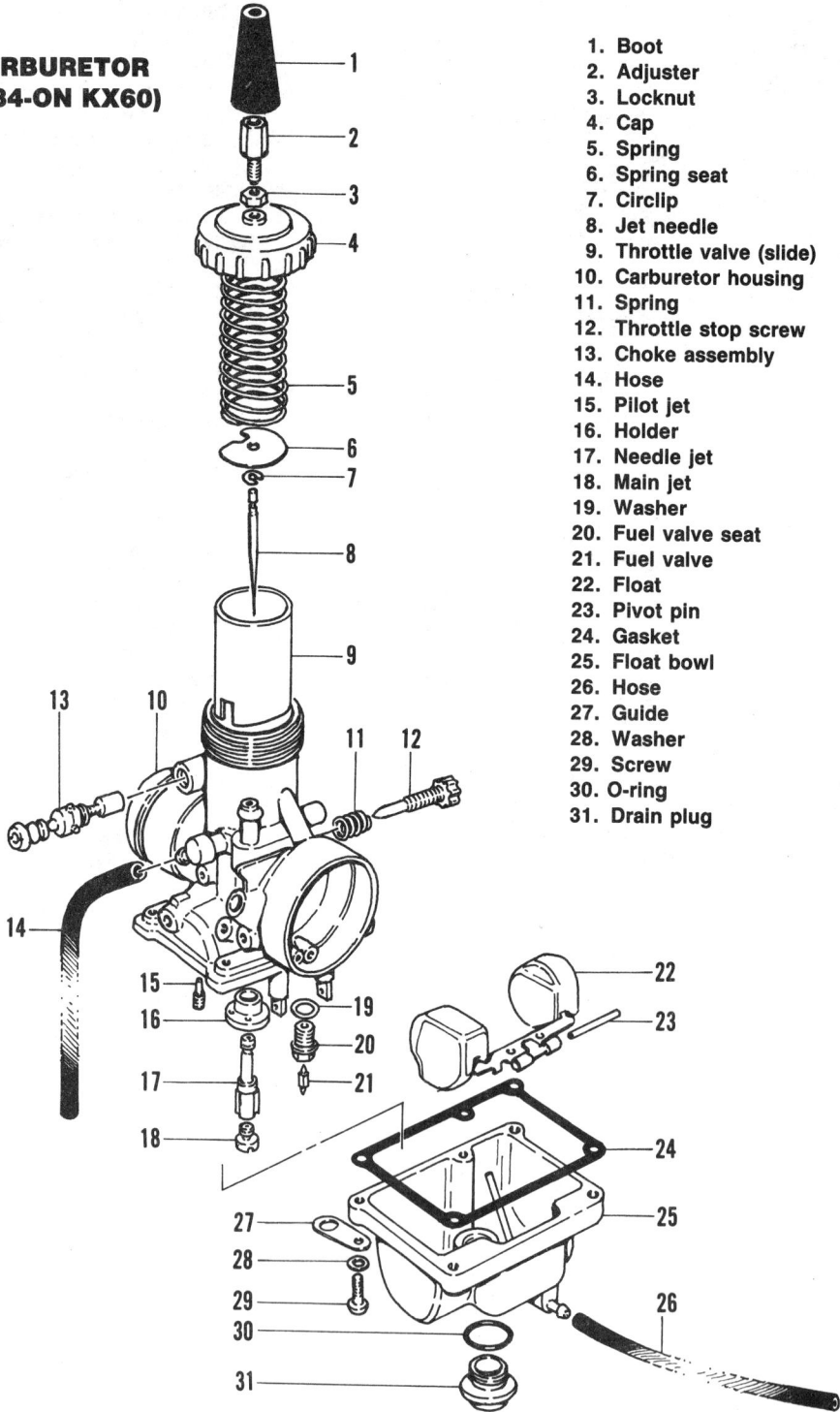

1
2
3
4
5
6
7
8
9
13 10
11 12
14
15
16
19
20
17
21
18

1. Boot
2. Adjuster
3. Locknut
4. Cap
5. Spring
6. Spring seat
7. Circlip
8. Jet needle
9. Throttle valve (slide)
10. Carburetor housing
11. Spring
12. Throttle stop screw
13. Choke assembly
14. Hose
15. Pilot jet
16. Holder
17. Needle jet
18. Main jet
19. Washer
20. Fuel valve seat
21. Fuel valve
22. Float
23. Pivot pin
24. Gasket
25. Float bowl
26. Hose
27. Guide
28. Washer
29. Screw
30. O-ring
31. Drain plug

22
23
24
25
27
28
29
30
31
26

(10)

CARBURETOR
(1983-1985 KX80)

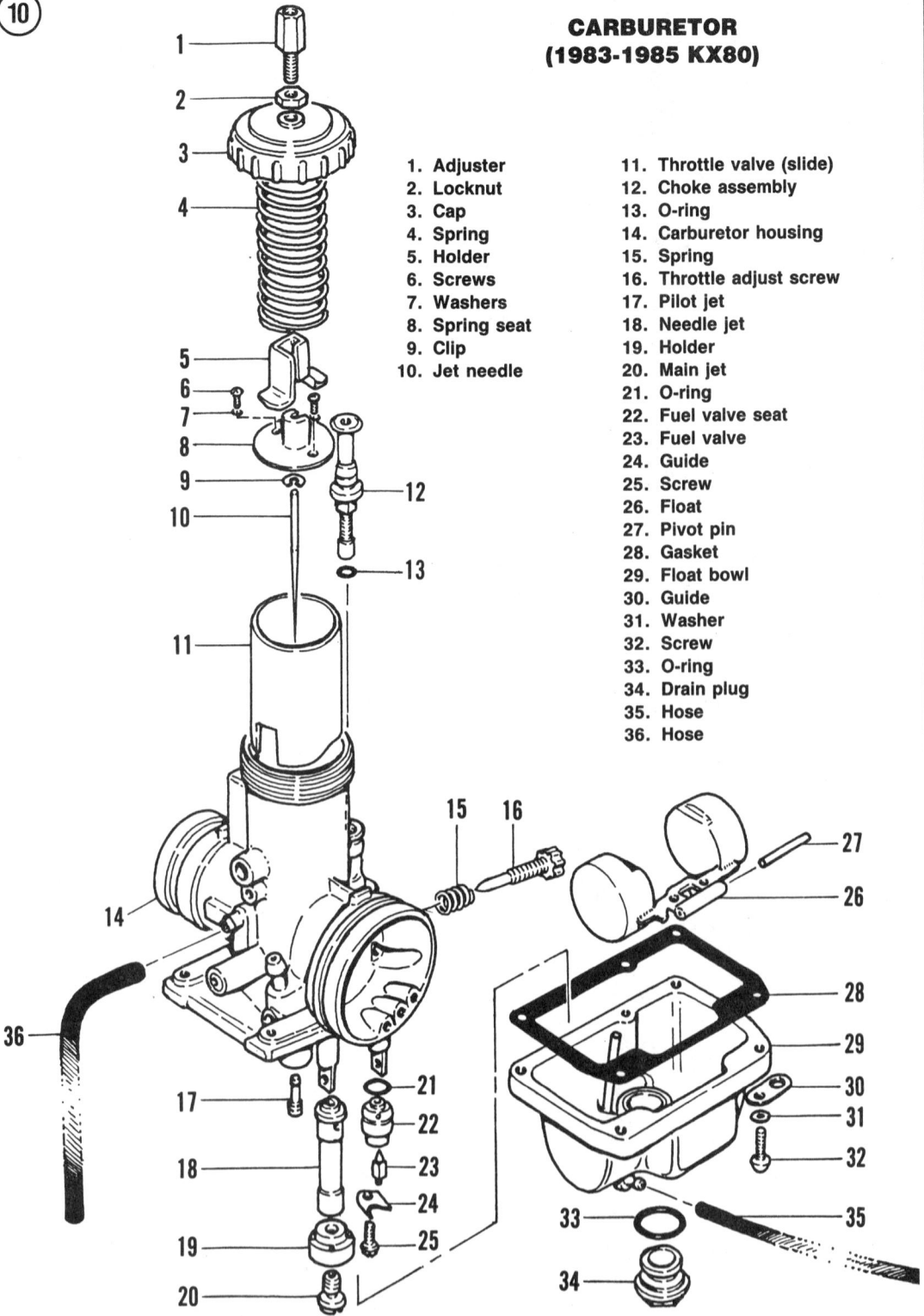

1. Adjuster
2. Locknut
3. Cap
4. Spring
5. Holder
6. Screws
7. Washers
8. Spring seat
9. Clip
10. Jet needle
11. Throttle valve (slide)
12. Choke assembly
13. O-ring
14. Carburetor housing
15. Spring
16. Throttle adjust screw
17. Pilot jet
18. Needle jet
19. Holder
20. Main jet
21. O-ring
22. Fuel valve seat
23. Fuel valve
24. Guide
25. Screw
26. Float
27. Pivot pin
28. Gasket
29. Float bowl
30. Guide
31. Washer
32. Screw
33. O-ring
34. Drain plug
35. Hose
36. Hose

8

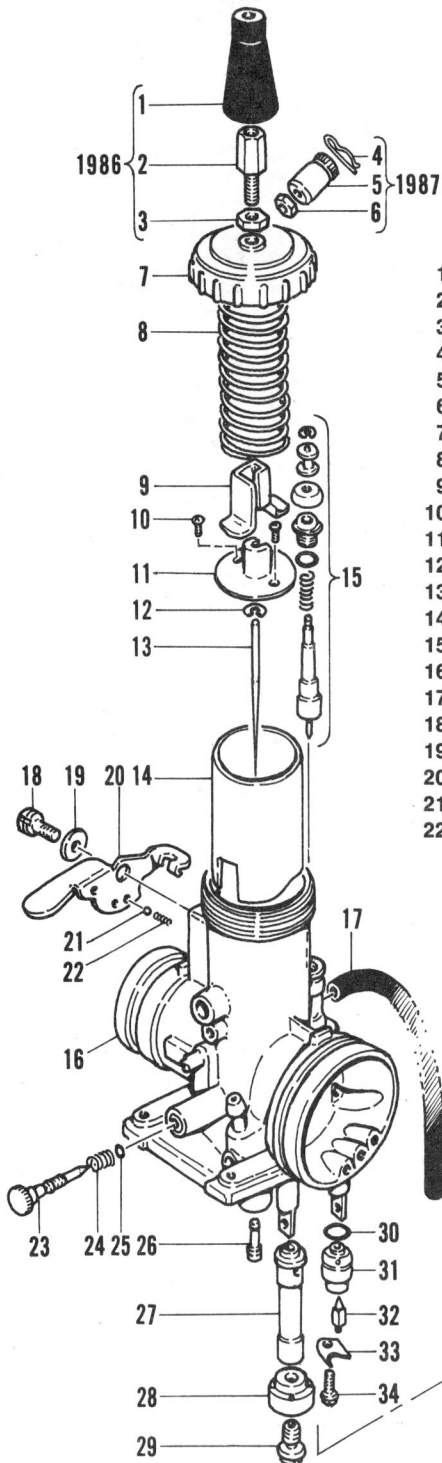

**CARBURETOR
(1986-1987 KX80)**

1. Cover (1986)
2. Adjuster (1986)
3. Locknut (1986)
4. Clip (1987)
5. Adjuster (1987)
6. Locknut (1987)
7. Cap
8. Spring
9. Holder
10. Screw
11. Spring seat
12. Clip
13. Jet needle
14. Throttle valve (slide)
15. Choke assembly
16. Carburetor housing
17. Hose
18. Screw
19. Collar
20. Choke lever
21. Ball
22. Spring
23. Throttle adjust screw
24. Spring
25. O-ring
26. Pilot jet
27. Needle jet
28. Holder
29. Main jet
30. O-ring
31. Fuel valve seat
32. Fuel valve
33. Holder
34. Screw
35. Pivot pin
36. Float
37. Gasket
38. Float bowl
39. Guide
40. Washer
41. Screw
42. Hose
43. O-ring
44. Drain plug

3. Remove the screws securing the float bowl (**Figure 13**) and remove it.

4. See **Figure 14**. Remove the float pin (A) and remove the float (B).

5. Remove the fuel valve (**Figure 15**).

6. Remove the main jet (**Figure 16**).

7A. *KX60:* Remove the needle jet and holder (**Figure 17**).

7B. *KX80:* Remove the holder from the top of the needle jet. Then remove the needle jet through the top of the carburetor (**Figure 18**).

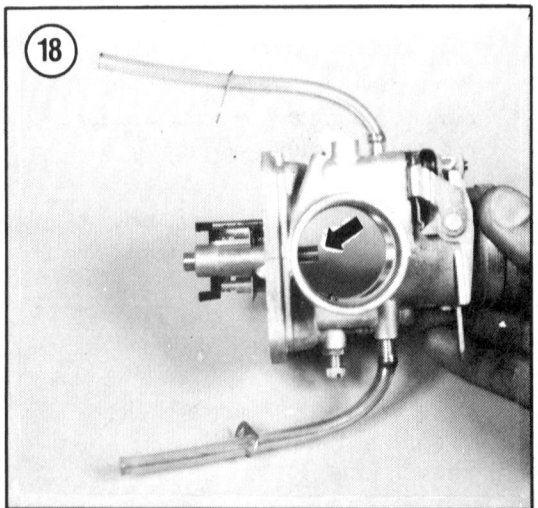

8

8. Remove the pilot jet (**Figure 19**).

9A. *KX60:* Remove the fuel valve seat and gasket (**Figure 20**).

9B. *KX80:* Remove the screw securing the fuel valve holder clamp. Remove the clamp, fuel valve and gasket.

10. Remove the float bowl gasket from the carburetor housing before cleaning. Replace the gasket if damaged.

11. Clean and inspect the carburetor components as described in this chapter.

12. After all parts have been cleaned and dried, reverse these steps to assemble the carburetor. Note the following.

13. Check the float height and adjust if necessary. Refer to *Float Height Adjustment* in this chapter.

14A. *KX60:* Slip the jet needle over the holder before installation (**Figure 21**).

14B. *KX80:* When installing the jet needle (**Figure 18**), align the slot in the side of the jet needle with the pin in the carburetor bore.

15. After the carburetor has been assembled, adjust the idle speed. Refer to *Idle Speed Adjustment* in Chapter Three.

Cleaning/Inspection

1. Carburetor components should be cleaned in hot soapy water. Then rinse with clean water and dry thoroughly.

2. Blow out the jets with compressed air. *Do not use a piece of wire to clean them as minor gouges in the jet can alter flow rate and upset the fuel/air mixture.* If compressed air is not available, use a piece of straw from a broom to clean the jets.

> *NOTE*
> *Photography dealers sell small cans of compressed air that can be used for cleaning jets and carburetor air passages.*

3. Be sure to clean out the float bowl overflow tube from both ends.

4. Inspect the tip of the float valve (**Figure 22**) for wear or damage. Replace the valve and seat as a set.

5. O-ring seals tend to become hardened after prolonged use and heat and therefore lose their ability to seal properly. Inspect all O-rings and replace if necessary.

6. Check the floats for leaks. Fill the float bowl with water and try to push the floats down. There should be no signs of bubbles. Replace the floats if they leak.

7. Check the idle stop screw for tip wear or thread damage. Replace the screw and/or spring as required.

8. Check all of the choke components for excessive wear or damage.

CARBURETOR SERVICE (1988-ON)

Major carburetor service (removal and cleaning) should be performed after every race on competition bikes. On a bike that is used for fun

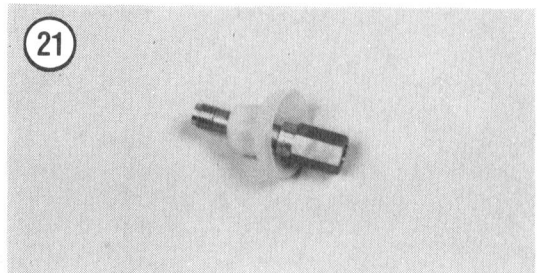

on weekends, it should be performed whenever the engine is decarbonized or when poor engine performance, hesitation, and little or no response to mixture adjustment is observed. The service interval time will become natural to you after owning and running the bike for a period of time.

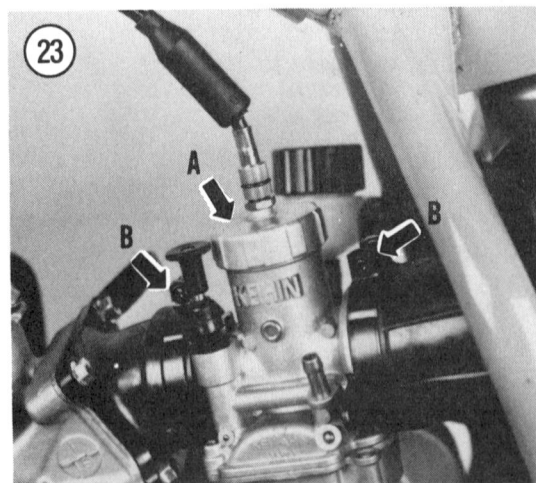

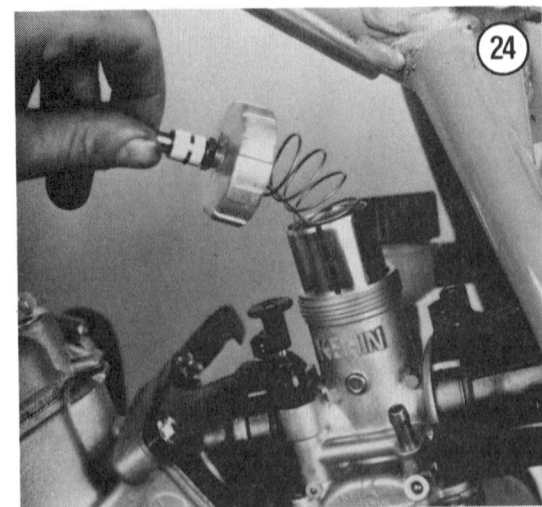

Carburetor Identification

Refer to **Table 3** at the end of this chapter for carburetor specifications.

Removal/Installation

1. Support the bike on a bike stand.
2. Turn the fuel shutoff valve to the OFF position and remove the fuel line to the carburetor.
3. If necessary, remove the fuel tank as described in this chapter.

> *NOTE*
> *Before removing the top cap, thoroughly clean the area around it so no dirt will fall into the carburetor.*

4. Unscrew the carburetor top cap (A, **Figure 23**) and pull the throttle valve assembly up and out of the carburetor (**Figure 24**).

> *NOTE*
> *If the top cover and throttle valve assembly are not going to be removed for cleaning, wrap them in a clean shop cloth or place them in a plastic bag to help keep them clean.*

5. Loosen the screws on both clamps on the rubber boots (B, **Figure 23**). Slide the clamps away from the carburetor.
6. Make sure all overflow and drain tubes are free.
7. Carefully work the carburetor free from the rubber boots and remove it.
8. Take the carburetor to a workbench for disassembly and cleaning.
9. Install by reversing these removal steps. Install the throttle valve so that the groove in the valve (**Figure 24**) aligns with the pin in the carburetor bore. Operate the throttle grip and check throttle valve operation. It should move smoothly with no signs of sticking or dragging.

> *WARNING*
> *Do not ride the bike if the throttle valve does not operate correctly. Remove the carburetor cap and pull the throttle valve back out. Check parts before starting the bike.*

8

**CARBURETOR
(1988-ON KX80)**

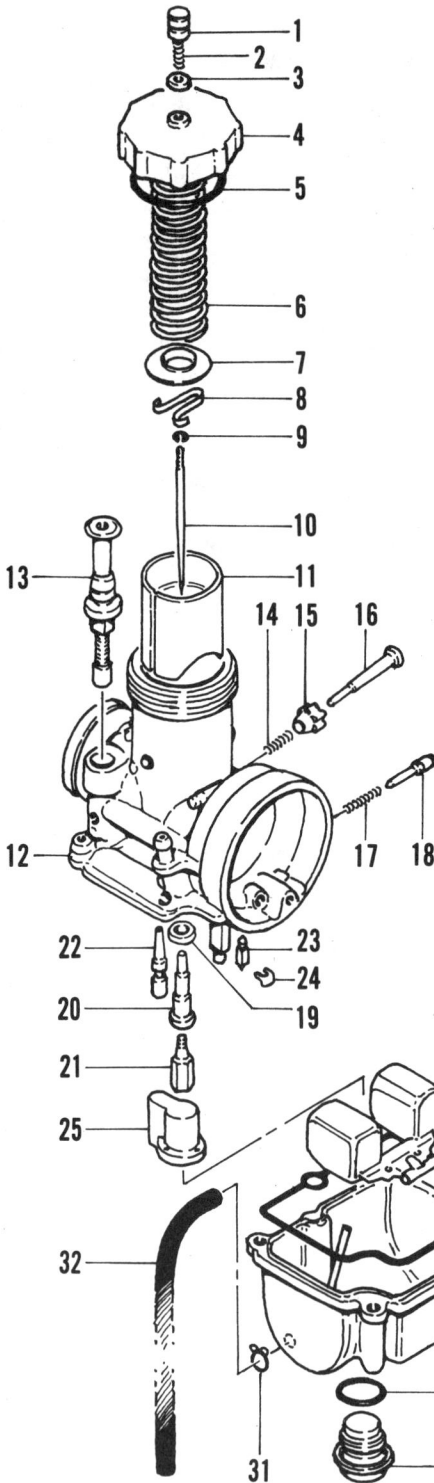

25

1. Clip
2. Adjuster
3. Locknut
4. Cap
5. O-ring
6. Spring
7. Spring seat
8. Clip
9. Circlip
10. Jet needle
11. Throttle valve (slide)
12. Carburetor housing
13. Choke assembly
14. Spring
15. Knob
16. Throttle stop screw
17. Spring
18. Pilot screw
19. Nut
20. Needle jet
21. Main jet
22. Pilot jet
23. Fuel valve*
24. Clip
25. Holder
26. Float
27. Pivot pin
28. O-ring gasket
29. Float bowl
30. Screw
31. Clamp
32. Hose
33. O-ring
34. Drain plug

* The fuel valve seat is an integral part of the carburetor housing.

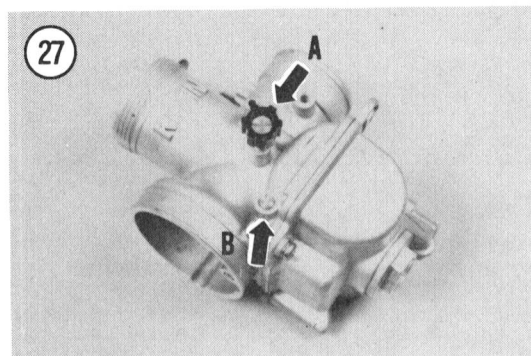

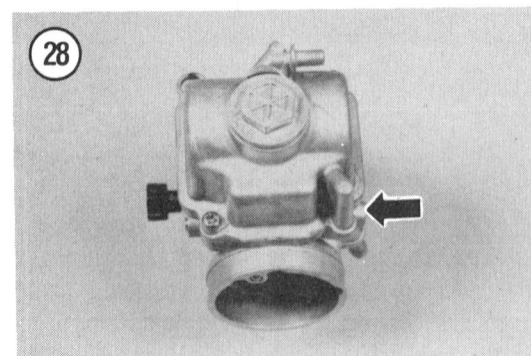

Disassembly/Reassembly

Refer to **Figure 25** for this procedure.

1. Remove the fuel line and all drain and overflow tubes.

2. Loosen the choke knob nut and remove the choke assembly (**Figure 26**).

3. Remove the idle adjust screw and spring (A, **Figure 27**).

NOTE
Before removing the pilot adjust screw in Step 4, turn the screw clockwise and count the number of turns required to seat the screw. Record this number for reassembly.

4. Remove the pilot adjust screw and spring (B, **Figure 27**).

5. Remove the screws securing the float bowl and remove it (**Figure 28**).

6. Remove the holder (**Figure 29**).

7. Remove the float pin (A, **Figure 30**) and lift the float assembly (B, **Figure 30**) out of the housing. The fuel valve (**Figure 31**) will come out with the float.

8

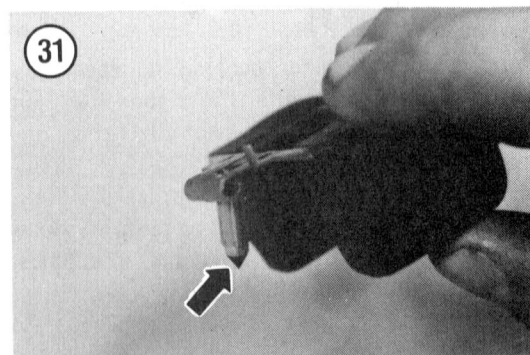

8. Remove the pilot jet (**Figure 32**).

9. Remove the main jet (**Figure 33**).

10. Remove the needle jet (**Figure 34**).

11. Clean and inspect the carburetor components as described in this chapter.

12. After all parts have been cleaned and dried, reverse these steps to assemble the carburetor. Note the following.

13. Make sure the fuel valve is attached to the float arm (**Figure 31**) before installing the float assembly.

14. Check the float height and adjust if necessary. Refer to *Float Height Adjustment* in this chapter.

15. Make sure the float bowl O-ring fits in the float bowl snugly (**Figure 35**).

16. After the carburetor has been assembled, adjust the idle speed and the pilot air screw. Refer to Chapter Three.

Cleaning/Inspection

1. Carburetor components should be cleaned in hot soapy water. Then rinse with clean water and dry thoroughly.

2. Blow out the jets with compressed air. *Do not use a piece of wire to clean them as minor gouges in the jet can alter flow rate and upset the fuel/air mixture. If compressed air is not available, use a piece of straw from a broom to clean the jets.*

> *NOTE*
> *Photography dealers sell small cans of compressed air that can be used for cleaning jets and carburetor air passages.*

3. Be sure to clean out the float bowl overflow tube from both ends.

4. Inspect the tip of the float valve (**Figure 22**) for wear or damage. Replace the valve and seat as a set.

5. O-ring seals tend to become hardened after prolonged use and heat and therefore lose their ability to seal properly. Inspect all O-rings and replace if necessary.

6. Check the floats (**Figure 36**) for leaks. Fill the float bowl with water and try to push the floats down. There should be no signs of bubbles. Replace the floats if they leak.

7. Check the choke valve assembly. Check the plastic parts for wear or damage. Check the

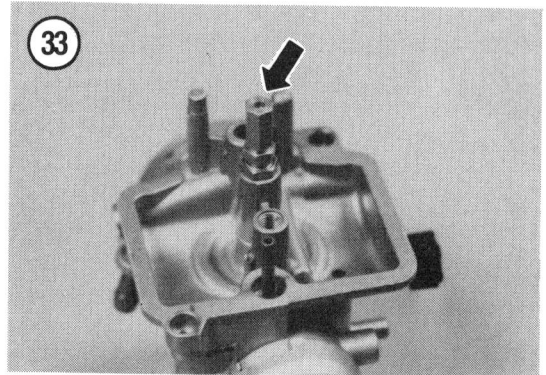

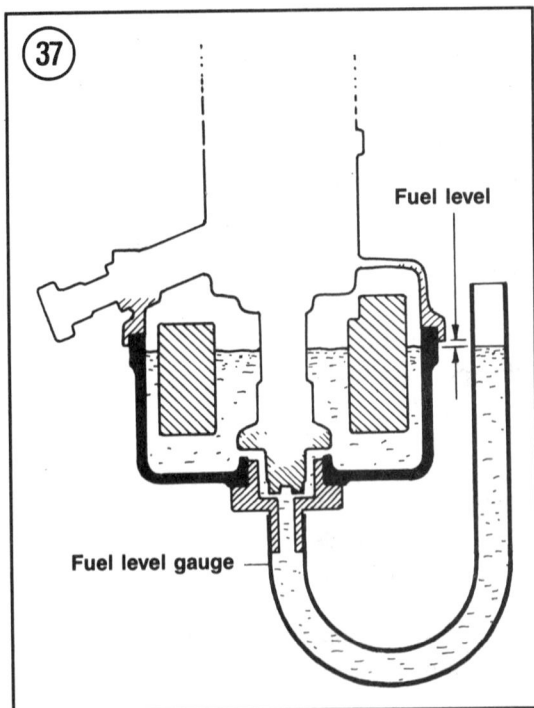

Fuel level

Fuel level gauge

plunger assembly for spring damage or plunger scoring. The plunger should move smoothly. Replace the choke valve is necessary.

8. Check the pilot screw and the idle stop screw for tip wear or thread damage. Replace the screw and/or spring as required.

CARBURETOR ADJUSTMENT

Fuel Level Adjustment

The fuel level in the carburetor float bowl is critical to proper performance. The fuel flow rate from the bowl up to the carburetor bore depends not only on the vacuum in the throttle bore and the size of the jets, but also upon the fuel level. Kawasaki gives a specification of actual *fuel level*, measured from the top edge of the float bowl with the carburetor held level (**Figure 37**).

The measurement is more useful than a simple float height measurement because actual fuel level can vary from bike to bike, even when their floats are set at the same height. However, fuel level inspection requires a special fitting with a numbered hose that screws into the bottom of the carburetor. You can get the proper fitting at your Kawasaki dealer. **Figure 37** shows the special tool in use.

The fuel level is adjusted by bending the float arm tang.

> *WARNING*
> *Some fuel may spill from the carburetor when performing this procedure. Because gasoline is an extremely flammable and explosive petroleum, perform this procedure away from all open flames (including pilot lights) and sparks. Do not smoke or allow someone who is smoking in the work area. Always work in a well ventilated area. Wipe up any spills immediately.*

1. Remove the fuel tank and carburetor as described in this chapter.
2. Set the fuel tank on wood blocks so that it will be higher than the carburetor. Then reconnect the fuel hose so that the carburetor is attached to the fuel tank. Make sure the fuel valve is turned OFF.
3. Remove the drain plug (**Figure 38**) from the bottom of the float bowl and install the special tool onto the carburetor (**Figure 37**).

4. Hold the numbered hose against the carburetor body so that the "0" mark on the hose is higher than the top of the float bowl. With the carburetor level to the ground, turn the fuel valve ON. Continue to hold the tube until the fuel in the hose stabilizes. Then lower the hose until the "0" mark on the hose aligns with the bottom edge of the carburetor body (**Figure 37**). Read the fuel level beside the number on the hose. Refer to **Tables 1-3** for your bike's fuel level specification.

NOTE
Take your readings just after the fuel level has risen to its maximum in the tube. If you raise the tube (and the fuel drops in the tube) you'll probably get a faulty level reading. Try it again, forcing the fuel level to rise against surface tension within the tube.

5. If the fuel level is incorrect, adjust the float/arm height setting as described in Step 6 for your model. Then recheck the fuel level. Readjust if necessary.

NOTE
Decreasing the float height raises the fuel level; increasing the float height lowers it.

6. Adjust the float by performing the following:
   a. Remove the float bowl and float as described in this chapter.
   b. Adjust the float by bending the tang (**Figure 39**) with a screwdriver.
7. Reinstall the float and float bowl. Recheck the adjustment.

NOTE
If the fuel level cannot be adjusted properly, the fuel valve or float may be damaged.

Float Height Adjustment

Kawasaki gives a float height specification for some KX60 and KX80 models. See **Tables 1-3** for available specifications. While the float height adjustment is not as accurate as the fuel level adjustment previously described, knowing how to check the float height may prove useful should it become necessary to adjust, troubleshoot or service your carburetor while at the track or when along side a trail.

1. Remove the carburetor as described in this chapter.
2. Remove the screws holding the float bowl to the carburetor. Remove the float bowl (**Figure 28**) and gasket.
3. Holding the carburetor upside down, measure the distance from the float bowl mating surface (without gasket) to the top of the float (**Figure 40**). Compare your float height with the specifications in **Tables 1-3**.
4. If necessary, adjust the float by performing the following:
   a. Remove the float as described in this chapter.
   b. Adjust the float by bending the tang (**Figure 39**) with a screwdriver.
5. Reinstall the float and recheck the float height. Recheck the adjustment.

**Pilot Screw and
Idle Speed Adjustment**

Refer to Chapter Three.

CARBURETOR REJETTING

Changes in altitude, temperature, humidity and track conditions can noticeably affect engine performance. To obtain maximum performance from the KX, jetting changes may be necessary. Before attempting to rejet the engine, be sure the engine is in good running condition.

NOTE
If the bike is now running poorly under the same weather, altitude and track

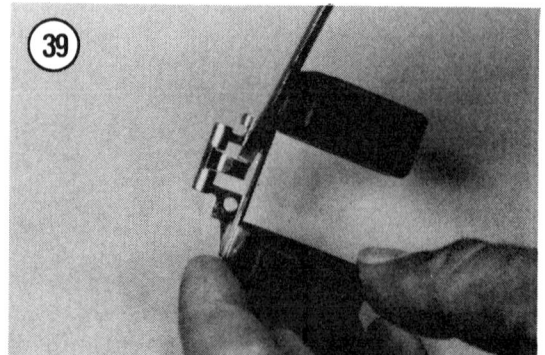

conditions where it once ran properly, it is unlikely the carburetor jetting is at fault. Attempting to tune the engine by rejetting the carburetor would only complicate matters.

NOTE
Changes in port shape and smoothness, expansion chamber, carburetor, etc., will also require jetting changes because these factors alter the engine's ability to breathe. When installing aftermarket equipment or when the engine has been modified, equipment manufacturers often include a tech sheet listing suitable jetting changes to correspond to their equipment or modification. This information should be taken into account along with altitude, temperature, humidity and track conditions previously mentioned.

If the bike shows evidence of one of the following conditions, rejetting may be necessary:
a. Poor acceleration (too rich).
b. Excessive exhaust smoke (too rich).
c. Fouling spark plugs (too rich).
d. Engine misfire at low speeds (too rich).
e. Erratic acceleration (too lean).
f. Ping or rattle (too lean).

NOTE
Engine ping can also be caused by old gasoline or by using a gasoline with a too low octane rating. See Chapter Three.

g. Running hot (too lean).

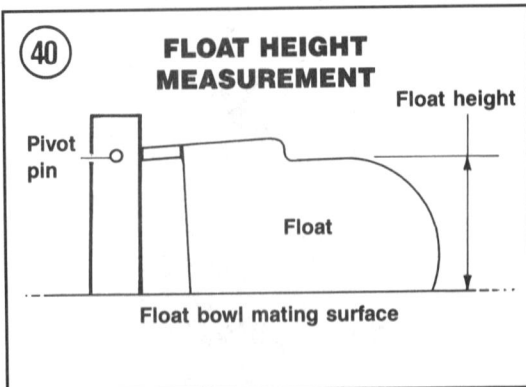

FLOAT HEIGHT MEASUREMENT

Float height

Pivot pin

Float

Float bowl mating surface

h. Engine revs okay then cuts out like it is running out of fuel (too lean).

Before checking the carburetor for one of the previously listed operating conditions, consider the following maintenance procedures:
a. The float level in the carburetor must be properly adjusted. If the float level is incorrect, it will be difficult to accurately jet the carburetor.
b. The air filter element should be clean. A dirty air filter element will cause the engine to run rich. Attempting to rejet the engine with a dirty air filter element will only complicate engine tuning.
c. The ignition timing should be correct.
d. The engine top end should be routinely decarbonized.

If the previously mentioned service items are correctly performed, carburetor rejetting may be required if any of the following conditions hold true:
a. A nonstandard air filter element is being used.
b. A nonstandard exhaust system is being used.
c. Any of the top end parts (piston, porting, compression ratio, etc.) have been modified.
d. The motorcycle is in use at considerably higher or lower altitudes, or in a markedly hotter or colder, or wetter or drier climate than in the past.
e. The motorcycle is being operated at considerably high speeds than before (faster track conditions) and changing to a colder spark plug does not solve the problem.
f. A previous owner changed the jetting or the needle positions in the motorcycle.
g. The motorcycle has never held a satisfactory engine tune.

The original jets, jet needle and throttle slide are listed in **Tables 1-3**.

Carburetor Variables

The following parts of the carburetor may be changed to vary the fuel mixture.

Pilot Jet

The pilot jet and air screw setting (if so equipped) control the fuel mixture from 0 to about 1/8 throttle. As the pilot numbers increase, the fuel mixture gets richer.

8

Throttle Valve

The throttle valve cutaway (**Figure 41**) affects airflow at small throttle openings. Cutaway sizes are numbered, and larger numbers result in a leaner mixture.

Jet Needle

The jet needle controls the mixture at medium speeds, from approximately 1/4 to 3/4 throttle. The jet needle has 2 operating ends. The top of the jet needle has 5 evenly spaced circlip grooves. The bottom half of the jet needle is tapered; this portion extends into the needle jet. While the jet needle is fixed into position by the circlip, fuel cannot flow through the space between the needle jet and jet needle until the throttle valve is raised approximately 1/4 open. As the throttle valve is raised, the jet needles tapered portion moves out of the needle jet. The grooves permit adjustment of the mixture ratio. If the clip is raised (thus dropping the needle deeper into the jet), the mixture will be leaner; lowering the clip (raising the needle) will result in a rich mixture.

If changing the jet needle clip position does not provide the desired results, it may be necessary to change to a smaller or larger needle jet.

Needle Jet

The needle jet works in conjunction with the jet needle.

On Mikuni carburetors, the letter and number stamped on the side of the needle jet indicates the jet's inside diameter. The mixture gets richer in large steps as the letter increases (from "N" through "R"), and in small steps within the letter range as the number increases (from "0" through "9"). Some needle jets have a tab extending 2 to 8 mm into the throttle bore, indicated by "/2" through "/8" following the letter and number mark. This is called the primary choke, and it causes the mixture to be leaner at low speeds and richer at high speeds.

On Keihin carburetors installed on models in this manual, the needle jet is an integral part of the carburetor housing.

Main Jet

The main jet controls the mixture from 3/4 to full throttle, and has some effect at lesser throttle openings. Each main jet is stamped with a number. Larger numbers provide a richer mixture, smaller numbers a leaner mixture. Most main jets can be reached by removing the float bowl drain plug (**Figure 42**).

Rejetting

> *CAUTION*
> *A too-lean mixture caused by running a too small main jet can cause serious engine damage in a matter of seconds. When determining proper jetting, always start out rich and progress toward a more lean mixture, one step at a time.*

The engine must be at full operating temperature when checking jetting. Attempting to rejet an

engine not up to temperature can result in a too-lean mixture when the engine reaches full operating temperature.

When rejetting a carburetor, basic procedures must be followed to assure consistent results. Note the following before carburetor jetting:

a. Referring to **Figure 43**, note the different jetting circuits and how they overlap with each other in regards to throttle position. Then determine the throttle position at which the adjustment should be made at. Too often, the main jet is changed when the adjustment calls for a jet needle adjustment.

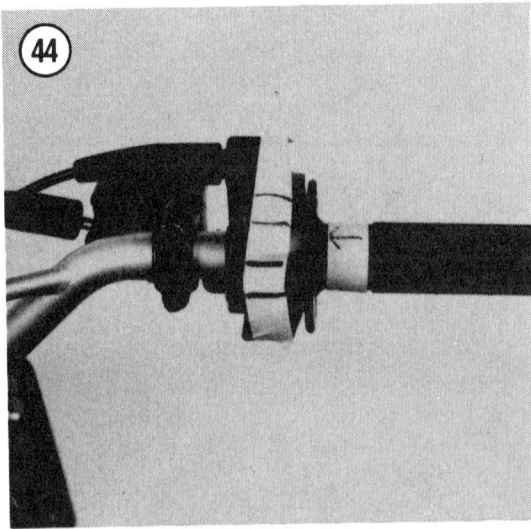

b. An accurate way to determine throttle position is by marking the throttle housing and throttle grip with tape and a marking pen (**Figure 44**). The mark on the throttle grip can be used as a pointer to align with the throttle positions marked on the throttle housing when riding the bike. Make 4 marks on the throttle housing to represent closed, 1/4, 3/4 and full open throttle positions.

CAUTION
To prevent expensive engine damage when removing the spark plug, refer to **CAUTION** *under* **Spark Plug Removal** *in Chapter Three.*

c. When checking the jetting, the bike should be run on a track or on a private road where it can be run at top speed for a distance of 1/2 to 1 mile. Keep accurate records as to weather, altitude and track conditions.

d. The jetting should be checked in the following order: Pilot air screw, main jet and jet needle.

1. Adjust the pilot air screw (if so equipped) and idle as described in Chapter Three.

2. Because the main jet controls the mixture from 3/4 to full throttle, the bike should be run a full throttle for a long distance. Stop the engine with the kill button while still under full throttle. Pull in on the clutch lever and coast to a stop. Remove and examine the spark plug after each test. The insulator should be a light tan color. If the insulator

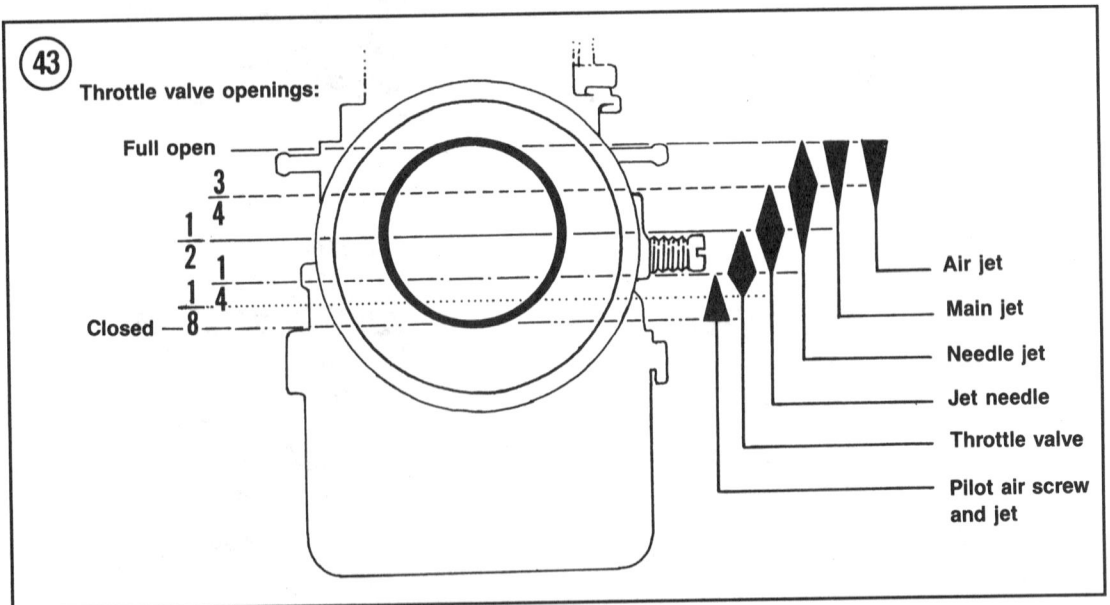

43 Throttle valve openings:

Full open
3/4
1/2
1/4
Closed — 1/8

Air jet
Main jet
Needle jet
Jet needle
Throttle valve
Pilot air screw and jet

⑤

SPARK PLUG CONDITIONS

NORMAL USE

OIL FOULED

CARBON FOULED

OVERHEATED

GAP BRIDGED

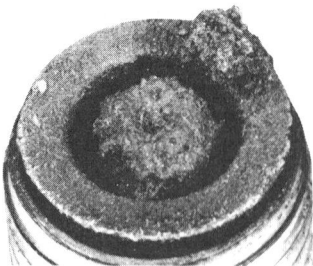

SUSTAINED PREIGNITION

WORN OUT

is soot black, the mixture is too rich; install a smaller main jet as described in this chapter. If the insulator is white, or blistered, the mixture is too lean; install a larger main jet. See **Figure 45**. Refer to *Main Jet Replacement* in this chapter.

3. Using the marked throttle housing, repeat the jetting check in Step 2 at different throttle positions. You may find that the full open throttle position is correct but that the 1/4 to 3/4 position is too rich or too lean. Refer to *Carburetor Variables*. If it is necessary to change the jet needle clip position, refer to *Jet Needle Adjustment* in this chapter.

Main Jet Replacement

Refer to **Tables 1-3** at the end of this chapter, for standard main jet sizes.

WARNING
If you are taking spark plug readings, the engine will be HOT! Use caution as the fuel in the float bowl will spill out when the main jet cover is removed from the bottom of the float bowl. Have a fire extinguisher and an assistant standing by when performing this procedure.

1. If you have never removed the main jet while the carburetor is mounted on the bike, make a dry run while the engine is cold. When taking spark plug readings, the engine will be hot.
2. Turn the fuel shutoff valve to the OFF position.
3. Loosen the main jet cover (float bowl plug) and drain out all fuel in the bowl. See **Figure 38**.
4. The main jet is directly under the cover (**Figure 42**). Remove it and replace it with a different one. Remember, change only one jet size at a time.
5. Install the main jet cover; tighten it securely.

Jet Needle Adjustment

The top of the carburetor must be removed for this adjustment, but the carburetor does not have to be removed from the engine.

NOTE
The circlip securing the jet needle can be easily lost. Before making a series of spark plug readings, order a few replacement circlips from your Kawasaki dealer to have on hand.

1. If necessary, loosen the carburetor clamp screws and turn the carburetor to gain access to the carburetor cap.

NOTE
Before removing the top cap, thoroughly clean the area around it so no dirt will fall into the carburetor.

2A. *Mikuni carburetor:* Perform the following:
   a. Unscrew the top cap and pull the throttle valve assembly (**Figure 46**) up and out of the carburetor.
   b. At the end of the throttle cable, push up on the throttle valve spring and hold it (**Figure 47**).

8

c. *KX60:* Lift up on the jet needle and remove the spring seat (**Figure 48**). Remove the jet needle. If necessary, disconnect the throttle cable from the throttle valve (**Figure 49**) and remove the throttle valve (**Figure 50**).

d. *KX80:* Remove the clip holding the throttle cable in place (**Figure 51**). Remove the clip and disconnect the cable from the throttle valve. Remove the screws holding the jet needle plate to the throttle valve. Remove the plate and jet needle. See **Figure 52**.

2B. *Keihin carburetor:* Perform the following:

a. Unscrew the top cap and pull the throttle valve assembly (**Figure 53**) up and out of the carburetor.

b. At the end of the throttle, push up on the throttle valve spring and spring seat and hold it (**Figure 54**).

c. Disconnect the throttle cable from the throttle valve and remove the throttle valve (**Figure 55**).

d. Pull the clip out of the throttle valve. Then remove the spring seat and jet needle.

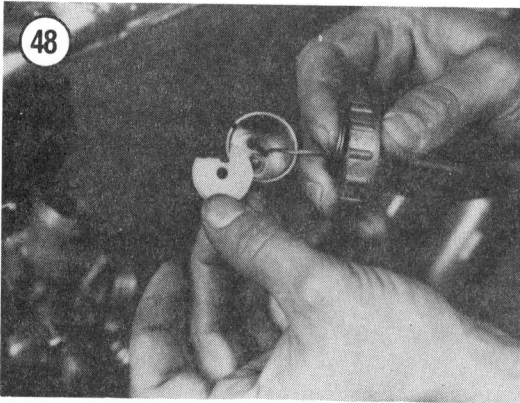

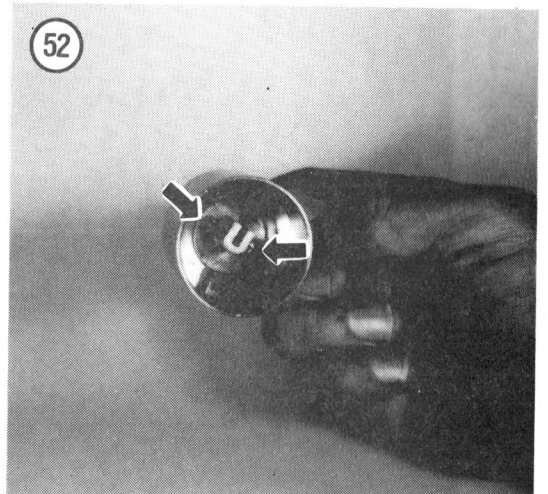

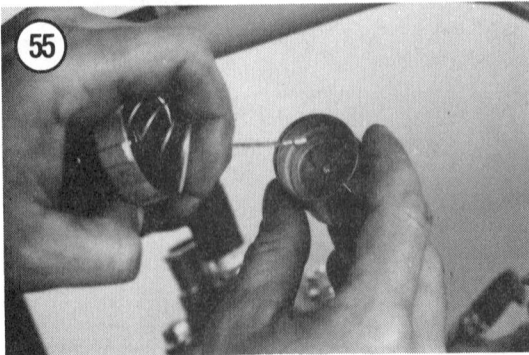

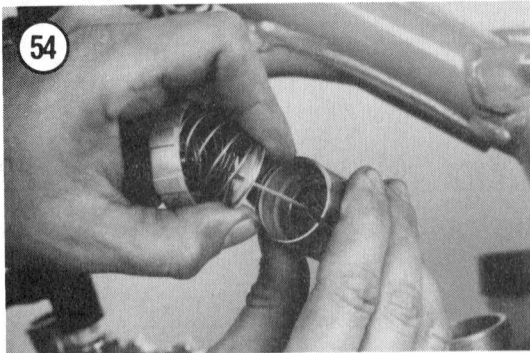

3. Note the position of the clip. Raising the needle (lowering the clip) will enrich the mixture during mid-throttle opening, while lowering it (raising the clip) will lean the mixture. Refer to **Figure 56**.

4. Refer to **Tables 1-3** at the end of the chapter for standard clip positions.

5. Installation is the reverse of these steps.

NOTE
*An O-ring is installed inside the carburetor cap (**Figure 57**). Before installing the cap, make sure the O-ring is in good condition; replace the O-ring if necessary.*

FUEL TANK

Removal/Installation

1. Support the bike on a bike stand.

2. Turn the fuel shutoff valve to the OFF position (**Figure 58**) and remove the fuel line to the carburetor.

8

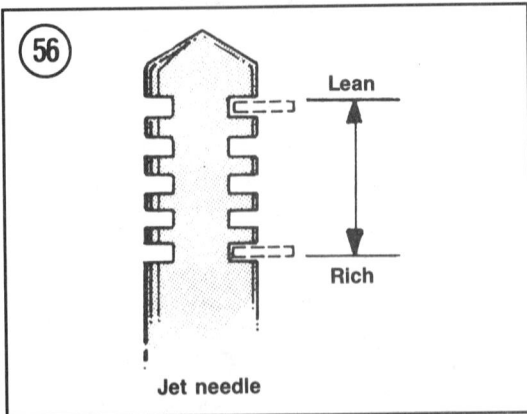

Lean

Rich

Jet needle

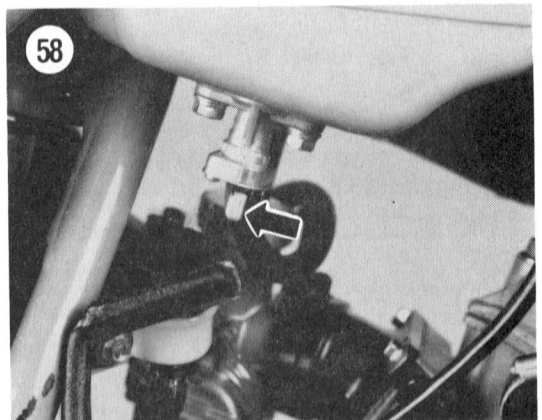

3. Remove the seat.

4. Pull the fuel fill cap vent tube free from the steering head area.

5. *Liquid-cooled models:* Remove all air collectors from the fuel tank (**Figure 59**) as required.

6. Remove all bolts (**Figure 60**) or straps securing the fuel tank to the frame. Remove the fuel tank.

7. Check for missing or damaged fuel tank rubber dampers. See **Figure 61**, typical.

8. Install by reversing these removal steps.

FUEL SHUTOFF VALVE

Removal/Installation

> *WARNING*
> *Some fuel may spill from the fuel tank when performing this procedure. Because gasoline is an extremely flammable and explosive petroleum, perform this procedure away from all open flames (including pilot lights) and sparks. Do not smoke or allow someone who is smoking in the work area. Always work in a well ventilated area. Wipe up any spills immediately.*

1. Remove the fuel tank as described in this chapter.

2. Drain the fuel into a fuel storage container.

3. Remove the bolts holding the fuel shutoff valve to the bottom of the fuel tank. Remove the shutoff valve.

4. Remove the screw above the handle or on the handle and disassemble the valve. Clean all parts in solvent with a medium soft toothbrush, then dry. Check the small O-ring within the valve and the O-ring gasket; replace if they are starting to deteriorate or get hard. Make sure the spring is not broken or getting soft; replace if necessary.

5. Reassemble the valve and install it on the tank. Don't forget the O-ring gasket between the valve and the tank.

EXHAUST SYSTEM

The exhaust system (**Figure 62**) on a 2-stroke motorcycle engine is much more than a means of routing the exhaust gases to the rear of the bike.

It's a vital performance component and frequently, because of its design, it is a vulnerable piece of equipment.

Check the exhaust system for deep dents and fractures and repair them as described under *Exhaust System Repairs* at the end of this chapter. Check the expansion chamber frame mounting flanges for fractures and loose bolts and bushings.

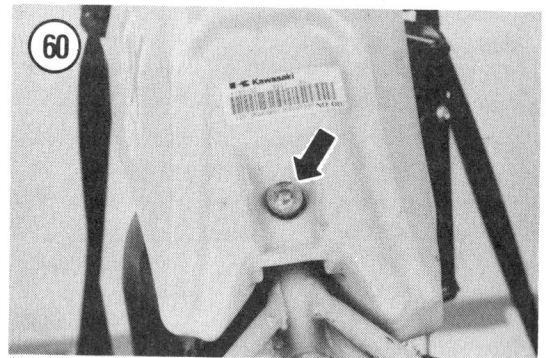

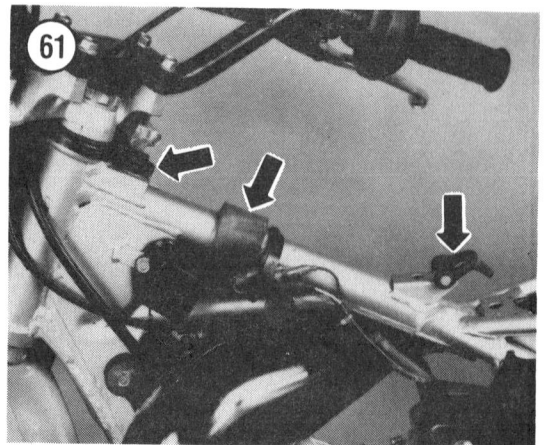

Check the cylinder mounting flange or collar for tightness. A loose headpipe connection will not only rob the engine of power, it could also damage the piston and cylinder.

The exhaust system consists of an exhaust pipe assembly (head pipe and expansion chamber) and a silencer. This system varies slightly with different models and years. All attachments are basically the same but they all vary a little.

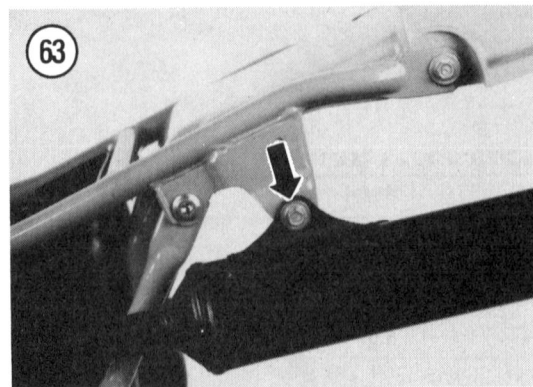

Removal/Installation

1. Support the bike on a bike stand.
2. Remove the seat, fuel tank and both frame side cover/number plates.
3. Remove the bolts securing the silencer (**Figure 63**). Also loosen the clamping band and remove the silencer if it is a separate assembly.
4. Use a pair of Vise Grips or a spring removal tool and disconnect the springs at the front of the exhaust pipe.
5. Remove the bolts securing the exhaust pipe (**Figure 64**) and remove the exhaust pipe.
6. Installation is the reverse of these steps. Note the following:
   a. Replace the rubber O-ring at the head pipe and apply grease from the edge of the pipe to the O-ring. If the joint leaks in spite of a good O-ring and grease, clean the surfaces with solvent and use high temperature silicone sealant to seal the joint.
   b. Make sure the spark plug wire, fuel line and throttle cable protection spring are properly positioned to prevent damage from a hot exhaust pipe.

EXHAUST SYSTEM DECARBONIZING

Refer to Chapter Three for complete details on engine and exhaust system decarbonization.

EXHAUST SYSTEM REPAIR

A dent in the headpipe or expansion chamber of a 2-stroke exhaust system will alter the system's flow characteristics and degrade performance. Minor damage can be easily repaired if you have welding equipment, some simple body tools, and a bodyman's slide hammer.

Small Dents

1. Drill a small hole in the center of the dent. Screw the end of the slide hammer into the hole.
2. Heat the area around the dent evenly with a torch.
3. When the dent is heated to a uniform orange-red color, operate the slide hammer to raise the dent.

8

4. When the dent is removed, unscrew the slide hammer and weld or braze the drilled hole closed.

Large Dents

Large dents that are not crimped can be removed with heat and a slide hammer as previously described. However, several holes must be drilled along the center of the dent so that it can be pulled out evenly.

If the dent is sharply crimped along the edges, the affected section should be cut out with a hacksaw, straightened with a body dolly and hammer and welded back into place.

Before cutting the exhaust pipe apart, scribe alignment marks over the area where the cuts will be made to aid correct alignment when the pipe is rewelded.

After the welding is completed, wire brush and clean up all welds. Paint the entire pipe with a high-temperature paint to prevent rusting.

Table 1 CARBURETOR SPECIFICATIONS (KX60)

	1983	1984
Type	Mikuni	Mikuni
Size	VM24SS	VM24SS
Main jet	125	180
Jet needle/clip position	513/3	5L14/3
Needle jet	0-2	0-2
Slide cutaway	1.5	2.0
Pilot jet	45	35
Float height	20.1-22.1 mm	—
	(0.79-0.87 in.)	—
Fuel level	0.5-2.5 mm	0.5-2.5 mm
	(0.02-0.10 in.)	(0.02-0.10 in.)
	1985-on	
Type	Mikuni	
Size	VM24SS	
Main jet	200	
Jet needle/clip position	5L14/3	
Needle jet	N-8	
Slide cutaway	2.0	
Pilot jet	20	
Float height	20.1-22.1 mm (0.79-0.87 in.)	
Fuel level	0.5-2.5 mm (0.02-0.10 in.)	

Table 2 MIKUNI CARBURETOR SPECIFICATIONS (1983-1987 KX80)

	1983	1984
Size	VM29SS	VM29SS
Main jet	120R	200
Jet needle/clip position	53J36/2	6EJ3/3
Needle jet	P-0	P-2
Slide cutaway	3.0	2.0
Pilot jet	30	35
Float height	21.9 mm (0.86 in.)	21.9 mm (0.86 in.)
Fuel level	4.5-6.5 mm (0.18-0.26 in.)	4.5-6.5 mm (0.18-0.26 in.)
	1985	**1986**
Size	VM29SS	VM29SS
Main jet	200	210
Jet needle/clip position	6EJ3/3	6DK2/3
Needle jet	P-2	P-2
Slide cutaway	2.0	2.0
Pilot jet	30	30
Float height	21.9 mm (0.86 in.)	21.9 mm (0.86 in.)
Fuel level	4.5-6.5 mm (0.18-0.26 in.)	4.5-6.5 mm (0.18-0.26 in.)
	1987	
Size	VM29SS	
Main jet	200	
Jet needle/clip position	6EJ3/4	
Needle jet	P-2	
Slide cutaway	2.0	
Pilot jet	30	
Float height	21.9 mm (0.86 in.)	
Fuel level	4.5-6.5 mm (0.18-0.26 in.)	

8

Table 3 KEIHIN CARBURETOR SPECIFICATIONS (1988-ON KX80)

	1988	1989
Size	PE28	PE28
Main jet	155	132
Jet needle/clip position	F3045F/2	F1342H/4
Slide cutaway	5.0	6.0
Slow jet	58	55
Float height	18-20 mm (0.71-0.79 in.)	18-20 mm (0.71-0.79 in.)
Fuel level	0.5-2.5 mm (0.02-0.10 in.)	0-2 mm (0-0.078 in.)

CHAPTER NINE

IGNITION SYSTEM

This chapter describes service and testing procedures for the ignition system. **Tables 1-3** are found at the end of the chapter.

CAPACITOR DISCHARGE IGNITION

All KX models are equipped with a capacitor discharge ignition (CDI) system. This solid state system, unlike conventional ignition system, uses no contact breaker points or other moving parts.

Alternating current from the magneto is rectified and used to charge the capacitor. As the piston approaches the firing position, a pulse from the pulser coil is rectified, shaped and then used to trigger the silicone controlled rectifier. This in turn allows the capacitor to discharge quickly into the primary side of the high-voltage ignition coil where it is increased, or stepped up, to a high enough voltage to jump the gap between the spark plug electrodes.

CDI Cautions

Certain measures must be taken to protect the capacitor discharge system. Damage to the semiconductors in the system may occur if the following is not observed.

1. Keep all connections between the various units clean and tight. Be sure that the wiring connectors are pushed together firmly.

2. Never disconnect any of the electrical connections while the engine is running.

3. Do not substitute another type of ignition coil.

4. The CDI unit is mounted on a rubber vibration isolator. Always be sure that the CDI unit is mounted correctly.

CDI Troubleshooting

Refer to Chapter Two.

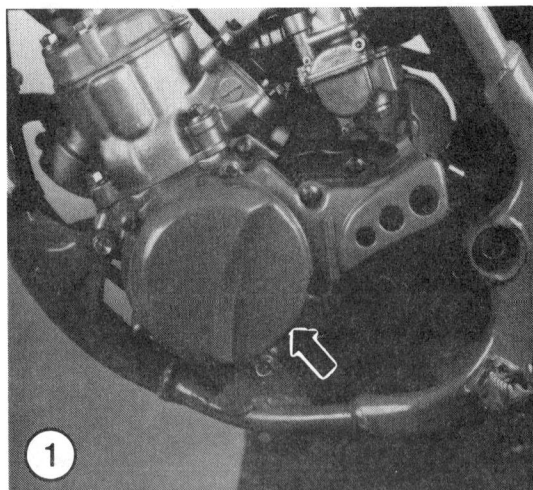

1

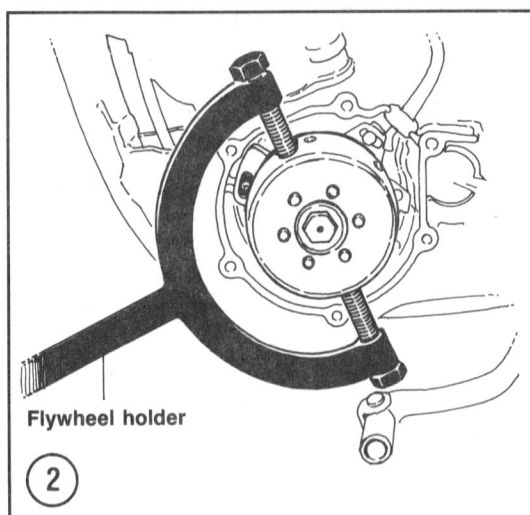

Flywheel holder

2

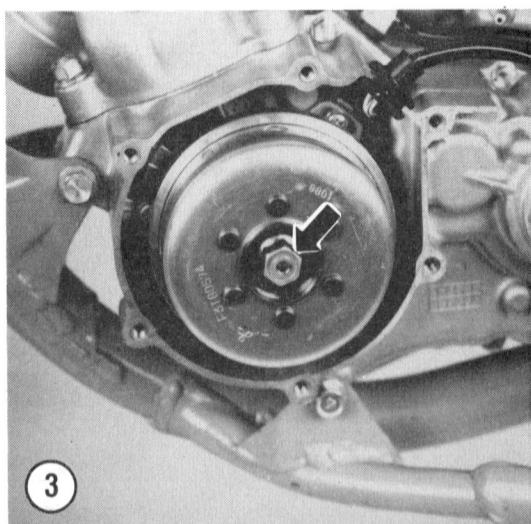

3

FLYWHEEL

Removal/Installation

1. Place the bike on a stand to support it securely.

2. Remove the screws holding the left-hand crankcase side cover to the crankcase. Remove the cover (**Figure 1**).

3. Secure the flywheel with a strap wrench or use the Kawasaki flywheel holder (**Figure 2**) (part No. 57001-308) and loosen the flywheel nut (**Figure 3**).

4. Remove the nut and plain washer. On some models, a lockwasher is installed between the nut and plain washer.

> *NOTE*
> *The Kawasaki flywheel puller (part No. 57001-252) (or equivalent) will be required to remove the flywheel (**Figure 4**).*

> *NOTE*
> *The flywheel puller has left-hand threads. During installation, turn the puller counterclockwise.*

5. Thread the flywheel puller into the flywheel by turning it *counterclockwise*. Turn the puller until it almost bottoms out.

> *CAUTION*
> *Do not strike the puller screw with excessive force in Step 6 or crankshaft, flywheel and/or bearing damage may result. Do not use heat during removal, as it may cause the flywheel to seize on the crankshaft.*

9

4

6. Hold the puller body with a wrench (**Figure 5**) and tighten the center screw. If flywheel does not pop off from crankshaft taper, lightly tap the puller center screw with a brass hammer.

> *CAUTION*
> *Don't pry or hammer on the flywheel in any way. Damage is sure to result, and you may destroy the flywheel magnetism. Use the proper type of puller assembly described.*

> *CAUTION*
> *If normal flywheel removal attempts fail, do not force the puller as the threads may be stripped out of the flywheel causing expensive damage. Take it to a dealer and have them remove it.*

7. Remove the flywheel and puller. Remove the puller from the flywheel.

> *NOTE*
> *The Woodruff key may fall out of the crankshaft keyway as the flywheel is removed in Step 7. Be sure to locate and retrieve the key of it comes out.*

8. Remove the Woodruff key (**Figure 6**) from the crankshaft slot if it does not come off with the flywheel.
9. Inspect the flywheel as described in this chapter.
10. Inspect the crankshaft and flywheel tapers. They must be perfectly dry and free of oil. Swab the tapered surfaces with solvent and blow dry.

> *CAUTION*
> *Carefully inspect the inside of the flywheel (Figure 7) for small bolts, washers or other metal "trash" that may have been picked up by the magnets. These small metal bits can cause severe damage to the magneto stator plate components.*

11. To install, place the Woodruff key in the crankshaft slot (**Figure 6**). Position the flywheel over the crankshaft with the flywheel keyway (A, **Figure 8**) aligned with the Woodruff key in the crankshaft (B, **Figure 8**). Install the flywheel.

12. Install the flywheel washer (or lockwasher) and nut. Tighten the flywheel nut (**Figure 3**) to the torque specification in **Table 3**. To keep the flywheel from turning, hold it with the same tool used during removal.
13. Reinstall the left-hand crankcase side cover and tighten the screws securely.

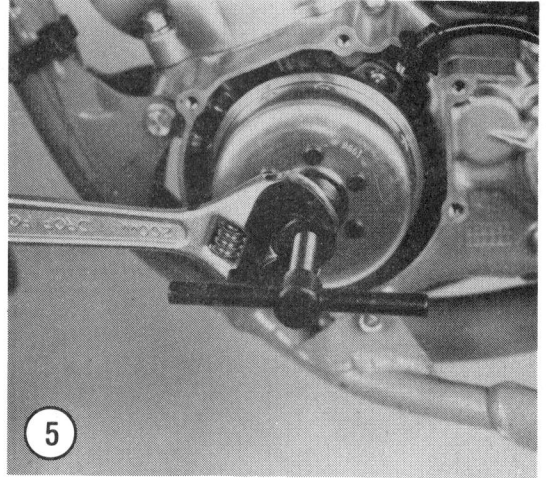

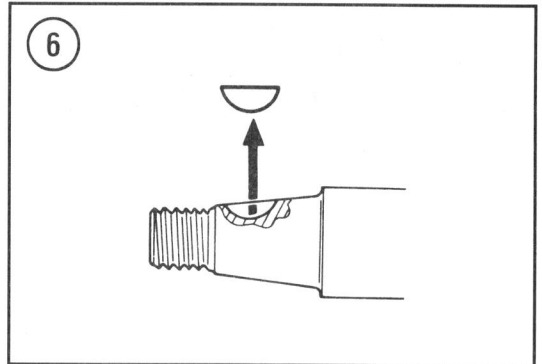

Inspection

1. Check the flywheel (**Figure 7**) carefully for cracks or breaks.

> *WARNING*
> *A cracked or chipped flywheel must be replaced. A damaged flywheel may fly apart at high rpm, throwing metal fragments over a large area and injure the rider. Do not attempt to repair a damaged flywheel.*

2. Check the tapered bore of the flywheel and the crankshaft taper for cracks or other abnormal conditions.

3. Check the crankshaft and flywheel nut threads for wear or damage.

4. Replace the flywheel, crankshaft half and/or flywheel nut as required.

Stator Assembly
Removal/Installation

1. Remove the flywheel as described under *Flywheel Removal/Installation* in this chapter.

2. Remove the fuel tank as described in Chapter Eight.

3. Disconnect the electrical wire connectors from the stator plate to the CDI unit. See **Figure 9**, typical.

> *NOTE*
> *If there are additional timing marks other than the original marks, refer to **Ignition Timing** in Chapter Three. Additional marks may have been added by a previous owner.*

4. Note the timing marks on the stator plate and on the crankcase (**Figure 10**). These must be realigned during installation.

5. Loosen and remove the screws securing the stator plate.

6. Carefully pull the electrical harness out along with the rubber grommet from the crankcase and any holding clips on the engine.

7. Remove the stator plate assembly (**Figure 11**).

8. Install by reversing these removal steps while noting the following.

9. Route the electrical wires in the same way it was. Make sure to keep it away from the exhaust system.

10. Realign the stator plate and crankcase timing marks for correct ignition timing (**Figure 10**).

Stator Coil Testing

The stator coils (**Figure 12**) can be inspected for continuity without removing them from the bike. With the engine turned off, disconnect the connector from the magneto and measure the resistance between the pairs of leads listed in **Table 1**.

If the resistance is zero (short circuit) or infinite (open circuit), check the wiring to the coils, and replace the coils if the wiring is okay.

CAPACITOR DISCHARGE IGNITION UNIT

Removal/Installation

1. Support the bike on a bike stand.
2. Remove the seat and fuel tank.
3. Disconnect the CDI electrical connector.
4. Remove the bolts holding the CDI unit to the frame. Remove the CDI unit (**Figure 13**, typical).
5. Installation is the reverse of these steps.

Testing

The capacitor discharge ignition unit can only be tested with special electrical equipment. Refer all testing to a Kawasaki dealer.

IGNITION COIL

Removal/Installation

1. Support the bike on a bike stand.
2. Remove the seat and fuel tank.
3. Disconnect the electrical wires to the ignition coil.
4. Remove the screws securing the ignition coil to the frame and remove it. See **Figure 14**, typical.
5. Install by reversing these removal steps. Make sure all electrical connectors are tight and free of corrosion. Make sure the ground wire is secured tightly.

Testing

If the functional condition of the coil is in doubt, there are several checks which should be made. Disconnect the coil wires before testing.

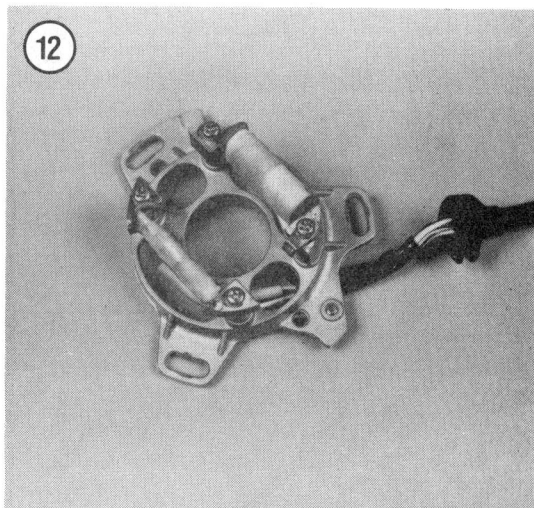

1. Measure the coil primary resistance using an ohmmeter set at R × 1 (**Figure 15**). Measure the resistance between the coil terminals. See **Table 2** for test specifications.

2. Measure the secondary resistance using an ohmmeter set at R × 1,000 (**Figure 15**). Measure the resistance between the secondary lead (spark plug lead) and the ground lead terminal. See **Table 2** for test specifications.

3. If the meter indicates an open circuit (no continuity) in Step 2, unplug the high-tension lead (spark plug wire) from the coil and test it again with the meter lead connected directly to the contact pin in the coil cap. If there is continuity now, the trouble is in the high-tension lead. It may be a bad connection at the spark plug or an internal break in the wire. Make sure the connection is good and check the lead for continuity. If an open circuit is still indicated, replace the high-tension lead.

4. If the high tension lead has continuity, the coil itself is defective and must be replaced.

NOTE
Continuity in both the primary and secondary windings in the coil is not a guarantee that the unit is in top working order; only an operational test can tell if a coil is producing an adequate spark from the input voltage. Your motorcycle dealer or auto electrical repair shop may have the equipment to test the coil's output. If not, substitute a known good coil to see if the problem goes away.

SPARK PLUG

The spark plugs recommended by the factory are usually the most suitable for your machine. If riding conditions are mild, it may be advisable to go to spark plugs one step hotter than normal. Unusually severe riding conditions may require slightly colder plugs. See Chapter Three for details.

ENGINE STOP SWITCH

Testing

1. Remove the fuel tank as described in Chapter Eight.

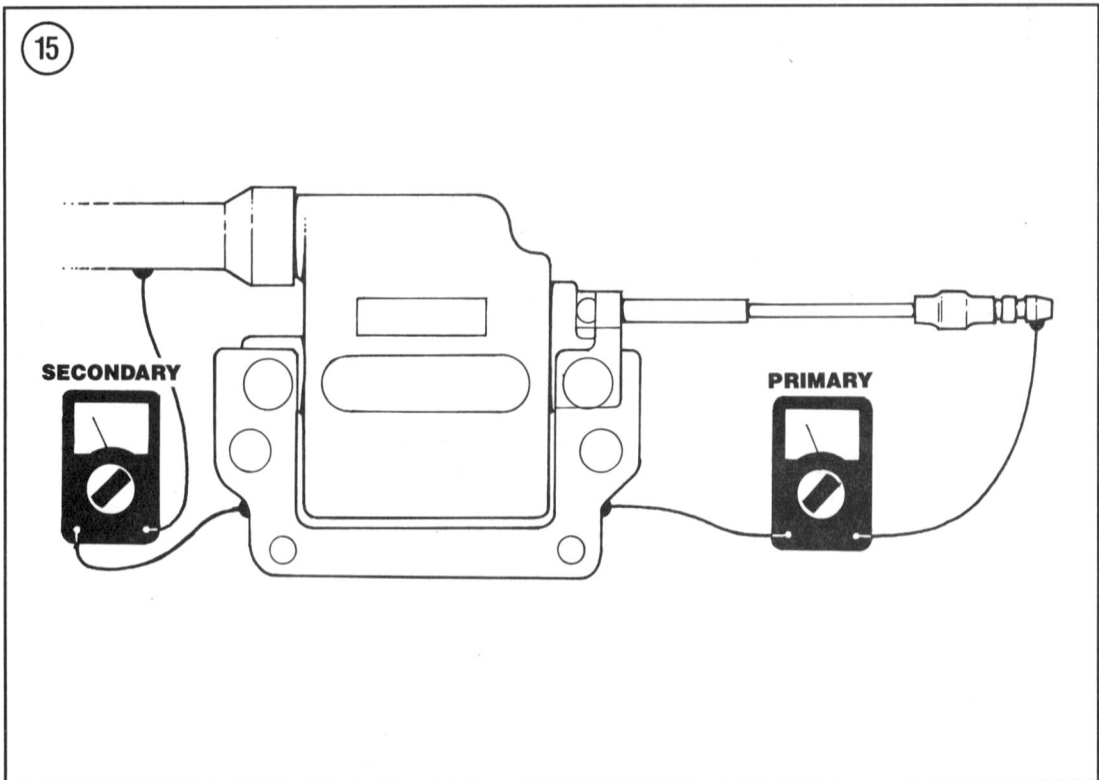
SECONDARY   PRIMARY

2. Disconnect the black stop switch connector at the CDI unit.

3. Use an ohmmeter set at R × 1 and connect the 2 leads of the ohmmeter to the 2 electrical wires of the switch.

4. Push the stop switch button—if the switch is good there will be continuity (resistance).

5. If the needle does not move (no continuity) the switch is faulty and must be replaced.

6. Remove the screw securing the switch (**Figure 16**) and remove it. Reverse to install a new switch.

WIRING DIAGRAMS

Wiring diagrams for all models are located at the end of this book.

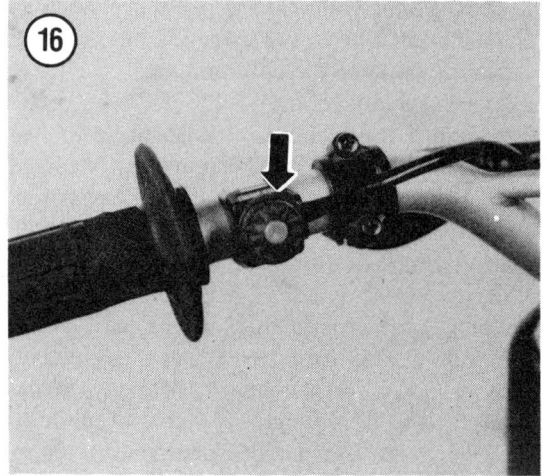

Table 1 STATOR COIL TEST SPECIFICATIONS

KX60	
Black/red to black/yellow	368-552 ohms
White/red to black/yellow	10-14.5 ohms
KX80	
1983-1985	
Black/red to black/yellow	432-648 ohms
White/red to black/yellow	7.7-11.5 ohms
1986-on	
Black/red to black/yellow	432-648 ohms
White/red to white/green	4.0-6.0 ohms

Table 2 IGNITION COIL TEST SPECIFICATIONS

Primary	1.0 ohm ±15%
Secondary	5.9K ohms ±15%

Table 3 TIGHTENING TORQUES

	N·m	ft.-lb.
Flywheel nut		
KX60	29	22
KX80	29	22

CHAPTER TEN

LIQUID COOLING SYSTEM

The liquid cooling system used on 1985 and later KX60 and all KX80 models consists of a radiator, water pump, radiator cap and hoses (**Figure 1**). During operation, the coolant heats up and expands, thus pressuring the system. The radiator cap is used to seal the system. Water cooled in the radiator is pumped down through the radiator and into the cylinder head where it passes through the cylinder water passages and back into the radiator at the top. The water then runs down through the radiator where it is cooled and the cycle is repeated.

This chapter describes repair and replacement of the liquid cooling system components.

> *WARNING*
> *Do not remove the radiator cap (Figure 2) when the engine is hot. The coolant is very hot and is under pressure. Severe scalding could result if the coolant comes in contact with your skin.*

The cooling system must be cooled prior to removing any component of the system.

COOLING SYSTEM INSPECTION

1. Check the radiator for clogged or damaged fins. If more than 20% of the radiator fin area is damaged, repair or replace the radiator.
2. To clean a clogged radiator, blow compressed air from the rear (engine side).
3. Check all coolant hoses for cracks or damage. Replace all questionable parts. Make sure the hose clamps are tight, but not so tight that they cut the hoses.
4. Pressure test the cooling system as described in Chapter Three.

RADIATOR

Removal/Installation

Refer to **Figure 3** (1985-on KX60), **Figure 4** (1983-1984 KX80) or **Figure 5** (1985-on KX80) for this procedure.
1. Place the bike on a bike stand.
2. Remove the fuel tank as described in Chapter Eight.

10

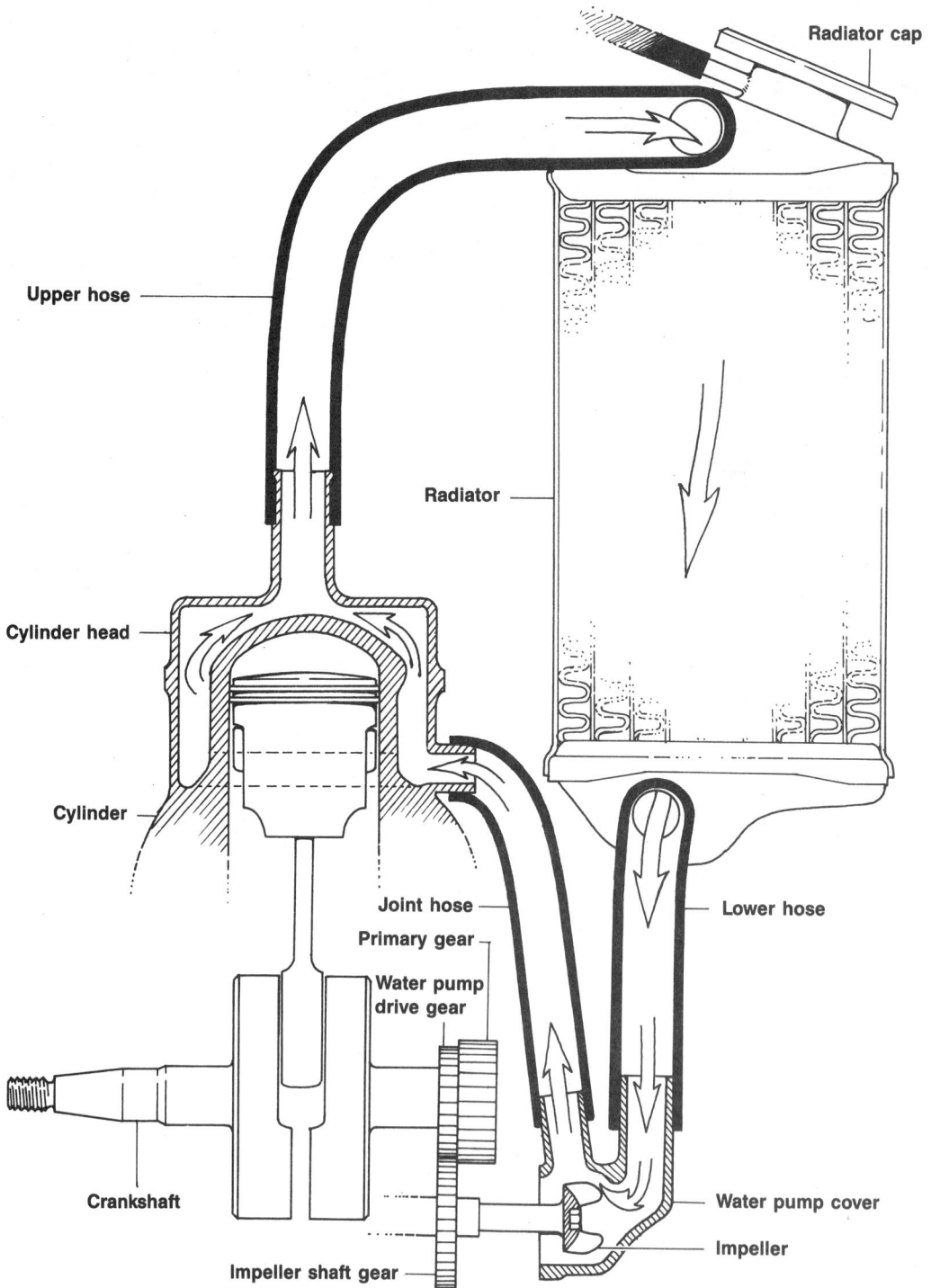

COOLING SYSTEM

- Radiator cap
- Upper hose
- Radiator
- Cylinder head
- Cylinder
- Joint hose
- Primary gear
- Water pump drive gear
- Lower hose
- Crankshaft
- Water pump cover
- Impeller
- Impeller shaft gear

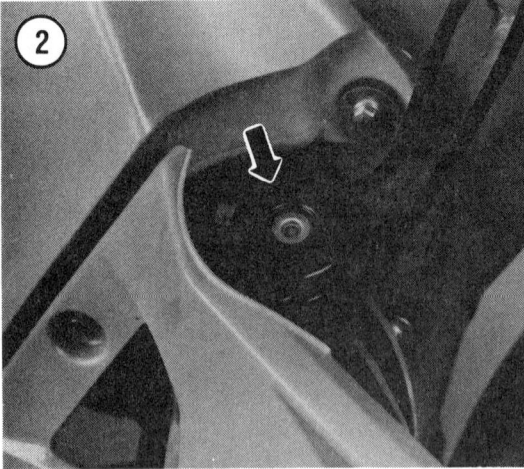

3. Drain the cooling system as described in Chapter Three.

4. Loosen the hose clamps and disconnect the hoses at the radiator. See **Figure 6** and **Figure 7**, typical.

5. Remove the bolts securing the radiator and remove the radiator.

6. Installation is the reverse of these steps.

7. Refill the coolant as described in Chapter Three.

Inspection

1. Examine the radiator cooling surface for damage. Also check along the sides at the lower mounting bushings. If the radiator is damaged,

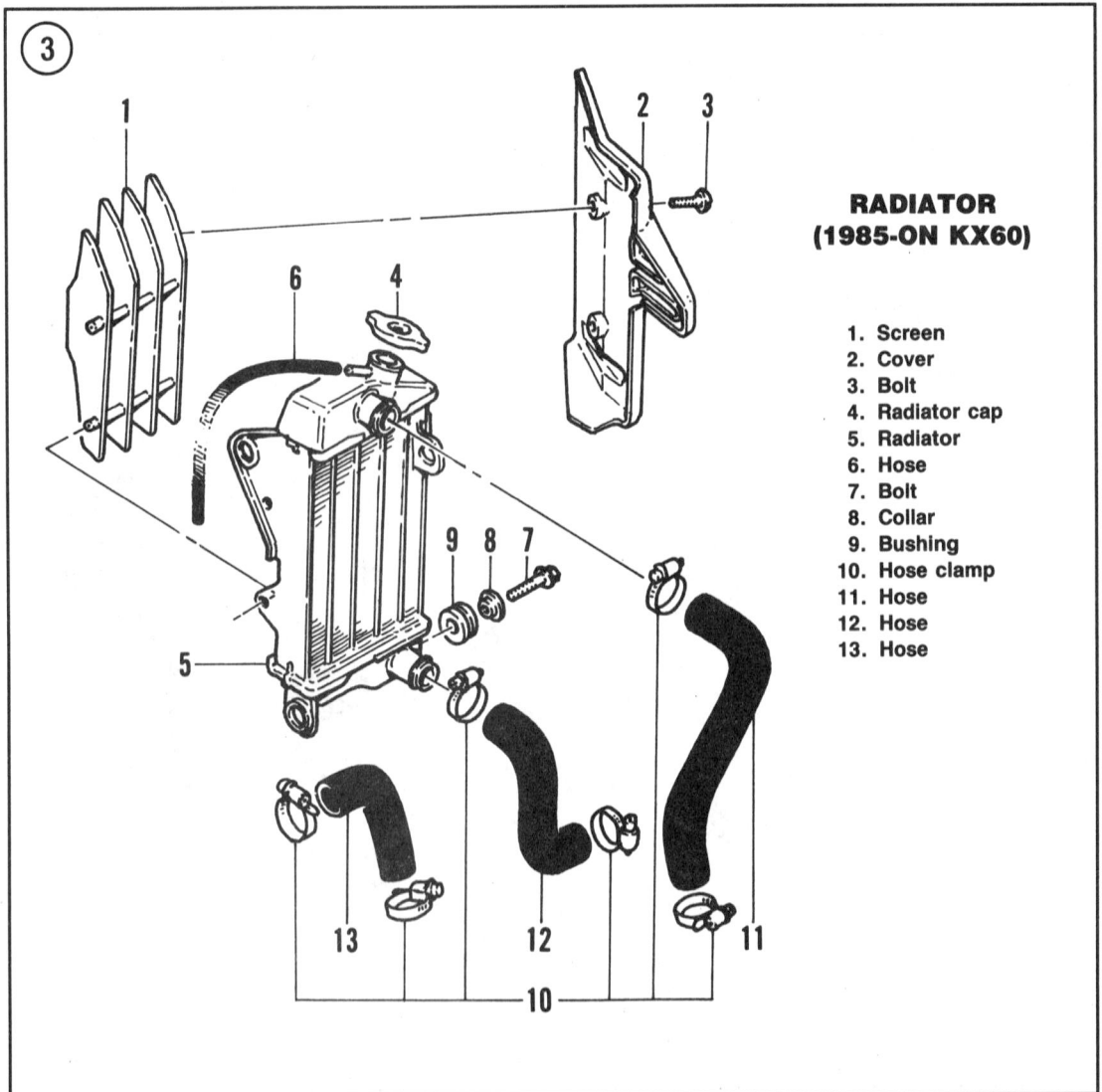

RADIATOR (1985-ON KX60)

1. Screen
2. Cover
3. Bolt
4. Radiator cap
5. Radiator
6. Hose
7. Bolt
8. Collar
9. Bushing
10. Hose clamp
11. Hose
12. Hose
13. Hose

10

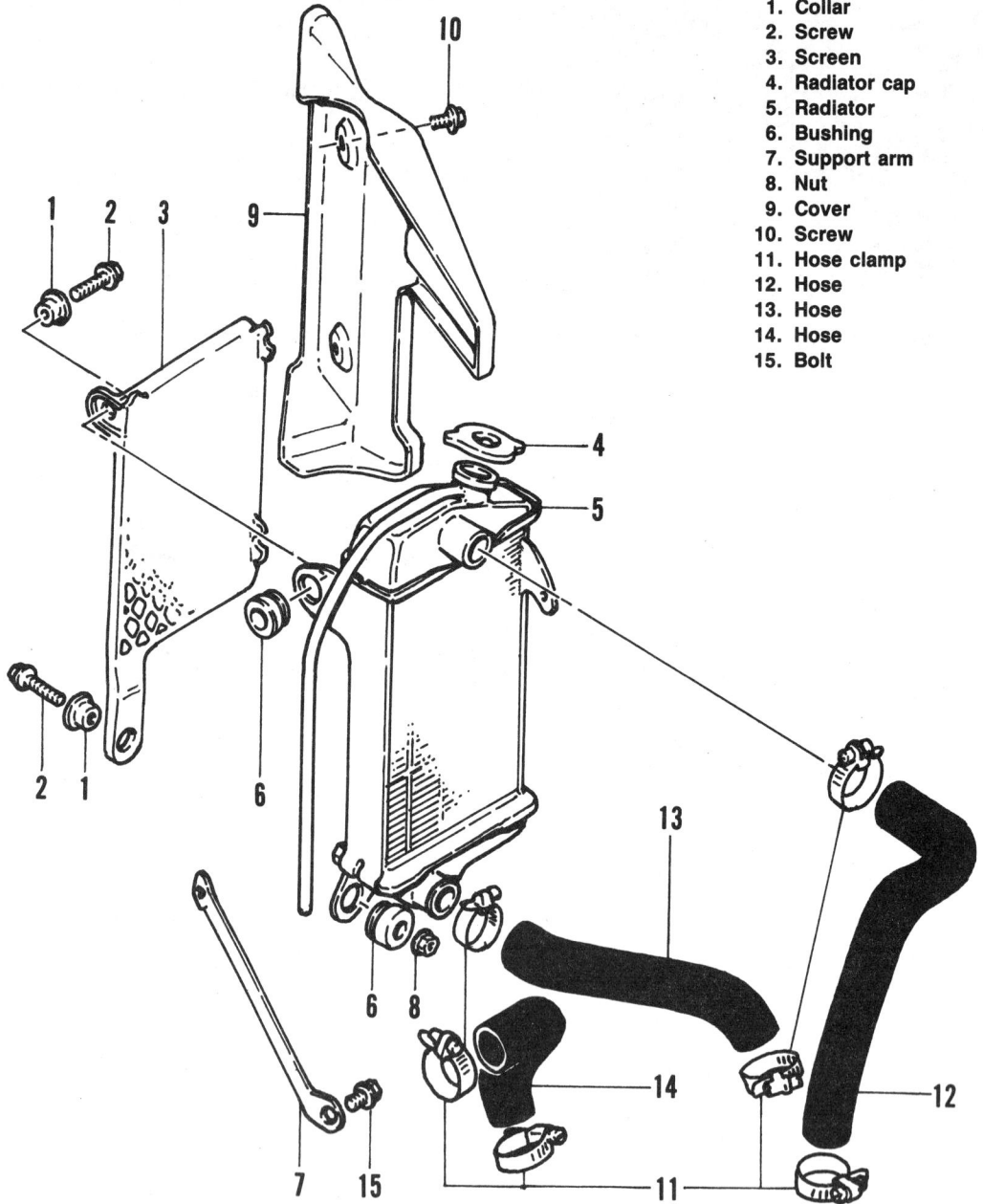

**RADIATOR
(1983-1984 KX80)**

1. Collar
2. Screw
3. Screen
4. Radiator cap
5. Radiator
6. Bushing
7. Support arm
8. Nut
9. Cover
10. Screw
11. Hose clamp
12. Hose
13. Hose
14. Hose
15. Bolt

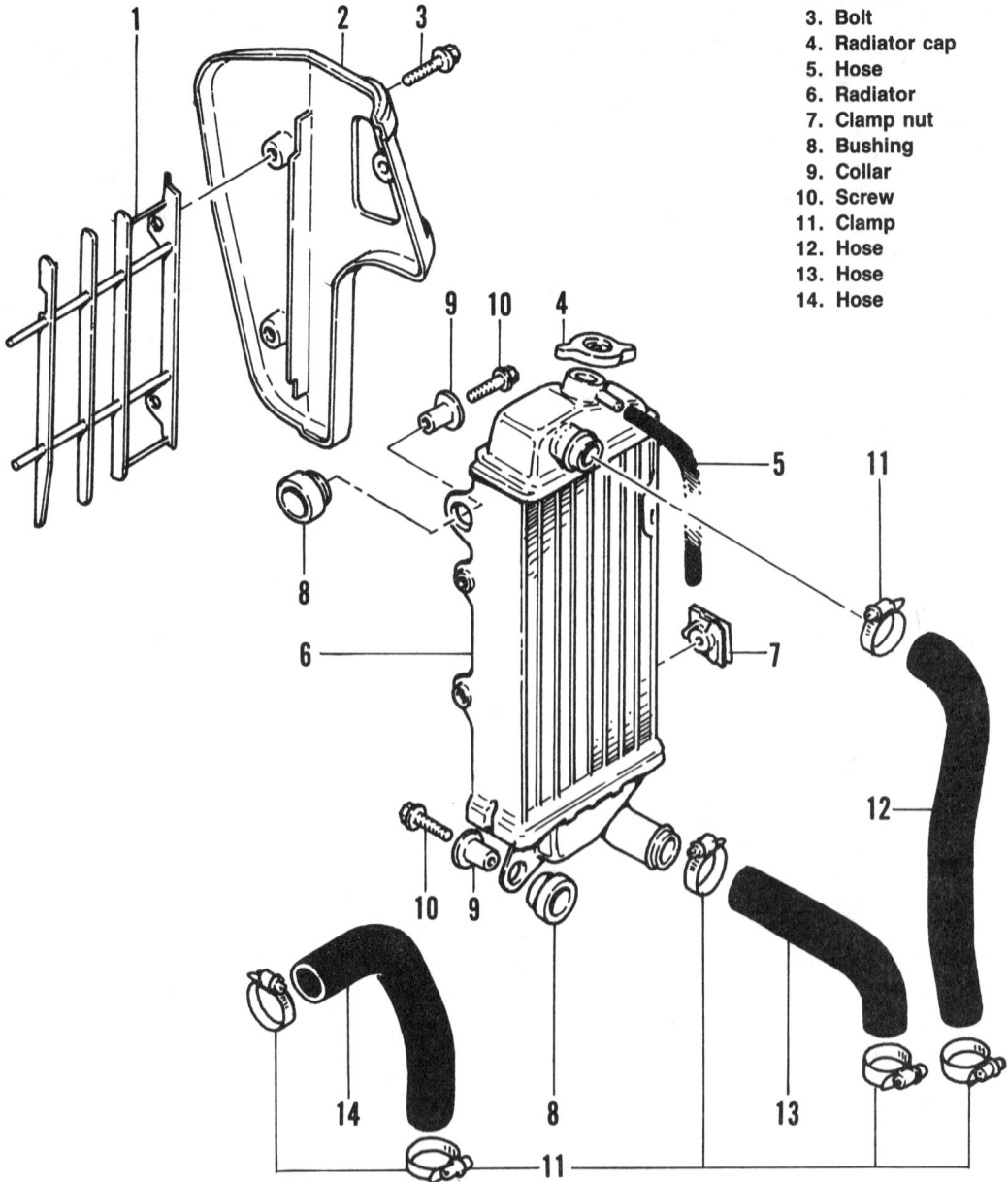

⑤

**RADIATOR
(1985-ON KX80)**

1. Screen
2. Cover
3. Bolt
4. Radiator cap
5. Hose
6. Radiator
7. Clamp nut
8. Bushing
9. Collar
10. Screw
11. Clamp
12. Hose
13. Hose
14. Hose

10

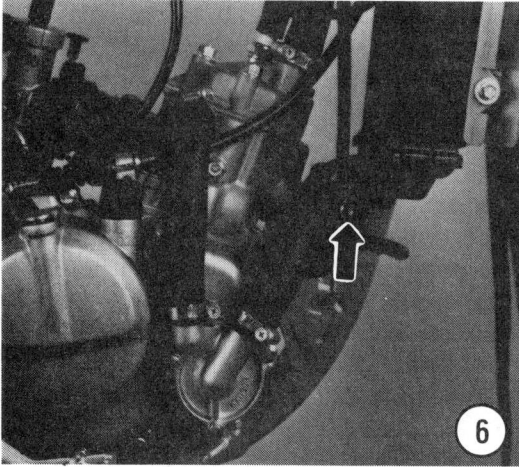

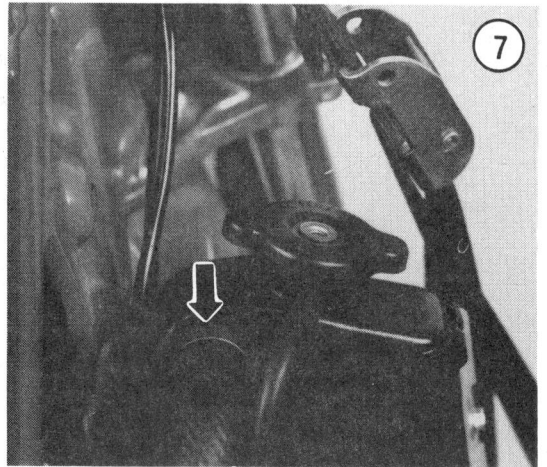

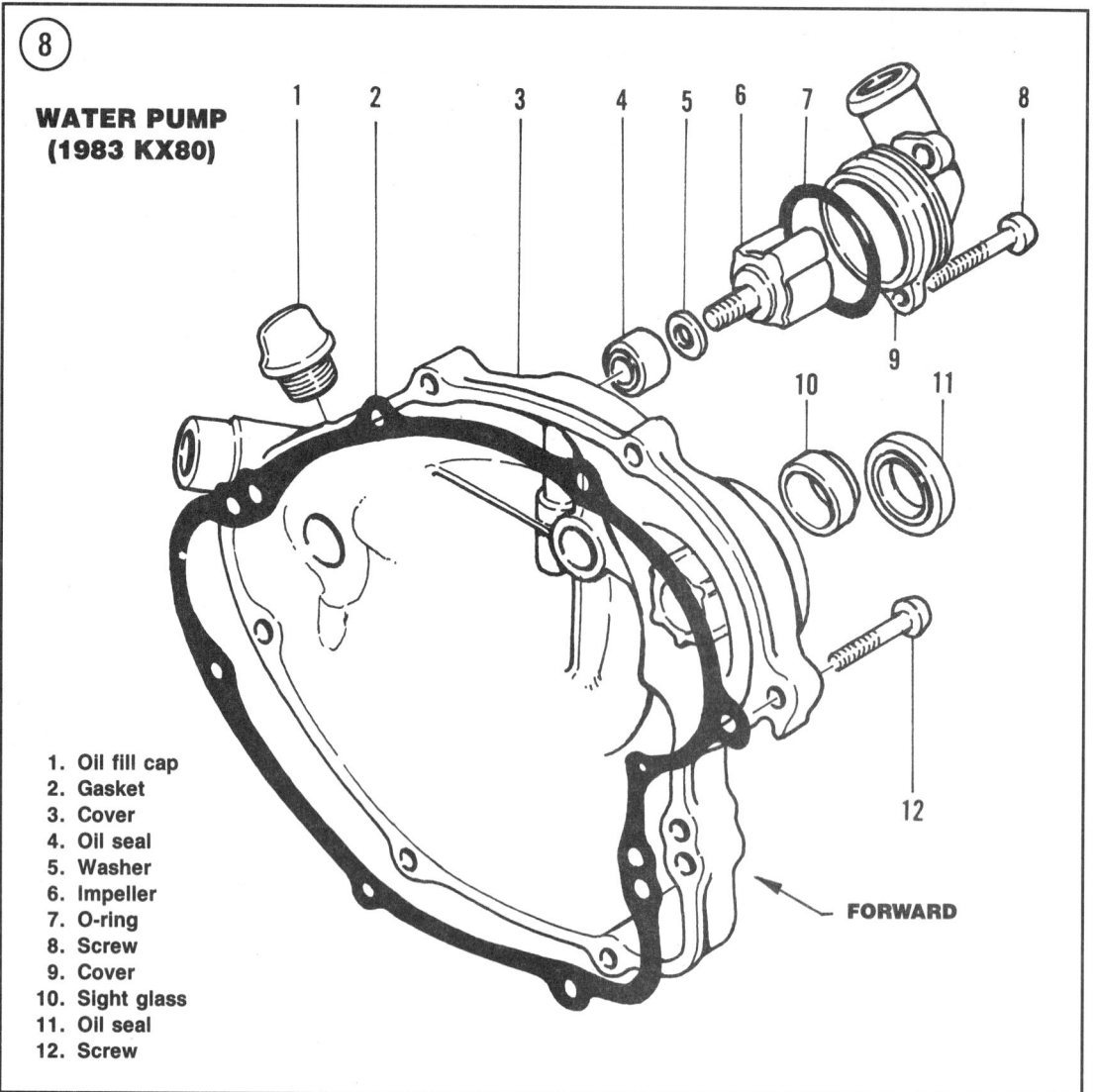

WATER PUMP
(1983 KX80)

1. Oil fill cap
2. Gasket
3. Cover
4. Oil seal
5. Washer
6. Impeller
7. O-ring
8. Screw
9. Cover
10. Sight glass
11. Oil seal
12. Screw

FORWARD

refer repair to a radiator repair shop. If damage is severe, replace the radiator.

2. Check the radiator coolant hoses and hose clamps for damage; replace if required.

WATER PUMP

The water pump is mounted in the clutch cover on all models. Under normal operating conditions, disassembly of the water pump should not be necessary. However, if the engine overheats or if the coolant level changes, the water pump should be removed and examined.

Disassembly/Assembly (1983-1984 KX80)

Refer to **Figure 8** (1983 KX80) or **Figure 9** (1984 KX80) for this procedure.

1. Drain the radiator as described under *Coolant Change* in Chapter Three.

2. Disconnect the coolant hoses on the water pump.

NOTE
On models equipped with Phillips screws, an impact driver with a

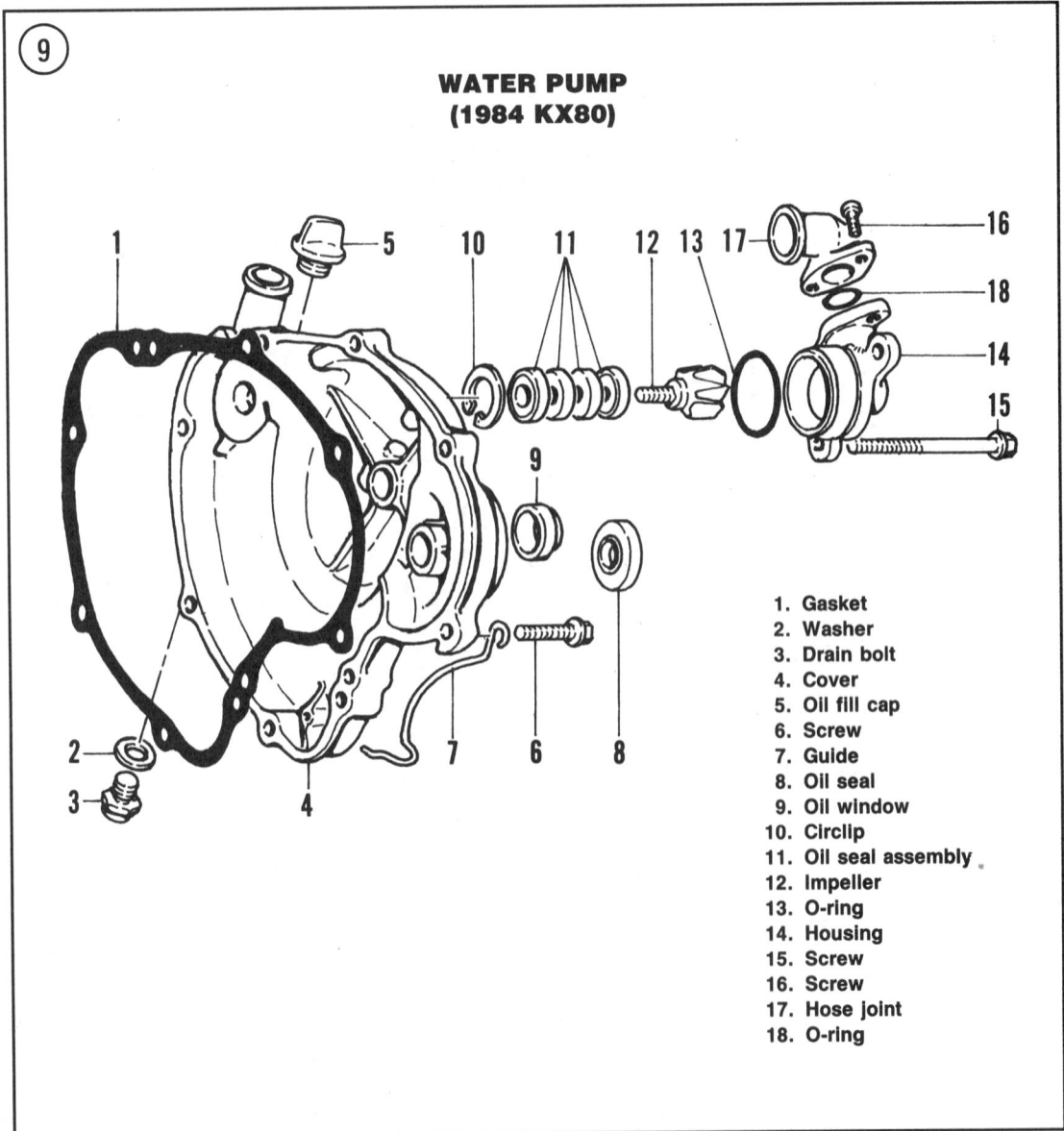

WATER PUMP (1984 KX80)

1. Gasket
2. Washer
3. Drain bolt
4. Cover
5. Oil fill cap
6. Screw
7. Guide
8. Oil seal
9. Oil window
10. Circlip
11. Oil seal assembly
12. Impeller
13. O-ring
14. Housing
15. Screw
16. Screw
17. Hose joint
18. O-ring

Phillips bit is necessary to loosen the water pump cover screws in Step 3.

3. Remove the Phillips screws or bolts holding the water pump cover onto the clutch cover. Remove the water pump cover. Remove the dowel pins (if so equipped).

4. Remove the impeller mounting bolt and remove the impeller (**Figure 10**).

NOTE
If it is necessary to replace the water pump oil seal, perform Step 5.

5. Remove the clutch cover as described under *Clutch Cover Removal/Installation* in Chapter Six.

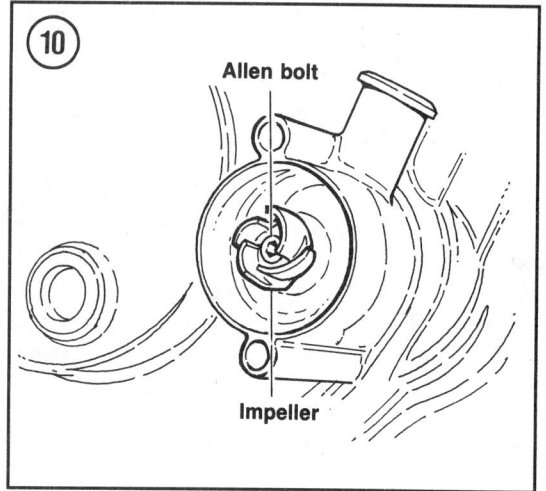

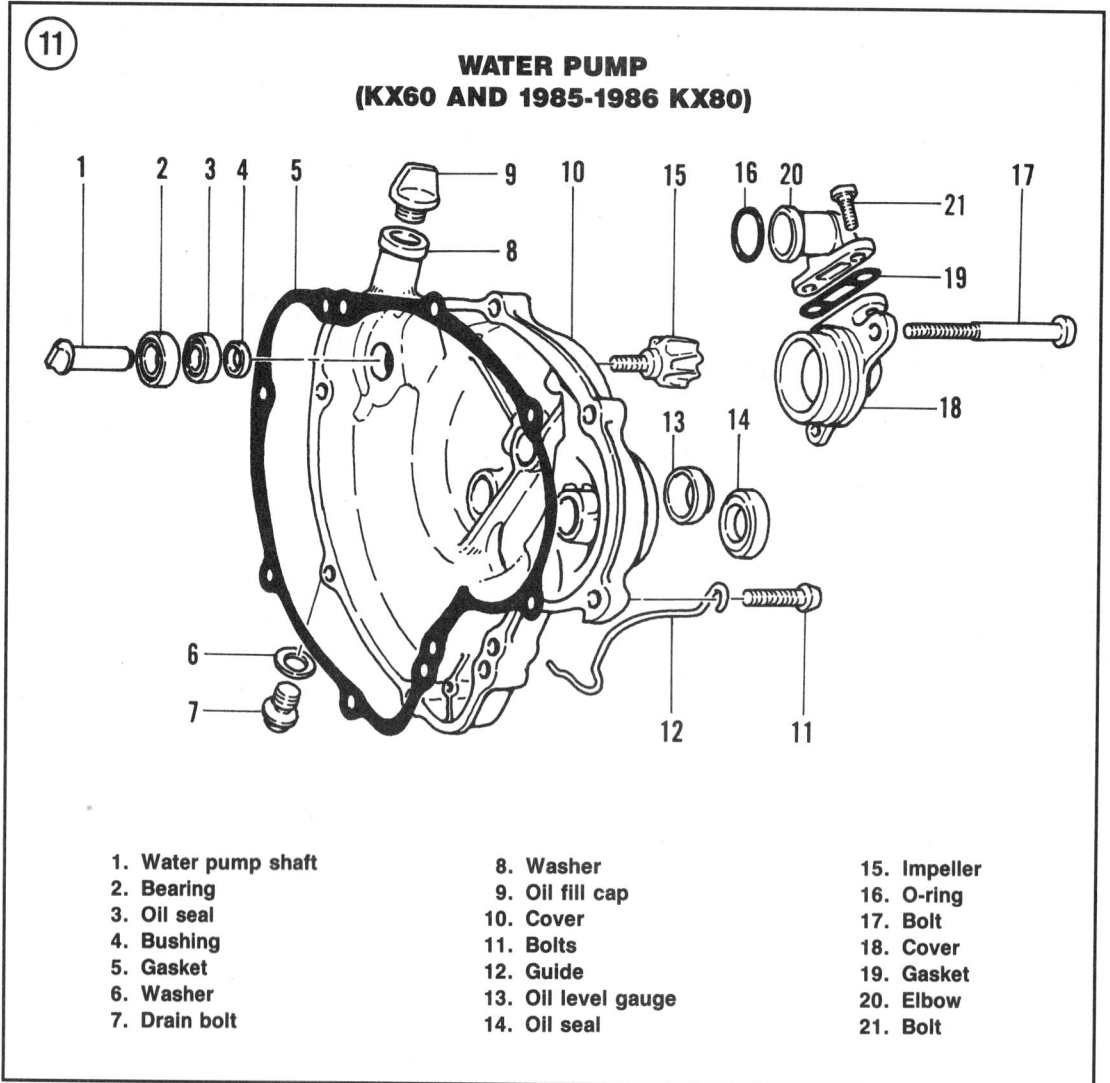

WATER PUMP
(KX60 AND 1985-1986 KX80)

1. Water pump shaft	8. Washer	15. Impeller
2. Bearing	9. Oil fill cap	16. O-ring
3. Oil seal	10. Cover	17. Bolt
4. Bushing	11. Bolts	18. Cover
5. Gasket	12. Guide	19. Gasket
6. Washer	13. Oil level gauge	20. Elbow
7. Drain bolt	14. Oil seal	21. Bolt

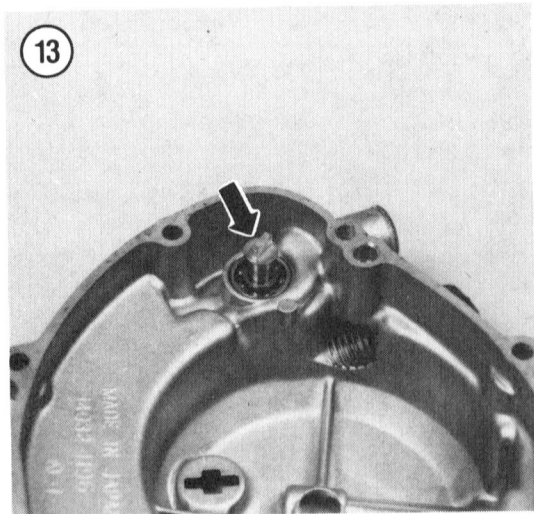

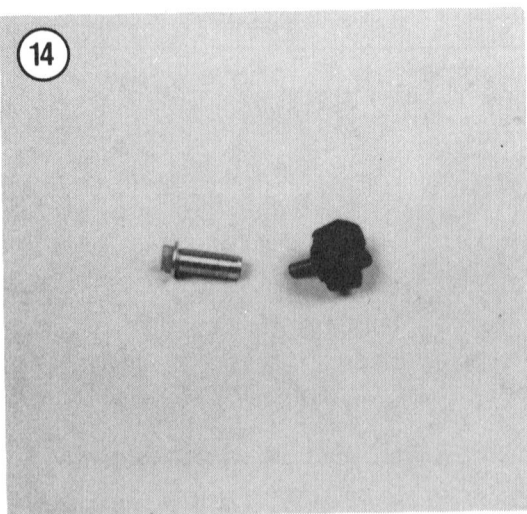

6. Inspect the water pump as described in this chapter.

7. Installation is the reverse of these steps. Note the following:

 a. Tighten the impeller bolt securely.

 b. Install a new water pump cover O-ring.

 c. Refill the cooling system as described under *Coolant Change* in Chapter Three.

 d. Refill the clutch/transmission oil as described in Chapter Three.

Removal/Installation
(KX60 and 1985-1986 KX80)

Refer to **Figure 11** for this procedure.

1. Drain the radiator as described under *Coolant Change* in Chapter Three.

2. Drain the clutch/transmission oil as described in Chapter Three.

3. Disconnect the coolant hoses on the water pump. See **Figure 12**.

> *NOTE*
> *On models equipped with Phillips screws, an impact driver with a Phillips bit is necessary to loosen the water pump cover screws in Step 4.*

4. Remove the Phillips screws or bolts holding the water pump cover onto the clutch cover. Remove the water pump cover. Remove the dowel pins (if so equipped).

5. Remove the impeller (**Figure 10**).

6. Remove the clutch cover as described under *Clutch Cover Removal/Installation* in Chapter Six.

7. Remove the water pump shaft from inside the clutch cover (**Figure 13**).

8. Inspect the water pump as described in this chapter.

9. Installation is the reverse of these steps. Note the following:

 a. Apply molybdenum disulfide grease to the water pump shaft (**Figure 14**) before installation.

 b. Tighten the impeller bolt securely.

 c. Install a new water pump cover O-ring.

 d. Refill the cooling system as described under *Coolant Change* in Chapter Three.

 e. Refill the clutch/transmission oil as described in Chapter Three.

10

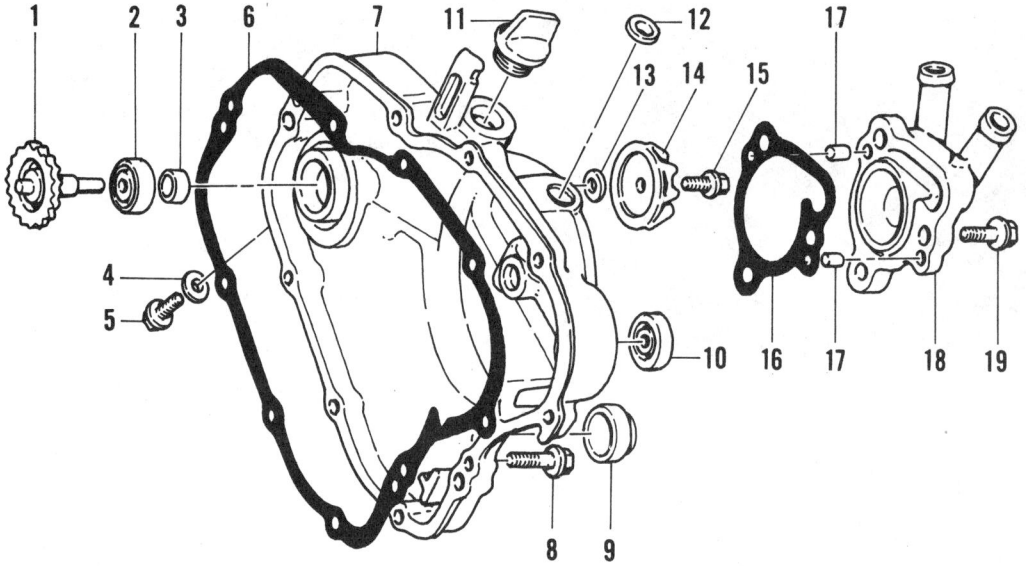

**WATER PUMP
(1987-ON KX80)**

1. Water pump shaft
2. Bearing
3. Oil seal
4. Washer
5. Drain bolt
6. Gasket
7. Cover
8. Bolt
9. Oil level gauge
10. Oil seal
11. Oil fill plug
12. Washer
13. Washer
14. Impeller
15. Bolt
16. Gasket
17. Dowel pins
18. Cover
19. Bolt

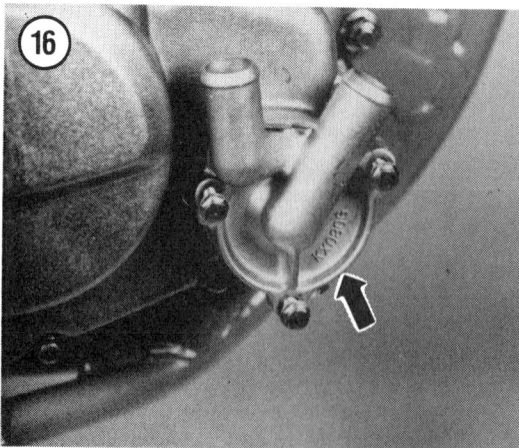

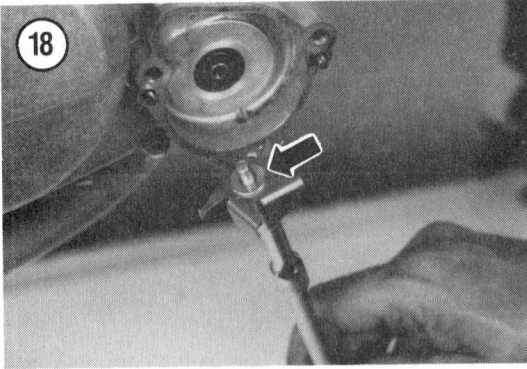

**Removal/Installation
(1987-on KX80)**

Refer to **Figure 15** for this procedure.

1. Drain the radiator as described under *Coolant Change* in Chapter Three.

2. Drain the clutch/transmission oil as described in Chapter Three.

3. Disconnect the coolant hoses on the water pump.

4. Remove the bolts holding the water pump cover onto the clutch cover. Remove the water pump cover (**Figure 16**). Remove the dowel pins and gasket.

5. Loosen and remove the impeller mounting bolt (**Figure 17**), impeller and washer (**Figure 18**).

6. Remove the clutch cover as described under *Clutch Cover Removal/Installation* in Chapter Six.

7. Remove the circlip securing the primary drive gear to the crankshaft. Remove the primary drive gear (**Figure 19**).

8. Remove the water pump shaft (**Figure 20**).

9. Remove the water pump drive gear (**Figure 21**).

10. Inspect the water pump as described in this chapter.

11. Installation is the reverse of these steps. Note the following:

    a. Apply molybdenum disulfide grease to the water pump shaft (**Figure 22**) before installation.

    b. Tighten the impeller bolt securely.

    c. Install a new water pump cover O-ring or gasket.

    d. Refill the cooling system as described under *Coolant Change* in Chapter Three.

    e. Refill the clutch/transmission oil as described in Chapter Three.

10

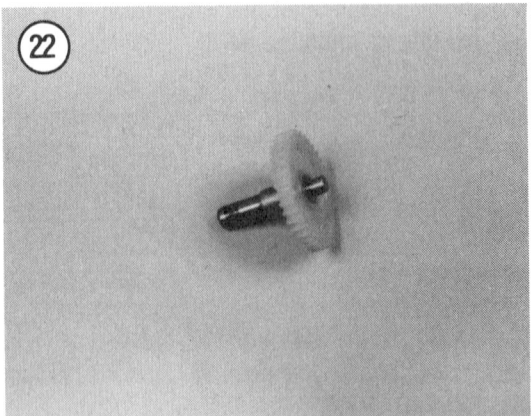

Inspection

1. Check the impeller for coolant crust and clean if necessary.
2. Check the water pump shaft surface for cracks, deep scoring or excessive wear. On late model KX80 models, check the nylon gear (**Figure 22**) for cracks or other damage.
3. Check the water pump seal and bearing for wear or damage (**Figure 23**, typical). If necessary, replace the bearing and seal as described in this chapter.
4. Check the water passages in the water pump cover (**Figure 24**) for coolant buildup. Clean thoroughly.

Water Pump
Bearing and Seal Replacement

1. Remove the water pump as described in this chapter.
2. *1984*: Remove the circlip (**Figure 9**).
3. Insert a drift through the bearing and tap the oil seal out of the cover. Work the drift around the oil seal during removal so that the seal does not become cocked in the seal bore.
4. Using a press, remove the bearing. If a press is not available, use a socket placed on the inner bearing race and drive the bearing out of the cover.
5. Wash the cover thoroughly in solvent.
6. Install the oil seal as follows:
   a. Place the cover on the workbench so that the inside of the cover faces up.
   b. Apply a high temperature grease to the inside of the seal lips.
   c. Drive the oil seal into the cover so that the marked side of the oil seal faces down. Drive the oil seal in until the seal is flush with the bearing mounting surface.
7. Install the bearing as follows:
   a. Place the cover on the workbench so that the inside of the cover faces up.
   b. Align the bearing with the bearing bore and drive the bearing into the cover until it bottoms on the cover step.

HOSES

Hoses deteriorate with age and should be replaced periodically or whenever they show signs

of cracking or leakage. To be safe, replace the hoses every 2 years. The spray of hot coolant from a cracked hose can cause rider injury. Loss of coolant will also cause the engine to overheat and result in severe damage.

Whenever any component of the cooling system is removed, inspect the hoses(s) and determine if replacement is necessary.

Inspection

1. With the engine cool, check the cooling hoses for brittleness or hardness. A hose in this condition will usually show cracks and must be replaced.
2. With the engine hot, examine the hoses for swelling along the entire hose length. Eventually a hose will rupture at this point.
3. Check area around hose clamps. Signs of rust around clamps indicate possible hose leakage.

Replacement

Hose replacement should be performed when the engine is cool.
1. Drain the cooling system as described under *Coolant Change* in Chapter Three.
2. Loosen the hose clamps from the hose to be replaced. Slide the clamps along the hose and out of the way.
3. Twist the hose end to break the seal and remove from the connecting joint. If the hose has been on for some time, it may have become fused to the joint. If so, cut the hose parallel to the joint connections with a knife or razor. The hose then can be carefully pried loose with a screwdriver.

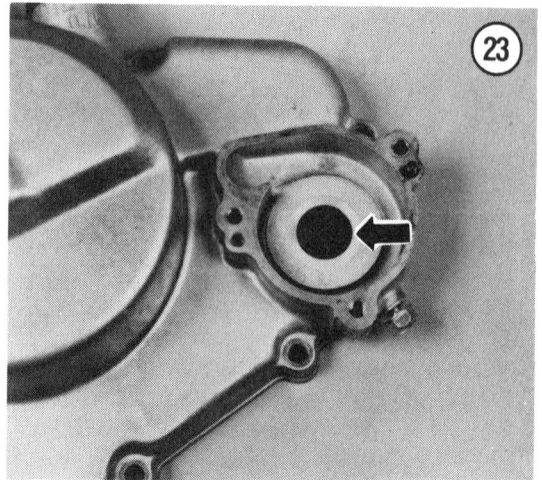

CAUTION
Excessive force applied to the hose during removal could damage the connecting joint especially the radiator.

4. Examine the connecting joint for cracks or other damage. Repair or replace parts as required. If the joint is okay, remove rust with sandpaper.

5. Inspect hose clamps and replace as necessary.
6. Slide hose clamps over outside of hose and install hose to inlet and outlet connecting joint. Make sure the hose clears all obstructions and is routed properly.

NOTE
If it is difficult to install a hose on a joint, soak the end of the hose in hot water for approximately 2 minutes. This will soften the hose and ease installation.

7. With the hose positioned correctly on joint, position clamps back away from end of hose slightly. Tighten clamps securely, but not so much that hose is damaged.
8. Refill cooling system as described under *Coolant Change* in Chapter Three. Start the engine and check for leaks. Retighten hose clamps as necessary.

10

CHAPTER ELEVEN

FRONT SUSPENSION
AND STEERING

This chapter describes repair and maintenance on the front wheel, forks and steering components.

Steering specifications are listed in **Table 1**. Front suspension service specifications are listed in **Table 2**. **Tables 1-4** are at the end of the chapter.

FRONT WHEEL

Removal/Installation
(KX60 and 1983 KX80)

> *WARNING*
> *When removing the wheels or working on the brakes, wear a protective mask to keep from inhaling any dust from the brake linings. The brake linings contain asbestos fiber; asbestos has been connected with lung scarring and cancer. Do not use compressed air to clean the brake drums or linings; dump any dust onto a newspaper and place in a resealable plastic bag. Dispose of it in the trash. Wash your hands thoroughly after handling the brake parts.*

1. Support the motorcycle on a bike stand so that the front wheel is off the ground.
2. If it is necessary to remove the front brake hub, loosen the brake cable adjuster (A, **Figure 1**) at the front hub and disconnect the cable from the hub.
3. Loosen and remove the front axle nut (B, **Figure 1**).

4. Remove the front axle (**Figure 2**) from the left-hand side. Then pull the wheel forward and remove it.

5. Remove the spacer from the right-hand side (**Figure 3**).

6. Pull the brake hub out of the front wheel and remove the wheel.

7. To install the front wheel, reverse the removal steps. Note the following:

   a. Clean the axle and axle spacer in solvent and thoroughly dry. Make sure all axle contact surfaces are clean and free of dirt and old grease prior to installation. If these surfaces are not cleaned, the axle may be difficult to remove later on.

   b. When installing the wheel in the forks, make sure the anchor boss on the left-hand fork leg (**Figure 4**) fits between the lugs cast into the brake panel (**Figure 5**). This is necessary for proper brake operation.

   c. Apply a light coat of grease to the axle, bearings and grease seals.

   d. To center the brake shoes in the drum, tighten the axle nut lightly, spin the wheel and apply the brake forcefully, then tighten the axle nut.

   e. Tighten the axle nut to the torque specification in **Table 3** or **Table 4**.

   f. Adjust brake cable play. Refer to Chapter Three.

**Removal/Installation
(1984-on KX80)**

1. Support the motorcycle with the front wheel off the ground.

2. Loosen and remove the front axle nut (**Figure 6**).

11

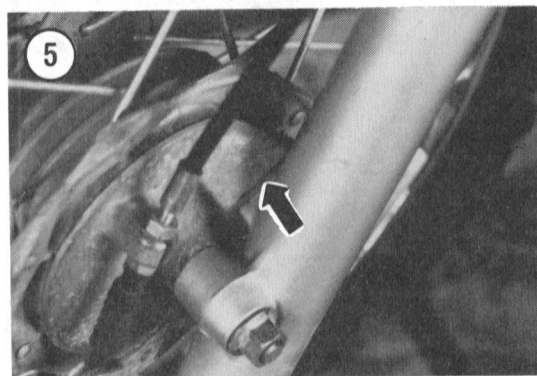

3. Slide the axle (**Figure 7**) out from the left-hand side and lower the front wheel.

NOTE
After removing the front wheel, insert a piece of wood or hose in the caliper between the brake pads. That way, if the brake lever is accidently squeezed, the piston will not be forced out of the brake caliper cylinder. If the brake lever is squeezed and the piston comes out, the caliper might have to be disassembled to reseat the piston and the system will have to be bled.

4. Remove the left- and right-hand axle spacers. See **Figure 8**.
5. Install the axle spacers and axle nut on the axle to prevent their loss when servicing the wheel.
6. To install the front wheel, reverse the removal steps. Note the following:
   a. Clean the axle and axle spacers in solvent and thoroughly dry. Make sure all axle contact surfaces are clean and free of dirt and old grease prior to installation. If these surfaces are not cleaned, the axle may be difficult to remove later on.
   b. Apply a light coat of grease to the axle, bearings and grease seals.
   c. Carefully insert the disc between the brake pads when installing the wheel.
   d. Install the axle nut. Tighten the axle nut to the torque specification in **Table 4**.
   e. After the wheel is completely installed, rotate the front wheel and apply the brake. Do this a couple of times to make sure the front wheel and brake are operating correctly.

Inspection

Spokes loosen with use and should be checked prior to each race or a weekend ride. The "tuning fork" method for checking spoke tightness is simple and works well. Tap each spoke with a spoke wrench or the shank of a screwdriver and listen for a tone. A tightened spoke will emit a clear, ringing tone, and a loose spoke will sound flat. All the spokes of the same length in a correctly tightened wheel will emit tones of similar pitch but not necessarily the same precise tone.

Bent, stripped or broken spokes should be replaced as soon as they are detected, as they can cause the destruction of an expensive hub. Unscrew the nipple from the spoke and depress the nipple into the rim far enough to free the end of the spoke, taking care not to push the nipple all the way in. Remove the damaged spoke from the hub and use it to match a new spoke of identical length. If necessary, trim the new spoke to match the original and dress the end of the thread with a thread die. Install the new spoke in the hub and screw on the nipple; tighten it (**Figure 9**) until the spoke's tone is similar to the tone of the other spokes in the wheel. Periodically check the new spoke; it will stretch and must be retightened several times before it takes its final set.

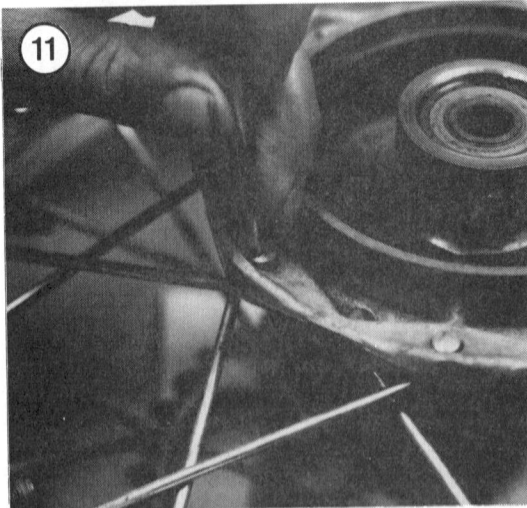

CAUTION
When spokes loosen or when installing new spokes, the head of the spokes (Figure 10) should be checked for proper seating in the hub. Improperly seated spokes can cause severe hub damage. If one or more spokes required seating, hit the head of the spoke with a punch and hammer as shown in Figure 11.

Wheel rim runout is the amount of "wobble" a wheel shows as it rotates. You can check runout with the wheels on the bike by simply supporting the wheel off the ground and turning the wheel slowly while you hold a pointer solidly against a fork leg. Just make sure any wobble you observe isn't caused by your own hand.

Off the motorcycle, runout can be checked with the wheel installed on a truing stand.

The maximum allowable axial (side-to-side) and radial (up and down) play is listed in **Table 2**. Tighten or replace any bent or loose spokes.

1. Draw the high point of the rim toward the centerline of the wheel by tightening the spokes in the area of the high point and on the same side as the high point and loosening the spokes on the side opposite the high point.

2. Rotate the wheel and check runout. Continue adjusting until the runout is within specification. Be patient and thorough, adjusting the position of the rim a little at a time. If you tighten 2 spokes at the high point 1/2 turn, tighten the adjacent spokes 1/4 turn. Loosen the spokes on the opposite side equivalent amounts.

FRONT HUB

Refer to **Figure 12** (KX60 and 1983 KX80) or **Figure 13** (1984-on KX80) for this procedure.

Disassembly/Reassembly

Do not remove bearings for periodic inspection as bearing removal normally damages the first bearing removed. Always replace bearings as a set.

1. Remove the front wheel as described in this chapter.

2. *KX60 and 1983 KX80:* Remove the right-hand oil seal (**Figure 12**) by carefully prying it out of

⑫

**FRONT HUB
(KX60 AND 1983 KX80)**

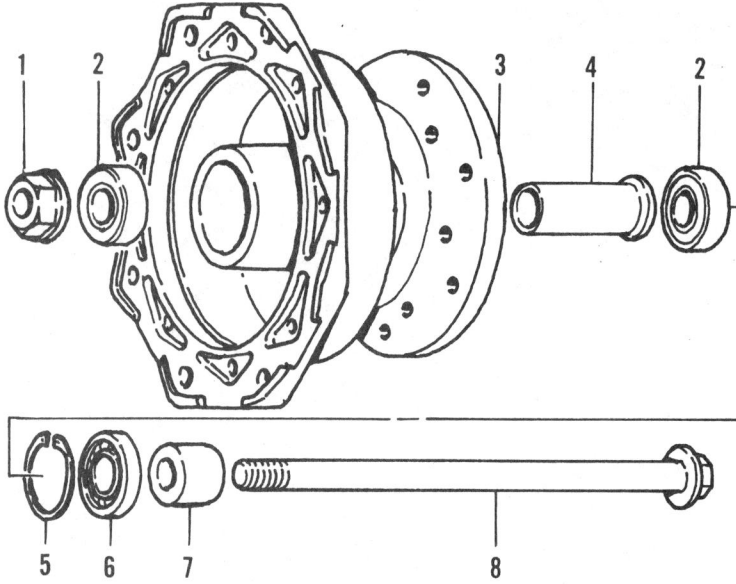

1. Axle nut
2. Bearing
3. Hub
4. Spacer
5. Circlip
6. Oil seal
7. Spacer
8. Front axle

⑬

**FRONT HUB
(1984-ON KX80)**

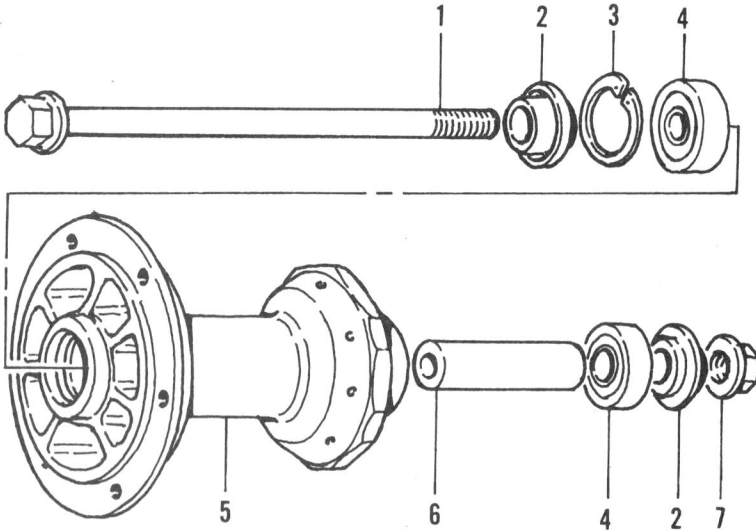

1. Front axle
2. Spacer
3. Circlip
4. Bearing
5. Hub
6. Spacer
7. Axle nut

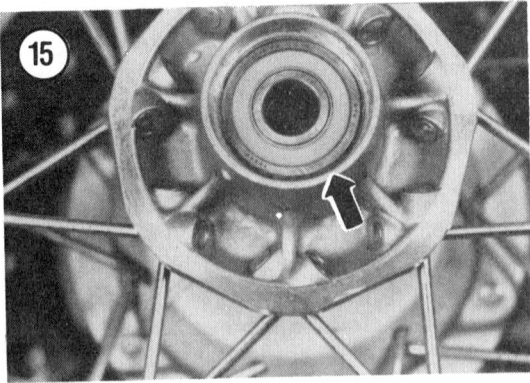

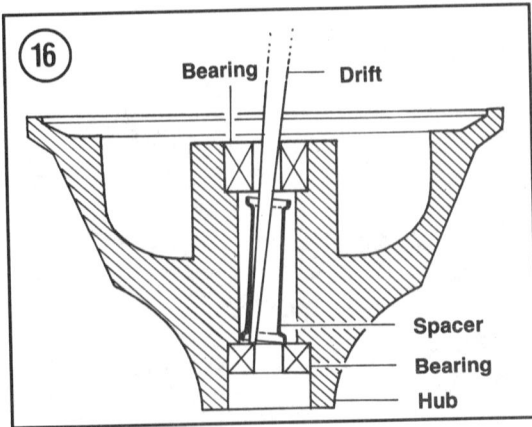

Bearing — Drift

Spacer
Bearing
Hub

the hub with a flat-bladed screwdriver. Prop a piece of wood or rag underneath the screwdriver to prevent damaging the hub.

NOTE
If the seal is tight, work the screwdriver around the seal every few degrees until the seal pops out of the hub.

3A. *KX60 and 1983 KX80:* Remove the circlip (**Figure 12**) from the right-hand side.
3B. *1984-on KX80:* Remove the circlip (**Figure 14**) from the left-hand side.
4. Remove the left- and right-hand bearings (**Figure 15**) and spacer. To remove the bearings, insert a soft-aluminum or brass drift into one side of the hub. Push the spacer over to one side and place the drift on the inner race of the lower bearing (**Figure 16**). Tap the bearing out of the hub with a hammer, working around the perimeter of the inner race.
5. Remove the spacer and tap out the opposite bearing.
6. Thoroughly clean out the inside of the hub with solvent and dry with compressed air or a shop cloth.

NOTE
Avoid getting any greasy solvent residue on the brake drum or brake disc during this procedure. If this happens, clean it off with a shop cloth and lacquer thinner.

NOTE
Fully sealed bearings are available from many good bearing specialty shops. Fully sealed bearings provide better protection from dirt and moisture that may get into the hub.

NOTE
*When checking axle runout with V-blocks in Step 7, place the V-blocks 100 mm (4.0 in.) apart (**Figure 17**).*

7. Check the axle for wear and straightness. Use V-blocks and a dial indicator (**Figure 17**). If the runout exceeds the service limit in **Table 2**,

11

straighten the axle with a press. If the runout exceeds the repair limit (**Table 2**), replace the axle.

8. Pack non-sealed bearings with good-quality bearing grease. Work the grease in between the balls thoroughly. Turn the bearing by hand a couple of times to make sure the grease is distributed evenly inside the bearing.

9. Pack the spacer with multipurpose grease.

> *NOTE*
> *If a bearing has only one sealed side, install the bearing with the sealed side facing out.*

> *CAUTION*
> *When installing the bearings in the following procedures, tap the bearings squarely into place and tap on the outer race only. Use a socket (**Figure 18**) that matches the outer race diameter. Do not tap on the inner race or the bearing might be damaged. Be sure that the bearings are completely seated.*

10. Install the left-hand bearing.
11. Install in the spacer.
12. Install the right-hand bearing.
13A. *KX60 and 1983 KX80:* Install the circlip (**Figure 12**) into the hub groove on the right-hand side.
13B. *1984-on KX80:* Install the circlip (**Figure 14**) into the hub groove on the left-hand side.
14. *KX60 and 1983 KX80:* Install a new right-hand grease seal. Lubricate it with multipurpose grease and tap it squarely into the hub. Install the oil seal until it seats against the circlip.

TIRE CHANGING

Removal

1. Remove the valve core and deflate the tire.
2. Loosen the rim lock nut (**Figure 19**).
3. Press the entire bead on both sides of the tire into the center of the rim.
4. Lubricate the beads with soapy water.

> *NOTE*
> *Use only quality tire irons without sharp edges (**Figure 20**). If necessary, file the ends of the tire irons to remove rough edges.*

5. Insert the tire iron under the bead next to the valve (**Figure 21**). Force the bead on the opposite side of tire into the center of the rim and pry the bead over the rim with the tire iron.
6. Insert a second tire iron next to the first to hold the bead over the rim. Then work around the tire with the first tire iron, prying the bead over the rim. Be careful not to pinch the inner tube with the tire irons.

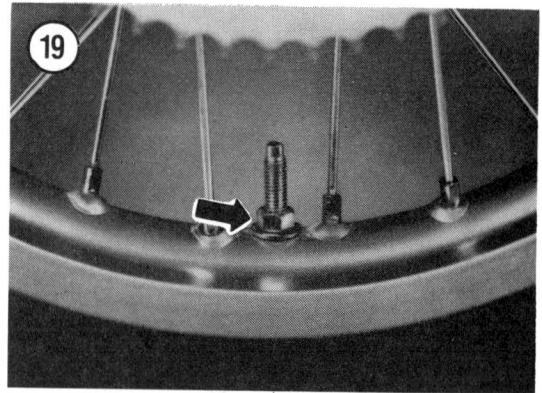

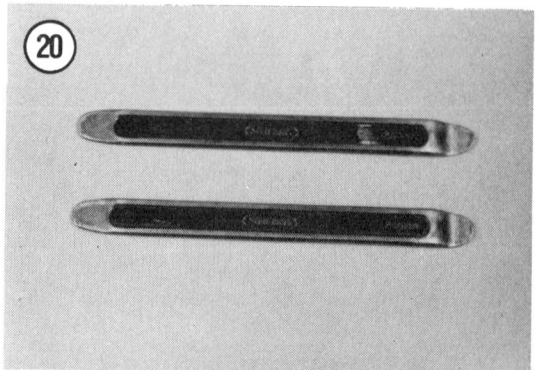

7. Remove the valve from the hole in the rim and remove the tube from the tire.

NOTE
Step 8 is required only if it is necessary to completely remove the tire from the rim, such as for tire replacement.

8. Stand the tire upright. Insert the tire iron between the second bead and the side of the rim

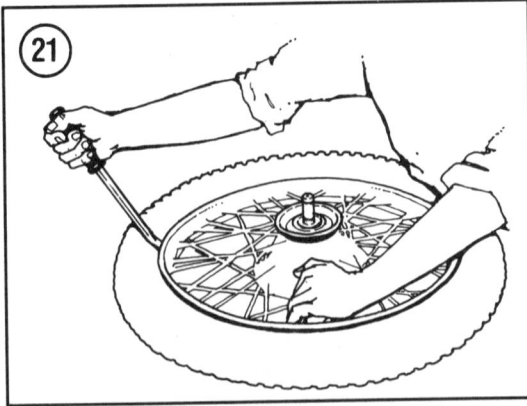

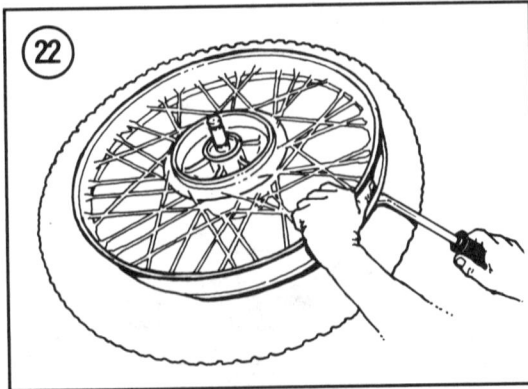

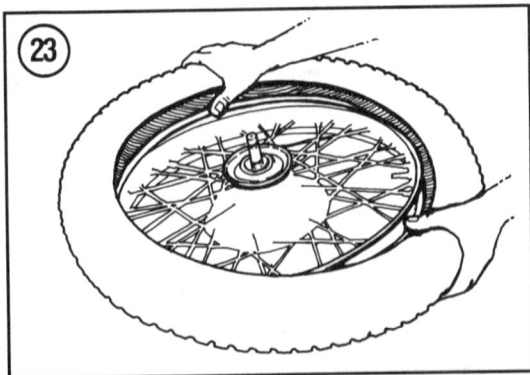

that the first bead was pried over (**Figure 22**). Force the bead on the opposite side from the tire iron into the center of the rim. Pry the second bead off of the rim, working around as with the first.

Installation

1. Carefully check the tire for any damage, especially inside. On the front tire, carefully check the sidewall as it is very vulnerable to damage from rocks and other riders footpegs.
2. Check that the spoke ends do not protrude through the nipples into the center of the rim to puncture the tube. File off any protruding spoke ends.

NOTE
If you are having trouble with water and dirt entering the wheel, remove and discard the rubber rim band. Then wrap the rim center with 2 separate revolutions of duct tape. Punch holes through the tape at the rim lock and valve stem mounting areas.

3. Install the rim lock if removed.
4. If you are using the rubber rim band, be sure the band is in place with the rough side toward the rim. Align the holes in the band with the holes in the rim.
5. Liberally sprinkle the inside tire casing with talcum power. This helps to minimize tube pinching because the power reduces chafing between the tire and tube.
6. If the tire was removed, lubricate one bead with soapy water. Then align the tire with the rim and push the tire onto the rim (**Figure 23**). Work around the tire in both directions (**Figure 24**).

11

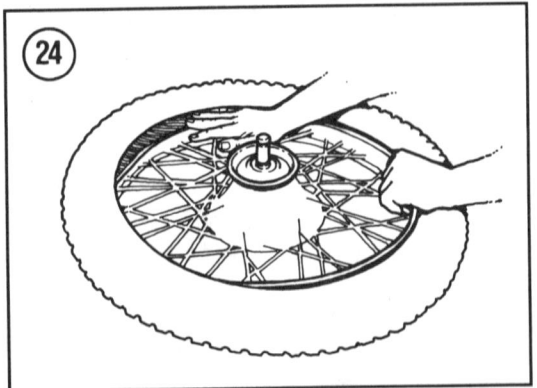

7. Install the core into the inner tube valve. Put the tube in the tire and insert the valve stem through the hole in the rim. Inflate just enough to round it out. Too much air will make installing it in the tire difficult, and too little will increase the chances of pinching the tube with the tire irons.

8. Lubricate the upper tire bead and rim with soapy water.

9. Press the upper bead into the rim opposite the valve. Pry the bead into the rim on both sides of the initial point with your hands and work around the rim to the valve. If the tire wants to pull up on one side, either use a tire iron or one of your knees to hold the tire in place. The last few inches are usually the toughest to install and it is also where most pinched tubes occur. If you can, continue to push the tire into the rim with your hands. Relubricate the bead if necessary. If the tire bead wants to pull out from under the rim, use both of your knees to hold the tire in place. If necessary, use a tire iron for the last few inches (**Figure 25**)—but be careful that the tire iron does not puncture the tube when the tire finally slides under the rim.

10. Wiggle the valve to be sure the tube is not trapped under the bead. Set the valve squarely in its hole before screwing on the valve nut.

NOTE
*Make sure the valve stem is not cocked in the rim as shown in **Figure 26**.*

11. Check the bead on both sides of the tire for an even fit around the rim. Inflate the tire to approximately 25-30 psi to ensure the tire bead is seated properly on the rim. If the tire is hard to seat, relubricate both sides of the tire and reinflate.

12. Tighten the rim lock nut (**Figure 19**).

13. Bleed the tire back down to between 10 and 14 psi. Never tighten the valve stem nut against the rim. It should always be installed finger-tight, near the valve stem cap rather than flush against the rim (**Figure 27**).

TIRE REPAIRS

Every dirt rider eventually experiences trouble with a tire or tube. Repairs and replacement are fairly simple, and every rider should know how to patch a tube.

Patching a motorcycle tube is only a temporary fix, especially on a dirt bike. The tire flexes too much and the patch could rub right off.

NOTE
If a regular standard inner tube is used, replace it every 10 races. A stronger heavy-duty tube will last longer and is not as easy to puncture. The stronger tube weighs more where you least need it (unsprung weight) but it's a sacrifice that's worth the durability.

Tire Repair Kits

Tire repair kits can be purchased from motorcycle dealers and some auto supply stores. When buying, specify that the kit you want is for motorcycles.

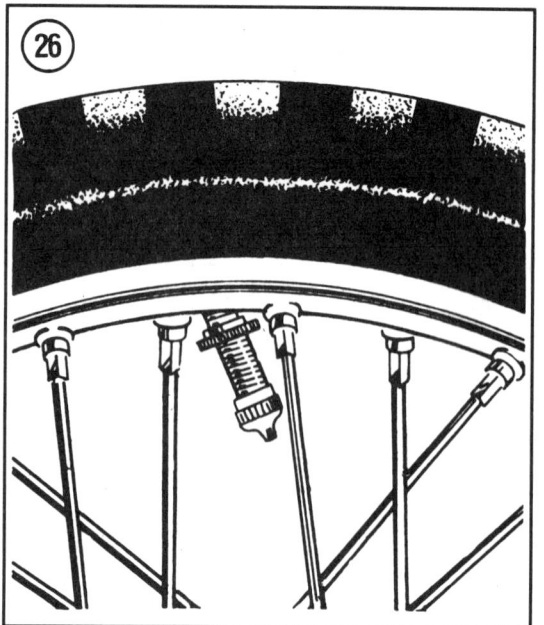

There are 2 types of tire repair kits:

a. Hot patch.

b. Cold patch.

Hot patches are stronger because they actually vulcanize to the tube, becoming part of it. However, they are far too bulky to carry for trail repairs, and the strength is unnecessary for a temporary repair.

Cold patches are not vulcanized to the tube; they are simply glued to it. Though not as strong as hot patches, cold patches are still very durable. Cold patch kits are less bulky than hot and more easily applied out on a dusty trail or in the pits. A cold patch kit contains everything necessary and tucks easily in with your emergency tool kit.

Tube Inspection

1. Remove the tube as described under *Tire Changing* in this chapter.
2. Install the valve core into the valve stem and inflate the tube slightly. Do not overinflate.
3. Immerse the tube in water a section at a time. Look carefully for bubbles indicating a hole. Mark each hole and continue checking until you are certain that all holes are discovered and marked. Also make sure that the valve core is not leaking. Tighten it if necessary.

NOTE
If you do not have enough water to immerse sections of the tube, try running your hand over the tube slowly and very close to the surface. If your hand is damp, it works even better. If

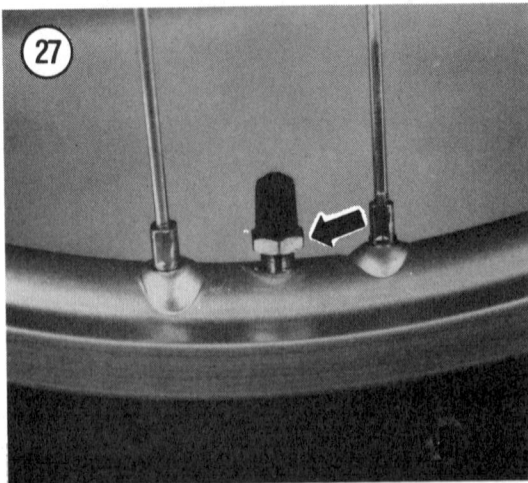

you suspect a hole anywhere, apply some saliva to the area to verify it.

4. Apply a cold patch using the techniques described under *Cold Patch Repair*, following.
5. Dust the patch area with talcum powder to prevent it from sticking to the tire.
6. Carefully check the inside of the tire casing for small rocks, sand or twigs which may have damaged the tube. If the inside of the tire is split, apply a patch to the area to prevent it from pinching and damaging the tube again.
7. Check the inside of the rim. Make sure the rubber rim band is in place, with no spoke ends protruding, which could puncture the tube.
8. Deflate the tube prior to installation in the tire.

Cold Patch Repairs

1. Remove the tube from the tire and inspect it as previously described.
2. Roughen an area around the hole slightly larger than the patch, using a cap from the tire repair kit or a pocket knife. Do not scrape too vigorously or you may cause additional damage.
3. Apply a small amount of the special cement from the kit to the puncture and spread it evenly with the tube container.
4. Allow the cement to dry until tacky—usually 30 seconds or so is sufficient.
5. Remove the backing from the patch.

CAUTION
Do not touch the newly exposed rubber with your fingers or the patch will not stick firmly.

6. Center the patch over the hole. Hold patch firmly in place for about 30 seconds to allow the cement to set.
7. Dust the patched area with talcum powder to prevent sticking.
8. Install the tube as previously described.

HANDLEBAR

Removal/Installation

1. Remove the plastic straps on the engine kill switch wire.

11

2. Remove the kill switch and the clutch lever assembly from the left-hand side. See **Figure 28**.

NOTE
Step 3 describes disassembly and removal of the throttle assembly. If it is not necessary to disassemble the throttle assembly when removing the handlebar, loosen the throttle assembly screws only. When the handlebar bolts and handlebar are removed from the steering stem, slide the throttle assembly off the handlebar.

3. Remove the screws securing the throttle assembly (A, **Figure 29**) and remove it.

NOTE
Carefully lay the throttle assembly and cable over the front fender, or back over the frame, so the cable does not get crimped or damaged.

4A. *Front drum brake models:* Remove the screws securing the front brake assembly and remove it.
4B. *Disc brake models:* Remove the bolts securing the master cylinder to the handlebar and remove the master cylinder (B, **Figure 29**). Support the master cylinder so that it does not hang by the hydraulic hose.
5. Remove the bolts (**Figure 30**) securing the handlebar holders and remove the holders.
6. Remove the handlebar.
7. Install by reversing these removal steps while noting the following.
8. To maintain a good grip in the handlebar and to prevent them from slipping down, clean the knurled section of the handlebar with a wire brush. It should be kept rough so it will be held securely by the holders. The holders should also be kept clean and free of any metal that may have been gouged loose by handlebar slippage.
9. Tighten the clamp bolts securing the handlebar to the torque specification listed in **Table 3** or **Table 4**.

NOTE
After tightening the handlebar clamp bolts, check the position of the clamp. When properly tightened, there should not be a gap at the front of the clamp.

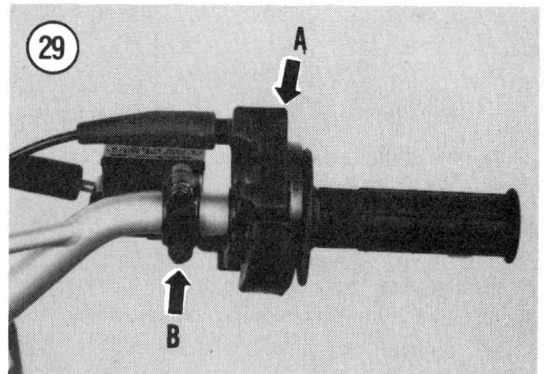

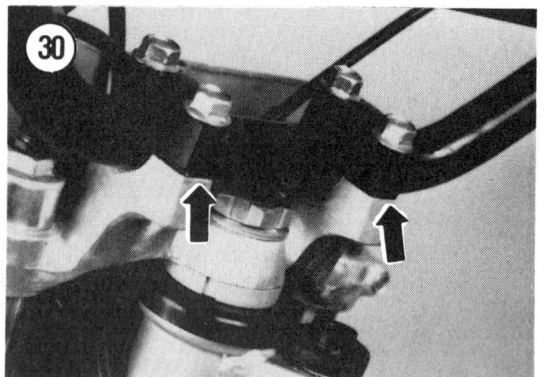

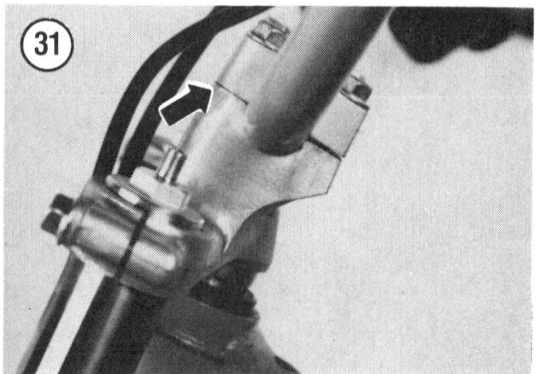

Figure 31 shows a properly tightened clamp.

10. Apply a light coat of light machine oil to the throttle grip area on the handlebar prior to installation.

> *WARNING*
> *After installation is completed, make sure the brake lever does not come in contact with the throttle grip assembly when it is pulled on fully.*

11. Adjust the front brake (drum brake models) and clutch as described in Chapter Three.

> *WARNING*
> *Make sure the front brake and clutch operate properly before riding the bike.*

STEERING HEAD (KX60 AND 1983-1985 KX80)

The steering head on these models uses loose ball bearings. Refer to **Figure 32** when performing procedures in this section.

Disassembly

1. Remove the front wheel as described in this chapter.

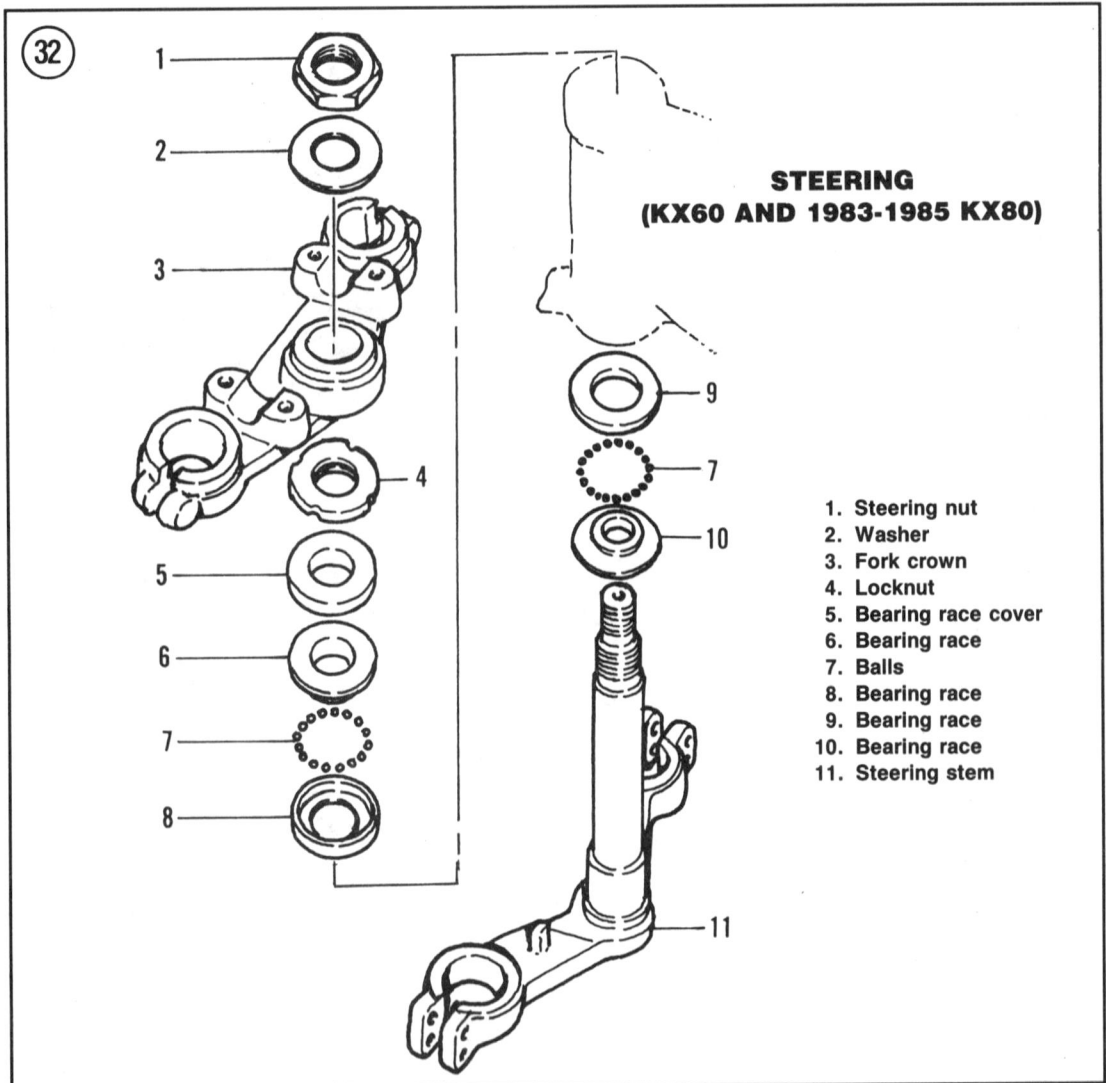

STEERING (KX60 AND 1983-1985 KX80)

1. Steering nut
2. Washer
3. Fork crown
4. Locknut
5. Bearing race cover
6. Bearing race
7. Balls
8. Bearing race
9. Bearing race
10. Bearing race
11. Steering stem

11

2. Remove the front fender.

3. Remove the handlebar as described under *Handlebar Removal/Installation* in this chapter.

> NOTE
> *Before removing the fork tube, measure the distance from the top of the fork tube to the top of the fork crown (Figure 33). Record this distance so that the fork tubes can be reinstalled to the same position.*

4. Remove the front forks as described in this chapter.

5. Loosen and remove the steering nut and washer.

6. Remove the fork crown.

7. Remove the fork crown locknut (**Figure 34**) and washer. Use a large drift and hammer or a spanner wrench (**Figure 35**).

> NOTE
> *The upper and lower bearing balls are the same diameter (3/16 in.) and the quantity is the same for the upper and lower races (23 balls).*

8. Lower the steering stem assembly down out of the steering head.

> NOTE
> *Have an assistant hold a large pan under the steering stem to catch the loose ball bearings and carefully lower the steering stem.*

9. Remove the upper bearing race cover and bearing inner race.

10. Remove the upper ball bearings (**Figure 36**).

11. Remove the lower ball bearings from the steering stem (**Figure 37**).

Inspection

1. Clean the bearing races in the steering head, the steering stem races, and the ball bearings with solvent.

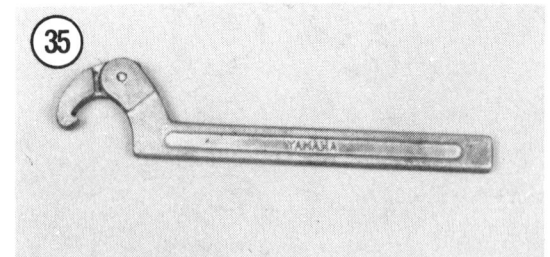

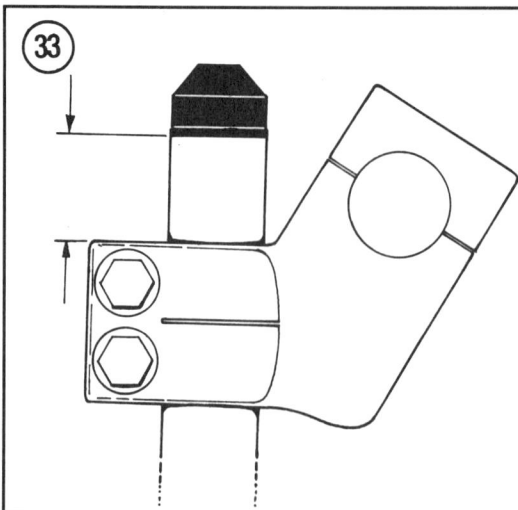

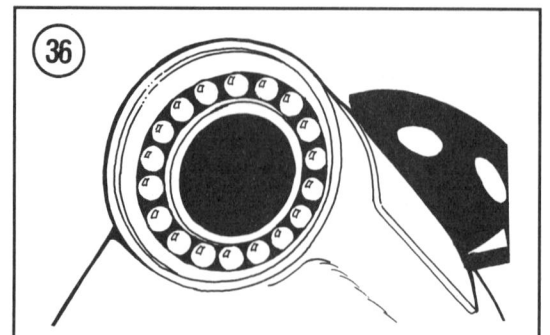

2. Check the welds around the steering head for cracks and fractures. If any are found, have them repaired by a competent frame shop or welding service.

3. Check the balls for pitting, scratches, or discoloration indicating wear or corrosion. Replace them in sets if any are bad.

4. Check the races for pitting or galling, and corrosion. If any of these conditions exist, replace the races as described under *Headset Race Replacement* in this chapter.

5. Check the steering stem for cracks and check its race for damage or wear. If this race or any race is damaged, they should be replaced as a complete bearing set. Take the old races and bearings to your dealer to ensure accurate replacement.

Headset Race Replacement

To remove the headset race, insert a hardwood stick or soft punch into the head tube (**Figure 38**) and carefully tap the race out from the inside. After it is started, tap around the race so that neither the race nor the head tube is damaged.

To install the headset race, tap it in slowly with a block of wood or suitable size socket or piece of pipe (**Figure 39**). Make sure they are squarely seated in the race bores before tapping them in. Tap them in until they are flush with the steering head.

> *NOTE*
> *The upper and lower bearings and races are not the same size. Be sure that you install them at the proper ends of the head tube.*

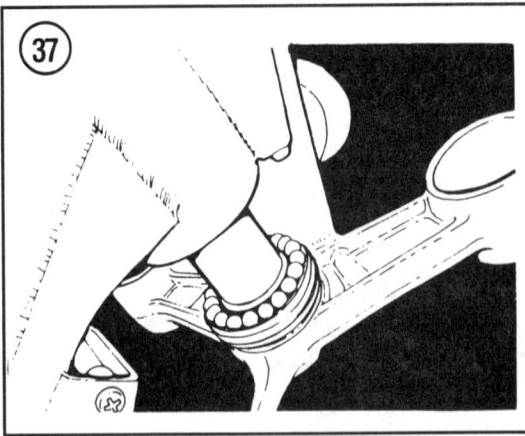

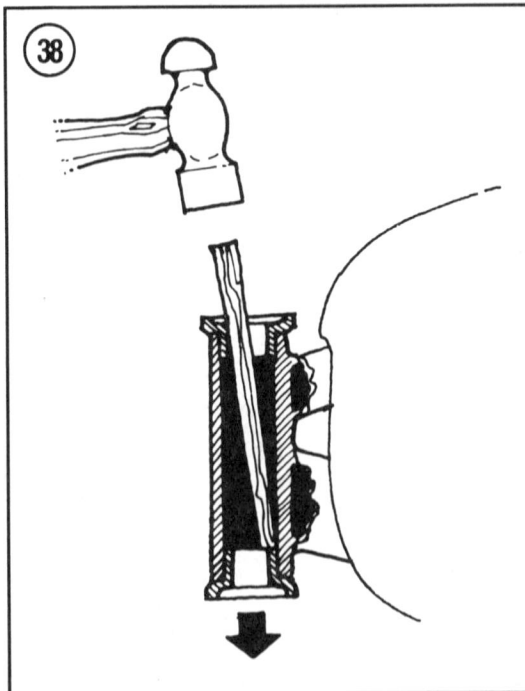

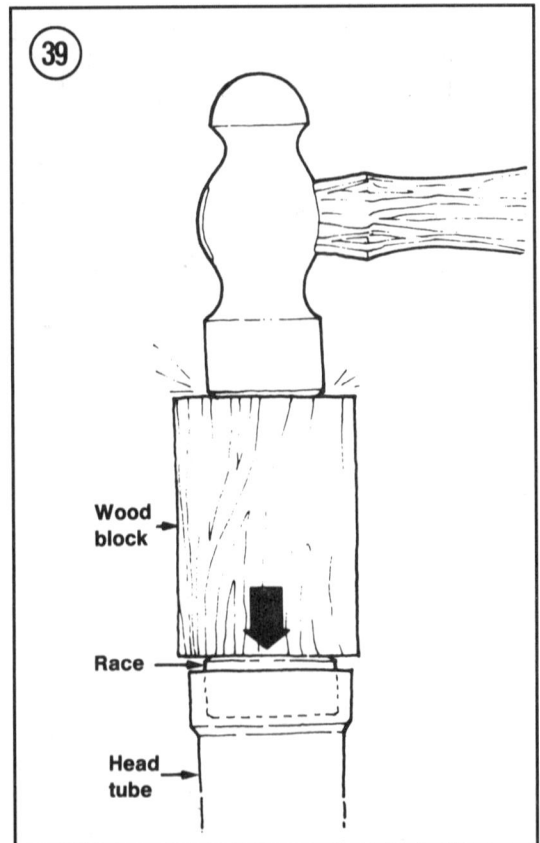

11

Steering Stem Race Replacement

To remove the steering stem race, try twisting and pulling it up by hand. If it will not come off, carefully pry it up with a screwdriver, while working around in a circle, prying a little at a time. Remove the race from the steering stem.

Slide the race over the steering stem with the bearing surface pointing up. Tap the race down with a piece of hardwood; work around in a circle so that the race will not be bent. Make sure it is seated squarely and all the way down.

Steering Head Assembly

Refer to **Figure 32** for this procedure.

1. Make sure the steering head and stem races are properly seated.

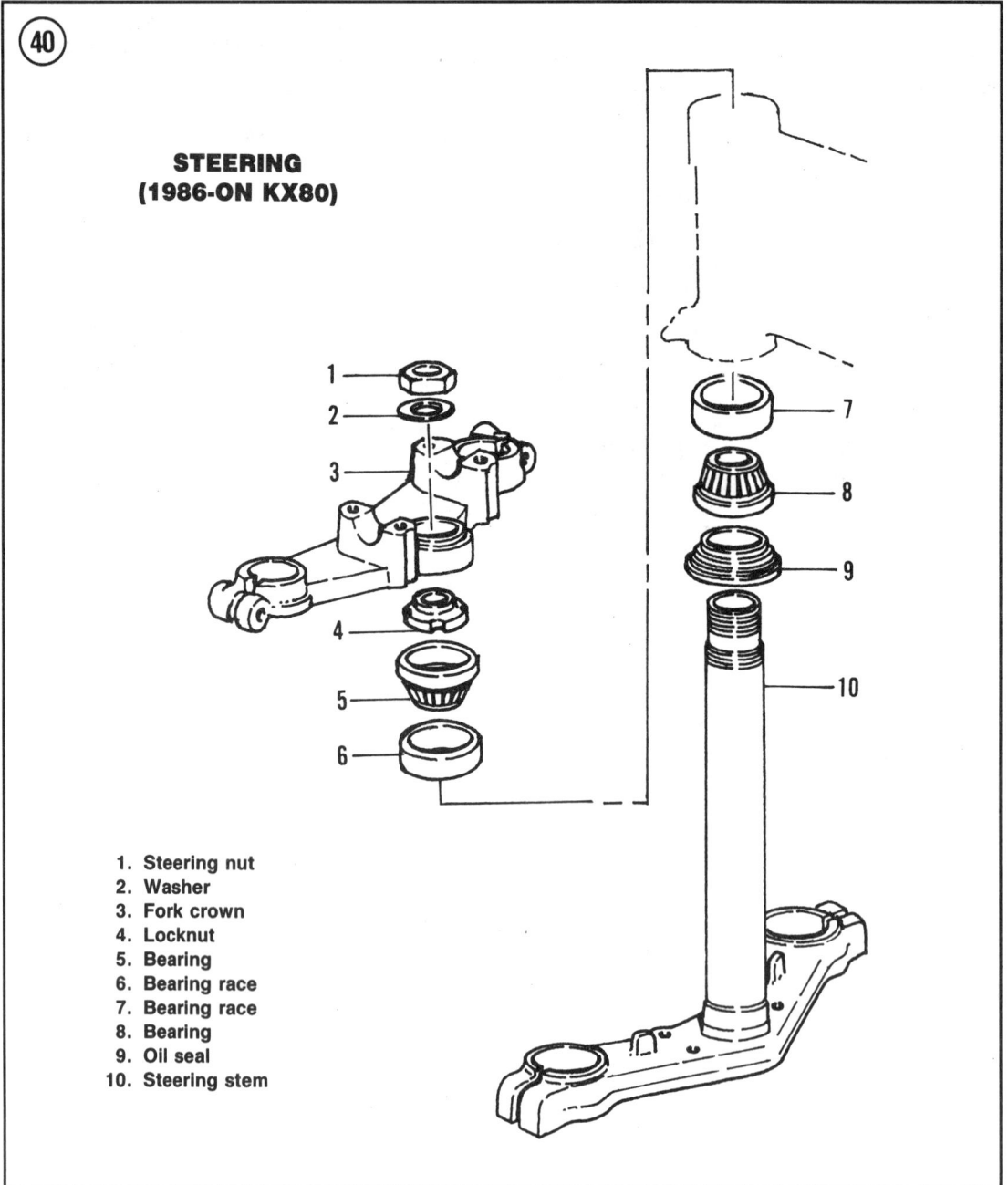

**STEERING
(1986-ON KX80)**

1. Steering nut
2. Washer
3. Fork crown
4. Locknut
5. Bearing
6. Bearing race
7. Bearing race
8. Bearing
9. Oil seal
10. Steering stem

2. Apply a coat of bearing grease to the lower bearing race cone and fit 23 ball bearings (3/16 in. diameter) around it (**Figure 37**).

3. Apply a coat of bearing grease to the upper bearing race cone and fit 23 ball bearings (3/16 in. diameter) around it (**Figure 36**).

4. Install the steering stem into the head tube and hold it firmly in place.

5. Install the upper bearing inner race and race cover.

6. Install the steering stem locknut (**Figure 34**) and tighten it until it is snug against the upper race. Then tighten the locknut to the torque specification in **Table 3** or **Table 4**.

NOTE
The adjusting nut should be just tight enough to remove play, both horizontal and vertical, yet loose enough so that the assembly will turn to both lock positions under its own weight after an assist.

7. Install the upper fork crown. Then install the washer and the steering nut finger-tight.

NOTE
Steps 8-10 must be performed in this order to assure proper upper and lower fork bridge to fork alignment.

8. Slide both fork tubes into position and tighten the lower front fork clamp bolts to the torque specification in **Table 3** or **Table 4**.

NOTE
Install the fork tube the same distance up from the top of the upper fork crown; see NOTE after Step 3, Disassembly.

9. Tighten the steering nut to the torque specification in **Table 3** or **Table 4**.

10. Tighten the upper front fork clamp bolts to the torque specification in **Table 3** or **Table 4**.

11. Continue assembly by reversing Steps 1-4, *Steering Stem Disassembly.*

12. After a few hours of riding, the bearings have had a chance to seat; readjust the free play in the steering stem with the steering locknut. Refer to Step 6.

STEERING HEAD
(1986-ON KX80)

The steering head on these models uses tapered roller bearings at the top and bottom pivot positions. Refer to **Figure 40** when performing procedures in this section.

Disassembly

1. Remove the front wheel as described under *Front Wheel Removal* in this chapter.

2. Remove the front fender.

3. Remove the handlebar as described under *Handlebar Removal/Installation* in this chapter.

NOTE
Before removing the fork tube, measure the distance from the top of the fork tube to the top of the fork crown (Figure 33). Record this distance so that the fork tubes can be reinstalled to the same position.

4. Remove the front forks as described in this chapter.

5. Loosen and remove the steering nut (**Figure 41**). Remove the washer (**Figure 42**).

11

6. Remove the fork crown (**Figure 43**).

7. Remove the locknut (**Figure 44**). Use a large drift and hammer or a spanner wrench (**Figure 35**).

8. Lower and remove the steering stem (**Figure 45**).

9. Remove the upper bearing (**Figure 46**).

Inspection

1. Clean the bearing races (**Figure 47**) in the steering head, the steering stem races and the tapered roller bearings (**Figure 48**) with solvent.

2. Check the welds around the steering head (**Figure 49**) for cracks and fractures. If any are found, have them repaired by a competent frame shop or welding service.

3. Check the races (**Figure 47**) for pitting or galling and corrosion. If any of these conditions exist, replace the races as described under *Headset Race Replacement* in this chapter.

4. Check the steering nut, adjust nut and washer (**Figure 50**) for cracks or damage. Replace if necessary.

6. Check the steering stem (**Figure 51**) for cracks and damage.

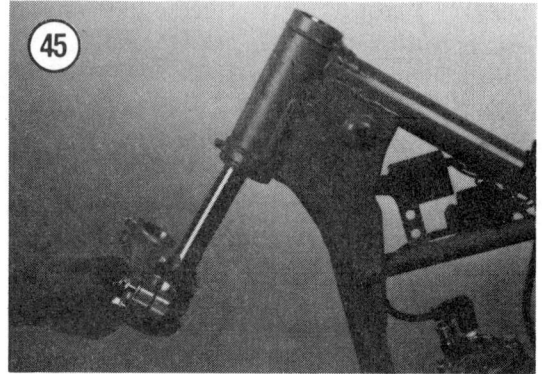

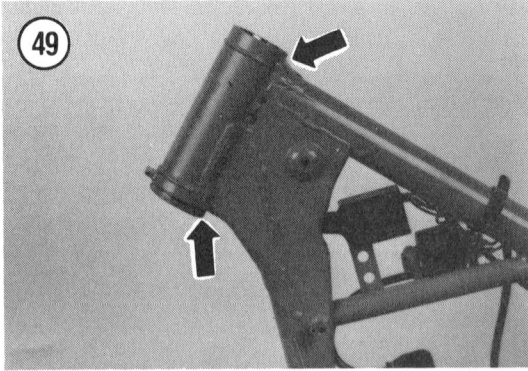

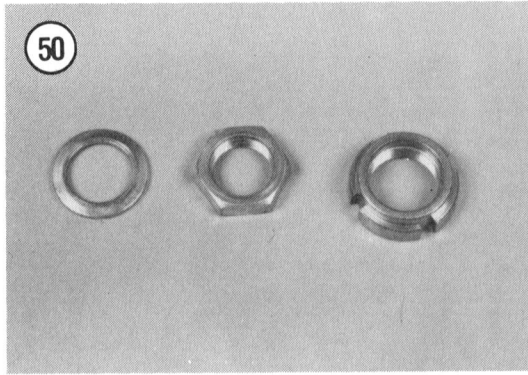

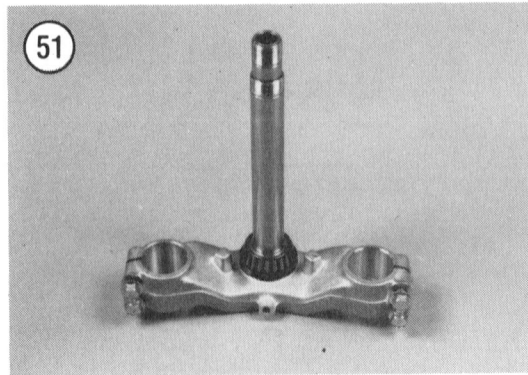

7. Check the tapered roller bearings (**Figure 52**) for pitting, scratches or discoloration indicating wear or corrosion. If necessary, replace the lower bearing as follows:

a. Install a bearing puller onto the steering stem and bearing.

b. Pull the bearing off of the steering stem.

c. Clean the steering stem thoroughly in solvent.

d. Slide a new bearing onto the steering stem until it stops.

e. Align the bearing with the machined portion of the shaft and slide a long hollow pipe over the steering stem until it seats against the inner bearing race. Drive the bearing onto the shaft until it bottoms out.

8. Check the upper (**Figure 53**) and lower fork crowns (**Figure 51**) for cracks or damage, especially where the fork tubes mount.

Headset Race Replacement

To remove an upper or lower headset race (**Figure 47**), insert a hardwood stick or soft punch into the head tube (**Figure 54**) and carefully tap

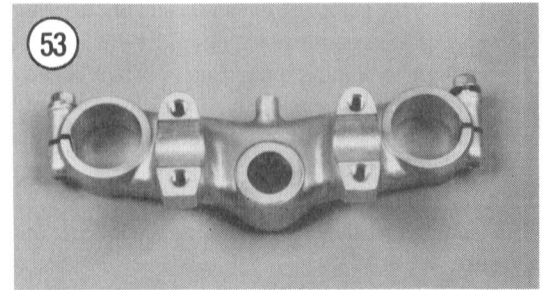

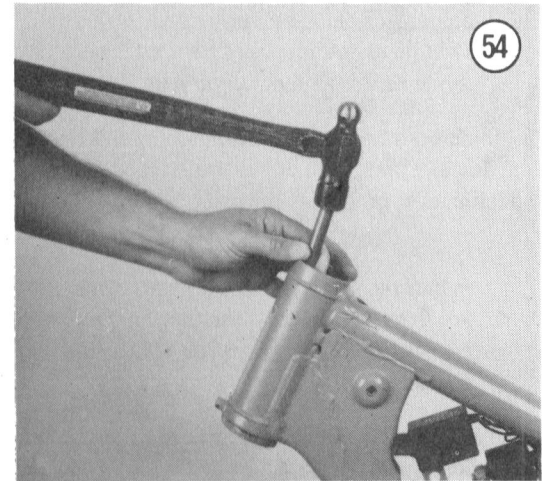

11

the race out from the inside. After it is started, tap around the race so that neither the race nor the head tube is damaged.

To install the headset race, tap it in slowly with a block of wood or suitable size socket or piece of pipe (**Figure 39**). Make sure they are squarely seated in the race bores before tapping them in. Tap them in until they are flush with the steering head.

Steering Head Assembly

Refer to **Figure 40** for this procedure.

1. Make sure the steering head and stem races are properly seated.
2. Apply a coat of bearing grease to the tapered roller bearing on the steering stem (**Figure 51**). Carefully work the grease into the rollers.
3. Install the steering stem (**Figure 45**) into the head tube and hold it firmly in place.
4. Install the upper bearing (**Figure 46**). Push the bearing down to seat it in the race (**Figure 55**).
5. Install and tighten the locknut as follows:
   a. Install the steering stem locknut (**Figure 44**).
   b. Tighten the locknut securely (**Figure 56**) to seat the bearings.
   c. Loosen the adjusting nut and check the bearing play. The adjusting nut should be just tight enough to remove play, both horizontal and vertical yet loose enough so that the assembly will turn to both lock positions under its own weight after an assist.
6. Install the fork crown (**Figure 43**).
7. Install the washer (**Figure 42**) and steering nut (**Figure 41**).

> *NOTE*
> *Steps 8-10 must be performed in this order to assure proper upper and lower fork bracket to fork alignment.*

8. Slide both fork tubes into position and tighten the lower front fork clamp bolts to the torque specification in **Table 4**.

> *NOTE*
> *Install the fork tube the same distance up from the top of the upper fork crown; see NOTE after Step 3, **Disassembly.***

9. Tighten the steering nut to the torque specification in **Table 4**.

10. Tighten the upper front fork clamp bolts to the torque specification in **Table 3** or **Table 4**.
11. Continue assembly by reversing Steps 1-4, *Steering Stem Disassembly.*
12. After a few hours of riding, the bearings have had a chance to seat; readjust the free play in the steering stem with the steering locknut. Refer to Step 5.

STEERING ADJUSTMENT

1. Raise the front wheel off the ground. Support the motorcycle securely under the engine.
2. Loosen the lower fork tube pinch bolts.

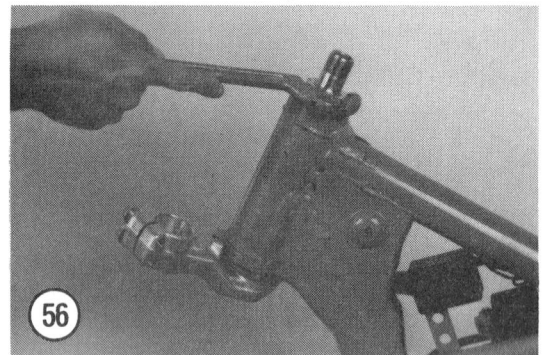

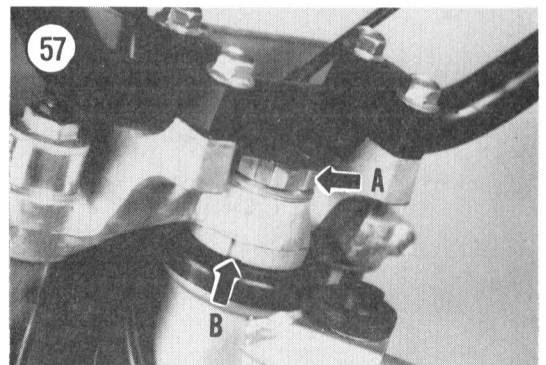

3. Loosen the steering nut (A, **Figure 57**).

4. Turn the locknut (B, **Figure 57**) with a spanner wrench or punch until you just feel the steering play taken up.

5. Tighten lower fork tube pinch bolts and steering nut to the torque specifications in **Table 3** or **Table 4**.

6. Recheck the steering play.

FRONT FORK

The Kawasaki front fork is spring-controlled and hydraulically damped. The damping rate is determined by the viscosity (weight) of the oil used and the spring rate can be altered by varying the amount of oil used and by air pressurization of the forks.

Before suspecting major trouble with the front fork, drain the fork oil and refill with the proper type

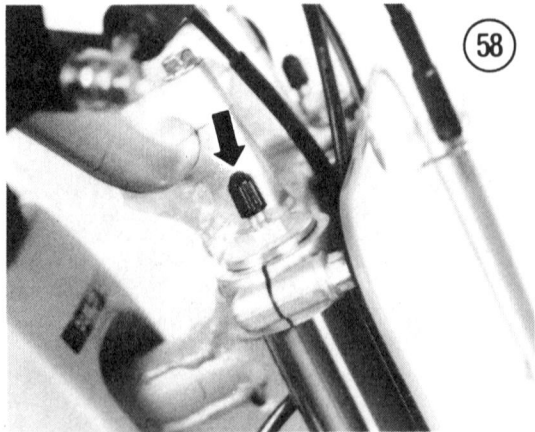

and quantity. If you still have trouble, such as poor damping, tendency to bottom out or top out, or leakage around the rubber seals, then follow the service procedures in this section.

To simplify fork service and to prevent the mixing of parts, the legs should be removed, serviced and reinstalled individually.

Each front fork leg consists of the fork tube (inner tube), slider (outer tube), fork spring, damper rod with its damper components and bushings.

If the front fork is going to be removed without disassembly, perform the *Removal/Installation* procedures in this chapter. If the front forks are going to be disassembled, refer to *Disassembly* in this chapter.

Removal/Installation

1. Remove the front wheel as described in this chapter.

2. Disconnect the front brake cable or hose at the left-hand fork tube.

3. *1984-on KX80:* Without disconnecting the brake hydraulic hose, remove the brake caliper as described under *Front Caliper Removal/ Installation* in Chapter Thirteen.

> *NOTE*
> *Insert a piece of wood or hose in the caliper in place of the disc. That way, if the brake lever is inadvertently squeezed, the piston will not be forced out of the calipers. If it does happen, the calipers might have to be disassembled to reseat the piston.*

> *WARNING*
> *When performing Step 4, release the air pressure gradually. If released too fast, oil may spurt out with the air. Protect your eyes accordingly.*

4. Remove the air valve cap and depress the valve (**Figure 58**) to release fork air pressure from both fork tubes.

> *NOTE*
> *Before removing the fork tube, measure the distance from the top of the fork tube to the top of the fork crown (**Figure 59**). Record this distance so*

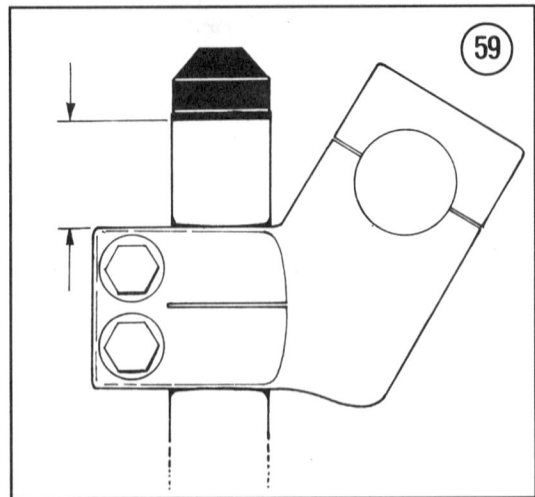

11

that the fork tubes can be reinstalled to the same position.

5. Loosen the upper and lower fork tube clamp bolts (**Figure 60**).

6. Twist the fork tube and remove it.

7. Install by reversing these removal steps. Note the following.

8. Tighten the fork tube clamp bolts to the torque specification in **Table 3** or **Table 4**.

9. *1984-on KX80:* Perform the following:
   a. Install the brake caliper as described in Chapter Thirteen.
   b. After installing the front wheel, squeeze the front brake lever. If the brake lever feels

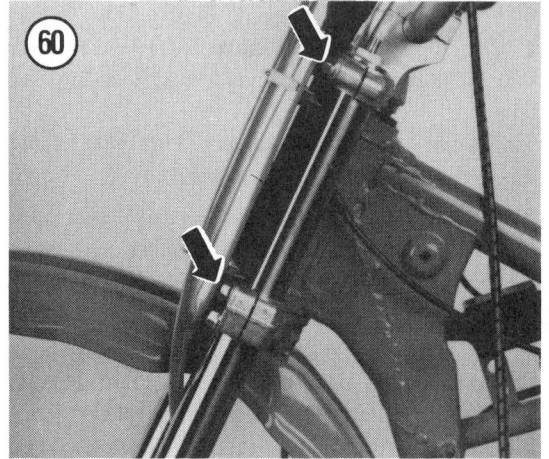

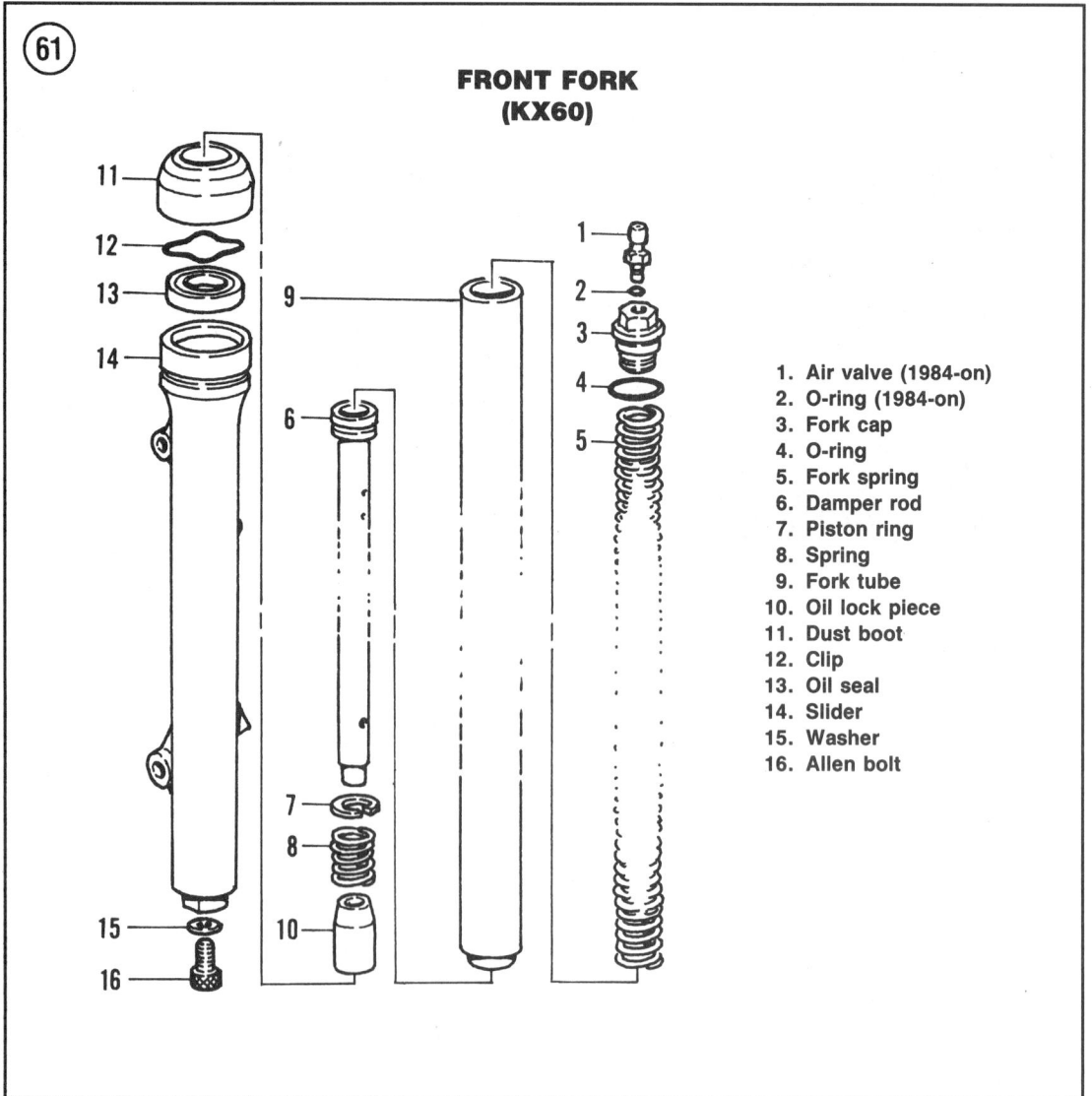

**FRONT FORK
(KX60)**

1. Air valve (1984-on)
2. O-ring (1984-on)
3. Fork cap
4. O-ring
5. Fork spring
6. Damper rod
7. Piston ring
8. Spring
9. Fork tube
10. Oil lock piece
11. Dust boot
12. Clip
13. Oil seal
14. Slider
15. Washer
16. Allen bolt

spongy, bleed the brake as described under *Brake Bleeding* in Chapter Thirteen.

10. Refill the front fork air pressure as described in Chapter Three.

Disassembly
(KX60 and 1983 KX80)

Refer to **Figure 61** (KX60) or **Figure 62** (1983 KX80).

NOTE
Prior to removing the fork tube, measure the distance from the top of the fork tube to the top of the fork

crown *(Figure 59)*. *Record this distance so that the fork tubes can be reinstalled to the same position.*

1. Perform Steps 1-3 described under front fork *Removal/Installation*.

WARNING
When performing Step 2, release the air pressure gradually. If released too fast, oil may spurt out with the air. Protect your eyes accordingly.

2. Depress the air valve(s) (**Figure 58**) to release all fork air pressure.

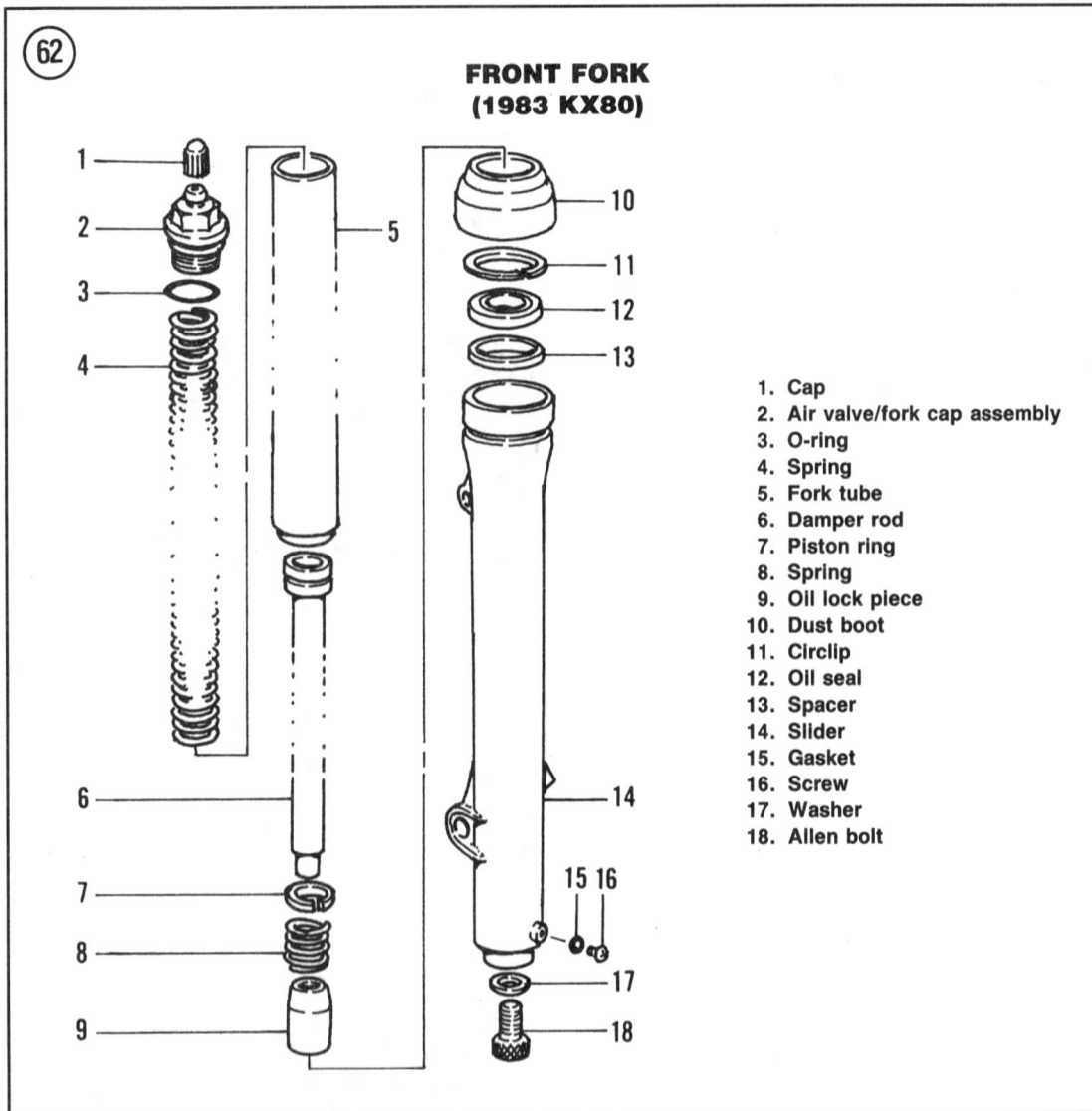

**FRONT FORK
(1983 KX80)**

1. Cap
2. Air valve/fork cap assembly
3. O-ring
4. Spring
5. Fork tube
6. Damper rod
7. Piston ring
8. Spring
9. Oil lock piece
10. Dust boot
11. Circlip
12. Oil seal
13. Spacer
14. Slider
15. Gasket
16. Screw
17. Washer
18. Allen bolt

11

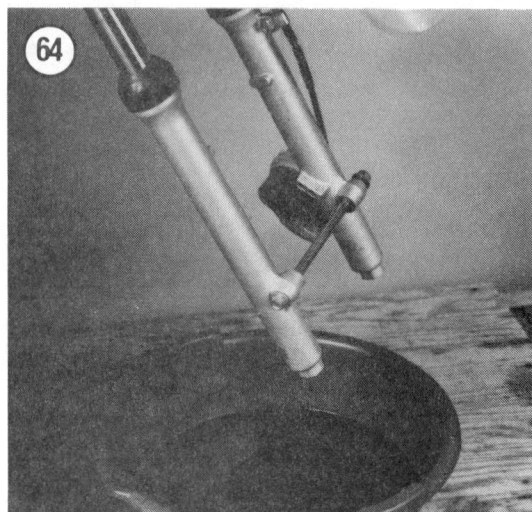

NOTE
The Allen bolt that threads into the damper rod at the bottom of the fork tube is normally secured with a thread locking agent and can be difficult to remove because the damper rod may turn inside the lower fork tube when the bolt is turned. The Allen bolt can be removed easily with an air impact driver. If you do not have access to an air impact driver, loosen the Allen bolt before removing the fork tube cap and spring. Spring pressure may prevent the damper rod from turning when the Allen bolt is loosened.

*If these methods are not successful, you will have to keep the damper rod from turning with a special tool. Kawasaki sells a long T-handle (part No. 57001-183) and adapter (part No. 57001-1257). See **Figure 63**. You can substitute the long T-handle with a short T-handle and a number of 3/8 in. drive extensions.*

3. Insert the axle through the fork tubes (**Figure 64**) to hold them in place when loosening the Allen bolt.

4. Place a drain pan underneath the fork tubes. Then loosen and remove the Allen bolt and washer (**Figure 65**).

5. Slide the dust boot (**Figure 66**) up the fork tube.

6. Remove the slider (**Figure 67**) from the fork tube.

7. Remove the oil lock piece from the end of the damper rod.

8. Loosen the upper fork tube clamp bolt. Then loosen and remove the fork cap (**Figure 68**).

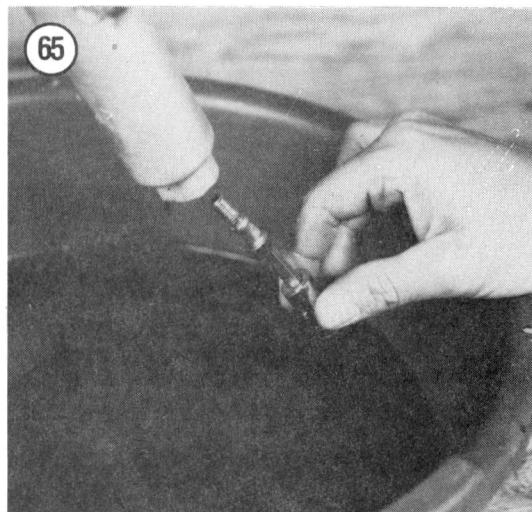

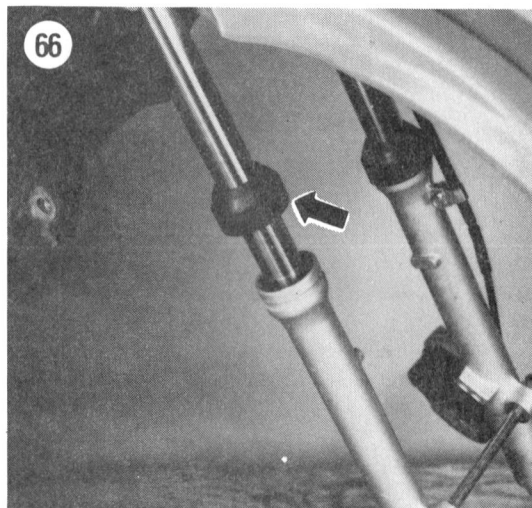

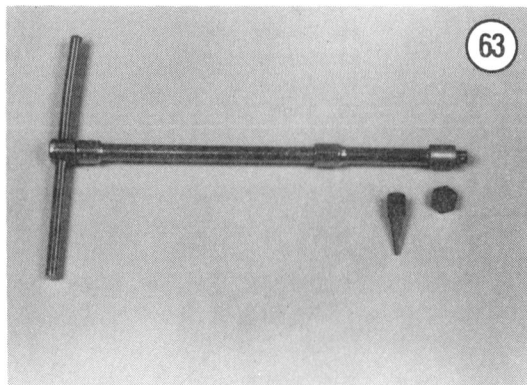

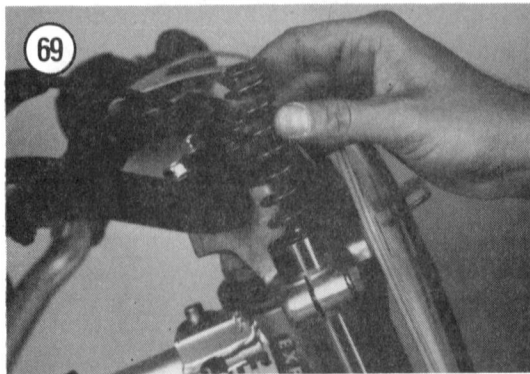

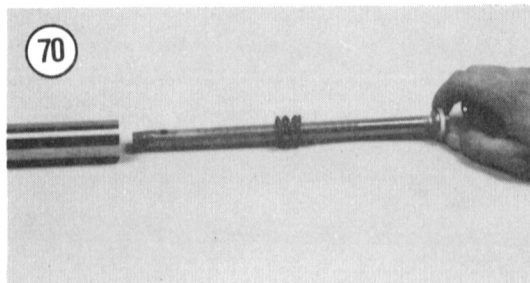

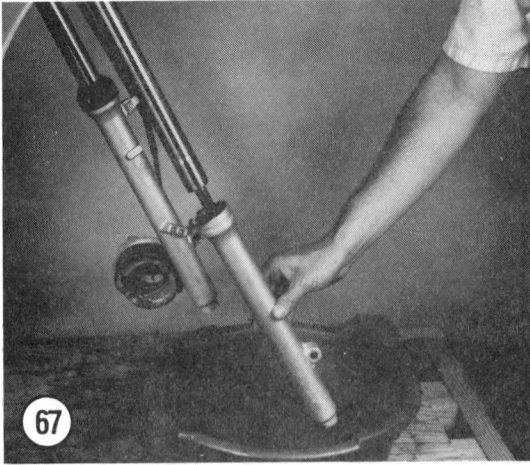

9. Remove the fork spring (**Figure 69**). Place the spring on a clean newspaper spread over the workbench.

10. Remove the lower fork tube clamp bolt and slide the fork tube out of the steering stem assembly.

11. Turn the fork tube over and remove the damper rod and spring (**Figure 70**).

12. Carefully inspect the fork assembly as described under *Inspection* in this chapter.

Oil Seal Replacement

1. Remove the circlip from its groove in the slider (**Figure 71**).

2. Carefully pry the oil seal out of the slider with a large flat-tipped screwdriver (**Figure 72**). Place a rag underneath the screwdriver to prevent from damaging the edge of the slider. It may be necessary to lift the screwdriver and work it around the oil seal during removal.

3. Check the lip of the slider for nicks or gouges.

4. Clean the slider with solvent and thoroughly dry.

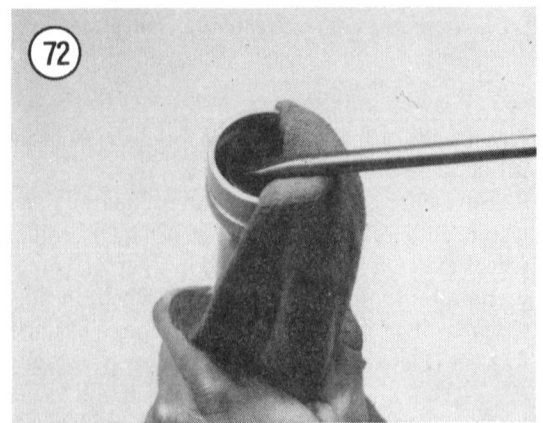

11

5. Install a new oil seal by driving it into the slider with a suitable size socket placed on top of the seal (**Figure 73**). Drive the oil seal in until it bottoms or when it is below the circlip groove.

6. Reinstall the circlip into the slider (**Figure 71**). Make sure the circlip seats in the groove completely.

Assembly
(KX60 and 1983 KX80)

Refer to **Figure 61** (KX60) or **Figure 62** (1983 KX80) for this procedure.

1. Slide the spring onto the damper rod (**Figure 74**) and insert the damper rod and spring into the upper fork tube. See **Figure 70**.

2. Slide the oil lock piece (**Figure 75**) onto the end of the damper rod.

3. Insert the damper rod/fork tube into the slider (**Figure 76**).

4. Make sure the gasket is on the Allen bolt (**Figure 77**).

5. Apply Loctite 242 (blue) to the threads on the Allen bolt. Install the Allen bolt (**Figure 78**) finger tight at this time.

6. Tighten the Allen bolt (installed in Step 5) securely.

NOTE
Use the same tool and procedure as during disassembly to prevent the damper rod from turning when tightening the Allen bolt. If the fork tube was assembled when the Allen bolt was loosened, temporarily install the fork spring and fork cap to apply tension to the damper rod. Remove these parts after tightening the Allen bolt.

7. Slide the dust boot down the fork tube and seat it onto the slider (**Figure 79**).

8. Fill the fork tube with the correct quantity and weight fork oil as described in Chapter Three. Check the oil level as described in Chapter Three.

9. Install the fork tubes as described in this chapter. Then install the spring (**Figure 69**) and fork cap (**Figure 68**). Tighten the fork cap securely.

10. Tighten the upper fork tube clamp bolt to the torque specification listed in **Table 3** or **Table 4**.

Disassembly
(1984-on KX80)

Refer to **Figure 80** (1984 KX80), **Figure 81** (1985-1987 KX80) or **Figure 82** (1988-on KX80).

1. Perform Steps 1-3 described under front fork *Removal/Installation*.

CAUTION
When performing Step 2, release the air pressure gradually. If released too fast, oil may spurt out with the air. Protect your eyes accordingly.

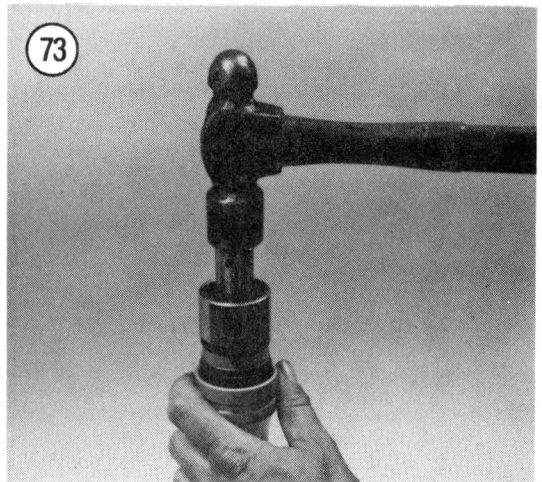

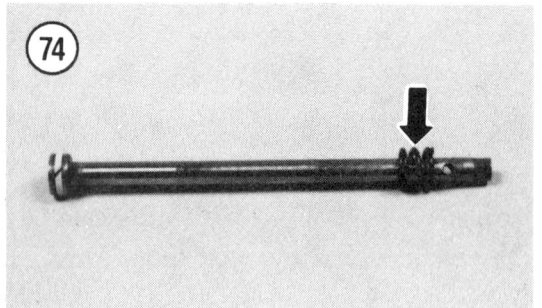

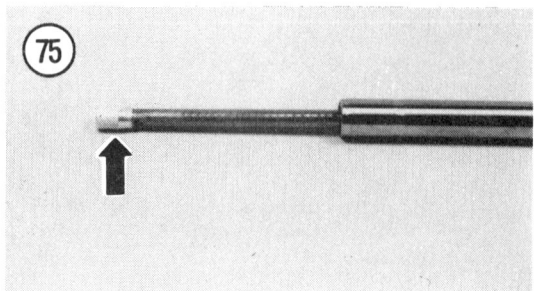

2. Depress the air valve(s) to release all fork air pressure (**Figure 83**).

NOTE
The Allen bolt that threads into the damper rod at the bottom of the fork

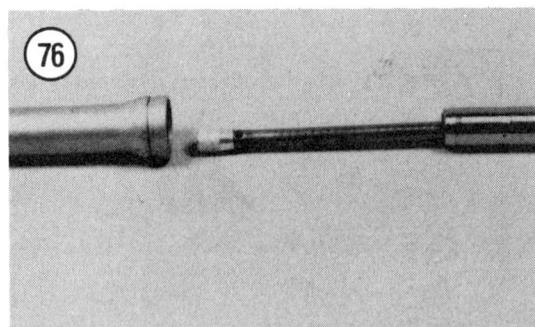

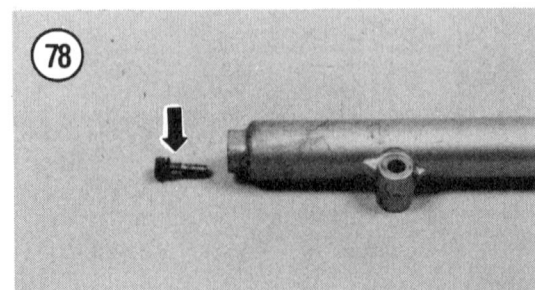

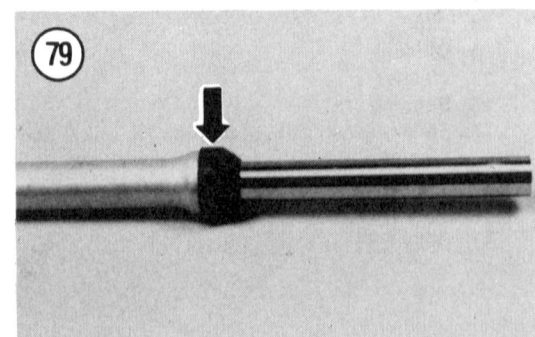

tube is normally secured with a thread locking agent and can be difficult to remove because the damper rod may turn inside the lower fork tube when the bolt is turned. The Allen bolt can be removed easily with an air impact driver. If you do not have access to an air impact driver, loosen the Allen bolt before removing the fork tube cap and spring. Spring pressure will prevent the damper rod from turning when the Allen bolt is loosened.

If these methods are not successful, you will have to keep the damper rod from turning with a special tool. Kawasaki sells a long T-handle (part No. 57001-183) and adapter (part No. 57001-1257). See **Figure 84.** *You can substitute the long T-handle with a short T-handle and a number of 3/8 in. drive extensions.*

3. Insert the axle through the fork tubes (**Figure 85**) to hold them in place when loosening the Allen bolt.

4. Place a drain pan underneath the fork tubes. Then loosen and remove the Allen bolt and washer (**Figure 86**).

5. Slide the dust boot (A, **Figure 87**) up the fork tube.

6. Carefully pry the circlip (B, **Figure 87**) out of the slider groove with a screwdriver.

7. There is an interference fit between the bushing in the fork slider and the bushing on the fork tube. In order to remove the slider from the fork tube, pull hard on the slider (**Figure 88**) using quick up-and-down strokes. Doing this will withdraw the oil seal, washer and bushing (**Figure 89**).

8. Remove the oil lock piece (**Figure 90**) from the end of the damper rod if it hasn't already dropped off into the oil pan.

9. Loosen the upper fork tube clamp bolt (A, **Figure 91**). Then loosen and remove the upper fork cap (B, **Figure 91**) with a socket and a speeder bar or long T-handle.

10A. *1984-1987 KX80:* Remove the following parts:
  a. Spacer.
  b. Spring seat.
  c. Fork spring.

11

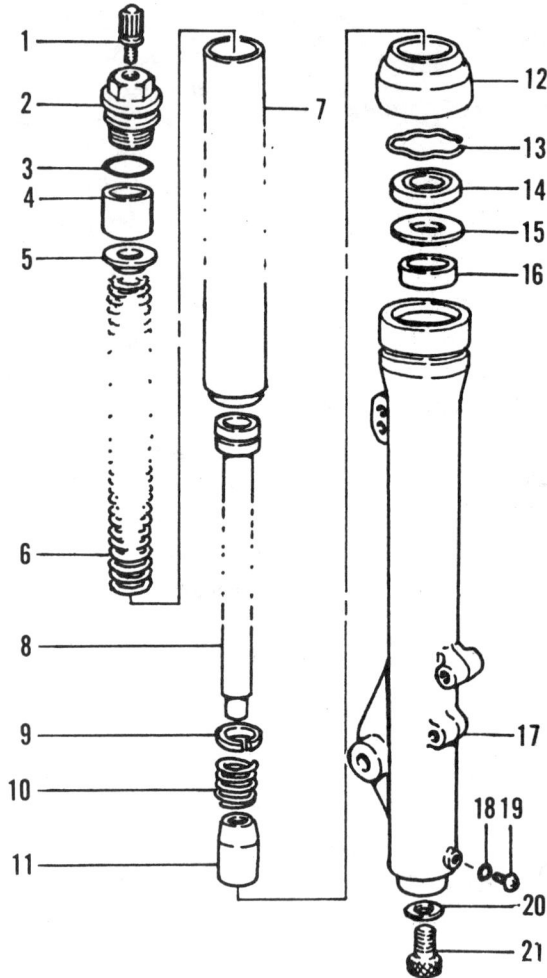

**FRONT FORK
(1984 KX80)**

1. Air valve
2. Fork cap
3. O-ring
4. Spacer
5. Spring seat
6. Spring
7. Fork tube
8. Damper rod
9. O-ring
10. Spring
11. Oil lock piece
12. Dust boot
13. Clip
14. Oil seal
15. Washer
16. Bushing
17. Slider
18. Washer
19. Drain screw
20. Washer
21. Allen bolt

(81)

**FRONT FORK
(1985-1987 KX80)**

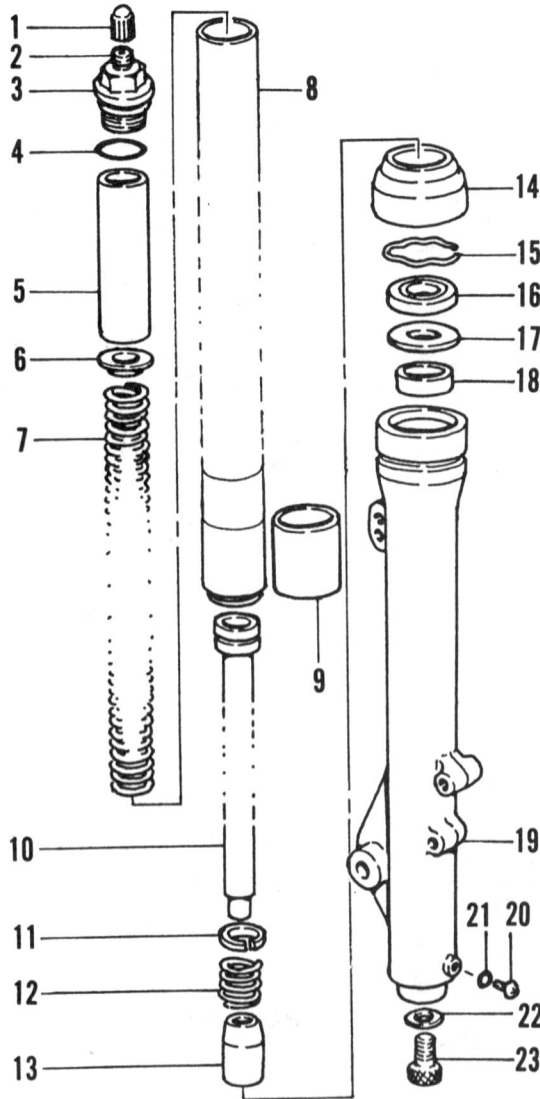

1. Cap
2. Air valve
3. Fork cap
4. O-ring
5. Spacer
6. Spring seat
7. Spring
8. Fork tube

9. Bushing
10. Damper rod
11. Piston ring
12. Spring
13. Oil lock piece
14. Dust boot
15. Clip
16. Oil seal

17. Washer
18. Bushing
19. Slider
20. Drain screw
21. Gasket
22. Washer
23. Allen bolt

11

⑧²

FRONT FORK
(1988-ON KX80)

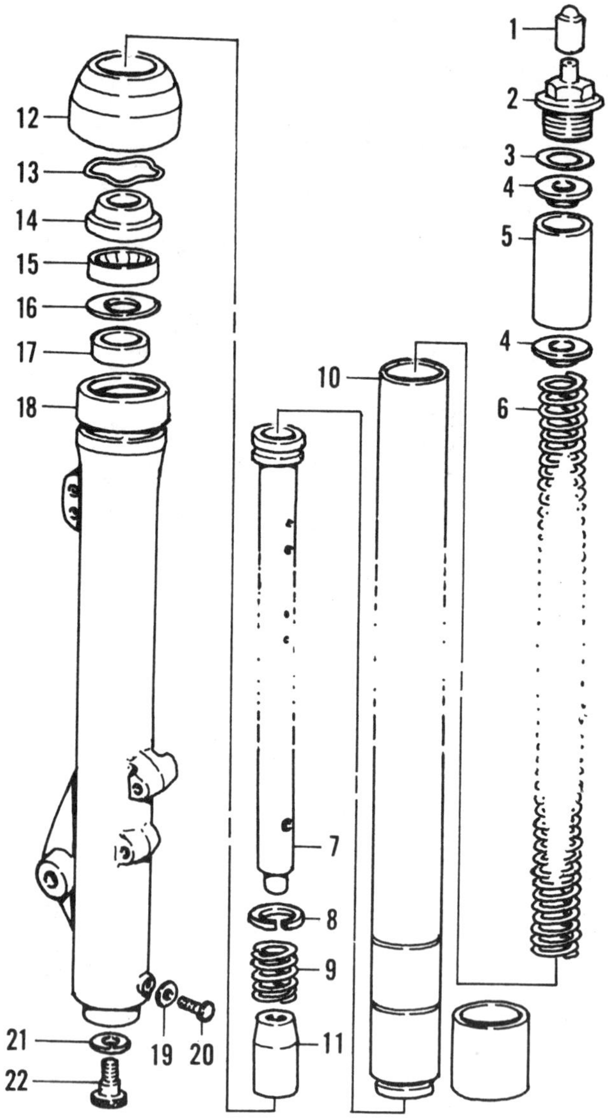

1. Air valve cap
2. Air valve/fork cap
3. O-ring
4. Spring seat
5. Spacer
6. Fork spring
7. Damper rod
8. Piston ring
9. Spring
10. Fork tube
11. Oil lock piece
12. Dust boot
13. Clip
14. Oil seal
15. Oil seal
16. Washer
17. Bushing
18. Slider
19. Gasket
20. Drain bolt
21. Washer
22. Allen bolt

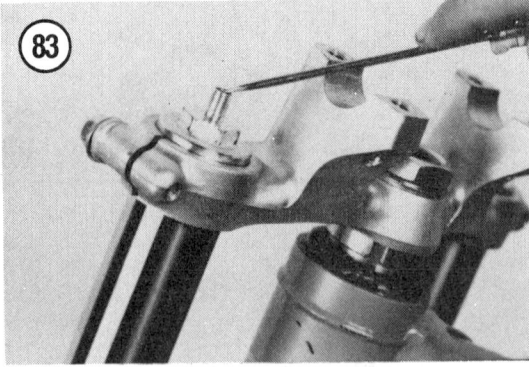

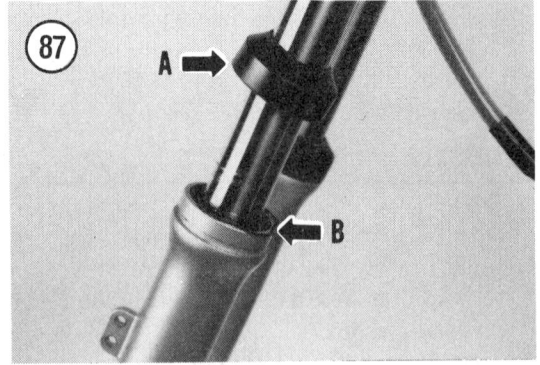

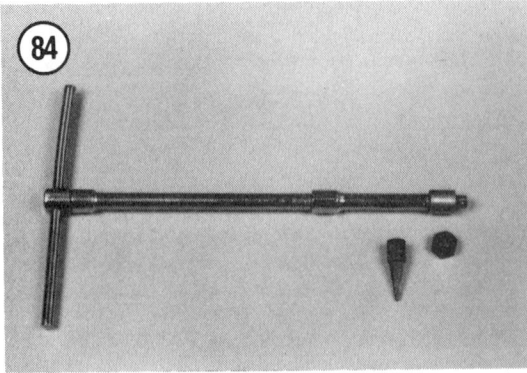

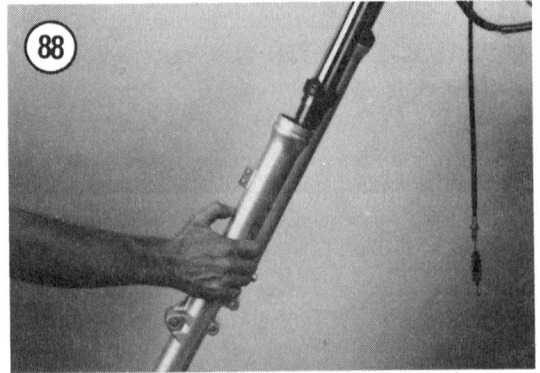

11

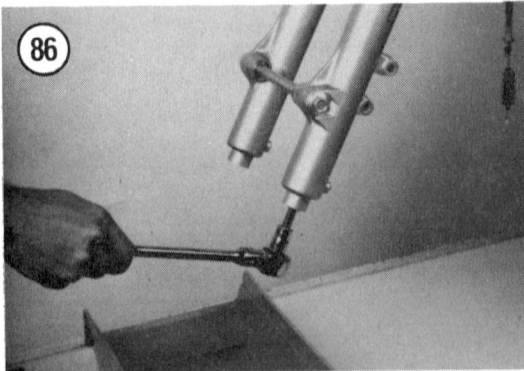

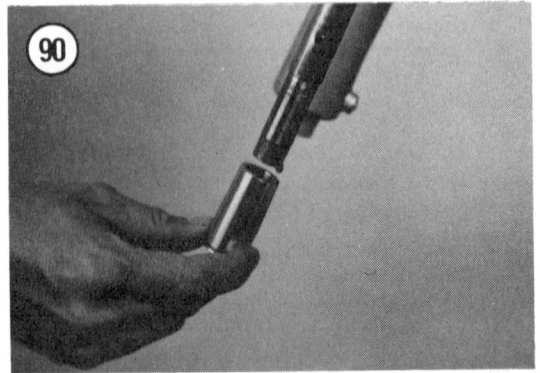

10B. *1988-on:* Remove the following parts:
   a. Spring seat (**Figure 92**).
   b. Spacer (**Figure 93**).
   c. Spring seat (**Figure 94**).
   d. Fork spring (**Figure 95**).

11. Immediately wrap the end of the spring with a rag to prevent oil from dripping onto the floor or the bike. Place the fork spring on newspapers laid over the workbench.

12. Remove the fork tube lower clamp bolt and remove the fork tube.

13. Turn the fork tube over and remove the damper rod and spring (**Figure 96**).

14A. *1984-1987:* Referring to **Figure 80** or **Figure 81**, remove the following parts in order:
   a. Dust cap.
   b. Clip.
   c. Oil seal.
   d. Washer.
   e. Bushing.

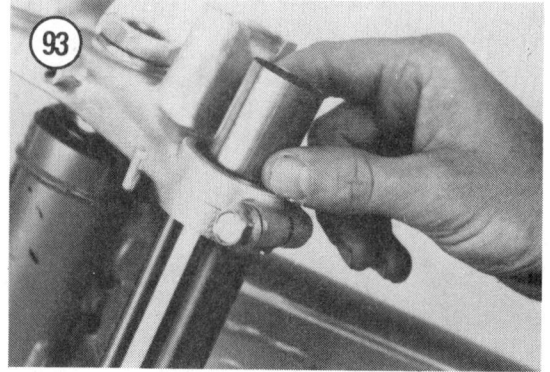

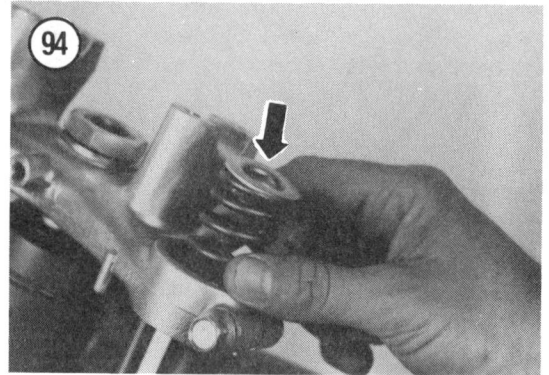

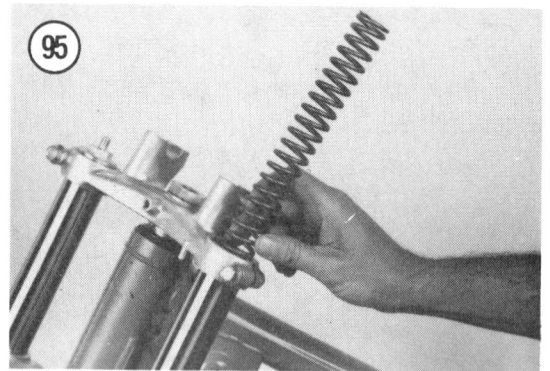

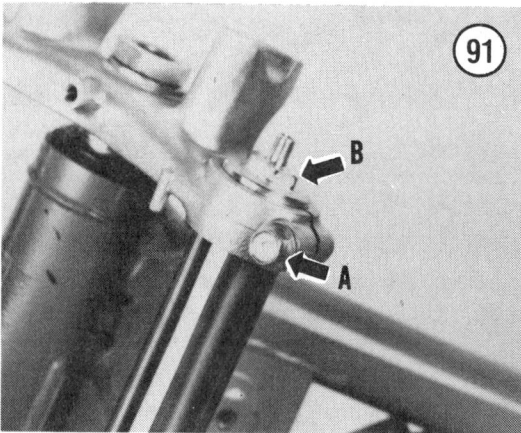

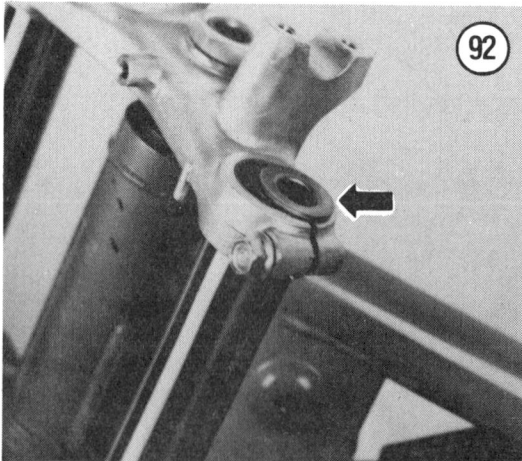

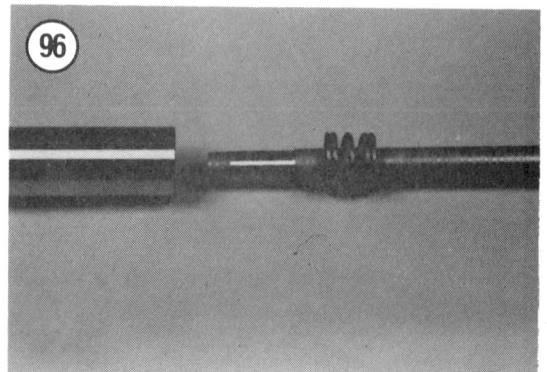

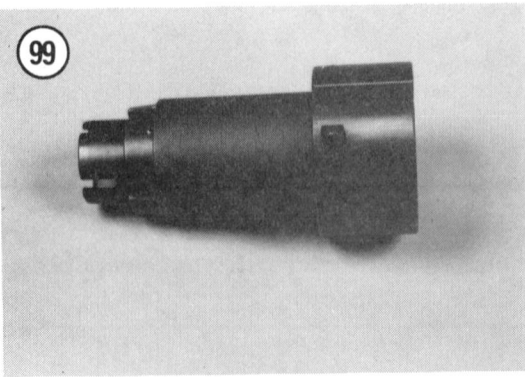

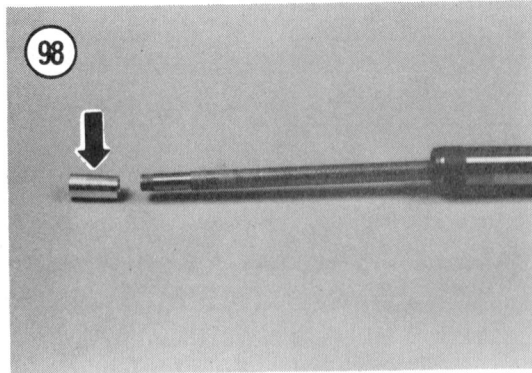

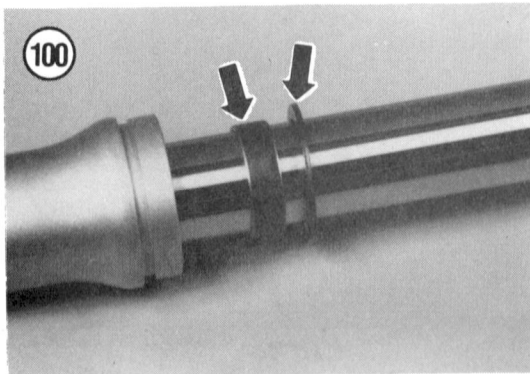

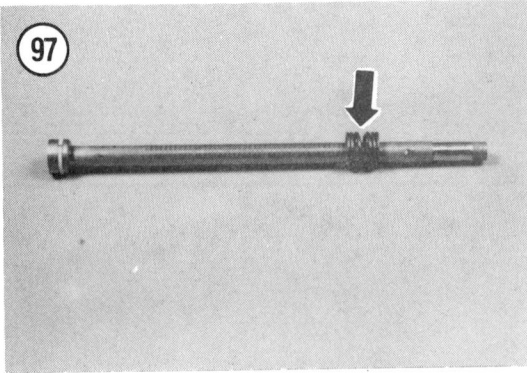

14B. *1988-on KX80:* Referring to **Figure 82**, remove the following parts in order:
  a. Dust cap.
  b. Clip.
  c. Dust seal.
  d. Oil seal.
  e. Washer.
  f. Bushing.
15. Carefully inspect the fork assembly as described under *Inspection* in this chapter.

Assembly
(1984-on KX80)

  Refer to **Figure 80** (1984 KX80), **Figure 81** (1985-1987 KX80) or **Figure 82** (1988-on KX80).
1. Slide the spring (**Figure 97**) onto the damper rod and insert the damper rod and spring into the upper fork tube (**Figure 96**).
2. Slide the oil lock piece (**Figure 98**) onto the end of the damper rod.
3. Insert the damper rod/fork tube into the slider.

NOTE
Some type of driver will be required to install the bushing, oil seal and dust seal in the following steps. The front fork oil seal driver (part No. 57001-1219) and weight (part No. 57001-1218) (Figure 99) can be ordered through Kawasaki dealers or a tool can be made from a piece of aluminum pipe.

4. Slide the guide bushing and washer (**Figure 100**) over the fork tube. Tap the guide bushing into the lower fork tube until it bottoms (**Figure 101**).

11

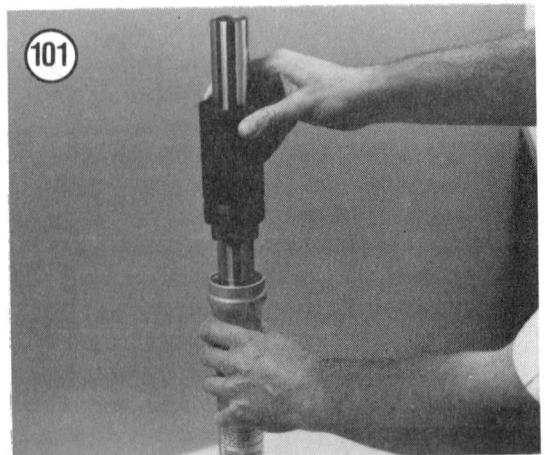

5. Position the oil seal (**Figure 102**) with the marking facing upward and slide down onto the fork tube. Drive the seal into the lower fork tube with the same tool used in Step 4 (**Figure 101**). Drive the oil seal in until it rests against the washer.

6. *1988-on:* Position the dust seal (**Figure 103**) with the lip facing upward and slide down onto the fork tube. Drive the seal into the lower fork tube with the same tool used in Step 5 (**Figure 101**). Drive the dust seal in until it rests against the oil seal.

> *NOTE*
> *Make sure the groove in the fork slider çan be seen above the oil seal (1984-1987) or dust seal (1988-on). If not, the seal will have to driven into the slider.*

7. Slide the clip (**Figure 104**) down the fork tube and seat it in the slider groove. Make sure the clip is completely seated in the groove.

8. Slide the dust boot (**Figure 105**) down the fork tube and seat in the slider.

> *NOTE*
> *Use the same tool and procedure as during disassembly to prevent the damper rod from turning when tightening the Allen bolt. If the fork tube was assembled when the Allen bolt was loosened, temporarily install the fork spring, spacer spring seat and fork cap to apply tension to the damper rod. Remove these parts after tightening the Allen bolt.*

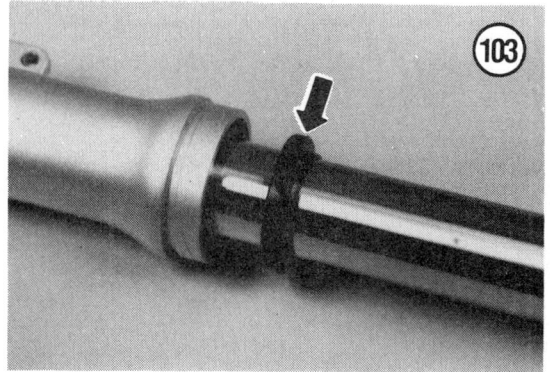

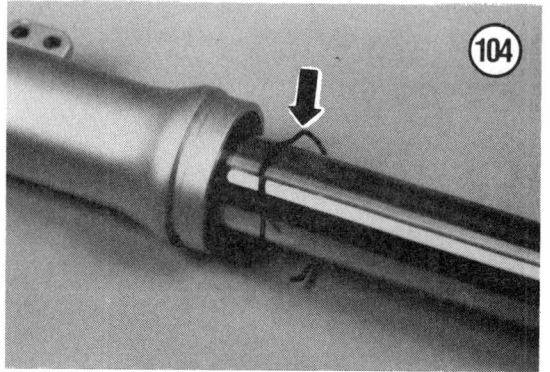

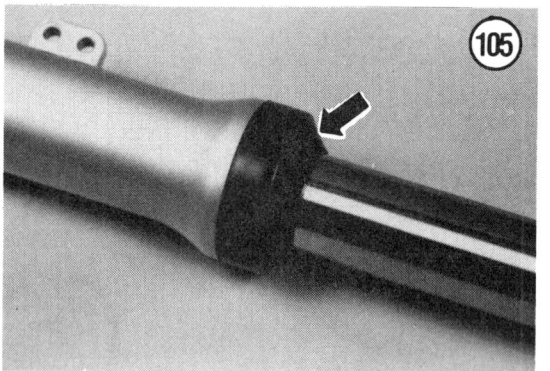

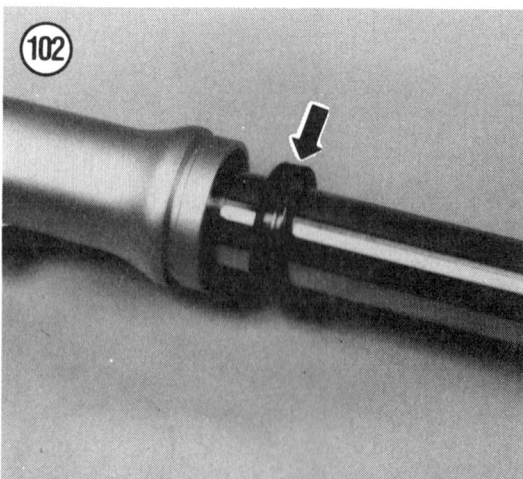

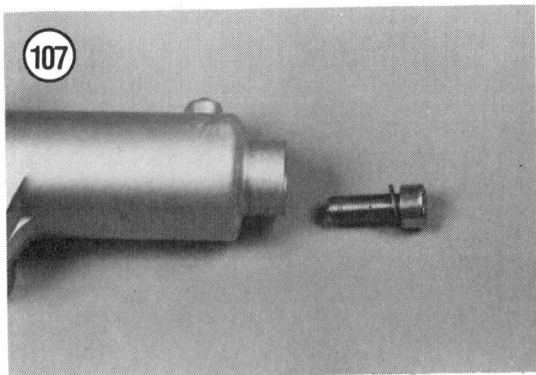

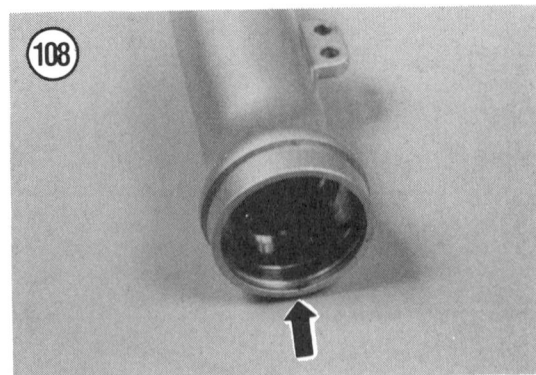

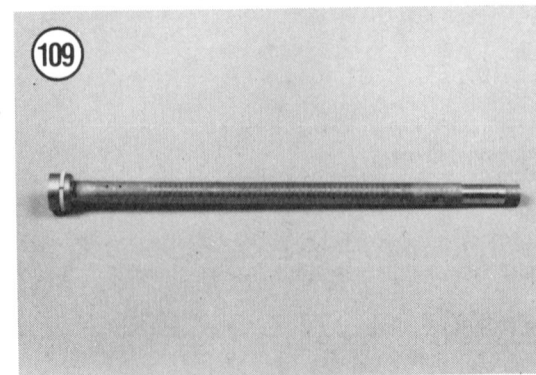

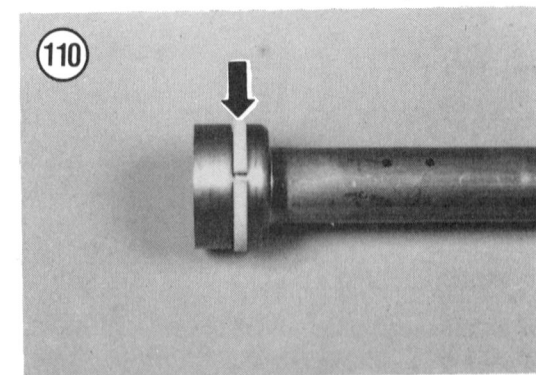

9. Make sure the gasket is on the Allen bolt (**Figure 106**).

10. Apply Loctite 242 (blue) to the threads on the Allen bolt. Install the Allen bolt (**Figure 107**) and tighten securely.

11. Fill the fork tube with the correct quantity and weight fork oil as described in Chapter Three. Check the oil level as described in Chapter Three.

12. Install the fork tubes onto the motorcycle as described in this chapter.

13A. *1984-1987 KX80:* Install the following parts:
   a. Fork spring.
   b. Spring seat.
   c. Spacer.

13B. *1988-on:* Install the following parts:
   a. Fork spring (**Figure 95**).
   b. Spring seat (**Figure 94**).
   c. Spacer (**Figure 93**).
   d. Spring seat (**Figure 92**).

14. Install the fork cap. Tighten it securely.

15. Tighten the fork tube upper clamp bolt to the torque specification in **Table 4**.

Inspection

1. Thoroughly clean all parts in solvent and dry them.

2. Check the fork tube and slider for wear or scratches. Check the fork tube for straightness. If bent, refer service to a Kawasaki dealer.

3. Check the fork tube for chrome flaking or creasing; this condition will damage oil seals. Replace the fork tube if necessary.

4. *1984-on:* Check the slider oil seal area (**Figure 108**) for dents or other damage that would allow oil leakage. Replace the slider if necessary.

5. Check the damper rod (**Figure 109**) for straightness by rolling it on a surface plate or thick piece of glass. Any clicking noise indicates a bent rod.

6. Check the damper rod piston ring (**Figure 110**) for tearing, cracks or damage.

7. Check the guide bushing on the fork tube (A, **Figure 111**) for scoring, nicks or damage. Replace if necessary by pulling off the fork tube.

8. Check the mating guide bushing (B, **Figure 111**) for scoring, nicks or damage. Replace if necessary.

9. Measure the uncompressed length of the fork spring (**Figure 112**) with a tape measure and compare to specifications in **Table 2**. Replace any spring(s) that are too short.

11

NOTE
If one fork spring is replaced, compare the measurement of the new and the remaining old spring. If the length difference is great between a new spring and the old usable spring, it is best to replace both springs to keep the forks balanced.

10. Replace the fork cap O-ring (**Figure 113**) if damaged.

11. Check the oil and dust seals for wear or damage. Replace if necessary.

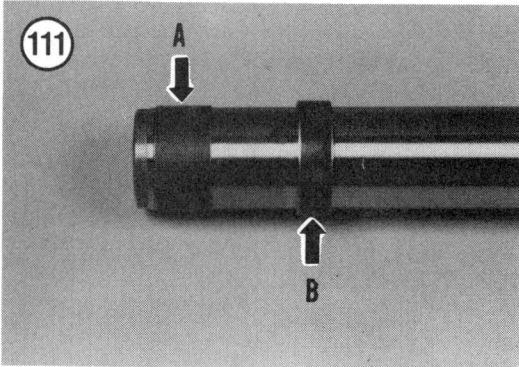

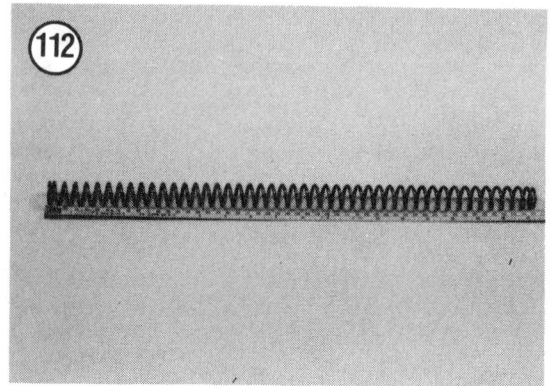

Table 1 STEERING SPECIFICATIONS

Steering angle	45°
Castor	28°
Trail	
KX60	65 mm (2.56 in.)
KX80	
1983-1986	90 mm (3.5 in.)
1987	
G, H	90 mm (3.5 in.)
J, K	108 mm (4.3 in.)
1988-on	
L, M	95 mm (3.74 in.)
N, P	113 mm (4.45 in.)
Front fork travel	
KX60	200 mm (7.9 in.)
KX80	
1983-1985	255 mm (10.04 in.)
1986	275 mm (10.8 in.)
1987	
G, H	275 mm (10.8 in.)
J, K	230 mm (9.1 in.)
1988-on	
L, M	275 mm (10.8 in.)
N, P	265 mm (10.4 in.)

Table 2 FRONT SUSPENSION SERVICE SPECIFICATIONS

	New mm (in.)	Service Limit mm (in.)
Axle		
Runout	0-0.1 (0-0.004)	0.2 (0.008)
Repair limit	—	0.7 (0.028)
Rim runout		
Axial play	0-0.5 (0-0.02)	2.0 (0.08)
Radial play	0-0.8 (0-0.03)	2.0 (0.08)
Front fork spring free length		
KX60	487.9 (19.21)	478 (18.8)
KX80		
1983	549.1 (21.62)	538 (21.18)
1984	490.6 (19.31)	478 (18.82)
1985	467.6 (18.41)	455 (17.91)
1986	497.5 (19.59)	487 (19.17)
1987-1988		
G, H, L, M	497.5 (19.6)	487 (19.2)
J, K, N, P	470 (18.5)	461 (18.1)
1989	497.5 (19.6)	461 (18.1)

Table 3 FRONT SUSPENSION TIGHTENING TORQUES (KX60)

	N·m	ft.-lb.
Front axle nut	49	36
Upper front fork clamp bolt	20	14.5
Lower front fork clamp bolt	25	18
Front fork cap bolt	22	16
Handlebar clamp bolts	21	15
Steering stem nut	34	25
Steering stem locknut		
1983-1986	29	22
1987-on	19	14

Table 4 FRONT SUSPENSION TIGHTENING TORQUES (KX80)

	N·m	ft.-lb.
Front axle nut		
1983-1985	49	36
1986-on	69	51
Front fork clamp bolts or nuts		
Upper		
1983	20	14.5
1984	17-20	12.3-14.5
1985	17	12.3
1986-1987	20	14.5
1988-on	17	12.3
Lower		
1983-1985	28	18
1986-1987	20	14.5
1988-on	17	12.3
Front fork cap bolt		
1983	22	16
1984	21-22	15-16
1985-on	—	—

(continued)

11

Table 4 FRONT SUSPENSION TIGHTENING TORQUES (KX80) (continued)

	N·m	ft.-lb.
Handlebar clamp bolts	21	15
Steering stem		
1983-1985		
Nut	34	25
Locknut		
1983	—	—
1984	—	—
1985	29	22
1986-on		
Nut	44	33
Locknut	4.0	35 in.-lb.

CHAPTER TWELVE

REAR SUSPENSION

This chapter contains repair and replacement procedures for the rear wheel and hub and rear suspension components. Service to the rear suspension consists of periodically checking bolt tightness, replacing swing arm bushings, and checking the condition of the spring/gas shock unit and overhauling (KX80 models) it as required.

Rear suspension specifications are listed in **Table 1** and **Table 2**. **Tables 1-6** are found at the end of the chapter.

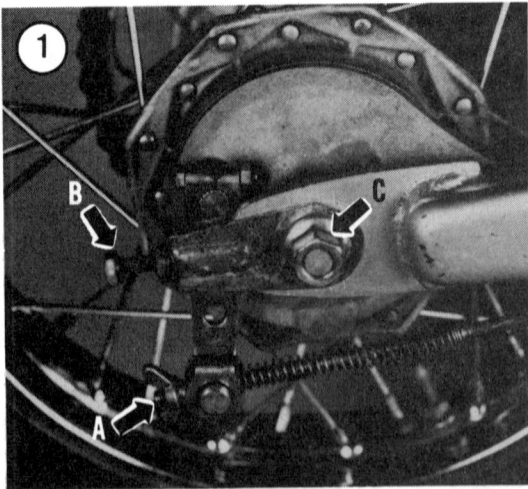

REAR WHEEL

WARNING
When removing the wheels or working on the brakes, wear a protective mask to keep from inhaling any dust from the brake linings. The brake linings contain asbestos fiber; asbestos has been connected with lung scarring and cancer. Do not use compressed air to clean the brake drums or linings; dump any dust onto a newspaper and place in a resealable plastic bag. Dispose of it in the trash. Wash your hands thoroughly after handling the brake parts.

Removal/Installation
(KX60 and 1983-1987 KX80)

1. Support the bike on a stand so that the rear wheel is off of the ground.
2. Unscrew the rear brake adjusting nut completely from the brake rod (A, **Figure 1**). Withdraw the brake rod from the brake lever and pivot it down out of the way. Reinstall the adjusting nut to avoid misplacing it.

3. Loosen the left- and right-hand chain adjusters (B, **Figure 1**).

4. *KX80:* Disconnect the brake rod at the rear hub.

5. Loosen and remove the axle nut (C, **Figure 1**). Remove the left-hand chain adjuster.

6. Push the wheel forward to provide as much chain slack as possible. Then, rotate the rear wheel and slip the drive chain off of the driven sprocket.

7. Remove the axle (**Figure 2**) and chain adjuster from the left-hand side.

8A. *KX60:* Pull the wheel back as required to disconnect the brake panel from the tab welded to the swing arm and remove the rear wheel.

8B. *KX80:* Remove the rear wheel.

9. Remove the axle spacer (**Figure 3**) from the left-hand side.

10. Remove the brake panel (**Figure 4**) from the right-hand side.

11. Install by reversing these removal steps. Note the following:

  a. Clean the axle and axle spacers in solvent and thoroughly dry. Make sure all axle contact surfaces are clean and free of dirt and old grease prior to installation. If these surfaces

are not cleaned, the axle may be difficult to remove later on.

  b. Apply a light coat of grease to the axle, bearings and grease seals.

  c. Be sure to install the axle spacer on the left-hand side of the wheel (**Figure 3**).

  d. *KX60:* Make sure to align the groove in the brake panel with the tab welded to the swing arm (**Figure 5**).

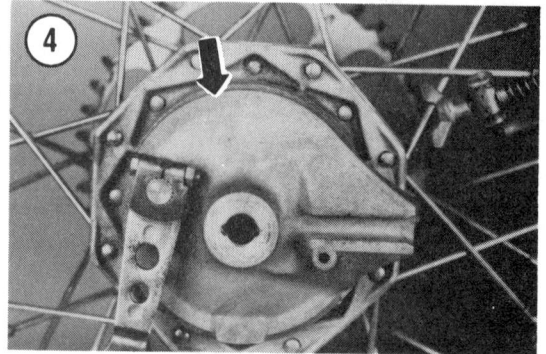

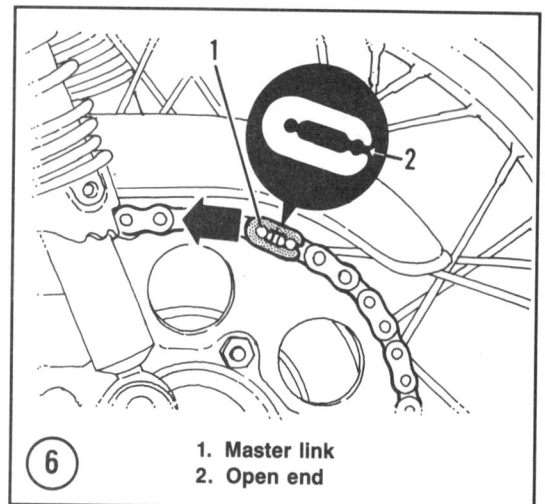

1. Master link
2. Open end

e. If the drive chain was disconnected, install the drive chain master link so that its closed end is facing the direction of chain travel (**Figure 6**).

f. Adjust the drive chain as described in Chapter Three.

g. Tighten the axle nut to the torque specification in **Table 3** or **Table 4**.

h. After the wheel is completely installed, rotate it several times to make sure it rotates smoothly. Apply the brakes several times to make sure it operates correctly.

i. Adjust the rear brake as described under *Rear Brake Pedal Adjustment* in Chapter Three.

Removal/Installation (1988-on KX80)

1. Support the bike on a stand so that the rear wheel is off of the ground.

2. Remove the brake caliper cover (**Figure 7**).

3. Remove the caliper mounting bolts and lift the brake caliper (**Figure 8**) off of the brake disc. Support the brake caliper with a Bunjee cord.

4. Remove the holder from the brake caliper (A, **Figure 9**).

> *CAUTION*
> *Do not allow the caliper to hang by the brake hose or damage to the hose may occur.*

> *NOTE*
> *After removing the brake caliper. Insert a piece of wood or hose in the caliper between the brake pads (B, Figure 9). That way, if the brake lever is accidently squeezed, the piston will not be forced out of the brake caliper cylinder. If the brake pedal is inadvertantly applied and the piston comes out, the caliper might have to be disassembled to reseat the piston and the system will have to be bled.*

5. Loosen and remove the rear axle nut.

6. Push the wheel forward to provide as much chain slack as possible. Then rotate the rear wheel and slip the drive chain off of the driven sprocket.

7. Remove the axle (**Figure 10**) and slide the rear wheel assembly out of the swing arm (**Figure 11**).

12

8. Remove the left- (**Figure 12**) and right-hand (**Figure 13**) axle spacers.

9. Install the axle spacers and axle nut on the axle to prevent their loss while servicing the wheel.

10. To install the rear wheel, reverse the removal steps. Note the following:

a. Clean the axle and axle spacers in solvent and thoroughly dry. Make sure all axle contact surfaces are clean and free of dirt and old grease prior to installation. If these surfaces are not cleaned, the axle may be difficult to remove later on.

b. Apply a light coat of grease to the axle, bearings and grease seals.

c. Install the brake holder (A, **Figure 9**) into the rear brake caliper assembly.

d. Carefully insert the brake pads between the disc when installing the brake caliper. Tighten the brake caliper mounting bolts to the torque specification in **Table 4**.

e. If the drive chain was disconnected, install the drive chain master link so that its closed end is facing the direction of chain travel (**Figure 6**).

f. Install the axle nut. Tighten the axle to the torque specification in **Table 4**.

g. After the wheel is completely installed, rotate the rear wheel and apply the brake. Do this a couple of times to make sure the rear wheel and brake are operating correctly.

Inspection

Spokes loosen with use and should be checked prior to each race or a weekend ride. The "tuning fork" method for checking spoke tightness is simple and works well. Tap each spoke with a spoke wrench or the shank of a screwdriver and listen for a tone. A tightened spoke will emit a clear, ringing tone, and a loose spoke will sound flat. All the spokes of the same length in a correctly tightened wheel will emit tones of similar pitch but not necessarily the same precise tone.

Bent, stripped or broken spokes should be replaced as soon as they are detected, as they can cause the destruction of an expensive hub. Unscrew the nipple from the spoke and depress the nipple into the rim far enough to free the end of the spoke, taking care not to push the nipple all the way in. Remove the damaged spoke from the hub and use it to match a new spoke of identical length. If

necessary, trim the new spoke to match the original and dress the end of the thread with a thread die. Install the new spoke in the hub and screw on the nipple; tighten it (**Figure 14**) until the spoke's tone is similar to the tone of the other spokes in the

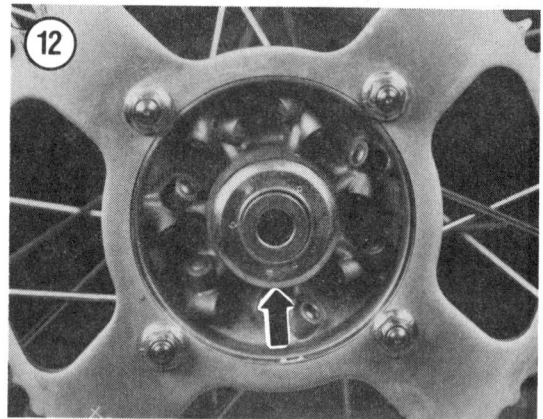

wheel. Periodically check the new spoke; it will stretch and must be retightened several times before it takes its final set.

CAUTION
When spokes loosen or when installing new spokes, the head of the spokes

(Figure 15) should be checked for proper seating in the hub. Improperly seated spokes can cause severe hub damage. If one or more spokes required seating, hit the head of the spoke with a punch and hammer as shown in Figure 16.

Wheel rim runout is the amount of "wobble" a wheel shows as it rotates. You can check runout with the wheels on the bike by simply supporting the wheel off the ground and turning the wheel slowly while you hold a pointer solidly against the swing arm. Just make sure any wobble you observe isn't caused by your own hand.

Off the motorcycle, runout can be checked with the wheel installed on a truing stand.

The maximum allowable axial (side-to-side) and radial (up and down) play is listed in **Table 2**. Tighten or replace any bent or loose spokes.

1. Draw the high point of the rim toward the centerline of the wheel by tightening the spokes in the area of the high point and on the same side as the high point and loosening the spokes on the side opposite the high point.

2. Rotate the wheel and check runout. Continue adjusting until the runout is within specification. Be patient and thorough, adjusting the position of the rim a little at a time. If you tighten 2 spokes at the high point 1/2 turn, tighten the adjacent spokes 1/4 turn. Loosen the spokes on the opposite side equivalent amounts.

REAR HUB

Refer to **Figure 17** (KX60 and 1983-1985 KX80), **Figure 18** (1986-1987 KX80) or **Figure 19** (1988-on KX80) when performing procedures in this section.

Inspection

1. The grease seals are normally damaged during removal. When checking grease seals, look for hardening, discoloration or internal rib damage. If a seal has hardened or the ribbing damaged, seal to axle clearance will be excessive. This condition allows dirt and moisture to enter the bearing. Always replace questionable oil seals.

2. Do not remove bearings for periodic inspection as bearing removal normally damages the first

12

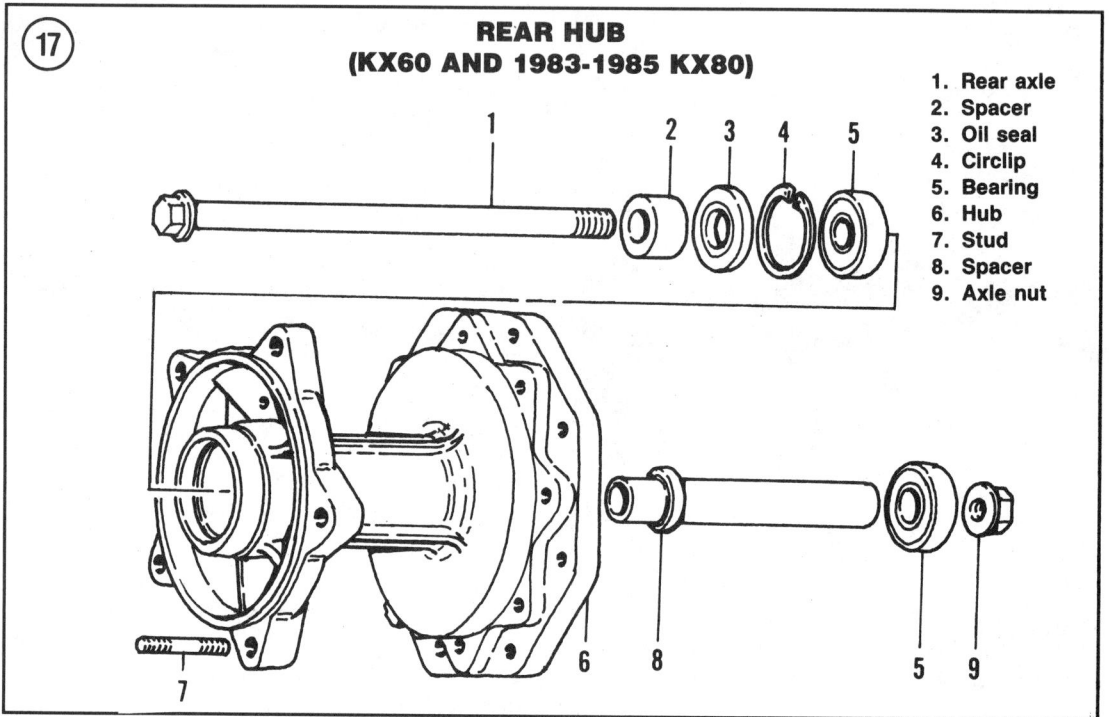

**REAR HUB
(KX60 AND 1983-1985 KX80)**

1. Rear axle
2. Spacer
3. Oil seal
4. Circlip
5. Bearing
6. Hub
7. Stud
8. Spacer
9. Axle nut

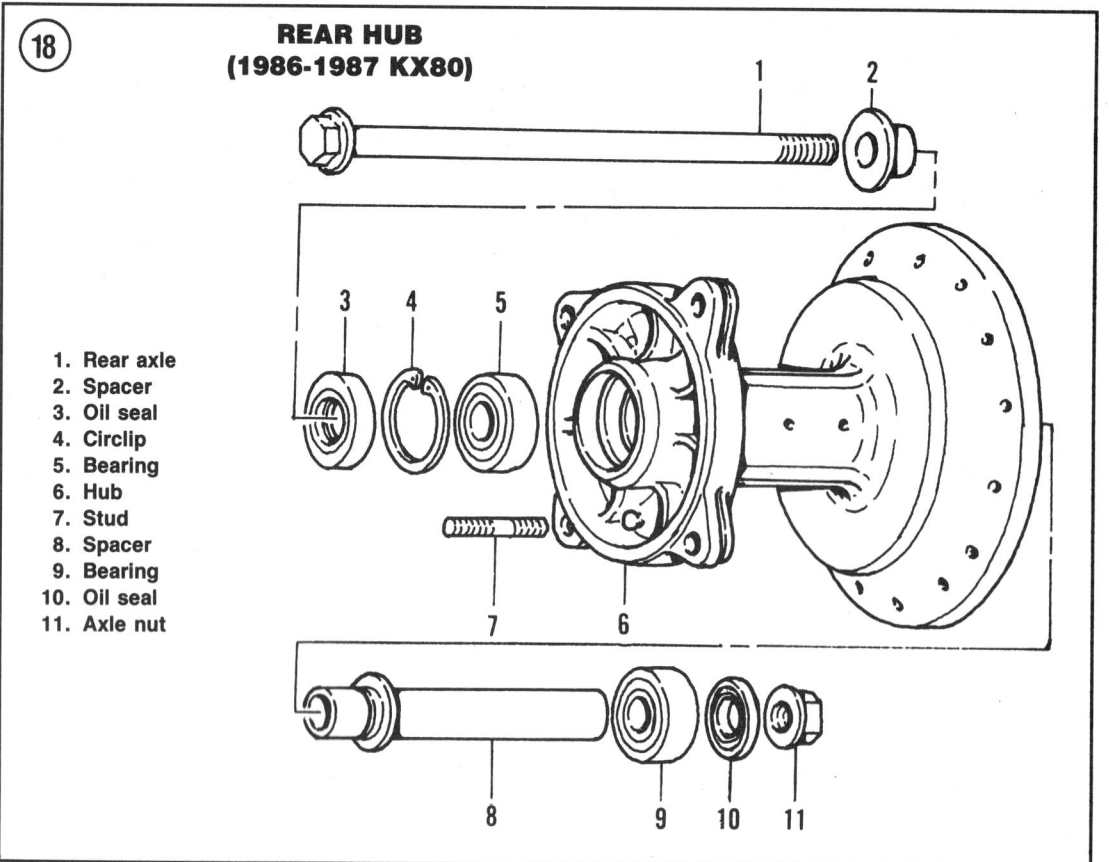

**REAR HUB
(1986-1987 KX80)**

1. Rear axle
2. Spacer
3. Oil seal
4. Circlip
5. Bearing
6. Hub
7. Stud
8. Spacer
9. Bearing
10. Oil seal
11. Axle nut

bearing removed. Turn the inner bearing race and check for any roughness, binding or excessive noise that would indicate bearing damage.

3. Replace worn or damaged grease seals and bearings as described in this chapter.

Disassembly/Reassembly

Always replace bearings and seals as a set.

1. Remove the rear wheel as described in this chapter.

2. Remove the axle spacer(s) from the wheel, if so equipped.

3. *Drum brake models:* Pull the brake panel (**Figure 4**) straight up and out of the drum.

4. Remove the oil seals (**Figure 20**) by carefully prying them out of the hub with a flat-bladed

screwdriver. Prop a piece of wood or rag underneath the screwdriver to prevent damaging the hub.

NOTE
If the seal is tight, lift the screwdriver and work it around the seal every few degrees until the seal pops out of the hub.

5. Remove the circlip from the left-hand side.

6. Remove the left- and right-hand bearings and spacer. To remove the bearings, insert a soft-aluminum or brass drift into one side of the hub. Push the spacer over to one side and place the drift on the inner race of the lower bearing (**Figure 21**).

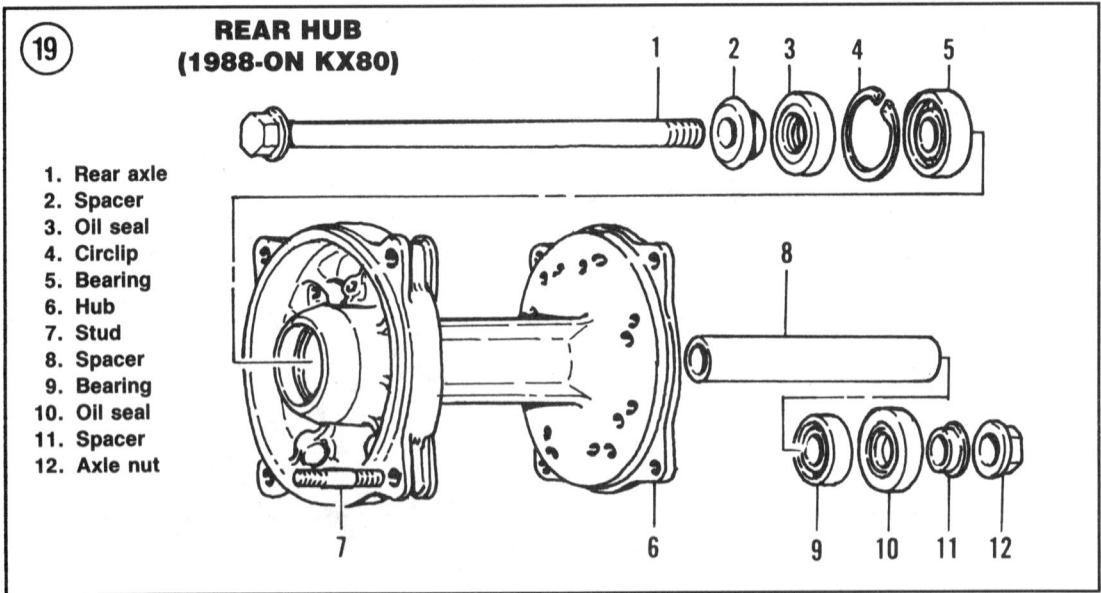

**REAR HUB
(1988-ON KX80)**

1. Rear axle
2. Spacer
3. Oil seal
4. Circlip
5. Bearing
6. Hub
7. Stud
8. Spacer
9. Bearing
10. Oil seal
11. Spacer
12. Axle nut

12

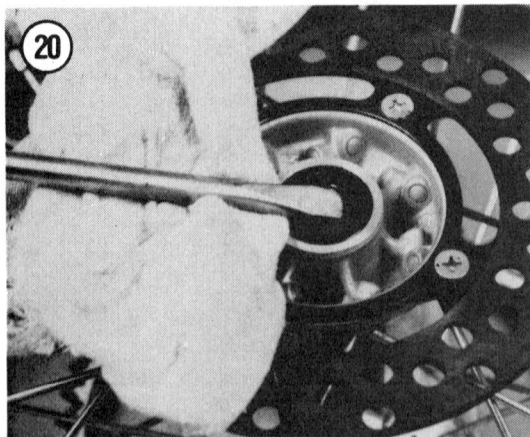

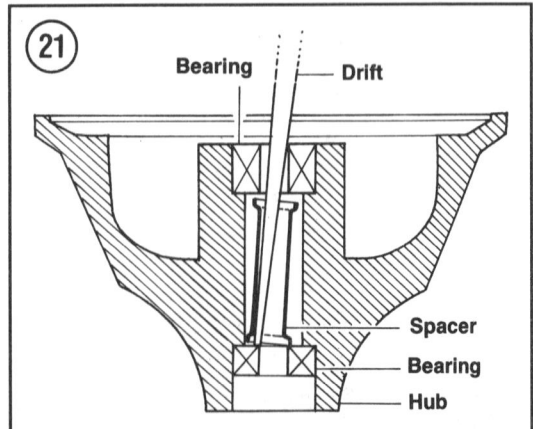

Bearing   Drift

Spacer
Bearing
Hub

Tap the bearing out of the hub with a hammer, working around the perimeter of the inner race.

7. Remove the spacer and tap out the opposite bearing.

8. Thoroughly clean out the inside of the hub with solvent and dry with compressed air or a shop cloth.

NOTE
Avoid getting any greasy solvent residue on the brake drum or brake disc during this procedure. If this happens, clean it off with a shop cloth and lacquer thinner.

NOTE
Fully sealed bearings are available from many good bearing specialty shops. Fully sealed bearings provide better protection from dirt and moisture that may get into the hub.

9. Check the axle for wear and straightness. Use V-blocks and a dial indicator (**Figure 22**). If the runout exceeds the service limit in **Table 2**, straighten the axle with a press. If the runout exceeds the repair limit in **Table 2**, replace the axle.

10. Pack non-sealed bearings with good-quality bearing grease. Work the grease in between the balls thoroughly. Turn the bearing by hand a couple of times to make sure the grease is distributed evenly inside the bearing.

11. Pack the distance collar with multipurpose grease.

NOTE
If a bearing has only one sealed side, install the bearing with the sealed side facing out.

CAUTION
When installing the bearings in the following procedures, tap the bearings squarely into place and tap on the outer race only. Use a socket (Figure 23) that matches the outer race diameter. Do not tap on the inner race or the bearing might be damaged. Be sure that the bearings are completely seated.

12. Install the right-hand bearing.
13. Install the spacer.
14. Install the left-hand bearing.
15. Install the left-hand circlip.
16. Install new grease seals. Lubricate them with multipurpose grease and tap squarely into the hub. Install the oil seal until it is at least flush with the hub (**Figure 24**).

DRIVEN SPROCKET

Removal/Installation

1. Remove the rear wheel as described in this chapter.
2. Loosen then remove the sprocket nuts or bolts.
3. Remove the sprocket (**Figure 25**).
4. Assemble by reversing these disassembly steps. Tighten nuts or bolts to the torque specification in **Table 3** or **Table 4**.

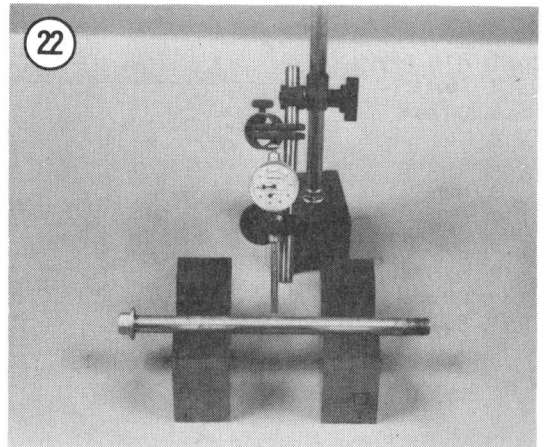

Inspection

Inspect the sprocket teeth. If they are visibly worn, replace the sprocket.

If the sprocket requires replacement, the drive chain is probably worn also and may need replacement. Refer to *Drive Chain Cleaning/ Lubrication* in Chapter Three.

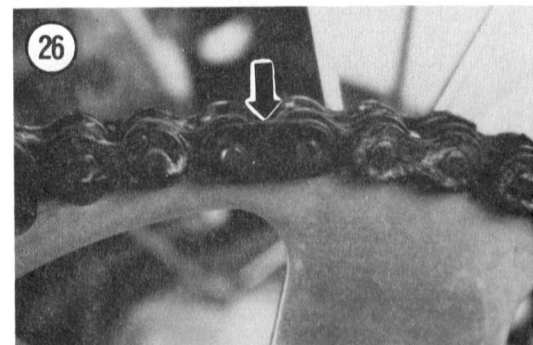

DRIVE CHAIN

Removal/Installation

1. Support the bike on a stand so that the rear wheel is off the ground.
2. Turn the rear wheel and drive chain until the master link is accessible.
3. Remove the master link clip (**Figure 26**) and remove the master link.
4. Slowly rotate the rear wheel and pull the drive chain off the drive sprocket.
5. Install by reversing these removal steps.
6. Install the clip on the master link so that the closed end of the clip is facing the direction of chain travel (**Figure 6**).

Service and Inspection

For service and inspection of the drive chain, refer to *Drive Chain Cleaning/Lubrication* in Chapter Three.

TIRE CHANGING AND TIRE REPAIRS

Refer to Chapter Eleven.

UNI-TRAK LINKAGE

The Uni-Trak linkage has a rocking arm (or suspension arm) mounted on the frame and connecting the top of the shock to the suspension rod. The vertical link or suspension rod assembly connects the rocking arm to the swing arm. The bearings at all these joints must be inspected and lubricated according to the maintenance schedule (Chapter Three) and replaced when worn past the specified limits.

NOTE
Grease fittings (Zerk fittings) are installed on some models. These can be used to periodically lubricate the bushings. Other models will require disassembly of the Uni-Trak linkage for periodic lubrication.

Uni-Trak Linkage Disassembly/Inspection/Lubrication (KX60 and 1983-1985 KX80)

Refer to **Figure 27** for this procedure.

12

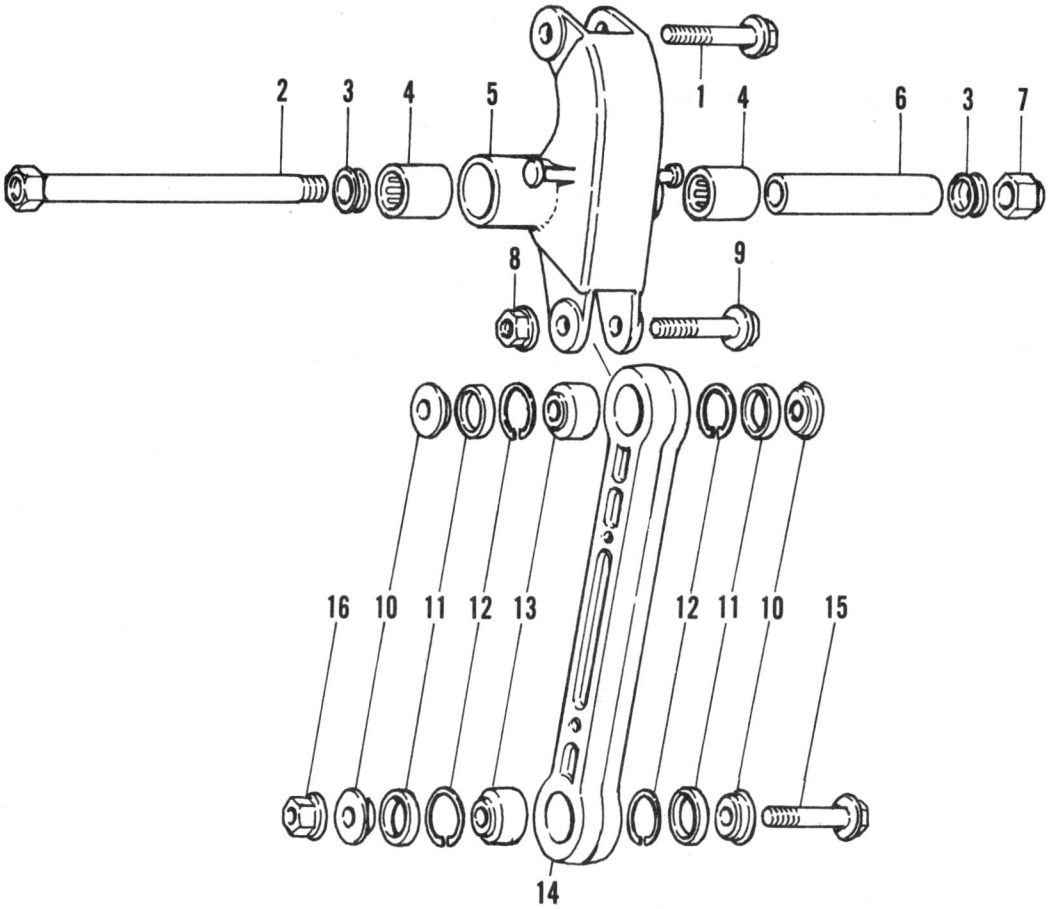

**REAR SUSPENSION
(KX60 AND 1983-1985 KX80)**

1. Bolt
2. Pivot bolt
3. End cap
4. Bearing
5. Rocking arm
6. Sleeve bushing
7. Nut
8. Nut
9. Pivot bolt
10. End cap
11. Oil seal
12. Circlip*
13. Bearing
14. Vertical link
15. Pivot bolt
16. Nut

* Circlip used on 1983-1984 KX60 and 1983-1984 KX80.

1. Support the motorcycle on a stand with the rear wheel off the ground.
2. Remove the seat and side covers.
3. Remove the vertical link as follows:
   a. Remove the 2 bolts (A, **Figure 28**) securing the vertical link.
   b. Remove the vertical link (B, **Figure 28**) and the 4 end caps.
4. Remove the rocking arm as follows:
   a. Remove the vertical link bolt at the rocking arm (A, **Figure 28**), if not previously removed.
   b. Remove the shock absorber upper pivot bolt (A, **Figure 29**) at the rocking arm.
   c. Remove the rocking arm pivot shaft nut and bolt (B, **Figure 29**) and remove the rocking arm (C, **Figure 29**).

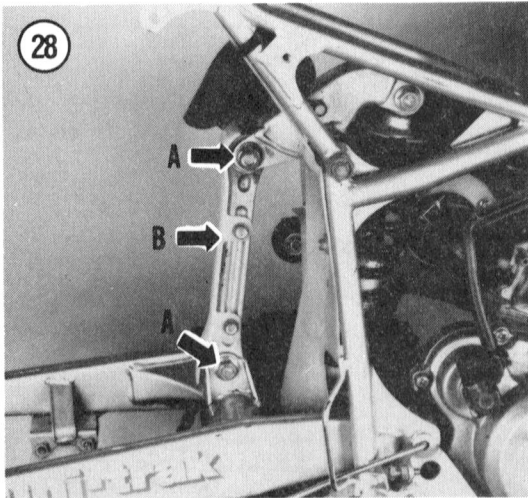

5. Inspect the vertical link as follows:
   a. Remove the oil seals and circlips.
   b. Clean the vertical link assembly in solvent and dry thoroughly.
   c. Inspect the bearings and pivot bolts. Maximum bearing wear is 0.7 mm (0.028 in.). Replace any bearings that show excessive wear. Bearing replacement requires a press. If you do not have access to a press, refer service to a Kawasaki dealer or machine shop.
6. Inspect the rocking arm as follows:
   a. Remove the end caps.
   b. Remove the sleeve bushing.
   c. Clean the rocking arm assembly in solvent and dry thoroughly.
   d. Inspect the bearings, sleeve bushing and pivot bolt. Replace any bearings that show excessive wear or damage. Bearing replacement requires a press. Refer this service to a Kawasaki dealer or machine shop.
7. Measure the sleeve bushing outside diameter with a micrometer and compare to the specification in **Table 2**. Replace the sleeve bushing and its bearings if the OD meets or exceeds the wear limit.
8. Lubricate all bearings, bushings and pivot bolts with molybdenum disulfide grease.
9. To assemble the linkage, reverse the disassembly procedure. Note the following:
   a. Be sure to install the end caps during assembly.
   b. Tighten all pivot bolts to the torque specifications in **Table 3** or **Table 4**.

Uni-Trak Linkage Disassembly/Inspection/Lubrication (1986-on KX80)

Refer to **Figure 30** (1986-1988 KX80) or **Figure 31** (1989-on KX80).

1. Support the motorcycle with the rear wheel off the ground.
2. Remove the tie rods (**Figure 32**) as follows:
   a. Loosen the tie rod front pivot bolt and nut.
   b. Loosen and remove the tie rod rear pivot bolt and nut. Repeat for both tie rods.
   c. Remove the tie rod front pivot bolt and nut and remove the tie rod assemblies.
3. Remove the rocking arm as follows:
   a. Loosen the shock absorber lower pivot shaft nut at the rocking arm. Remove the pivot bolt and nut.

12

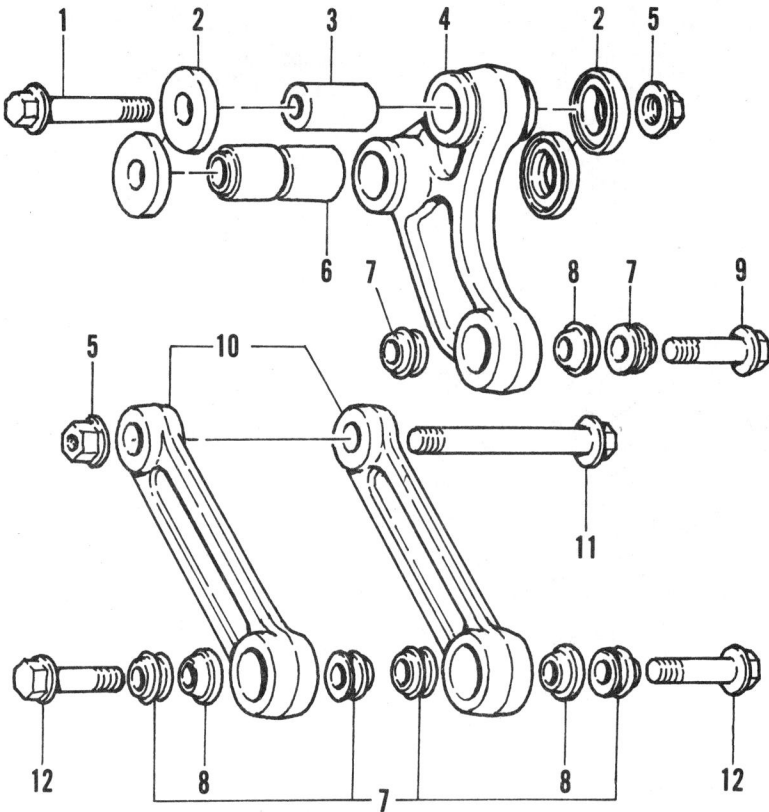

**REAR SUSPENSION
(1986-1988 KX80)**

1. Pivot bolt
2. Oil seal
3. Sleeve
4. Rocking arm
5. Nut
6. Sleeve
7. Oil seal
8. Ball-joint
9. Pivot bolt
10. Tie rod
11. Pivot bolt
12. Pivot bolt

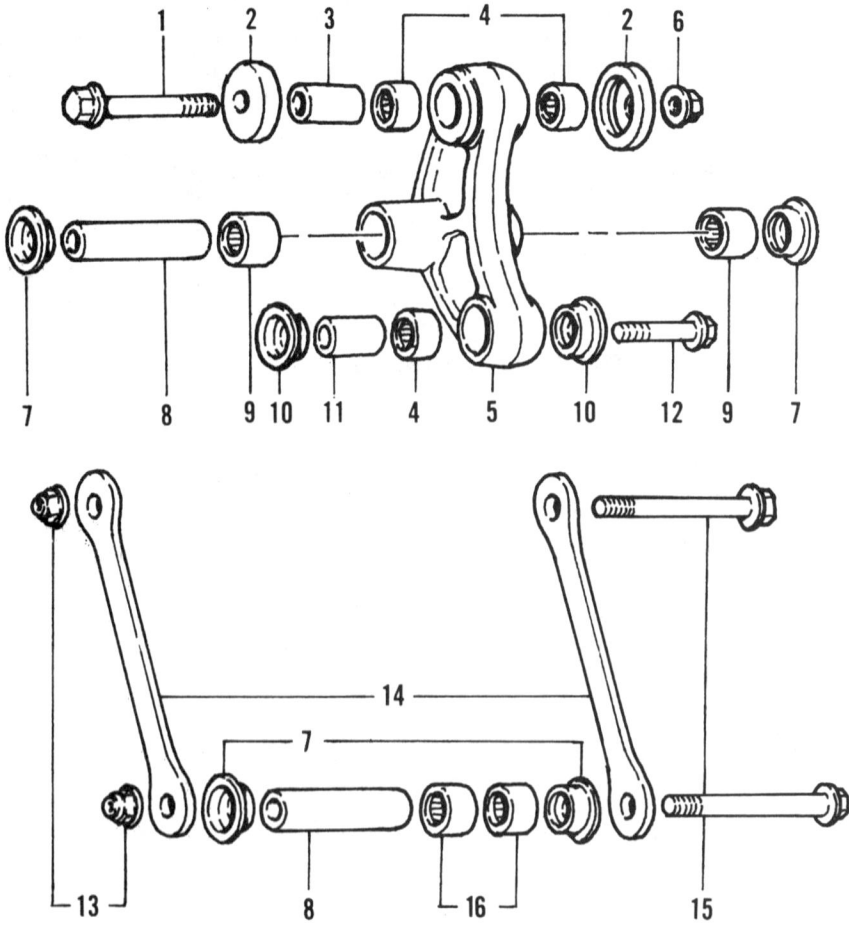

**REAR SUSPENSION
(1989-ON)**

1. Pivot bolt
2. End cap
3. Sleeve bushing
4. Bearing
5. Rocking arm
6. Nut
7. Oil seal
8. Sleeve bushing
9. Bearing
10. Oil seal
11. Sleeve bushing
12. Pivot bolt
13. Nut
14. Tie rod
15. Pivot bolt
16. Bearing

12

b. Loosen the rocking arm pivot bolt nut. Remove the nut, pivot bolt and rocking arm.

4. Inspect the tie rods as follows:

   a. Remove the end caps or oil seals.

   b. Clean the tie rods in solvent and dry thoroughly.

   c. Inspect the bearings and pivot bolts. Maximum bearing wear is 0.7 mm (0.028 in.). Replace any bearings that show excessive wear. Bearing replacement requires a press. Refer this service to a Kawasaki dealer or machine shop.

5. Inspect the rocking arm as follows:

   a. Remove the end caps.

   b. Remove the sleeve bushings.

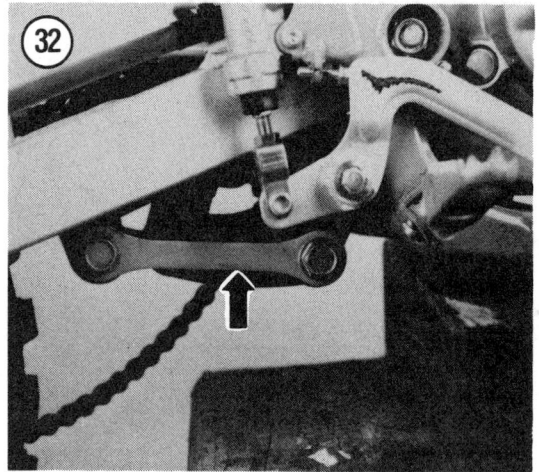

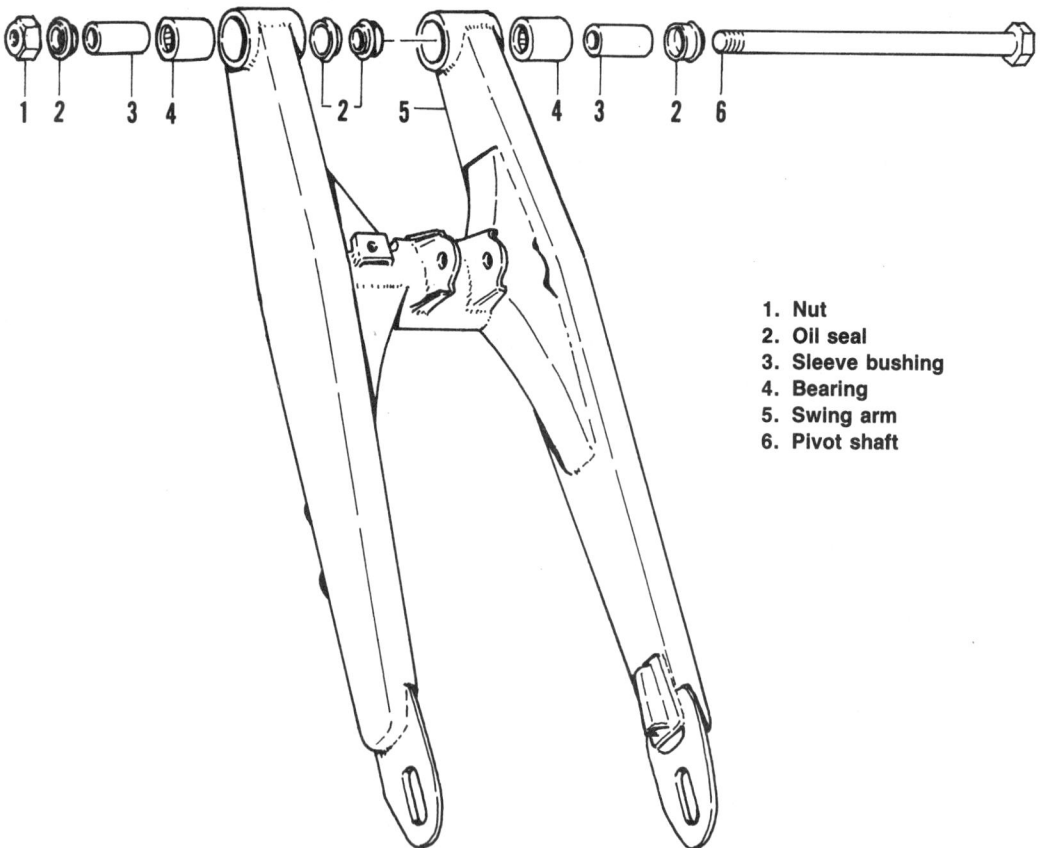

**REAR SWING ARM
(KX60 AND 1983-1984 KX80)**

1. Nut
2. Oil seal
3. Sleeve bushing
4. Bearing
5. Swing arm
6. Pivot shaft

c. Clean the rocking arm assembly in solvent and dry thoroughly.

d. Inspect the bearings, sleeve bushings and pivot bolt. Replace any bearings that show excessive wear or damage. Bearing replacement requires a press. Refer this service to a Kawasaki dealer or machine shop.

6. Measure the sleeve bushing outside diameter with a micrometer and compare to the specification in **Table 2**. Replace the sleeve bushing and its bearings if the OD is worn to the wear limit or less.

7. Check the rocking arm pivot bolt runout with a V-block and dial indicator and compare to the specification in **Table 2**. If the special tools are not available, roll the pivot bolt on a flat surface and check the bolt for excessive bending. Replace the bolt if the runout exceeds the wear limit in **Table 2** or if the bolt appears damaged.

8. Lubricate all bearings, sleeve bushings and pivot bolts with molybdenum disulfide grease.

9. To assemble the linkage, reverse the disassembly procedure. Note the following:

a. Be sure to install the end caps or oil seals during assembly.

b. Install the tie rods so that the small end with the protruding side faces in.

c. Tighten all pivot bolts to the torque specifications in **Table 4**.

REAR SWING ARM

In time the bearings will wear beyond service limits and must be replaced. The condition of the bearings can greatly affect handling performance and if not replaced they can produce erratic and dangerous handling.

The rear swing arm used on the various models differ in construction and design.

Removal/Installation

Refer to **Figure 33** (KX60 and 1983-1984 KX80), **Figure 34** (1985-1987 KX80) or **Figure 35** (1988-on KX80).

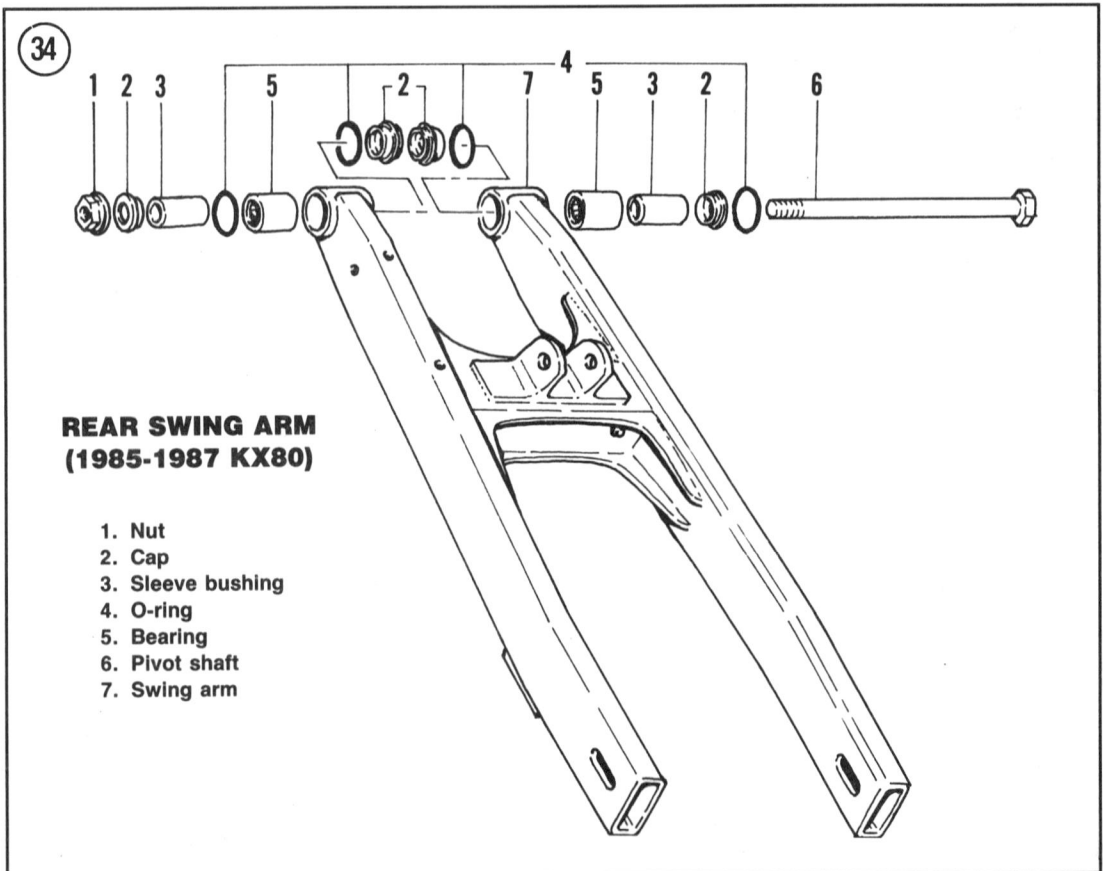

**REAR SWING ARM
(1985-1987 KX80)**

1. Nut
2. Cap
3. Sleeve bushing
4. O-ring
5. Bearing
6. Pivot shaft
7. Swing arm

(35)

**REAR SWING ARM
(1988-ON KX80)**

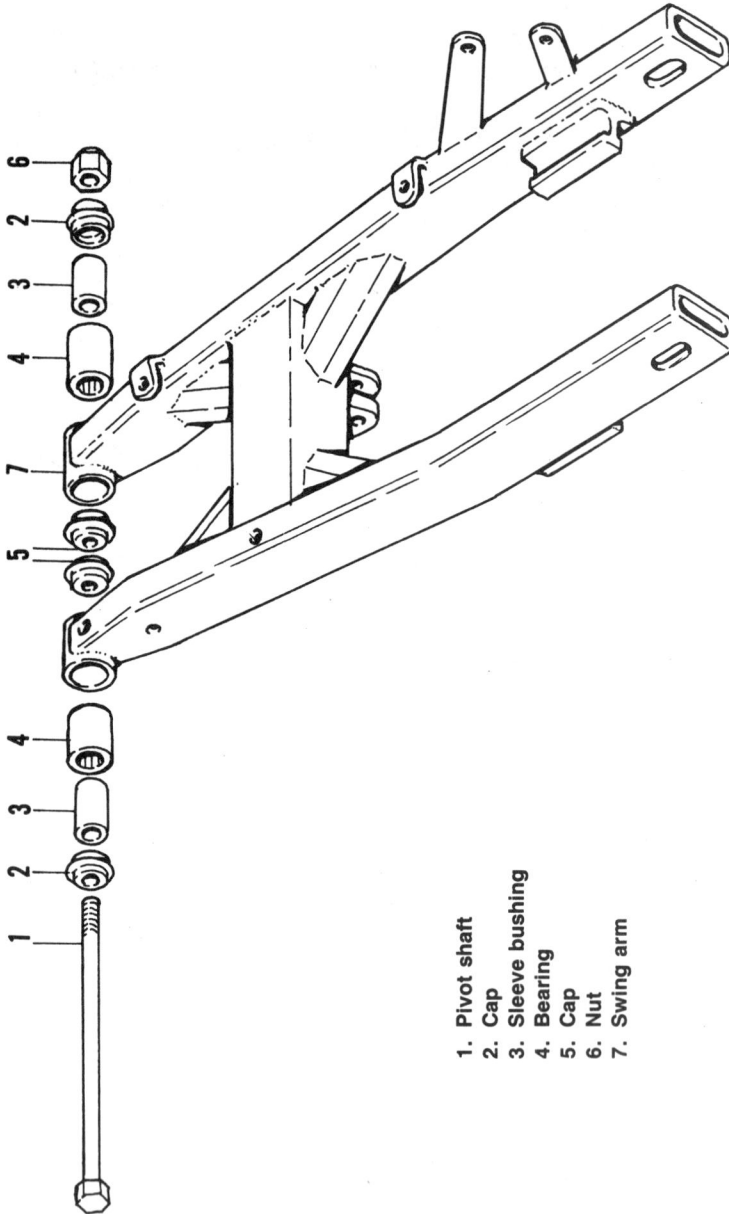

1. Pivot shaft
2. Cap
3. Sleeve bushing
4. Bearing
5. Cap
6. Nut
7. Swing arm

1. Remove the bolts securing the seat and remove it.

2. Remove both frame number/side panels.

3. Remove the rear wheel and drive chain as described in this chapter.

4A. *KX60 and 1983-1985 KX80:* Perform the following:

   a. Remove the rear brake pedal assembly.

   b. Loosen the vertical link lower pivot bolt nut at the swing arm (A, **Figure 28**). Remove the nut and pivot bolt.

4B. *1986-on KX80:* Loosen the left- and right-hand tie rod pivot bolt nuts at the swing arm. Remove the pivot bolts and nuts and lower the tie-rods away from the swing arm.

5. Grasp the swing arm as shown in **Figure 36** and try to rock it back and forth, pulling the top and pushing the bottom, then reversing. If you feel any more than a very slight movement of the swing arm, and the pivot bolt is correctly tightened, the bearings should be replaced.

6. Loosen the swing arm pivot shaft nut and remove it. Grasp the swing arm in one hand and

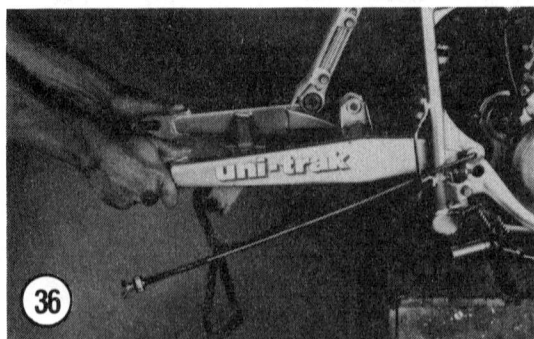

pull the pivot shaft out of the swing arm. If the pivot shaft is tight, carefully drive it out with a brass or aluminum drift.

7. Remove the swing arm along with any external washers, shims or seals. See **Figure 33** (KX60 and 1983-1984 KX80), **Figure 34** (1985-1987 KX80) or **Figure 35** (1988-on KX80).

8. Inspect the bearings. If necessary, replace them as described in this chapter.

9. Inspect the chain guards and plates for wear or damage. Replace worn parts before the drive chain starts to wear into the swing arm.

10. Clean the old grease from all parts. After the parts have been cleaned and dry, apply a liberal amount of molybdenum disulfide grease to the bearings, sleeves and pivot shaft.

11. Installation is the reverse of these steps. Note the following.

12. Tighten the swing arm pivot shaft nut to the torque specification in **Table 3** or **Table 4**.

13A. *KX60 and 1983-1985 KX80:* Perform the following:

   a. Reinstall the vertical link pivot bolts and nut. Tighten to the torque specification in **Table 3**.

   b. Install the rear brake pedal assembly.

13B. *1986-on KX80:* Reinstall the left- and right-hand tie rod pivot bolts and nuts at the swing arm. Tighten the pivot bolt nuts to the torque specification in **Table 4**.

14. Adjust the drive chain as described in Chapter Three.

REAR SUSPENSION BEARING REPLACEMENT

Refer to **Figure 33** (KX60 and 1983-1984 KX80), **Figure 34** (1985-1987 KX80) or **Figure 35** (1988-on KX80).

1. Remove the swing arm as described in this chapter.

2. Secure the swing arm in a vise with soft jaws.

CAUTION
Do not remove the bearings just for inspection as they are usually damaged during removal.

3. Carefully tap out the bearing. Use a suitable size drift or socket and extension and carefully drive the bearing out from the opposite end (**Figure 37**).

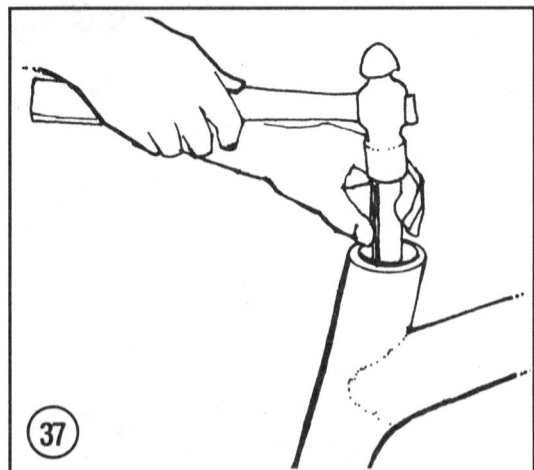

12

4. Clean the swing arm thoroughly in solvent. Check the bearing mounting areas for cracks, wear or other damage.

NOTE
A press is be required to accurately and safely install the bearings.

5. Apply a light coat of molybdenum disulfide grease to all parts before installation.
6. Using a press, install the new bearings into each side of the swing arm.
7. After installing the bearings, liberally coat them with molybdenum disulfide grease.
8. Install the swing arm as described in this chapter.

UNI-TRAK REAR SUSPENSION

All models use a single rear shock absorber/spring unit. The single shock controls swing arm movement through a compound linkage system with spherical bearings.

The single shock/spring unit minimizes swing arm flex caused by unequal damping and spring tension between dual shocks. However, several suspension bushings carry a great load in the Uni-Trak system. Frequent lubrication and inspection are necessary to preserve good handling and prevent premature component wear.

REAR SHOCK ABSORBER (KX60)

Removal/Installation

1. Support the bike with its sidestand.
2. Remove the seat and both frame side covers.
3. Loosen but do not remove the shock absorber upper (A, **Figure 29**) and lower (**Figure 38**) nuts.
4. Place the bike on a stand so that the rear wheel clears the ground.

NOTE
Mark the rear of the shock absorber with a piece of tape so that the shock absorber can be reinstalled with the correct orientation.

5. Remove the shock absorber upper and lower mounting nuts and bolts and remove the shock absorber from the left-hand side.
6. Installation is the reverse of these steps.
7. Tighten the shock absorber bolts and nuts to the torque specification in **Table 3**.

Spring
Removal/Installation

Refer to **Figure 39**.
1. Remove the shock absorber as described in this chapter.
2. Secure the bottom of the shock absorber in a vise with soft jaws.
3. Using a shock hook wrench, turn the shock adjuster to its softest position.

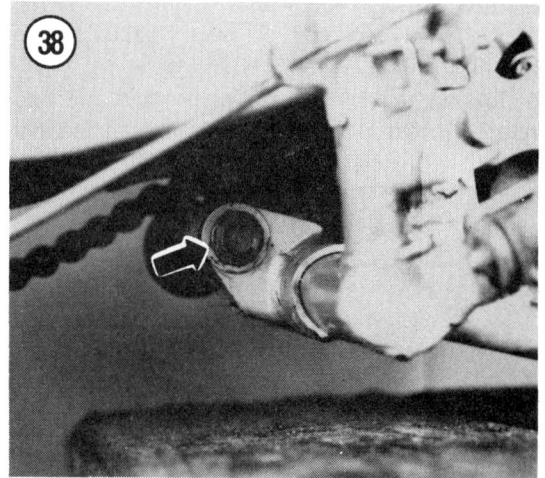

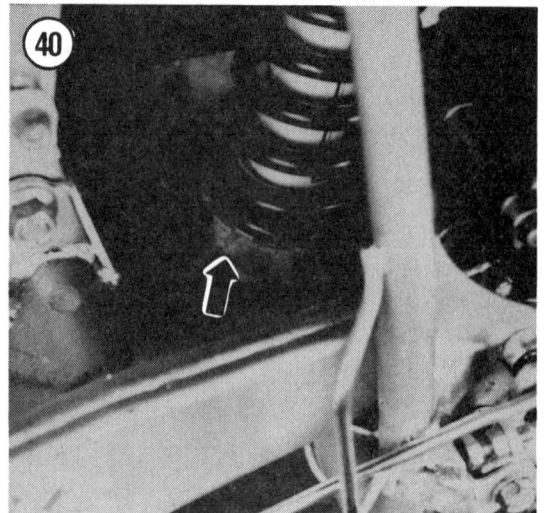

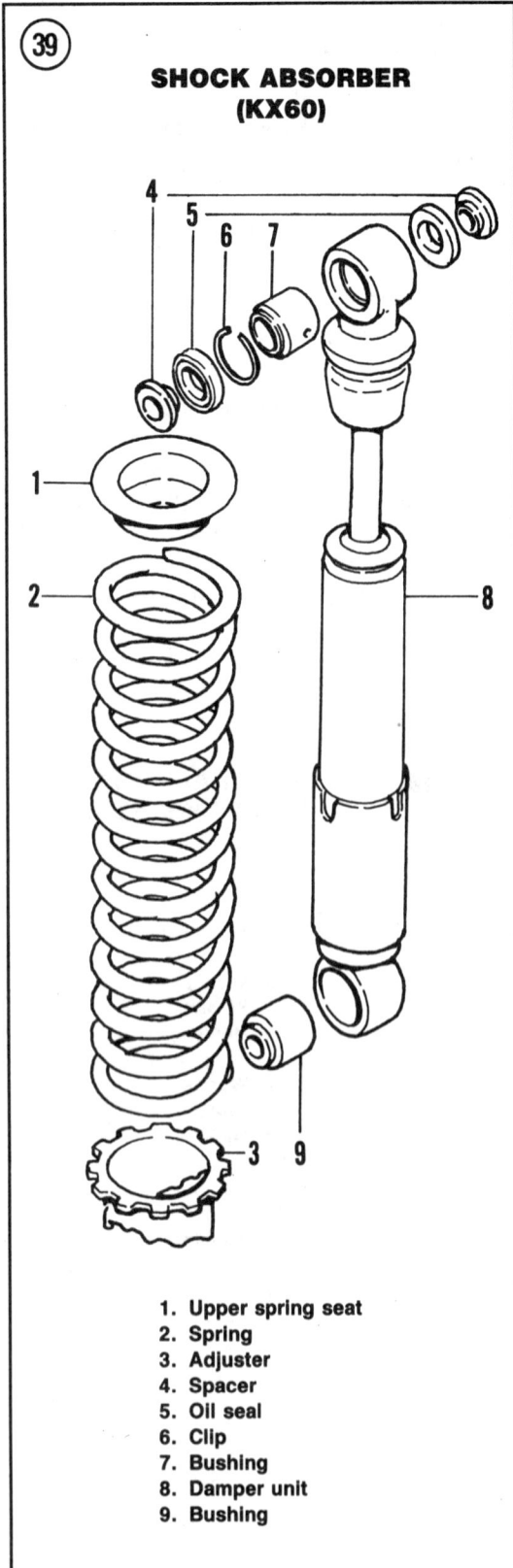

**SHOCK ABSORBER
(KX60)**

1. Upper spring seat
2. Spring
3. Adjuster
4. Spacer
5. Oil seal
6. Clip
7. Bushing
8. Damper unit
9. Bushing

4. Slide the rubber bumper down the shock shaft.

5. Install a spring compressor onto the shock absorber following the manufacturer's instructions. Then compress the spring with the tool and remove the spring retainer clip from the top of the shock. Remove the retainer upper spring seat, the spring and the adjuster.

6. Installation is the reverse of these steps. Make sure the spring retainer clip secures the spring completely.

7. Adjust the spring preload as described in this chapter.

Shock Adjustment

Spring preload is the only adjustment available on the KX60 stock shock absorber. There is no damping adjustment.

The spring adjuster installed at the bottom of the spring has 5 spring adjustment positions (**Figure 40**). If the shock's spring action feels too hard or too soft, adjust the spring as follows.

1. Remove the seat and both frame side covers.

2. Remove the pivot bolt and nut at the top of the vertical link and slide the link towards the back of the bike.

3. Remove bolts holding the shock flap cover to the frame. Remove the cover.

4. Reposition the vertical link and install the upper pivot bolt and nut. Tighten the nut finger-tight.

5. Using a shock hook wrench, turn the spring adjuster to adjust the spring preload.

6. Remove the vertical link pivot bolt and nut and reinstall the shock flap cover. Secure the cover with the mounting bolts.

7. Reposition the vertical link and install the pivot bolt and nut. Tighten the vertical link to the torque specification in **Table 3**.

**REAR SHOCK ABSORBER
(1983-1985 KX80)**

Removal/Installation

1. Loosen the shock absorber upper and lower pivot shaft nuts.

2. Support the bike on a stand so that the rear wheel clears the ground.

WARNING
Do not disconnect the shock absorber reservoir hose when performing Step

12

3. In addition, do not drop the reservoir or lay it in a position where it could be damaged. The shock and the reservoir are under extreme pressure and eye damage could occur if these components are damaged in any way.

3. Remove the shock absorber reservoir from its mount on the right-hand side of the frame.
4. Remove the upper and lower pivot shaft nuts and shafts.
5. Remove the shock absorber through the left side of the frame.
6. To install, reverse the removal procedures. Note the following:
   a. Tighten the nuts to the torque specification in **Table 4**.
   b. Make sure the shock reservoir is properly mounted on the right-hand side of the frame.

Spring
Removal/Installation

Refer to **Figure 41**.
1. Remove the shock absorber as described in this chapter.

CAUTION
Support the shock reservoir when performing this procedure to prevent its damage.

2. Secure the bottom of the shock absorber in a vise with soft jaws.
3. Using a shock hook wrench, turn the shock adjuster to it lightest position (**Figure 42**).
4. Slide the rubber bumper down the shock shaft.
5. Install a spring compressor onto the shock absorber following the manufacturer's instructions.

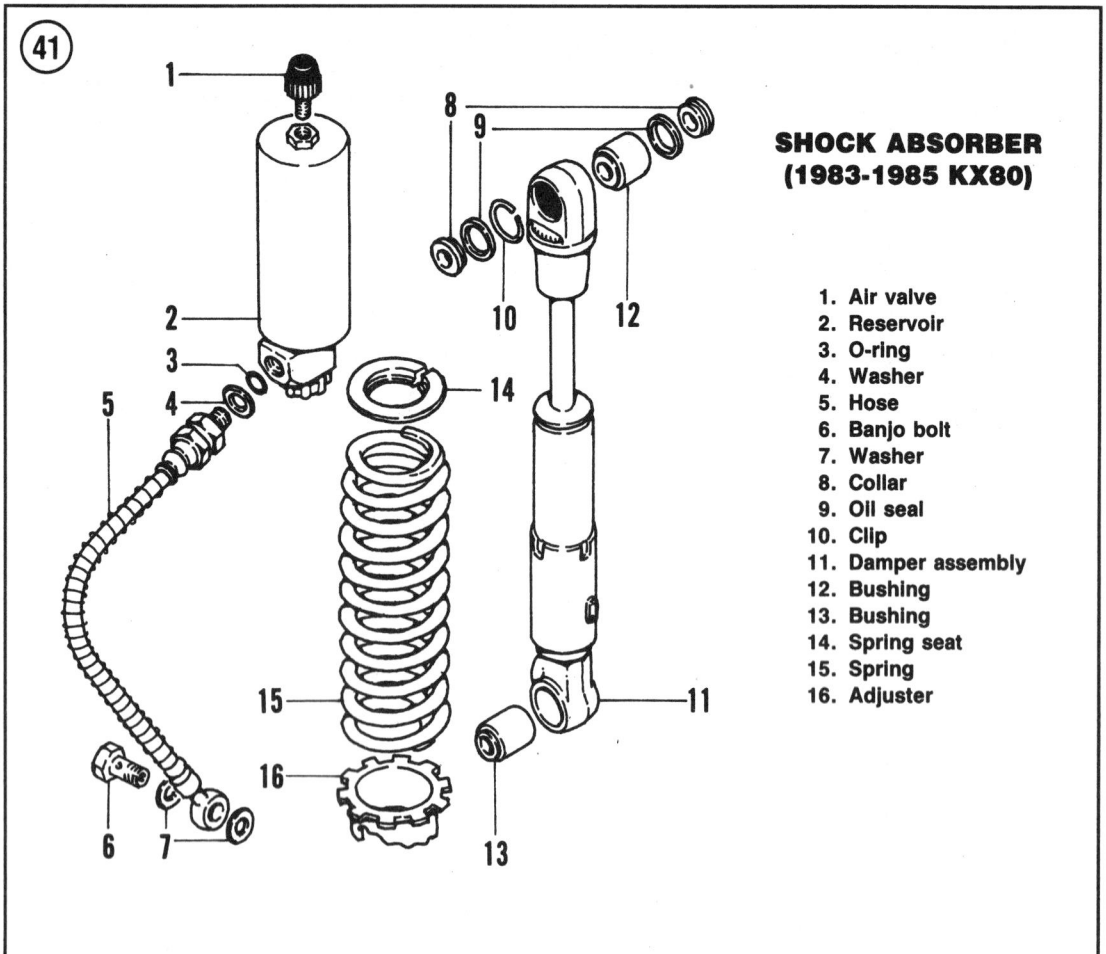

SHOCK ABSORBER (1983-1985 KX80)

1. Air valve
2. Reservoir
3. O-ring
4. Washer
5. Hose
6. Banjo bolt
7. Washer
8. Collar
9. Oil seal
10. Clip
11. Damper assembly
12. Bushing
13. Bushing
14. Spring seat
15. Spring
16. Adjuster

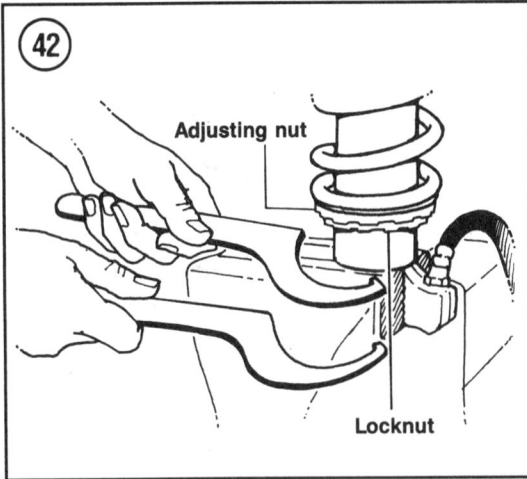

Adjusting nut

Locknut

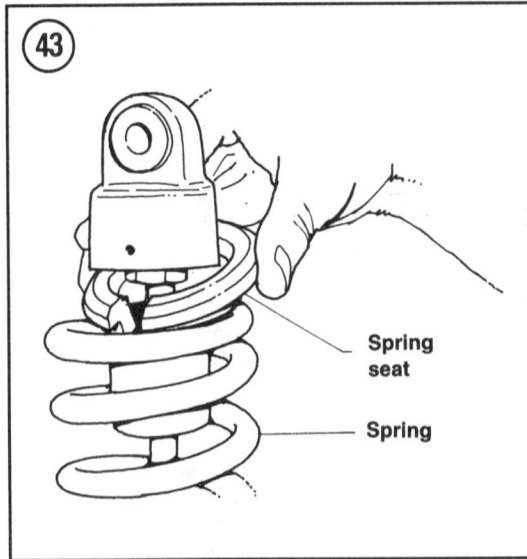

Spring seat

Spring

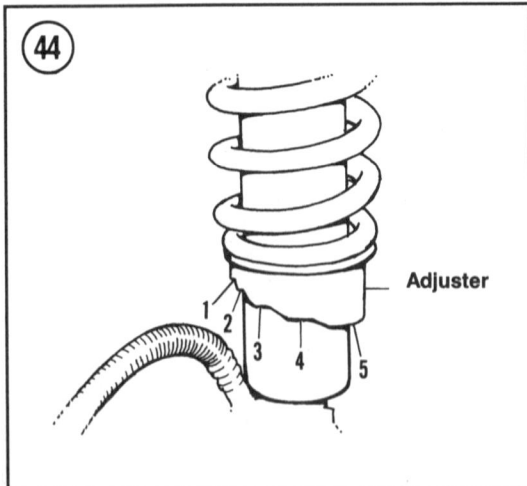

Adjuster

1
2
3 4
5

Then compress the spring with the compressor tool and remove the spring retainer clip from the top of the shock (**Figure 43**). Remove the retainer, the spring seat, spring and adjuster.

6. Installation is the reverse of these steps. Make sure the spring retainer clip secures the spring completely.

7. Adjust the spring preload as described in this chapter.

Shock Adjustment

The stock shock absorber can be adjusted as follows:

   a. Spring preload.
   b. Rebound damping adjustment.
   c. Compression damping adjustment (1985).

Spring preload

The spring adjuster installed at the bottom of the spring has 5 spring adjustment positions (**Figure 44**). If the shock's spring action feels too hard or too soft, adjust the spring as follows.

1. Remove the shock absorber as described in this chapter.

> *CAUTION*
> *Support the shock reservoir when performing this procedure to prevent its damage.*

2. Secure the bottom of the shock absorber in a vise with soft jaws (**Figure 42**).

3. Using a shock hook wrench, turn the spring adjuster to adjust the spring preload.

4. Reinstall the shock absorber as described in this chapter.

Rebound damping adjustment

The stock shock absorber is equipped with a 4-way damping adjuster. The adjuster is a round slotted wheel marked with the numbers 1, 2, 3 and 4 at the adjustment positions (**Figure 45**). The adjuster is located at the top of the shock directly underneath the mounting boss. To change the damping, use a flat-tipped screwdriver to turn the damping adjuster. Turn the adjuster until it clicks into position. Read the number off the top of the adjuster to determine the adjustment position. The

12

minimum damping adjustment is No. 1. The maximum damping adjustment is No. 4.

Compression damping adjustment (1985)

The gas reservoir on the stock 1985 KX80 shock absorber is equipped with a 4-way compression damping adjuster. The adjuster is mounted at the bottom of the gas reservoir housing (**Figure 46**). To change the damping, turn the damping adjuster by hand until it clicks into position. Read the number off the side of the adjuster to determine the adjustment position. The minimum damping adjustment is No. 1. The maximum damping adjustment is No. 4.

Shock Oil Change

Refer to **Figure 41** for this procedure.
1. Remove the shock absorber as described in this chapter.
2. Wash the outside of the shock absorber with aerosol electrical contact cleaner and allow to dry thoroughly. Especially clean the threads at the bottom of the shock.
3. Secure the bottom shock absorber mount in a vise with soft jaws (**Figure 42**).
4. Using a shock hook wrench, turn the shock adjuster to its lightest preload position.
5. Slide the rubber bumper down the shock shaft.
6. Install a spring compressor onto the shock absorber following the manufacturer's instructions.

Then compress the spring with the compressor tool and remove the spring retainer clip from the top of the shock (**Figure 43**). Remove the retainer, the spring seat, spring and adjuster.

> **WARNING**
> *When discharging the nitrogen pressure in Step 7, make sure to wear eye protection. In addition, make sure to point the reservoir air valve away from your body or face. Failure to observe this warning may cause severe eye damage.*

7. Remove the air valve cap from the air valve on the reservoir. Then depress the air valve with a

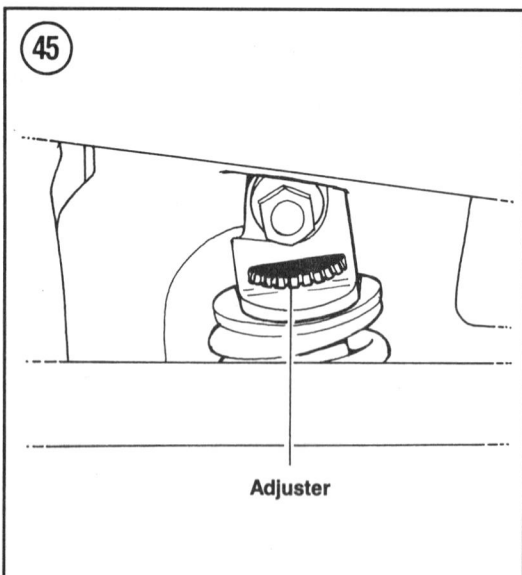

Damper adjuster

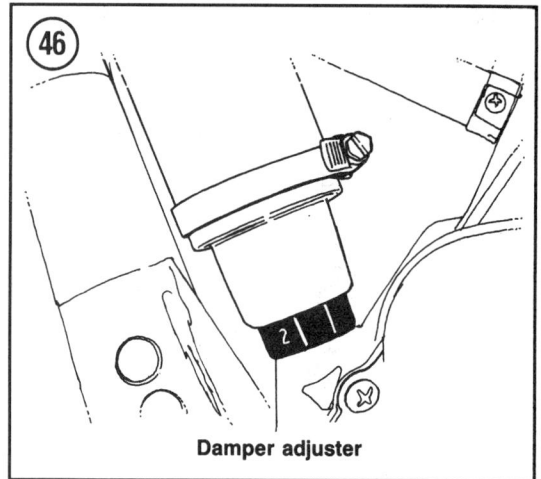

Adjuster

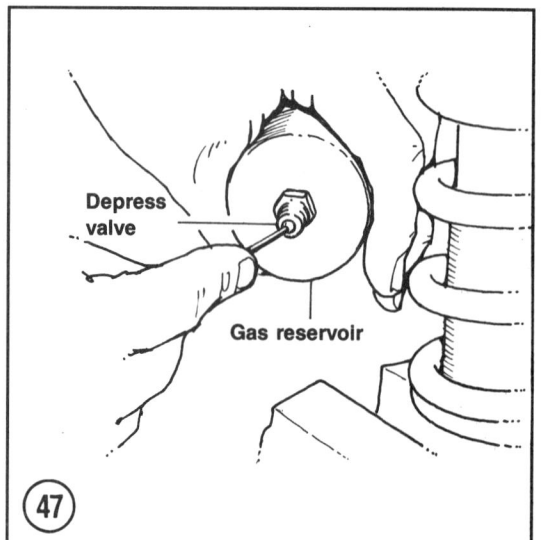

Depress valve

Gas reservoir

small screwdriver (**Figure 47**) to release all nitrogen from the shock absorber.

8. Secure the reservoir in a vise (with padded jaws) as shown in **Figure 48**. Then loosen and remove the banjo bolt and 2 washers at the reservoir and disconnect the reservoir from the hose.

9. Pour the oil out of the reservoir and the shock body.

10. Inspect the O-ring at the hose fitting. Also check the hose for cracks or other damage. Replace the hose and O-ring if necessary.

11. Remove the air valve from the reservoir.

12. Using a rod through the air valve hole, push the piston until it is 55 mm (2.17 in.) from the bottom edge of the reservoir (dimension A) as shown in **Figure 49**.

13. Reinstall the air valve and O-ring.

14. Invert the reservoir, then slowly fill it through the hose threads with 57 cc (1.9 oz.) of SAE 5W shock oil. Set the reservoir aside in an upright position to prevent oil from leaking out.

15. Secure the shock body in a vise and angle it as shown in **Figure 50**.

16. Compress the shock shaft so that it is completely bottomed.

17. Attach a clean empty container to the shock hose as shown in **Figure 50**. Then fill the container with 129 cc (4.4 oz.) of SAE 5W shock oil.

18. Pump the shock shaft until all of the oil is drawn into the shock absorber. Continue until there are no signs of air bubbles in the hose.

19. Remove the container attached to the shock hose. Keep the shock hose up to prevent oil from draining out.

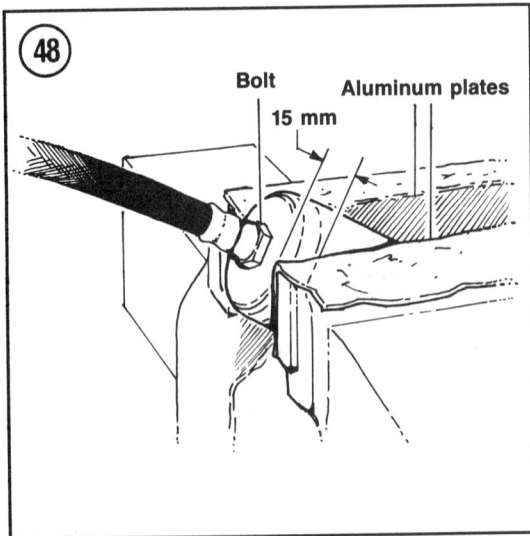

(48)

Bolt   Aluminum plates

15 mm

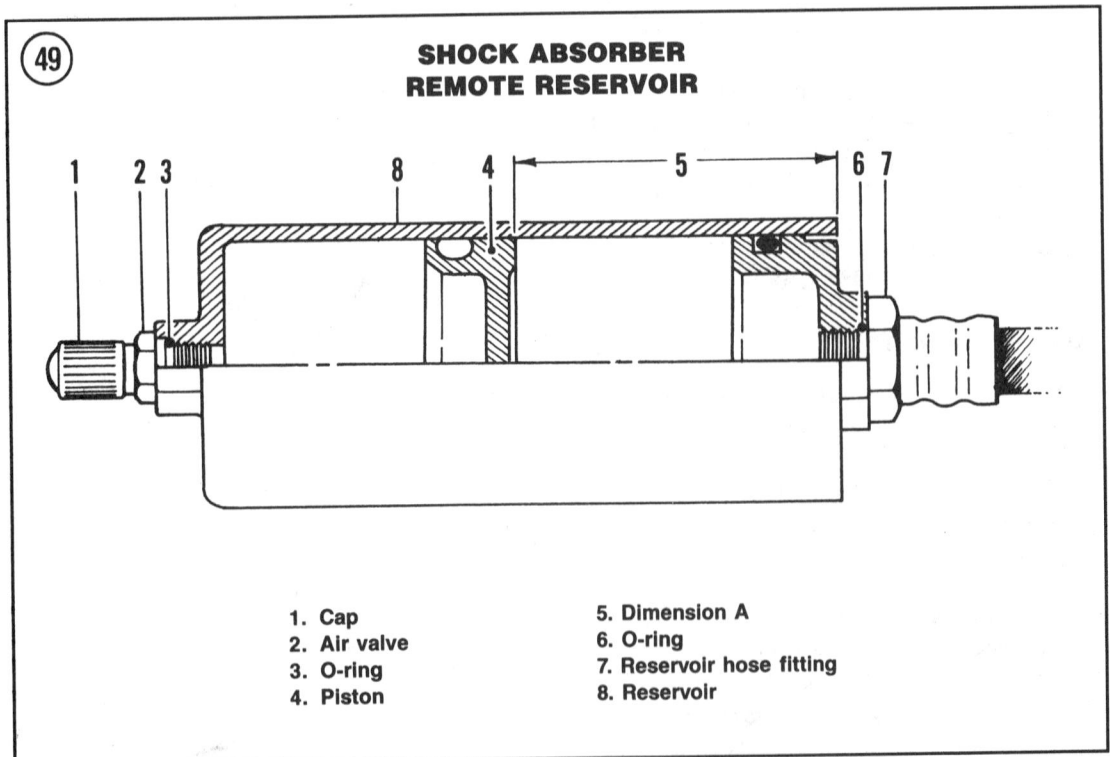

(49) **SHOCK ABSORBER REMOTE RESERVOIR**

1   2 3   8   4 |⟵   5   ⟶| 6 7

12

1. Cap
2. Air valve
3. O-ring
4. Piston
5. Dimension A
6. O-ring
7. Reservoir hose fitting
8. Reservoir

20. Attach the hose to the reservoir with the 2 washers and banjo bolt. Tighten the bolt by hand.

WARNING
Use only nitrogen or air—DO NOT use any other type of compressed gas as an explosion may result. Never heat the shock absorber with a torch or place them near an open flame or extreme heat.

WARNING
Working with high pressure is dangerous. Have the shock pressurized by a Kawasaki dealer or qualified suspension specialist.

21. Have the dealer or shock specialist inject approximately 10 kg/cm² (142 psi) of nitrogen into the reservoir. Then check the shock body, hose and reservoir for leaks. If the shock leaks, bleed the nitrogen out and repair the problem. When the shock assembly holds the nitrogen, proceed with Step 22.
22. When having your shock pressurized, note the following:
  a. Adjustment range: 10-15 kg/cm² (142-213 psi).
  b. Standard factory pressure: 10 kg/cm² (142 psi).
23. After the shock absorber has been safely pressurized with nitrogen, perform Step 24.
24. Install the adjuster, spring and spring seat onto the shock absorber and install the clip. Adjust the spring preload as described in this chapter.

SHOCK ABSORBER
(1986-1987 KX80)

Removal/Installation

1. Support the bike with its sidestand.
2. Loosen the upper and lower shock absorber pivot shaft nuts.
3. Support the bike on a stand so that the rear wheel clears the ground.

WARNING
Do not disconnect the reservoir to shock absorber hose when performing Step 4. In addition, do not drop the reservoir and lay it in a position where it could be damaged. The shock and

reservoir is under extreme pressure and eye damage could occur if these components are damaged in any way.

4. Remove the shock absorber reservoir from its mount on the right-hand side of the frame.
5. Remove the shock absorber through the left side of the frame.
6. To install, reverse the removal procedures. Note the following:
  a. Tighten the nuts to the torque specification in **Table 4**.
  b. Make sure the shock reservoir is properly mounted on the right-hand side of the frame.

Spring
Removal/Installation

Refer to **Figure 51**.
1. Remove the shock absorber as described in this chapter.

CAUTION
Support the shock reservoir in a soft-jawed vise when performing this procedure to prevent its damage.

2. Clean the threads on the shock absorber before loosening the locknut.

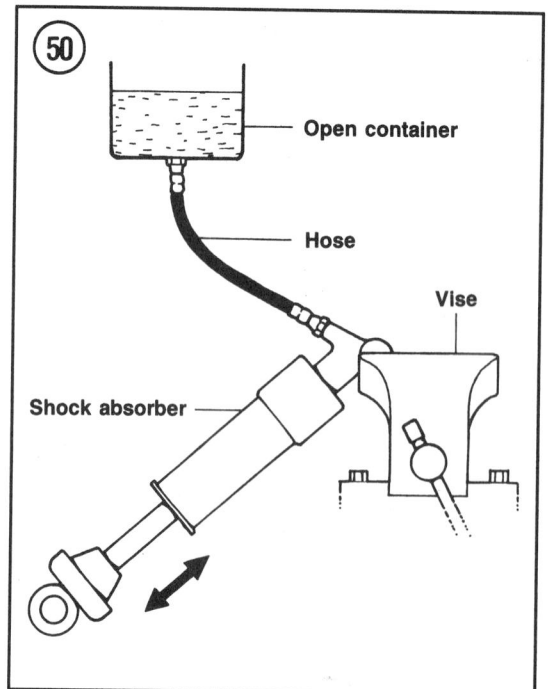

(51)

**SHOCK ABSORBER
(1986-1987 KX80)**

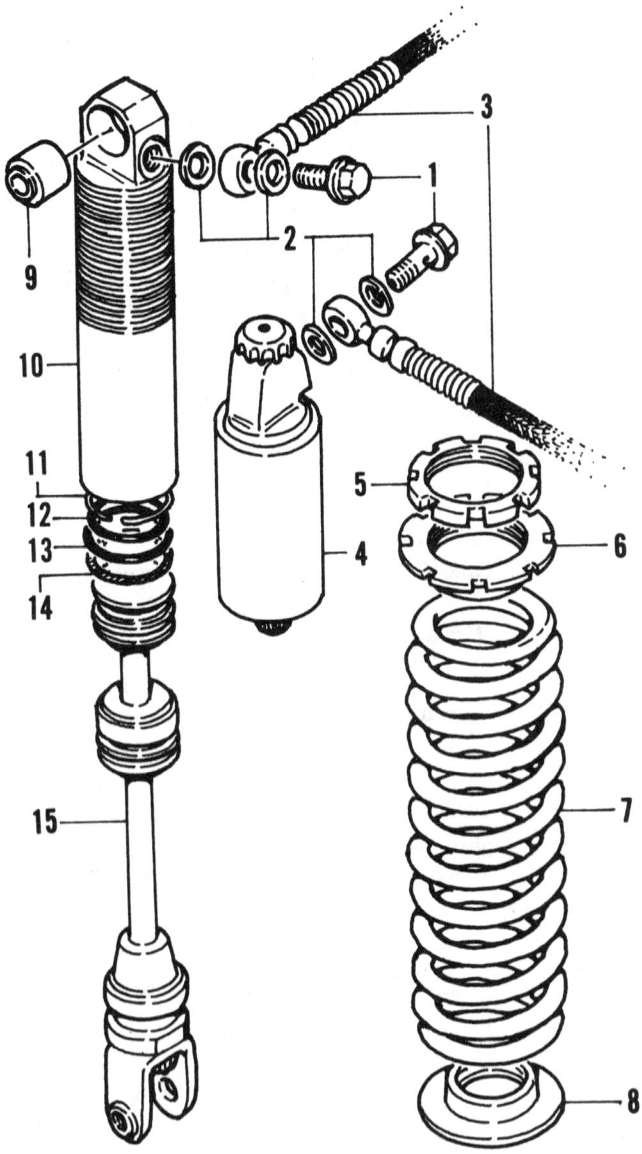

1. Banjo bolt
2. Washer
3. Hose
4. Reservoir
5. Locknut
6. Adjusting nut
7. Spring
8. Spring seat
9. Bushing
10. Damper unit body
11. Circlip
12. O-ring
13. O-ring
14. Packing
15. Pushrod assembly

12

3. If the original spring is going to be reinstalled, measure the installed spring length (**Figure 52**).

4. Secure the bottom of the shock absorber in a vise with soft jaws (**Figure 42**).

5. Using a shock hook wrench, loosen the locknut and the adjusting nut until the spring is loose.

6. Slide the rubber bumper down the shock shaft.

7. Disconnect the spring retainer clip at the opposite end of the shock absorber (**Figure 43**). Remove the retainer clip and remove the spring seat and spring from the shock absorber.

8. Installation is the reverse of these steps. Make sure the spring retainer clip secures the spring completely.

9. After installing the spring, turn the adjusting nut until the spring installed length is the same as recorded in Step 3 or within the range listed in **Table 5**. When turning the adjusting nut, make sure the retainer clip at the top of the spring engages the spring properly. Tighten the locknut against the adjusting nut.

CAUTION
Do not turn the spring preload adjuster in excess of the minimum or maximum settings listed in **Table 5**.

Shock Adjustment

The stock shock absorber can be adjusted as follows:

a. Spring preload.
b. Rebound damping adjustment.
c. Compression damping adjustment.

Spring preload

If the shock's spring action feels too hard or too soft, adjust the spring as follows.

1. Remove the seat and both frame side covers.

2. Remove the air filter case. Place a rag over the carburetor to prevent dirt from entering it.

3. Remove the rear frame assembly.

4. Support the bike on a stand so that the rear wheel is off the ground.

5. Measure the distance from the center of the upper shock bolt hole to the top of the spring adjuster flat surface (**Figure 52**). Record this measurement and compare to the standard, minimum and maximum specifications listed in **Table 5**.

6. Using a hook wrench, loosen the locknut.

7. Using a hook wrench, turn the spring adjuster to adjust the spring preload as required. Remeasure the spring preload length (**Figure 52**). For every 1 complete turn of the adjuster, spring length changes the preload by the following:

a. 1986 KX80: 14 lb.
b. 1987 KX80G and H: 14 lb.
c. 1987 KX80 J and K: 9.0 lb.

CAUTION
Do not turn the spring preload adjuster in excess of the minimum or maximum settings listed in **Table 5**.

8. Tighten the locknut against the adjusting nut.

9. Remove the stand from the bike so that the rear wheel touches the ground. Push on the rear end of the bike and make sure the shock spring is seated correctly.

10. Reinstall the rear frame assembly. Tighten the mounting bolts to the torque specification in **Table 4**.

11. Reinstall the air filter case. Install all mounting bolts and tighten securely.

12. Reinstall the frame side covers and seat.

Rebound damping adjustment

The stock shock absorber is equipped with a 4-way damping adjuster. The adjuster is a round slotted wheel marked with the numbers 1, 2, 3 and 4 at the adjustment positions. The adjuster is located at the top of the shock directly underneath the mounting boss. To change the damping, use a flat-tipped screwdriver to turn the damping

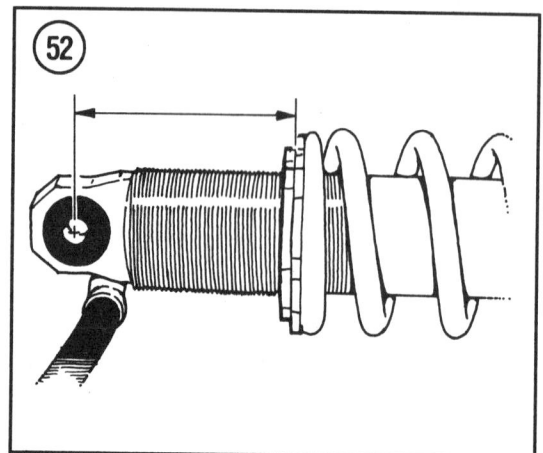

adjuster. Turn the adjuster until it clicks into position. Read the number off the top of the adjuster to determine the adjustment position. The minimum damping adjustment is No. 1. The maximum damping adjustment is No. 4.

Compression damping adjustment

The gas reservoir on the stock shock absorber is equipped with a 4-way damping adjuster. The adjuster is mounted at the bottom of the gas reservoir housing (**Figure 53**). To change the damping, turn the damping adjuster by hand until it clicks into position. Read the number off the side of the adjuster to determine the adjustment position. The minimum damping adjustment is No. 1. The maximum damping adjustment is No. 4.

Nitrogen Pressure Adjustment

An air valve is mounted at the bottom of the gas reservoir to allow adjustment of the shock's nitrogen pressure to better suit track and riding conditions. **Table 6** lists the standard, minimum and maximum nitrogen pressures.

> *NOTE*
> *The shocks nitrogen pressure should be checked and adjusted when the gas reservoir is cold (before riding the bike).*

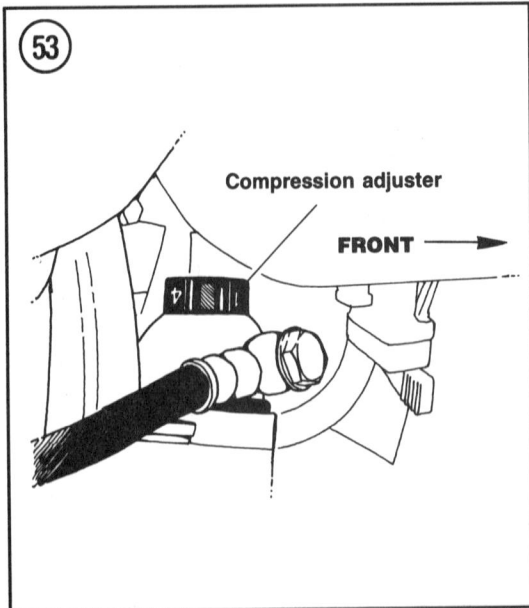

Compression adjuster

FRONT ———▶

> *WARNING*
> *Use only nitrogen or air—DO NOT use any other type of compressed gas as an explosion may result. Never heat the shock absorber assembly with a torch or place them near an open flame or extreme heat.*

1. Support the bike on a stand so that the rear wheel is off the ground.
2. Remove the valve cap at the bottom of the gas reservoir.
3. Check the nitrogen pressure with an air pressure gauge.
4. If necessary, add nitrogen gas from a suitable tank.
5. Recheck the air pressure.
6. Reinstall the air valve cap before riding the bike.

Disassembly

Refer to **Figure 51**.
1. Remove the shock absorber as described in this chapter.
2. Wash the outside of the shock absorber with aerosol electrical contact cleaner and allow to dry thoroughly. Especially clean the threads at the bottom of the shock.
3. Measure the installed spring length (**Figure 52**).
4. Secure the bottom of the shock absorber in a vise with soft jaws (**Figure 42**).
5. Using a hook wrench, loosen the locknut and the adjusting nut until the spring is loose.
6. Slide the rubber bumper down the shock shaft.
7. Disconnect the spring retainer clip at the opposite end of the shock absorber (**Figure 43**). Remove the retainer clip and remove the spring seat and the spring from the shock absorber.

> *WARNING*
> *When discharging the nitrogen pressure in Step 8, make sure to wear eye protection. In addition, make sure to point the reservoir air valve away from your body or face. Failure to observe this warning may cause severe eye damage.*

8. Remove the air valve cap from the air valve on the reservoir. Then depress the air valve with a small screwdriver (**Figure 47**) to release all nitrogen from the shock absorber.

12

9. Secure the reservoir in a vise (with padded jaws) as shown in **Figure 48**. Then loosen the hose bolt at the reservoir and disconnect the reservoir from the hose. Pour oil out of the reservoir.

10. Secure the bottom of the shock absorber in a vise.

11. Remove the banjo bolt and washers securing the hose to the shock body.

12. Referring to **Figure 54**, pry up the packing with 2 small punches or screwdrivers until the stop is clear of the shock body. Slide the stop up the shock shaft and out of the way.

13. A bearing is now visible in the shock body. Lightly tap the bearing downward approximately 20 mm (0.8 in.) or until the circlip in the shock body is exposed.

14. Remove the circlip from the shock body.

CAUTION
Check the edge of the circlip groove. If it is flared or burred, remove this material with a bearing knife or emery paper. Failure to remove this material could result in damage to the shock piston ring when the shock shaft is withdrawn from the shock body.

15. Move the pushrod up and down and carefully remove it from the shock body.

16. Pour any remaining shock oil out of the shock body.

17. Further disassembly of the shock assembly is not recommended.

Inspection

1. Clean all parts in contact cleaner and dry thoroughly.

2. Check the O-rings for wear or damage.

3. Check the gas reservoir for dents or other damage that would prevent the internal piston from operating freely.

4. Replace all worn or damaged parts as required.

Assembly

Refer to **Figure 51** for this procedure.

1. Do not assemble the shock assembly until all of the parts have been cleaned and allowed to dry thoroughly.

2. Mount the bottom end of the shock body in a vise with soft jaws.

3. Turn the gas reservoir damping adjuster to the number 1 position.

4. If the air valve was removed from the reservoir, apply Loctite 242 (blue) to the valve threads. Install the valve and tighten securely.

5. Attach the hose to the shock body and reservoir. Make sure to install washers on both sides of the hose fitting as shown in **Figure 51**. Hand tighten the banjo bolt.

6. Fill the shock body with SAE 5W shock oil until it is just level with the circlip groove.

7. Soak the piston end of the rod/piston assembly in shock oil. Slowly turn it in the oil to allow any air bubbles to escape.

8. Carefully insert the rod/piston assembly into the shock body until the bearing is just below the top edge of the shock body.

9. Loosen the hose banjo bolt at the reservoir. Compress the shock about 25 mm (1 in.). Excess oil and air will ooze out of the loose hose joint. Tighten the hose banjo bolt to 18 N·m (13 ft.-lb.).

10. Repeat Step 9 for the hose joint at the shock body but tighten the hose banjo bolt by hand.

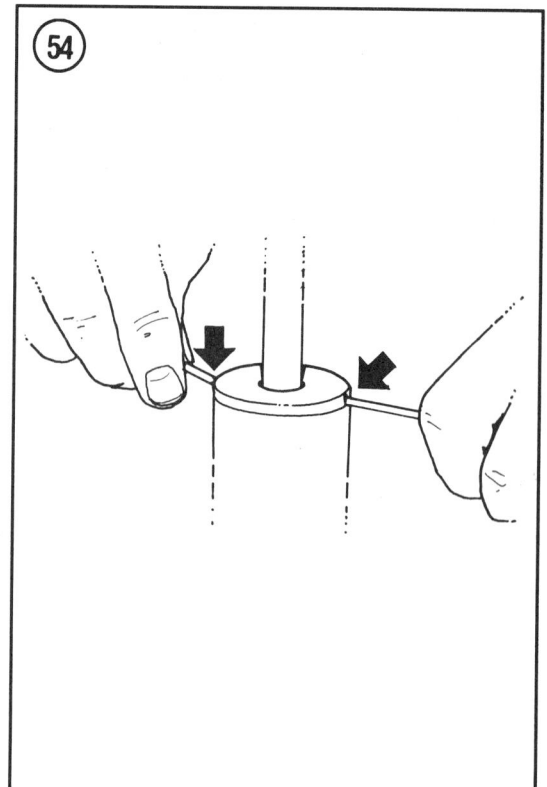

11. Slowly pump the shock rod up and down. Begin with short strokes and gradually increase stroke length.

12. Push the shock rod into the shock body until the circlip groove is visible. Install the circlip. Make sure the circlip seats fully in the groove. Tap the stop over the shock body until it bottoms.

13. Clamp the shock in a vise so the oil banjo bolt on the shock is pointing straight up. Remove the oil banjo bolt at the shock. Keep the hose end elevated to avoid losing too much oil.

14. Extend the shock rod to full extension. Pour oil into the oil bolt hole until it is topped off.

15. Carefully reinstall the oil banjo bolt, 2 washers and oil hose. Hand tighten the banjo bolt.

16. Add about 10-15 psi air to the reservoir's air valve. This will allow the diaphragm to assume its

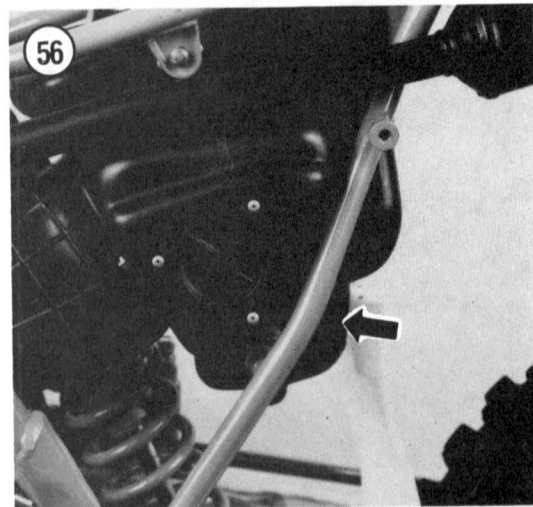

normal shape and will also force any excess oil and air from the hand-tightened oil banjo bolt.

17. Tighten the oil banjo bolt to 18 N·m (13 ft.-lb.).

18. Stroke the shock rod back and forth in full strokes. If all the air has been bled from the shock, resistance will be consistent. If there is still some air in the shock, resistance will be inconsistent.

WARNING
Use only nitrogen—DO NOT use any other type of compressed gas as an explosion may result. Never heat the shock absorber with a torch or place them near an open flame or extreme heat.

WARNING
Working with high pressure is dangerous. Have the shock pressurized by a Kawasaki dealer or qualified suspension specialist.

19. Have the dealer or shock specialist inject approximately 0.5 kg/cm² (7 psi) of nitrogen into the reservoir. Then check the shock body, hose and reservoir for leaks. If the shock leaks, bleed the nitrogen out and repair the problem. When the shock assembly holds nitrogen, proceed with Step 20.

20. When having the shock pressurized, note the following:
   a. Adjustment range: 10-15 kg/cm² (142-213 psi).
   b. Standard factory pressure: 10 kg/cm² (142 psi).

21. After the shock absorber has been safely pressurized with nitrogen, perform Step 22.

22. Install the spring and spring seat over the pushrod and install the clip. Adjust the spring preload as described in this chapter.

SHOCK ABSORBER (1988-ON)

Removal/Installation

1. Support the motorcycle on a stand with the rear wheel off the ground.

2. Remove the seat and both frame side covers.

3. Remove the rear frame assembly (**Figure 55**).

4. Remove the air cleaner element and box (**Figure 56**).

5. Remove the tie rod front pivot bolt (**Figure 57**).

6. Remove the shock absorber lower pivot bolt.

7. Remove the shock absorber upper pivot bolt (**Figure 58**) and remove the shock absorber.

8. To install, reverse the removal procedures. Tighten the bolts and nuts to the torque specification in **Table 4**.

Spring
Removal/Installation

Refer to **Figure 59**.

1. Remove the shock absorber as described in this chapter.

> *CAUTION*
> *Support the shock reservoir when performing this procedure to prevent its damage.*

2. Clean the threads on the shock absorber before loosening the locknut.

3. If the original spring is going to be reinstalled, measure the installed spring length (**Figure 52**).

4. Secure the bottom of the shock absorber in a vise with soft jaws (**Figure 42**).

5. Using a hook wrench, loosen the locknut and the adjusting nut until the spring is loose.

6. Slide the rubber bumper down the shock shaft.

7. Disconnect the spring retainer clip at the opposite end of the shock absorber (**Figure 43**). Remove the retainer clip and remove the spring seat, and spring from the shock absorber.

8. Installation is the reverse of these steps. Make sure the spring retainer clip secures the spring completely.

9. After installing the spring, turn the adjusting nut until the spring installed length is the same as recorded in Step 3. When turning the adjusting nut, make sure the retainer clip at the top of the spring engages the spring properly. Tighten the locknut against the adjusting nut.

> *CAUTION*
> *Do not turn the spring preload adjuster in excess of the minimum or maximum settings listed in Table 5.*

Shock Adjustment

The stock shock absorber can be adjusted for the following:

a. Spring preload.

b. Rebound damping.

c. Compression damping.

d. Shock nitrogen pressure.

Spring preload adjustment

If the shock's spring action feels too hard or too soft, adjust the spring as follows.

1. Remove the seat and both frame side covers.

2. Loosen the air filter housing hose clamp at the carburetor.

3. Remove the rear frame mounting bolts and remove the rear frame assembly (**Figure 55**).

4. Remove the air filter housing assembly (**Figure 56**).

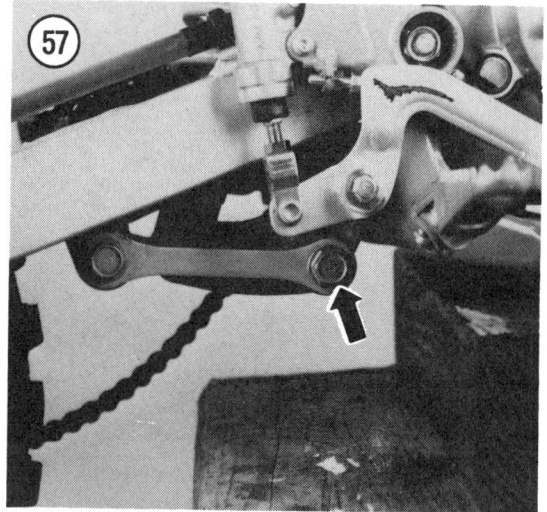

5. Support the bike on a stand so that the rear wheel is off the ground.

6. Clean the threads at the bottom of the shock absorber with aerosol electrical contact cleaner.

CAUTION
The fine threads at the bottom of the shock absorber are used for spring preload adjustment. Because fine threads are used, it is important to clean the threads before loosening and turning the locknut and spring adjuster. Dirt or mud packed between the threads can cause thread damage when the locknut and adjuster are turned.

7. Measure the distance from the center of the upper shock bolt hole to the top of the spring

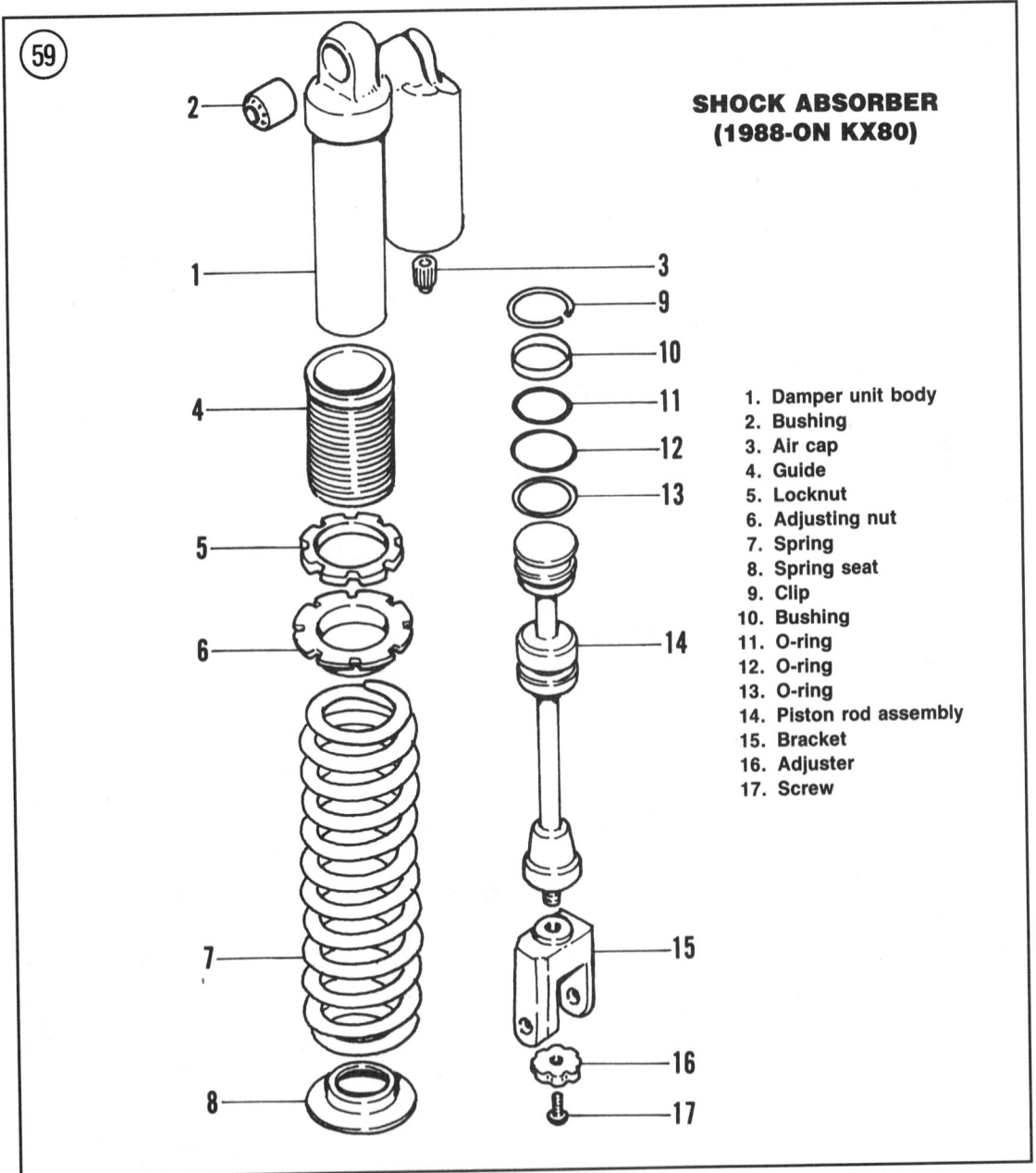

**SHOCK ABSORBER
(1988-ON KX80)**

1. Damper unit body
2. Bushing
3. Air cap
4. Guide
5. Locknut
6. Adjusting nut
7. Spring
8. Spring seat
9. Clip
10. Bushing
11. O-ring
12. O-ring
13. O-ring
14. Piston rod assembly
15. Bracket
16. Adjuster
17. Screw

12

adjuster flat surface (**Figure 52**). Record this measurement and compare to the standard, minimum and maximum specifications listed in **Table 5**.

8. Using a hook wrench, loosen the locknut.

9. Using a hook wrench, turn the spring adjuster to adjust the spring preload as required. Remeasure the spring preload length (**Figure 52**). Spring length changes the preload 14 lbs. (KX80M) or 10.6 lbs. (KX80N and P) for every 1 complete turn of the adjuster.

> *CAUTION*
> *Do not turn the spring preload adjuster in excess of the minimum or maximum settings listed in **Table 5**.*

10. Tighten the locknut securely. Then lower the rear wheel to the ground and push on the bike's rear end to bounce compress the rear shock absorber a few times. Check to make sure the spring is seated in the shock correctly.

11. Record the spring preload setting so that you can refer to it when making additional adjustments later on.

12. Reinstall the air filter housing.

13. Reinstall the rear frame assembly. Tighten the mounting bolts to the torque specifications in **Table 4**.

Rebound Damping Adjustment

The stock shock absorber is equipped with a 4-way rebound damping adjuster. The adjuster is a knob located at the bottom of the shock absorber. Turn the adjuster until one of the four adjuster position numbers are visible at the rear of the shock absorber. The number represents the rebound damping adjustment.

Compression Damping Adjustment

The compression adjuster can be adjusted 4-ways. To change the compression damping, turn the damping adjuster at the top of the shock absorber with a screwdriver (**Figure 60**) until it clicks into position. Read the number off the side of the adjuster at the rear of the shock absorber to determine the adjustment position. The minimum damping adjustment is No. 1. The maximum damping adjustment is No. 4.

Nitrogen Pressure Adjustment

An air valve is mounted at the bottom of the gas reservoir to allow adjustment of the shock's nitrogen pressure to better suit track and riding conditions. **Table 6** lists the standard, minimum and maximum nitrogen pressures.

> *NOTE*
> *The shocks nitrogen pressure should be checked and adjusted when the gas reservoir is cold (before riding the bike).*

> *WARNING*
> *Use only nitrogen—DO NOT use any other type of compressed gas as an explosion may result. Never heat the shock absorber with a torch or place them near an open flame or extreme heat.*

1. Support the bike on a stand so that the rear wheel is off the ground.

2. Remove the valve cap at the bottom of the gas reservoir (**Figure 61**).

3. Check the nitrogen pressure with an air pressure gauge.

4. If necessary, add nitrogen gas from a suitable tank.

> *WARNING*
> *Do not exceed the maximum nitrogen pressure listed in **Table 6** when filling the shock absorber.*

5. Recheck the pressure.

6. Reinstall the air valve cap before riding the bike.

Disassembly

Refer to **Figure 59**.

1. Remove the shock absorber as described in this chapter.

2. Wash the outside of the shock absorber with an aerosol electrical contact cleaner and allow to dry thoroughly. Especially clean the threads at the bottom of the shock.

3. Measure the installed spring length (**Figure 52**).

4. Secure the bottom of the shock absorber in a vise with soft jaws.

5. Using a hook wrench, loosen the locknut and the adjusting nut until the spring is loose.

6. Slide the rubber bumper down the shock shaft.

7. Disconnect the spring retainer clip at the opposite end of the shock absorber (**Figure 43**). Remove the retainer clip, spring seat and the spring from the shock absorber.

WARNING
When discharging the nitrogen pressure in Step 8, make sure to wear eye protection. In addition, make sure to point the reservoir air valve away from your body or face. Failure to observe this warning may cause severe eye damage.

8. Remove the air valve cap from the air valve on the reservoir. Then depress the air valve with a small screwdriver (**Figure 47**) to release all nitrogen from the shock absorber.

9. Referring to **Figure 54**, pry up the stop with 2 small punches or screwdrivers until the stop is

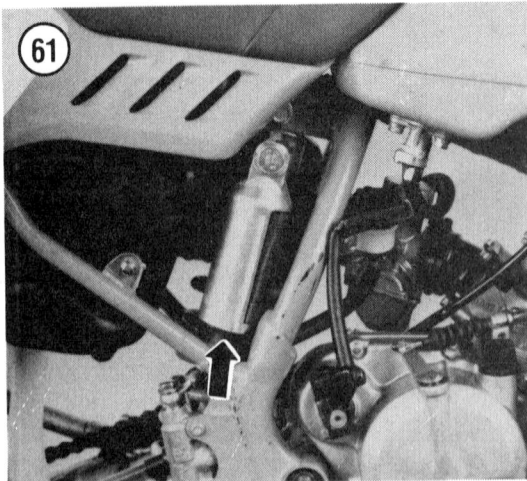

clear of the shock body. Slide the stop up the shock shaft and out of the way.

10. A bearing is now visible in the shock body. Lightly tap the bearing downward approximately 10 mm (0.4 in.) or until the circlip in the shock body is exposed.

11. Remove the circlip from the shock body.

CAUTION
Check the edge of the circlip groove. If it is flared or burred, remove this material with a bearing knife or emery paper. Failure to remove this material could result in damage to the shock piston ring when the shock shaft is withdrawn from the shock body.

12. Move the pushrod up and down and carefully remove it from the shock body.

13. Pour the shock oil out of the shock body.

14. Further disassembly of the shock assembly is not recommended.

Inspection

1. Clean all parts in contact cleaner and dry thoroughly.

2. Check the O-rings for wear or damage.

3. Check the gas reservoir for dents or other damage that would prevent the internal piston from operating freely.

4. Replace all worn or damaged parts as required.

Assembly

Refer to **Figure 59** for this procedure.

1. Do not assemble the shock assembly until all of the parts have been cleaned and allowed to dry thoroughly.

2. Mount the shock body in a vise with soft jaws.

3. Turn the gas reservoir damping adjuster to the number 1 position.

4. Fill the shock body with SAE 5W shock oil until it is just level with the circlip groove.

5. See **Figure 62**. Slide the seal assembly on the pushrod and up the rod so that it cannot enter the shock body in Step 6. Soak the piston end in shock oil. Then insert the piston end into the shock body. Slowly turn it in the oil to allow any air bubbles to escape. Do not remove the pushrod from the shock body.

12

6. Slide the seal assembly (**Figure 62**) down the pushrod until it just clears the circlip groove in the shock body.

7. Install the circlip. Make sure the circlip seats fully in the groove. Pull the pushrod assembly up so that the piston seats against the circlip.

8. Tap the stop over the shock body until it bottoms.

9. Add about 10-15 psi air to the reservoir's air valve. This will allow the diaphragm to assume its normal shape and will also force any excess oil and air from the hand-tightened oil banjo bolt.

10. Stroke the shock rod back and forth in full strokes. If all the air has been bled from the shock, resistance will be consistent. If there is still some air in the shock, resistance will be inconsistent.

> *WARNING*
> *Use only nitrogen—DO NOT use any other type of compressed gas as an explosion may result. Never heat the shock absorber with a torch or place them near an open flame or extreme heat.*

> *WARNING*
> *Working with high pressure is dangerous. Have your shock pressurized by a Kawasaki dealer or qualified suspension specialist.*

11. Have the dealer or shock specialist inject approximately 0.5 kg/cm² (7 psi) of nitrogen into the reservoir. Then check the shock body, hose and reservoir for leaks. If the shock leaks, bleed the nitrogen out and repair the problem. When the shock assembly holds nitrogen, proceed with Step 12.

12. When having the shock pressurized, note the following:

   a. Adjustment range: 10-15 kg/cm² (142-213 psi).
   b. Standard factory pressure: 10 kg/cm² (142 psi).

13. After the shock absorber has been safely pressurized with nitrogen, perform Step 14.

14. Install the spring and spring seat over the pushrod and install the clip. Adjust the spring preload as described in this chapter.

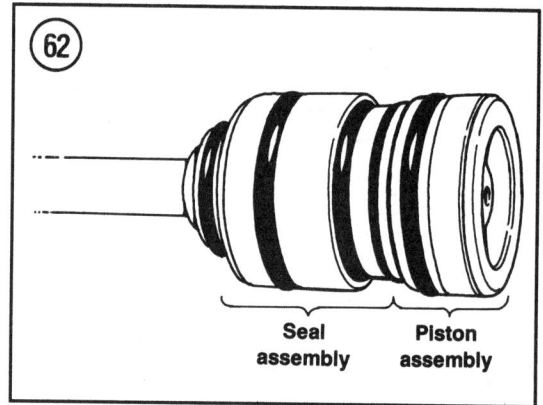

Table 1 REAR WHEEL TRAVEL

KX60	200 mm (7.9 in.)
KX80	
1983-1984	255 mm (10.04 in.)
1985	260 mm (10.25 in.)
1986	275 mm (10.8 in.)
1987	
G, H	275 mm (10.8 in.)
J, K	245 mm (9.6 in.)
1988-on	
L, M	275 mm (10.8 in.)
N, P	250 mm (9.8 in.)

Table 2 REAR SUSPENSION SERVICE SPECIFICATIONS

	New mm (in.)	Wear Limit mm (in.)
Axle		
Runout	0-0.1 (0-0.004)	0.2 (0.008)
Repair limit	—	0.7 (0.028)
Rim runout		
Axial play	0-0.5 (0-0.02)	2.0 (0.08)
Radial play	0-0.8 (0-0.03)	2.0 (0.08)
Rear shock spring free length*		
KX60		
1983-1984	234 (9.2)	229 (9.0)
1985-1987	235.5 (9.3)	232 (9.1)
KX80		
1983-1987	268.5 (10.57)	263 (10.35)
Sleeve bushing outside diameter		
KX60	16.989-17.000 (0.6689-0.6693)	16.95 (0.6673)
KX80		
1983-1985	16.989-17.000 (0.6689-0.6693)	16.95 (0.6673)
1986-on	15.987-16.000 (0.6294-0.6299)	15.85 (0.624)
Rocker arm pivot bolt runout		
1986-on	0-0.1 (0-0.004)	0-0.2 (0.008)

* Spring specifications are not available for 1988 and later models.

Table 3 REAR SUSPENSION TIGHTENING TORQUES (KX60)

	N·m	ft.-lb.
Swing arm pivot shaft nut	69	51
Rear axle nut	69	51
Rear shock absorber bolts and nuts	49	36
Rear sprocket bolts	21	15
Uni-Trak rocking arm center pivot bolt	69	51
Uni-Trak tie rod and vertical link bolts	49	36

12

Table 4 REAR SUSPENSION TIGHTENING TORQUES (KX80)

	N·m	ft.-lb.
Swing arm pivot shaft nut	69	51
Rear axle nut	69	51
Rear shock absorber bolts or nuts		
1983-1986	49	36
1987	31	23
1988	54	40
1989-on	39	29
Rear sprocket		
Bolts		
1983-1986	21	15
Nuts		
1987-on	29	22
Uni-Trak		
1983-1985		
Vertical link	69	51
Rocking arm pivot bolt	69	51
Tie rod bolts	49	36
1986		
Rocker arm pivot bolt	49	36
Tie rod bolts	49	36
1987-on		
Rocker arm pivot bolts	49	36
Tie rod pivot bolts		
1987-1988		
Front	59	43
Rear	34	25
1989-on	49	36
Rear frame bolts		
1986-on	25	18
Rear brake caliper mounting bolts		
1988-on	25	18

Table 5 REAR SHOCK SPRING PRE-LOAD LENGTH (1986-ON KX80)

Model	Standard mm (in.)	Minimum mm (in.)	Maximum mm (in.)
1986	73 (2.87)	63 (2.48)	91 (3.58)
1987			
G and H	76 (3.04)	63 (2.48)	91 (3.58)
J and K	65 (2.56)	63 (2.48)	91 (3.58)
1988			
M	83 (3.27)	73 (2.87)	96 (3.78)
N and P	86 (3.39)	76 (3.04)	96 (3.78)
1989-on	88 (3.46)	71 (2.80)	96 (3.78)

Table 6 REAR SHOCK ABSORBER NITROGEN PRESSURE (1986-ON KX80)

	Standard kg/cm^2 (psi)	Minimum kg/cm^2 (psi)	Maximum kg/cm^2 (psi)
1986-on	10.0 (142)	10.0 (142)	15.0 (213)

BRAKES

The KX60 and the 1983 KX80 uses drum brakes on the front and rear. The 1984-1987 KX80 uses a disc brake on the front and a drum brake on the rear. All 1988 and later KX80 models are equipped with front and rear disc brakes.

Brake specifications are listed in **Tables 1-3** at the end of this chapter.

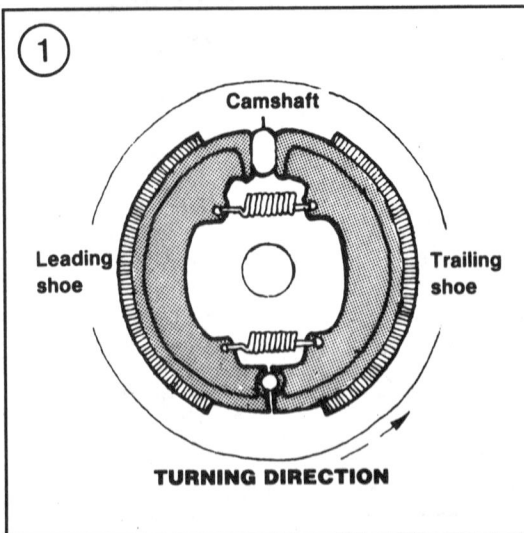

DRUM BRAKES

Figure 1 illustrates the major components of a typical drum brake assembly. Activating the brake hand lever or foot pedal pulls the cable or rod which in turn rotates the camshaft. This forces the brake shoes out into contact with the brake drum.

Lever and pedal free play must be maintained on both brakes to minimize brake drag and premature brake wear and maximize braking effectiveness. Refer to *Front Brake Lever Adjustment* and *Rear Brake Pedal Free Play* in Chapter Three, for complete adjustment procedures.

Glaze buildup on the brake shoes reduces braking effectiveness. The brake shoes should be removed and cleaned regularly to assure maximum brake shoe contact.

The front brake cable must be inspected and replaced periodically as it will stretch with use and can no longer be properly adjusted.

> *WARNING*
> *When removing the wheels or working on the brakes, wear a protective mask*

13

to keep from inhaling any dust from the brake linings. The brake linings contain asbestos fiber; asbestos has been connected with lung scarring and cancer. Do not use compressed air to clean the brake drums or linings; dump any dust onto a newspaper and place in a resealable plastic bag. Dispose of it in the trash. Wash your hands thoroughly after handling the brake parts.

Disassembly

Refer to the illustration for your model when performing this procedure:

Figure 2: Front drum brake (KX60 and 1983 KX80).

Figure 3: Rear drum brake (KX60).

Figure 4: Rear drum brake (1983-1985 KX80).

Figure 5: Rear drum brake (1986-1987 KX80).

1A. Remove the front wheel as described in Chapter Eleven.

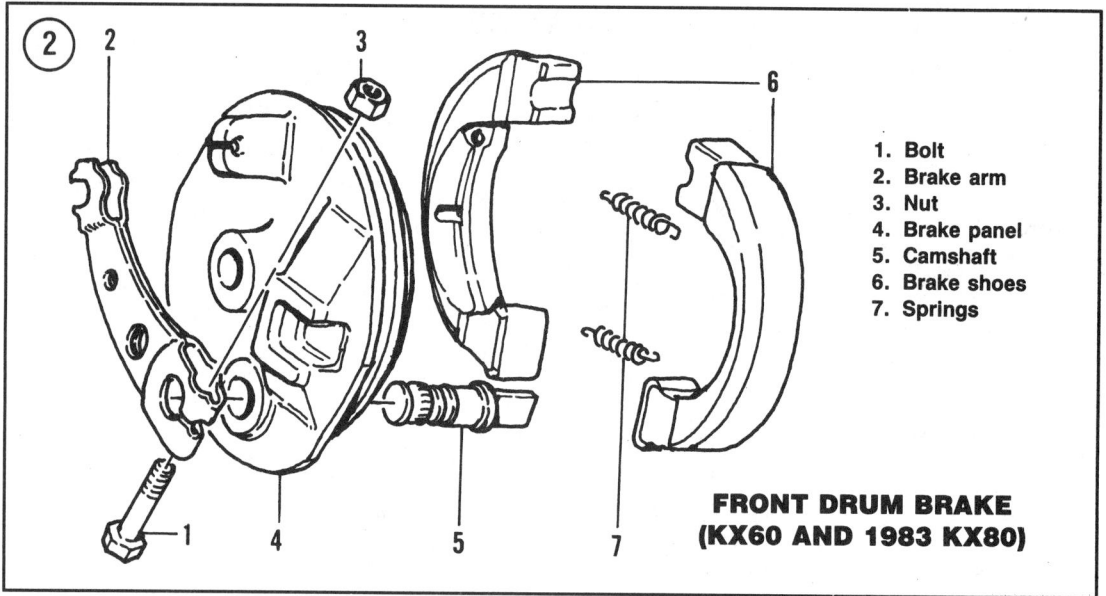

1. Bolt
2. Brake arm
3. Nut
4. Brake panel
5. Camshaft
6. Brake shoes
7. Springs

**FRONT DRUM BRAKE
(KX60 AND 1983 KX80)**

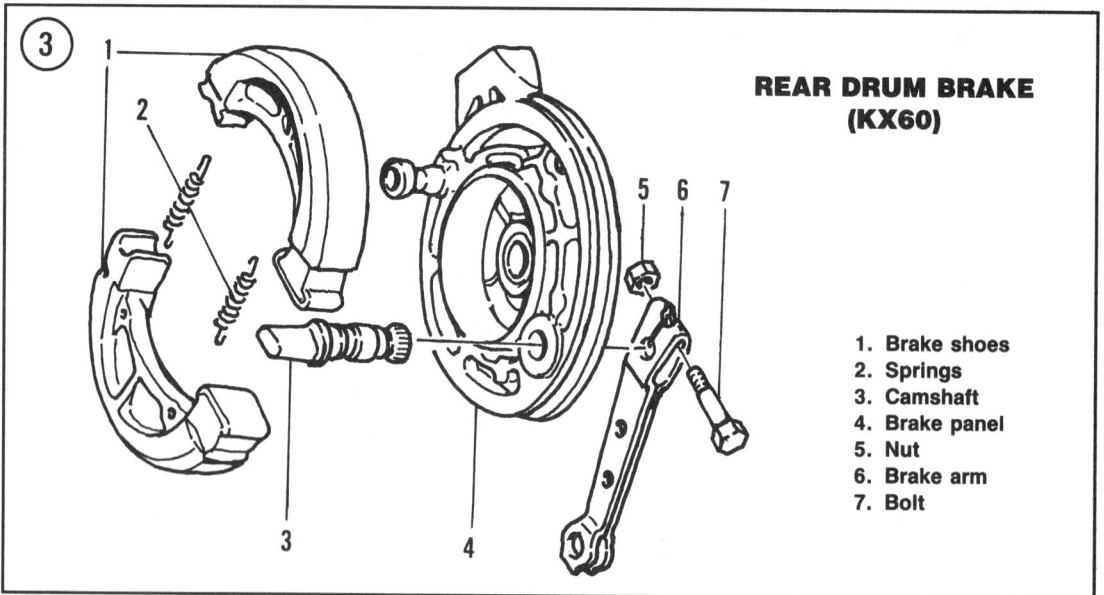

**REAR DRUM BRAKE
(KX60)**

1. Brake shoes
2. Springs
3. Camshaft
4. Brake panel
5. Nut
6. Brake arm
7. Bolt

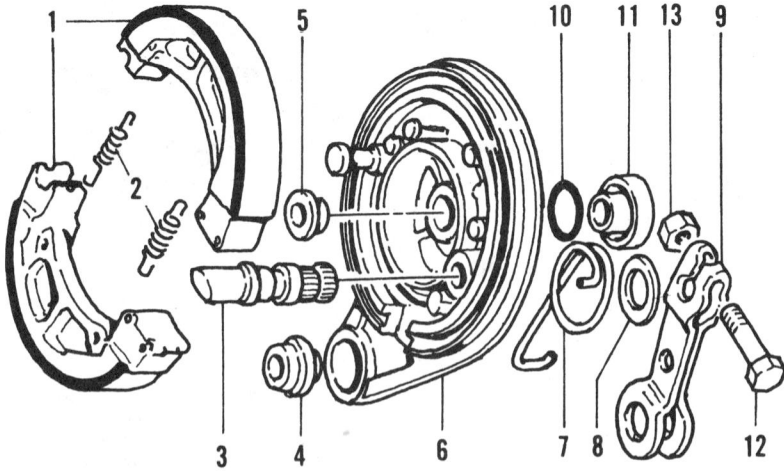

**REAR BRAKE DRUM
(1983-1985 KX80)**

1. Brake shoes
2. Springs
3. Camshaft
4. Bushing
5. Spacer
6. Brake panel
7. O-ring
8. Spacer
9. Brake arm
10. Bolt
11. Nut

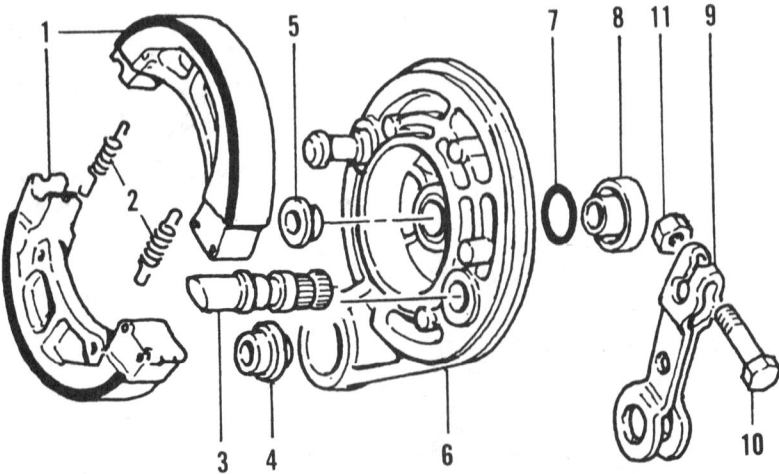

**REAR BRAKE DRUM
(1986-1987 KX80)**

1. Brake shoes
2. Springs
3. Camshaft
4. Bushing
5. Spacer
6. Brake panel
7. Spring
8. Washer
9. Brake arm
10. O-ring
11. Spacer
12. Bolt
13. Nut

13

1B. Remove the rear wheel as described in Chapter Twelve.

2. Pull the front or rear brake panel out of the wheel. See **Figure 6**.

NOTE
*Mark each brake shoe (**Figure 7**) for position before removing them in Step 3. In addition, place a clean shop rag on the linings to protect them from oil and grease during removal.*

3. Remove the brake shoe assembly, including the return springs, from the brake panel. Pull both brake shoes from the panel (**Figure 8**).

4. See A, **Figure 9**. Remove the return springs and separate the shoes.

5. Mark the position of the brake lever (**Figure 10**) as it is installed on the camshaft so it can be reinstalled in the same position.

6. Loosen the bolt and nut securing the brake lever to the cam. Remove the lever and camshaft. Remove the spring, if so equipped.

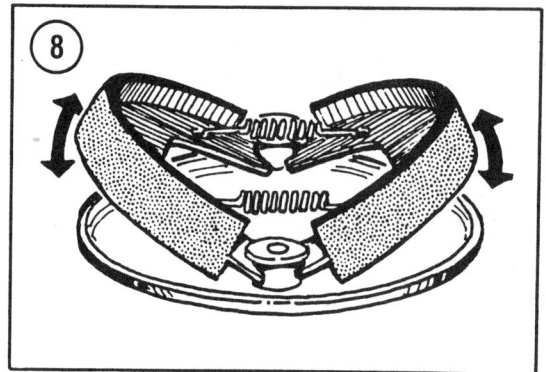

Inspection

1. Read the *Warning* in the introduction of this section before cleaning the brake shoes and drum. Wear a dust mask when handling the brake shoes and linings.

2. Thoroughly clean and dry all parts except the linings.

3. Check the contact surface of the drum (A, **Figure 11**) for scoring. If there are deep grooves or the drum surface is severely damaged, the hub will have to be replaced. This type of wear can be

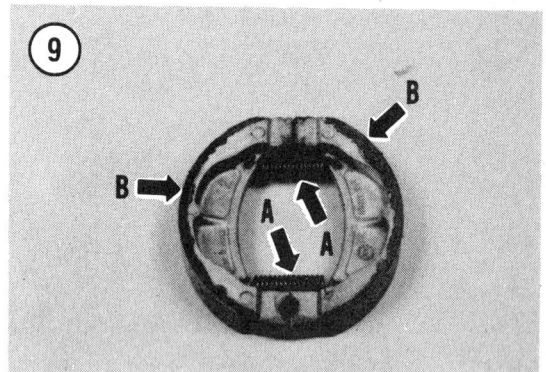

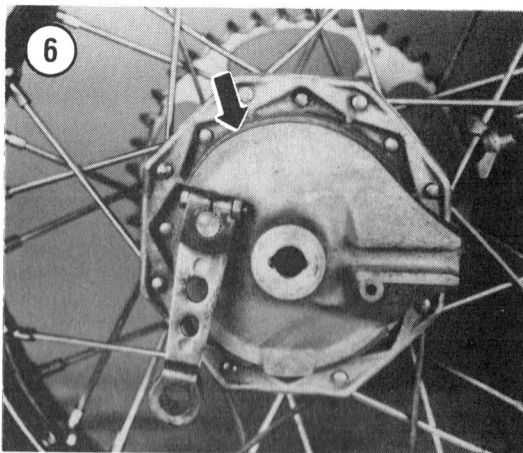

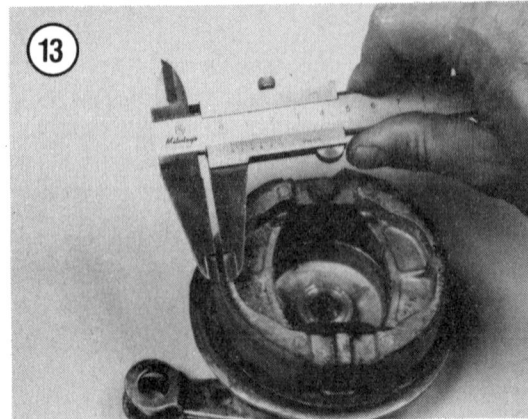

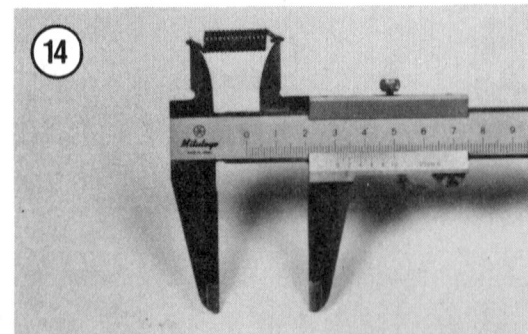

avoided to a great extent if the brakes are disassembled and thoroughly cleaned after the bike has been ridden in mud or deep sand, or after each race.

NOTE
If oil or grease is on the drum surface, clean it off with a clean rag soaked in lacquer thinner—do not use any solvent that may leave an oil residue.

4. Check the sealed bearing (B, **Figure 11**) on the brake drum side for damage that would allow grease to enter the brake drum and contaminate the drum and brake shoes. Replace the bearing or seal as described in Chapter Eleven (front wheel) or Chapter Twelve (rear wheel).
5. Use vernier calipers (**Figure 12**) and measure the inside diameter of the drum for out-of-round or excessive wear. Refer to **Table 1** for brake specifications.
6. Inspect the linings for imbedded foreign material. Dirt can be removed with a stiff wire brush. Check the lining surface for a glazed appearance or for traces of oil or grease. Glaze buildup and small traces of oil or grease can be removed by sanding the lining surface with a coarse grade sandpaper. If the linings are contaminated, they must be replaced.

NOTE
Do not include the metal pad thickness when measuring lining thickness.

7. Measure the brake lining thickness with a vernier caliper as shown in **Figure 13**. Replace the linings if worn to the wear limits in **Table 1**.
8. Inspect the cam lobe and the pivot pin area of the shaft for wear and corrosion. Minor roughness can be removed with a fine emery cloth.
9. Measure the length of the brake shoe spring with a vernier caliper as shown in **Figure 14**. Replace the springs if they exceed the wear limit specifications in **Table 1**. If the brake shoe springs are stretched, they will not fully retract the brake shoes from the drum, resulting in a power-robbing drag on the drums and premature wear of the linings.
10. Check the bushing in the rear brake panel, if so equipped. Replace the bushing if it is starting to deteriorate or if cracked or worn.

13

Assembly

Refer to the illustration for your model when performing this procedure:

Figure 2: Front drum brake (KX60 and 1983 KX80).

Figure 3: Rear drum brake (KX60).

Figure 4: Rear drum brake (1983-1985 KX80).

Figure 5: Rear drum brake (1986-1987 KX80).

1. Grease the shaft, cam and pivot post with a light coat of thick wheel bearing grease. Avoid getting any grease on the brake plate where the linings come in contact with it.

2. Install the brake lever onto the brake cam. Make sure to align the 2 marks made during disassembly.

3. Hold the brake shoes (B, **Figure 9**) in a V-formation with the return springs attached (**Figure 8**) and snap them in place on the brake panel. Make sure they are firmly seated on it.

4. Install the brake panel assembly into the brake drum. See **Figure 6**.

5A. Install the front wheel as described in Chapter Eleven.

5B. Install the rear wheel as described in Chapter Twelve.

6A. Adjust the front brake as described in Chapter Three.

6B. Adjust the rear brake as described in Chapter Three.

FRONT BRAKE CABLE

Brake cable adjustment should be checked periodically as the cable stretches with use and increases brake lever free play. Free play is the distance that the brake lever travels between the released position and the point when the brake shoes come in contact with the drum.

If the brake adjustment, as described in Chapter Three, can no longer be achieved, the cable must be replaced.

Replacement

1. At the hand lever, loosen the locknut (A, **Figure 15**) and turn the adjusting barrel (B, **Figure 15**) all the way toward the cable sheath.

2. Disconnect the front brake cable at the wheel as follows:

  a. Loosen brake cable adjuster locknut (**Figure 16**).

  b. Disconnect the end of the brake cable at the brake arm.

3. Pull the hand lever all the way to the grip, remove the cable nipple from the lever and remove the cable.

4. Withdraw the cable from the plastic holders on the front fork clamps.

NOTE
Before removing the cable, make a drawing (or take a Polaroid picture) of the cable routing through the frame. It is very easy to forget how it was once it has been removed. Replace it exactly as it was, avoiding any sharp turns.

5. Install by reversing these removal steps.

6. Adjust the brake as described under *Front Brake Lever Adjustment* in Chapter Three.

DISC BRAKE
(1984-ON)

The front and rear disc brake is actuated by hydraulic fluid and controlled by a hand or foot lever on the master cylinder. As the brake pads wear, the brake fluid level drops in the reservoir and automatically adjusts for wear.

When working on hydraulic brake systems, it is necessary that the work area and all tools be absolutely clean. Any tiny particles of foreign matter and grit in the caliper assembly or master cylinder can damage the components.

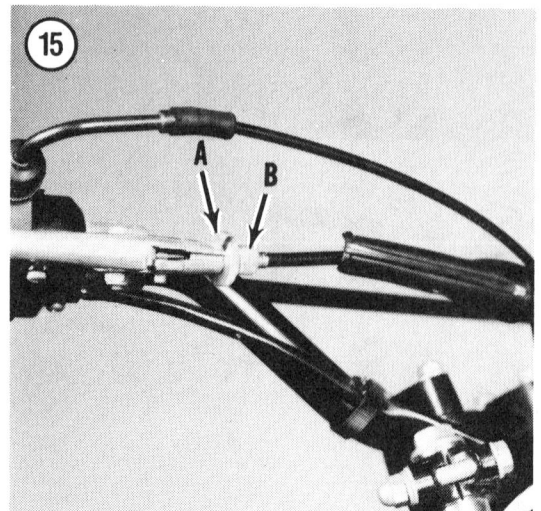

Consider the following when servicing the front disc brake.

1. Use only DOT 3 brake fluid from a sealed container.

2. Do not allow disc brake fluid to contact any plastic parts or painted surfaces as damage will result.

3. Always keep the master cylinder reservoir and spare cans of brake fluid closed to prevent dust or moisture from entering. This would result in brake fluid contamination and brake problems.

4. Use only disc brake fluid (DOT 3) to wash parts. Never clean any internal brake components with solvent or any other petroleum base cleaners.

5. Whenever *any* component has been removed from the brake system the system is considered "opened" and must be bled to remove air bubbles. Also, if the brake feels "spongy," this usually means there are air bubbles in the system and it must be bled. For safe brake operation, refer to *Bleeding the System* in this chapter for complete details.

CAUTION
Disc brake components rarely require disassembly, so do not disassemble unless absolutely necessary. Do not use solvents of any kind on the brake systems internal components. Solvents will cause the seals to swell and distort. When disassembling and cleaning brake components (except brake pads), use new DOT 3 brake fluid.

BRAKE PAD REPLACEMENT

There is no recommended time interval for changing the friction pads in the front or rear disc brake. Pad wear depends greatly on riding habits and conditions.

To maintain an even brake pressure on the disc, always replace both pads in the caliper at the same time.

Front Brake Pads
Removal/Installation

Refer to **Figure 17** for this procedure.

1. Read the information listed under *Disc Brake 1984-On* in this chapter.

2. Place the bike on a stand so the front wheel clears the ground.

3. Remove the brake caliper mounting bolts (A, **Figure 18**) and pull the brake caliper off of the brake disc (B, **Figure 18**).

4. Push the caliper holder toward the piston. Then remove the outer brake pad (**Figure 19**) from the caliper holder shaft.

5. Remove the inner brake pad (**Figure 20**).

6. Remove the anti-rattle spring (**Figure 21**).

7. Measure the brake pad friction thickness with a vernier caliper or ruler. Compare to the specifications in **Table 2**. Replace the brake pads if the friction thickness is worn to the limit thickness or less.

8. Carefully remove any rust or corrosion from the disc.

9. When new brake pads are installed in the caliper the master cylinder brake fluid will rise as the caliper pistons are repositioned. Clean the top of the master cylinder of all dirt. Remove the cap (**Figure 22**) and diaphragm from the master cylinder and slowly push the caliper piston into the caliper. Constantly check the reservoir to make sure brake fluid does not overflow. Siphon fluid, if necessary, prior to it overflowing. The piston should move freely in the caliper bore. If the piston doesn't move smoothly and there is evidence of it sticking in the caliper, the caliper should be removed and serviced as described under *Front Caliper Rebuilding* in this chapter.

10. Perform the following to install the brake pads:
   a. With your hand, push the piston into the caliper as far as it will go.

13

(17)

FRONT BRAKE CALIPER
(1984-ON KX80)

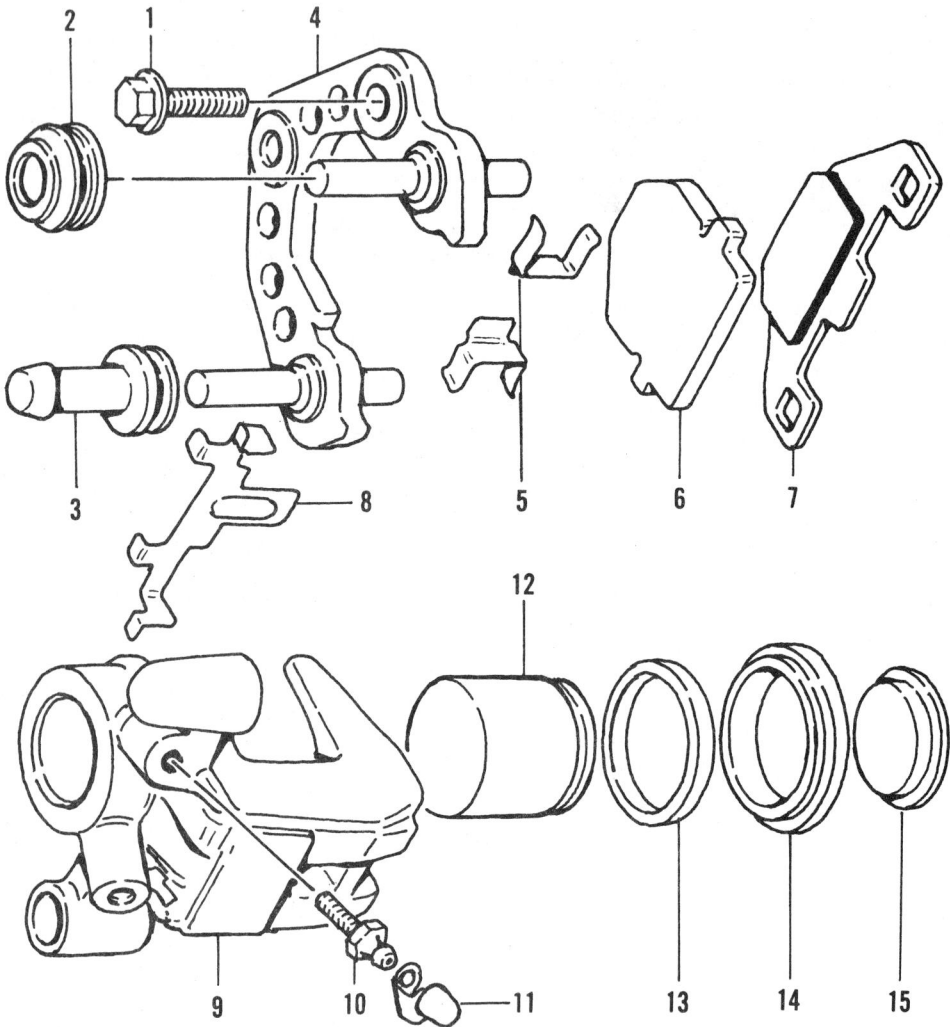

1. Bolt
2. Boot
3. Boot
4. Caliper bracket
5. Pad stopper guide
6. Brake pad
7. Brake pad
8. Anti-rattle spring
9. Caliper housing
10. Bleed valve
11. Cover
12. Piston
13. Piston seal
14. Dust seal
15. Pad

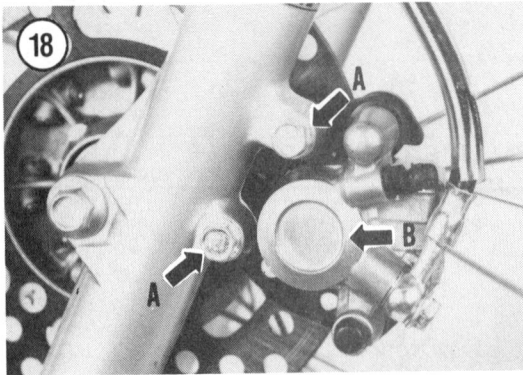

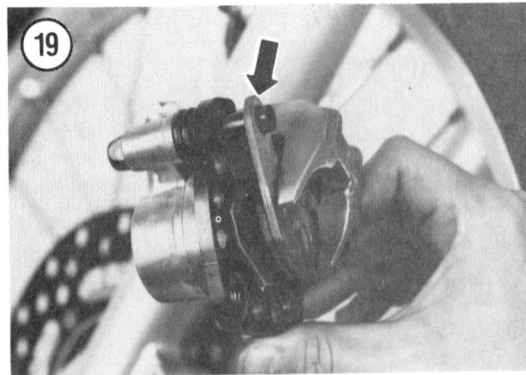

b. Install the anti-rattle spring (**Figure 21**) into the caliper.

c. Install the inner brake pad (**Figure 20**).

d. Coat the support bracket pivot rods and holes with PBC (Poly Butyl Cuprysil) grease.

11. Install the outer brake pad into the caliper behind the support bracket (**Figure 19**).

12. Align the holes in the inner brake pad with the caliper support bracket arms and install the brake pad (**Figure 19**).

13. Align the brake caliper with the brake disc. The brake shoes should be on each side of the brake disc with the brake friction material facing against the disc.

14. Install the brake caliper mounting bolts (A, **Figure 18**) and tighten them to the torque specification in **Table 3**.

15. Spin the front wheel and activate the brake lever as many times as necessary as it takes to refill the cylinder in the caliper and correctly locate the pads.

> *WARNING*
> *Use brake fluid clearly marked DOT 3 from a sealed container. Other types may vaporize and cause brake failure. Always use the same brand name; do not intermix as many brands are not compatible.*

16. Refill the master cylinder reservoir, if necessary, to maintain the correct brake fluid level. Install the diaphragm and top cover (**Figure 22**).

> *WARNING*
> *Do not ride the motorcycle until you are sure the brake is operating correctly with full hydraulic advantage. If necessary, bleed the brake system as described in this chapter.*

13

(23)

REAR BRAKE CALIPER
(1988-ON KX80)

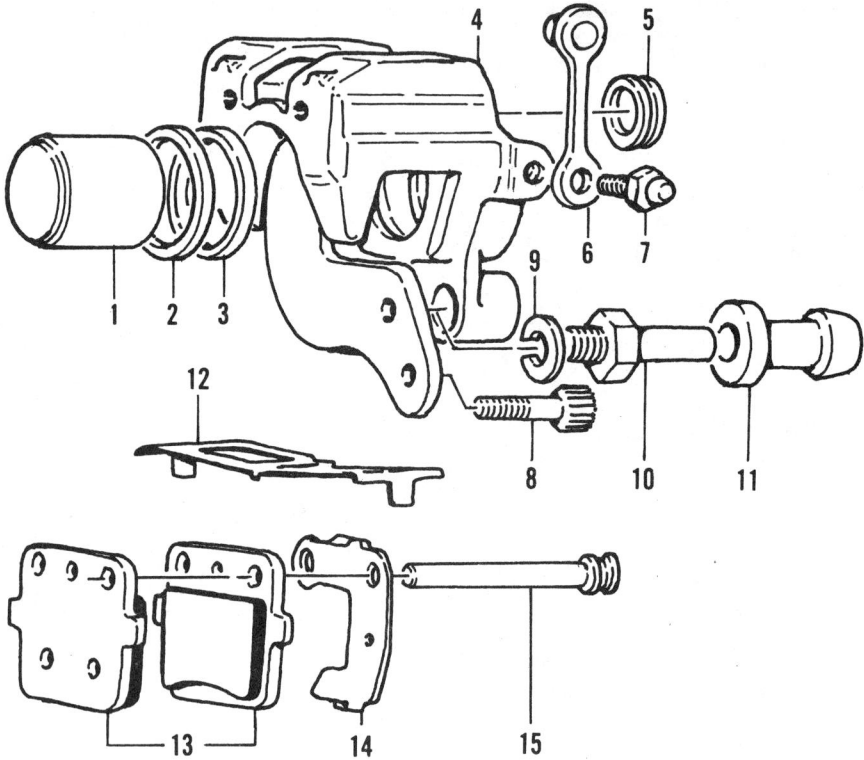

1. Piston
2. Dust seal
3. Piston seal
4. Caliper housing
5. Damper
6. Cap
7. Bleed valve
8. Bolt
9. Lockwasher
10. Shaft
11. Boot
12. Anti-rattle spring
13. Brake pads
14. Shim
15. Brake pad Allen bolt

Rear Brake Pads
Removal/Installation
(1988-on KX80)

Refer to **Figure 23** for this procedure.

1. Read the information listed under *Disc Brake 1984-On* in this chapter.

2. Place the bike on a stand so the rear wheel clears the ground.

3. Remove the brake caliper master cylinder cover screws and remove the cover (**Figure 24**).

4. Loosen the 2 brake pad Allen bolts (A, **Figure 25**).

5. Remove the brake caliper mounting bolts (B, **Figure 25**) and lift the brake caliper off of the brake disc. See **Figure 26**.

6. Remove the 2 brake pad Allen bolts loosened in Step 4 (**Figure 27**).

7. Remove the outer (**Figure 28**) and inner (**Figure 29**) brake pad.

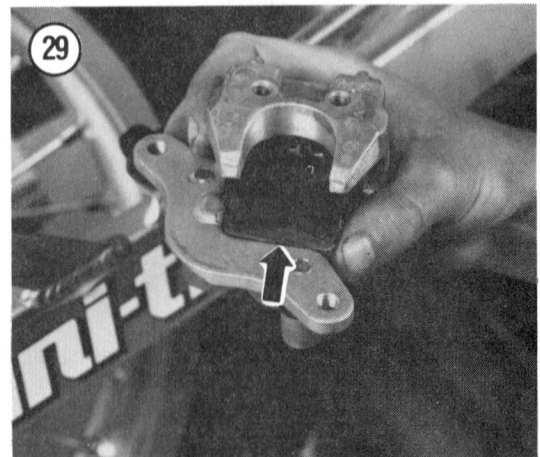

13

NOTE
The inner brake pad has a shim mounted on the backside (Figure 30). Don't loose it.

8. Remove the anti-rattle spring (**Figure 31**) from the caliper housing.

9. Measure the brake pad friction thickness with a vernier caliper or ruler. Measure the thickness of the brake pad material only. Do not include the thickness of the pad's metal plate. See **Figure 32**. Compare to the specifications in **Table 2**. Replace the brake pads if the friction thickness is worn to the wear limit or less.

NOTE
Always replace both pads at the same time.

NOTE
Before installing the brake pads, check the end of the piston (Figure 33) for corrosion buildup or signs of fluid leakage. If there is any doubt as to the condition of the piston or seal assembly, rebuild the caliper as described in this chapter.

10. Carefully remove any rust or corrosion from the disc.

11. When new brake pads are installed in the caliper, the master cylinder brake fluid will rise as the caliper pistons are repositioned. Clean the top of the master cylinder of all dirt. Remove the cap (**Figure 34**) and diaphragm from the master cylinder and slowly push the caliper piston (**Figure 33**) into the caliper. Constantly check the reservoir to make sure brake fluid does not overflow. Siphon fluid, if necessary, prior to it overflowing. The piston should move freely in the caliper bore. If the piston doesn't move smoothly and there is evidence of it sticking in the caliper, the caliper should be removed and serviced as described in this chapter.

12. With your hand, push the piston (**Figure 33**) into the caliper as far as it will go.

13. Install the anti-rattle spring into the caliper (**Figure 31**).

14. Install the shim on the backside on the inner brake pad (**Figure 30**).

15. Install the inner brake pad next to the piston so that the holes in the pad face to the top of the caliper (**Figure 29**).

16. Partially insert the 2 brake pad Allen bolts (**Figure 27**) so that they contact the inner brake pad holes.

17. Install the outer brake pad (**Figure 28**).

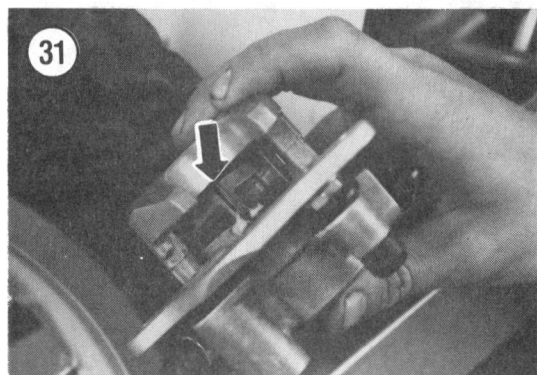

BRAKE PAD LINING THICKNESS

1 mm

18. Push the 2 brake pad Allen bolts through the outer brake pad and thread the bolt into the caliper. Tighten the bolts finger-tight a this time.

19. Align the brake caliper with the brake disc. The brake shoes should be on each side of the brake disc with the brake friction material facing against the disc.

20. Install the brake caliper mounting bolts (B, **Figure 25**) and tighten to the torque specification in **Table 3**.

21. Tighten the brake pad Allen bolts (**Figure 27**) to the torque specification in **Table 3**.

22. Spin the front wheel and activate the brake lever as many times as necessary as it takes to refill the cylinder in the caliper and correctly locate the pads.

WARNING
Use brake fluid clearly marked DOT 3 from a sealed container. Other types may vaporize and cause brake failure. Always use the same brand name; do not intermix as many brands are not compatible.

23. Refill the master cylinder reservoir, if necessary, to maintain the correct brake fluid level. Install the diaphragm and top cover (**Figure 34**).

24. Reinstall the brake caliper cover (**Figure 24**).

WARNING
Do not ride the motorcycle until you are sure the brake is operating correctly with full hydraulic advantage. If necessary, bleed the brake system as described in this chapter.

FRONT CALIPER

Removal/Installation

1. Place the bike on a stand so the front wheel clears the ground.

2. Place a pan underneath the brake caliper.

3. Loosen the brake hose banjo bolt at the caliper (**Figure 35**). Remove the banjo bolt and the 2 washers. Support the hose so that the fluid will drain into the pan. Discard the brake fluid.

4. Remove the brake pads as described in this chapter. Remove the brake caliper.

NOTE
If the caliper is going to be disassembled, the piston will have to be removed. Normally the piston is removed by directing compressed air through the caliper banjo bolt hole after the hose has been

13

disconnected and the caliper taken to the workbench. However, if you do not have access to compressed air, you can remove the piston as follows. First remove the brake pads and anti-rattle spring as described in this chapter. Then wrap a large disposable cloth around the brake caliper assembly. Hold the caliper so that your hands are away from the piston/brake pad area.

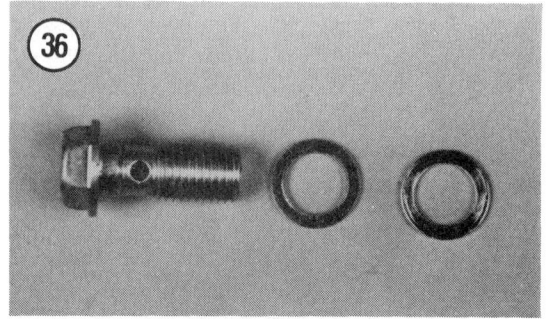

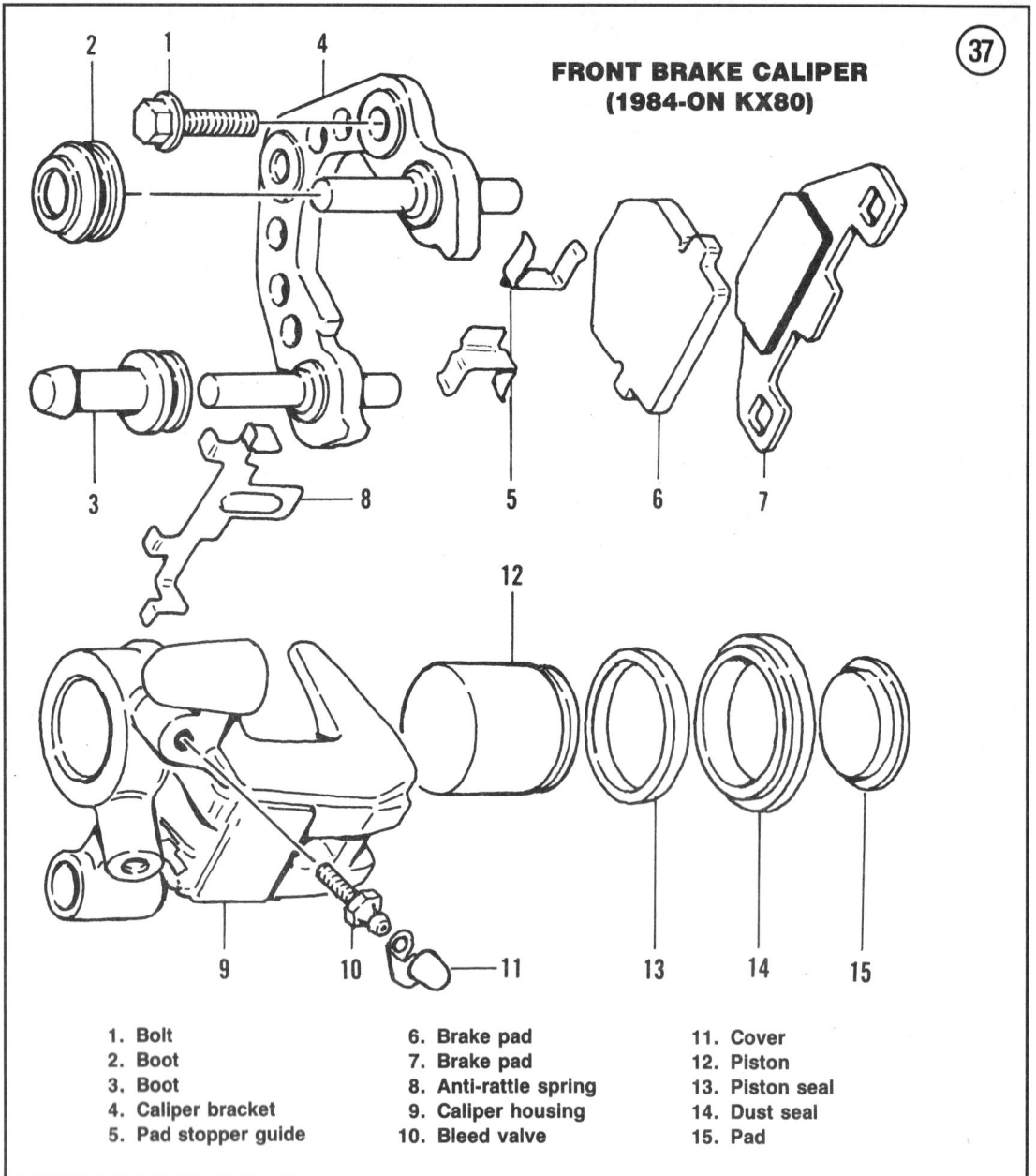

**FRONT BRAKE CALIPER
(1984-ON KX80)**

1. Bolt
2. Boot
3. Boot
4. Caliper bracket
5. Pad stopper guide
6. Brake pad
7. Brake pad
8. Anti-rattle spring
9. Caliper housing
10. Bleed valve
11. Cover
12. Piston
13. Piston seal
14. Dust seal
15. Pad

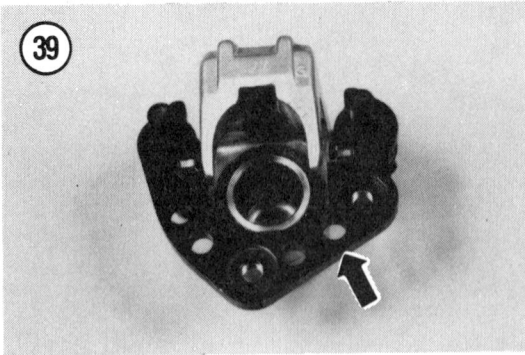

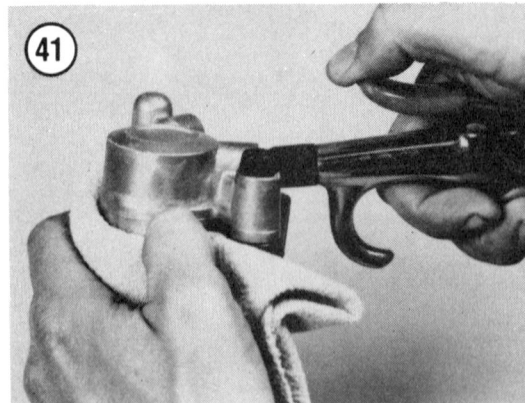

Operate the front brake lever to force the piston out of the caliper bore. Immediately wipe up any brake fluid.

5. Install by reversing these removal steps. Note the following.

6. Install the brake hose, with a sealing washer on each side of the fitting, onto the caliper (**Figure 36**). Install the banjo bolt and tighten to the torque specification in **Table 3**.

7. Install the brake pads and tighten the caliper bolts as described in this chapter.

8. Bleed the brake as described in this chapter.

> *WARNING*
> *Do not ride the motorcycle until you are sure the brake is operating properly.*

Disassembly/Inspection/Reassembly

Refer to **Figure 37** for this procedure.

1. Remove the pad from the front of the piston (**Figure 38**).

2. Pull the caliper bracket out of the housing (**Figure 39**).

3. Remove the dust seal (**Figure 40**) from around the piston.

> *WARNING*
> *Cushion the piston with a shop rag. Do not try to cushion the piston with your fingers, as injury could result.*

4. Cushion the caliper pistons with a shop rag. Then apply compressed air through the brake line port to remove the piston (**Figure 41**).

5. Remove the piston seal (**Figure 42**) from the piston bore.

13

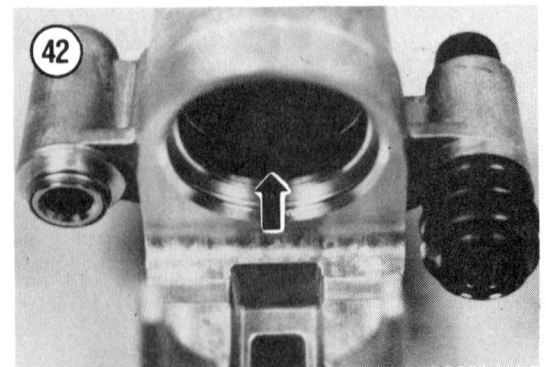

6. Check the piston (**Figure 43**) and the piston bore (**Figure 44**) for deep scratches or other obvious wear marks. If either part is less than perfect, replace it.

7. *1985-1987:* Measure the piston outside diameter (**Figure 45**) and the brake caliper piston bore inside diameter. Compare with the service wear limits in **Table 2**. Replace the piston and caliper housing as a set if any one part is worn to or past the wear limits.

8. Remove the bleed valve assembly (**Figure 46**) and check for damage or blockage.

9. Check the banjo bolt threads in the caliper. Check thread condition by screwing the banjo bolt into the caliper.

10. Check the caliper bushings for wear or damage; replace by pulling out of caliper. Reverse to install.

11. Check the caliper bracket for cracks or other damage.

12. Check the anti-rattle spring for cracks or damage. Replace if necessary.

13. Measure the brake pad friction thickness with a vernier caliper or ruler (**Figure 32**). Compare to the specifications in **Table 2**. Replace the brake pads as a set (**Figure 47**) if the friction material is worn to the wear limit or less.

14. See **Figure 48**. Replace the piston (A) and dust (B) seals.

15. Clean all parts (except brake pads) with DOT 3 brake fluid.

16. Soak the new piston seal in fresh brake fluid. Coat the inside of the cylinder with fresh brake fluid prior to the assembly of parts.

17. Install the piston seal (A, **Figure 41**) into the second groove in the cylinder bore. See **Figure 42**.

NOTE
Check that the seal fits squarely in the cylinder bore groove. If the seal is not installed properly, the caliper assembly will leak and braking performance will be reduced.

18. The piston (**Figure 43**) has one open and one closed end. Insert the piston into the cylinder so that the open end faces out. Push the piston in all the way.

19. Install the dust seal around the piston (**Figure 49**). Make sure the dust seal fits into the groove completely. See **Figure 40**.

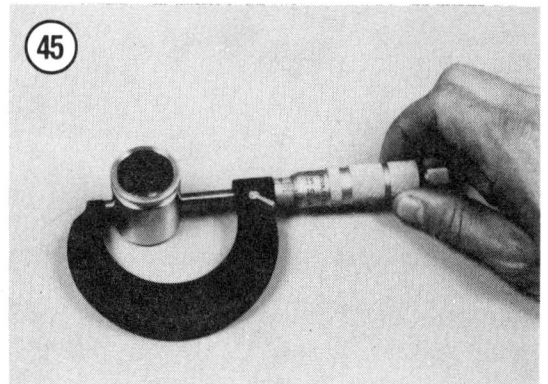

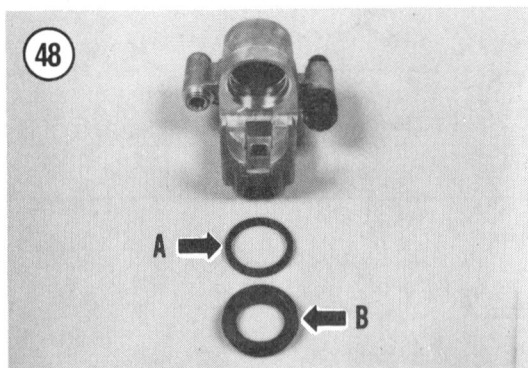

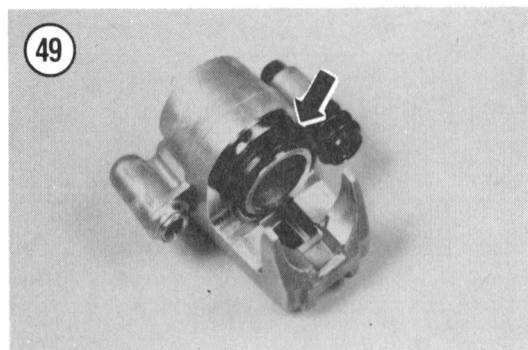

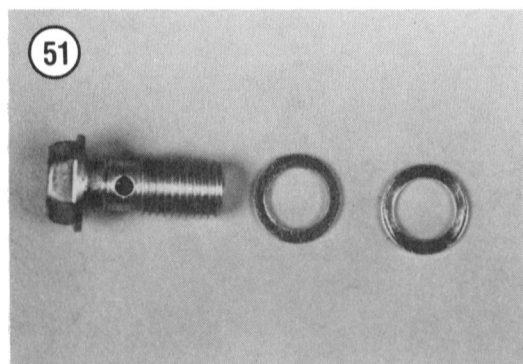

20. Apply a thin coat of PBC (Poly Butyl Cuprysil) grease to the caliper bracket shafts and caliper holder holes. Install the caliper bracket (**Figure 39**).

21. Install the pad into the end of the piston (**Figure 38**).

22. Install the brake caliper assembly as described in this chapter.

REAR CALIPER
(1988-ON KX80)

Removal/Installation

1. Place the bike on a stand so the rear wheel clears the ground.

2. Remove the brake caliper cover screws and remove the cover (**Figure 24**).

3. Place a pan underneath the brake caliper.

4. Loosen the brake hose banjo bolt at the caliper (**Figure 50**). Remove the banjo bolt and the 2 washers. Support the hose so that the fluid will drain into the pan. Discard the brake fluid.

5. Remove the brake pads as described in this chapter. Remove the brake caliper.

NOTE
If the caliper is going to be disassembled, the piston will have to be removed. Normally the piston is removed by directing compressed air through the caliper banjo bolt hole after the hose has been disconnected and the caliper taken to the workbench. However, if you do not have access to compressed air, you can remove the piston as follows. First remove the brake pads and anti-rattle spring as described in this chapter. Then wrap a large disposable cloth around the brake caliper assembly. Hold the caliper so that your hands are away from the piston/brake pad area. Operate the rear brake pedal to remove the piston. Immediately wipe up any brake fluid.

6. Install by reversing these removal steps. Note the following.

7. Install the brake hose, with a sealing washer on each side of the fitting, onto the caliper (**Figure 51**). Install the banjo bolt and tighten to the torque specification in **Table 3**.

13

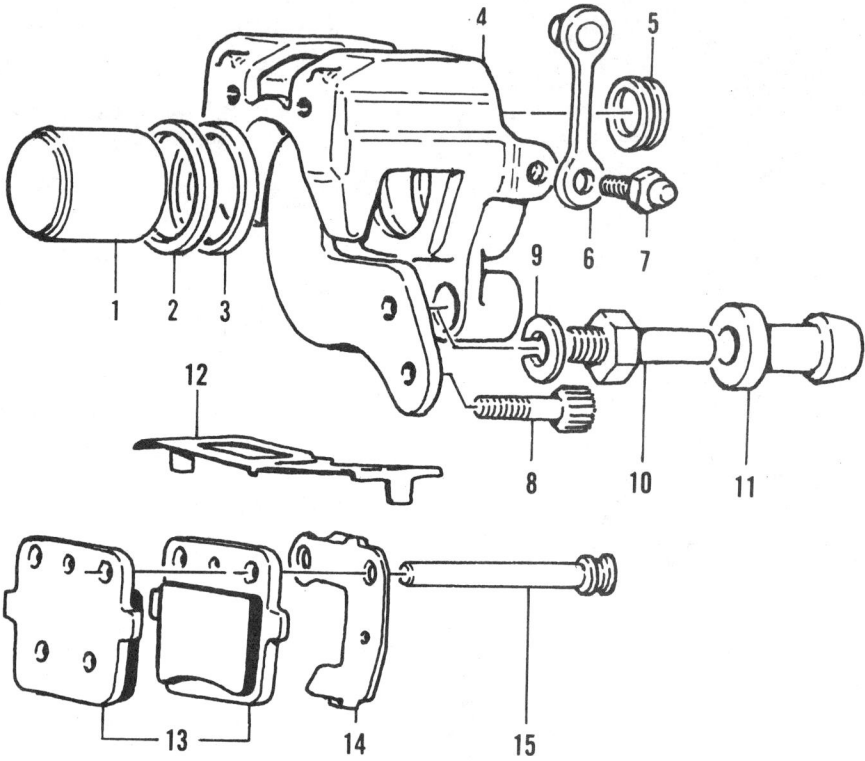

**REAR BRAKE CALIPER
(1988-ON KX80)**

1. Piston
2. Dust seal
3. Piston seal
4. Caliper housing
5. Damper
6. Cap
7. Bleed valve
8. Bolt
9. Lockwasher
10. Shaft
11. Boot
12. Anti-rattle spring
13. Brake pads
14. Shim
15. Brake pad Allen bolt

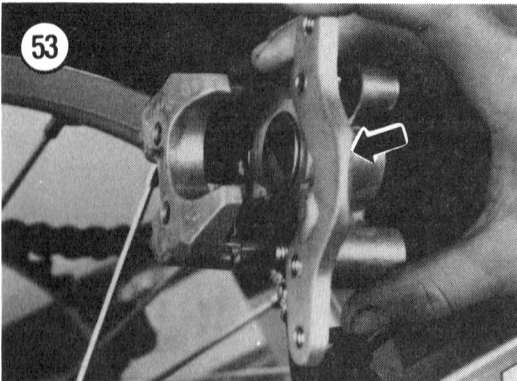

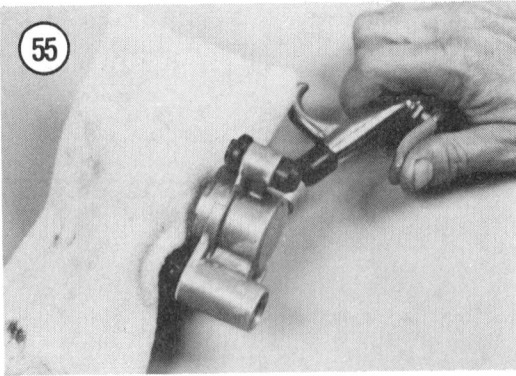

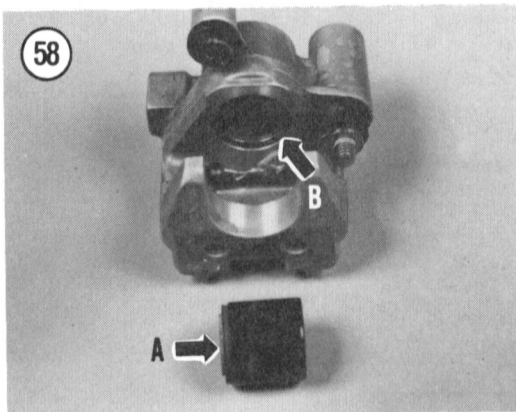

8. Install the brake pads and tighten the caliper bolts as described in this chapter.

9. Bleed the brake as described in this chapter.

WARNING
Do not ride the motorcycle until you are sure the brake is operating properly.

Disassembly/Inspection/Reassembly

Refer to **Figure 52** for this procedure.

1. Remove the caliper bracket from the housing (**Figure 53**).

2. Remove the pad from the front of the piston (**Figure 54**).

WARNING
Cushion the piston with a shop rag. Do not try to cushion the piston with your fingers, as injury could result.

3. Cushion the caliper piston with a shop rag. Then apply compressed air through the brake line port (**Figure 55**) and remove the piston. See **Figure 56**.

4. Remove the dust and piston seals (**Figure 57**) from the piston bore.

5. See **Figure 58**. Check the piston (A) and the piston bore (B) for deep scratches or other obvious wear marks. If either part is less than perfect, replace it.

6. Remove the bleed valve assembly (**Figure 46**) and check for damage or blockage.

7. Check the banjo bolt threads in the caliper. Check thread condition by screwing the banjo bolt into the caliper.

8. Check the bushings in the caliper for wear or damage; replace by pulling out of caliper. Reverse to install.

9. Check the caliper bracket (**Figure 59**) for cracks or other damage.

13

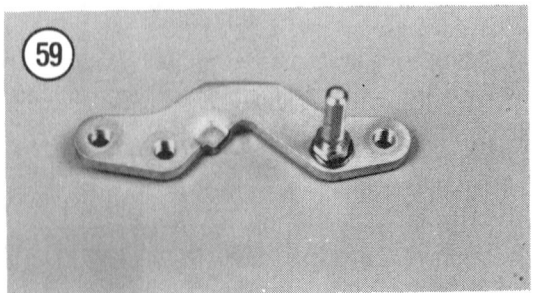

10. Check the brake pad Allen bolts (**Figure 60**) for scoring or thread damage.

11. Check the pad anti-rattle spring for cracks or damage. Replace if necessary.

12. Measure the brake pad friction thickness with a vernier caliper or ruler (**Figure 32**). Compare to the specifications in **Table 2**. Replace the brake pads as a set (**Figure 61**) if the friction material is worn to the wear limit or less.

13. Replace the piston and dust seals.

14. Clean all parts (except brake pads) with DOT 3 brake fluid.

15. Soak the new piston seal in fresh brake fluid. Coat the inside of the cylinder with fresh brake fluid prior to the assembly of parts.

16. Install the piston seal (**Figure 57**) into the second groove in the cylinder bore. Install the dust seal (**Figure 57**) into the first groove.

NOTE
Check that the seals fit squarely in the cylinder bore groove. If the seals are not installed properly, the caliper assembly will leak and braking performance will be reduced.

17. Insert the piston into the caliper so that the cork end (**Figure 56**) faces out. Push the piston in all the way.

18. Install the pad onto the end of the piston (**Figure 54**).

19. Apply a thin coat of PBC (Poly Butyl Cuprysil) grease to the caliper bracket shafts and caliper holder holes. Install the bracket (**Figure 53**).

20. Install the brake caliper assembly as described in this chapter.

FRONT MASTER CYLINDER

Removal/Installation

1. Place the bike on a stand so the front wheel clears the ground.

2. Loosen the brake hose banjo bolt (**Figure 62**) at the master cylinder. Remove the banjo bolt and washers (**Figure 51**).

NOTE
Wrap the end of the brake hose in a plastic bag to prevent brake fluid from dripping onto other parts.

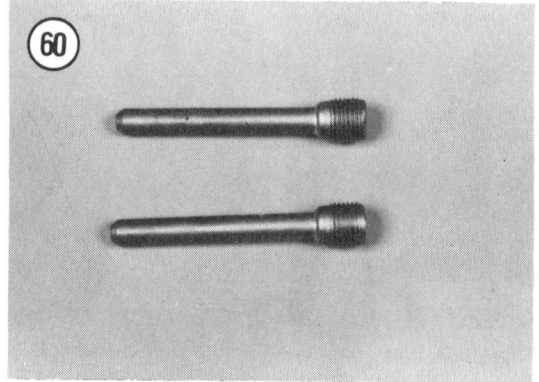

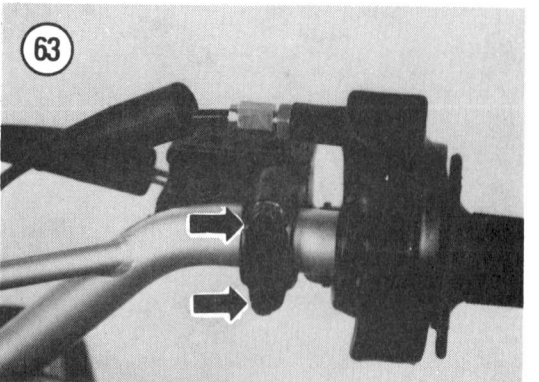

3. Remove the bolts (**Figure 63**) holding the master cylinder to the handlebar. Remove the clamp and master cylinder.

4. If necessary, service the master cylinder assembly as described in this chapter.

5. Mount the master cylinder housing onto the handlebar assembly. Install the clamp and the 2 bolts (**Figure 63**). Tighten the bolts securely.

6. Remove the end of the brake hose from the plastic bag and discard the bag.

7. Insert the banjo bolt and the 2 washers through the brake hose. Install the banjo bolt (**Figure 62**) and tighten to the torque specification in **Table 3**.

8. Refill the master cylinder and bleed the brake as described in this chapter.

WARNING
Do not ride the bike until the front brake is working properly.

Disassembly

Refer to **Figure 64** (1984-1987 KX80) or **Figure 65** (1988-on KX80) when performing this procedure.

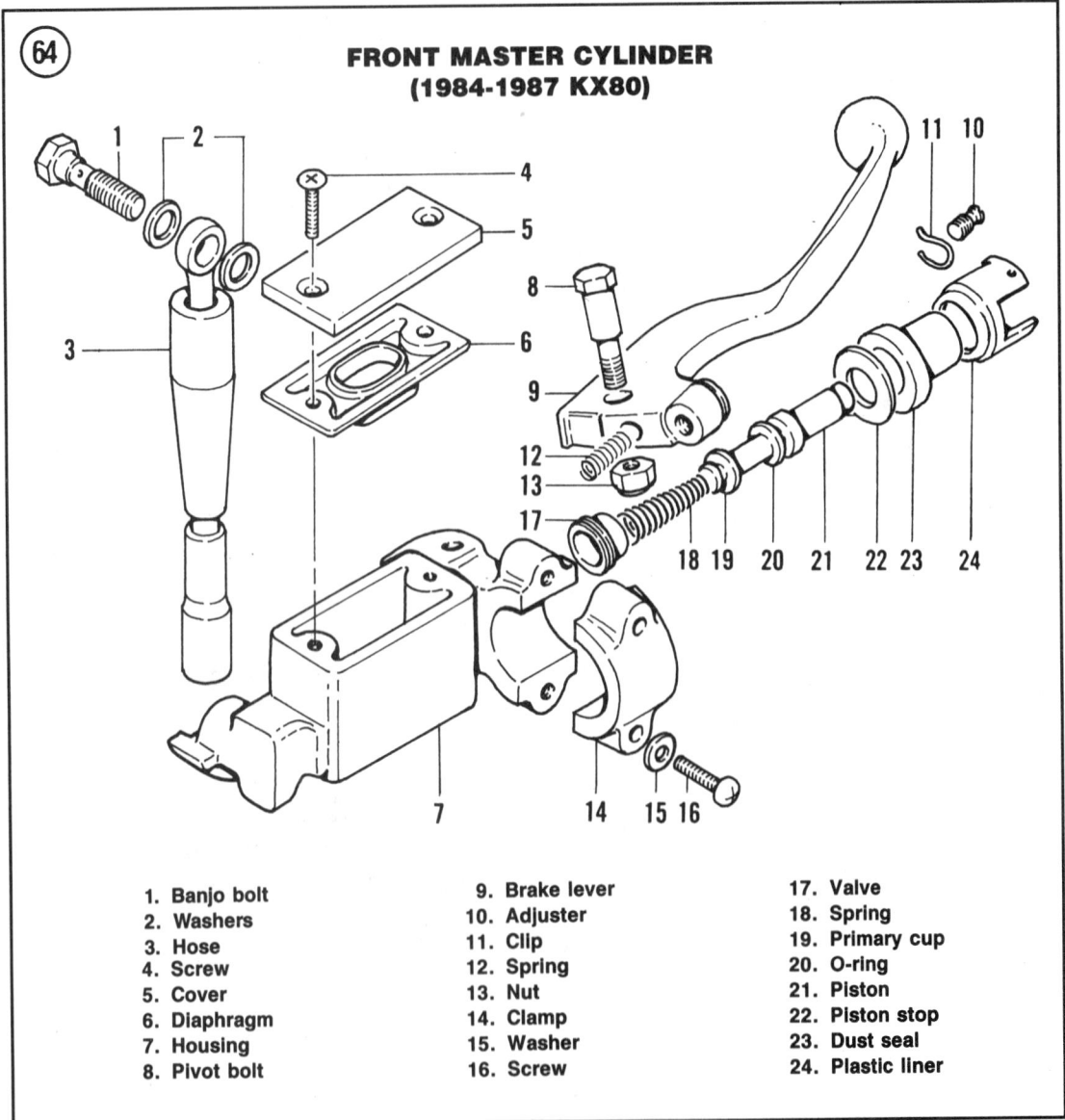

FRONT MASTER CYLINDER (1984-1987 KX80)

1. Banjo bolt
2. Washers
3. Hose
4. Screw
5. Cover
6. Diaphragm
7. Housing
8. Pivot bolt
9. Brake lever
10. Adjuster
11. Clip
12. Spring
13. Nut
14. Clamp
15. Washer
16. Screw
17. Valve
18. Spring
19. Primary cup
20. O-ring
21. Piston
22. Piston stop
23. Dust seal
24. Plastic liner

13

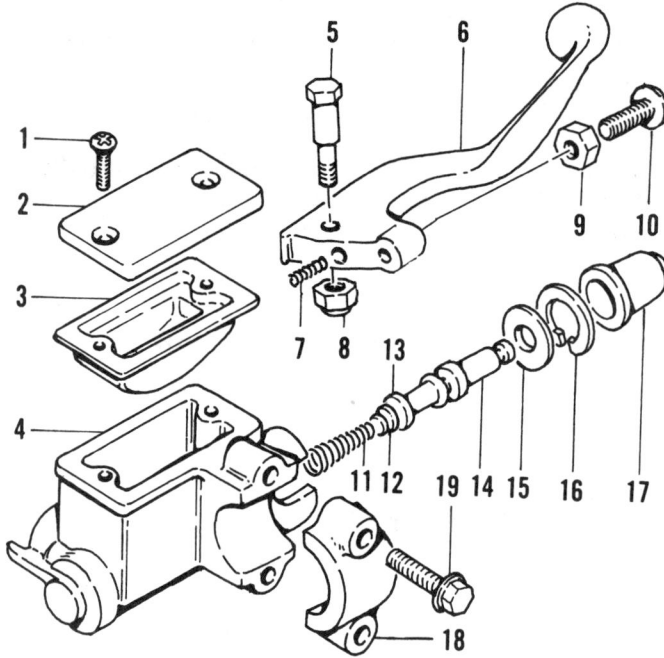

FRONT MASTER CYLINDER (1988-ON KX80)

1. Screw
2. Cover
3. Diaphragm
4. Housing
5. Pivot bolt
6. Brake lever
7. Spring
8. Nut
9. Locknut
10. Adjust bolt
11. Spring
12. Primary cup
13. O-ring
14. Piston
15. Washer
16. Circlip
17. Dust seal
18. Clamp
19. Bolt

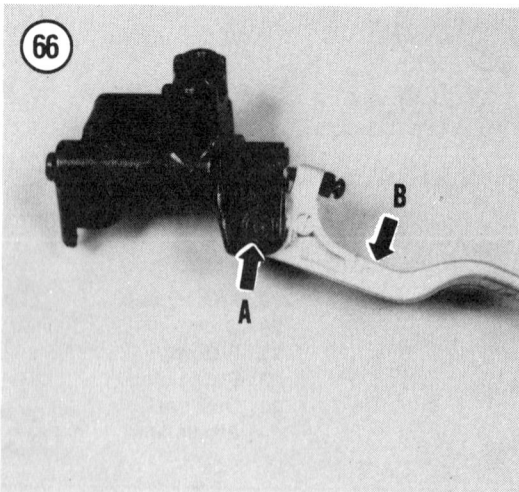

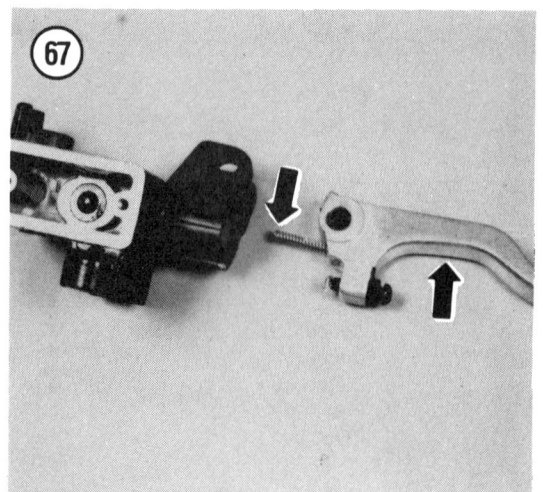

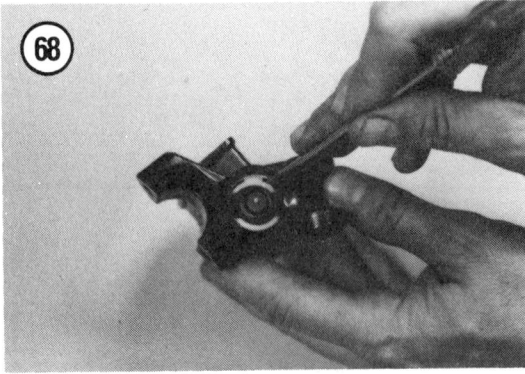

1. Remove the master cylinder cover and diaphragm and pour the brake fluid into a disposable container.

2. Remove the nut and bolt (A, **Figure 66**) securing the brake lever (B) to the housing. Remove the lever and spring (**Figure 67**).

3A. *1984-1987 models:* Perform the following to remove the piston assembly:

   a. Using a small tipped screwdriver (**Figure 68**), press the plastic liner tabs out of the master cylinder housing grooves and remove the liner (**Figure 69**).

   b. Remove the piston assembly (**Figure 70**).

3B. *1988-on:* Perform the following to remove the piston assembly:

   a. Carefully remove the dust cover (**Figure 71**) from the end of the master cylinder.

   b. Stand the master cylinder so that the piston assembly faces up. Then have an assistant compress the piston assembly (with a small wooden dowel) and remove the circlip (**Figure 72**) from the end of the master cylinder. Remove the washer.

   c. Remove the piston assembly (**Figure 73**).

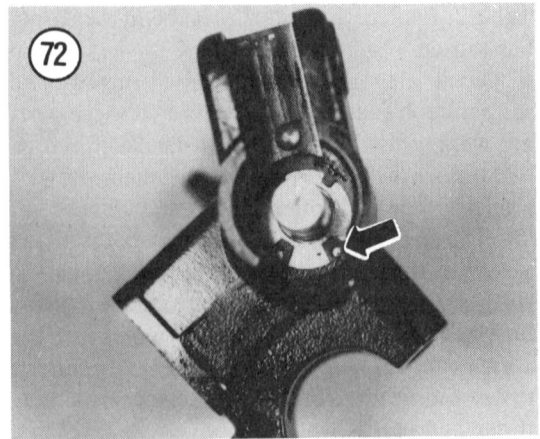

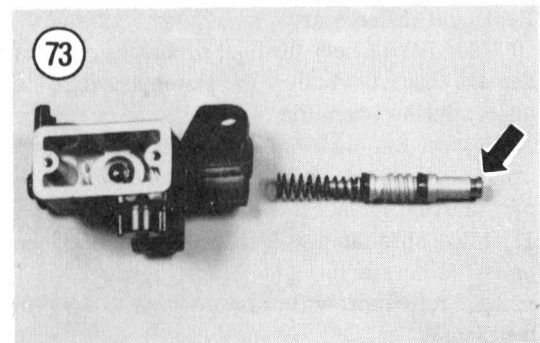

13

Inspection

Refer to **Figure 64** or **Figure 65** for this procedure.

1. Clean all parts in fresh DOT 3 brake fluid.
2. The piston assembly is shown in **Figure 64** (1984-1987) and **Figure 65** (1988-on). See **Figure 74** (1984-1987) or **Figure 75** (1988-on).

> *CAUTION*
> *Do not attempt to remove the primary cup off of the piston. The primary cup will be damaged and the piston assembly must be replaced.*

3. Check the piston assembly for wear or damage. The piston assembly must be replaced as a set if any one part is worn or damaged. Individual replacement parts are not available from Kawasaki.
4. Inspect the cylinder bore (**Figure 76**) and piston contact surfaces for scratches, pitting or rust. If either part is less than perfect, replace it.
5. Check the spring for cracks or damage. If the spring appears okay, measure its length with a vernier caliper and compare to the wear limit in **Table 2**. Replace the piston assembly if the spring has sagged.
6. Check the primary cup and O-ring on the piston. Replace the piston assembly if these parts are worn, softened, swollen or damaged.
7. Measure the primary cup outside diameter with a micrometer or vernier caliper and compare to the dimensions listed in **Table 2**. Replace the piston assembly if the primary cup outside diameter is worn to the wear limit or less.
8. Measure the piston outside diameter and the master cylinder bore inside diameter and compare to the specifications in **Table 2**. Replace both parts if any one part is worn excessively.
9. *1984-1987:* Check the piston stop for cracks. Replace it if necessary.
10. *1984-1987:* Check the liner for cracks or other damage that would allow the piston assembly to unseat during operation.
11. Inspect the pivot hole in the hand lever and master cylinder. If worn or elongated, the worn part must be replaced.
12. Make sure the passages in the bottom of the brake fluid reservoir are clear (**Figure 77**). A plugged relief port will cause the pads to drag on the disc.

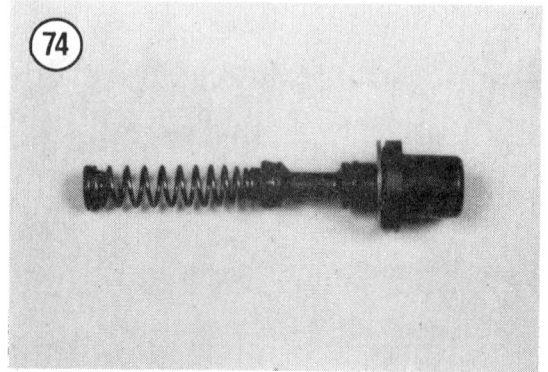

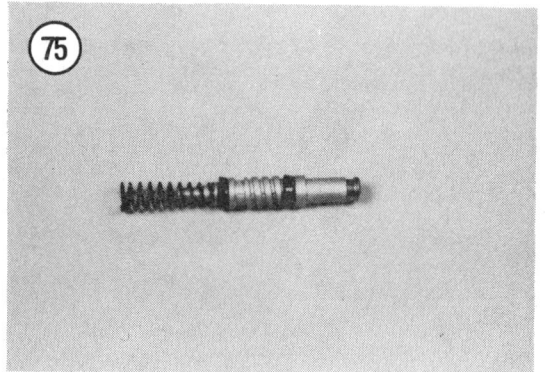

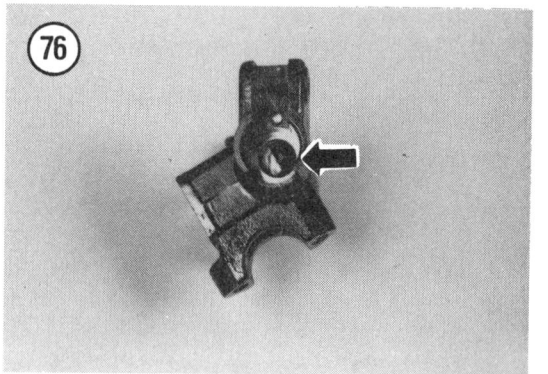

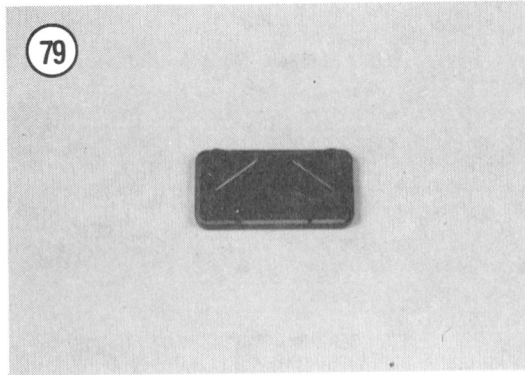

13. Check the banjo bolt threads in the master cylinder housing (**Figure 78**). Repair the threads with a tap if necessary. Flush the housing with DOT 3 brake fluid after using the tap.

14. Check the reservoir cap and diaphragm (**Figure 79**) for damage and deterioration and replace as necessary.

Assembly

Refer to **Figure 64** (1984-1987 KX80) or **Figure 65** (1988-on KX80) when performing this procedure.

1. Soak the piston assembly in fresh DOT 3 brake fluid. Coat the inside of the cylinder bore with fresh brake fluid prior to the assembly of parts.

2. Assemble the piston assembly as shown in **Figure 64** or **Figure 65**.

3A. *1984-1987:* Install the piston assembly (**Figure 74**) as follows:

    a. Insert the piston assembly into the bore in the direction shown in **Figure 70**.

> *CAUTION*
> *Make sure the primary cup does not turn inside out when installing the piston.*

    b. Compress the piston assembly (**Figure 80**) and install the liner around the dust seal (**Figure 69**). Push the liner into the bore until it snaps into position. Check that the piston cannot fly out of the bore.

3B. *1988-on:* Install the piston assembly (**Figure 75**) as follows:

    a. Insert the piston assembly into the bore in the direction shown in **Figure 73**.

> *CAUTION*
> *Make sure the primary cup does not turn inside out when installing the piston.*

    b. Have an assistant compress the piston assembly and install the washer and circlip (**Figure 81**). Make sure the circlip seats in the master cylinder groove completely (**Figure 72**).

    c. Install the dust seal (**Figure 71**).

4. Insert the spring (**Figure 67**) into the brake lever. Then align the brake lever with the master

13

cylinder pivot hole and install the lever (B, **Figure 66**). Install the pivot bolt and nut (A, **Figure 66**). Tighten the nut securely. Operate the lever to make sure the pivot bolt is not too tight.

5. Refill the master cylinder and bleed the brake as described in this chapter.

WARNING
Do not ride the bike until the front brake is working properly.

REAR MASTER CYLINDER
(1988-ON KX80)

1. Place the bike on a stand so the rear wheel clears the ground.
2. Remove the right-hand frame side cover.
3. Disconnect the master cylinder pushrod at the rear brake lever (**Figure 82**). Remove the circlip, washer and cotter pin. Discard the cotter pin.
4. Disconnect the brake hose at the master cylinder nipple (A, **Figure 83**).

NOTE
Wrap the end of the brake hose in a plastic bag to prevent brake fluid from dripping onto other parts.

5. Remove the banjo bolt securing the reservoir (**Figure 84**) and the 2 bolts securing the master cylinder (B, **Figure 83**). Remove the master cylinder assembly.
6. If necessary, service the master cylinder assembly as described in this chapter.
7. Mount the master cylinder and reservoir assembly onto the frame. Install and tighten the mounting bolts securely.
8. Remove the end of the brake hose from the plastic bag and discard the bag.
9. Reconnect the hose at the master cylinder nipple (A, **Figure 83**). Make sure it is on all the way and that the hose clamp is properly seated.
10. Assemble the master cylinder pushrod at the brake lever (**Figure 82**). Install the pin, washer and a new cotter pin. Bend the cotter pin over to lock it.
11. Refill the master cylinder reservoir and bleed the brake as described in this chapter.

WARNING
Do not ride the bike until the rear brake is working properly.

Disassembly

Refer to **Figure 85** when performing this procedure.

1. Remove the master cylinder cover and diaphragm and pour the brake fluid into a disposable container.
2. Disconnect the brake hose from the master cylinder hose fitting and disconnect the reservoir.

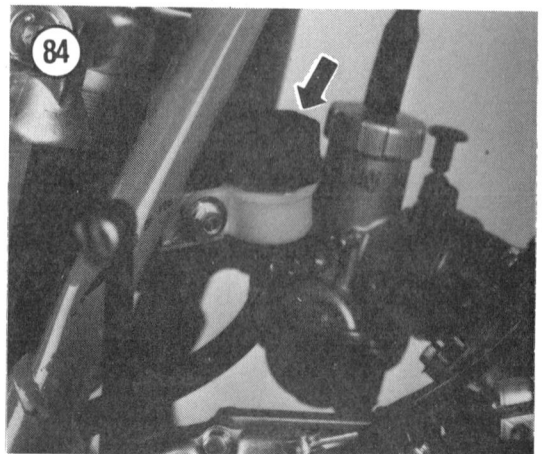

85

**REAR MASTER CYLINDER
(1988-ON KX80)**

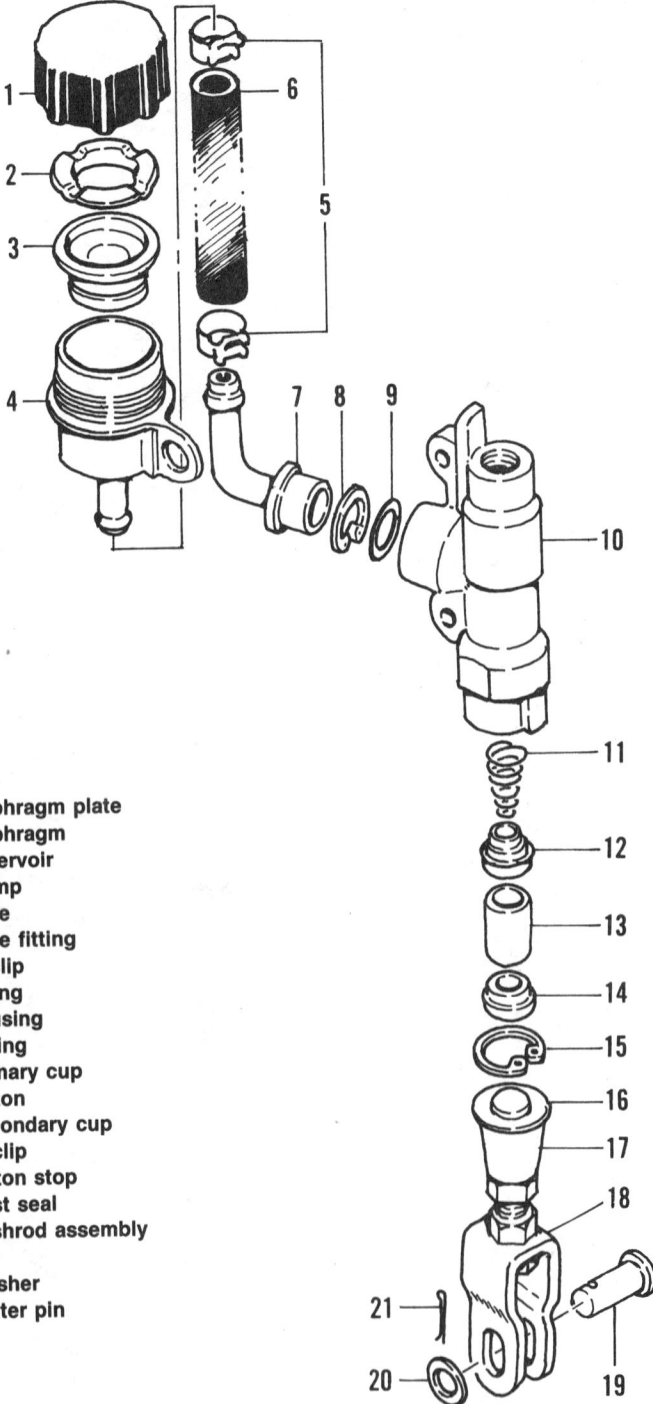

1. Cap
2. Diaphragm plate
3. Diaphragm
4. Reservoir
5. Clamp
6. Hose
7. Hose fitting
8. Circlip
9. O-ring
10. Housing
11. Spring
12. Primary cup
13. Piston
14. Secondary cup
15. Circlip
16. Piston stop
17. Dust seal
18. Pushrod assembly
19. Pin
20. Washer
21. Cotter pin

13

3. Remove the circlip and remove the hose fitting (**Figure 86**) and O-ring from the master cylinder. See **Figure 87**.

4. Carefully pry the dust seal (**Figure 88**) out of the master cylinder.

5. Stand the master cylinder on end so that the piston assembly faces up. Then have an assistant compress the piston assembly and remove the circlip (**Figure 89**) from the end of the master cylinder. Remove the pushrod assembly (**Figure 90**).

6. Remove the piston assembly (**Figure 91**).

Inspection

Refer to **Figure 85** for this procedure.

1. Clean all parts in fresh DOT 3 brake fluid.

2. The piston assembly is identified in **Figure 85**. See **Figure 92**.

> *CAUTION*
> *Do not attempt to remove the primary cup from the piston. The primary cup will be damaged and the piston assembly must be replaced.*

3. Check the piston assembly (**Figure 85**) for wear or damage. The piston assembly must be replaced as a set if any one part is worn or damaged. Individual replacement parts are not available from Kawasaki.

4. Inspect the cylinder bore (**Figure 93**) and piston contact surfaces for scratches, pitting or rust. If either part is less than perfect, replace it.

5. Check the spring (**Figure 92**) for cracks or damage. Replace the piston assembly if the spring is damaged.

6. Check the secondary and primary cups on the piston (**Figure 92**). Replace the piston assembly

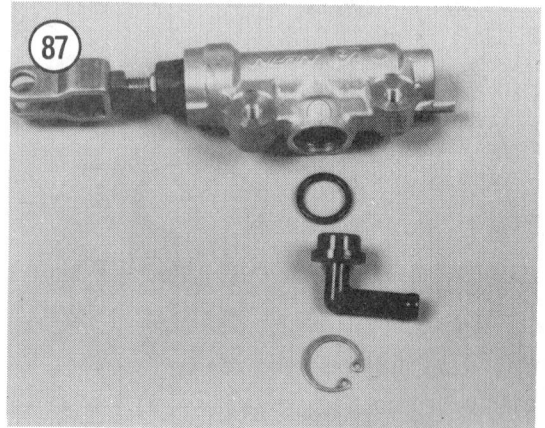

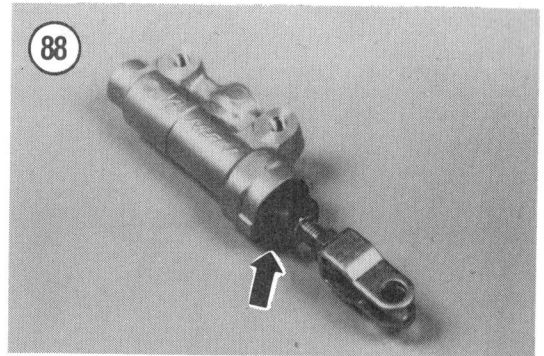

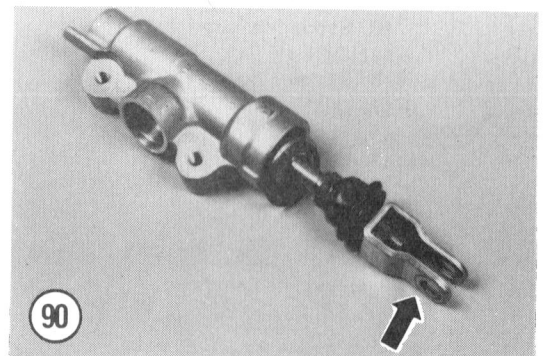

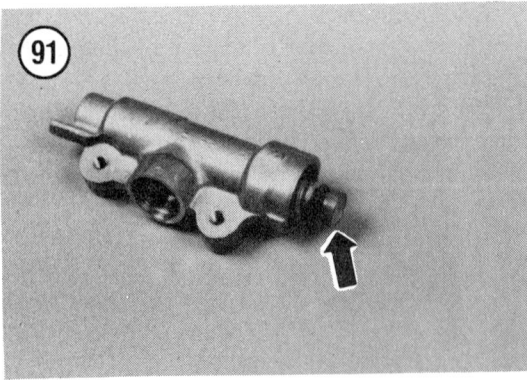

if these parts are worn, softened, swollen or damaged.

7. Make sure the passages in the bottom of the brake fluid reservoir are clear (**Figure 94**). A plugged relief port will cause the pads to drag on the disc.

8. Check the banjo bolt threads in the master cylinder housing. Repair the threads with a tap if necessary. Flush the housing with DOT 3 brake fluid after tap use.

9. Flush the reservoir with DOT 3 brake fluid.

10. Check the reservoir cap and diaphragm for damage and deterioration and replace as necessary.

11. Check the pushrod assembly (**Figure 95**) for excessive wear or damage. Check the dust seal on the pushrod for wear, cracks or other damage. If the dust seal is damaged, replace the pushrod assembly. Individual parts are not available.

Assembly

Refer to **Figure 85** for this procedure.

1. Soak the piston assembly in fresh DOT 3 brake fluid. Coat the inside of the cylinder bore with fresh brake fluid prior to the assembly of parts.

2. Assemble the piston assembly as shown in **Figure 92**.

3. Insert the piston assembly into the bore in the direction shown in **Figure 96**.

> *CAUTION*
> *Make sure the primary cup does not turn inside out when installing the piston.*

4. Align the pushrod with the end of the piston (**Figure 96**) and compress the piston assembly (**Figure 90**).

13

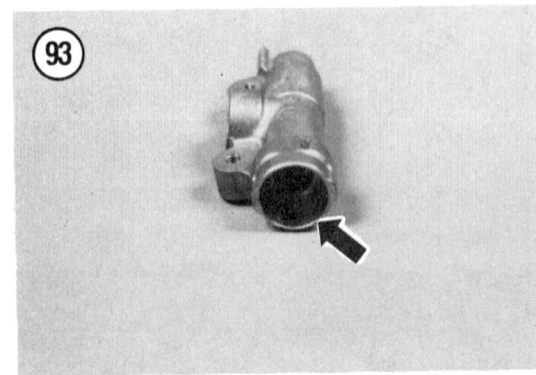

5. Slide the washer down the pushrod and install the circlip (**Figure 89**). Make sure the circlip seats in the master cylinder groove completely.

6. Seat the pushrod dust boot (**Figure 88**) into the end of the master cylinder.

7. Install the hose fitting and O-ring (**Figure 87**). Secure the nozzle with the circlip (**Figure 86**).

8. Reconnect the reservoir-to-master cylinder hose.

BRAKE HOSE REPLACEMENT

Under racing conditions, the brake hose(s) should be replaced whenever it shows signs of wear or damage.

1. Place a container under the brake line at the caliper. Remove the banjo bolt and sealing washers at the caliper assembly.

2. Place the end of the brake hose in a clean container. Operate the front brake lever or rear brake pedal to drain the master cylinder and brake hose of all brake fluid. Dispose of this brake fluid—never reuse brake fluid.

3. Remove the banjo bolt and sealing washers at the master cylinder.

4. Install a new brake hose in the reverse order of removal. Install new sealing washers and banjo bolts (**Figure 97**) if necessary.

5. Tighten the banjo bolts to torque specification listed in **Table 3**.

6. Refill the master cylinder with fresh brake fluid clearly marked DOT 3. Bleed the brake as described in this chapter.

WARNING
Do not ride the motorcycle until you are sure that the brakes are operating properly.

BRAKE DISC

Inspection

It is not necessary to remove the disc from the wheel to inspect it. Small marks on the disc are not important, but radial scratches deep enough to snag a fingernail reduce braking effectiveness and increase brake pad wear. If these grooves are found, the disc should be resurfaced or replaced.

1. Measure the thickness around the disc at several locations with vernier calipers or a micrometer (**Figure 98**). The disc must be replaced if the thicknesses at any point is less than the wear limit specified in **Table 2**.

2. Make sure the disc bolts are tight prior to performing this check. Check the disc runout with

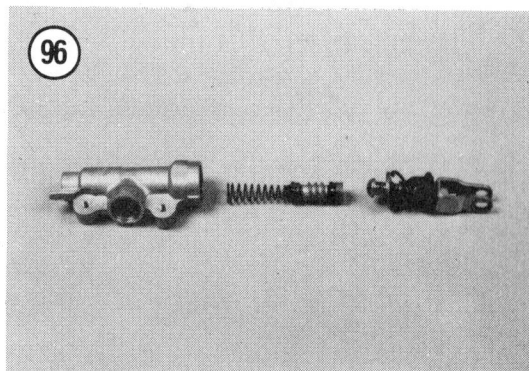

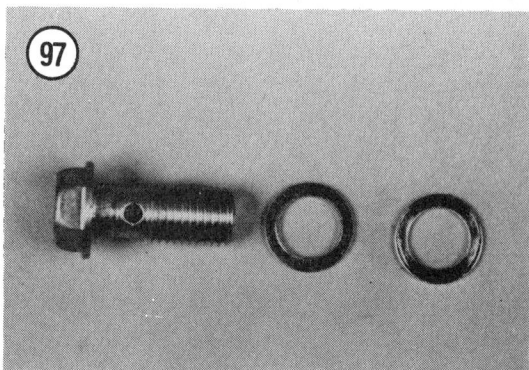

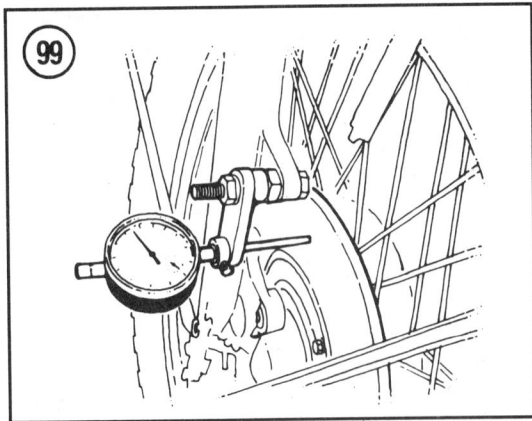

a dial indicator as shown in **Figure 99**. Slowly rotate the wheel and watch the dial indicator. If the runout exceeds the limit in **Table 2**, the disc must be resurfaced or replaced.

3. Clean the disc of any rust or corrosion and wipe clean with lacquer thinner. Never use an oil based solvent that may leave an oil residue on the disc.

Removal/Installation

1. Remove the front (Chapter Eleven) or rear (Chapter Twelve) wheel.

NOTE
Place a piece of wood or hose in the caliper in place of the disc. This way, if the brake lever or pedal is inadvertently applied, the piston will not be forced out of the cylinder. If this does happen, the caliper might have to be disassembled to reseat the piston and the system will have to be bled.

2. Remove the screws securing the disc to the wheel and remove the disc (**Figure 100**).
3. Install by reversing these removal steps. Tighten the screws to the torque specification in **Table 3**.

BRAKE BLEEDING

This procedure is necessary only when the brakes feel spongy, there is a leak in the hydraulic system, a component has been replaced or the brake fluid has been replaced.

NOTE
During this procedure, all the hose junctions in the brake system will be bled of air. It is important to frequently check the fluid level in the master cylinder. If the reservoir runs dry, air will enter the system which will require starting over.

1. Flip off the dust cap from the brake bleeder valve.
2. Connect a length of clear tubing to the bleeder valve on the caliper (**Figure 101**). Place the other end of the tube into a clean container. Fill the container with enough fresh brake fluid to keep the end of the tube submerged. The tube should be long enough so that a loop can be made higher than the

13

bleeder valve to prevent air from being drawn into the caliper during bleeding.

CAUTION
Cover all parts which could become contaminated by the accidental spilling of brake fluid. Wash any spilled brake fluid off of any surface immediately, as it will destroy the finish. Use soapy water and rinse completely.

3. Clean the top of the front master cylinder or the reservoir cap of all dirt and foreign matter. Remove the cap and diaphragm. Fill the reservoir to about 10 mm (3/8 in.) from the top. Insert the diaphragm to prevent the entry of dirt and moisture.

WARNING
Use brake fluid clearly marked DOT 3 only. Others may vaporize and cause brake failure. Always use the same brand name; do not intermix the brake fluids, as many brands are not compatible.

NOTE
During this procedure, it is important to periodically check the reservoir fluid level to make sure it doesn't run dry. If the reservoir should run dry, air will enter the system and you'll have to start over.

4. If the master cylinder was drained, it must be bled before bleeding the entire system. Perform the following:
   a. Remove the banjo bolt and hose at the master cylinder. See **Figure 102** (front) or **Figure 103** (rear).
   b. Hold your thumb over the bolt hole and fill the reservoir with DOT 3 brake fluid. Do not remove your thumb.
   c. While holding your thumb over the bolt hole, pump the brake lever or brake pedal several times. Then hold the lever or pedal in the depressed position.
   d. Reduce thumb pressure on the banjo bolt hole. Some fluid and air bubbles will leak out. Reapply thumb pressure.

   e. Repeat sub-steps c and d until no air bubbles bleed out of the banjo bolt hole and you can fell resistance at the lever or pedal.
   f. Check the reservoir fluid level and top-off if necessary.
   g. Reconnect the hose, installing the 2 washers and banjo bolt. Tighten the banjo bolt to the torque specification in **Table 3**.
   h. Turn the handlebar so that the banjo bolt is at its lowest position.
   i. Pump the lever or pedal several times and hold it depressed.
   j. Loosen the banjo bolt 1/4 turn. Some fluid and air bubbles will leak out. Tighten the banjo bolt.
   k. Repeat sub-steps i and j until no more air bubbles bleed out of the banjo bolt hole and you can feel resistance at the lever or pedal.

1. Wipe up any spilled brake fluid before continuing.

5. Slowly apply the brake lever or pedal several times. Hold the lever or pedal in the applied position and open the bleeder valve about 1/2 turn (**Figure 101**). Allow the lever to travel to its limit. When this limit is reached, tighten the bleeder screw. As the brake fluid enters the system, the level will drop in the master cylinder reservoir. Maintain the level at about 10 mm (3/8 in.) from the top of the reservoir to prevent air from being drawn into the system.

6. Continue to pump the lever or pedal and fill the reservoir until the fluid emerging from the hose is completely free of air bubbles. If you are replacing the fluid, continue until the fluid emerging from the hose is clean.

NOTE
If bleeding is difficult, it may be necessary to allow the fluid to stabilize for a few hours. Repeat the bleeding procedure when the tiny bubbles in the system settle out.

7. Hold the lever or pedal in the applied position and tighten the bleeder valve. Remove the bleeder tube and install the bleeder valve dust cap.

8. If necessary, add fluid to correct the level in the master cylinder reservoir. It must be above the level line.

9. Install the cap and tighten the screws (front master cylinder).

10. Test the feel of the brake lever or pedal. It should feel firm and should offer the same resistance each time it's operated. If it feels spongy, it is likely that air is still in the system and it must be bled again. When all air has been bled from the system and the brake fluid level is correct in the reservoir, double-check for leaks and tighten all fittings and connections.

WARNING
Before riding the motorcycle, make certain that the brake is working correctly by operating the lever or pedal several times. Then make the test ride a slow one at first to make sure the brake is working correctly.

Table 1 DRUM BRAKE SPECIFICATIONS

	New mm (in.)	Wear Limit mm (in.)
Brake drum inside diameter		
KX60		
Front and rear	90.000-90.087 (3.543-3.547)	90.75 (3.573)
KX80		
Front		
1983-1984	94.00-94.087 (3.701-3.704)	94.75 (3.73)
1985-on	—	—
Rear		
1983-1987	90.000-90.087 (3.543-3.547)	90.75 (3.573)
Brake shoe lining thickness	2.7 (0.11)	1.5 (0.06)
Brake shoe spring free length		
1983-1987		
Front and rear	32.2 (1.23)	32.8 (1.29)
1988-on		
Front	30.8-31.2 (1.21-1.22)	32.8 (1.29)
Rear	32-33 (1.26-1.29)	34.5 (1.35)

13

Table 2 DISC BRAKE SPECIFICATIONS (1984-ON KX80)

	New mm (in.)	Wear Limit mm (in.)
Brake pad friction thickness		
Front	3.7 (0.15)	1.0 (0.04)
Rear	4.2 (0.17)	1.0 (0.04)
Disc runout	0-0.15 (0-0.006)	0.3 (0.01)
Disc thickness	— —	2.5 (0.10)
Brake caliper (1984-1987)*		
Bore inside diameter	33.94-33.98 (1.336-1.338)	34.00 (1.339)
Piston outside diameter	33.887-33.900 (1.3341-1.3346)	33.85 (1.333)
Master cylinder (1986-1987)*		
Bore inside diameter	11.000-11.063 (0.4331-0.4356)	11.08 (0.436)
Piston outside diameter	10.823-10.850 (0.4261-0.4272)	10.80 (0.425)
Primary cup diameter	11.3-11.7 (0.445-0.461)	11.2 (0.441)
Spring free length	38.3-42.3 (1.51-1.67)	36.4 (1.43)
* Specifications not provided for 1988 and later models.		

Table 3 DISC BRAKE TIGHTENING TORQUES

	N·m	ft.-lb.
Banjo bolts		
1984-1987	29	21.7
1988-on	25	18
Caliper mounting bolts		
1984-1985	23	16.5
1986-on	25	18
Rear master cylinder mounting bolts		
1988-on	25	18
Rear brake pad Allen bolts	25	18

INDEX

14

14

1983 KAWASAKI KX60

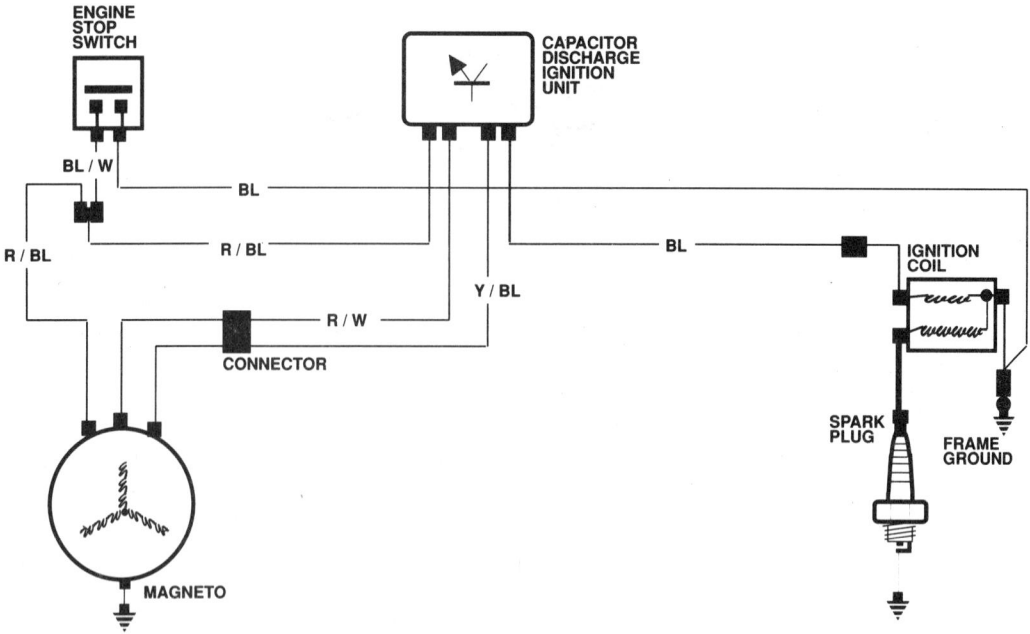

ENGINE STOP SWITCH

CAPACITOR DISCHARGE IGNITION UNIT

BL / W

BL

R / BL

R / BL

BL

IGNITION COIL

R / W

Y / BL

CONNECTOR

SPARK PLUG

FRAME GROUND

MAGNETO

1984-1990 KAWASAKI KX60

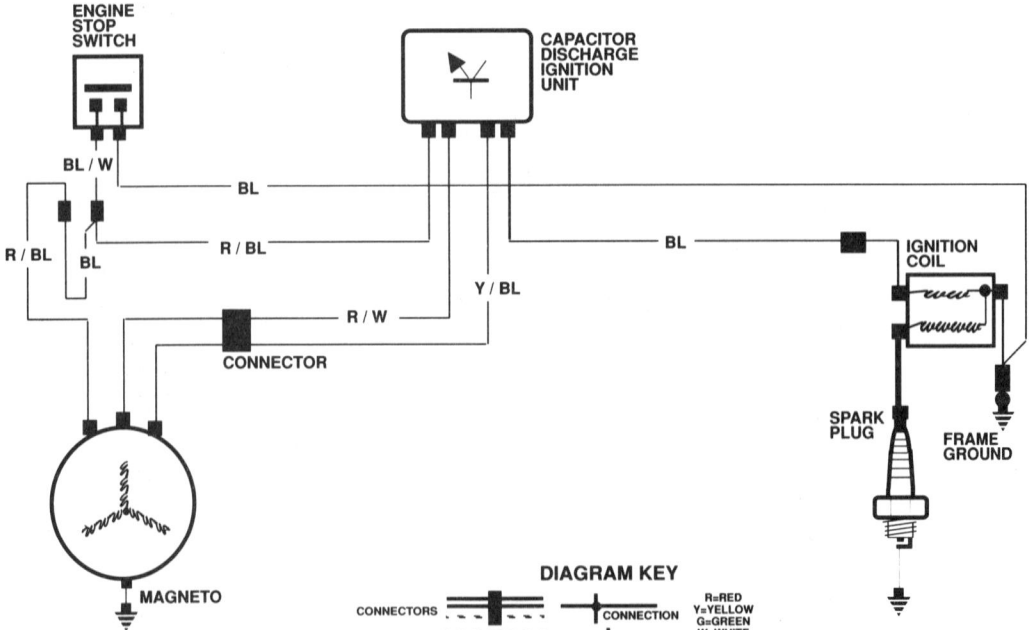

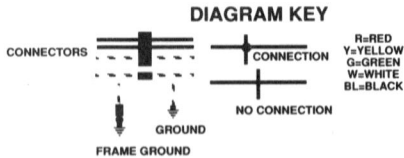

ENGINE STOP SWITCH

CAPACITOR DISCHARGE IGNITION UNIT

BL / W

BL

R / BL

R / BL

BL

IGNITION COIL

BL

R / W

Y / BL

CONNECTOR

SPARK PLUG

FRAME GROUND

MAGNETO

DIAGRAM KEY

CONNECTORS

CONNECTION

R=RED
Y=YELLOW
G=GREEN
W=WHITE
BL=BLACK

GROUND

NO CONNECTION

FRAME GROUND

15

1983 KAWASAKI KX80

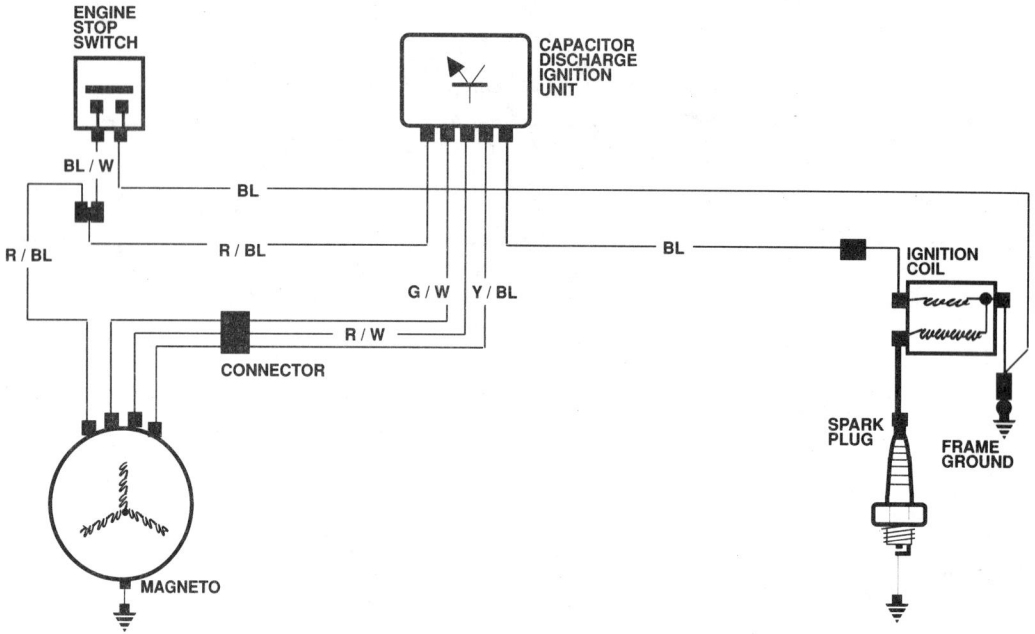

1984-1990 KAWASAKI KX80

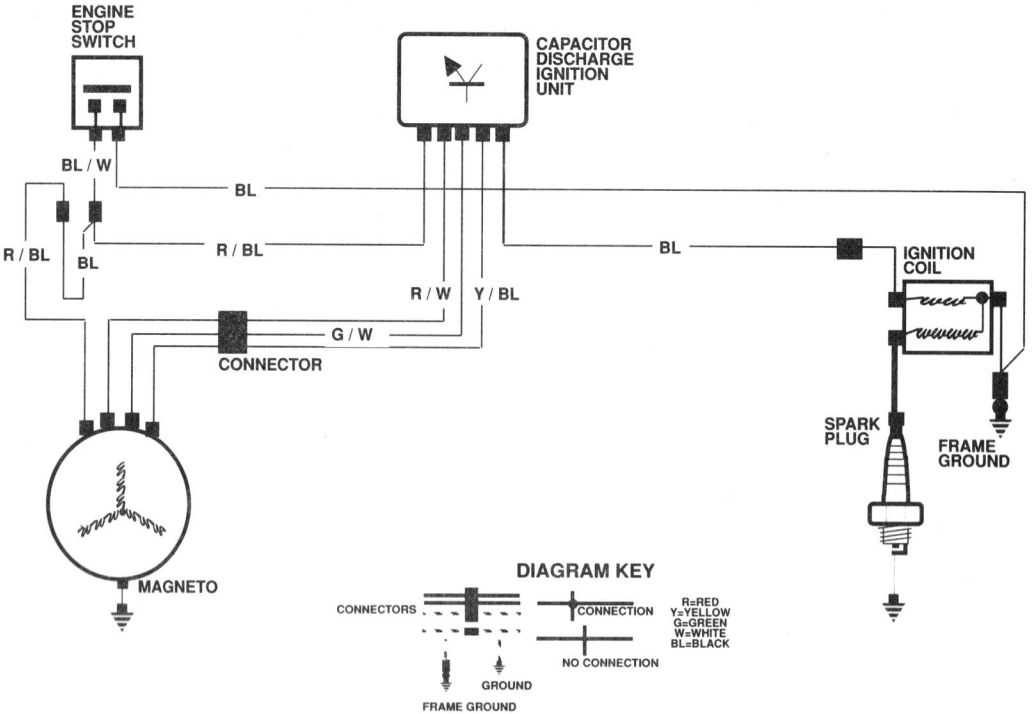

DIAGRAM KEY

CONNECTORS

CONNECTION

NO CONNECTION

GROUND

FRAME GROUND

R=RED
Y=YELLOW
G=GREEN
W=WHITE
BL=BLACK

NOTES

NOTES